With
the
Word

Warren W. Wiersbe

With
the
Word

OLIVER
NELSON

A Division of Thomas Nelson Publishers
Nashville

Copyright 1991 by Warren W. Wiersbe

Published in Nashville, Tennessee, by Oliver-Nelson Books, a division of Thomas Nelson, Inc., Publishers, and distributed in Canada by Lawson Falle, Ltd., Cambridge, Ontario.

Printed in the United States.

Senior Editor: Lila Empson
Senior Copy Editor: Dimples Kellogg
Manuscript Coordinator: Marie Sennett
Interior Design: William Parsons
Production Manager: Brenda White

Typesetting by ProtoType Graphics, Inc.

Library of Congress Cataloging-in-Publication Data

Wiersbe, Warren W.
    With the word / Warren W. Wiersbe.
      p.   cm.
    ISBN 0-8407-9108-9
    1. Bible—Commentaries. I. Title.
BS491.2W52 1991
220.7—dc20   91–15086
                                   CIP

Contents

Getting the Most Out of This Book

With the Word is designed to be a supplement to your Bible and not a substitute for it. Its main purpose is to assist you in discovering and applying some of the basic spiritual lessons found in Scripture. Where needed, explanations of difficult texts are given, but this is not an "explanatory commentary" as such.

The Bible is God's truth (John 17:17), and that truth is given on several "levels." The foundation is *historical truth*, the record of facts and words that involve real people and real events. From these facts we learn *doctrinal truth* concerning God, man, sin, salvation, and a host of other subjects. Of course, the end result must be *practical truth*, for we get God's blessing by *doing* His Word and not simply by *learning* it (James 1:22–25). Learning must lead to living.

The Bible was written for the heart as well as for the mind and the will, which is where *devotional truth* comes in. We use the Bible devotionally when we allow it to speak to us personally as we are taught by the Spirit of God (John 14:26; 15:26; 16:13–15). All Scripture was not written *to* us, but it was written *for* us (2 Tim. 3:16–17); and it can enlighten, enable, enrich, and encourage us if we will only let it.

Charles Haddon Spurgeon, the famous British preacher, said, "No Scripture is of private interpretation; no text has spent itself upon the person who first received it. God's comforts are like wells, which no one man or set of men can drain dry, however mightily may be their thirst."

When we read the Bible devotionally, we focus on the spiritual essentials, not the historical or geographical accidentals. God has often encouraged me from the first chapter of Joshua, but this does not mean I can walk into the Jordan River and expect it to open up before me. However, I have seen

Him "open up" difficult situations in ministry as I have trusted Him.

The Word of God is given to warn us (1 Cor. 10:1–12) and to offer hope to us (Rom. 15:4). It can do these things for us only if we receive the Word personally and let it work in our lives (1 Thess. 2:13).

Christian biography is filled with examples of God's "speaking" to His servants from the Word and giving them just the truth they needed for making hard decisions or facing difficult challenges. My wife and I have experienced this in our ministry. God has revealed His mind to us at just the right time through a portion of Scripture that was a part of our regular daily reading. People who "just open the Bible anywhere" and ask for help are turning God's Word into a magic book and are tempting God, not trusting Him.

A word of caution here: we must be very careful of saying, "God told me to do this." God does not address us today as He did Moses and Joshua and Paul. It is far better to say, "This is what the Spirit revealed to me from the Word, and I'm praying about what God wants me to do." After all, Satan also knows how to use the Bible (Matt. 4:5–7). "It is written" must be balanced by "*Again* it is written."

If you want to get the most out of this book, I suggest that you do the following:

1. Have a program for reading the Bible, a definite time and place and a schedule to follow. Random Bible reading is better than no reading at all, but it is rarely edifying.

2. Read the passage carefully, asking the Spirit to instruct you. Meditate on it, and seek the truths God has for you. You may want to write down in a devotional journal what you discover in the Word.

3. Read the comments in *With the Word,* think about them, and assimilate whatever truths God impresses on your heart. Trace the cross-references; compare Scripture with Scripture, and see how one passage sheds light on another.

4. Pray the truth into your inner being, and ask the Spirit to help you put it into practice. True Bible knowledge, properly assimilated, will lead to a "burning heart" that wants to obey (Luke 24:32) and not to a "big head" that wants to show off (1 Cor. 8:1).

To benefit from this book, you do not have to agree with everything I have written. My comments on the Word are not the meal; they are the menu that describes the meal. They are not the road but signal lights that help point the way. If this book ever takes the place of your Bible, or of your own meditation on the Bible, you will cease to grow. Bible knowledge alone is not spiritual nutrition.

I have been reading the Bible faithfully ever since I became a Christian in 1945. Many comments in this book have come from material that I wrote in notebooks I have kept for the past twenty years. When my good friend and editor, Dr. Victor Oliver, suggested that I write a devotional commentary, I had the opportunity to examine those notebooks again and "mine" from them the truths that I thought would help fellow pilgrims on the path of life. At least they have helped me, and for this, I am grateful to the Lord.

WARREN W. WIERSBE

THE PENTATEUCH

$\blacklozenge$

Pentateuch means "five books" in Greek and is the title for the first five books of the Bible, all written by Moses. These five books tell the history of the nation of Israel: its beginnings in the call of Abraham and the birth of Jacob's twelve sons (Genesis); its birth as a nation at Sinai (Exodus); its walk as a separated people (Exodus; Leviticus); its unbelief and disobedience (Numbers); and its preparation for conquering the Promised Land (Deuteronomy).

From Israel's experiences, Christians today can learn about God and the life of faith (1 Cor. 10:1-13). The nation's history presents both encouragement and warning, and we need both (Rom. 15:4). A knowledge of the Pentateuch provides a foundation for understanding the whole Bible. The God of Abraham, Isaac, Jacob, Joseph, and Moses is our God, and we can trust Him to do what He promises to do.

GENESIS

◆

Genesis is a book of *beginnings:* creation (chap. 1); human history, including marriage (chap. 2); sin and death (chap. 3); the promise of the Redeemer (3:15); human civilization (4:16ff.); Babylon (chap. 11); and the Jewish nation (chap. 12). Things that start in Genesis are carried through the Bible narrative and are fulfilled in the book of Revelation.

It is a book of *begetting,* describing the family tree from Adam to the founding of the nation of Israel. Ten different genealogies are recorded in Genesis. The account focuses on six persons and their families: Adam (chaps. 1—5); Noah (chaps. 6—10); Abraham (chaps. 11:1—25:18); Isaac (chaps. 25:19—27:46); Jacob (chaps. 28—36); and Joseph (chaps. 37—50). These genealogies may be boring to us, but they are important for tracing the Redeemer's ancestry.

It is a book of *believing.* Noah believed God and built an ark. Abraham believed God and left home for the Promised Land. Abraham and Sarah believed God, and He gave them a son. God gave His promises and then acted on behalf of those who trusted Him, just as He does today. (See Heb. 11:1–22.)

It is a book of *becoming.* God patiently worked with His people to make them what He wanted them to be. They failed Him often, but God did not give up on them. He is still the God of Abraham, Isaac, and Jacob, and He can accomplish in your life all that He has planned for you.

GENESIS 1

We are conscious every day of the visible world around us. We need to remember that this world speaks to us of God, His existence, His wisdom, and His power (Rom. 1:20; Ps. 19:1–3).

God creates. Everything begins with God and fulfills His

purposes for His glory (Col. 1:16–17; Rev. 4:11). He works by the power of His Word (Ps. 33:6–9), the same Word that can work in our lives (1 Thess. 2:13). He works according to a plan: first He forms, then He fills. He formed the earth and filled it with plants and animals. He formed the firmament and filled it with stars and planets. He formed the seas and filled them with living creatures. He can form and fill our lives today if we will yield to Him. Persons who have trusted Jesus Christ are a part of the new creation (2 Cor. 4:6; 5:17; Eph. 2:8–10).

God names. He named what He made, and we have no right to make changes: "Woe to those who call evil good, and good evil; who put darkness for light, and light for darkness" (Isa. 5:20). God calls things by their right names; if we use His vocabulary, we must also use His dictionary. (See Prov. 17:15.)

God divides. He separated the light from the darkness, the dry land from the waters, and the waters above from the waters beneath. This principle of separation is basic in all the Bible: He separated Abraham from Ur, the nation of Israel from the Gentiles, His church from the world (John 17:14–16). He wants His people today to be separated from all that defiles (2 Cor. 6:14—7:1).

God blesses. The first man and woman were the only part of creation especially blessed by God. Because we are created in the image of God, we are different from the other creatures God has made, and we must be careful how we treat one another (Gen. 9:6; James 3:9). Sin has marred that divine image, but one day all true believers will bear the image of Christ (Rom. 8:29). The more we are like Christ, the more we will enjoy His blessing (2 Cor. 3:18).

GENESIS 2

Now we are given the details concerning the creation of man and woman and their place in God's plan. The account does not contradict chapter 1; it complements it. We see the man involved in several activities.

Resting (1–3). God's rest was the rest of completion, not the rest of exhaustion, for God never gets weary (Ps. 121:4). Adam must have rested also, fellowshiped with the Lord, and worshiped Him. The seventh day, the Sabbath, became a sign to Israel that they were God's special people (Exod. 31:13–17). It is also a symbol of the eternal rest God's people will have with Him (Heb. 4:9–11).

Working (4–15). Rest and work must be in balance. Human history involves three gardens: the Garden of Eden, where man took of the tree and sinned; the Garden of Gethsemane, where the Savior took the cup and went to the tree to die for our sins; and the "garden city" of glory where God will take all His children to live forever (Rev. 21—22).

Work is not a curse. God gave Adam the task of guarding the Garden and tilling it. It was a fulfilling ministry for him. Man and God must work together to produce the harvest. St. Augustine said, "Pray as though everything depended on God, and work as though everything depended on you."

Submitting (16–17). The Creator has the right to govern His creatures. Love sets limits for the good of man. God calls us to obey Him because we want to, not because we have to. He wants children, not machines. Note especially the word *freely* in verse 16.

Naming (18–25). Man's naming the animals was a part of his "dominion" as the head of creation (1:26–28). He lost this dominion because of sin (Ps. 8), but we have regained it through Christ (Heb. 2:5ff.).

Adam also named his mate; he called her "Woman." Later, he would call her "Eve." God established marriage to meet man's need for companionship (2:18) and to provide for the rearing of children (1:28). In addition it served as a picture of Christ and His church (Eph. 5:25–32). Adam gave of himself for his bride, and Jesus gave of Himself for His bride (John 19:31–37).

GENESIS 3

The voice of deception (1–6). Up to this point, God's word is the only word that has been at work, creating and commanding. Now another "word" enters the scene, the word of Satan, the deceiver. He is a serpent that deceives (2 Cor. 11:1–3), a liar, and a murderer (John 8:44). He questioned God's word and God's goodness (v. 1), denied God's warning (v. 4), and then substituted a lie for God's truth (v. 5). "You will be like God" is his master lie (Isa. 14:12–14; Rom. 1:21–25), and people still believe it.

Eve was deceived when she ate, but Adam was not; he sinned with his eyes wide open (1 Tim. 2:14). He would rather forfeit his dominion than be separated from his wife.

The voice of love (7-13). Guilt produces fear, and fear makes us want to run and hide. Ordinarily, Adam and Eve would have run to meet God, but they had become sinners (Rom. 3:10-12). Sinners cannot cover their sins by their own works, nor can they hide from God.

The Father sought the lost sinners, as Jesus did when He was on earth (Luke 19:10), and as the Holy Spirit does today through His people (Acts 8:29ff.). God wants to use *us* to call men and women to salvation (Acts 1:8).

Overcoming Temptation

God tests us to bring out the best in us, but Satan tempts us to bring out the worst in us (James 1:1-15). Satan "baits the hook" with what seems good, and we take the bait and end up doing something bad. We can overcome the tempter by having faith and putting on the armor God provides (Eph. 6:10-18), by using the Word of God, by praying, by trusting God for the way of escape (1 Cor. 10:13), and by depending on the power of the Spirit.

The voice of judgment (14, 16-19). God cursed the serpent and the ground, but He did not curse Adam and Eve. The consequences of man's fall are all around us, and we suffer because of them. The ultimate judgment is death. Man can overcome a difficult environment to some extent, but he can do nothing about "the last enemy," death (1 Cor. 15:26). His only victory over death is through faith in Jesus Christ (John 11:25-26; 1 Cor. 15:57-58).

The voice of grace (15, 20-24). In verse 15, God declared war on Satan and gave the first promise of the Redeemer. Satan would bruise Christ's heel, but Christ would bruise Satan's head and defeat him (John 12:31; Col. 2:15).

Adam believed the promise that his wife would bear children, and his faith saved him. He called her *Eve*, which means "life-giver." In response to their faith, God shed innocent blood and clothed them. The only way sinners can be saved is by faith in the shed blood of Christ (Heb. 9:22; see also Isa. 61:10; Eph. 2:8–9).

Jesus Christ is "the last Adam" (1 Cor. 15:45–49). The first Adam's disobedience plunged us into sin, but the Last Adam's obedience brought salvation (Rom. 5:12–21). The first Adam was a thief and was cast out of Paradise. The Last Adam told a thief he would enter paradise (Luke 23:43). In Adam we die; in Christ we have eternal life.

GENESIS 4

Satan is a serpent that deceives and a lion that devours (1 Pet. 5:8–9). He used Eve to tempt Adam and Cain to destroy Abel. The two "seeds" of Genesis 3:15 came into conflict, for Cain was a child of the devil (1 John 3:10–12), while Abel was a child of God (Matt. 23:35). Like his father, the devil, Cain was a liar and a murderer (John 8:44).

The marks of God's children are faith, hope, and love (1 Cor. 13:13; 1 Thess. 1:3–4). The marks of the devil's seed are unbelief, despair, and hatred, and they are evident in Cain.

Unbelief (1–7). When God killed animals and clothed Adam and Eve (3:21), He taught the significance of blood sacrifice (Heb. 9:22). Cain brought the wrong sacrifice in his hands and had the wrong attitude in his heart. His was not a sacrifice of faith, and God rejected it. God also warned Cain that sin was lying at his door, waiting to pounce on him.

Hatred (8). Cain's anger slowly became envy and hatred, and then it led to murder (Matt. 5:21–26). When you start to play with temptation, you will soon be caught (James 1:13–16). Cain was guilty of every sin that God hates (Prov. 6:16–19).

Despair (9–24). God's question to Adam and Eve was, "Where are you?" His question to Cain was, "Where is Abel your brother?" Do we know where our brothers and sisters are? Do we care? Or are we making excuses, as Cain did?

Now God curses a man! But Cain was not convicted about

his sin; he was concerned only about his punishment. Cain's unbelief, hatred, and deceit destroyed every relationship in his life: his relationship with his brother, God, himself, and the world around him. All of us are pilgrims on this earth, but Cain became a fugitive, a wanderer. "Thou hast made us for Thyself," said St. Augustine, "and our hearts are restless until they rest in Thee."

Hope (25–26). Cain tried to compensate for his despair by building a "civilization" in the land of Nod ("wandering"). Since Adam and Eve had many children, Cain must have married a relative. He had many fine things in his city, but God rejected the whole thing and gave Adam another son, Seth ("appointed"), to carry on the godly line.

Controlling Anger

We may have righteous anger against sin (Mark 3:5; Eph. 4:26), but too often our anger is itself sinful. Jesus warned that anger could be the first step toward murder (Matt. 5:21–26). We must ask the Holy Spirit to help us control anger (Prov. 15:18; 16:32), manifest love to those who offend us (Matt. 5:43–48), and learn to practice forgiveness (Eph. 4:26–32).

GENESIS 5

The Old Testament is "the book of the genealogy of Adam" (v. 1). It tells us about Adam's descendants, and the story is not a happy one. In fact, the Old Testament closes with "lest I come and strike the earth with a curse" (Mal. 4:6).

The New Testament is "the book of the genealogy of Jesus Christ" (Matt. 1:1); before it ends, it declares, "And there shall be no more curse" (Rev. 22:3). The first Adam brought the curse; the Last Adam bore the curse (Gal. 3:13). Adam's sin caused thorns to grow (Gen. 3:18), but Jesus wore those thorns as a crown (Matt. 27:29).

God made man in His likeness, but sinful man now begets children in his likeness (v. 3). We are all born sinners (Ps. 51:5). But when a sinner is born again through faith in Christ, he or she begins to grow into the likeness of the Last Adam (Rom. 8:29; 2 Cor. 3:18).

Eight times in chapter 5 you find the sobering phrase "and he died." Death is an appointment, not an accident. Because sin was reigning, death was also reigning (Rom. 5:14, 17), but in the life of Enoch, *God's grace was reigning* (Rom. 5:20–21). He believed God (Heb. 11:5–6), walked with God in the midst of a godless society, and witnessed for God (Jude 14–15). Enoch did not die; God raptured him away to heaven. This is the "blessed hope" of all Christians (Titus 2:11–14; see also 1 Thess. 4:13–18).

Noah means "rest." Mankind was in misery and longed for the promised Redeemer to come. He *has* come, and we can come to Him and find true rest (Matt. 11:28–30).

GENESIS 6—8

The account of a flood is written into the history of many ancient peoples, and the results of a flood are seen in many places on the earth. Jesus believed in the Flood (Matt. 24:37–39), and so did Peter (1 Pet. 3:20) and the author of Hebrews (11:7).

The holiness of God (6:1–7). God saw a world of people who were inwardly corrupt, outwardly violent, and upwardly rebellious. Noah was the tenth generation from Adam. It didn't take long for sin to spread in the human race. When the world is again as it was in Noah's day, watch for the return of the Lord (Matt. 24:37–39).

The grace of God (6:8—7:10). Noah was saved just as any sinner is saved, by grace (Gen. 6:8), through faith (Heb. 11:7). (See Eph. 2:8–9.) He heard God's Word, believed God's promise of protection, and proved his faith by his works. There was only one way to be saved from destruction, and that was by entering the ark; and the ark had only one door. It is a picture of the salvation we have in Christ.

The wrath of God (7:11–24). God was very patient and gave the world at least 120 years of opportunity to be saved (Gen. 6:3; 1 Pet. 3:20; 2 Pet. 2:5). The world refused Noah's witness and rejected God's grace up to the very day Noah and his family went into the ark. God waited another week (how the neighbors must have laughed at Noah!), but then the judgment came. As David proclaimed, "The LORD sat enthroned at the Flood" (Ps. 29:10). He is sovereign in all things! The next worldwide judgment will be with fire, not water (2 Pet. 3:1–12).

The faithfulness of God (8:1–22). Noah had faith in God's promises, and God did not disappoint him. (See 1 Kings 8:56.) True faith does not get in a hurry (Isa. 28:16); Noah waited until the word of God told him what to do. The first thing Noah and his family did on the cleansed earth was to worship the God who had faithfully cared for them (Ps. 116:12–19; Rom. 12:1–2). God gave them a covenant that assured them of the continuity of creation despite man's evil heart. This covenant makes possible the sustaining of life on earth. God has been faithful to His covenant, but man has not been faithful in his stewardship of the earth. (See Rev. 11:18.)

Faithfulness to God

Noah and his family were the only believers on earth, yet they witnessed courageously for God and against the evil of their day. They were faithful to God when everything seemed to be against them. God still calls His people to stand alone if needs be, and He promises never to forsake us (Heb. 13:5–6). God will judge us not on the basis of our popularity but on our faithfulness to Him (1 Cor. 4:2). God needs courageous witnesses today.

GENESIS 9

Government (1–7). God gave some new rules for life on the cleansed earth. He always guides His redeemed and shows them His will. Noah and his family could now eat animal flesh (Gen. 1:29), *but they were forbidden to eat the blood* (Lev. 17:11–14). The sanctity of human life was affirmed in the ordaining of human government (Rom. 13). God established government because man is basically a sinner and must be kept under control. Murder is a terrible crime because man is made in the image of God, and to kill a human being is to attack God's image. All people are not children of God, but all belong to one human family because God made us of one blood (Acts 17:26).

Grace (8–17). God gave assurance that He would never send another flood to destroy life on the earth. The covenant included not only man but also birds, cattle, and the beasts of the field (Ezek. 1:10; Rev. 4:7). The sign of the covenant was the rainbow, a bridge of beauty that joins heaven and earth. Whether we look at the rainbow or not, *God* looks upon it and remembers His promises. Noah saw the rainbow *after* the storm; Ezekiel saw it *in the midst* of the storm (Ezek. 1:4ff.); and John saw it *before* the storm of judgment (Rev. 4:1–3).

Guilt (18–29). Imagine, a "preacher of righteousness" (2 Pet. 2:5), who was over six hundred years old, *getting drunk!* (See Gen. 6:5; 8:21; 1 Cor. 10:12.) Ham should have grieved over his father's sins, not gloated over them (Prov. 14:9). His brothers did what love always does: "covers all sins" (Prov. 10:12; 12:16; 17:9; 1 Pet. 4:8).

Noah's words must not be interpreted to mean that certain races are inferior and destined to be enslaved. In fact, history shows that some of Canaan's descendants were mighty nations with great empires. For that matter, even the Jews, the descendants of Shem, have had their share of captivity. His words were a prophecy: the sin of Ham would be visited on his son Canaan, who must have been involved in some way; Shem would have God's blessing (Rom. 9:1–5); Japheth (the Gentiles) would multiply and would worship the God of Shem. John wrote, "Salvation is of the Jews" (John 4:22). People who trust Christ for salvation are all one in Him (Gal. 3:28; Col. 3:11).

GENESIS 10—11

From Noah's three sons, God made a new beginning in human history. He set apart Shem to be His special channel of blessing, and it was through Shem that Abraham, the father of the Jewish nation, was born (11:10ff.).

Sin always separates: man from God (chap. 3); brother from brother (chap. 4); family from family (chap. 9); and now nation from nation.

Note the name of Nimrod (10:8–10). The phrase "mighty hunter" implies that he was a rebel against God and a tyrant against his fellowman. He founded two cities important in Bible history: Babylon and Nineveh.

Man seeks unity and notoriety, and he tries to accomplish these things by his own wisdom and strength. Lucifer wanted to be like God (Isa. 14:14), and man wanted to make a name for himself. But only God can make a person's name truly great (Gen. 12:2; Josh. 3:7).

Babel means "confusion," and "God is not the author of confusion" (1 Cor. 14:33; see also James 3:16). Babylon will appear often in the biblical record as the enemy of God's people. Wherever there is confusion, the spirit of Babylon—the world and the flesh—is at work. Ultimately, the whole "Babylonian system" will be destroyed (Rev. 17–18).

The confusion of tongues that began at Babel was reversed at Pentecost (Acts 2:7–8). A descendant of Ham, an Ethiopian, was saved in Acts 8; a descendant of Shem, Paul, was saved in Acts 9; and the gentile descendants of Japheth were saved in Acts 10. Unity is not worked up by man; it is sent down by God (Ps. 133; Eph. 4:1–6). As we share the gospel with others, we are helping to unite what sin has torn apart (Eph. 1:10–11). Christians are indeed the peacemakers of the world.

GENESIS 12

God's Word leads to faith (1–3). Abram was an idolater when God called him (Josh. 24:2), revealed His glory to him (Acts 7:2), and spoke to him. Abram turned from vain idols to walk with the Lord, and all of this was by God's grace. The hearing of the Word creates faith (John 5:24; Rom. 10:17). Again God's creative Word is at work.

Faith leads to obedience (4–6). The New Testament states, "By faith Abraham obeyed" (Heb. 11:8). "I will show you, I will make you, I will bless you!" were God's promises, and Abram believed. It has well been said that faith is not believing in spite of evidence; it is obeying in spite of consequences. The proof of faith is obedience, for true faith always leads to works (James 2:14ff.). Hearing leads to heeding.

Obedience leads to blessing (7–9). We are told nothing about the journey, which must have been very difficult; but we are told that God met Abram when he arrived and gave him a new promise. God always goes before us and has His Word ready to encourage us. From now on, Abram's life will be marked by the presence of the *tent* (a pilgrim on earth) and the *altar* (a citizen of heaven).

Am I Living by Faith?

When you live by faith, you make your decisions on the basis of the Word of God (Rom. 10:17), and you seek to glorify God alone (Rom. 4:19–20). True faith is not in a hurry; it is willing to wait (Isa. 28:16; Heb. 6:12).

Faith obeys God in spite of circumstances or consequences, and it is not afraid of what others may say or do (Heb. 11:29–30).

Blessing leads to testing (10–20). Faith is always tested for at least three reasons: to prove whether our faith is real; to help our faith grow; and to bring glory to the Lord (1 Pet. 1:6–9; James 1:1–8). Imagine a famine in the very land where God led him! We can be in the will of God and still suffer trials. It has been said that "faith is living without scheming," but Abram began to scheme. He was walking by sight and not by faith, and it cost him his testimony—and almost his wife! Note that Abram had neither a tent nor an altar in Egypt. "Going down to Egypt" is Bible language for getting out of the will of God.

God blessed Abram *that he might be a blessing*. Through Abram and his descendants, the whole world has been blessed. Whenever God gives you a blessing, it's so that you might be a blessing to others. God's blessings are not luxuries; they are opportunities.

GENESIS 13

A new beginning (1–4). God chastened Abram in Egypt, and Abram returned to the land he never should have left. He was a very wealthy man, but his tent and altar were the most valuable things he possessed. When we fail, the Lord is ready to forgive and restore (1 John 1:5—2:2). "The victorious Christian life is a series of new beginnings," said Alexander Whyte.

A new burden (5–13). While in Egypt, Lot acquired wealth and a taste for the world, and his temporal interests were partly Abram's fault. God forgave Abram's sin, but He did not prevent the sad consequences. We reap what we sow, even after we are forgiven. Abram's first test of faith came from a famine; his second test came from his own family. Family tests are the hardest tests of all.

Abram was a peacemaker because he lived by faith; Lot was a troublemaker because he lived by sight. Abram chose a heavenly city (Heb. 11:13–16); Lot chose an earthly city, and a wicked one at that. The city appeared to be ideal, but it was headed for destruction. You can move your tent nearer and nearer to sin, *but you cannot take your altar with you*. Lot left God behind and destroyed his home.

A new blessing (14–18). The man of faith always receives a special word from God after a time of testing. Let others take what they want; our God gives us far more than they can ever imagine (Pss. 16:5; 33:12). Abram lifted up his eyes and saw the land. He lifted up his feet and claimed it by faith (Josh. 1:3). Then he lifted up his heart and worshiped God. Lot had broken Abram's heart, but God blessed Abram's heart—and made him a blessing.

GENESIS 14

Abram won three victories.

A victory over Lot. It would have been easy for Abram to let Lot suffer the sad consequences of his own foolish decision. But a man of faith is called "to be a blessing," so Abram went to the rescue. Lot was not a very dedicated believer, but he was still a brother and needed help. When a brother or a sister creates problems for you, remember Abram and the words of Romans 12:21. Lot went right back into Sodom, but Abram did what he did for the Lord; and that's what really counts.

A victory over the kings. Abram the pilgrim would never have gotten involved in the war except to rescue Lot. Abram did not have a large army, but he battled by faith; that is what gave him the victory (1 Sam. 14:6; 1 John 5:4–5).

A victory over himself. "Let us be as watchful after the victory as before the battle," said Andrew Bonar. Abram was tempted to use God's victory for personal gain, but he refused the offer. The king of Sodom came with a bargain, but the king of Salem (a picture of our Lord Jesus Christ [Heb. 7:1–3]) came with a blessing. Even a shoelace from Sodom would have defiled Abram's godly walk! After every battle, give God the glory; and beware the devil's bargains. If you aren't careful, you may win the war and lose the victory.

GENESIS 15

Abram's reward was not the applause of the people he rescued but the approval of the God he served. This is the first of many "fear nots" in the Bible. Fear after a battle is not unusual, but fear and faith cannot live very long in the same heart (Matt. 8:26). Abram's fears were quieted by three revelations from God.

What God is (1). God is our protection and provision, so we need not fear the enemy without or our feelings within. God is the great I AM, and He can meet every need. With Him, we have everything; without Him, nothing we have is sufficient.

What God says (2–7). Abram looked at himself and realized how old he was getting. Then he looked at his steward, Eliezer, and thought perhaps God could use him. But God told him to stop looking at himself and at others and to start looking up to God. This is the second time he lifted up his eyes to see what God had for him (Gen. 13:14; see also 13:10). Verse 6 makes it clear that Abram was saved by faith in God's word (Rom. 4:3; Gal. 3:6; James 2:23), and that is the *only* way to be saved.

What God does (8–21). God sealed His promise with a covenant. In those days, to walk between the divided parts of an animal was one way to seal an agreement. *But God was the only One who passed between the pieces!* Abram was asleep! God's covenants are all of grace (Eph. 2:8–9), and our works are but evidence of our faith.

When you find yourself afraid or impatient with God's will, look toward heaven and remember His covenant and His promises. When you bring your offering to God, be sure the enemy doesn't steal it. When you can do nothing, rest assured God is at work.

Fear   *There is a godly fear, a reverence for the Lord, that must be in every heart (1 Pet. 1:17; 2:17). If we fear God, we need not fear anyone or anything else (Ps. 112; Isa. 8:13). The fear of man trips us up (Prov. 29:25), but if we fear God, we need not fear the words or threats of men (Matt. 10:26–33).*

GENESIS 16

Faith and patience always go together (Heb. 6:12; James 1:1–5). Isaiah declared, "Whoever believes will not act hastily" (Isa. 28:16). We must trust God not only for His plan but also for His timing. Before He could send the promised son, God had to wait until Abram and Sarai were as good as dead (Rom. 4:19–21; Heb. 11:11–12). Sarai leaned on human understanding instead of God's promises (Prov. 3:5–6). She trusted a woman from Egypt instead of the God of heaven.

Sarai was not a strong *believer,* but she was a capable *blamer.* She blamed God for her barrenness, then blamed Abram when Hagar created problems in the home. The wisdom from God is pure and peaceable, but the wisdom of the flesh is always divisive (James 3:13–18). Abram abdicated his spiritual leadership in the home, and the result was confusion.

When we walk by sight and not by faith, we get impatient; we scheme and blame others. Then when things go wrong, we try to get rid of our mistakes. God sent Hagar and Ishmael back to Abram and Sarai, and they had to live with their mistake for at least another seventeen years.

Abram and Sarai greatly wronged Hagar, and they suffered for it; but God stepped in and cared for her and her son. Abram obeyed God and gave the appointed name to his son: "Ishmael—God shall hear." Had Abram and Sarai waited on God instead of running ahead of God, they would have avoided all that pain.

GENESIS 17

New revelations. As far as the record is concerned, God waited thirteen years before He revealed Himself again to Abram. During those quiet intervening years, Abram continued to walk with God and serve Him. He did not need constant special revelations to do God's will, nor do we. God reaffirmed His covenant and then gave Abram the sign of circumcision as the mark of that covenant. How unfortunate that many of the Jews trusted in the sign rather than in the Lord (Acts 15:5; Rom. 4:10; Gal. 5:6)! God wanted an inward change of the heart, not just surgery on the body (Deut. 10:16; Jer. 4:4).

New names. In Bible history, a new name means a new beginning, a step forward in faith. (See Gen. 32:28; John 1:40–42.) *Abram* means "exalted father"; it became *Abraham,* "father of a multitude." *Sarai* ("contentious") became *Sarah,* "a princess." God even revealed a new name for Himself: God Almighty. The only name that did not change was Ishmael, for what is born of the flesh remains flesh and cannot be changed (John 3:6).

New joy. At last, the long-awaited son would be born, and his name would be "Isaac—laughter." No wonder Abraham laughed (John 8:56). Abraham wanted to cling to his past mistake (v. 18) instead of looking to the future miracle that God would perform. Abraham and Sarah's impatient act of unbelief had brought sorrow and division into the home, but God's miracle of faith brought joy and peace (Rom. 15:13). It pays to trust God's way and wait for God's time.

> ## God Almighty!
>
> *The Bible affirms our need to rely on God, for whom nothing is impossible (Luke 1:37): "Is anything too hard for the LORD?" (Gen. 18:14). "There is nothing too hard for You" (Jer. 32:17); God is "able to do exceedingly abundantly above all that we ask or think" (Eph. 3:20). So, we may say, "I can do all things through Christ who strengthens me" (Phil. 4:13). Lay hold of God's power!*

GENESIS 18

Resting (1). Resting in the afternoon is a normal practice in the East, and don't forget that Abraham was nearly a hundred years old. Sometimes the most spiritual thing we can do is take a nap! The believer's body is God's temple and must be cared for (1 Cor. 6:19–20). (See Mark 6:31.)

Serving (2–8). Abraham had no trouble noticing the pilgrims because it was unusual for people to travel in the heat of the day. The visitors were two angels and the Lord Jesus Christ, in one of His preincarnation appearances. Even though he had 318 servants, Abraham served Him personally, and fourteen times he called Him "Lord." Abraham ran from place to place to make certain the meal they were preparing was the very best.

Listening (9–15). Abraham stood nearby as the visitors ate, ready to serve them whatever they wanted. But the Lord gave Abraham something better than food: He announced that the promised son would be born within the year. "Where is Sarah your wife?" is the last of three key questions in Genesis (3:9; 4:9; 18:9). The question "Is anything too hard for the LORD?" has been answered by Job (Job 42:2), Jeremiah (Jer. 32:17), and Gabriel (Luke 1:37).

Interceding (16–33). Because Abraham was both the friend of God and the servant of God, he shared God's secrets. (See Ps. 25:14; John 15:15; James 2:23.) Lot had been rescued by Abraham's intervention (chap. 14); now he would be rescued by Abraham's intercession. Abraham prayed for the city on the basis of the justice of God, but God saved Lot on the basis of His mercy and grace (19:16, 19). Interceding for the lost and for needy saints is a high and holy privilege that we must not neglect.

GENESIS 19

Because Jesus did not "feel at home" with Lot in Sodom, He sent the two angels to look into the situation for Him. The angels didn't walk the streets or visit the public places of amusement. *They visited a professed believer to see what his home was like.* Lot's wife and family were far from the Lord. The salt had lost its flavor (Matt. 5:13), so what hope was there for the city?

Abraham was visited when it was light, but Lot received the angels at evening (1 John 1:5–10). Abraham's household obeyed his word as he served the Lord, but Lot's family only laughed at Lot's words. Abraham hastened, but Lot lingered and had to be dragged out of the city. Abraham, who lived outside Sodom, had more influence than Lot, who lived in the city.

Lot tried first to plead with the men at the door, and then to bargain with them. God's approach was to judge them. They loved darkness rather than light (John 3:19).

God did not find ten righteous people, but He spared Lot and his wife and daughters for the sake of Abraham. While we may hate the sins of Sodom, keep in mind that all those people went to eternal judgment. (See Jude 23.)

Lot had no tent or altar, and he ended up in a cave committing terrible sins. Were it not for 2 Peter 2:7–8, we might doubt that he was a believer at all. (See Ps. 1:1.)

GENESIS 20

Relapse. The man of faith started walking by sight (v. 11), became frightened (Prov. 29:25), and began scheming (Gen.

12:10ff.). This time, even Sarah lied (v. 5)! Whatever we carry with us from the old life (v. 13) will create problems in the new life. It is one thing to *confess* our sins but another thing to *judge* them before God and forsake them (Prov. 28:13). When a marriage must be protected by a lie, the home is in danger.

Revelation. God spoke to the heathen king but not to His own friend, Abraham! Although God kept the king from sinning, He allowed Abraham to lie! God called Abraham to be a blessing, but now he had become a curse in the land. God was protecting Sarah, Isaac, and His great plan of salvation.

Rebuke. What a humiliating thing to be openly rebuked by a pagan king. God sometimes uses the unsaved to chasten the saved. The fact that Abraham was a believer did not give him license to sin. Unfortunately, years later, Abraham's son Isaac would imitate his father's sin (Gen. 26).

Restoration. In those days, the paying of a large sum of money was public "atonement" for guilt; however, sin is never profitable. God did not forsake His friend (Ps. 105:15; 2 Tim. 2:12-13) but honored him in the end and answered his prayer. Financially, Abraham was richer; spiritually, he was poorer. He lost character as well as opportunity to witness and glorify God.

GENESIS 21

Family joys (1-7). God kept His promises, followed His schedule, and did not fail. This time, Sarah's laughter was open and sincere, not hidden and skeptical (Gen. 18:12). The name *Isaac* means "laughter," and the boy brought much joy to the aged couple. Through him, joy has come to the world. God makes "everything beautiful in its time" (Eccles. 3:11).

Family sorrows (8-21). Abraham reaped the sad consequences of forgiven sin. He had lived with Ishmael for perhaps seventeen years, and he loved the lad, so the parting was painful. There comes a time when we must "cut off" the past and make a new beginning. The apostle Paul saw this as a picture of law and grace (Gal. 4:21-31). For Abraham's sake, God blessed the lad and made him a great nation.

Family testimony (22-34). Abraham's unsaved neighbors could tell that he was a man whom God had blessed. Abraham didn't try to lie his way out of this problem; he boldly told the truth and trusted God to work. The possession of water is an important thing in the East, and people will fight over wells. God's people must be careful in their relationships with "those who are outside" the faith (Col. 4:5; 1 Thess. 4:12).

Life is a balance of joys and sorrows, problems and blessings. We must learn to accept what God gives us and walk by faith.

GENESIS 22

Offering Isaac on the altar was the hardest test Abraham ever faced, but he came through victoriously because he trusted God (Heb. 11:17–19). He had experienced resurrection power in his own body (Rom. 4:19–21), so he knew what God could do. It was a test of *faith,* far more difficult than the previous tests involving Lot and Ishmael.

It was also a test of *hope,* for God's plan of salvation for the world was wrapped up in Isaac. If Isaac died, how could the Jewish nation be built and the Savior be born? But Abraham had a living hope because he trusted in the living God (1 Pet. 1:3).

Certainly it was a test of *love.* In verse 2, you find the first use of the word *love* in the Bible. Abraham loved his son, but he loved God more. Isaac was God's gift to Abraham, but the gift had to become a sacrifice to God. If the gift becomes more important than the Giver, it becomes an idol.

After He tests us, God reveals Himself to us in a new way (John 14:21–23). The name *Jehovah-Yireh* means "the Lord will see to it" or "the Lord will provide." The ram was God's provision for Isaac, and Jesus Christ is God's provision for the whole world. In this experience, Abraham saw Christ by faith and rejoiced (John 8:56).

Why this "family news" in verses 20–24? To introduce us to Rebekah who will become the bride of Isaac (chap. 24). Isaac was a "living sacrifice" (Rom. 12:1–2), and God was working out His perfect will for him.

GENESIS 23

Abraham the mourner. Sarah is the only woman named in the Bible whose age is given and burial described. It was the death of a princess, a woman of faith (Heb. 11:11–13; 1 Pet. 3:6). Abraham felt the pain of his loss and openly expressed his grief. Faith is not the enemy of tears, for we sorrow as those who have hope (1 Thess. 4:13–18). Jesus wept (John 11:35) even though He knew He would raise His friend from the dead.

Abraham the sojourner. Ephron did not plan to *give* Abraham a valuable piece of land, but that is how typical Eastern bargaining always begins. The land already belonged to Abraham (15:7), but he could never explain that to his unbelieving neighbors. He was a pilgrim and did not claim any of it for himself.

Abraham the owner. He paid a high price for what became one of the most famous tombs in Bible history, and eventually six people were buried there (49:31–32). Abraham owned only one thing on earth: a grave. Genesis ends with a full tomb, but the gospel story ends with an empty tomb! And because Jesus Christ lives, we who trust in Him never need fear death.

GENESIS 24

This is the longest chapter in Genesis, and it focuses on faith, hope, and love.

The father (1–9) loved his son and wanted a bride for him. He had faith that God would keep His promise (Gen. 12:2) and provide the bride. Note that the bride could not be an outsider (1 Cor. 7:39). Is this whole event not a picture of the heavenly Father getting a bride for His Son?

The servant (10–49) loved his master's son and asked for God's guidance. He knew how to "watch and pray" and discern God's leading. He was not disappointed, for God rewarded his faith. Little did Rebekah realize that a small act of kindness would open up an exciting new life for her. "Make every occasion a great occasion, for you can never tell when someone may be taking your measure for a larger place," advised Marsden. The servant talked about his master and not about himself, and he would not eat until he had given his message (John 4:31–32).

The bride (50–60) had nothing to go on but the treasures she saw and the words she heard from the servant. In spite of those who urged her to delay, she made a decision of faith and said, "I will go!" This is an illustration of personal salvation.

The Spirit speaks to us about Christ and shows us His treasures, and we trust Christ even though we have never seen Him (1 Pet. 1:8).

The bridegroom (61–67) was last seen on the mountain with his father (chap. 22), but now he comes to meet his bride at eventide. That is what Jesus Christ will do when He returns for His church. Then we shall see Him and be like Him (1 John 3:1–2).

GENESIS 25

The center of attention now shifts from Abraham to Isaac.

Isaac the heir. God's resurrection power continued to work in Abraham; he married again and begat six more sons. God is not likely to do this for people today, but the spiritual lesson is clear: we should be fruitful even in old age (Ps. 92:14). Abraham distinguished Isaac from his other sons: he gave them generous gifts, but he made Isaac his heir (v. 5; 24:35). God gives good things to unsaved people (Matt. 5:45; Acts 14:17; 17:25), but only those who are His children, through faith in Christ, can claim their inheritance. (See Rom. 8:17; Eph. 3:6; Heb. 1:2.)

Isaac the orphan. Abraham lived by faith and died by faith (Heb. 11:13), and God kept His word (Gen. 15:15). Isaac and Ishmael together mourned their father's death, for death is a human experience that binds all men together. Unsaved relatives share in times of sorrow, but their grief is hopeless without Jesus Christ. Compare Ishmael's death (v. 17) with that of Abraham.

Isaac the intercessor. Isaac was forty years old when he married Rebekah. For twenty years, they waited for a family that did not come. God blessed Isaac in everything but the thing he wanted most. He and Rebekah knew that God had promised descendants (Gen. 15:5), so Isaac laid hold of the promise and prayed. True prayer lays hold of God's Word (John 15:7) and seeks to accomplish God's purposes.

Isaac the father. God gave them twin boys who were opposite each other in every way. He also gave them a revelation that the younger one, Jacob, would carry on the messianic line. For that reason, you would think that Isaac would have favored Jacob, but the physical won over the spiritual. Esau pictures the man of the world who despises the eternal and lives for the temporal.

GENESIS 26

Faith cannot grow apart from trials, and this chapter records several trials that Isaac endured and shows how he responded to them.

Escape (1–6). Like Abraham, Isaac started for Egypt (12:10ff.); but God stopped him at the border (10:19) and reassured him. Isaac was blessed because of Abraham (vv. 5, 24). We must never forget our debt to spiritual leaders (and relatives) who have gone before us.

Deception (7–14). While in enemy territory, Isaac resorted to the "family lie" that twice got Abraham into trouble (12:10ff.; 20:1ff.). It is sad when the new generation imitates the sins of the old generation. God blessed Isaac in a material way, but we wonder what his spiritual life was like. Did his neighbors trust him after hearing about his lie?

Surrender (15–25). Water is a very precious commodity in desert country, and possessing a well is almost the same as having a deed to the land. Instead of defending what his men had done, Isaac moved to new locations. He may have been practicing Romans 12:18.

Confrontation (26–35). In contrast to his father Abraham, who dared to declare war, Isaac was a quiet, meditative man who tried to avoid trouble. He boldly faced his neighbors with their bad conduct—and he won! Note that he went the extra mile and entertained the men at a feast. (See Rom. 12:18–21.)

GENESIS 27

A wrong decision. It was only a matter of time before the divided home would start to self-destruct, and it all began with Isaac. He knew that God had chosen Jacob, the younger son, to receive the blessing (Gen. 25:23–26); but he announced that he would give it to Esau. It seems that Isaac was more interested in his physical appetite than in spiritual things. He was not the spiritual person he once had been.

A wrong solution. Rebekah knew what God's promise was

to Jacob, and she should have let God work it out in His own way. "Faith is living without scheming," and who can hinder the Lord from accomplishing His purposes (Dan. 4:35)? Instead, she made her son a liar and deceived her husband. If Isaac had trusted the Lord instead of his physical senses (vv. 21, 22, 25, 27), he would not have been fooled.

A wrong attitude. Esau had made it clear years before that he was not interested in spiritual things (Gen. 25:29–34), and certainly he knew God's word about the blessing. He wept (Heb. 12:17) and begged for a blessing, and then he plotted to kill his brother! His heart was not right with God or man. We are reminded of Cain (Gen. 4).

Rebekah's "a few days" (v. 44) became over twenty years! Despite all her scheming, she never saw her son on earth again.

GENESIS 28

A day of disappointment (1–9). Jacob was a lonely fugitive, forced to flee from home. Even though he left with his father's blessing (and Isaac knew what he was doing), Jacob faced an unknown future, and his brother still wanted to kill him. Not an encouraging beginning for a new chapter in his life! But God was still in control (Rom. 8:28).

A night of discovery (10–15). Jacob was literally between a rock and a hard place. But that night, Jacob made several discoveries that helped to change his life. He discovered that God was with him and working for him and had a perfect plan for his life. Jacob may have been separated from home, but he was not separated from heaven. (See John 1:51.) The very angels of God were caring for him (Heb. 1:13–14). "When the night is the darkest, you see the stars the brightest."

A morning of dedication (16–22). Jacob began his day worshiping God and turning his hard pillow into a holy altar. He gave the place a new name: "house of God." Wherever God meets us, that place becomes a holy sanctuary. Jacob's faith as yet was weak, but he did lay hold of God's promises, even if there is a bit of "the bargainer" in his vow to give God the tithe. Jacob was making a new beginning, and twenty years later he would return to Bethel a more mature believer.

GENESIS 29

Abraham's faithful servant had found a wife for Isaac, but Jacob had to find his own wife. God's plans are different for each of us, and we must accept His will (Phil. 2:12–13).

The guest (1–14). God's providence brought Jacob to the well just as Rachel was arriving. (See Gen. 24:27.) True to his scheming nature, Jacob tried to get rid of the shepherds so he could have her all to himself! It was love at first sight. That first month in Uncle Laban's home must have been heaven on earth to Jacob, but it didn't take long for things to change.

The worker (15–30). Jacob was not wealthy as Isaac was when he got his wife (Gen. 24:36, 53), so he had to work for his uncle to have the woman he loved. But love takes the burden out of work and makes time pass quickly. Jacob the schemer met his match in Laban and soon began to reap what he had sown. Jacob had deceived his father, and his father-in-law deceived him.

The father (31–35). The building of Jacob's family was vitally important to God's plan of salvation, for God would use the nation of Israel to give the world the Bible and the Redeemer. Although Rachel had great beauty, she was unable to conceive, while Leah gave birth to four sons: Reuben ("see, a son!"), Simeon ("hearing"), Levi ("joined"), and Judah ("praise"). The Lord was in control and had a special purpose for each son (Ps. 139:14–16; Eccles. 3:2).

GENESIS 30

There are two major themes in this chapter: the building of Jacob's family (vv. 1–24), and the building of Jacob's fortune (vv. 25–43). Various people (including Jacob) thought they were in control of the situation, but all of it was in the hands of God.

Having grown up his mother's favored son (25:28), Jacob was accustomed to a woman telling him what to do. But now he had *four* different women involved in his life! When he came home from the fields, he never knew which one he would be living with! The schemer discovered the pain that people feel when their lives are selfishly manipulated by others.

Rachel will have only two sons, Joseph and Benjamin, and Joseph will save the whole family from destruction.

Laban tried to trick Jacob and make him poor, but God overruled and made Jacob a very wealthy man. In fact, God even blessed Laban because of Jacob, and the old trickster admitted it (v. 27)! It was God's blessing and not Jacob's schemes that increased the flocks. God was keeping the promises He had made at Bethel (28:13–15). When we are in difficult situations, we can trust God to care for us.

GENESIS 31

Escape. The family situation was not at all comfortable for Jacob or his wives, but he patiently waited for God's instructions before making a move. The seeking heart will always get a word from God when decisions have to be made. Read Psalm 25 in the light of Jacob's situation. Like his mother before him, Jacob did a right thing in a wrong way, and God had to intervene to protect him (v. 24).

Encounter. Jacob had a three-day lead on Laban, but his father-in-law finally caught up with him. No one can successfully run away from problems. Laban accused Jacob of a breach of social custom, while Jacob accused Laban of breaking his promises for twenty years. There was also the matter of the household gods, for whoever had them could claim possession of Laban's property.

Expedience. The two men never did agree, and their problems were not solved. Instead, they declared a truce and made a pile of stones the boundary beyond which neither would pass. It was called "the heap of witness" to remind Jacob and Laban that God was watching both of them. (The word *Mizpah* means "watchtower.") The so-called Mizpah benediction is not a correct interpretation or application of this passage.

It is better to declare a truce than to wage a war, but the best decision of all is for brethren to "dwell together in unity" (Ps. 133:1). See Ephesians 4:25–32 for directions.

GENESIS 32

Jacob expected a battle and his concern was escape, not reconciliation (v. 8). He saw the army of angels protecting him, but even that didn't encourage his faith. *Mahanaim* means "double camp"—his camp and the camp of God's angels. Had Jacob recalled his experience with God at Bethel, he would not have been afraid of Esau (28:13–15).

One minute Jacob prayed for God's help, and the next minute he devised some new way to appease his angry brother. He reminded God of His great promises and then acted as though God had never spoken. This is the conduct of a believer who needed to be broken before God. He prayed to be delivered from Esau (v. 11), but his greatest need was to be delivered from himself.

Jacob was broken to be healed and weakened to be strengthened. When he surrendered, he won and became a "prince with God." His limp would be a constant reminder that God would be in control of his life. "God fights *against* us with His left hand and *for* us with His right hand," wrote John Calvin. When we let God have His way, it is the dawning of a new day (v. 31).

GENESIS 33

Jacob had seen God and been given a new name, but the benefits of his experience didn't appear immediately. Sometimes he acted like Jacob ("the heel-catcher") and sometimes like Israel ("the prince with God"). Many of God's people fail to live up to their new life in Christ because they don't claim what they have by faith. God had to give Jacob a limp to encourage him to walk by faith.

In his attempt to appease Esau, the old schemer used several devices: bowing (vv. 1–7), bribery (vv. 8–11), outright lying (vv. 12–16), and then moving off in another direction (vv. 17–20). Esau went south and Jacob went east! Princes are not supposed to bow, and what about God's promise in Genesis 25:23 and 27:29?

One mistake often leads to another. Jacob ceased to be a pilgrim, purchased the land he was already given by God, built a house, and settled down. He built an altar and called on "God, the God of Israel" (note the new name); but that didn't prevent him from getting into trouble with the neighbors. Far better had he pressed on to Bethel.

GENESIS 34

Defilement. Lot pitched his tent toward Sodom and lost his daughters (19:30ff.), and Jacob moved too close to Shechem and lost Dinah. She was the daughter of Leah (30:21), which explains why Simeon and Levi became so angry (35:23). Had nobody warned her? Was she out looking for opportunities to sin? Or was she completely overpowered by the prince? It may have been love at first sight, but that didn't lessen the guilt or tragedy of the sin.

Deception. Note the twofold attempt at deception: Simeon and Levi deceived Hamor, and Hamor thought he deceived them. Jacob's sons had learned much from watching their father. Dinah's two brothers were preparing for war while the men of Shechem were preparing for wealth. When the men of the city were unable to fight, Simeon and Levi killed all the men and took the spoils. It was another case of promoting a holy cause in an unholy way and being motivated by hatred of the enemy instead of love for the truth.

Disgrace. Jacob was more concerned about his safety and his reputation than he was the character and conduct of his ruthless sons. Although Jacob was not to blame for their deed, had he not settled near Shechem, this tragedy would not have occurred. On his deathbed, Jacob brought the matter up again (49:5–7). How gracious of God to make the tribe of Levi the priestly tribe! (See Rom. 5:20.)

GENESIS 35—36

New beginnings. God once more appeared and told Jacob what to do. This was a part of the Bethel promise (28:13–15). We walk by faith when we obey God in spite of circumstances or consequences. But a change in geography does not guarantee a change in life, so Jacob told the whole family to bury the past and get rid of their heathen charms and idols. At Bethel, Jacob built a new altar and worshiped "the God of the house of God."

New sorrows. Three deaths are recorded in chapter 35, for death is one of the facts of life. Jacob's obedience to God did not prevent him for experiencing trials. He lost a friend,

Deborah; a favorite wife, Rachel; and then his beloved father. (In spite of what he said in 27:2, Isaac lived for forty-three years after that!) Perhaps the greatest sorrow of all was the sin of his firstborn son Reuben. Sin is expensive, and this one cost Reuben the birthright (49:3–4; 1 Chron. 5:1).

New joys. The birth of Benjamin cost Rachel her life (30:1). Jacob wisely changed the name from "son of my sorrow" to "son of my right hand" (the place of honor). It was an act of faith at a time when Jacob's heart was broken. Like Benjamin, our Lord Jesus is a Son of sorrow (Isa. 53:3) and a Son of the right hand (Ps. 110:1; Mark 16:19). The tribe of Benjamin gave us the apostle Paul (Phil. 3:5), so the mother's sacrifice bore a rich harvest for the whole world (John 12:24–25).

Since the family was complete, the sons and mothers were listed. Esau's family tree is much more imposing than Jacob's, but this is the last we hear of it. Despite their failures, the sons of Israel are the chosen instruments to accomplish God's will on earth.

GENESIS 37

As you read the life of Joseph, you see in him a picture of the Lord Jesus Christ. Joseph was greatly loved by his father (v. 3; Matt. 3:17), hated and envied by his brothers (John 15:25; Mark 15:10), plotted against, sold as a slave, arrested unjustly, and made to suffer. But he went from suffering to glory and became the savior of the people who had rejected him.

God's goal for all His children is that we become like His Son (Rom. 8:29). The goal is glorious, but the process is painful. Both Jesus and Joseph had to suffer before they could enter into their glory (Luke 24:26; 1 Pet. 5:10). Had Joseph remained at home, his father probably would have pampered him and ruined his character. God knew what was best.

Joseph's dreams were to him what God's Word is to us today: they gave him the assurance he needed when the going was hard.

Again, Jacob reaped what he had sown. He had killed a beast and lied to his father (27:9ff.), and his own sons lied to him.

GENESIS 38

Marrying a Canaanite woman was disobedience on Judah's part (24:3; 2 Cor. 6:14—7:1). When one gets away from the family of God, it is easy to fall into temptation and sin (Ps. 1:1). Two of his sons were slain by God, and then his wife died. What tragedy!

It was expected that the next son would marry the widow and thus preserve the family, but Judah probably did not intend to keep his promise (v. 11). Tamar's purpose was good, but her plan was wicked. Leaving the signet and staff was like leaving fingerprints, because each man's was distinctive. Judah was quick to condemn Tamar for sinning, but what about his own sins toward Joseph and Tamar?

Why is this sordid chapter in the Bible? For one thing, we see the contrast between Judah's sin and Joseph's victory (chap. 39), and we realize the importance of purity. But the main reason is to add another link in the Redeemer's family tree (v. 29; Ruth 4:18-22; Matt. 1:3). How gracious God is to mention a prostitute like Tamar in the genealogy of the Savior!

GENESIS 39—40

The key to Joseph's conduct was his godly character, and the basis for that character was his recognition that he belonged to God and served Him (39:9). "The LORD was with Joseph" is often repeated (39:2, 3, 21, 23).

The Lord is with us as we work, and we should do our work as unto Him (Eph. 6:5-8). He is with us when we are tempted and will show us the way to escape (1 Cor. 10:13). We must keep away from temptation (Rom. 13:14); and if it gets too close, we must run away (2 Tim. 2:22). It is better to flee and lose your garment than fall and lose your character.

God is with us as we wait. Joseph spent two difficult years working in the prison, but he held to his faith and did what he could to serve others. The experience helped to "put iron into his soul" (Ps. 105:17-22). If the Lord controls us, it makes little difference who commands us.

The fact that Joseph could interpret the dreams of the

baker and butler indicates that he understood the meaning of his own dreams. He knew that one day his eleven brothers would have to bow before him. What an encouragement that was to his faith!

GENESIS 41

Explanation. For two years, Joseph was forgotten by the chief butler, but he was not forgotten by the Lord. It is disappointing to depend on people, for often their help never comes (Pss. 60:11; 146:3). Speaking to the world's greatest ruler, Joseph was careful to give all the glory to God (vv. 16, 25, 28, 32).

Exaltation. God always exalts the humble "in due time" (1 Pet. 5:6). Joseph started as a servant, but then God made him a ruler (Matt. 25:21). He experienced suffering before God gave him glory (1 Pet. 5:10). God invested thirteen years in making a man out of Joseph; when it comes to building character, God is never in a hurry.

Expectation. Joseph's new name probably means "the one who furnishes nourishment to the land." He married an Egyptian wife, and she bore him two sons who were given significant names: Manasseh ("one who forgets") and Ephraim ("double fruit"). Joseph determined to forget the past and live for the future. In the Bible, *forgetting* means "not holding it against another." Joseph certainly did not forget what his brothers did, but he did not hold it against them. Instead, he concentrated on living a fruitful life to the glory of God.

GENESIS 42—44

These chapters describe Joseph's dealings with his brothers and the brothers' consequent confrontations with their father. The ten brothers had sinned against both Jacob and Joseph, but they thought that Joseph was dead and their sin was safely hidden. Joseph had to deal with them patiently, honestly, and decisively, just the way the Lord works with us when we have tried to cover our sins.

Joseph's immediate goal was to get all eleven brothers to Egypt so they could bow before him and fulfill the dream God had given him more than twenty years before. His ultimate goal was to get them to confess their sins and be reconciled to him and Jacob. The men had to come to the place where their mouths were stopped (44:16; Rom. 3:19).

In a masterful way, Joseph wove these two purposes together as he spoke roughly to them, accused them of crimes, and insisted on their bringing Benjamin to Egypt. Outwardly, he was a stern ruler; but behind the scenes, he was a weeping brother.

Jacob's responses mirror our responses to God's providential disciplines: "Everything is against me!" (42:36); "Why didn't you do it differently?" (43:6); "Take a gift along" (43:11 [always the schemer!]); "If it has to be, it has to be!" (43:14). From pessimism to fatalism, and very little faith.

GENESIS 45

Recognition. When Joseph saw that his brothers' hearts were humble, and when he heard them confess their sins, he knew it was safe to reveal his identity to them. Had he done it earlier, they would not have been ready for the blessings he had for them; and had he waited longer, the men might have been in total despair. Our Lord knows just how to work in our lives to bring us to submission. Joseph could have fed them and their father without going through this lengthy procedure, but it would only have further ruined their character.

Reconciliation. Joseph said, "Please come near to me" (v. 4). He had forgiven them, but they were still afraid. In fact, they would still be afraid seventeen years later (50:15–21). In Jesus Christ, we have been reconciled to God, and we need not fear judgment (Rom. 8:1; 2 Cor. 5:18; Col. 1:20). God wants us to draw near to Him (Heb. 10:19–25; James 4:8).

Reassurance. Joseph explained to them that God had sent him before them to preserve the nation so that Israel could be a blessing to all the earth (12:1–3). God's providential purpose did not minimize their sins or negate their responsibility (Acts 2:23; 3:13–18), but it did help to ease their fear and sorrow. Joseph further reassured them by giving them rich gifts and promising to care for the whole family. The gifts he sent home helped to give Jacob the assurance he needed that Joseph indeed was alive.

Joseph knew his brothers, so he admonished them: "Don't be angry with yourselves!" (v. 5), and "Don't quarrel on the journey!" (v. 24). We quickly lose the blessing when we fail to accept Christ's forgiveness and then love one another. (See 1 John 4:7ff.)

GENESIS 46—47

It would not be easy for Jacob, now 130 years old, to leave the land God gave him and go to Egypt. Moving to a new home is usually a difficult experience, and the older we are, the more difficult it is. Furthermore, Abraham got into trouble in Egypt (12:10ff.), and God had stopped Isaac from going there (26:2ff.).

But Jacob was able to go with confidence and peace because he was sure of God's promise and presence (46:1–4). In the crisis hours of life, God speaks to us and assures us when we take time to worship. Furthermore, Jacob knew that God had gone before him and that Joseph was there making everything ready for him. The future is your friend when Jesus is your Lord and you follow Him.

Jacob was a blessing in Egypt. He blessed Pharaoh (47:7, 10), Joseph and Joseph's sons (48:15, 20), and all twelve of the sons of Israel (49:1ff.). God blesses us that we might be a blessing. Circumstances change, but God never changes.

Egypt was a haven for Jacob and his family, and there God protected them and built of them a great people. But Jacob knew that Egypt was not his home, Canaan was; and he wanted to be buried there with the others who had made the same pilgrimage of faith. He was a testimony in life, and he wanted to be a testimony in death. Despite his mistakes and failures in life, Jacob ended well.

GENESIS 48—49

What should believers do for their family before God takes them in death? Just what Jacob did.

He praised God for the past. He told his family what God had done for him and how God had blessed him. God had redeemed him and shepherded him all his life (48:15–16). Jacob had been in some hard places, but the "Stone of Israel" had been his refuge and defense (49:24). At the end of life, may we be able to say, "Come, you children, listen to me; I will teach you the fear of the LORD" (Ps. 34:11).

He gave a blessing while he could. Reuben's sin cost him the blessing of the firstborn, which went to Joseph's sons. (See Gen. 35:22; 1 Chron. 5:1–2.) Again, God changed the birth order as Jacob put Ephraim ahead of Manasseh. Joseph was disturbed by the move, but Jacob was right. We must never try to tell God how to bless other people. Note that Jacob crossed his arms. Is this perhaps a picture of the Cross that sets aside the first birth and gives us a second birth?

He warned about the future. Chapter 49 is not a father's blessing on his sons. Rather, it is a prophecy of what the sons could expect in the future because of their individual characters and the decisions they had made. Reuben was the lustful prodigal son, but Levi and Simeon were angry elder brothers. Judah would be the royal tribe, for the Messiah (Shiloh, "the peace-bringer") would come from Judah. Joseph was the vine that went over the wall separating Jews and Gentiles. He was shot at by his brethren, which often happens to those who are especially blessed of God. But the Lord was with him, strengthened him, and extended his boundaries of blessing (v. 26). Joseph suffered, and his sons were blessed by God. Reuben sinned, and his sons lost the blessing of God.

GENESIS 50

Three burials are mentioned in this final chapter of Genesis, and each is significant.

Burying a beloved father. It is instructive to contrast the simple Jewish funerals with the elaborate burial customs of the Egyptians. There is certainly nothing wrong with caring for the body and expressing grief, so long as we keep things in perspective. Jacob died in faith and was a pilgrim to the very end (Heb. 11:21). He started with his staff and ended with his staff (32:10; 1 Tim. 6:7).

Burying the past. Joseph's brothers did not really believe that Joseph had forgiven them, even though they had heard his words, seen his tears, felt his kisses, and received his gifts (45:1–15). Like the prodigal son, they offered to work their way into his favor (Luke 15:19). Their attitude grieved Joseph, who had endured so much for them, just as we grieve our Lord when we doubt His forgiveness and love (Rom. 8:31–39).

Burying a devoted brother. Like his father, Joseph knew what he believed and where he belonged. If we consider all the difficulties he had experienced in life, it is remarkable that Joseph had any faith at all. He knew God's promise to Abraham that the nation would be delivered from Egypt (15:12–16), and he reiterated that promise to his family. Joseph had brought them to Egypt and cared for them in Egypt. His coffin reminded them that God would bring them out of Egypt. What an encouragement that was during the dark days of their bondage. Our encouragement today is not a coffin but an empty tomb (1 Pet. 1:3ff.).

EXODUS

Exodus means "going out." The book has three main themes.

Liberation (1—18). This section describes Jehovah's victory over the gods of Egypt and the deliverance of His people from bondage. The emphasis is on *the hand of God.* (See 3:20; 7:4-5; 9:3, 15; 13:3, 9, 14, 16.) The Exodus is a picture of the redemption we have through faith in Jesus Christ, the Lamb of God (John 1:29; 1 Cor. 5:7; 1 Pet. 1:18-21).

Separation (19—24). God and Israel entered into covenant relationship at Sinai. God gave them His law that they might be separated from the other nations and devoted wholly to Him. The emphasis is on *the holiness of God.* While God's people today are not obligated to obey all these precepts, the basic principles are timeless and apply to holy living today.

Habitation (25—40). God had walked with His people in Genesis, but now He wanted to dwell with them. The emphasis is on *the house of God* and the priests who ministered there. The book of Hebrews in the New Testament explains how the tabernacle ministry foreshadowed the work of Jesus Christ and His present ministry in heaven as High Priest. Today, God's people are His temple (1 Cor. 6:19-20; Eph. 2:20-22).

EXODUS 1

The nation growing. God promised that the descendants of Abraham would multiply greatly, and they did (Gen. 13:16; 15:5). God keeps His word and accomplishes His purposes in His time. Over the centuries, nations have tried to destroy Israel but have not succeeded. God gave Israel a special promise in Genesis 12:3, and He is keeping it. God's children today should pray for Israel (Ps. 122:6), share the gospel with them

(Rom. 1:16), and minister to them in practical ways (Rom. 15:25–27).

The nation groaning. God told Abraham that his people would experience suffering (Gen. 15:13–14). It is easy for nations and local churches to forget the heroes of yesterday (Heb. 13:7–8). Although we must not "embalm" the past, we certainly must not forget those who helped to make our future possible.

The new Pharaoh was more concerned about national security than human decency. When people become a means to an end instead of an end in themselves, we are not treating them as God wants us to. Enslaving the men and killing the baby boys were Egypt's solution to "the Jewish problem."

The midwives believed in obeying God rather than men (Acts 5:29). Thank God for concerned people who will courageously defend the little ones! God rewarded the women, not by making them sterile (which would have been safer), but by *giving them families!* This shows how valuable children are in the sight of God (Ps. 127:3–5). Ponder the words of our Lord in Matthew 18:1–6.

Obeying God

Moses' parents and the Jewish midwives are not the only ones in Bible history who had the courage to put God's will ahead of man's law. Daniel and his friends (Dan. 1), the three Hebrew men (Dan. 3), and the apostles (Acts 4:19–20; 5:29) are other examples. Their aim was not to oppose a bad law but to uphold the glory and truth of God.

EXODUS 2

Moses' parents, Amram and Jochebed (Exod. 6:20), knew that the times were difficult, but they had faith to get married and have a family (Acts 7:20; Heb. 11:23). Aaron and Miriam were already in the home when Moses was born. It was not easy to provide for another child, but God enabled them, as He still does parents today.

It also took faith for the parents to put their son into the river, obeying at least the spirit of the Egyptian law. God rewarded their faith. Jochebed not only got her son back, but she was paid to take care of him!

Moses had a splendid education (Acts 7:22), but he was lacking in faith. He fought the wrong enemy at the wrong time with the wrong weapon. When you start to look around and ask yourself "Is it safe?" and not "Is it right?" you have stopped living by faith. Sometimes God has to "set us aside" to teach us what we need to know—and to help us forget the way the world does things. Moses' impulsive deed sent him to the back of the desert for forty years, just as his impulsive words would keep him out of the Promised Land (Num. 20:9–13). An impatient spirit is a dangerous thing.

Impulsive People—Prov. 19:2

Moses	Exod. 2:11–14; Num. 20:9–13
David	1 Sam. 25:1–13
Elijah	1 Kings 19:1–3
Peter	John 18:10
Mary Magdalene	John 20:1–2

EXODUS 3

You never know what a day may bring, so keep your eyes and ears open to the leading of the Lord. Childlike curiosity completely changed Moses' life. God calls busy people to serve Him, and He reveals Himself to them.

God is faithful. He called Abraham, cared for Isaac, guided and protected Jacob, and He would be with Moses. He is the God of the individual as well as the nation, and He does not change from generation to generation.

God is concerned and compassionate. He saw the afflic-
tion of His people, and He heard their cries. Then why didn't
He act sooner? Because He was following a perfect timetable
(Gen. 15:13–16). You must learn to wait on the Lord. (See Ps. 37.)

God is long-suffering. The Lord answered all of Moses' ob-
jections and gave one assurance after another to encourage
him. Moses said, "I am not!" and God replied, "I AM!" Faith
lays hold of what God is and obeys what God says. Faith sees
the opportunities while unbelief sees the obstacles. Are you
arguing with God about something He wants you to do?

EXODUS 4

Forty years before, Moses was sure he could solve his people's problems; but now that God had called him, he was sure
he would fail. He could give no reasons for disobeying God,
but he certainly had plenty of excuses. "An excuse is the skin
of a reason stuffed with a lie," observed Billy Sunday. But God
gave Moses everything he needed for success. All he had to do
was trust the great I AM.

Credentials. If we give God what we have, He can use it for
His glory: a rod, a sling (1 Sam. 17:40), a net (Luke 5:1–11), or a
little lunch (John 6:9). He can even use the hand if *nothing* is in
it!

Companion. God already had Aaron prepared and on his
way to meet Moses. While Aaron at times created some problems for Moses, he was still a valued helper in the work. He
was the speaker, and Moses was the doer. But in time, Moses
himself became a great orator.

Commission. God spoke to Moses and gave him the instructions and encouragement he needed (vv. 19–23). Before he
arrived in Egypt, Moses knew that his work would be difficult
and that Pharaoh would oppose him.

Chastening. Moses was chastened by God and almost
died because he had failed to make his child a son of the covenant (Gen. 17:10). How could Moses lead Israel if his own family was not dedicated to God? (See 1 Tim. 3:5.)

Conviction. Moses was sure nobody would believe him;
however, when the elders saw the signs and heard the message, they believed and bowed to worship God.

When you face a tough job and you are afraid that you will

fail, remember Moses. God keeps His promises, no matter how you feel or how people respond.

EXODUS 5—6

When Moses and Aaron began their work in Egypt, their first problem was with Pharaoh (5:1-9). Not only did Pharaoh refuse to let the people leave Egypt, but he made their work more difficult. That gave Moses a second problem—his own people, who blamed him for their plight (5:20-21). He had a foretaste of the criticism and rebellion he would experience for the next forty years. Often the people you help the most appreciate you the least.

Moses' third problem was with the Lord Himself (5:22-23)! God had promised success but Moses had failed. Even the Jews didn't believe him! Madame Guyon spoke of these kinds of difficulties: "In the commencement of the spiritual life, our hardest task is to bear with our neighbor; in its progress, with ourselves; and in its end, with God."

But God gave Moses the assurance that he needed (6:1-8) and told him to return to his job and stay with it. God doesn't solve every problem immediately, nor does He follow your schedule. When you think you have failed, even when you have obeyed God's will, ponder Isaiah 55:8-9 and Jeremiah 29:11.

EXODUS 7—8

If men will not obey His words of warning, God must speak by His works of judgment. When God speaks, people either obey and submit their hearts or disobey and harden their hearts (Heb. 3:7-13). From the human point of view, Pharaoh resisted God's will and thus hardened his own heart. From the divine point of view, God sent the judgments and therefore caused his heart to harden. The same sun that melts the ice also hardens the clay.

The court magicians were able to imitate Aaron's miracle. Satan is a counterfeiter, and that is one way he opposes God's work today (2 Tim. 3:8-9). Some miracles are lying wonders (2 Thess. 2:9-10). Be sure you can tell the difference (1 John 2:18-27; 4:1-6).

The plagues were God's declaration of war against the false gods of Egypt (12:12). He proclaimed, "I am the LORD" (7:5). They were also a declaration that God had put a difference between the Jews and the Egyptians (8:23).

How sad that Israel saw God's wonders in Egypt and yet did not trust Him (Ps. 106:6–7). They even wanted to return to Egypt after they had been delivered! Great experiences are no guarantee that one has grown spiritually. It all depends on what happens to your heart.

EXODUS 9—10

All Moses wanted was Pharaoh's permission to take the people on a three-days' journey to a place where they could worship God. God had put a difference between His people and the people of Egypt, just as today He has put a difference between the people of God and the people of the world (2 Cor. 6:14–18).

But the world doesn't want believers to be too radical, so it offers various compromises: "Sacrifice in the land" (8:25); "Don't go too far away" (8:28); "Don't take your children" (10:8–11); and "Don't take your possessions to serve God" (10:24–26). Have you been tempted by any of these compromises lately?

God's judgments had practically ruined the land, yet Pharaoh would not give in. In so doing, Pharaoh thought he was showing great strength; actually, God was using him to display His own sovereignty (9:16; see also Rom. 9:17–18). God is greater than any ruler, so we need never fear (Dan. 4:34–37).

Pharaoh's "confession of sin" (9:27) was not sincere; he only wanted Moses to stop the plagues. True repentance involves a change of mind that leads to a change of life. Balaam (Num. 22:34), Saul (1 Sam. 15:24), and Judas (Matt. 27:4) were all guilty of insincere confession of sin.

EXODUS 11—12

Life. "One more plague!" The words sounded ominous, and they were, for the last plague was death to the firstborn. When you trust in the Lord, it means the difference between light and darkness (10:21–23) and life and death. God made this difference (11:7), and His people must maintain it (Rom. 12:1–2).

Lamb. Observe the sequence: "*a* lamb" (12:3), "*the* lamb" (12:4), "*your* lamb" (12:5). The Passover lamb is a picture of Jesus Christ who died for the sins of the world (John 1:29; 1 Cor. 5:6–7). Do you call Him "*a* Savior," "*the* Savior," or "*my* Savior" (Luke 1:47)?

Jesus is the perfect Lamb (1 Pet. 1:18–19) who had to die to save us. We are saved not by admiring His example or by studying His teaching, but by applying His blood to our own hearts by faith. The lamb saved the Jews and it also sustained them for their journey. You "feed" on Jesus Christ when you meditate on His Word and make its truths a part of your inner person.

Leaven. Yeast is a picture of sin: it begins small but spreads quickly; it puffs up; and it works secretly. When you are saved by the blood of Christ, you want to have a life that is pure and free from known sin. The Jews were not saved by getting rid of the leaven; they got rid of the leaven because God had saved them (2 Cor. 7:1; 2 Tim. 2:19). Note how Paul applied these truths in 1 Corinthians 5.

EXODUS 13

Remembering. God wanted Israel to remember what His hand had done for them (vv. 3, 9, 14, 16), lest in the future they forget to trust Him and serve Him. The setting apart of the firstborn would remind them that the firstborn sons of Israel had been redeemed by the Lord. The annual Passover would remind them to keep their lives pure. When you consider that Jesus Christ has redeemed us by His blood, surely we should give ourselves to Him and obey His Word.

Instructing. The younger generation cannot know the works of the Lord unless the older generation tells them. The Word of God must control our lips (v. 9), our eyes, and our hands (v. 16), and we must share it with others. The Jews took this literally and wore portions of the Law on the forehead and hand, but the Lord was surely speaking in a metaphorical way.

Following. God frees us from bondage, and He also guides us to the inheritance He has prepared for us. His Word is like that pillar of cloud and fire, and He will show us the way if we will trust Him.

EXODUS 14

God sees before (1–19). God knew Pharaoh's plans and saw to it that Israel was cared for. This is *providence,* which means "to see before." He is Jehovah-Jireh (Gen. 22:14), "the Lord will see to it." No matter what the enemy plans to do to you, God has already taken care of it and will tell you what to do.

God comes between (19–20). The pillar that brought light to Israel brought darkness to the enemy. The people of the world are walking in darkness, but God's people have "the light of life" (John 8:12). The enemy cannot touch you without first encountering God.

God goes ahead (21–25). He opens the way and does the impossible. The next time you are in a seemingly impossible situation, remember what God did for Israel at the Red Sea. The people of Israel never forgot this victory (Pss. 66:6; 106:9; 136:13–14). Recalling God's past help can encourage you as you face future challenges to your faith.

God comes behind (26–31). Isaiah stated, "And the God of Israel will be your rear guard" (Isa. 52:12). The defeat was complete; the Egyptian army was no more. There is much truth in these words: "And this is the victory that has overcome the world—our faith" (1 John 5:4).

EXODUS 15

The Lord who triumphs (1–21). When they walked by sight, Israel complained (14:10–12); but when they believed God and saw His mighty hand at work, they praised Him. Redemption should lead to rejoicing (Luke 15:1–24).

This first recorded song in Scripture is a pattern for true worship, for it emphasizes the Lord, who He is, and what He has done for His people. He saves His people (vv. 1–10), guides them to their inheritance (vv. 11–13), glorifies His name (vv. 14–17), and reigns forever (v. 18). Today, let God be your strength, your song, and your salvation (v. 2; see also Ps. 118:14; Isa. 12:2).

The Lord who heals (22–26). The people went from rejoicing to complaining! It is easy to sing when the circumstances are comfortable, but it takes faith to sing when you are suffering. God tests us in the everyday experiences of life to see whether we will obey Him. He is able to change our circumstances, but He would rather change us (Phil. 4:10–13).

The Lord who refreshes (27). Life is not always battles and bitter waters. God brings us to the refreshing oases from time to time, and for this we should praise Him. However, we can never claim our inheritance if we linger at Elim. We are pilgrims, not residents.

Praise Him with Song

Singing is an important part of the Christian life, for it enables us to praise God and bear witness to others. Our praise should come from the Holy Spirit within (Eph. 5:18–20) and be based on Scripture (Col. 3:16). In this way, we worship Him "in spirit and truth" (John 4:24).

EXODUS 16

The redeemed Jews were acting like unsaved Gentiles, for they asked, "What shall we eat? What shall we drink?" (Matt. 6:25–34). God did not rescue them from bondage in order to kill them with hunger! (See Rom. 8:31–32.) Their real problem was that they still had the old appetite and needed to learn to enjoy the new food God had for them.

The manna is a picture of Jesus Christ (John 6:30ff.). The manna came only to Israel, and all it could do was sustain physical life. But the Savior came for the whole world, and He gives spiritual life. If the Jews did not appropriate the manna, they died. Sinners must believe on Jesus Christ to receive life.

Feeding on the manna is also a picture of your daily appropriation of Christ through the Word of God. Just as your food becomes a part of your very being, so the Word strengthens your inner person when you read it, meditate on it, and obey it. Just as the Jews could not live on yesterday's manna, so you cannot live on yesterday's spiritual diet. Begin each day with the Lord, and He will give you what you need for facing the burdens and battles ahead.

Spiritual Food

God's Word is food for the inner person. It is milk (1 Pet. 2:2), bread (Matt. 4:4), meat (1 Cor. 3:1–2; Heb. 5:11–14), and honey (Ps. 119:103). Feeding on the Word should bring joy to our hearts (Jer. 15:16), and we should desire spiritual food more than physical food (Job 23:12; Luke 10:38–42).

EXODUS 17

Another test (1–7). You never solve your problems by blaming other people. Israel's real problem was unbelief and a desire to go back to the old life. Every difficulty you meet is an opportunity for testing yourself and trusting your Lord, for going forward or going backward. The rock pictures Jesus Christ who was smitten for us (1 Cor. 10:4) that we might have the living water of the Holy Spirit within (John 7:37–39).

Another enemy (8–13). The Egyptian army had been drowned, but the Amalekites were very much alive and did not want Israel in their territory. It was Esau fighting Jacob again (Gen. 36:12). It takes intercession on the mountain as well as intervention in the valley for God's people to win the victory. Israel watched God defeat Egypt, but now they had to enter the battle themselves and trust God for victory. Our High Priest intercedes in heaven for us (Heb. 4:14–16). This is the first mention of Joshua in Scripture. Little did he know that one day he would take Moses' place as leader of God's people.

Another assurance (14–16). Each test can tell you something new about yourself and about the Lord (Gen. 22:14; Exod. 15:26). When you face the battles of life, remember that He is your banner and can give you victory (John 16:33; 1 John 5:4–5).

EXODUS 18

Balance. Moses experienced some exciting things after leaving Egypt, but now he returns to the everyday duties of life. God balances our lives and gives us enough burdens to keep us humble and enough blessings to keep us happy. Moses returned to his family, told them all that God had done, and then worshiped the Lord with them.

Counsel. Sometimes an outsider can see things more clearly than those who are doing the work, and we must always be open to counsel (Prov. 12:15; 13:10). Moses was trying to do all the work himself, and he was not making a distinction between major matters and minor problems. He needed assistants, and he needed priorities. Note that Jethro expected Moses to seek God's will in the matter (v. 23). What seems like good counsel from men might be bad counsel in God's sight, so we must always ask for God's directions (Acts 27:9–14).

Leadership. Verse 21 describes the kind of leaders God needs, people characterized by ability, the fear of God, honesty, and a hatred for covetousness. (See Acts 6:3 for additional leadership qualities.) Moses was a great man, but he could not do the job alone. God may not call you to be a leader, but He may want you to help a leader do a better job.

EXODUS 19

A special people. At the Red Sea, God separated His people from their old life; at Sinai, He brought them into a new life, a covenant relationship with Himself. It was like a wedding ceremony, with God as the Husband and Israel as the wife. Whenever the nation turned from God to idols, God accused them of committing adultery (Isa. 1:21; Jer. 3:1–5). Believers today must also beware this sin (James 4:4). The church is a nation of kings and priests (1 Pet. 2:5, 9) called to glorify God.

A sanctified people. Because we belong to God, we must be separated from sin (vv. 10, 14, 22). God's people are set apart from the world and unto the Lord.

A submissive people. To impress the people with the fear of the Lord, God demonstrated His power at Sinai and warned them not to come near. It was the childhood of the nation, and the people, like children, learned from rewards and punishments. Hebrews 12:18–29 contrasts this experience with that of the New Testament believer today. We must still fear the Lord and respect the boundaries He establishes, but we are invited to "draw near" (Heb. 10:19–25). The Israelites were not saved from Egypt by obeying the Law, but their obedience enabled them to enjoy all the blessings God had for them.

We Are Set Apart

To be sanctified means to be set apart for God's exclusive use and pleasure. Christians are set apart by the death of Christ (Heb. 10:10), the indwelling Spirit (Rom. 15:16), and the Word of God (John 17:17; Eph. 5:26).

EXODUS 20

The Law does not save sinners (Gal. 2:21; 3:21); it reveals God's holiness and man's need for salvation (Rom. 3:20). It is a mirror that shows us how dirty we are (James 1:22—2), but it does not provide the cleansing we need. Only Christ can do that.

Under the old covenant, God's law was written on tables of stone (Exod. 24:12), but under the new covenant, God writes His word on our hearts (2 Cor. 3:1–3). As you meditate on the Word, the Spirit makes it a part of your inner being, and you become more like the Lord Jesus Christ (2 Cor. 3:18). The Holy Spirit enables us to fulfill the righteous demands of God's law (Rom. 8:1–4).

The first four commandments deal with our relationship with God, while the last six deal with our relationship with others. If we love God and obey Him, we will also love others and serve them. (See Matt. 22:34–40.)

Some people obey God because of fear (vv. 18–21). Others obey only because they want His blessing. The highest motive for obedience is our love for the Lord. But what if we disobey the Lord? God made provision for Israel in the prescribed sacrifices (vv. 22–26). He has made provision for believers today through the work of Christ (1 John 1:9—2:2). Believers are not under law but under grace. This is not an excuse for sin but an encouragement for loving obedience to His will. Ponder Romans 6.

EXODUS 21

Having stated His basic law, God then told Moses how to apply it to specific situations so that everybody would receive equal justice, which is the principle in verses 22–25. No person was to take the law into his or her own hands. When it comes to *personal* retaliation, we must obey Matthew 5:38–48.

God's law shows that He is concerned about everything: men, women, children, the unborn, property, and even animals. This is His creation, and He has the right to tell us how to manage it. The Law did not change people's hearts, but it did help to control their conduct and give order to the nation. Laws and government have been instituted by God, and we should respect them (Rom. 13).

Some penalties given here may seem harsh to us; but keep in mind that the nation was in its "childhood" (Gal. 4:1–7), and children learn best through rewards and punishments. Forty years later, when the new generation was on the scene, Moses emphasized love when he repeated the Law (Deut. 4:37; 6:4–6; 7:6–13). Love is the fulfilling of the Law (Rom. 13:8–10).

EXODUS 22

Property (1–15). God wants us to respect personal property, and the key idea here is *restitution* (vv. 3, 5, 6, 12). It is not enough to admit the crime and show sorrow over it. There must also be a readiness to make things right with those who have been hurt (Prov. 6:30–31; Luke 19:8). David knew verse 1 and could apply it to others (2 Sam. 12:1–6), but he did not apply Exodus 20:13–14 to himself.

Persons (16–27). These many laws reveal the holiness of God and His desire that we be a holy people (v. 31). When obeyed, these laws protected the people from violence, extortion, oppression, and affliction. God has compassion on widows and orphans, poor workers (James 5:1–4), and strangers. Do we?

Principles (28–31). Respect God and put Him first in everything. Jesus summarized it in Matthew 6:33. If we truly love God with all our hearts, we will have no desire to hurt others. But if God is not first, we will start exploiting people to get what we want.

EXODUS 23

Consideration (1–9). Treating people justly would seem to be an easy thing to do, but the sinful human heart can lead us astray with rumors (2 Cor. 13:1), false witnesses, crowds, and money. The fact that a person is rich or poor, a friend or an enemy, must not blind us to the truth. Integrity must not be for sale.

Conservation (10–13). The Sabbath was God's special gift to Israel to mark the nation as His holy people (Exod. 31:13–17). It was also His gift to man and beast to provide needed rest. The Sabbatical Year showed His concern for the land and the poor. It is unfortunate that people today have forgotten these lessons and are destroying creation by their exploitation of resources.

Celebration (14–19). God wants His people to celebrate and rejoice in His goodness. If our celebration ignores the Lord, we are guilty of idolatry. (See 1 Tim. 6:17.)

Consecration (20–33). The nation would be entering enemy territory and would be tempted to compromise with the wicked people of the land. They must not even speak about the false gods (v. 13) lest they would be led to bow down and serve those gods (v. 24) and make covenants with them (v. 32). Do not talk yourself into disobeying God!

EXODUS 24

There are degrees of nearness to God. The people remained at a distance because of their fear of the Lord. Moses, Joshua, Nadab, Abihu, Aaron, and seventy of the elders went up the mountain to meet God. Then Moses and Joshua went further, and finally Moses went into the glory cloud alone.

J. Oswald Sanders wisely commented, "We are at this moment *as close to God as we really choose to be.*" God invites us to draw near (James 4:8), but often we are unwilling to do what is necessary to meet Him. The people below had the Book and the blood, and they made promises to obey God; but they did not have the vision of the glory of the Lord that Moses had on the mount.

You would think verse 11 would read, "So they saw God, and they fell down and prayed." But it says, "They ate and drank." The vision of God's glory should not make us careless or impractical. We can eat and drink to His glory (1 Cor. 10:31). But beware lest nearness to God lead to careless familiarity, for "our God is a consuming fire" (Heb. 12:28–29). Nadab and Abihu would find that out (Lev. 10:1ff.)

EXODUS 25

An offering. God could have made the whole tabernacle in an instant of creative power, but instead He asked the people to bring Him their offerings. They were privileged to make a sanctuary for God. Today, we are helping to build His church, and we must use only the best materials (1 Cor. 3:9–23). Are you giving willingly to God what He has given to you?

A pattern. God gave Moses the pattern for the tabernacle just as He later gave David the pattern for the temple (1 Chron. 28:19). When God wants a work done on earth, He has a plan for His people to follow. It is dangerous to turn from God's plan and follow the wisdom of this world (1 Cor. 3:18–20).

The ark was the throne of God in the Holy of Holies, and God's glory dwelt between the cherubim on the mercy seat (Ps. 99:1). Our mercy seat is in heaven (Heb. 4:11–16), and the way is always open to God.

The table reminds us that God is the source of our suste-

nance (Matt. 6:11). The bread also speaks of the spiritual nourishment we have in His Word (Deut. 8:3; Matt. 4:4). The golden
candlestick tells us that "God is light" (1 John 1:5) and that we
are to be lights in this dark world (Matt. 5:14–16). Just as the
lamps were fed by the oil, so we must have the power of the
Spirit to be effective witnesses for the Lord (Acts 1:8).

EXODUS 26

Ten curtains, fifty loops, fifty clasps, forty sockets, twenty
boards, two veils—yet it was one sanctuary: "That it may be
one tabernacle" (v. 6); "That it may be one" (v. 11). Diversity,
yes; but unity in diversity.

There was only *one plan* for the tabernacle, and it came
from God (v. 30). Man's cleverness and wisdom may bring success in the things of the world (Luke 16:8), but they will destroy
the work of the Lord (1 Cor. 3:16–23). Be sure you get your plans
from heaven and not from the world.

There was *one set of measurements* for the building (v. 2).
When we measure ministry by God's standards, we will have
unity, but if we use our own standards, there will be division.

They used only *the materials* that God told them to use. In
1 Corinthians 3:10–16, read about building with the proper
materials that will endure. Note the emphasis on gold in chapter 37, silver in chapter 38, and precious stones in chapter 39.

The sanctuary was indwelt by *one glory,* the glory of God.
When man brings in his glory, there is division.

Jesus prayed that His people might be one (John 17:20–23).
Are you helping to answer that prayer?

EXODUS 27

The tabernacle was not a gathering place for worship but a
place for sacrifice and holy service.

Sacrifice. The first thing one saw was the brazen altar, for
no one can come into the presence of God until sin has been
dealt with (Lev. 17:11).

Separation. The tent was surrounded by a fence of linen
hangings, for only the priests and Levites could enter the sacred courts. The common people were kept out of the courts

and the priests out of the Holy of Holies. God wanted *all* His people to be priests (Exod. 19:5–6), but that would not happen until the finished work of Christ on the cross (1 Pet. 2:5, 9). We today have open access to the presence of God through Jesus Christ (Heb. 10:19–25).

Shining. The lampstand stood in the holy place and helped the priests to see as they served. It did not illumine the camp; the glory of God did that (Exod. 40:38). God's people (Phil. 2:15) and His churches (Rev. 1:12, 20) are lights in this dark world. Be sure you keep your lamp trimmed and your light shining (Matt. 5:16).

EXODUS 28

The priesthood was both a privilege and a responsibility. It was wonderful to wear the glorious garments and be in the holy courts, but being a priest also brought serious obligations.

They ministered first to the Lord. Four times in this chapter, God emphasized this point (vv. 1, 3, 4, 41). God's servants must seek to please Him alone (1 Cor. 4:1–7). We must be "bondservants for Jesus' sake" (2 Cor. 4:5).

They ministered to the people. God's people are like jewels to Him (Mal. 3:17). Our great High Priest carries us over His heart and on His shoulders. He represents us before the throne of God so that we are "accepted in the Beloved" (Eph. 1:6).

They ministered together. God supplied their needs as they served the people. There was no competition or confusion in the holy tabernacle because they served the same Lord and obeyed the same Word. God has a ministry for each of us, and He will equip us to do it.

EXODUS 29

We dedicate, but God consecrates. We surrender, but He sanctifies and sets us apart for His exclusive use. As God's priesthood, His people have experienced *spiritually* what Aaron and his sons experienced physically.

We have been washed. The blood of Christ has cleansed us (Rev. 1:5–6), and our past is gone (1 Cor. 6:9–11). Sinful hearts are purified not by religious rites but by faith in Jesus Christ (Acts 15:9; Titus 3:5).

We have been clothed. We stand in the very righteousness of Christ (Isa. 61:10; 2 Cor. 5:21) and wear the garments of God's grace (Col. 3:1ff.).

We have been anointed. We have the Holy Spirit living within (2 Cor. 1:21; 1 John 2:27), and He enables us to minister.

We belong to God. The priests were "marked" by the blood on the ear (hear God), the hand (serve God), and the foot (walk with God). The "continual burnt offering" morning and evening was a reminder of their complete and constant devotion to God. Don't forget your daily presentation of yourself to God (Rom. 12:1–2).

EXODUS 30

Remember to pray. The golden altar before the veil symbolized the ministry of prayer (Ps. 141:1–3; Rev. 5:8). God's people today don't stand before the veil: they enter the very presence of God. We need the "fire" of the Holy Spirit or our prayers are heartless (Rom. 8:23–27). Prayer is special, and we must not treat it as common (vv. 34–38).

Remember you are ransomed. They were not redeemed by paying money, nor are we (1 Pet. 1:18ff.); but paying the annual half-shekel reminded them of what God had done for them. The silver was used to make the sockets for the posts of the tabernacle (38:25–37). The foundation for everything is redemption.

Remember to keep clean. Like the priests, we are washed once at redemption, but we must keep clean in our daily walk. If they became defiled even while serving the Lord in the holy tabernacle, what must happen to us as we serve in an evil world!

Remember to honor the Holy Spirit. The holy anointing oil symbolizes the Spirit of God. We must beware trying to duplicate His work by human effort or treating Him in a common way (vv. 32–33). (See Eph. 4:30–32.)

EXODUS 31

Work. When God wants to get a job done, He calls workers, equips them, and gives them the plan for the task. He also calls people to help them and to provide the needed resources. Bezalel and Aholiab were gifted artisans, but they needed God's calling and enabling before they could do the work to please Him.

Rest. Why did God mention the Sabbath at this point? Perhaps He wanted to remind His people that even the building of the sacred tabernacle was not a reason for breaking the Sabbath law. They needed a day of rest, and since the Sabbath was a sign between God and His people, they needed to honor Him. God wants us to be balanced: work, rest, worship.

Law. Luke 11:20 suggests that "the finger of God" signifies the Holy Spirit, who wrote the Word of God (2 Tim. 3:16; 2 Pet. 1:21). He now writes it on the hearts of those who trust Christ and worship Him (2 Cor. 3:1ff.).

EXODUS 32

Unbelief. Despite all that God had said and done, and all that Israel had promised to do (19:8), the nation did not know how to live by faith. Moses had been gone forty days (Deut. 9:11ff.), and the people had become impatient. They still had the fire and cloud to assure them of God's presence, but that was not enough. They wanted another visible representation of Jehovah to encourage them. It was unbelief: "Whoever believes will not act hastily" (Isa. 28:16).

Compromise. Aaron was supposed to be the spiritual leader in the absence of Moses, but instead he gave in and let the people have their way. When confronted with his sin, Aaron blamed the people, Moses, and the furnace (vv. 22–24), but he did not blame himself.

Intercession. Had Moses been a selfish man, he could have become the founder of a new nation, but he loved the people and prayed for their forgiveness. (See Luke 23:34; Rom. 9:1–3.) He reminded God of His covenant and of the glory He would lose if the nation were destroyed. When you pray, remind God of His promises and seek to magnify His glory.

Discipline. We all should heed the psalmist's wise words: "You who love the LORD, hate evil" (Ps. 97:10). God in His grace forgives the sinner, but in His government, He must punish the sin. This judgment may seem cruel to us, but the people had been warned against idolatry and had willfully disobeyed God. God had to teach them early not to act like the heathen nations around them. Israel had to remain a separated people, or God could not work out His great purposes through them.

EXODUS 33

God's friendship. The tabernacle had not yet been built, so the structure referred to here was probably a tent where Moses met with God and over which the cloud rested. God spoke to Moses as with a friend because Moses obeyed God (Deut. 34:10; John 15:14–16). God could not dwell with a rebellious people, but He could fellowship with Moses (2 Cor. 6:14–18).

God's Glory	*The glory of God is the manifestation of all His attributes and character, all that He is and says and does. Everything about God is glorious, and the highest activity of man is to glorify God (Matt. 5:16; 1 Cor. 10:31). All who trust Christ share His glory today and will see His glory in heaven (John 17:22–24).*

God's presence. The Jews *watched* things happen, but Moses *made* things happen. He knew God's ways (Ps. 103:7) and prayed for God's presence to go with them. Moses could not pray on the basis of Israel's obedience to the Law, but he could plead the grace of God. Believers today are sure of

God's presence because He has promised to stay with us (Heb. 13:5–6).

God's glory. Many believers pray, "Show me Your way," but not many pray, "Show me Your glory." No man can see God in His fullness and live, but God can reveal some of His glory. He did that for Moses "in the secret place of the Most High" (Ps. 91:1–4). Our experience of glory today is explained in 2 Corinthians 3:18.

EXODUS 34

A gracious God (1–9). Because He is gracious and long-suffering, God gave His people another opportunity, just as He does with us today (1 John 2:1–2). He gave a "second chance" to Abraham (Gen. 13:1ff.), Jonah (Jon. 3:1), and Peter (John 21:15ff.). The enemy accuses us and wants us to quit, but God is ready to forgive when we turn to Him (Pss. 103:10–14; 130:3–4).

A jealous God (10–29). God works for us, but He expects us to walk with Him. He will keep His covenant, but we must beware not to compromise with evil. It is easy to get into sin gradually. First there is agreement in worship (vv. 12–13), then sacrifice (v. 15), then marriage (v. 16); and the result is the loss of our children to false gods. Note the emphasis on putting God first (vv. 19–22, 26).

A glorious God (30–35). Moses not only sought God's glory and saw it on the mount, but he shared it as it reflected from his own face. However, this glory faded away, just like the glory of the Law. As we see Christ in the Word, and the Spirit makes us more like Him, we go "from glory to glory" (2 Cor. 3:12–18; see also Prov. 4:18; Matt. 17:1–8; Acts 6:15).

EXODUS 35—39

Each aspect of the making of the tabernacle is mentioned in detail because each part was important to God. The smallest wooden peg had to conform to the pattern God gave Moses on the mount. If we expect God to be concerned about the details of our lives, we must pay attention to the details of His instructions.

The construction of the tabernacle involved God's pattern and man's provision. The people had plundered the Egyptians (12:35–36), and they willingly brought that wealth to the Lord. It was an act of spontaneous generosity and not something that was forced from them (35:5, 21–22, 26, 29). Christians today should give in the same way (2 Cor. 8:1–12).

God gave the plan, and He also gave the workers the wisdom needed to do the job right (35:10, 25, 34–35). There is nothing wrong with dedicated artistry, for God built beauty into His tabernacle. God wants skillful hands as well as dedicated hearts (Ps. 78:72).

Moses was careful to inspect the work to see that it was just what God had commanded. (The word *commanded* is found seventeen times in these chapters.) Moses was faithful as the servant of God to do what God told him to do (Heb. 3:5).

Chapter 39 ends by saying, "And Moses blessed them" (v. 43). Have you taken time lately to bless those who have done the will of God in serving you? (See Ruth 2:4.)

EXODUS 40

Finished. All the framework, hangings, and pieces of furniture were completed, along with the priests' garments; but Moses waited for the Lord to tell him what to do next. Wise is the leader who gets his orders from God.

Furnished. God told Moses what to do and when to do it. First they were to set up the tent and then put in the six special pieces of furniture, starting with the ark in the Holy of Holies. The right order was as significant as the right furnishings. When he finished with the tent and the furniture, he put up the court around it and set it apart from the rest of the camp.

Fragrant. Everything in the tabernacle was anointed with the holy oil, which set it all apart for God's use. Is there a fragrance about our lives that makes people think of heaven?

Filled. Two things made the tabernacle a special building: the pattern was given by God, and God's glorious presence filled it when He came to dwell with His people. What a gracious God that He should consent to dwell with such a rebellious people!

God's Dwelling Places

First, God walked with man (Gen. 5:24; 6:9); then He desired to dwell with him (Exod. 25:8). His glory came to the tabernacle (Exod. 40:34), but when Israel sinned, the glory departed (1 Sam. 4:21–22). The glory dwelt in the temple (1 Kings 8:10–11), but then departed again because of the sins of the people (Ezek. 11:22–23). The glory came in the person of Jesus Christ (John 1:14) and dwells now in believers individually (1 Cor. 6:19–20) and the church collectively (Eph. 2:20–22). One day God's glory will be revealed in a new heaven and earth and a perfect city where His people will dwell forever (Rev. 21—22).

LEVITICUS

◆

The name of this book means "pertaining to the Levites." Exodus and Leviticus were guidebooks for the priests in their ministry. Israel today has neither priesthood nor temple, so the nation cannot obey these laws (Hos. 3:4), but Leviticus has great value to the Christian. It illustrates the sacrificial work of Jesus Christ and stresses the importance of a life of separation and obedience.

Jesus Christ in the Sacrifices

1. Burnt offering	He showed perfect dedication to God.	John 10:17; Rom. 5:19; Heb. 10:10
2. Grain offering	He had a perfect character, a fragrance to God.	Eph. 5:2
3. Peace offering	He made peace between God and man and between Jew and Gentile.	Rom. 5:1; Eph. 2:14, 17; Col. 1:20
4. Sin offering	He was made sin for us on the cross.	2 Cor. 5:17; 1 Pet. 2:24
5. Trespass offering	He assumed the debt for our sins and paid it.	Luke 7:36–50

The book emphasizes *sacrifice* (chaps. 1—10), for man must deal with his sins if he expects to have fellowship with a holy God. These five sacrifices are fulfilled in Jesus Christ and picture His perfect life and atoning work on the cross (Heb. 10:1–14).

Leviticus also emphasizes *separation* (chaps. 11—24), for a redeemed people should walk in God's holy will. These various laws touch on many aspects of everyday life and illustrate principles of holy living that God's children should follow today.

Finally, since God anticipated the nation's entrance into the Promised Land, He gave them some rules for *success* (chaps. 25—27). The land was theirs because of God's covenant, but they could enjoy it only if they obeyed God's will. Obedience by faith always brings blessing.

LEVITICUS 1

"All on the altar" (v. 9) is the key to this sacrifice, for it speaks of complete dedication to the Lord. The animal was an involuntary sacrifice that died, but God's people are to be willing *living* sacrifices (Rom. 12:1–2). Do you put *your* "all on the altar" at the beginning of each day (Lev. 6:8–13)?

The offering must be brought to the Lord, and its purpose must be to please the Lord as a "sweet aroma" (vv. 9, 13, 17). People may not understand you, but if you seek to please Him, He will accept it (1 Pet. 2:5).

No matter how poor we may feel, or how little we think we have to give Him, He will receive what we have and bless it (vv. 14–17). The important thing is that we give our all to Him each day.

The priest started each day by sacrificing a burnt offering. It became the foundation for all the other offerings put on the altar (Exod. 29:38–42; Lev. 3:5). Unless we have our "all on the altar," our other sacrifices will not mean much to the Lord.

LEVITICUS 2

There was no shedding of blood involved in the grain offering, for it focused on the life and character of our Lord Jesus Christ rather than on His death. In Him was perfect balance;

nothing was ever in excess. His life on earth pleased God (Matt. 17:5). As we become more like Him, we shall become more and more balanced in character.

The oil symbolizes the Holy Spirit who has anointed each believer (2 Cor. 1:21–22). The oil *mixed* with the offering (v. 4) reminds us that our Lord was born of the Spirit with a perfect nature (Luke 1:35). The oil *poured* on the offering (v. 6) speaks of the power of the Spirit given to the Savior (Acts 10:38). We need the fruit of the Spirit (Gal. 5:22–23) and the power of the Spirit (Acts 1:8) if we are to please God in character and service.

Note that God never wants leaven (a picture of sin [1 Cor. 5:6–8]) or honey (man's glory and not God's [Prov. 25:27]). But He does want salt, which speaks of purity (Col. 4:6), and frankincense, which is praise to God. What a privilege it is to build a Christian life that brings glory to God!

LEVITICUS 3

Religion is man's attempt to make peace with God on his own terms. Redemption is God's offer of peace through Jesus Christ. But this is "peace through the blood of His cross" (Col. 1:20). The animal sacrifice had to die and the blood had to be sprinkled on the altar before God could declare peace.

Peace with God is a precious blessing that we must never take for granted: "Therefore, having been justified by faith, we have peace with God through our Lord Jesus Christ" (Rom. 5:1).

After the sacrifice, the worshiper and his family would eat what remained once the priest had taken his rightful share (7:11–18). It was to be a joyful feast of fellowship. In fact, the Jews were to consider it a peace offering whenever they slaughtered an animal for food (17:1–9). Do you strive to make each meal an occasion of fellowship and praise to God? If we would present ourselves and the food to Him as an act of worship, our meals might become much happier occasions.

LEVITICUS 4

The sin offering was for unintentional sins of ignorance and not for deliberate sins of disobedience. For deliberate sins,

God made no provision for a sacrifice (Num. 15:30–31). All the offender could do was plead the mercy of God (Ps. 51:16–17).

But ignorance is no excuse in God's sight! Once we know that we have sinned, we must come to God for forgiveness. Jesus Christ was the sin offering for the whole world, including ignorant Israel (Luke 23:34; Acts 3:17). Our Lord's prayer on Calvary did not automatically forgive their sins, because the people did not repent; but it did postpone the outpouring of God's wrath for nearly forty years.

The priest's sacrifice was the same as that of the whole congregation (vv. 3, 14), for the higher the privilege, the greater the responsibility (Luke 12:48). But when the offerings were brought by faith, God promised to forgive (vv. 20, 26, 31, 35). Of course, the final and complete atonement was wrought by Jesus Christ on the cross (Heb. 10:1–14).

When we sin, it affects our prayer life. This is why the priest had to cleanse the golden altar (v. 7). (See Ps. 66:18.)

LEVITICUS 5

The trespass offering could involve both sacrifice and restitution. It reminds us that sin harms others (v. 16) and that true repentance ought to result in our making right the things we have done wrong.

The sin offering deals with the fact that we are sinners by nature, while the trespass offering deals with individual acts of sin. We must be honest with God about both what we are and what we do (1 John 1:8, 10).

Sometimes we commit sin by keeping quiet (v. 1), or we may cover up (vv. 2–3) or speak out (v. 4). Our sins may be unintentional, and we may be ignorant of them; but once we know about them, we must come to God for cleansing. Sin is *not* "deliberate disobedience to a *known* law." If we disobey God, we are guilty whether we realize it or not.

Have you claimed 1 John 1:9 lately?

LEVITICUS 6—7

Let's follow the example of the priest and each morning get rid of the old ashes, stir up the fire, and offer a burnt offering to the Lord (Rom. 12:1–2). The phrase "stir up" in 2 Timothy 1:6

means "stir up the flame into life again." Is the flame burning high on the altar of your heart (Luke 24:32), or are you getting lukewarm (Rev. 3:15–16) or cold (Matt. 24:12)?

Let's also keep the leaven out of our lives (6:14–18), which includes hypocrisy (Luke 12:1), false doctrine (Gal. 5:8–9), and corrupt living (1 Cor. 5:6ff.).

The sin offering was so holy that it could not remain in the defiled camp; it had to be taken outside the camp (5:11–12; see also Heb. 13:10–13). The priests were permitted to eat their share, but only in the holy court of the tabernacle because whatever the offering touched was made holy. Fellowship with God and one another depends on purity (7:19–21).

LEVITICUS 8—9

Altar is a key word in these chapters; it is used twenty-three times. Without an altar, there can be no acceptable sacrifice; without a sacrifice, man cannot approach a holy God. But there must also be a priesthood to serve at the altar. In the Old Testament, God's people *had* a priesthood, but in the New Testament, God's people *are* a priesthood (1 Pet. 2:5, 9).

What made the priests acceptable to God? Water (8:6), oil (8:10–12), blood (8:14–29), and garments (8:7–9). We have been washed (1 Cor. 6:11), anointed by the Spirit (1 John 2:20, 27), redeemed by Christ's blood (1 Pet. 1:18ff.), and dressed in His righteousness (Isa. 61:10).

The day of dedication began a week of consecration (8:31–36), and the week ended with Aaron's blessing the people and the Lord's accepting the sacrifices (9:22–24). The glory of the Lord appeared (9:6, 23), which is the purpose of sacrifice and service. Can people say of our worship, "God is truly among you" (1 Cor. 14:25)?

LEVITICUS 10

It did not take long for sin to enter the priestly family. After a great experience with the Lord, beware the enemy's attack. Elijah ran away after the great victory at Mount Carmel (1 Kings 19), and Jesus was tempted after His baptism at the Jordan (Matt. 3:13—4:11). Great blessings sometimes mean great temptations.

Eleven times in chapters 8—9 you find the phrase "the LORD commanded." Nadab and Abihu did what the Lord had *not* commanded, and the fire of God killed them (Heb. 12:29). At the beginning of new periods in redemptive history, God judged sin in a dramatic way so that the people would learn to fear Him (Josh. 7; Acts 5:1–11).

Did their sin have something to do with strong drink (vv. 8–11)? Paul's admonition in Ephesians 5:18ff. is appropriate here, for there is no acceptable substitute in ministry for the power of the Holy Spirit.

Aaron obeyed the spirit of the commandment but not the letter. Had he obeyed the letter, he would have been insincere before God, and God would have known that his heart was not in it. Moses looked at the outward appearance, but God looked on the heart (1 Sam. 16:7). God knows your heart and understands you, even when others are critical (1 John 3:20–21).

LEVITICUS 11

Defilement. Chapters 11—15 focus on the concept of "clean" and "unclean" in the areas of food (11), birth (12), disease (13—14), and normal bodily functions (15). Although the laws certainly served a practical hygienic purpose, there was also a spiritual principle involved. As God's people, Israel had to be separated from everything that God called unclean. Other nations might be able to do those things, but the Jews could not (vv. 44–45). Defilement spreads, and one person's carelessness could affect many people.

Discernment. If they wanted to be pleasing to God, the people had to exercise discernment (vv. 46–47); the priests were supposed to teach them God's will (Ezek. 44:23). The dietary laws were temporary (Mark 7:14–23; Acts 10:9–18; 1 Tim. 4:1–5), but the principle is permanent: believers must have discernment and avoid what is unclean (2 Cor. 7:1; Phil. 1:9–11; Heb. 5:14).

LEVITICUS 12

Birth. There is no suggestion here that either conception or birth is an act of sin. After all, God created sex and told us to be fruitful and multiply (Gen. 1:28). God reminds us that we are conceived sinners (Pss. 51:5; 58:3) and therefore need His grace.

Compassion. Is a female child twice as unclean as a male child? Of course not, for there were no degrees of uncleanness. God was giving the mother extra time to care for a daughter in a masculine society that preferred sons. He was also giving her time to recuperate before the next pregnancy. A husband to whom she bore a daughter might be anxious to try again for a son.

Grace. Even the poorest could bring an acceptable sacrifice, and God would receive it (v. 8). This is the sacrifice that Joseph and Mary brought when they dedicated Jesus (Luke 2:22–24). Truly, He became poor that we might be rich (2 Cor. 8:9).

LEVITICUS 13

Concern. Leprosy was a feared disease for which there was no known cure. God had concern for the leper and made certain he or she was treated with dignity. God gave the priest all the information needed to detect the disease and make sure it did not spread. How tragic it would be to isolate someone who was not really infected or to declare clean somebody who was unclean.

Characteristics. There is more to this law than a lesson in symptoms; in the Bible, leprosy is a picture of sin (Isa. 1:4–6). The disease was not on the surface; like sin, it was "deeper than the skin." (The phrase is used ten times.) Leprosy spreads in the system and makes the person unclean, so much so that he or she had to be isolated: "He shall dwell alone" (v. 46). How like sin!

Compassion. Our Lord had compassion on the lepers, touched them, and made them clean (Mark 1:40–45); and He gave His disciples power to cleanse the lepers (Matt. 10:8). What Jesus did for all of us is beautifully pictured in the next chapter.

LEVITICUS 14

This ceremony of restoration for the healed leper pictures our Lord's work of redemption. Jesus went outside the camp to

meet us and to die for us (Luke 19:10; Heb. 13:10–13). He identified Himself with the outcasts (Matt. 9:10–13)! Whatever is infected with leprosy is fit for the fire (13:52), but He rescued us.

Birds don't belong in clay jars; they ought to be flying in the
heavens. This is a picture of our Lord's incarnation, when He
took upon Himself a human body that He might die for our
sins. Their turning the living bird loose pictured His resurrection from the dead. The former leper was treated like a priest!
(Compare vv. 14–20 with Lev. 8:22–24.) God has made us
"kings and priests" through the blood of Christ (Rev. 1:6). Hallelujah, what a Savior!

LEVITICUS 15

The key words in this chapter are *discharge* (twenty-four
times), *unclean* (twenty-nine times) and *bathe in water* (eleven
times). Verses 1–15 refer to discharges from infections, while
verses 16–30 refer to the discharges from the normal functions
of the body. No doubt sanitation and health were parts of
these laws, but fundamentally God was teaching His people
how to live separate from defilement (vv. 31–33).

The body is not sinful, and bodily functions are not morally
defiling. But man's nature (what the Bible calls "the flesh") is
sinful and produces what is sinful and defiling (Mark 7:20–23;
Gal. 5:19–21). If we are not careful, what we say and do, and
what we are, will touch others and defile them as well (vv. 5–
12; Matt. 23:25–28).

God made provision for Israel's ceremonial uncleanness,
and He has made provision for us. Our heavenly Advocate
cleanses us when we come in contrition and confession (1 John
1:5—2:2; see also John 13:1–11). He keeps us clean through His
blood (1 John 1:7) and through the cleansing power of His
Word (John 15:3; Eph. 5:25–27).

LEVITICUS 16

The most important day. The annual Day of Atonement
was the most significant of Israel's special days because on it
their sins were atoned for. It was the only time the high priest
was allowed to enter the Holy of Holies. Nadab and Abihu
tried to do it their own way and were judged (Lev. 10), so this
ceremony was a matter of life and death.

The most important person. You can see the Lord Jesus illustrated in the high priest. He did the work alone. He laid aside His garments of glory (Phil. 2:5–8), and He sanctified Himself for us (John 17:19). The difference is that Jesus did not offer any sacrifices for Himself because He is sinless. He Himself *is* the perfect and final sacrifice for the sins of the world (Heb. 7:23–28).

The most important reason. The high priest entered the Holy of Holies three times: (1) with the incense (vv. 12–14), (2) with blood for his sins, and (3) with blood for the sins of the people. The cloud of incense speaks of the glory of God, which is the whole purpose of redemption (John 17:1; Eph. 1:6, 12, 14).

Scapegoat may come from an Aramaic word that means "to remove." The setting free of the live goat pictured God's forgiveness of their sins (Ps. 103:10–13), but this required the death of the other goat. Salvation is free, but it is not cheap.

LEVITICUS 17

One price. The only price for sin that God will accept is blood, for the blood is the life of the creature. The sacrifice of blood means one life given for another. We should respect all life and not treat the blood as something common. The Jews were not to bring sacrifices of game (v. 13), because those cost them nothing. (See 2 Sam. 24:24.) The animals shed their blood involuntarily, but Jesus gave His life willingly for the sins of the world.

One place. While in the wilderness, the Jews had to do all their slaughtering at the brazen altar and make each animal a peace offering to the Lord. (This law was modified when they entered the land [Deut. 12:20–28].) No other place was acceptable to God. The blood of Jesus Christ, shed at Calvary, is the only acceptable sacrifice for sin in God's sight.

Do you look upon each meal as an offering to the Lord, and do you eat and drink to His glory (1 Cor. 10:31)?

LEVITICUS 18

Standards. God could not accept the moral standards of either Egypt or Canaan, and the Jews were not to follow them.

Instead, they were to obey the laws of God. "I am the LORD" appears twenty-one times in chapters 18 and 19, and the statement reminds us that we are under His authority. (See Rom. 12:2.)

Sexuality. Sex is a wonderful gift of God to the human family. When it is used according to His will, it is creative and brings rich blessing. Used apart from His will, sex is destructive and brings tragic consequences. Illicit sex defiles the persons involved (vv. 20–30), whole nations (v. 24) and the land itself (vv. 25, 27).

Sickness. Sexual perversions are abominable to God and make a nation sick. The nations in Canaan were devoted to such practices, and the land "vomited them out" to make room for God's people. God can forgive sexual sins (1 Cor. 6:9–11), but God warns His people not to practice them (1 Thess. 4:1–8; Heb. 13:4).

LEVITICUS 19

God's command for His people to be holy applies to us today (1 Pet. 1:16). The declaration "I am the LORD," found fifteen times in this chapter, reminds us that He must control every area of life.

The home (3a). Holiness should start in the home as we show respect for our parents (Eph. 6:1–3).

Time (3b). All of our time belongs to God, and we must not waste it (Eph. 5:15–17). But we must also take care to devote special times to Him in worship and service.

Food (5–8). Yes, we must eat and drink to the glory of God (1 Cor. 10:31). Our table should be an altar for peace offerings, but too often it is a field for battles!

Labor (9–10). We should think of others as we enjoy what God has given to us. If He is Lord in our work, we cannot be selfish.

Business (11–13). Making dishonest deals, telling lies, holding back money, and using God's name to cover frauds are all out of the question when He is Lord.

Neighbors (14–18). Unkindness, injustice, gossip, grudges, and hatred (note the sequence) are evil. "Love your neighbor as yourself" is the second greatest commandment (Mark 12:31).

Read the entire chapter carefully and find other areas of practical application.

LEVITICUS 20

The ominous phrase "put to death" is found nine times in this chapter, for "the wages of sin is death" (Rom. 6:23). But fear of death is not the highest motive for holy living. "I am the LORD who sanctifies you" (v. 8) ought to be motivation enough (Phil. 2:12–13).

Idolatry (1–5). Molech was the Ammonite god whom the people worshiped by sacrificing their children on the altar or presenting them as temple prostitutes. The modern idols of money, possessions, success, and position have cost many parents their children.

Spiritism (6–8). Idolatry and spiritism go together (1 Cor. 10:19–22). The increasing interest in satanism in our own day is frightening, and no Christian ought to joke about Satan or have anything to do with satanic practices.

Dishonoring parents (9). This verse emphasizes the fifth commandment (Exod. 20:12) and repeats the law given in Exodus 21:17. (See Prov. 20:20; 30:11, 17; 2 Tim. 3:1–4.)

Immorality (10–21). Adultery, incest, homosexuality, and bestiality are condemned, for these things are contrary to nature (Rom. 1:24–27). God created sex and marriage, and we should abide by His laws regarding them.

If Israel allowed these sins, the nation would forfeit its inheritance. (See Eph. 5:5.)

LEVITICUS 21

Privilege always brings responsibility. If the nation was to be sanctified, the spiritual leaders had to set the example. God had a word for the priests (1–9), the high priest (10–15), and those who could not be priests (16–24). Note the admonitions in this chapter.

"Don't defile yourself!" (1, 3, 4, 11). Anyone who touched a dead body was ceremonially unclean, so the priests had to be extra careful. They were expected to mourn, but not like the hopeless pagans (v. 5; see also 1 Thess. 4:13–18).

"Don't profane God's name!" (6). If we adopt pagan practices, people think we are worshiping pagan gods, and we dishonor the name of the Lord. "Hallowed be Your name" is the first petition in the Lord's Prayer (Matt. 6:9).

"Don't profane My sanctuary!" (12, 23). A defiled or disqualified priest would profane God's holy sanctuary, and God would have to judge. Holy men must minister in holy courts.

"Don't profane your posterity!" (15). So special was the high priest that he could not take anyone but a virgin for a wife to assure the nation that his firstborn was truly a descendant of Aaron. Any sons born with physical defects could not serve, but they received their share of the offerings. The priest who offers a faultless sacrifice (Lev. 22:20–25) must himself be faultless. God wants servants today to be blameless (1 Tim. 3:2, 10).

LEVITICUS 22

The chapter begins and ends with the solemn admonition, "You shall not profane My holy name" (vv. 1, 32). In chapter 21, God warned the priests not to be defiled by the unclean things; now He warns them not to defile the clean things.

Defective serving (1–9). It was dangerous for the priests to serve God if they knew they were unclean. They were insulting God, who knows all things, and deceiving the people who depended on them to present their offerings. The prophet Isaiah advised, "Be clean, you who bear the vessels of the LORD" (Isa. 52:11).

Defective sharing (10–16). The priests fed their families from the sacrifices the people brought, and that holy food could not be given to outsiders, not even a house guest. It is good to be generous, but not if our generosity dishonors God's gifts (Matt. 7:6).

Defective sacrificing (17–33). We must give God the best, for that is what He deserves. Since they pictured the coming Savior, the sacrifices had to be perfect. How easy it is to give to the Lord something we don't want anymore! Ponder Malachi 1:6–8.

LEVITICUS 23

The Hebrew calendar was organized around a series of sevens. The seventh day of the week was the Sabbath. They celebrated seven annual feasts, three of which occurred in the seventh month. The seventh year was their Sabbatical Year, and after forty-nine years (seven times seven), they celebrated the Year of Jubilee.

The Seven Feasts Picture Salvation History

Passover	*Christ, the Lamb, who died for us*	John 1:29; 1 Cor. 5:7
Unleavened Bread	*The Christian life of fellowship, separation from sin, and feeding on Christ*	1 Cor. 5:6–8
Firstfruits	*The resurrection of Christ*	1 Cor. 15:20–23
Pentecost	*The coming of the Holy Spirit*	Acts 2:1ff.
Trumpets	*The gathering together of God's people*	Isa. 27:12–13; Matt. 24:29–31; 1 Thess. 4:13–18
Day of Atonement	*The future cleansing of God's people*	Zech. 13:1–2; Rom. 14:10
Tabernacles	*The future joy of God's people in His kingdom*	Zech. 14:16–21

God invites us to remember. Passover and the Feast of Unleavened Bread reminded them of their miraculous deliverance from Egypt by the mighty hand of God. The Feast of Tabernacles reminded the people that their ancestors had lived in booths during their wanderings. Each new generation must be taught what God has done for His people; otherwise, they may take their blessings for granted. Specific times of remembering can be good for all of us.

God invites us to rejoice. At least three of the seven feasts (Firstfruits, Pentecost, and Tabernacles) were tied to the agricultural life of the people, reminders that God was the Giver of all that they needed and enjoyed.

God invites us to repent. The great Day of Atonement (chap. 16) required the people to confess their sin and trust God for cleansing. It was followed by Tabernacles, a week of joy and feasting. True joy comes only when we know we are right with God (Ps. 51:8, 12).

LEVITICUS 24

Three important responsibilities "before the LORD" (vv. 3, 6, 8) are given in this chapter.

Providing the oil (1-4). Only God and the priests saw the light, but the lamps had to be kept shining, for there was no other source of light in the Holy of Holies. The purest olive oil had to be used, supplied by the people themselves. Do we today, as God's people, help the light of the church to keep shining continually (Rev. 1:20)?

Presenting the bread (5-9). Twelve loaves were put on the table each Sabbath, and then the old loaves were given to the priests to eat. They were a reminder that God fed the twelve tribes both physically and spiritually, and that they in turn were to feed the world the truth about the Lord.

Protecting the name (10-23). The man could not be blamed for his parentage, but he could be blamed for blaspheming. Would someone with Egyptian ancestry glorify Israel's God? (See Exod. 5:2.) Like Moses, we should wait on God for direction (James 1:5). It was a capital offense, and the man was stoned to death. God emphasized again the basic principle that He stated in Exodus 21: equal justice and not personal vengeance.

LEVITICUS 25

Resources. The Sabbatical Year (vv. 1–7) and the Year of Jubilee (vv. 8–55; *jubal* means "to blow a trumpet") were based on two propositions: "The land is Mine" (v. 23), and "The children of Israel are My servants" (vv. 42; 55). God owns the land; we are stewards of what He has shared with us. We must use His resources wisely for His glory, for one day we must give an account of our stewardship (Luke 16:1ff.).

Rest. There was also an ecological purpose behind these laws, for obedience to them would grant rest to the land, to the beasts who helped work the land, and to the people. Along with the weekly Sabbath, the two events reminded Israel that rest and work go together and that people and God-given resources must not be exploited.

Riches. There was an economic purpose, for God had a concern for the poor and afflicted (vv. 25, 35, 39, 47). Had Israel obeyed the law of the Year of Jubilee, it would have helped to balance the economy, and the rich would have had difficulty exploiting the poor.

Responsibility. But the overriding purpose was spiritual, a reminder that Jehovah was Lord of both the land and the people, and that Israel had the responsibility to trust Him for everything. They could not sow during either the forty-ninth or fiftieth year but had to wait for the harvest of the fifty-first year. That would take faith (vv. 18–22)!

Redemption. Jesus used the Year of Jubilee to picture salvation (Luke 4:16–21). Today He offers rest and freedom to all who will trust Him. We are living now in the Year of Jubilee!

LEVITICUS 26

Covenant (1–13). God used the word *covenant* eight times in this chapter. It reminded the people of their special relationship with Him and the responsibilities belonging to that relationship. If they obeyed the terms of the covenant, they would remain in the Promised Land and enjoy His blessings. God does not promise material success to His new covenant people today, but He does promise to be with us and meet our every need.

Chastening (14–39). God's covenant included both blessing

and chastening, for God will not share His goodness with rebellious children. Enjoying the gifts while insulting the Giver is both selfish and idolatrous. We should obey God, not to "deserve" His blessings or even to avoid His chastenings, but to show our love to Him and our desire to please His heart.

Confession (40–46). A gracious God always leaves the door open for restoration. That is one loving purpose of His chastening hand (Heb. 12:1–13). The people may break their promises to God (v. 15), but God will never break His promises to His people (v. 44). God forgets our sins but remembers His covenant! This is not an excuse for sin, but it is an encouragement for sinners to repent and return to the Lord.

LEVITICUS 27

If you have ever found it difficult or impossible to fulfill a promise, the message of this chapter is for you.

In a moment of extreme joy or trial, a Jew might make a vow to God, offering to give Him something valuable in return for His blessing. (See Judg. 11:29–40; Jon. 2:9.) The vow might involve people (vv 1–8), animals (vv. 9–13, 26–27), property (vv. 14–25), or produce (vv. 30–33).

If the person could not fulfill the vow, he was not permitted to back out, nor could he offer a cheaper substitute. He had to give the priest the equivalent in money, plus one-fifth more. This chapter tells the priest how to evaluate the gift so that the Lord would receive the right amount, for the money was used for the work of the sanctuary. The word *valuation* is used nineteen times.

Talk is not "cheap"; rash promises can be very expensive. It behooves us to be careful when we experience great joy or great sorrow, lest we make promises to God that we cannot keep. (See Prov. 20:25; Eccles. 5:4–5.) Yes, you can give God something else, but be sure it is equivalent to the original offer—and let Him do the evaluating.

NUMBERS

◆

Numbers gets its name from the numberings of Israel's men of war. The old generation was numbered at Mount Sinai (chaps. 1—4) and the new in the plains of Moab (chaps. 26—27). This is a book of *transition*. God set aside the old generation because of their unbelief (chaps. 1—20) and then prepared a new generation to inherit the Promised Land (chaps. 21—36).

It is a book of *wanderings*, for God made His people wander in the wilderness for forty years until the old generation, twenty years and older, died off. They did not believe God, and their unbelief cost them the inheritance. The New Testament commentary on this event is the book of Hebrews. Unless by faith you enter into your spiritual inheritance in Christ (Eph. 1:3), you will "wander" in unbelief and rob yourself of the blessings God has planned for you (Eph. 2:10).

Bible geography is instructive. Israel in Egypt pictures our lost condition of bondage to the world. Israel in Canaan illustrates our claiming our inheritance by faith and enjoying the fullness of God's provision. Israel in the wilderness pictures carnal Christians whose unbelief and disobedience prevent them from entering into all that God has for them.

NUMBERS 1—2

Genesis pictures God's people as pilgrims and strangers, looking for their inheritance. Exodus and Leviticus depict Israel as a holy nation of priests, worshiping the Lord. The book of Numbers emphasizes God's people as warriors, overcoming the enemy and claiming the promised inheritance.

They counted the men, twenty years and older, who were able to go to war. They did not ask for volunteers. When you enter the family of God by faith in Jesus Christ, you automatically become one of His soldiers (2 Tim. 2:3–4). Every believer is a soldier, either a good one or a bad one.

The army was organized, each tribe with its leaders and its standard. There was unity in diversity. Perhaps the camp of Israel pictures the church. There are different "tribes" and standards, with their different leaders, but it is one army, following one Commander and fighting one enemy: "And this is the victory that has overcome the world—our faith" (1 John 5:4).

NUMBERS 3—4

The priests were also a part of the battle, for without the blessing of the Lord, there could be no victory. Some of God's people are in the front lines of the battle, while others are behind the lines, interceding to the Lord.

It was important that the tabernacle of the Lord go with the people, so God instructed the priests and Levites exactly how to dismantle it and carry it. Each detail about the Lord's work is significant and must not be left to mere human wisdom.

And each person is vital to the work of the Lord, no matter what task God assigns. No task is trivial, not even taking care of the pegs (3:37). Some Levites had heavier burdens than others, but God had given them the assignments and He would enable them.

The putting up and taking down of the tabernacle were tasks as essential as the offering of the sacrifices or the burning of the incense. Spiritual ministry is no place for idle spectators or careless workers, for it is a matter of life and death (4:17–20).

NUMBERS 5

Defiling (1–4). Not everybody in Israel was a soldier or a priest, but each individual was responsible to please the Lord and keep from defilement. Israel was to be holy to the Lord; otherwise He could not bless the nation with victory. You may not think you are important to the spiritual battles going on in today's world, but you are; and you must keep clean.

Defrauding (5–10). If the soldiers are not loyal to one another, how can they defeat the enemy? It was not enough to confess the sin; there had to be restitution as well. The people were also reminded to care for the priests because their ministry was important to the victory. Again, each individual had to be sure he or she was obedient to the Lord.

Discovering (11–31). This unusual law protected the woman as well as sanctified the marriage relationship. Husbands and wives must be faithful to each other. Marriage is an intimate relationship, and even *hidden* unfaithfulness can create a spirit of jealousy and doubt. If the wife was guilty, the truth would come out; if not, the husband could trust her, and they could live together and have a family. We have no such laws today, but we have an all-seeing God to whom we will answer one day.

NUMBERS 6

Separation (1–12). *Nazirite* comes from a word that means "to dedicate." Nazirites were men and women dedicated to the Lord, either for a brief period or for a lifetime (Judg. 13:1–5). Their separation was twofold: *to* the Lord (v. 2) and *from* what defiled (vv. 3–8). Even little things could defile, like the seeds and skins of grapes! When God says something is wrong, it is wrong, no matter how small a thing it may seem to be.

Termination (13–21). The Nazirite stated at the beginning how long the vow would last, but our separation to the Lord must be for life. However, it is not wrong occasionally to set aside periods of time for special devotion to the Lord, just as the Nazirites did. If the Nazirite became defiled, all the days of the dedication were lost (v. 12). It is a costly thing to disobey the Lord. Even though the Nazirite had lived in dedication, it was still necessary to bring sacrifices to the Lord, for nobody is perfect before Him.

Benediction (22–27). What a privilege it was for the priests to bless the people, and what a privilege it is for us to share God's blessing with others. He blesses us so that we may be a blessing (Gen. 12:1–3). The people were about to enter into war, yet God told them how to have peace. No matter how trying your circumstances may be, you can have God's peace as you live under the blessing of His smile.

NUMBERS 7

The longest chapter in Numbers deals with a generous offering brought by the leaders of the tribes just after the tabernacle was set up. Leaders certainly ought to set the example in giving, and those men did.

The gifts were identical, presented on twelve successive days; and yet in God's eyes, the gifts were individual. If what we give is from the heart, presented for God's glory, He sees it, and He will reward in His own time. Each of those twelve leaders was precious to God. He received their gifts individually.

The gifts were practical, to be used for the service of the tabernacle. When we supply ministry tools for God's servants, we also bring gifts to the Lord.

Everybody but the Kohathites could use the carts for their work. The sons of Kohath had to carry the tabernacle furniture on their shoulders (3:30–31; 4:15). Although there are some burdens others can help us bear, "each one shall bear his own load" (Gal. 6:1–5). David disobeyed this law and brought judgment from God (2 Sam. 6:1–15). Don't refuse the burdens; God will enable you to carry them.

NUMBERS 8

Not everybody is called to be a priest or a leader. Some are called to be helpers, such as the Levites. The gift of helps (1 Cor. 12:28) is important in God's work and must never be despised. God considered the Levites as His gift to Aaron (v. 19). We should be thankful for those God gives to help us in our work.

Substitutes. The Levites were first of all given to the Lord as substitutes for all the firstborn in Israel (vv. 16–18; 3:11–13). The firstborn belonged to God, but He allowed them to be redeemed (Exod. 13:1, 11–13). You have your work to do for Christ, but don't forget those who represent you as they serve the Lord in different places.

Servants. The Levites were given to Aaron as workers (vv. 11, 19). They could not do all that the priests did, but they had their tasks and were expected to fulfill them faithfully.

Sacrifices. They were presented to God as "living sacrifices," wave offerings to the Lord (vv. 11, 13, 15, 21). No matter what work you do for the Lord, it should be like offering up a sacrifice of worship to Him (Phil. 4:10–20).

NUMBERS 9

God teaches us in different ways. There are *commandments to obey* (vv. 1–5), and we must know them and do them. Passover was the annual reminder that God had redeemed Israel from bondage and they belonged to Him. Think of the thousands of lambs that were slain so that the people might obey God! Think of the Lamb of God who died for the whole world (John 1:29)!

There are also *exceptions to consider* (vv. 6–14). The legalist makes no exceptions, and the anarchist makes everything an exception; but the child of God waits on the Lord for His orders. Each problem in life is an opportunity to learn how to wait on God and discover His will. Let's not fear exceptions. Our job is to be obedient even if what we do does not always appear to be consistent.

The Will of God

Never be afraid of the will of God; God's will is the expression of God's love, and it comes from His heart (Ps. 33:11). It is food, not medicine (John 4:31–34), and nourishes us as we obey. Oswald Chambers was correct when he said, "Doing God's will is never hard. The only thing that is hard is not *doing His will." Are you doing His will* now?

There are *leadings to follow* (vv. 15–23). Note the sequence: obeying the Lord, waiting on the Lord, following the Lord. God has His times and His routes, and we must watch for His leading. Perhaps the most difficult time for us is when God tarries and we have to wait (v. 19). It is also the most dangerous time, for human nature wants to rush ahead. We must "rest in the LORD, and wait patiently for Him" (Ps. 37:7).

NUMBERS 10

The people of Israel were to set out for their God-appointed inheritance. They would go through an unknown land that was dangerous, but God gave them the help they needed.

His command (1–13). The priests used the two silver trumpets to communicate God's will to the people. The blowing of the silver trumpets would gather them together, move them forward, summon them to battle, or call them to enjoy the feasts of the Lord. They heard the trumpets and watched the cloud, and they were safe.

His word (14–28). God had already told them how to organize the march, and all they had to do was obey. If we don't obey in the things God has told us, He will not reveal anything new to us (John 7:17).

Experience (29–32). Hobab was a brother of Zipporah, Moses' wife; and Moses asked him to come with Israel and share his "wilderness wisdom." Hobab's wisdom did not take the place of God's leading. Rather, Hobab assisted in the everyday problems of a people who were not accustomed to wilderness life. God promises to guide us, but that doesn't mean we should be deaf to the wisdom of experienced people. Hobab did Israel good, and Israel brought good to him (Judg. 1:16; 4:11).

Prayer (33–36). The ark represented God's presence and His throne. Moses prayed to God when the people marched forward and when God told them to stop. That's a good example for us to follow as we move through each day.

NUMBERS 11

This is a chapter of complaining!

Complaining about bread (1–9). God was leading them, so the people had all they needed; yet they complained again. (See Phil. 2:14–15.) Their grumbling was evidence of the unbelief that would keep them out of the Promised Land. Had they been grateful for God's goodness and obedient to God's guidance, they would have saved themselves a great deal of misery. Let's remember that the next time we are tempted to complain about the providence of God. "The slaves of sin rarely grumble at that slavery; it is their slavery to God they grumble at," said George MacDonald.

Complaining about burdens (10–25). Moses was grieved when they criticized both him and God. Could they improve upon the manna that came from heaven? Why did they crave food from Egypt? Had they forgotten their bondage in that land? Moses did what you must do when people disappoint you: he took it to God in prayer and told God just how he felt. God met the need, encouraged His servant, and punished the rebels.

Complaining about blessing (26–35). Zealous for Moses and his position, Joshua told him to stop the two men from prophesying. James and John made a similar mistake, and Jesus had to rebuke them (Luke 9:49–50). If all of God's people were praising God by the Spirit, they would not be complaining! The Jews got what they asked for, but they lost the spiritual enrichment that comes when people walk by faith (Ps. 106:15). Have you learned to be grateful for *unanswered* prayer?

NUMBERS 12

The leader denounced (1–3). If you are in a place of leadership, expect criticism, even from members of your family. It happened to Moses, David (2 Sam. 6:20–23), and the Lord Jesus (Mark 3:20–21). Moses' wife was not the real reason for their criticism. Aaron and his sister were jealous of the authority God had given Moses, and they wanted him to share it. Perhaps they were reacting to what God did for the seventy elders (chap. 11).

The Lord displeased (4–10). Moses did not defend himself; he waited for God to act. If we defend ourselves, we may hinder the Lord from defending us. Next to death, becoming a leper was the worst thing that could have happened to Miriam.

The nation delayed (11–16). How often people turn for help to the very ones they have criticized! In his meekness, Moses did not rejoice at his sister's punishment; instead, he prayed for her (Matt. 5:43–48). Because of their sin, Aaron and Miriam delayed the march of the nation for a whole week. The sin of criticism is far more serious than most people realize (Matt. 7:1–5; James 4:12).

NUMBERS 13

Seeing the opportunities (1–25). The people thought they should spy out the land before conquering it, and Moses let them do it (Deut. 1:19–25). God had already told them what the Promised Land was like, so why did they have to investigate? Faith takes God at His word and needs no other evidence (Heb. 11:1). The spies discovered that the land was indeed all that God had promised it to be.

Seeing the obstacles (26–33). Ten spies emphasized the obstacles instead of the opportunities and concluded that Israel was too weak to conquer the enemy. They walked by sight and not by faith. The people of the land were giants, the city walls were high, and the men felt like grasshoppers! Unbelief blinds you to God's greatness and magnifies your own weakness.

Seeing the Lord (30). Caleb was a man of faith who didn't worry about the size of the problem because he trusted a great God. The important question in life is not, "How big is the problem?" or "How big am I?" The major question is, "How big is my God?" The Lord saw the Canaanites as grasshoppers (Isa. 40:22), but the unbelieving spies were not looking at the situation from God's point of view. When you walk by faith, the future is your friend, and every enemy is defeated.

NUMBERS 14

The report of the majority of the spies brought about a destructive chain reaction in the camp of Israel.

Unbelief led to rebellion (1–10). The people wept, complained, looked back to Egypt, wanted a new leader, and even threatened to stone Caleb and Joshua. Such are the evidences of unbelief. Faith looks ahead with courage; unbelief looks back with complaint. Faith unites the people of God; unbelief looks for somebody to blame. There was still time to repent and seek God's face, but the people refused to listen to Caleb and Joshua.

Rebellion led to intercession (11–19). Moses once again

stood between God's people and God's judgment and turned down God's offer to make him the founder of a new nation (Exod. 32). Moses interceded for the people on the basis of the character and glory of God.

Intercession led to pardon (20–38). God pardoned the people, but at the same time He judged their sins (Gal. 6:7–8). The ten spies died in a plague, and the nation was consigned to forty years of wandering until the people who were twenty years old or older died. Faith brings life, but unbelief brings defeat and death.

Pardon led to presumption (39–45). The people had acted stubbornly like the mule, and now they acted impetuously like the horse (Ps. 32:9). God forgives us that we might fear Him (Ps. 130:4), not that we might tempt Him. The flesh can never accomplish what only faith can do. (See Deut. 1:41–44.)

When You Are Outnumbered

Caleb and Joshua were a minority on the Search Committee and yet they did not give in, even when the nation turned against them and their lives were in danger. They had faith in God, they knew God's will for the people, and they stood their ground. It is not important that we please others, but it is important that we please God. Like Caleb and Joshua, sometimes we must suffer because of the sins of others; but in the end, God will vindicate those who trust Him. (See Acts 20:24; 1 Cor. 15:58.)

NUMBERS 15

Assurance (1–21). God gave the people a word of assurance when He said, "*When* you have come into the land" (italics added). In spite of the nation's sins, the new generation would make it to Canaan and possess the land. (See 2 Tim. 2:11–13.) When they did, they were expected to take time to thank God and worship Him. Do you pause to thank God for sharing His blessings with you?

Obedience (22–29). God made provision for the forgiveness of unintentional sins. Of course, innocent animals had to die to provide forgiveness, just as Jesus had to die to make our cleansing possible.

Arrogance (30–36). In His law, God made no provision for presumptuous sin, for such sinners were despising God's Word and defying His authority. God in His mercy could forgive such sins, as He did with David (2 Sam. 12), but He did not put Himself under obligation. The man who deliberately violated the Sabbath discovered that God is not mocked.

Remembrance (37–41). The tassels were small things, yet they carried a big message: Israel belonged to God and must respect and obey His commandments. It is not wrong to have reminders that point us to God, provided they don't replace God or His Word. We are to "seek those things which are above" (Col. 3:1).

NUMBERS 16

A successful leader is often accused of exalting himself, especially by those who are jealous of him and want to take his place. It is true that all of God's people are set apart by Him and for Him, but it is also true that God calls some of His people to be leaders in special places of service. Without leadership, we would have chaos.

Leaders often get blamed for things they did not do (vv. 12–14). Moses wanted to lead the nation into their inheritance, but the unbelief of the people kept them out. It is easier for rebels to find a scapegoat than to confess their own sins. They said that *Egypt* was a "land flowing with milk and honey." Their statement showed where their hearts really were.

The opposition was impressive: 250 leaders, all united against Moses. But Moses was not intimidated; he took the matter to the Lord and let Him be the judge. God will vindicate His servants better than they can vindicate themselves. Once again, the love and intercession of Moses saved the very people who had created problems for him. (See Rom. 12:14–21.)

Nearly fifteen thousand people died because of four men who wanted to promote themselves. That danger is still with us, and we must heed Proverbs 16:18; 18:12; and 1 Peter 5:5–6.

NUMBERS 17

God had disciplined the people because of their murmuring and rebelling, but the problem was not yet solved. One of Israel's besetting sins was *murmuring* (1 Cor. 10:10), a sin that we must avoid today (Phil. 2:14).

Complaining God's people are commanded not to complain (Phil. 2:14); therefore, complaining is a sin. When we complain, we give evidence of unbelief in our hearts and lack of gratitude toward God. If we were truly "giving thanks always for all things" (Eph. 5:20), we would not be complaining. The best way to overcome a complaining spirit is to accept God's will by faith and thank Him for His goodness, even if we don't see anything good happening. Romans 8:28 is still there for us to claim!

Korah, a Levite, was not satisfied to serve in the tabernacle according to God's will; he wanted a "promotion" so he could enjoy all the privileges of the priests. It is good to desire spiritual growth and progress, but we must beware selfish ambition that glorifies the servant and not the Master (Phil. 2:3–4). "Selfish ambition" is one of the works of the flesh (Gal. 5:20), and it brings destruction.

God vindicated His servants by bringing *death* to some of their opponents and by giving *life* to Aaron's rod. By the power of God, the dead rod produced beauty and fruit. Spiritual leadership will be recognized by its life and fruitfulness, which come from being in the Holy of Holies with God.

How unpredictable is human nature! One day, the people wanted to serve in the tabernacle; the next day, they were afraid to get near it! They did not sincerely fear God; they feared only His judgment. They *needed* leadership far more than they realized.

NUMBERS 18

The emphasis in this chapter is on *gifts*. God gives *helpers* (v. 6) to assist us in our work, and we must accept them and be grateful for them. Some of the Levites had rebelled against Moses and Aaron, but God still gave them the privilege of serving Him and helping the priests.

God gives us *work to do* (v. 7). If we are in the will of God, our work is a divine vocation, and we must do it for His glory.

God gives us *what we need* (v. 8ff.). He fed the priests from the sacrifices brought to the altar and also from the tithes (v. 21). His action reminds us that "the laborer is worthy of his wages" (Luke 10:7; 1 Cor. 9:14; 1 Tim. 5:18).

God gives us *Himself* (v. 20). The priests and Levites were assigned places to live in Israel, but they did not have property from which they could get income (Josh. 13:14). They had to trust God to meet their needs. But when God is your inheritance, what more do you need? (See Ps. 16:5–6.)

NUMBERS 19

As a holy and separated people, the Jews had to avoid ritual uncleanness of all kinds, especially contamination from dead bodies. No doubt there were hygienic purposes behind this law, but it also reminded the people to avoid sin because of the defilement it brings. God dwelt in the camp and no one was to defile it. The application for today is found in 2 Corinthians 6:14—7:1.

God made provision for restoring persons who became defiled. Blood had to be shed, for the heifer was a sin offering (v. 9). The ashes from the sacrifice were ceremonially clean and were used to make "water of purification." The defiled person could be ceremonially cleansed by obeying God's instructions and using the water of purification.

Water for washing is a picture of the Word of God (John 15:3; Eph. 5:25–27). The Word promises us cleansing because the blood of God's Son was shed for us on the cross (1 John 1:5—2:2). The Word also provides cleansing for the inner person as we read it, meditate on it, and apply it to our lives.

Why should we be defiled and defile others when God's gracious cleansing is available?

NUMBERS 20

Leaders are often discouraged as they go through one trial after another. First, Miriam died, and Moses and Aaron mourned their only sister. Then the people began to complain again, for Egypt was still in their hearts. In the will of God, no place is an "evil place"; but when your inner desires are not spiritual, no place is a good place—except Egypt!

Leaders sometimes disobey God, as Moses did when he was angered by the people (Ps. 106:32–33). Water for drinking is a picture of the Holy Spirit (John 7:37–39), and the rock is a symbol of Christ (1 Cor. 10:4). Christ was smitten on the cross for us that we might receive the gift of the Spirit. He died but once, so Moses should not have smitten the rock again. Instead, he should have spoken to the rock.

Leaders are disciplined by God, for with privilege goes responsibility. Neither Moses nor Aaron was permitted to enter the Promised Land, although Moses was allowed to see the land from afar (Deut. 3:21–29).

Leaders are sometimes disappointed. Edom would not permit Israel to pass through the land despite the promises Moses gave. The Edomites were the descendants of Esau, Jacob's brother, and were therefore blood relatives to Israel; but they did not act like brethren.

It is not easy to be a leader, and we must pray for those whom God has made leaders in His service.

NUMBERS 21

In the journeys of life, God can meet every need.

God gives victory. The nation of Israel was on the move as God gave the people one victory after another over strong kings and armies. Israel could have had this experience *in Canaan* had they trusted God and entered the land. These battles helped to train the younger men for the time when they would conquer Canaan.

God gives healing. Israel murmured not about the battles but about their lack of food and water in the wilderness. It was the old "Egyptian appetite" asserting itself again. Instead of meeting the need immediately, God first disciplined the people until they cried out for help. Jesus used the uplifted brazen serpent to picture His own death on the cross (John 3:14–16). He became the very thing that was killing us—*sin* (2 Cor. 5:21). And the only way to be saved is to look to Christ by faith.

God gives water. This time the water did not come from a rock, for God is not limited to one way of meeting our needs. He provided a well for them in a miraculous way. This shows the grace and goodness of the Lord, for just a short time before, the people had complained about the way He was leading them. Give thanks for Psalm 103:10 and Philippians 4:19!

NUMBERS 22

The reports of Israel's victories brought fear to Balak. He knew that the army of Israel could never be defeated by human means because the Jews were *God's* people and the battle was a spiritual one. That is why he asked Balaam to curse the nation. Our battle today is not against flesh and blood but against spiritual wickedness, and we will win the victory only if we use spiritual weapons (Eph. 6:10–18; 2 Cor. 10:3–6).

Balaam was a hireling prophet who finally succumbed to the pressure of greater honor and more money. He was willing to look at things "from another viewpoint" in hopes he could find a loophole in the revealed will of God. It is a dangerous thing to bargain over the will of God. Using one's gifts to make money is "the way of Balaam" (2 Pet. 2:15–16), a sin that God condemns.

Thomas Merton has said that "the greatest evil is found where the greatest good has been corrupted." And Paul warned, "For the love of money is a root of all kinds of evil" (1 Tim. 6:10). Balaam and Judas Iscariot know how true this is!

NUMBERS 23

God did not shut Balaam's mouth. He let him speak, *but He turned the curse into a blessing* (Neh. 13:2). Whenever you feel that people and circumstances are cursing you, remember what God did for Israel, and trust Him (Rom. 8:28).

Balaam's descriptions of Israel remind us of the privileges we have as the children of God. We are *safe* (v. 8; Rom. 8:31–39) because we are *separated from the world* (v. 9; John 17:14–16) and belong to the Lord who never lies (v. 19). We have *strength* like an ox (v. 22) and a lioness (v. 24).

Balaam wanted very much to die the death of the righteous (v. 10), but he did not want to live the life of the righteous. Read Psalm 37:37, Proverbs 14:32, and Revelation 14:13, and contrast Paul's testimony in Philippians 1:19–23.

NUMBERS 24

Balak could not silence Balaam no matter how he tried. In his third oracle (vv. 1–9), Balaam saw Israel in Canaan, conquering their enemies and enjoying their inheritance. His statement in verse 9 about blessing and cursing reminds us of God's covenant with Abraham (Gen. 12:3). Balaam was actually condemning himself when he spoke. God does not defend His people's sins, but He always defends His people, for they are dear to Him.

In his fourth oracle (vv. 15–24), Balaam saw Israel's future glory in the coming of the Messiah (v. 17). God used a covetous prophet to give a beautiful picture of the Savior and the victories He would win.

Satan and his followers do their best to curse God's people today. However, through it all, God's grace still works, God's people are still blessed, and God's name is glorified, for God can turn the curse into a blessing.

NUMBERS 25—26

Balaam could not destroy Israel with his curses, but he could defile Israel with his counsel. He seduced the Jews into disobeying God by suggesting that Balak invite Israel to the religious feasts of the Moabites (31:16). There the Jews quickly fell into sin.

Moses had commanded the people to separate themselves from the nations around them and to avoid their abominable religious practices (Exod. 34:10–17). Israel abandoned its special position (Num. 23:9) and compromised with sin. The result? Twenty-four thousand Jews died from a plague God sent to the camp.

It was not Moses, the leader, or Eleazer, the high priest, who stopped the plague, but Phinehas, the son of Eleazer. His devotion to the Lord brought him a special commendation and reward from the Lord. (See Ps. 106:28–31.)

God's people must beware compromising with the enemy (2 Cor. 6:14–18). If Satan does not succeed as the devouring lion (1 Pet. 5:8), he will come as the deceiving serpent (2 Cor. 11:3).

The taking of the second census was a sign that the nation's wanderings were soon to end. Note the people in this list who are given special attention: Dathan and Abiram, who rebelled against the Lord (26:9–11); Nadab and Abihu, who defied the Lord (26:61); and Joshua and Caleb, who believed the Lord (26:65).

NUMBERS 27

Claiming the land (1–11). New problems give us new opportunities to seek God's wisdom and learn new truths: "Yet you do not have because you do not ask" (James 4:2). The five daughters had the courage and faith to ask for their inheritance, and they got it. They also had a part in establishing a law that helped other families in Israel get their inheritance.

Seeing the land (12–14). Moses saw the Promised Land but (as far as we know) did not enter it until he appeared with Elijah on the Mount of Transfiguration (Matt. 17:1–8). The land of Canaan is a picture, not of heaven but of the believer's inheritance in Christ in the heavenlies (Eph. 1:3). A whole generation died and never saw the land. Ten of the spies saw the land for forty days and then died in their unbelief. Moses saw the land but could not enter it. The new generation, along with Caleb and Joshua, entered the land and claimed their promised inheritance. To which group do you belong?

Conquering the land (15–23). As always, Moses' greatest concern was the people and not himself, and God gave him his assistant Joshua to be his successor (Matt. 25:21). Joshua was God's general who would conquer the land and give the people their inheritance. He is a type of Jesus Christ (*Joshua* means "Jehovah is salvation") who conquered our enemies for us and opened the way for us to claim all the blessings God has for us.

NUMBERS 28—29

The new generation had to be taught the "religious calendar," which would govern their lives after they entered the land. The older generation should see to it that those coming after understand the traditions. They were instructed about the regular offerings and also about the annual feasts. (See Lev. 23.)

All time belongs to God, but it is good for us to set aside special times to remind us of what He has done for us. The Jews presented their worship at the the beginning of each day (28:1–8), at the end of the week (28:9–10), and on the first of the month (28:11–15). We do not bring animal sacrifices. Instead, we present our bodies to the Lord as "living sacrifices" (Rom. 12:1–2).

The special annual feasts could not take the place of the regular offerings. The way to become more spiritual is to strengthen the regular worship day after day, and then the special times of worship will do us more good. Never neglect the "regular burnt offering" (28:3). The word *regular* is used seventeen times in Numbers 28—29, a reminder that the daily routine is important to God and to us.

NUMBERS 30

The power of words. God takes our promises and pledges seriously, and so should we (Ps. 50:14; Eccles. 5:4–5). If we promise God that we will do something, or not do something, we must keep our word. We must also recognize that *willing* and *doing* are two different things (Rom. 7:18–25). We need the wisdom of God in making our promises and the power of God in keeping them (Phil. 2:12–13). Words are powerful things and must be used carefully. The Quakers say, "Of your unspoken words, you are the master; of your spoken words, the servant; of your written words, the slave."

The power of authority. God acknowledges the presence of authority. A wife's vow may be canceled by her husband and a daughter's vow by her father. The wife and the daughter should consider this before making promises to God. Although Moses does not instruct the man of the house this way, certainly the husband and father would want to consider the whole family before making any promises to God.

The power of silence. If the father or the husband says nothing, this is considered to be approval of the vow. Silence can sometimes be more powerful than words and have much greater consequences. (See Ps. 141:3.)

NUMBERS 31

The last battle Moses directed was against the Midianites who, at Balaam's suggestion, had seduced Israel into both idolatry and immorality (chap. 25). Each tribe sent one thousand soldiers, and the high priest went before the army with the ark of the covenant. It was God's battle, and He would give victory.

Balaam did not have long to enjoy whatever rewards Balak gave him because he was killed in the battle (v. 8). Alas, he did not "die the death of the righteous" (23:10)! As Mark wrote, "For what will it profit a man if he gains the whole world, and loses his own soul?" (Mark 8:36).

Israel won the war but almost lost the victory, for the leaders brought some Midianite women into the camp along with the spoils. Incomplete obedience always leads to further temptation. (See 1 Sam. 15.) If we do not defeat the enemy, the enemy will defeat us.

They had fought a "holy war," but the army was defiled in the slaying of the Midianites. They had to purify themselves and the spoils to be clean before God (chap. 19). Some of the spoils were cleansed by fire. The Lord wants clean soldiers as well as conquering soldiers.

NUMBERS 32

Some people choose to live on the border of God's blessing. They make their decisions on the basis of material gain and not spiritual blessing. The two and a half tribes did not claim their inheritance in Canaan, though they were very close to it.

They assured Moses that they would help conquer the land, but the tribes still brought division to Israel. In fact, when the land was fully conquered, the two and a half tribes had to put up an altar to let people know, "We belong to Israel!" (See Josh. 22.) Had they gone over the Jordan and claimed their inheritance, everybody would have known their citizenship.

"Do not take us over the Jordan!" (v. 5) is as much an expression of failure as "Take us back to the land of Egypt!" or "Let us die in the wilderness!" When material gain, not the glory of God, governs our decisions, we will make the wrong decisions. (See Ps. 47:4.)

NUMBERS 33

Reviewing the past (1–49). Dr. A. T. Pierson said, "History is His story." It is good to review the past and discern the hand of the Lord at work. God delivered them from Egypt and brought them to Sinai, where they entered into a covenant with Him (vv. 1–15). Then He brought them to the border of the Promised Land, where they refused to go in (vv. 16–36). They wandered for forty years and then ended up on the plains of Moab (vv. 37–49). Unbelief means wasted time, wasted lives, and wasted opportunities, but God is gracious and long-suffering with His people.

Anticipating the future (50–56). "When you have crossed the Jordan into the land of Canaan" was a word of promise and assurance that would encourage the nation in their new venture of faith. What a privilege to claim their God-given inheritance! But God also gave some responsibilities: drive out the enemy, destroy their idols, dispossess the people, and then divide the land. First you conquer, then you claim. First the obedience, then the blessing.

NUMBERS 34

God assigned the tribes their inheritance and set their boundaries, but He used human leaders to do it. What a privilege it is to help people claim their inheritance from God!

We must accept what God assigns to us and not complain or covet what others possess. Some land fronted on wilderness (v. 3), and other portions faced the Great Sea (v. 6). Some tribes had mountains in their territory. Like Canaan, the Christian life is "a land of hills and valleys" (Deut. 11:11), and our God is a God of both the hills and the valleys (1 Kings 20:23ff.). He knows what is best for us, and He is always with us.

When you are tempted to complain about what God has assigned to you, ponder John 3:27 and 1 Corinthians 4:7; 12:4–7, 11. Through faith in Christ, we can be content with our lot (Phil. 4:11–13).

NUMBERS 35

Residence. The fact that the Levites were servants of God did not make them any less citizens of the land. They needed places to live and care for their families when they were not ministering at the tabernacle. The tribes' provision of forty-eight cities for them was done in a fair way (v. 8). God's people should care for God's work and should share as God has provided for them (2 Cor. 8:1–15).

Refuge. Six of the Levitical cities were designated cities of refuge. God makes a distinction between murder and manslaughter, the intentional and the accidental. In that day, the nation had no police force to investigate crimes and prosecute criminals, so the innocent had to be protected from angry family members who might want to take justice into their own hands. In the city of refuge, the fugitive was safe until the congregation decided whether he was guilty of murder or not (Deut. 19:11–13).

Redemption. Jesus Christ is our "city of refuge" (Heb. 6:18).

When we trust Him, our sins are all forgiven and judgment is past (Rom. 8:1). Salvation is not probation. If the fugitive left the city, he was in danger of death. In Jesus Christ, we have eternal life (John 5:24). Our High Priest will never die; therefore, we are saved eternally (Heb. 7:23–28).

NUMBERS 36

Moses had already decreed that a man's inheritance must go to his daughters if he had no sons (27:1–11), but that did not completely solve the problem. Some men of the tribe of Manasseh (Zelophehad's tribe) had discussed and pondered the matter and were concerned about the distribution of their tribal land. What if the daughters married into other tribes? Would the inheritance eventually be confused or even lost?

It is good to think about decisions and see their practical ramifications in everyday life. It is good to think about the future and ask, "What may happen?"

The simple solution was to require the women who inherit property to marry only within their own family clan. It is good to inherit wealth, but with the inheritance may come restrictions and responsibilities. If we want the one, we must accept the other. The daughters of Zelophehad married their cousins, so the inheritance remained intact.

DEUTERONOMY

◆

Deuteronomy means "second law." It records the second giving of the Law by Moses as he prepared the nation to enter their promised inheritance. But Moses did more than simply repeat the Law to a new generation. He applied it to their new life in the land and stressed the importance of their loving God and obeying Him from the heart.

Some key words in Deuteronomy are *land* (190 times), *hear* (54 times), *possess* and *possession* (57 times), *heart* (53 times), and *love* (25 times).

The nation *owned* the land by God's grace and *possessed* the land by God's power, but they could not *enjoy* the land unless they obeyed God's Word. When the nation disobeyed, God chastened them *in the land* (book of Judges) and then took them *from the land* into Babylonian captivity.

In the addresses, Moses first reminded the people of God's past leading (chaps. 1—4). The word *remember* is used 14 times in the book. Then he restated and applied the Law (chaps. 5—26), and closed his message with words of warning and blessing (chaps. 27—33) In chapter 34, we read how Moses passed from the scene and Joshua took over.

DEUTERONOMY 1

The Kadesh Barnea event is recorded in Numbers 14, and the New Testament commentary is in Hebrews 3—4. God warns against "an evil heart of unbelief" (Heb. 3:12). An *evil* heart! Why is the sin of unbelief so evil?

To begin with, unbelief makes God a liar and questions the dependability of His Word. Our responsibility is not to question God but to believe God and do what He commands.

Unbelief wastes time. An eleven-day journey turned into

forty years of wandering and death! Unbelief robs us of God's best blessings. God cared for His people those forty years, but how much more He would have done had they claimed their inheritance.

When you come to those Kadesh Barnea places in your pilgrimage, don't look around at the problems and dangers. Look up to the God who is leading you, and walk by faith.

DEUTERONOMY 2

God assigns our battles. He instructed the nation not to meddle with the Edomites, the Moabites, or the Ammonites. The people were to behave themselves as godly pilgrims and avoid creating trouble. For a nation that enjoyed great victory in war, His instructions were probably hard to take, but God had better things for His people than the spoils of those nations. (See Rom. 12:18; Col. 4:5.) It is unwise to meddle in things that God commands us to avoid.

God assures our victory. When the Lord leads us into battle, we need not fear, for His commandment is His enablement. Israel defeated Sihon, and "there was not one city too strong" (v. 36) for God's people. (See 1 John 5:1–4.)

God assigns our inheritance. God promised to give the Trans-Jordan territory to the tribes of Reuben and Gad (Num. 32), and He kept His promise. (See Ps. 47:4; Acts 20:32; 1 Pet. 1:3–5.) God promises—we possess by faith!

DEUTERONOMY 3

A possession to claim (1–11). Guided by God's will and fortified by God's promises, the people marched from victory to victory. Were it not for their unbelief, the former generation could have won the victories in Canaan forty years earlier. The high walls and gates were no problem to God (Num. 13:26–33). He is limited only by our unbelief.

A promise to keep (12–22). The tribes to be settled east of the Jordan had promised to cross the river and help conquer Canaan (Num. 32:16–23). Now that their land was subdued, Reuben and Gad might have settled down and avoided a lot of danger, but they kept their word. God hears our promises and takes them seriously (Num. 30:2; Eccles. 5:1–5).

A penalty to endure (23–29). Because of his pride at Kadesh (Num. 20:1–13), Moses was not allowed to enter Canaan, even though he prayed earnestly for God to relent. He did see the land and give the people a leader to take them into the land. He also visited the land centuries later when Jesus was transfigured (Matt. 17:1–3). Some of the disappointments of life will have their compensations when the glory comes. Be patient!

DEUTERONOMY 4

Before he repeated the Law to Israel, Moses reminded them of their holy relationship with God and of their privileges as His chosen people. What other nation had heard the voice of God, had seen His power and glory, and had received His Word as their wisdom and their very life (vv. 1, 4, 25, 40)? When we take our blessings for granted, we are in danger of disobeying God.

On the basis of these privileges, Moses warned them to *take heed* lest they forget what God had done for them (v. 9), how God had come to them (v. 15), what God had said to them (v. 19), and what God expected of them because of His covenant (v. 23). To whom much is given, much shall be required.

He also warned them that disobedience would bring chastening. God forgives His people when they repent (vv. 29–31), but read Hebrews 12:25–29 before making plans to disobey God. He is a merciful God (v. 31), but He is also a jealous God (v. 24); He will not permit His children to sin successfully.

DEUTERONOMY 5

God's people have three responsibilities when it comes to His commandments: hear them, learn them, and do them (v. 1). When we read the Word of God, we should hear the voice of God as the Spirit speaks to us personally. We must allow the Spirit to teach us God's truth and then empower us to obey it. The blessing comes in the *living* of the Word and not in the *learning* (James 1:21–25).

Most of Deuteronomy is an explanation and application of the commandments repeated here. God's laws are clear and simple; man's laws are complex. As we walk in love, we fulfill God's law in the power of the Holy Spirit (Rom. 8:1–4; 13:8–10).

Beware a mere outward obedience to the laws of God (Matt. 5:20ff.). We must have a true fear of God in our hearts as well as a love for Him (vv. 28–29). "Hear" and "fear" are not contradictory commands; in fact, they belong together (Deut. 4:10).

DEUTERONOMY 6

Verse 4 is called "the Shema," from the Hebrew word for "hear." The devout Jew recites it several times a day to affirm his faith in Jehovah. The worship of foreign gods was always a threat to Israel, and this statement of faith reminded the Jews that Jehovah is the true and living God who alone deserves worship and obedience. (See 1 John 5:21.)

We must love the Lord with *all* our hearts by keeping *all* His Word *all* the days of our lives (v. 2). He cannot accept half-hearted worship or obedience (Eph. 6:6; 1 John 5:3).

How do we show our love to Him? By hearing and obeying His Word and by sharing it with others. If we love God, His truth will be a part of our normal daily conversation. We also show our love to Him by appreciating His blessings. Times of prosperity become times of temptation if we receive the gifts but fail to thank the Giver (vv. 10–15). (See Phil. 4:11–13; James 1:17.)

DEUTERONOMY 7

Israel had experienced the wrath of God when they allowed themselves to be seduced by the Moabites (Num. 25). Now they were entering a land where they would be surrounded by pagan worship. There could be no compromise. If the nation were defiled by the awful sins of the Canaanites, it would jeopardize the fulfilling of God's promise of the Savior. Israel had to be a separated people if they were to bless the whole world (Gen. 12:1–3).

Moses gives us some motives for personal obedience. To begin with, God has commanded us (vv. 1–5), and we belong to Him (vv. 6–8). He is faithful (vv. 9–11); what He promises, He will fulfill (vv. 12–26).

Believers today must maintain a separated position (2 Cor.

6:14–18; 1 John 2:15–17) while at the same time loving the lost and seeking to win them to Christ. How do we demolish the strongholds of the enemy? Read 2 Corinthians 10:1–6 and Ephesians 6:10–20.

DEUTERONOMY 8

If we will trust Him, God will bring us out (v. 14), lead us through (v. 15), and bring us in (v. 7). Whatever He starts, He finishes (Ps. 138:8; Phil. 1:6).

As He guides us, God tests us. He tests us by His Word (v. 1). Will we hear *every* word that He speaks, and will we obey? He also tests us by His ways (vv. 2–9), putting us into situations that help us to know our own hearts. When we become proud, God has to humble us. When we neglect His Word, He must remind us that His Word is our very life.

God tests us by His wealth (vv. 10–20). If we love Him and feed on His Word, we will rejoice in Him and not just in His gifts. In times of prosperity, it is easy to forget the Lord who makes it possible for us to work and earn wealth.

Christians ask God's blessing on their food before they eat, but verse 10 tells us to bless God *after* we have eaten. This is one way to remember that God "gives us richly all things to enjoy" (1 Tim. 6:17).

DEUTERONOMY 9

Moses is pointing out dangers that God's people must avoid: forgetting God's goodness (chap. 6), compromising with the enemy (chap. 7), and becoming self-satisfied and complacent after great victory (chap. 8). In this chapter, he warns about a danger that all believers constantly face: the reappearance of an old sin. In Israel's case, that sin was rebellion against God.

"But we are a new generation!" the people might have argued. "The old generation that died in the wilderness was guilty of rebellion. We are different!"

But Moses warned *them*. He knew that human nature is the same from one generation to another and that people rarely learn from the mistakes of others. *The sin we think we have conquered is the one that will conquer us.* (See 1 Cor. 10:12.)

Your greatest fear may come before the battle (vv. 1–3), but your greatest danger may be after the battle (vv. 4–6). If the victory makes you proud, you will fall; but if God's blessing humbles you, you will succeed. God is able to make you stand (Rom. 14:4).

Self-Confident People Who Failed

A wealthy farmer (Luke 12:13–21). A courageous apostle (Matt. 26:31–35). A mighty ruler (Dan. 4). A self-satisfied church (Rev. 3:14–22). Some successful businessmen (James 4:13–17). All those people failed. They apparently did not take these words to heart: "Do you see a man wise in his own eyes? There is more hope for a fool than for him" (Prov. 26:12).

DEUTERONOMY 10

Moses balances the two important themes of *law* (vv. 1–11) and *love* (vv. 12–22). Because God loves His people, He gives them His Word to nourish and guide them. *We cannot fully experience God's love for us unless we are obedient to His will.* The will of God is the expression of the love of God (Ps. 33:11).

There is no question that God loves His people (vv. 15–18). He has stated it clearly in His Word and has proved it in many ways, especially in giving His Son to die for the sins of the world (Rom. 5:8). We should love God (vv. 12–14) and prove it by our obedient service and our worship. If we love God, we will also love others (v. 19; 1 John 4:7–12).

God wants to write His Word on our hearts and make it a part of the inner person (2 Cor. 3:1–3). If you love the Word, meditate on it daily, and obey it, the Spirit will perform this wonderful work and transform your life.

DEUTERONOMY 11

What God did (1-7). Moses reminded the people of God's past mercies by using the phrase "what He did" five times. *They* did not win the battle in their own strength; God gave the victory. Note that Moses selected two examples of God's judgment, one from outside the nation (Egypt) and one from within the nation (the rebellion of Dathan and Abiram). The second is more dangerous than the first (Acts 20:28-30).

What God asks (8-21). He asks that His people obey Him because their obedience is their strength and life (vv. 8-9). They could not prosper in the land without God's constant care and blessing (Matt. 6:33). The Word in the heart will control the hand, the eyes and the tongue and will protect and direct the household (vv. 18-19).

What God promises (22-32). God's "I will" is all the promise we need! If we choose to obey, God will bless, even though we may experience trials and burdens. If we choose to disobey, God will still keep His promise and chasten us. If we love Him (vv. 1, 13, 22), we will obey Him, and in that obedience is life.

DEUTERONOMY 12

Sometimes we think that a new location is the solution to all our problems, so we change jobs or addresses. It has well been said that a change in geography does not overcome a flaw in character. A change can bring out the best in us, but it might bring out the worst in us.

Moses warned that the new land could be a place of *entanglement* (vv. 1-4, 29-32) if the people disobeyed God. Today's pluralistic society tends to treat all religious faiths alike, but God demands that we worship and serve Him alone.

The land would be a place of *enjoyment* (vv. 5-19) if they followed the Lord, for God would give them safety, rest, and blessing. We receive our spiritual inheritance by God's grace (Eph. 1:3), and we claim it by faith; but we enjoy it only if we are obedient to His will.

The land was to be a place of *enlargement* (vv. 26-28) as the people trusted God to give them victory. God wants to enlarge our lives; however, we must be careful that enlargement does not result in estrangement from God. It is folly to gain ground materially but lose it spiritually.

DEUTERONOMY 13

In Moses' day, as in our day, some people who claimed to have miraculous gifts were not faithful to the Lord. The test is not the person's ability to perform miracles, for even Satan can do that (2 Cor. 11:13–15; 2 Thess. 2:9–12), but his or her fidelity to the truth of God. Any leader who tempts us away from the Lord and His Word is an enemy and must be rejected.

Success does not determine truth, nor does personal affection (vv. 6–11). We must love truth more than we love people, no matter how painful our differences may be (Prov. 1:10ff.).

Numbers do not determine truth (vv. 12–18). If an entire city turned away from God, that is no reason for us to do so. God will stand with us (Matt. 10:28–42). Our allegiance must be "to the law and to the testimony" (Isa. 8:20).

DEUTERONOMY 14

The children of the Lord must not be like the people of the world. The basic meaning of the Hebrew word translated "holy" is "to be different." God's people are different.

Although the Jewish dietary code does not apply to God's people today (1 Tim. 4:1–5), the spiritual principle remains: we must be a separated and obedient people. The lists of "clean" and "unclean" foods were reminders that the people must learn to distinguish between what God accepts and what He rejects. Review Leviticus 11:41–47.

We should glorify God in what we receive and also in what we give (vv. 22–29). A tithe was 10 percent of the produce, which could be used as a sacrifice for joyful feasting before the Lord. A special tithe every third year supported the Levites and helped the poor.

In our receiving and in our giving, we should glorify God and joyfully serve Him. (See 1 Cor. 10:31.)

DEUTERONOMY 15

The blessing of God ought to motivate us to be a blessing and a help to others. Note how often Moses mentions the blessing of God (vv. 4, 6, 10, 14, 18). God has opened His hand generously to us, and we should open our hands widely to others (v. 8). He blesses us so that we might be a blessing (Gen. 12:2).

Not only must we have generous hands, but we should cultivate glad hearts as we share (v. 10). Giving is an occasion not for shrewd calculation (v. 9) but for jubilation! Paul may have had this verse in mind when he wrote "not grudgingly or of necessity; for God loves a cheerful giver" (2 Cor. 9:7).

The greatest gift of all is the gift of ourselves because we love one another (vv. 16–17). First we give ourselves to the Lord (Rom. 12:1–2) and then to one another in loving service (2 Cor. 8:1–5). There is plenty of room in "The Fellowship of the Pierced Ear."

DEUTERONOMY 16

From the seven feasts on the Jewish calendar (Lev. 23), Moses selected three to emphasize, and they bear a message to the believer today.

Passover (1–8) looks to the past and reminds us that we have been redeemed by the blood of the Lamb of God (John 1:29; 1 Pet. 1:18–19). Redemption brings responsibility: feeding on the Lamb and removing from our lives all things that are wrong. (See 1 Cor. 5:1–8).

Pentecost (9–12) speaks of renewal and the coming of the Spirit of God to His people (Acts 2). It is a harvest festival that calls us to enter into His service and help reap the harvest (Luke 10:2; John 4:33–38; Acts 1:8).

Tabernacles (13–17) reminded the Jews that they had lived in booths as a pilgrim people in the wilderness. We are "sojourners and pilgrims" in this world (1 Pet. 2:11) and must not get too settled down. Tabernacles also looks to the future kingdom that God has promised His people when their pilgrim journey is ended.

We need these three reminders today, lest we forget our redemption responsibilities.

DEUTERONOMY 17

Presumption. God's Word reveals God's will and we must not go beyond what God permits. To *transgress* (v. 2) means to "cross the line," which is presumptuous sin. God says, "Thus far and no farther!" and we must obey. That obedience applied to sentences of judgment (vv. 8–13). The sinner who challenged the judgment of God's appointed leaders was destined to die. "Hear and fear!"

Pride. Israel did ask for a king, and God gave them Saul (1 Sam. 8—10). We do not know whether he obeyed verses 18–20, but we do know that he failed to obey God's will (1 Sam. 15). His successor David was a man of God's Word, but David's son Solomon committed all of the sins named in verses 16–17 (1 Kings 10—11). There was great prosperity for a time, but then the nation divided and turned from God.

Common citizens, priests, judges, and kings—all had an obligation to submit to God's Word and obey it. The higher the position, the greater the responsibility. "Hear and fear!"

DEUTERONOMY 18

God's people should be a *generous* people (vv. 1–8), sharing what they have with those who serve (1 Cor. 9:1–14; 3 John 5–8). The priests and Levites depended on the sacrifices and the tithes for their sustenance, and an unfaithful people meant neglected servants. (See Neh. 13:10–14.)

They should also be a *separated* people (vv. 9–14). This is one of the strongest warnings in Scripture against occult practices, and it must be heeded today. Israel did not obey this command, and the land was defiled and the nation disciplined.

God's people must be a *discerning* people (vv. 15–22), listening to the Word, receiving it and obeying it. The Prophet mentioned here is Jesus Christ (Acts 3:18–23), but when He came, they did not recognize Him or receive Him (John 1:10–11; 5:43). The mark of a true prophet is that *everything* predicted comes to pass. The prophet is not 75 percent correct, but 100 percent correct!

DEUTERONOMY 19

There was a court system in Israel but no police force. The innocent person had to be protected before the family of a victim attempted to take vengeance. The cities of refuge provided a place of escape where the manslayer could be tried to see whether the death was manslaughter or murder.

The cities picture the salvation we have in Jesus Christ, the One to whom we have "fled for refuge" because death is pursuing us (Heb. 6:18; Rom. 6:23). The cities were appointed by God, and no other cities would do (Acts 4:12). They were accessible and available to all (Josh. 20:9; John 6:37), but the person had to believe God's Word and act on it. The roads to those cities were clearly marked and kept in good repair. The way was open and free.

However, in Christ we have something far better! The manslayer was tried to see if he were a murderer, but those who trust Christ shall never face judgment (John 5:24; Rom. 8:1). Our High Priest lives forever and intercedes for us; therefore, we can never be refused (Heb. 7:23–28). We are indeed guilty, but He forgives us by His grace—and He takes our punishment for us!

DEUTERONOMY 20

Claiming our spiritual inheritance will involve battles as well as blessings, for the hosts of evil are against us (Eph. 6:10–13). God's words to Israel help us understand how to defeat the enemies we face.

Before the battle: courage. We walk by faith and not by sight (v. 1) and must never judge the victory by our own resources or the resources of the enemy. God gives us the power to overcome, so take courage from the fact that God is with us and fights for us. Read 2 Chronicles 20:1–23 for an exciting example of this truth.

During the battle: obedience. We must be totally devoted to the Lord if we are to win the battle (2 Tim. 2:4). The battlefield is no place for the fearful and fainthearted or the doubleminded. We must obey whatever battle plan God assigns to us, for the enemy often employs a different strategy.

After the battle: complete conquest. Even in defeat, the enemy is still the enemy and can entice us into sin. Remember what happened to Achan (Josh. 7) and King Saul (1 Sam. 15).

DEUTERONOMY 21

Man is made in the image of God, and human life is precious in His sight. People are not to be treated like animals or things, and the laws in this chapter illustrate this truth.

Murder (1–9). The unlawful taking of a life is a tragedy that cannot be erased simply by burying a corpse. The heifer died instead of the culprit (Gen. 9:5–6), but the sacrifice did not atone for the murderer's sin. Rather, the sacrifice kept the land from being defiled by innocent blood (Deut. 19:10–13), and it reminded the people that life is precious.

Marriage (10–17). Jews were forbidden to marry Canaanites (Deut. 7:1–4), so the captured wife mentioned in these verses had to come from another nation. Women in general, and captives in particular, had very little status in those days; but God protected her from abuse. No matter how much authority we have, we must not mistreat others or take advantage of them.

Rebellion (18–23). A rebellious son would grieve his parents, bring shame to his village, and be a bad example to other young men. The fear of death might deter some sons, or like the prodigal (Luke 15:11ff.), they might decide to leave home. To us, it seems like a drastic law, but God will not tolerate rebellion.

See our Lord in this chapter: He died for guilty sinners; He loved and married a foreign bride (Eph. 5:25ff.); He died for rebellious sinners; and He was hanged on a tree (Gal. 3:13).

DEUTERONOMY 22

Lost possessions (1–4). God honors private ownership and demands honesty in the handling of other people's goods, even when it is not convenient. He also has compassion for animals (Exod. 23:5). We are stewards of all that God gives us, and we must be faithful.

Lost distinctions (5–12). The Bible makes it clear that "God is not the author of confusion" (1 Cor. 14:33), but confusion results when we ignore the distinctions God has made be-

tween men and women, animals, and even seeds and fabrics.
Like the dietary laws, these rules reminded the Jews that they
were a separated people, and the tassels on their clothing
were an additional reminder.

Lost reputations (13–30). Here you see God's protection for
the helpless in the land. It is a serious thing to bear false witness, particularly in the matter of sexual purity. A reputation
can be ruined by people making false accusations. It is not
enough simply to love virtue; sometimes we must also "put
away the evil" (v. 21) and deal with sin.

DEUTERONOMY 23

The phrase "enter the assembly," used six times in this
chapter, refers to participation in religious activities rather
than citizenship in the nation. God has the right to decide who
shall approach Him in worship. (See Ps. 15; John 4:19–24.) Of
course, in Jesus Christ, these distinctions have been removed
(Gal. 3:26–29), and the gospel call is to "whoever" (Rev. 22:17).

These laws were required because God walked in the camp
(v. 14); therefore, the camp had to be clean. Even matters of
personal hygiene were important (vv. 9–14). Christ walks
among His churches (Rev. 1:13; 2:1) and wants to see a holy
people.

Verse 4 shows the sad consequences of sin, of both omis-
sion (the people did not help Israel) and commission (they
hired Balaam). The kindness that we show to others, we also
show to Christ (Matt. 25:31–46). One act of unkindness may
bring years of sorrow.

Even the source of our money is God's concern (vv. 17–18).
The pagan temples had religious prostitutes, male ("dogs")
and female, and God would not accept their money earned by
abominable means.

These miscellaneous regulations remind us that God is interested in the details of our lives. He wants us to be holy so
that we may fellowship with Him (2 Cor. 6:14–18).

DEUTERONOMY 24

Knowing the sinfulness of the human heart, God gave
these laws to promote happiness (v. 5) and to prevent oppression (v. 14) and the perversion of the law (v. 17).

Husbands and wives (1–5). God allowed divorced people to remarry; but this was a concession, not a commandment (Matt. 19:1–12). The divorced wife, protected by this law, could establish a new home, and she did not become a castaway. God wants happiness and holiness in our homes. We will enjoy those blessings if we obey Him and love one another.

Masters and servants (6–18). God sees how we treat those who depend on us for their living. We must never humiliate others because they have less money or authority than we do. When we start to get proud and insensitive, we should remember what we were before the Lord saved us (vv. 18, 22; Titus 3:3–8).

Helping Others	*When others have needs, don't close your eyes (Prov. 28:27), your ears (Prov. 21:13), your hand, or your heart (Deut. 15:7; 1 John 3:17). Good words are not a substitute for good works (James 2:14–17; 1 John 3:18). When we share with the poor, we give to the Lord, and He sees to it that there are dividends for them and for us (Prov. 19:17).*

Rich and poor (19–22). God had special concern for the poor, and He depended on the generosity of His people to meet their needs. He promised to bless all who showed compassion to aliens, widows, and orphans. We should ask ourselves where we would be if others helped us to the same degree that we help others.

DEUTERONOMY 25

The emphasis is on respecting people and treating them as fellow human beings, made in the image of God. It is wrong to humiliate others or take advantage of them (vv. 1–3, 11–12).

We also should have respect for animals (v. 4; see also Prov. 12:10). It would be frustrating for an ox to be in the midst of plenty and not be able to eat. The apostle Paul saw a much wider application of this verse (1 Cor. 9:1–14; 1 Tim. 5:17–18).

We should respect the family (vv. 5–10). This law was significant in Israel because of family and tribal inheritance. It does not apply today, but the principle is clear: the family carries on the life of the nation, and it must be protected.

We must have respect for truth (vv. 13–16) and not be devious in our business dealings. Read Proverbs 11:1 and 20:10, and heed the warning of Proverbs 21:6.

DEUTERONOMY 26

These two rituals were to be observed after the nation had entered Canaan and become an agricultural society. When they had reaped their first harvest, the people were to give the firstfruits to God to acknowledge Him as the Redeemer of the nation. God still wants us to put Him first and give Him glory for the blessings He freely bestows on us (Prov. 3:5–10).

They were also to present the "third-year tithe" to help support the Levites and the poor in the land. As with the ceremony of firstfruits, the people were to confess the Lord's goodness in blessing the land and giving the harvest.

There is nothing wrong with special times of ceremony and celebration, especially when we make new beginnings. However, we must focus on worshiping God and not just observing a ceremony.

These two events remind us of the two great commandments, to love God first and then to love our neighbor. Grateful obedience is a hallmark of God's special people (vv. 16–19).

DEUTERONOMY 27

This ceremony was observed only once, after Israel entered the land and began to conquer it (Josh. 8:30–35). It was a solemn reminder to them that obedience to God was the secret of success (Josh. 1:8).

The Law was written on large stones so that everyone could read it. Today, as we read and meditate on God's Word, the Spirit writes it on our hearts and transforms us from within (2 Cor. 3:1–3, 18).

The ceremony was a renewal of the nation's covenant with

God, for new beginnings deserve new acts of dedication. The burnt offering spoke of total dedication to God. The peace offerings, and the meal that followed, spoke of joyful fellowship with God.

The curses are related to the Law already given in the Ten Commandments and cover many aspects of personal life. Israel's obeying the Law did not deliver them from Egypt or take them into Canaan, but it did enable them to live together and enjoy the blessings of God.

None of us can wholly keep God's law or fully meet all His righteous demands. We give thanks for what Christ has done for us on the cross (Gal. 3:10–14) and what the Spirit does in our lives (Rom. 8:1–4).

DEUTERONOMY 28

God began with the blessings (vv. 1–14), but the major part of the address was given to the judgments. If this seems to be out of balance, just keep in mind that God knew their hearts (Deut. 5:29).

God promised to bless every area of their lives (vv. 2–6), including their political ventures (vv. 7, 13), their agriculture (vv. 8, 11–12), and their witness to the Gentiles (vv. 9–10). By being a separated and holy people, they would be a light to the Gentiles (Isa. 49:6), but they failed in their mission. Compare verse 10 with verse 25.

Obedience would lift them higher (vv. 1, 13), make them richer (vv. 3–6, 8), and keep them safer (v. 7). From a spiritual point of view, we can claim these promises today.

The curses are frightening, yet they eventually came upon the nation because the people turned from God to idols and disobeyed the Word of God. They did not *diligently* obey God, *carefully* observe His law, or *joyfully* do His will (vv. 1, 47). If we do not "serve the LORD with gladness" (Ps. 100:2), we will end up serving the enemy with sadness.

DEUTERONOMY 29

It is a serious thing to enter into a covenant with the Lord. He will keep His part of the agreement, but we are prone to disobey. If we are to be faithful, we need spiritual renewal for our eyes, ears, and hearts (v. 4). We need to see His hand at work, hear His Word, and love Him with all our hearts.

For forty years, the people saw miracles and heard words, yet they did not perceive what God was doing. They saw His acts but did not understand His ways (Ps. 103:7). They had seen God defeat the idols of Egypt, yet they still had idolatry in their hearts. What could have been spiritual experiences was only a series of historical events because they did not focus on the Lord.

Our responsibility is to obey what we know and not pry into what we do not know (v. 29). Ponder Matthew 13:10–17, and then examine your spiritual perception.

DEUTERONOMY 30

The purpose of chastening is restoration, not ruination. God knows what His people will do, so He makes provision for them to repent and return. He has done this for His people today (1 John 1:5—2.2).

Note the repetition of the little word *all*. God will send *all* His judgments among His people in *all* the nations (v. 1), so that with *all* their hearts and souls they will obey *all* He has commanded (v. 2). If we fail to deal with any sin, or if we ignore any word from God, our repentance will be incomplete.

The heart needs "spiritual surgery" if it is to love the Lord and obey Him (v. 6; Deut. 10:16; Jer. 4:4; Rom. 2:25–29). Every child of God has experienced this (Col. 2:11) and, by faith, can live victoriously. When we receive the Word in our hearts (vv. 11–14), we have both the desire and the dynamic to obey God and glorify Him. The heart of victory is the heart!

DEUTERONOMY 31

Moses could have closed his life under a dark cloud of discouragement. Instead, he gave encouragement to his people as they faced the challenge of a new life in a new land under a new leader.

He encouraged *the people* (vv. 1–6) not to be afraid of the enemy because the Lord would go before them and give them victory. He gave a similar word of encouragement to *Joshua* (vv. 7–8). It would not be easy for Joshua to take the place of a great man like Moses, but he still had the God of Moses as his help.

Moses encouraged *the Levites* (vv. 9–13, 24–29) to protect and proclaim the Word of God and to teach it to the whole nation. If Israel did not enjoy the Word, they could not enjoy the blessings of God in their inheritance.

God changes His workers, but His work goes on. No matter who our spiritual leaders are, we must love the Lord and live according to His Word. That is the secret of blessing and success. It is also the secret of being an encouragement to others.

DEUTERONOMY 32

God gave Moses this song to teach the people so that they would learn to love and obey Him (Deut. 31:19–30). Our songs today should follow this pattern by revealing the greatness and goodness of the Lord and thus encouraging us to live for Him (v. 3).

The key image for God is "the Rock." It speaks of His stability in a changing world and His dependability in a demanding world (v. 4). The Rock is our Savior (v. 15), Father (v. 18), and Deliverer (vv. 30–31). He is all that we need.

Israel is compared to young eagles that must leave the nest and learn how to fly (vv. 11–12). But Israel is also God's treasure, and He will protect His people (vv. 34–35). Moses reminded them not to forget their beginning (v. 18) or ignore their "latter end" (v. 29).

Moses compared God's Word to the rain and the dew (v. 2), which come down from heaven and bring life and refreshment to the earth. Much sharing of the Word may seem to be a waste, but the Word accomplishes God's purposes whether we see it or not (Isa. 55:10–11).

Much of this song is a warning to the people that they were prone to forget what God did for them and to turn from God to idols. We do not know how often they sang this song, but we do know that they did not take it to heart. Do God's people today pay attention to what they are singing?

DEUTERONOMY 33

Before viewing the land, Moses viewed the future and told the tribes what lay ahead. When Jacob gave his blessing before he died, he revealed some of the sins of his sons (Gen. 49), but Moses did not do that. Instead, he focused primarily on the relationship of the tribes with the Lord and how each one would have a distinctive character, blessing, and ministry.

God's people are privileged to be in His hand for safe-keeping (John 10:28–29) and at His feet for learning and obeying (v. 3). We are "between His shoulders," next to His heart (v. 12), and He bears us with His "everlasting arms" (v. 27). What more could we want?

Verse 25 is a good reminder to live a day at a time, as all creation lives (Matt. 6:25–34). The best way to destroy *today* is to regret *yesterday* and worry about *tomorrow*. Israel faced some difficult days, but God would be with them and help them *a day at a time*.

DEUTERONOMY 34

When your time comes to die, the important thing is not the grandeur of your funeral but the greatness of your life. In fact, how you live now will determine how you will die then.

Moses lived in the heights, and he died in the heights. He often met God on the mountain, saw His glory, and experienced His grace. Keep your mind and heart "in the heavenlies" as you live on earth (Col. 3:1ff.).

Moses lived in God's will and died in God's will. You never have to fear life or death if you walk in obedience to the Lord. Moses died "the death of the righteous" (Num. 23:10) because he lived the life of the righteous.

Finally, Moses lived with a forward vision, and he died with a forward vision as he viewed the Promised Land. The nation so often wanted to go back to Egypt, but he challenged them to go forward to the inheritance God prepared for them.

It is good to plan your funeral, but it is also good to live your life in such a way that you will be missed when you are gone.

THE BOOKS OF
HISTORY

◆

The books of Joshua through Esther record key events in the history of Israel: their conquest of Canaan (Joshua); compromise with the enemy (Judges); the establishment of the kingdom, ending with a divided nation (1 and 2 Samuel—2 Chronicles); the captivity; and the return from exile (Ezra—Esther).

Israel's besetting sin was idolatry, and these books record the decay of the nation both politically and spiritually because the people turned away from God and His Word. Throughout the turbulent history, God was faithful to His people, sending them prophets to call them to repentance and helping them in their crises. But the people repeatedly turned away from God to serve heathen idols, and the Lord finally had to chasten them and send them into captivity. God preserved His people so that He might send the promised Redeemer and fulfill His covenant to Abraham that through Israel all nations would be blessed.

Political systems change, as do means of war and international diplomacy, but human nature is the same today as in the days of Joshua, David, Solomon, and Hezekiah. As you read the history of Israel, you will discover how contemporary it really is: "Righteousness exalts a nation, but sin is a reproach to any people" (Prov. 14:34).

JOSHUA

$\blacklozenge$

The book of Joshua records the dedication of the nation (chaps. 1—5), the defeat of the enemy (chaps. 6—12), and the division of the land (chaps. 13—24). Joshua leads Israel from victory to victory as they follow the Lord and claim their promised inheritance.

The man Joshua is a picture of our Lord Jesus Christ who won the victory over sin and Satan and who gives rest to those who trust Him (Heb. 4; Matt. 11:28–30). Joshua knew that he was second in command (Josh. 5:13–15), and his career illustrates the victory we have through faith (1 John 5:1–5). Each of us has a spiritual inheritance to claim, a "land" to conquer, and Joshua tells us how to do it. The word *inheritance* is used fifty-eight times in Joshua. (See Eph. 1:11; Col. 1:12.)

JOSHUA 1

God equips us. Joshua was not in an easy situation, facing a difficult assignment and replacing a great leader like Moses. But God had equipped him and prepared him for this very work. Joshua had faithfully served with Moses and was now qualified to lead. The task that you faithfully do today gets you ready for what God is preparing for you (Matt. 25:21).

God encourages us. The inheritance can be claimed only by the obedience of faith (v. 3), but faith and obedience demand courage. God encouraged Joshua by giving His promise (v. 6) and the assurance of His presence (v. 9) and by reminding him that his success came from the Word (vv. 7–8). God also encouraged Joshua through the people (vv. 16–18). Are you an encouragement to your leaders?

God enables us. "Be strong!" is much more than an admonition (vv. 6, 7, 18), for God's commandments are God's enablements. It was not Joshua's experience or skill that brought the victory; more than once, he was defeated. The victory came from the power of God that was released when they obeyed Him by faith. God still does the impossible (Luke 1:37)!

Joshua— Training for Leadership

Joshua did not seek a place of leadership, but he was called and trained by God to be successor to Moses. Joshua knew the rigors of slavery in Egypt. He also knew how to obey orders as he served with Moses (Exod. 24:13). He had courage to face the enemy (Exod. 17:8–16) and faith to believe God for victory (Num. 14:1–10). His given name was Hoshea ("salvation"), but Moses changed it to Joshua ("Jehovah is salvation"). Even Joshua's name reminded people that he had faith in God.

JOSHUA 2

Joshua's sending the spies to Jericho was an act of wisdom, not unbelief (Prov. 20:18). The report of the two men encouraged Israel for the invasion (v. 24) and reminded them that God was fulfilling His promise to them (Deut. 2:25).

But the visit also meant the salvation of Rahab and her family. Although the Bible does not commend Rahab for her lies, it does commend her faith (Heb. 11:31) that revealed itself in works (James 2:25). Her faith saved her and her family from destruction (Josh. 6:17–19), and it resulted in her becoming an ancestress of the Messiah (Matt. 1:5). Once you begin to trust God and obey Him, you never know what He will do!

JOSHUA 3

Joshua was an early riser (v. 1; 6:12; 7:16; 8:10). He probably devoted that quiet time to praying and meditating on God's Word (Josh. 1:8; Ps. 63:1). This is a good example for us to follow today. (See Mark 1:35.)

We face an unknown future (v. 4) and need the Lord's presence as we step out each day. God goes before us and we must follow as He directs. God knows the way, leads the way and opens the way. He is "Lord of all the earth" (v. 11), and there is nothing for us to fear.

The priests had to get their feet wet before the nation could cross over, and that took faith. Your faith can encourage others in their walk with God. It takes great faith to walk through the water, but it takes even greater faith to walk *on the water* (Matt. 14:23–33). Are you still lingering on the banks or in the boat?

The future is your friend when you follow the Lord and trust His promises.

JOSHUA 4

It is good to memorialize the great acts of the Lord, provided that the memorials do not become idols. Each new generation must learn what God has done for His people so that they will obey His Word and trust Him for the future (Ps. 78:1–8). When you have living faith in a living God, the past is not "dead history." It throbs with living reality.

"Crossing the Jordan" is not a picture of dying and going to heaven despite what some songs say. It illustrates the teaching of Romans 6: death to the old self-life and identification with Christ in resurrection power. Nobody but God can see the stones in the middle of the Jordan, but the record bears witness that they are there. So it is with the death and resurrection of Christ: we believe the record and thus experience the miracle.

The stones on the shore reminded the people that the old life was buried and they should "walk in newness of life" (Rom. 6:4; Col. 3:1ff.). Have you crossed the Jordan and set up your memorial of faith?

JOSHUA 5

Israel had experienced a great miracle, the enemy was frightened, and God was at work. Now was the time for action! *But God told His people to wait.* Why? So that He might prepare them for the conquest of the land.

We must deal with the past (1–9). The new generation had not received the mark of the covenant (Gen. 17), so this ritual was a reaffirmation of their relationship with God. Circumcision symbolizes putting off what belongs to the sinful flesh (Rom. 8:13; Col. 2:11–12) and devoting the heart wholly to the Lord (Deut. 10:16; Jer. 4:4). The nation had experienced this *collectively* in crossing the Jordan, but it had to be made personal.

We must trust for the present (10–12). The nation stopped eating manna and started eating food that God naturally provided. There is a place for the miraculous, but God never wastes miracles. If we do the possible, He will do the impossible. The women baked unleavened bread for Passover, and the nation remembered how God had redeemed them from the land of Egypt.

We must submit for the future (13–15). Joshua met Jesus Christ and learned that the Lord already had a plan for taking Jericho. All Joshua had to do was obey and remember that he was on "holy ground." From that time, whenever Joshua took off his shoes, it reminded him that he was second in command. That was the secret of his victory (2 Chron. 20:15).

JOSHUA 6

If God calls you to do His work, He will tell you how to do it. His plans may seem foolish to you, but they always work if you obey by faith (Isa. 55:8–11).

As we today seek to conquer territory for the Lord, we do not follow the same procedure Joshua used, but we must obey the same principles of faith and obedience. We use spiritual weapons to break down the barriers in men's minds and to claim them for Christ (2 Cor. 10:1–6).

How could a holy, loving God command the killing of the entire population of a city? The people were wicked sinners with whom God had been patient for years (Gen. 15:16–21).

They knew that judgment was coming (Josh. 2:9–11) and could have followed the example of Rahab and been delivered if they had exercised faith.

God was wiping the land clean so that His people would not be defiled and His great plan of salvation frustrated (Deut. 7:1–11). The Canaanites sinned against a flood of light, *just as people are doing today!* Christ died for the sins of the world. Individuals who do not trust Him will die in their own sins. Are you sharing the good news of the gospel?

JOSHUA 7

We can be tempted in the midst of victory. The spies were tempted to be presumptuous and Achan to be covetous. Achan should have been attending to his military duties, but his eyes wandered and he walked into sin (v. 21; see also Gen. 3:6). He valued the spoils more than he valued obedience to God (Ps. 119:162). King Saul made the same mistake (1 Sam. 15).

We never sin alone. God sees His people as one, so the sin of Achan was the sin of the whole nation. (See 1 Cor. 12:12–27.) One man's sin caused the death of thirty-six soldiers.

Sin ultimately brings defeat. The secret of success is knowing and obeying God's Word (Josh. 1:8), and Achan knew that. But he deliberately disobeyed God and brought defeat to the army, disgrace to the Lord, and dismay to his commander. Joshua started looking back instead of looking ahead (v. 7)!

Sin cannot be hidden forever. There is a time to pray about a problem and a time to get up and deal with it. The punishment may seem severe to us, but Achan knew the rules. The main thing is the glory of God (v. 9).

The Jews raised another heap of stones, this time a witness to the trouble ("Achor") sin causes, but read Hosea 2:15 and rejoice.

JOSHUA 8

Never permit one failure to rob you of future victory. When God sees that we have obeyed His Word and sincerely dealt with sin, He comes with encouragement and guidance for the next step. It has well been said that the victorious Christian life is a series of new beginnings. (See Ps. 37:23–24.)

Had Achan only waited, he could have taken all the spoils he desired, but he ran ahead of God and lost everything. (See Matt. 6:33.)

Joshua knew how to bring victory from defeat, for he used the original battle plan to deceive the inhabitants of Ai. Now *they* were the ones who were presumptuous, and it cost them their lives. The strategy in verse 26 was learned from Moses (Exod. 17:8–13).

New victories ought to result in new steps of dedication (vv. 30–35). Joshua obeyed what Moses had commanded (Deut. 27), for obedience to the Word is the secret of success (Josh. 1:8).

JOSHUA 9

The Gibeonites knew that their neighbors were fighting a losing battle, for God was fighting for Israel, and no army could resist Him. So, they decided to use guile instead of muscle. If Satan does not defeat you by coming as the devouring lion (1 Pet. 5:8–9), he will try again as the deceiving serpent (2 Cor. 11:3). He never gives up.

The humiliating defeat at Ai should have taught Joshua and the leaders to take time to pray and seek the mind of the Lord. After all, the Lord was the Commander of the army (Josh. 5:13–15). But they walked by sight and not by faith, and unbelief has a hard time waiting (Isa. 28:16; 30:1–2).

Another defeat! The Lord lost glory, the leaders lost stature, and the nation lost a potential victory: "What agreement has the temple of God with idols?" (2 Cor. 6:16). But Joshua did not give up; rather, *he made his mistakes work for him* (vv. 21–27). That is the mark of a great leader.

JOSHUA 10

When you make an agreement with the enemy, there is no end to the problems you create for yourself. Israel had to defend the very people they should have defeated. Imagine the servants commanding the masters (v. 6)!

God could have said, "You got yourself into this, so you can get yourself out!" But instead, He gave His people encouragement (v. 8) and fought for them from heaven (vv. 10–11). When Joshua needed more time to finish the battle, God stayed the sun and moon in answer to prayer. The Canaanites worshiped the heavenly bodies, so this miracle must have impressed them greatly. If we are doing the will of God, prayer has tremendous power.

Victory over the five kings opened the way for Joshua to attack southern Canaan until he had subdued the whole region. What began as a humiliating defense maneuver ended up a glorious series of victories: "If God is for us, who can be against us?" (Rom. 8:31).

JOSHUA 11—12

The enemy in the north of Canaan united to resist Israel's advance, and their forces were formidable. But God assured Joshua that he would win the battle, and he did. God assures us before the battle (11:6), fights for us during the battle (11:8), and commands us after the battle (11:9, 15). How we follow orders after the victory is as important as what we do before the battle begins.

Joshua conquered the whole land and did it to provide each Israelite with his inheritance from the Lord (11:23). God helped him defeat thirty-one kings and claim their land and their wealth for the Lord and His people. Our Joshua, the Son of God, has defeated every spiritual enemy and now reigns in heaven (Eph. 1:15–23; Col. 2:9–15). Through Him, we can "reign in life" (Rom. 5:17) and claim the victory.

JOSHUA 13

Unlike some elderly people, Joshua lived in the future and not in the past. He had a job to do, and he wanted to complete it before he died. He was not satisfied to defeat thirty-one kings. He urged the tribes to possess the land they had conquered and claim it for the Lord.

No matter how much God has enabled you to accomplish in life, there is always much more land to possess. In the Christian life, we never stand still; we go either forward or backward. The challenge to the believer is Hebrews 6:1: "Let us go on!"

In all his ministry, Joshua was careful to follow the regulations laid down by Moses. Obedience to the Word guaranteed his success (Josh. 1:8).

Did the Levites feel left out? How could they, when God was their inheritance (v. 33)!

JOSHUA 14

Caleb illustrates the truth that "through faith and patience [we] inherit the promises" (Heb. 6:12). Along with Joshua, Caleb was eager to claim his inheritance over forty years before, but the nation had rebelled in unbelief. Patiently, Caleb endured the trials of the wilderness; he knew that his future was secure (Num. 14:24). That unbelieving generation had no hope, for they died in the wilderness, but Caleb had a "living hope" because of his faith (1 Pet. 1:3ff.).

What an example for us to follow! Age did not hinder him, the disappointments of the past did not embitter him, and giants did not frighten him! At a time in life when others were looking for security and ease, Caleb was saying, "Give me this mountain!" (v. 12). His secret? "He wholly followed the LORD God of Israel" (v. 14).

JOSHUA 15

Had the people chosen their inheritance, there no doubt would have been competition and conflict; but the Lord assigned the territory, and the tribes submitted to His will.

"For who makes you differ from another?" asked Paul. "And what do you have that you did not receive?" (1 Cor. 4:7). John the Baptist said, "A man can receive nothing unless it has been given to him from heaven" (John 3:27).

Whenever you envy another's achievements or abilities, you are forgetting this basic spiritual principle. Whenever you complain to God because of what you are *not,* instead of praising Him for what you are, you need to listen again to Paul and John the Baptist.

This is not to suggest that you become complacent. Caleb fought courageously to claim his God-given inheritance, and so did Othniel, his son-in-law. Caleb's daughter had faith to *ask* for additional blessings, and she received them. God gives—we possess by faith. We must accept whatever inheritance He grants us.

The people could rest on Psalm 47:4 and the Levites on Psalm 16:5. Are you happy with the perfect choices that God makes?

JOSHUA 16—17

Ephraim and Manasseh were Joseph's two sons, born to him in Egypt. Jacob adopted them as his own and gave them a special blessing from the Lord (Gen. 48), which explains why these two tribes were given such valuable land in the heart of Canaan. Joseph had kept the family alive during seven years of famine, and his descendants reaped the benefits. They were wealthy because of Joseph's faith and love and Jacob's special blessing.

However, we must not live only on what our ancestors have provided. We must also claim an inheritance for ourselves and our children (17:14-18). The two tribes did a lot of complaining but not much conquering! In the case of Zelophehad's daughters (17:3-6), they had not because they asked not (James 4:2). In the case of the two tribes, they had not because they claimed not. Are you guilty?

JOSHUA 18—19

Since it was centrally located, Shiloh was the ideal place for the tabernacle. During the years of Israel's wanderings, the tabernacle was in the center of the camp. Now it was at the center of the land, accessible to all and a reminder that the fear of God must be at the heart of the nation.

Beware the sin of neglect! It was not the enemy that prevented the tribes from claiming their inheritance; it was their own indifference and indolence. (See James 4:17.)

The surveyors gathered the facts, but God gave the guidance needed for the allocation of the land (18:8-10). We must cooperate with the Lord if we want to know His will. Although we must not *lean on* our own understanding (Prov. 3:6), we must have understanding in order for God to direct us.

Joshua saw to it that the distribution to the tribes was completed before he received his own inheritance (19:49-50). The city of Timnath was located in a mountainous region where life would not be easy. Joshua could have chosen the finest place in the land, but he put others first and let them take the best (1 Cor. 10:24; Phil. 2:1–4).

JOSHUA 20

The cities of refuge are mentioned in Exodus 21:12–13, Numbers 35, and Deuteronomy 19, so you may want to review those passages.

Jesus Christ is our "city of refuge" (Heb. 6:18–20), but the salvation He gives is in contrast to the refuge given to the manslayer. It is true that the sinner must come to Christ (Matt. 11:28–30), but it is also true that Christ first comes to us (Luke 19:10). The elders of the six cities did not go seeking for people to help.

When we come to Christ, there is no trial to determine our guilt. We know we are guilty! That is why we fled to Him! We did not stand at the door and wait; we entered the open door (John 10:9) and were welcomed by the Savior, knowing that we would never face condemnation (John 5:24; Rom. 8:1). The manslayer had to remain in the city, but we "go in and out and find pasture" (John 10:9).

JOSHUA 21

After the land was apportioned, the writer looked back and made one summary statement: *God keeps His promises* (v. 45).

God kept His promise and gave the land to Israel (v. 43). He had promised it first to Abraham (Gen. 13:14–17), and then to his descendants (Gen. 17:8). On the basis of that promise, Joshua entered Canaan, defeated the enemy, and claimed the land for Israel.

God kept His promise and gave them rest from war, enabling them to conquer all their enemies and enjoy their inheritance (v. 44). (See Deut. 12:10; 25:19; Josh. 1:13.) We have spiritual rest today through Christ (Heb. 3—4) and will one day enter into eternal rest.

God kept His promise and scattered the Levites throughout Israel (Gen. 49:7). He gave them forty-eight towns, including the cities of refuge. It should have been a blessing to Israel to have these servants of God living in many different places and sharing the truth of the Word with the people (Deut. 33:10).

Not one word of His promises has failed (v. 45; Josh. 23:14; 1 Kings 8:56). You can trust the Word of God.

JOSHUA 22

Not only had the Lord kept His promises to Israel, but Reuben, Gad, and the half tribe of Manasseh had kept their promise as well (Num. 32:25-32). It was time for them to cross the Jordan and join their families.

Joshua *commended* them for their faithful service, something that all of us should do for those who have ministered well (1 Thess. 5:12-13). He also *commanded* them to obey the Lord and serve Him sincerely. Finally, he *cautioned* them not to become selfish but to share the spoils with their brethren. Perhaps Achan came to mind as Joshua spoke to them.

The land was at rest, but the eastern tribes were restless because the Jordan River separated them from their brethren. Would their children grow up and think they were not truly Israelites? They should have considered that when they chose the boundary!

The building of the altar was at first misunderstood as a declaration of war, but then it became a witness of peace and unity. It is too bad when God's people are forced to manufacture evidence to bear witness of their unity. Before you declare war on the brethren, stop to find out what is going on. Maybe you agree after all! Ponder Proverbs 18:13 and James 3:13-18.

JOSHUA 23

No matter how great leaders may be, they cannot last forever, although their work is never lost (1 John 2:17). Like his predecessor Moses, Joshua gave a farewell address, first to his leaders (chap. 23) and then to the people as a whole (chap. 24).

He magnified the Lord and not himself. No one would question that Joshua was a gifted leader and a great general, but he gave the glory to God.

He challenged the people to keep trusting God and claiming their inheritance. In the book of Judges, you will discover how their incomplete obedience led to compromise and severe discipline from the Lord. Joshua had warned them (v. 16), but they forgot his words. Triumph was turned into tragedy.

He reminded them that God's Word never fails (v. 14) and must be obeyed completely if God is to continue His blessing on the land. Verse 7 explains how to wander from the Lord, and the nation did exactly that!

You are writing your own "farewell speech" right now. What will it sound like?

Family Faith

Joshua was a great leader and a courageous general, and he was also a godly father who led his family in serving the Lord. He took seriously the example of Abraham (Gen. 18:19) and the exhortation of Moses (Deut. 6:4–9). Parents today need to take these Scriptures seriously, and also what Paul wrote in Ephesians 5:22—6:4.

JOSHUA 24

Geography. Joshua chose a meaningful place for his final message, for Shechem held many memories for Israel. There God appeared to Abraham (Gen. 12:6–7), and there Jacob had a "family revival" as he went to Bethel (Gen. 35:1–4). Shechem was near Mount Ebal where the people had rededicated themselves to the Lord after entering the land (Josh. 8:30–35). Being in a special place can sometimes make it easier for us to meet with God.

History. Joshua reviewed the history of Israel and reminded the people of God's grace and goodness in calling Abraham, delivering Israel from Egypt, and giving them their land. It is good to review the past and remember the mercies of the Lord.

Sincerity. Our God is "a jealous God" in that He will not tolerate rivals. He will not be one of several gods in our lives; He must be Lord of all. Everybody serves some god, and if it is not the true God as revealed in Jesus Christ, it is a false god.

Joshua issued the challenge: "Choose for yourselves this day whom you will serve!" (v. 15). Have you chosen wisely?

Stones

Stones played an important role in the march of Israel through Canaan. The stones at the Jordan (4:1–9) reminded them of the miracle God performed as He opened the river; they also commemorated the people's death to the old life. The heap of stones in the Valley of Achor told of Achan's sin and the tragedy of covetousness and disobedience (7:25–26). The stones of the Law at Mount Ebal (8:31–32) spoke of Israel's dedication to God to obey His Word. The stone altar on the eastern bank of the Jordan was a witness to unity (22:10ff.), and the stone Joshua set up bore witness that the people promised to serve only the Lord (24:26–27). Over the years, those messengers became only monuments, and the people forgot what they meant. Today God's people still tend to forget what God would have us remember about our relationship with Him.

JUDGES

$\Diamond$

Judges is the book of "no king" (17:6; 18:1; 19:1; 21:25). God was their King, but the nation refused to obey Him. Their disobedience led to defeat (chaps. 1—2), discipline (chaps. 3—16) and decay (chaps. 17—21). Eight times we are told that the people "did evil" in God's sight and therefore had to be chastened. When God disciplined them, they cried out for mercy and were delivered, but then they lapsed back into their evil ways and had to be disciplined again.

In the book of Joshua, God was with *the whole nation* as they conquered the land. But in Judges, God turned from the nation and gave victory to *individuals* He called and empowered by His Spirit (3:10; 6:34; 11:29; etc.). Thirteen different judges are named in the book. Judges 2:16—19 is the best summary of Israel's history at this period—and a sad history it is.

We are living in a similar period today. God's people in general do not appear to be marching from victory to victory; but here and there, God enables selected servants, by the power of His Spirit, to accomplish great things for His glory. There will be no peace until there is a King in Israel.

JUDGES 1

After the death of Joshua and the move of the two and a half tribes to the east of the Jordan, the nation did not function as one great army. Individual tribes fought to claim their inheritance, and often the tribes worked together; but something was definitely lost in the transition. God's people must endeavor "to keep the unity of the Spirit in the bond of peace" (Eph. 4:3).

What began with conquest (vv. 1–26) soon became compromise (vv. 27–36) as the defeated tribes gave in to the enemy. If we do not defeat the enemy completely, the enemy will eventually defeat us. Israel learned their ways and worshiped their gods, and the Lord had to chasten His people to bring them back. They forgot the warnings of Moses (Deut. 7) and Joshua (Josh. 23).

It has well been said, "The one thing we learn from history is that we do not learn from history." Read 2 Corinthians 6:14—7:1 and take it to heart.

JUDGES 2

The tragedy of missed opportunities!

Opportunity for rededication (1–6). It was at Gilgal that Israel first camped after crossing the Jordan (Josh. 4:19), and there they "rolled away" the old life (Josh. 5). But all they did this time was weep, and their weeping was not a sign of true repentance. It was a passing emotional experience that brought no change to their hearts.

The Angel of the Lord

The Angel of the Lord in the Old Testament is generally agreed to be our Lord Jesus Christ who came to earth temporarily on occasion to deliver special messages or to accomplish special tasks. Among others, He ministered to Hagar (Gen. 16), Abraham (Gen. 22), Jacob (Gen. 31:11), and Moses (Exod. 3), and He appeared to Joshua (Josh. 5:13–15). Though we do not recognize them, the angels minister to God's people today (Heb. 1:14), and the Lord Jesus is with us as we walk with Him (Matt. 28:20; Heb. 13:5–6).

Opportunity for training (7–10). The older generation failed to teach the younger generation God's truth as Moses had commanded them (Deut. 6:1–9). It is bad enough that they forgot Joshua, their second greatest leader, but how could they forget the Lord? You will find the explanation in Deuteronomy 8.

Opportunity for witness (11–23). The nations in Canaan were in terrible bondage to ignorance, idolatry, and immorality, and they desperately needed to know the true God of Israel. But instead of giving illumination (Isa. 49:6), the Jews stooped to imitation and joined their neighbors in their sins. What an opportunity Israel missed, and what a price they paid!

In their relationship with God, the next generation, and their neighbors, Israel failed. Are we also failing in these ways today?

JUDGES 3

The presence of the enemy in the land was an opportunity for teaching, testing, and trusting. The younger generation could learn how to fight, and that would keep them from taking their inheritance for granted. God could test His people and encourage them to trust Him for victory. Even though the tribes had failed to drive out the enemy, God was still with His people and wanted to help them.

Chastening   The key passage is Hebrews 12:1–11. The word chastening means "child training" and refers to the process God uses to mature us and make us more like Jesus Christ. He tests us to bring out the best in us, but Satan tempts us to bring out the worst in us. If we persist in disobeying God, He will discipline us to bring us to submission. This is an act of love, a Father maturing a child and not a Judge punishing a criminal (Prov. 3:11–12).

God's people must live *in* the world, but they must not live *like* the world. Israel forgot the Lord and adopted the ways of the enemy. It began with intermarriage, which led to the worship of idols. After all, when you visit your in-laws, you must be polite to their gods!

How humiliating that the pagan nations Israel imitated were used as the instruments of God's discipline! The conquerors were now the conquered. They regretted their sufferings, but they did not repent of their sins. They experienced a painful cycle of disobedience, discipline, despair, and deliverance, only to go back into disobedience again.

JUDGES 4

The society of that day was strongly masculine, so it was humiliating when women had leadership in the land (Isa. 3:12). The pages of church history record the names of godly women like Deborah who knew God's will, rallied God's people, and won God's victories; and we are grateful for them.

In Hebrews 11:32, Barak is named as a man of faith, but Deborah enlisted him and saved the day. What a strange victory! God used two women, a jug of milk, a hammer, a tent peg, and a storm (Judg. 5:4–5, 20–21) to defeat the enemy! (See 1 Cor. 1:26–29.)

One person's faith and obedience can make a difference in history. Whether you are a leader like Deborah or a follower like Barak, be sure to be a *believer*, because faith makes the difference between defeat and victory.

JUDGES 5

Deborah and Barak cooperated in fighting the battle and also in praising the Lord (Ps. 149:6). Their song reveals some truths about our spiritual warfare in this world.

Be willing to fight (2, 9). Leaders cannot lead unless soldiers are willing to obey. Are you a willing soldier?

Know that the Lord goes before you (4–5, 31). The God of history can help you do exploits for Him today if you will trust Him and do His will. He is able!

Do not let others discourage you (13–18, 23). Not all the tribes responded with faith and courage; in fact, some refused to get involved in the battle. Some sacrificed their lives while others stayed home.

Victors turn darkness into light (31). Israel was in despair and darkness before Deborah took over (vv. 6–8), but she brought the dawning of a new day. Are you the kind of soldier who makes a difference in this world?

JUDGES 6

Gideon was an unlikely candidate for God's "Hall of Fame" (Heb. 11:32). When God called him, he was hiding. When God spoke to him, he raised problems instead of trusting promises. One of his favorite words was *if* (vv. 13, 17, 36; Mark 9:22–23). When Gideon did start to obey God, he worked at night (v. 27) and had to have repeated reassurance that the Lord was with him.

"Putting Out the Fleece"

"Putting out the fleece" (asking God to do some special thing to verify His will) is evidence of unbelief and not of faith. God stooped to Gideon's weakness and did what he asked, and He may do that for you; but this is not the level on which God wants to meet you. Immature faith needs signs for reassurance; mature faith takes God at His Word and obeys.

But God saw the potential in Gideon and even called him a "mighty man of valor" (v. 12). God sees the potential in you and says to you as He did to Simon, "You are . . . You shall be" (John 1:42). He knows your weaknesses and will accommodate Himself to your needs so that He might develop your faith.

For a man with a worried heart, "The-Lord-Is-Peace" was just what he needed (v. 24). You can enjoy God's peace today as you fight the battle (Phil. 4:4–9).

JUDGES 7

Imagine 32,000 Israelites facing 135,000 Midianites (Judg. 8:10), but it was the kind of situation that the Lord uses to glorify His name. When God is on your side, the size of the enemy is of no great concern, so keep your eyes on Him.

The really dangerous enemies were within the hearts of Gideon's soldiers. *Fear* was one of them (vv. 1–3), and it sent 22,000 men home (Deut. 20:1–9). *Overconfidence* was another enemy (vv. 4–8). God cut down the ranks from 10,000 to 300 so that the "army" had to trust completely in God. When God strips away your resources, it is not to impoverish your life but to enrich your faith.

Like Joshua, Gideon worshiped God before going to battle (v. 15; Josh. 5:13–15), for he knew the source of his power. God used weak weapons to defeat a great host because Gideon and his men were living by faith: "For nothing restrains the LORD from saving by many or by few" (1 Sam. 14:6).

Tests

We never know when God is using the everyday things of life to test our faith. The men in Gideon's army were tested by the way they drank water. Lot was tested by a disagreement over land (Gen. 13:6ff.). Israel was tested by thirst (Exod. 15:22–27), and Moses was tested by the complaining of the people (Num. 20:1–13). We must constantly be on guard because sometimes we do not know what the lesson was until we have failed the test!

JUDGES 8

It takes all kinds to make a nation (or a church), and a leader must know how to handle each one, especially after a great victory.

The critical (1–3). They were angry with Gideon because they were left out and did not share in the glory. Gideon tactfully gave them the "soft answer" that healed the wounds and prevented division (Prov. 15:1; Eph. 4:1–3). Better to do that than to start another war.

The cynical (4–9). They said, "You have not yet won the battle, so why should we help you?" The men of Succoth had no faith in God or appreciation for Gideon and his men, and their lack of love cost them dearly.

The cowardly (10–21). Executing two famous kings would be a great way to start a military career, but the lad was too immature to carry it out. We wonder if Gideon remembered his own fears and God's patience with him.

The compromising (22–35). Unlike Abraham, Gideon became covetous and asked for a generous share of the loot (Gen. 14:18–24). This led to idolatry and apostasy because the heart of man is ever ready to indulge in sin.

JUDGES 9

Gideon was a leader called of God, but Abimelech appointed himself and murdered his own brothers to become the leader. Absalom and Adonijah would make this mistake and pay for it dearly (2 Sam. 15; 1 Kings 1:5ff.).

Jotham's parable reveals that there is a price to pay for true leadership. *Others* had paid the price for Abimelech to rule, but he had sacrificed nothing himself. A true leader must often sacrifice richness (oil), sweetness, and joyfulness to serve the people. But if good men and women will not pay the price and lead, we have to settle for the bramble!

Abimelech's sin caught up with him, but he certainly did a lot of damage to his family and his people (Ps. 34:21; Prov. 11:3, 19).

JUDGES 10

No great deeds of valor are recorded for either Tola or Jair, but they gave the nation forty-five years of peace. No foreign invaders are named, so these two judges served by solving the internal problems of the nation. They were administrators rather than generals; we need both.

When there are no battles to fight, we tend to take our blessings for granted, which can lead to sin (Deut. 8:7–20). The people forsook God and worshiped the gods of the enemy, and God had to chasten them by an invasion of the Ammonites.

The confession in verse 10 was insincere, born out of suffering; but the confession in verse 15 was sincere because it was accompanied by repentance and a putting away of sin. (See 2 Cor. 7:8–11.) Remorse and regret are not the same as repentance. God is not impressed by hypocritical tears.

JUDGES 11

No person should be blamed for the circumstances surrounding his or her birth. Why permit the things you cannot control to burden your life? Learn to accept them, and the Lord will work out His purposes in His own time (Ps. 139:13–16). Opposition will one day give way to opportunity.

There is every evidence that Jephthah was a sincere worshiper of the Lord. He negotiated with the elders in the hearing of the Lord and he knew the Scriptures. He was a man of faith and courage (Heb. 11:32) who depended on God's power for victory (v. 29).

Jephthah knew that God's law prohibited human sacrifices, and certainly the Lord would not have given victory on the basis of such an offer. Jephthah's daughter was dedicated to serve the Lord at the tabernacle and therefore remained unmarried. As a result, Jephthah had no descendants to carry on his great name. If she had been sacrificed, it is not likely that the maidens would have been allowed to commemorate the event annually, for that would have been imitating the heathen around them.

JUDGES 12

The men of Ephraim could never rejoice in another's victory as long as they were left out (Judg. 8). Jephthah was not as patient and tactful as Gideon, and the result was a civil war that took 42,000 lives. "See how great a forest a little fire kindles!" (James 3:5). Proverbs 17:14 offers good counsel.

The word *shibboleth* is in the English dictionary and means "a test for determining if you belong." If you do not conform *exactly* to what a group demands, you are rejected. Some Christians make these minor matters a test of spirituality and fellowship and bring division to the church.

We do not even know where Jephthah was buried! No matter; the Lord keeps the records, and this brave man will get His reward.

JUDGES 13

Samson means "sunny," and initially he did bring sunshine to his home and to Israel at a dark period in their history. But his life ended in the darkness because he did not fully obey the Lord. He *began* to deliver Israel from the Philistines (v. 5), but Samuel and David would finish the job.

How could a man fail when he had so much in his favor? He was born to godly parents who feared the Lord, prayed for wisdom, and obeyed His will. Samson was dedicated to the Lord as a lifelong Nazirite (Num. 6). A godly home is no guarantee of a godly life if the spiritual influence is rejected by the children. The parents were not at fault; Samson was.

He began his ministry blessed by the Lord and closed his life mocked by a heathen crowd. Yes, in Samson's death, he killed many of the enemy, but how much better had he been a *living* sacrifice (Rom. 12:1–2) and not a dead one.

JUDGES 14

Samson's decision, opposed by his parents (Deut. 7:1–4), was used by the Lord in His campaign against the Philistines. When God is not allowed to rule, He will overrule (Prov. 16:33), but that is not an excuse for sin (Rom. 3:8).

Samson's next step of disobedience was in turning aside to contemplate a past victory (Prov. 4:27). The honey was defiled by the carcass, so Samson was defiled when he ate it (Num. 6:6). Beware defiled honey, no matter how sweet it is!

Then Samson defiled his parents by sharing the honey with them, and at the wedding, he made a joke out of the whole experience. His lack of seriousness in obeying the Lord eventually led to his ruin. When all his plans fell apart, he should have turned to the Lord for guidance; instead, he continued on his own determined way.

We may ignore our sins, but our sins will not ignore us. We eventually reap what we sow.

JUDGES 15

When life is motivated by retaliation, the consequences are usually painful. Responding to Samson's anger, his intended father-in-law retaliated by giving away Samson's bride. Then Samson retaliated by burning the Philistines' harvest, and the Philistines in turn burned the bride and her father. Who finally won?

Then the men of Judah became frightened and tried to get Samson out of the way. They would rather compromise with the enemy than declare war. Had Samson been a spiritual man, and not just a fighter, he could have led them forth to victory, but he preferred to work alone and not as the leader of a crusade.

All it took was *thirst* to remind Samson of his weakness and his total dependence on God. Had he prayed as earnestly for character as he did for physical help, he would have been a better man and a more successful judge. Like the prodigal son, he prayed, "Give me!" but he never did pray, "Make me!" (Luke 15:12, 19).

JUDGES 16

Defilement. God had rescued Samson from so many tight places that he was sure he was invulnerable, so he continued to play with sin and defile himself. A Spirit-filled God-called leader has no right doing what Samson did. His body belonged to God (1 Cor. 6:12–20).

Deception. The harlot in Gaza deceived him and so did Delilah. You would think that by then Samson would have been alert to danger, but his conscience was defiled and his moral senses were destroyed. Samson even deceived *himself* by thinking he had everything under control (v. 20), but he was wrong.

Destruction. Someone has said that verse 21 describes the "blinding, binding, and grinding effects of sin." Samson walked in the darkness and died in the darkness. God forgave him and restored his strength, but He did not restore his sight or his ministry. Samson may have died in victory, but he lived in moral and spiritual defeat. He destroyed God's enemies, but he did not live like God's friend (John 15:14). What a tragedy!

JUDGES 17

There is an old saying: "As goes the home, so goes the nation." If that is true, Israel was in trouble; for everything about this home violated the law of God.

The family was devoted to idolatry. The son had established his own priesthood and was a thief, and the mother was guilty of speaking both curses and blessings (James 3:9–10). She was concerned more about her money than about her son's character.

The Levite was far more guilty than they were because he was especially called of God and was trained in the Law. He was not God's servant; he was a hireling. When offered a better situation by the Danites, he took it!

What a vivid example of Do-It-Yourself Religion! But is the situation any different today? People still ignore Isaiah 8:20 and do what is right in their own eyes.

JUDGES 18

Corruption in the home will eventually spread to society; in this case, it spread to a whole tribe. False doctrine is like yeast: it grows quietly in secret and affects everything it touches (Gal. 5:7–9).

The Danites had claimed their inheritance (Josh. 19:40–48), but the enemy's invasion had forced them to relocate. Had the tribes stayed true to God, the enemy would not have dispossessed them, and they could have enjoyed their inheritance.

What a way to find a new home! The Danites kidnapped the hireling priest of the false religion and stole the idols. Then they killed innocent people who were living in ignorant isolation, a dangerous thing in that day. The climax came when they set up their own center of idolatrous worship, in open disobedience to the Word of God.

They were living in a place where there was "no lack of anything that is on the earth" (v. 10); yet they lacked everything that God wanted to give them from heaven. Their false prosperity gave them false security that could not last.

JUDGES 19

The sad history of Israel moves now from idolatry to immorality and civil war. If sin is not dealt with, it spreads like a plague and destroys. The basic cause of Israel's plight was their independence from God and their indifference to His law. Nothing can be right when every man does what is right in his own eyes. It was a time of moral and spiritual darkness (Isa. 8:20).

The Levite was not a good example of a spiritual leader. He had a concubine, which was permitted and regulated by law but not really approved by God. His main interests were eating, drinking, and enjoying life. Had he been a man of discipline and spiritual wisdom, he would never have caused all the trouble. He had no godly influence on the people whose lives he touched, and his evil treatment of his concubine was inexcusable.

When spiritual leaders fail to obey God and set godly examples, the church and the community suffer, and ultimately the whole nation decays. One incident of lawlessness can cause a national crisis. It makes a difference when God's people are truly salt and light in a decaying and dark society (Matt. 5:13–16).

JUDGES 20

The chapter is a good illustration of James 3:13–18. When we operate on the basis of human wisdom, we create one problem after another, but when we pause to pray and seek the mind of the Lord, He shows us what to do.

The Benjamites did not seek the Lord, admit their guilt, or repent of their sins. There can be no peace unless sin is put away, but the people of Benjamin would not judge their own people in Gibeah. "So shall you put away the evil person from among you" is repeated nine times in Deuteronomy, and God expected His people to obey.

God's people today need to deal with sin in their lives

(2 Cor. 7:1) and in the church family (1 Cor. 5). Unconfessed sin is like uncontrolled disease: it spreads and it kills. Charles Spurgeon said, "Sin is the mother and nurse of all evil, the egg of all mischief, the fountain of all bitterness, the root of misery."

JUDGES 21

After the tumult and the tempers calmed down, the nation discovered that their rash vow had created a new problem: a tribe in Israel was about to become extinct. If the people of Gibeah had dealt with sin as Moses had commanded, all of the trouble would have been avoided. The easy way always becomes the hard way.

The leaders of Israel became peacemakers (v. 13), and the tribes began working together to solve the problem. Their solution was a matter of semantics: Israel had vowed not to *give* them wives, but that did not prevent the men of Benjamin from going out and *taking* wives.

The apostle Paul came from the tribe of Benjamin. No doubt he was grateful for those four hundred women from Jabesh Gilead (v. 12) and the two hundred women who were kidnapped at Shiloh, for they kept the tribe alive.

RUTH

◆

It seems incredible that this beautiful love story could occur during the dark days of the judges, but such is the grace of God. We are living in trying days today; yet God is at work in His world, getting a bride for His Son and accomplishing His eternal purposes. Never permit the bad news of man's sin to rob you of the good news of God's love and grace.

You see the providence of God at work in the lives of Naomi, Ruth, and Boaz, and you see another important link in the genealogy of the Savior. In Ruth 4:17, David is mentioned for the first time in the Bible.

The four chapters of Ruth are four acts in a drama: (1) tears, (2) toil, (3) trust, and (4) triumph. The book begins with funerals and ends with a wedding. Naomi moves from bitterness to blessedness, and Ruth moves from loneliness to love. What a picture of the grace of God!

RUTH 1

Naomi and her husband sinned when they left Judah for enemy country. Better to be hungry in the will of God than to have a full stomach and be out of His will. They planned to stay in Moab a short time, but their "sojourn" was long enough for their sons to marry. Then the sons and father died. You can run away from famine, but you cannot escape death.

Naomi sinned by urging her daughters-in-law to go home. She did not want to take two Moabite women back to Bethlehem with her and reveal the family's disobedience to God (Deut. 23:3). Imagine a Jewess sending them back to their false gods! But Ruth had come to trust in the God of Israel (vv. 16–17; 2:12), and she refused to go back.

Naomi sinned by getting bitter and blaming God for her

plight. *Naomi* means "pleasant" and *Mara* means "bitter." But it was her decision to go to Moab, so why blame God? A "root of bitterness" can poison your life and the people around you (Deut. 29:18; Heb. 12:15), so avoid carrying grudges.

Although God does not prevent the painful consequences of our sins, He does overrule so that His purposes are fulfilled. By the grace of God, Naomi's emptiness will become fullness, and her sorrow will turn to joy.

RUTH 2

Ruth was a young believer, but she knew enough of the Word to understand that she was permitted to glean in the fields during the harvest (Lev. 19:9–10). She trusted the God who was concerned about widows and the poor (Exod. 22:22; Deut. 10:18), and He did not fail. When we trust God and obey Him, He begins to work on our behalf (Prov. 3:5–6).

Under His Wings (Ruth 2:12)

This image refers to the Holy of Holies in the tabernacle, where the wings of the cherubim overshadowed the mercy seat (Exod. 25:17–22). To be under His wings means to be in the place of security and fellowship with God (Pss. 36:7–8; 61:4; 91:1–4). Believers should abide in Him (John 15:1–10) and enter into the Holy of Holies (Heb. 10:19–25). God's people are "outside the camp" (Heb. 13:13) but living "inside the veil" in the Holy of Holies.

There were at least two men in Bethlehem who could permanently deliver Ruth and Naomi from their poverty and loneliness, and God providentially led Ruth to the field of one of them, Boaz. (See Ps. 25:9; Isa. 42:16.) It was not the bitterness of Naomi but the faithfulness of Ruth that changed the picture.

Boaz protected Ruth and provided for her even before she discovered who he was. (On his part, it was probably love at first sight!) Instead of living on leftovers, Ruth became a friend of "the lord of the harvest" who gave her generous gifts. Can you see in all of this a picture of what Christ has done for His own?

RUTH 3

Naomi got rid of her bitterness and began to think of others. She told Ruth how to approach Boaz, her kinsman-redeemer (Lev. 25:23–55). He was a near relative who was able to redeem, but was he *willing* to redeem? Ruth would find out that night.

The Kinsman-Redeemer (Lev. 25: 23–55)

This law helped to protect the poor from being exploited and the rich from taking property from one tribe to another. The redeemer had to be a near kinsman who was able to redeem and willing to redeem. He was not obligated to do so, but it was expected of him. To refuse was to hurt the family and tribe as well as his own reputation. By being born at Bethlehem, Jesus Christ became our near kinsman. He was able to save and willing to save; He saves all who will put their trust in Him.

She was already under the Lord's wings (2:12), but she requested to be under the wing of Boaz (v. 9). He was only too happy to comply! Up to that point, Ruth was doing all the work, but then Boaz went to work for Ruth (v. 18). It was time for Ruth to rest and wait, trusting her kinsman-redeemer.

Ruth is a good example for us to follow when we have needs to be met. She listened to instructions (vv. 1–4), obeyed (vv. 5–9), believed what her redeemer said (vv. 10–14), received his gifts (vv. 15–17), and waited in patience for him to do the rest (v. 18). When you are at the feet of your Redeemer, you have nothing to fear.

RUTH 4

Five times in the first two verses we read about people *sitting down*. It was to be a deliberate and final transaction; Boaz was to pay the price to redeem Ruth. When our Savior finished the work of redemption, He sat down (Mark 16:19; Heb. 1:3; see also John 19:30).

Boaz planned the marriage privately but paid the price publicly. The other kinsman was able to redeem but not willing. He was afraid of harming his own inheritance. Jesus has made us a part of His inheritance (Eph. 1:11–14). What a contrast between chapters 1—2 and chapter 4: from tears to joy, from hard labor to rest, from emptiness to fullness, from fear to peace and assurance. And the thing that made the difference was *obeying the Word of God*. When Ruth put herself at the feet of her redeemer and entrusted herself to him, he took over and changed everything.

In chapter 1, Ruth had nothing but her faith. In chapter 2, she lived on leftovers, and in chapter 3, she received generous gifts. But once she belonged to Boaz, *everything he owned belonged to her*. Ponder Ephesians 1:3 and 2 Corinthians 8:9.

THE BOOKS OF SAMUEL

———————◆———————

Three men are the center of attention in these books: Samuel (1 Sam. 1—7), Saul (1 Sam. 8—15) and David (1 Sam. 16—2 Sam. 24). Their careers overlap, of course, as the story of Israel's monarchy unfolds.

Samuel was the last of the judges, and Saul was the first of the kings. However, Saul was never meant to establish the dynasty because he was from the wrong tribe (Gen. 49:10). God chose David, from the tribe of Judah, to be His ruler. Saul was given to the people as a discipline because they rejected the Lord to have a king like other nations (Hos. 13:11).

These books show the hand of God at work in the affairs of men and nations. Men are free to make decisions, but God still guides and sees to it that His purposes are fulfilled.

1 SAMUEL

---◆---

1 SAMUEL 1

Grace. The name *Hannah* means "grace," and she needed God's grace to handle her burdens. Unfortunately, the home was divided, her rival provoked her, and she was childless. Out of this kind of sorrow and disappointment, God often builds great faith and sends special blessings. (See 1 Pet. 5:10.)

Faith. When you consider her situation at home and also the way Eli treated her, you find it remarkable that Hannah had any faith at all. But she did not become bitter against God, as Naomi had done (Ruth 1:19–22), nor did she create problems in the home. She asked God for a son, and God answered her prayer. No wonder Samuel ("heard by God") was a great man of prayer. Look at the mother God gave him!

Obedience. Hannah's vow was not a "bargain" with the Lord but an expression of devotion: she would *give* her first-born to God and not redeem him with a sacrifice (Exod. 13:11–16). A mother's prayers and a father's encouragement (vv. 21–23, 28) changed the destiny of an entire nation. Never underestimate the power of prayer or the value of one godly home.

1 SAMUEL 2

Singing (1–11). Most people would sing if they could *keep* their son, but Hannah sang because she could *give* her son to the service of the Lord. She glorified the Lord who does great things for His people. Mary's song is similar to Hannah's (Luke 1:46–55) because Mary had also made a sacrifice to the Lord (Luke 1:38). First the sacrifice, then the song (2 Chron. 29:27).

Sinning (12–17, 22–36). Eli had lost his influence over his sons and as a result caused his family to lose the priesthood (1 Kings 2:26–27, 35). (See 1 Tim. 3:4–5.) It has well been said that the greatest evil comes from the corruption of the greatest good, and Eli's sons illustrate this truth.

Serving (18–21). Blessed are those parents who realize that their children are growing and facing new needs and struggles, and blessed are those children who grow "before the Lord" (Luke 2:52). God kept Samuel pure in the midst of a defiled environment because he had parents who loved him and prayed for him. Jesus has a special love for children, and we must love them, too.

Children

Children are a gift from God (Gen. 48:8–9), a heritage and a reward (Ps. 127:3), weapons to use in fighting the enemy (Ps. 127:4–5), a source of joy (Ps. 113:9), and a crown in their parents' old age (Prov. 17:6). It is a serious thing to abuse children (Matt. 18:1–6) or to neglect their spiritual training (Eph. 6:1–4). Christian witness is always one generation short of extinction. If we fail to train the children for Christ, we forfeit the future.

---

1 SAMUEL 3

Sanctity. A godly life can develop in spite of ungodly influences surrounding it. So it was with Moses in Egypt, Daniel in Babylon, and our Lord in Nazareth. Samuel was not isolated, but he was separated. He belonged to the Lord. Daily, he was in contact with sin, and yet he was not contaminated by it. He was a "living sacrifice" and experienced God's transforming power (Rom. 12:1–2).

Authority. Even though Eli was not the most godly example or mentor, young Samuel submitted to his authority. We submit to man's authority "for the Lord's sake" (1 Pet. 2:13–25), for we serve God, not men. We trust Him to protect us and work out His will even in the lives of ungodly people.

Fidelity. God gave His message to Samuel because He knew Samuel was faithful. The lad was accustomed to being alert to Eli's voice and to obeying immediately, so when God spoke, Samuel was ready. Being faithful in a few small things prepares you for bigger things (Matt. 25:21). Hearing the voice of God did not keep Samuel from doing the work of God (v. 15); he went right back to the old tasks. The nation would now listen to Samuel's words, for they knew he was God's spokesman.

1 SAMUEL 4

Three tragedies are recorded here.

Defeat. Eli's two sons wanted God's help but not God's holiness. They wanted God for the crisis experiences of life but not in their daily ministry (1 Sam. 2:12–17). They thought that the presence of the ark would assure victory, but their superstitious faith had no foundation. Beware "using" God to solve your problems if your life is not yielded to Him.

Naming the Baby

Would you want your name to be Ichabod, "Where is the glory"? Or Ben-Oni, "Son of my sorrow" (Gen. 35:16–20)? Or Jabez, "He will cause pain" (1 Chron. 4:9–10)? Or Beriah, "Tragedy" (1 Chron. 7:23)? Our first birth identifies us with defeat, but the new birth identifies us with victory (1 John 5:1–5). When you trust Jesus Christ, your life changes in many wonderful ways.

Death. The bad news from the battlefield brought death to Eli and his daughter-in-law. In Eli's case, it was a judgment from God; in the mother's case, it was the result of her burden for the glory of God. Phinehas was an ungodly man, but his wife must have been a godly woman to speak as she did.

Departure. The glory of God dwelt with Israel (Exod. 40:34–35; Rom. 9:4), but their sin forced God to depart at an hour when they most needed Him (Ps. 78:56–64). Israel had neither the ark nor the glory of God; they were naked before their enemies. Had they been concerned about God's glory, they would have repented of their sins and obeyed Him, but it was too late.

1 SAMUEL 5

The glory may have departed from Israel, but God was still in control and well able to defend His name. If you get depressed because the enemy seems to have "captured" the glory, rest assured that God is still on the throne.

God can reveal His glory even in a heathen temple, and all false gods must fall before Him. How much better it would have been for His glory to be revealed on the battlefield, but He could not give victory to a disobedient people. It would only have encouraged them more in their sin.

Instead of confessing their sin and trusting the true God of Israel, the people of Philistia tried to get rid of the ark. What a great opportunity they were passing by! But then, would you want to trust the god of the defeated enemy? Israel was a poor witness to the other nations, so they rejected Israel's God.

1 SAMUEL 6

God chastened the Philistines because they kept the ark, but He killed some of His own people because they looked into the ark (v. 19). The Israelites knew the Law (Num. 4:15, 20) and therefore were more responsible than the Philistines. Curiosity is important to learning and progress, but it is unwise to be unduly curious about holy things.

The men of Beth Shemesh were reaping the harvest when the cart with the ark came into view. The ark had been gone for six months, but the men did not allow that to keep them from working. Even in times of defeat, there are jobs to be done and people to feed.

Abinadab's house will become a tabernacle of the Lord, but should not every home be a holy dwelling-place for Him? (See Isa. 4:4–5.)

1 SAMUEL 7

Cleaning up. The ark had been returned to Israel, but Israel had not returned to the Lord, so Samuel called them to repentance. They put away their foreign gods and then met at Mizpah to renew their covenant with the Lord. For years, God had been preparing Samuel for this strategic ministry, and he rescued the nation.

Looking up. The Philistines thought that the assembly at Mizpah was preparation for war; however, Israel was not equipped for battle. But God's people use spiritual weapons to defeat the enemy: Samuel prayed, and God sent the enemy back in confusion. Samuel was born in answer to prayer, and he lived in dependence on prayer.

Setting up. Ebenezer means "stone of help." It was a memorial to God's helping His people from the beginning to that very day. Missionary J. Hudson Taylor had a plaque in his home that read, EBENEZER and JEHOVAH-JIREH. That means, "Thus far the Lord has helped us—The Lord will see to it." This takes care of the past and the future, so why worry about the present? God is in control!

1 SAMUEL 8

It is possible to be faithful in ministry and yet close your life in disappointment. That is what happened to Samuel.

He was disappointed in his sons. They were not able to carry on their father's ministry because they did not follow their father's godly example. Eli's sons yielded to the lusts of the flesh (1 Sam. 2:12–17), while Samuel's sons were lovers of money.

He was disappointed in the nation, for they wanted a king. They used Samuel's sons as their excuse, but the real reason was their lack of faith in God. They wanted to be like the other nations and have a king lead them out to battle. Samuel's warnings about what the king would do made no impression on the people. Note the repetition of the phrase "he will take."

He was disappointed in King Saul who rebelled against God and forfeited the crown. Much that Samuel worked for and prayed for seems to have turned out differently from what he expected, and yet he remained faithful to the Lord to the end. Leaders who are faithful to God may not always appear successful to men.

1 SAMUEL 9

The donkey was a prized animal (Job 1:3) and was used by royalty (1 Kings 1:33–34), but would you expect to find a nation's first king out looking for lost donkeys? Saul's obedience to his father, his concern for his father (v. 5), and his willingness to persevere in a hard task seemed to indicate character and future success.

How strange that Saul did not know about Samuel, and how disappointing that the only reason they visited Samuel was to find their lost animals! People often "use" religion to solve their problems and not to strengthen their character or overcome their sins.

Nevertheless, God used all of this to bring Saul to Samuel. Faithfulness in a small task led Saul to a new friend, a new calling and a new opportunity to serve God. Had he remained a humble servant, things would have been different in his life and in Israel (v. 21; 1 Sam. 15:17). But good beginnings are no guarantee of good endings.

1 SAMUEL 10

Saul could not understand how a man like him could lead the nation of Israel, so God gave him a series of "signs" to assure him for his new responsibilities.

A leader must trust God to solve problems (vv. 1–2), to provide needs (vv. 3–4), and to give the power needed for service (vv. 5–7). He must know how to hear God's Word and wait obediently on the Lord (v. 8). Saul began his ministry in the strength of these assurances, but as time went on, he trusted more and more in himself and rebelled against God's Word.

His modesty in saying nothing about the kingdom (v. 16) and his self-control in not answering his critics (v. 27) are commendable, but what about his hiding on coronation day? Was he genuinely humble, or was he unwilling to take responsibility? This much is sure: he did a great deal of "hiding" in the years of his leadership, but God found him out. As the book of Proverbs warns, "He who covers his sins will not prosper" (28:13).

1 SAMUEL 11

It is one thing to have authority and ability, but quite something else to prove yourself a leader. People respond to a crisis in different ways: some give in (vv. 1–3), but others give up (v. 4). Saul responded with anger and action and rallied the troops for battle.

God empowered Saul to fight the battle and win (v. 6). He had *stature* as well as authority; he had proved himself a leader. But it can be as dangerous after the victory as it is during the battle, for Saul was tempted to get rid of his critics (vv. 12–13; see also 1 Sam. 10:27). He gave God the glory and did not use his authority and success as weapons to attack his own people.

Samuel had the right idea: it was time to renew their covenant with the Lord; and again, the nation met at historic Gilgal. Do the crises God permits in your life strengthen your faith? Do you use the victories He gives to glorify Him and help others?

1 SAMUEL 12

Samuel's message was the combination of a coronation address, a revival sermon, and a farewell speech. He pointed out the greatness of their sin in asking for a king and then called for new dedication. A key theme in the address is *witness* (vv. 3, 5).

The witness of a godly leader (1–5). The people had rejected a proven godly leader for a man who had won only one victory and whose devotion to the Lord was as yet unknown. Samuel was disappointed, but he left office knowing that his conscience was clear.

The witness of history (6–15). The hand of the Lord was with them when they obeyed, but it was against them when they rebelled. Verse 14 emphasizes the same secret of success that God gave to Joshua (Josh. 1:8). Rebellion became King Saul's besetting sin, and it cost him the kingdom (1 Sam. 15:23).

The witness of God's power (16–18). What a man of prayer Samuel was, for it was most unusual to have thunder and rain at that time of year.

The witness of the covenant (19–25). The people had forsaken God, but He would not forsake them, for He is true to His Word. They had the assurance of God's faithfulness as well as the prayers and ministry of Samuel. Had the king maintained his friendship with Samuel and obeyed the Word, he would have led the nation to victory.

1 SAMUEL 13

Saul's second crisis came after he started to build a standing army, and he failed in four ways in this crisis.

He failed to *act decisively* (vv. 1–4). It was Jonathan, not Saul, who declared war by attacking one of the Philistine garrisons. Saul took the credit and blew the trumpet to rally the people.

Excuses

Evangelist Billy Sunday defined an excuse as "the skin of a reason stuffed with a lie." Benjamin Franklin said, "I never knew a man who was good at making excuses who was good at anything else." Adam made the first excuse for sin (Gen. 3:12), and many have followed his bad example. Excuses only make matters worse.

He failed to *inspire the people* (vv. 5–7). Some ran away, some hid, and some left the country! (People still dodge military service in the same ways.) Those who were faithful were fearful and the future looked bleak.

He failed to *wait* (vv. 8–9; see also 1 Sam. 10:8). This was the first step in his rupture with Samuel and his rebellion against the Lord. Patience is a mark of character, and Saul's character was weak (James 1:1–8).

He failed to *tell the truth* (vv. 10–15). When David sinned, he came with confessions; when Saul sinned, he had only excuses. He lied to his best friend, and it cost him his crown. *And Saul would do it again* (1 Sam. 15:15). From that point, his course was downhill.

1 SAMUEL 14

Jonathan, not Saul, was the true leader in Israel. The contrast between the two is striking. Saul was sitting while Jonathan was attacking the enemy. Saul trusted his growing army, but Jonathan trusted God and did not depend on numbers (v. 6). Saul *watched* things happen, but Jonathan *made* things happen.

Saul tried to impress people with an oath, but Jonathan did what was necessary to fight the battle. Saul weakened the army; Jonathan strengthened the army and challenged it to new victories.

Saul was great on words but weak on deeds. (See Matt. 7:21–29.)

1 SAMUEL 15

God's orders were clear, but Saul's motives were mixed (James 1:8). Look at the losses Saul incurred because he disobeyed God's word.

He lost his *character,* for he lied to Samuel and tried to blame the people. Saul was very good at excuses.

He lost his *friend* Samuel (v. 35) who had anointed him, taught him, and prayed for him.

He lost his *crown.* God took the kingdom from Saul and gave it to David.

Saul had many advantages as he began his reign, but he failed God and the people because he did not cultivate his spiritual life. He became proud (vv. 12, 17); he feared men rather than God (v. 24); he blamed others for his own sins (v. 21); and he was concerned more about his reputation than about his character (v. 30). He tried to substitute sacrifice for obedience, but God rejected him.

Is there a King Agag in your life?

Obedience, Not Sacrifice

God's people face the constant temptation of substituting religious ritual for spiritual reality. Samuel's words (1 Sam. 15: 22–23) do not belittle sacrifices. Rather, they point out that the condition of the heart determines the value of the sacrifice (Ps. 51:16–17). God is not enriched by our gifts (Ps. 50:12–14), but we are enriched if our gifts to Him are backed by obedient hearts (Hos. 6:6; Mic. 6:7–8). He accepts the worship only if He can accept the worshiper (Isa. 1:10ff.).

---

1 SAMUEL 16

Reject what God rejects. You expect Samuel to mourn over Saul and his sin (1 Cor. 5:1–2), but mourning alone will not solve problems. There comes a time for action (Josh. 7:10ff.).

See as God sees. How strange that Samuel had not learned his lesson after the failure of Saul (1 Sam. 9:2; 10:23–24). God told Samuel that He would tell him the man of His choice (v. 3), but the old man was tempted to run ahead of the Lord. The heart determines the life (Prov. 4:23), and only God can see the heart (Acts 1:24–25).

Let God do the rest. Samuel anointed David to be king and then departed from Bethlehem, for his work there was done. How would a shepherd boy get from the fields to the throne? That was not Samuel's responsibility; God would see to it. God used David's musical skill to bring him into the king's presence. Empowered by the Spirit (v. 13), David had nothing to fear.

(The ominous statement in v. 14 should be compared with David's prayer in Ps. 51:11.)

God Sees the Heart

God not only sees our hearts, but He searches them (1 Chron. 28:9) and knows our thoughts and motives (Heb. 4:12–13). We think we know our own hearts, but we do not (Jer. 17:9), so we had better accept God's verdict. We should be careful not to judge others since we cannot know their hearts (John 7:24; 1 Cor. 4:5).

---

1 SAMUEL 17

Opportunities. God had prepared David for this occasion, for the private victories make possible the public victories (vv. 34–37). A seemingly trivial errand led to a challenging situation that brought glory to God and recognition to David. Be prepared; you never know when your opportunity will come.

Saul was losing strength, but David was growing in power; and Saul's diminishment would continue until Saul's tragic death. Saul stood head and shoulders above everybody else, but he was not big enough to meet Goliath. David was a man of faith, and God gave him spiritual stature. Great faith makes great men and women. David's only desire was to glorify the God of Israel (vv. 45–47).

Obstacles. Whenever you step out by faith, other people will often put obstacles in your way. David's brother ridiculed him (v. 28) and Saul bluntly told David, "You are not able!" (v. 33). Then Saul said, "If you must do it, do it my way," and he encumbered David with his heavy armor. David had to ignore the obstacles and keep his faith in the Lord. He had to do God's work in the way God wanted him to do it.

David and the Lord Jesus

David is a picture of the Lord Jesus Christ, the Son of David. He was born in Bethlehem and misunderstood by his family; he was an obedient son and a conquering hero. The name David *means "beloved," and Jesus is the Father's "beloved Son" (Matt. 3:17). David was anointed king long before he took the throne and ruled, and our Lord is King of kings even though He is not yet reigning on this earth. Like David, our Lord has had to experience rejection and exile before reigning.*

1 SAMUEL 18

As you read the history of Saul, you often find him with a spear in his hand. It was his symbol of authority and power, and he did not want anybody to forget that he was in charge. David had a harp in his hand—or a shepherd's crook or a sling or a sword. Whatever task God had for him to do, David was available to do it, and God received the glory.

When you are jealous over your authority and position, as Saul was, you become envious of others and sensitive to what people are saying about you. Saul became almost paranoid about David. First he was envious of David, then suspicious and afraid, then angry, and finally so hateful that he wanted to kill him.

In that difficult situation, David acted with wisdom from God and trusted God to help him. David never considered Saul his enemy, which kept David in the place of God's blessing. David remained a humble servant in spite of his great victories, for he knew that God's anointing was upon him. God used those difficult experiences of conflict to help make David a great man of faith.

1 SAMUEL 19

David was in constant danger, but God protected him, sometimes providentially (v. 10) and sometimes through the ministry of others. When the battles were all ended, David wrote, "He delivered me because He delighted in me" (Ps. 18:19). David's integrity before God was his strongest weapon during those years of persecution from Saul. You cannot control what people do to you, but you can control what you do with God.

Jonathan was David's dearest friend, and he kept David informed of Saul's plans. Faith in God does not exclude a commonsense approach to life. Michal, Saul's daughter, risked her life to protect her husband, and until the day of his death, Samuel stood by David.

The "ultimate weapon" of the believer is spiritual, the power of God at work changing people (vv. 18–24; 2 Cor. 10:3–6). Had Saul repented and yielded himself to the Lord, he would have saved himself and his family a great deal of sorrow and trouble.

1 SAMUEL 20

It has well been said that faith is living without scheming. In the midst of the trials of life, we must beware lest we become weary, stop trusting God, and start scheming. We may be inclined to judge David, but perhaps we have done some scheming ourselves.

David and Jonathan lied to Saul, and it almost cost Jonathan his life. Jonathan had been altogether too optimistic about his father, and this experience helped to open his eyes. Jonathan tried to mediate between David and Saul instead of taking his stand with God's anointed. After all, as far as God was concerned, Saul was a "has been" (v. 13).

Jonathan was also concerned about the future of his family (vv. 15, 42). David's promise to spare Jonathan's family made it possible for Mephibosheth to live (2 Sam. 9).

1 SAMUEL 21

Departure. David lived as an exile for about ten years, during which time Saul tried to kill him and Saul's followers lied about him. Many people in Israel actually believed that David was a rebel against the king and that David was trying to destroy Saul. David had to leave his reputation with God and trust Him to silence the accusers.

Deception. It is disappointing to see David depending on lies for protection. He lied to the priest and to the king, but he could not lie to Doeg: "For the sons of this world are more shrewd in their generation than the sons of light" (Luke 16:8). Whenever you think you have "pulled off" a smart deal, you will find a Doeg ready to give you trouble (1 Sam. 22:9ff.; see also Ps. 52).

"Lying lips are an abomination to the LORD, but those who deal truthfully are His delight" (Prov. 12:22).

Is It Ever Right to Lie?

Scripture commands us to tell the truth and warns about the consequences of lying. Jesus is our example, for there was no deceit in His mouth (1 Pet. 2:22). We must always speak the truth in love (Eph. 4:15). If our telling the truth endangers others, silence is our best response. When David ran ahead of God, he found himself in trouble and lied. The safest thing is to stay away from those situations and to pray, "Lead us not into temptation."

---

1 SAMUEL 22

What a motley group gathered around the exiled king (1 Cor. 1:26–30)! A. W. Tozer used to say, "Don't follow any leader until you see the mark of the oil on his forehead." David had the anointing of God, and he represented the future in Israel. Yes, he made mistakes and was sometimes discouraged, but he was God's man and God used him.

Contrast Saul's approach to leadership. He could not challenge his men to a holy cause, so he tried to bribe them (v. 7) and play on their sympathy (v. 8). He depended on spies like Doeg, and he was not afraid to murder innocent priests just to let people know who was in charge. Saul was unwilling to kill the wicked Amalekites, but he murdered God's priests. Saul was fighting a losing battle, and he was desperate.

God in His providence gave David two great gifts: the ephod (1 Sam. 23:6) and a priest. He could always seek the will of the Lord as he planned his strategy. You have the Word of God and an interceding High Priest in heaven. Do you seek the mind of the Lord as you make decisions?

1 SAMUEL 23

Guidance. A gifted leader like David might have been tempted to depend on his experience; instead, he turned to the Lord for the guidance he needed. Even the counsel of his men did not sway him once he knew the mind of the Lord.

Treachery. David rescued the citizens of Keilah, yet they planned to turn him and his men over to Saul! Do not expect everybody you help to appreciate what you have done. Do you appreciate what others have done for you?

Love. Although his father was out to kill David, Jonathan was brave enough to visit David and encourage him. That is what friendship is all about (Prov. 17:17). How tragic that Jonathan's hopes for the future were destroyed by his father's sins, but at least Jonathan was willing to be second man.

Providence. Ziph belonged to Judah (Josh. 15:24), so the citizens should have been loyal to David. They were obviously trying to curry favor with Saul, and they did not believe that David was their future king. God used an invasion of the Philistines to rescue David when it looked as if Saul's forces would win. No matter what men may do, God works out His purposes, and His providence does not fail.

1 SAMUEL 24

Circumstances. People interpret events differently, depending on what they have in their hearts. Saul thought circumstances were safe, so he laid aside his spear and went into the cave. David's men saw a great opportunity for David to avenge himself, but David saw an opportunity to show mercy (Matt. 5:10–12; Rom. 12:17–21). David may have been Saul's enemy, but Saul was not David's enemy (v. 19). Compare verse 5 with 1 Samuel 15:27. Another tear in the robe.

Conscience. David's conscience was so tender that he was troubled after he cut off a corner of Saul's robe. He was humiliating the king, and David knew what it meant to respect authority. A sensitive conscience is a great treasure and a valuable guide. Don't lose it!

Cowardice. Saul's tears were superficial and his conviction temporary; otherwise, he would have welcomed David and transferred the monarchy to him. He knew that David would be king, but he opposed it as long as he could. His greatest concern was that David spare his descendants, which David promised to do. However, it was Saul's sins, not David's revenge, that destroyed his family.

1 SAMUEL 25

These events remind us we can live on several levels.

We can return evil for good. Nabal did that when he refused to share his food with David's men. His name means "fool," and that is exactly what he was (Prov. 17:13).

We can return evil for evil. David planned to do that before he was stopped. It is the natural thing to do because most of the world lives that way, and our hurt feelings cry out for revenge. And yet David had just shown mercy to Saul who had treated him far worse than had Nabal! How easy it is to lose perspective in the heat of anger.

We can overcome evil with good. God used Abigail to prevent David from becoming a murderer. She reminded David of Nabal's true character (vv. 23–25) and of David's efforts to do *God's* work (vv. 26–29). She also told him he would suffer when he remembered the incident in the future (vv. 30–31). This is good counsel to heed the next time you consider seeking revenge. Ponder Proverbs 20:22 and 24:29.

1 SAMUEL 26

Saul's tearful words did not mean much, for he continued to pursue David. In His mercy, God gave Saul another opportunity to repent, but the king's heart was too hard. Even while he slept, Saul kept his spear next to him to remind everybody that he was king. David took the spear from him, a significant action.

Abishai, David's nephew, was a brave man; but brave men are not always wise. He said, "You missed your first opportunity, so don't miss this one!" But David knew that God's hand, not his own, would have to strike Saul.

David's speech was designed to make Saul examine his heart. Was Saul chasing David because *God* told him to do so, or because he believed the lies his flattering officers told about David? Twice before, Saul had said "I have sinned" (1 Sam. 15:24, 30), but his words were not sincere then or on this occasion. He was correct when he called himself a fool. He was a fool in the way he treated Jonathan, David, Samuel, his army, his nation, and his God. He lived like a fool, and he died like a fool. (See Proverbs 26:11–12.)

"I Have Sinned!" *King Saul is not the only one who made this confession. Pharaoh said it (Exod. 9:27) and so did Balaam (Num. 22:34), Achan (Josh. 7:20), David (2 Sam. 12:13; 24:10, 17; Ps. 51:4), Judas (Matt. 27:4), and the prodigal son (Luke 15:18, 21). Which of these men do you think were really sincere?*

---

1 SAMUEL 27

David won a great victory over Saul, only to be overwhelmed by despair. Such feelings are not unusual; you cannot have mountaintops without valleys. However, when you are feeling low, it is a dangerous thing to "talk to yourself" and make important decisions. David should have talked to the Lord. He and Abiathar could have sought the mind of God together.

David made some foolish decisions because he did not pause to inquire of the Lord. He stopped serving God and started thinking about survival: "For whoever desires to save his life will lose it" (Mark 8:35). He trusted the enemy for protection and did not trust the Lord. As a result, he had to scheme, kill, and lie to survive.

When you are discouraged, ask a trusted Christian friend to pray with you, and seek the Lord's direction. Take time to talk about your feelings with your friend. You will gain a clearer perspective. *Make no impulsive decisions about significant matters.* Follow this advice: "Wait on the LORD; be of good courage, and He shall strengthen your heart" (Ps. 27:14).

"When the outlook is discouraging, try the uplook!"

1 SAMUEL 28

Saul had been fighting the wrong enemy for so long that when the real enemy appeared, the king was unprepared. God was not with him, and prayer was not answered (Prov. 1:20–33). When Saul began his reign, it was "the dawning of the day" (1 Sam. 9:26), but now he was walking in the darkness. Saul did not disguise himself (v. 8); *he revealed his true self.* Throughout his reign, he had been pretending, and the truth was coming out.

Depending on demonic forces, the medium planned to impersonate Samuel, but the Lord permitted Samuel to appear. The friend Saul grieved in life, he called for in death. Too late do we learn to appreciate those who tried to help us. Too late do we humble ourselves.

Saul's disobedience in the past led to darkness in the present and defeat and death in the future. When God gave him opportunities to repent, he ignored them. He did not "seek the LORD while He may be found" (Isa. 55:6).

Christians and the Occult

God forbade Israel to dabble in the occult (Exod. 22:18; Lev. 19:31; 20:6; Deut. 18:9–14), and these warnings should be heeded today, too. Sorcery is one of the works of the flesh that must be rejected (Gal. 5:20). Both Peter (Acts 8:9ff.) and Paul (Acts 13:6ff.) had harsh words for sorcerers. Seemingly innocent games that border on the occult can open the door to serious problems. As for seances, read what see Isaiah 8:19 has to say.

1 SAMUEL 29

David was out of place, but God in His mercy cared for him. This is an encouragement to us when we sin, but it must not become an excuse for sin. That would be tempting God.

The king never once detected what was going on, so David must have been a gifted actor. However, what value is there in being successful at deception? Hypocrisy and lying destroyed King Saul.

The Lord used the song that got David into trouble with Saul (1 Sam. 18:7–9) to get him out of trouble with the Philistines. Saul was not David's enemy, and David did not want to meet him on the battlefield and fight against his own people. But when you fraternize with the enemy, you create difficult problems. Let us be grateful for Psalm 103:10–14.

1 SAMUEL 30

Relieved that he had been discharged from the war, David returned to Ziklag only to find tragedy. There are times when one problem follows hard on another. Had Saul slain the Amalekites as God commanded (1 Sam. 15), this raid would not have occurred. *Our* disobedience can cause problems for *others*.

A crisis does not make a person: it shows what a person is made of. Like his men, David wept and sorrowed, but unlike some of his men, he did not look for a scapegoat. In times of crisis, express your feelings honestly, but do not look for somebody to blame. Rather, get your strength from the Lord (v. 6) and seek His will (vv. 7–8). He is in complete control.

God uses the weak things of the world, even a sick boy who was left to die. When we do the possible, God does the impossible. The tragedy became victory, with profit for everybody.

1 SAMUEL 31

Defeat. David won a battle and divided the spoils; Saul lost a battle and was stripped by the enemy. Gideon camped near Gilboa before his great victory over the Midianites (Judg. 7:1), but Gilboa would forever be associated with the defeat of Saul. Are you leaving behind monuments to victory or to defeat?

Death. Death reigned over Israel: their soldiers died, Saul and his armorbearer died, and Saul's sons died. Such is the high cost of one man's rebellion:."For to be carnally minded is death" (Rom. 8:6).

Disgrace. Had Israel won, God would have been glorified. Instead, the pagan idols were honored, and the dead were desecrated. It is bad enough to die in a losing battle, but not to be buried was an even greater disgrace.

Devotion. The brave men of Jabesh Gilead risked their lives to give Saul and his sons a decent burial. After all, Saul had rescued their city forty years before, and they were showing their gratitude (1 Sam. 11:1–11). David later honored them for their feat (2 Sam. 2:4–7).

2 SAMUEL

◆

David the king is the central figure in this book that records his national victories (chaps. 1—10) and his personal defeats (chaps. 11—24). The turning point is his sin of adultery (chap. 11), the tragic consequences of which affected both his family and the nation. David confessed his sins, submitted to God's discipline, and spent the closing years of his reign preparing for the building of the temple. This book is an exposition of Proverbs 14:34 and 28:13.

2 SAMUEL 1

Saul began his career *standing* (1 Sam. 10:23), but he closed his career *falling* (vv. 4, 10, 12, 19, 25, 27): "Therefore let him who thinks he stands take heed lest he fall" (1 Cor. 10:12). Natural abilities and great opportunities do not guarantee success. Saul was head and shoulders above everybody else, but he was not heart and soul yielded to God. Robert Murray M'Cheyne said, "It is not great talents God blesses so much as great likeness to Jesus."

The Amalekite tried to deceive David and win his favor, for his account contradicts the inspired record (1 Sam. 31). He did not know David! Saul was not David's enemy, so David could not rejoice over Israel's inglorious defeat. Do you have enemies whose sorrows make you happy? If you do, carefully consider Proverbs 24:17 and Romans 12:14–15.

David said only good things about Saul and praised him as a mighty warrior. Saul's treatment of David had been diabolical, but David's treatment of Saul was always kind and considerate (Lev. 19:18; Prov. 20:22; 24:29). Saul listened to men's lies and lost his crown; David obeyed God's Word and gained a kingdom.

2 SAMUEL 2

David's tribe of Judah anointed him king and set up his headquarters in Hebron. But Abner, Saul's cousin (1 Sam. 14:50) and commander of his army, made Saul's son king in open defiance of God's will. Whenever we fail to submit to God's will, we cause division and bring destruction (James 3:13—4:1).

Three murders will occur before David becomes king of all the people: Asahel's (chap. 2), Abner's (chap. 3) and Ishbosheth's (chap. 4). All of that blood would not have been shed if the leaders had only submitted to God's chosen king instead of seeking their own advantage. Joab and Asahel were related to David (1 Chron. 2:16), so there were both family and national considerations. Had everybody put the glory of God and the good of the nation first, tragedies would have been avoided.

2 SAMUEL 3

Trusting in the Lord, David went "from strength to strength" (Ps. 84:7). He was God's anointed and knew that God would fulfill His promise and make him king over all Israel. When you walk by faith, you can wait on Him.

Abner also grew in strength (v. 6), not the strength of the Lord but political power. He had more authority than the king, for he had made Ishbosheth king. Abner's use of power to please himself was his downfall.

David's way of life was reconciliation; he was a peacemaker. But Abner and Joab lived by retaliation: "All who take the sword will perish by the sword" (Matt. 26:52). Abner had murdered Asahel, and his sin had found him out. But Joab's deed was wicked, and David dissociated himself from it. Imagine Joab avenging his brother's blood at Hebron, a city of refuge!

David was strong, yet he was weak (v. 39)! When we are weak in ourselves, the Lord can be strong through us (2 Cor. 12:7–10). We cannot control circumstances and people, but we can control what *we* say and do.

2 SAMUEL 4

Now for murder number three, committed by two men who did not know David's heart. When they heard that Abner was dead, they concluded that Ishbosheth would not remain king very long, so they murdered the king. They thought the act would please David and perhaps win them key positions in David's kingdom.

Verse 8 reveals the captains' stupidity. Saul was *not* David's enemy. *The Lord* did not avenge David. David was *not* pleased at what they did. What terrible things people do in the name of the Lord, thinking to please Him! How many "religious" wars and church conflicts have broken God's heart and disgraced His name!

When you are tempted to retaliate, keep in mind that God's people do not "do evil that good may come" (Rom. 3:8). Rather, they "overcome evil with good" (Rom. 12:21).

2 SAMUEL 5

When God's king ruled over His people, there was unity instead of division and civil war. All Israel submitted to God and to David, and there was peace among the brethren.

We should submit to Jesus Christ, the Son of David, for many reasons. He is God's Chosen One (v. 2), and we are "members of His body, of His flesh and of His bones" (Eph. 5:30). He is God's Anointed (the name *Christ* means "anointed one"), and He alone has the right to reign. He has proved Himself in battle and won the victory over our enemies.

As long as believers submit to someone other than the Lord Jesus Christ, division and dissension will exist among God's people. Unity comes not because we have a common enemy but because we obey a common King. (See 1 Cor. 1:10–31.)

2 SAMUEL 6

Fervor. David wanted to honor God by having the ark in the new capital of the land, Jerusalem (Matt. 6:33). The plan had all the marks of success: thirty thousand choice men assisted him, and the people were enthusiastic. David had lived among the Philistines so long that he unconsciously adopted their methods (1 Sam. 6) and ignored the law of God (Num. 4:15; 10:21). Why did he forget to consult God for the guidance he needed?

Fear. If the ark had been on the shoulders of the Levites, God would not have judged Uzzah, and David would not have been afraid. God's throne does not need man's hand to keep it steady and safe.

Faith. David was not one to quit because of a mistake, so he did it again—God's way. David expressed his worship and praise publicly, without shame, and God accepted them. Acts 3:1–10 is another example of fervent praise to God.

Folly. Full of joy, David came home to bless his family, only to have Michal ridicule him. Not everybody gets the blessing, and some people resent it when others get blessed. She was unspiritual and unsympathetic, and as a result, she became unfruitful. Michal was David's first wife, and she no doubt resented the other wives in the home (Deut. 17:17).

When all else fails, take time to read God's instructions.

Criticism Never be afraid of honest criticism. If it is correct, the critic has helped you. If it is incorrect, you can help the critic. Either way, somebody is helped. When criticism is cruel, as was Michal's, look beyond the critic and leave the matter with God (Ps. 37). Elbert Hubbard observed, "To escape criticism—do nothing, say nothing, be nothing."

---

2 SAMUEL 7

How would you respond if God said no to one of your greatest ambitions, something that you were sure would please Him? David wanted to build a house for the Lord (Ps. 132), but God would not permit him to do so. David was disappointed, and his responses show us how to handle the disappointments of life.

He submitted to God's will. David humbly accepted God's plan and did not try to change God's mind. He realized that God knows best.

He listened to God's word. God would build a house (family) for David! The immediate reference is to Solomon, but ultimately the promise refers to Jesus Christ, the Son of David. If God says no to something, it is so that He may say yes to something better.

He gave himself to worship. David's words in verses 18–29 emphasize the greatness and the grace of God. Who was David that God should call him and bless him? Who was Israel that God should choose them? And who are we that God should save us and bless us?

It has well been said, "Disappointments are His appointments." David believed that. Do you? Have you learned that there can be blessing in *un*answered prayer?

Forever!

Notice the "forevers" in 2 Samuel 7: a throne (v. 13), a kingdom (v. 16), a nation (v. 24), a promise (v. 25), and a blessing (v. 29).

---

2 SAMUEL 8

David's name is found twenty-one times in chapter 8. God magnified David's name because David did the will of God (v. 13). Exalt yourself and God will humble you, but humble yourself and God will exalt you (1 Pet. 5:5–6).

God gave David victory, and David used each victory to serve the Lord (v. 11). David knew that he would not build the temple, but he risked his life to gather the wealth Solomon would need to do the job. If God gives your dream to somebody else, help him or her fulfill it.

David recovered lost territory and gained new territory, a good example for us to follow in our spiritual walk and warfare.

2 SAMUEL 9

Kindness is the key theme (vv. 1, 3, 7) of this chapter. Kindness is a fruit of the Spirit (Gal. 5:22) and an evidence of love (1 Cor. 13:4). David was practicing what is taught in Ephesians 4:32.

This event illustrates God's kindness to us in Christ (Eph. 2:7; Titus 3:4). As a part of the family of Saul, Mephibosheth had no claims on the kingdom; yet David treated him like one of his own sons. He did it for the sake of Jonathan (v. 7) in order to keep his covenant (1 Sam. 20:12–16). God has saved us for the sake of His Son, a part of the eternal covenant of redemption (Eph. 4:32; Heb. 13:20–21).

Mephibosheth did not need to fear (v. 7) because David would keep his word. The lame prince would have all his needs met and sit with the king every day. There was nothing to worry about! In the light of Ephesians 1:3 and 2:4–10, why should you worry? Henry Drummond wisely stated, "The greatest thing a man can do for his Heavenly Father is to be kind to some of His other children."

2 SAMUEL 10

David's kindness to Mephibosheth was accepted, but his gesture of kindness to Hanun was rejected and led to the death of nearly fifty thousand men. Hanun's counselors were suspicious of David and questioned his motives because they judged David on the basis of *what they would have done*.

The King's servants are sometimes treated badly (Matt. 10:16ff.), but they need not fret: their King has everything in control, and some things heal with time. God cares for His own.

Verse 12 is a good illustration of the biblical balance between divine sovereignty and human responsibility. The same God who ordains the end (victory in battle) also ordains the means to the end (courageous men who do their job well). Faith and works must always go together.

2 SAMUEL 11

How we wish that "the matter of Uriah the Hittite" (1 Kings 15:5) were not in the Bible, but it is here for our warning and learning. Believers can thank God that *our* sins are not written down for everyone to read!

Disobedience. You start on the path to sin when you neglect duty. David was in more danger in Jerusalem than with his army on the battlefield. He laid aside his armor (Eph. 6:10ff.), allowed his eyes to wander, and lust took over (James 1:14–15).

Deception. Like our first parents, we try to cover our sins, but God will find us out (Gen. 3:7; Prov. 28:13). David the adulterer became a liar and a schemer, and then a murderer. Uriah was one of David's mighty men (2 Sam. 23:39). While David was sinning, Uriah and his fellow soldiers were risking their lives for him on the battlefield.

Displeasure. From the human point of view, the scheme worked, but God was not pleased. See what David wrote in Psalms 5:4 and 11:5, and note Proverbs 6:16–19 and 1 Thessalonians 4:1–8.

Before you yield to temptation . . . look back and recall God's goodness to you; look ahead and remember "the wages of sin"; look around and think of all the people who may be affected by what you do; look up and ask God for the strength to say no (1 Cor. 10:13).

2 SAMUEL 12

Chastening. For about a year, David hid his sins and suffered under the chastening hand of God (Ps. 32; Heb. 12:1–11). God gave David opportunity for repentance, but he refused to yield. Chastening proves God's love to us; our yielding proves our love to Him.

Conviction. How easy it is to condemn others! But beware: the sentence you pass on others will be passed on you (Matt. 7:1–5). David paid fourfold for his sins: the baby died, his daughter Tamar was raped, and his sons Absalom and Amnon were killed.

Confession. The Law said that both David and Bathsheba should die (Lev. 20:10). In His grace, God forgave their sins (Ps. 51); but in His government, He permitted them to reap what they had sown. First John 1:9 is a great promise, but it is not an excuse for sin. Remember, there are sad consequences of *forgiven* sin.

Comfort. God gave David another son and another crown. Saul lost his crown because he would not repent, but David always confessed his sin and rested on God's mercy (Rom. 5:20).

2 SAMUEL 13

David now begins to reap the harvest of sowing to the flesh, the painful consequences of *forgiven* sin (2 Sam. 12:10; Gal. 6:7–8). Of all the trials of life, the most difficult to bear are those that come from our own family because of our failures.

So possessed was he by lust that Amnon made arrangements to sin. He knew that he was breaking God's law by violating a virgin whom he could not wed (Deut. 22:28–29; Lev. 20:17). Lust was replaced by hatred, for both are born of violence, and hatred resulted in Tamar's being ostracized in Israel.

David's anger may have been restrained by his conscience, for he did nothing to punish Amnon. Absalom plotted, waited, and then avenged his sister by killing Amnon (James 1:15). David has now lost two sons to death and one to exile, and the situation will grow worse. The next time sin looks attractive to you, remember David's trials.

2 SAMUEL 14

Nathan had told a story to help David do a right thing, repent of his sins (2 Sam. 12:1–6). This woman told a story to encourage David to do a wrong thing, restore Absalom without first insisting on repentance.

Forgiveness that ignores justice is only a fiction. Even God does not restore a "banished one" (v. 13) without first paying the price to uphold His law. Forgiveness is not cheap; it is costly (Rom. 3:21–26). God demands that we repent and turn from sin. Jesus Christ had to die that we might be forgiven, for there is no other way.

God's forgiveness is complete; we can come into His presence and "see His face" (1 John 1:9—2:2). David restored Absalom's position, but he did not improve his character, so the young man returned to his sinful ways. The only thing weighty about Absalom was his hair; the rest of him was chaff. His good looks camouflaged a bad heart.

2 SAMUEL 15

Enticement. Absalom personified everything that God hates (Prov. 6:16–19). Unfortunately, many in Israel were deceived by him and believed his flattery and lies. They should have remained loyal to the Lord and to David, but recall what the crowd did to the Son of David (Matt. 27:15–26; Acts 3:14).

Escape. A crisis helps to reveal who our loyal friends really are. David's servants were ready to obey (v. 15) and ready to die (v. 21). Ittai was a foreigner, yet he stayed with the king. The priests and David's counselor returned to the place of danger. David was a man of prayer, but he also used wise strategy. Ahithophel abandoned David and joined the rebellion. But he was Bathsheba's grandfather (2 Sam. 11:3; 23:34), so he took the opportunity for revenge.

Read the following psalms that many Bible students believe David wrote during the time of Absalom's rebellion: 3–4, 39, 41, 55, 61–63, and 143.

2 SAMUEL 16

In times of crisis, people respond in various ways. Expect to meet the following:

The liar. Ziba was an opportunist who took advantage of both David and Mephibosheth. In situations like this, heed Proverbs 18:13.

The accuser. Shimei was related to Saul and blamed David for the destruction of Saul's family and kingdom. David patiently "took it" and left the matter with the Lord. There are times when silence and submission are your best responses (1 Pet. 2:18–25).

The avenger. Abishai was usually quick to declare war (1 Sam. 26:1–11), but David took the better approach. (See Luke 22:47–53.)

The traitor. Ahithophel had been David's esteemed counselor, but he turned traitor and sided with Absalom. He was the "Judas" in the camp (Ps. 55:12–14). David prayed about the problem (2 Sam. 15:31) and trusted God to work (Phil. 4:6-9), and He did.

2 SAMUEL 17

Hushai was a master of metaphors, and God used his skillful way with words to defeat Absalom. He compared David to an angry bear (v. 8) and a fierce lion (v. 10). Then he appealed to Absalom's pride by telling him to lead a large army ("like the sand" [v. 11]) and defeat David himself, coming upon David's men "as the dew falls" (v. 12). Absalom pictured himself as the conquering general, and pride did the rest (Prov. 16:18).

David owed his life to the brave men who stayed in Jerusalem and kept the king informed of Absalom's plans, and also to an anonymous woman who protected the messengers. The people who helped him at Mahanaim were a gift of God. Jacob saw angels at Mahanaim (Gen. 32:1-2), but David's "angels" were loving people who cared for him. Behind all great leaders are devoted people whom God rewards but whose names we too soon forget.

Ahithophel saw that Absalom would lose the battle, and like Judas, he committed suicide (Matt. 27:1-5). He could counsel others, but he did not wisely counsel himself.

2 SAMUEL 18

Two armies. There can be no neutrality when it comes to supporting and defending God's kingdom (Josh. 24:14-15; Matt. 12:30). We can understand a father's concern for his son, but there can be no gentleness when it comes to dealing with sin. David wanted love without justice, but with Joab it was justice without love. Only on the cross of Christ are love and justice both satisfied. God "did not spare His own Son" (Rom. 8:32).

Two monuments. Both Saul (1 Sam. 15:12) and Absalom set up monuments to their memory, but what do we remember about them? Joab and his men built the true monument: a heap of stones over the dead body of a proud rebel. The life you live is the monument you build, and ultimately the truth will come out.

Two messages. Ahimaaz had ambition and ability, but he lacked the maturity needed to minister to the king. Before you start to run, be sure you are the right person to deliver the message (Prov. 25:13).

2 SAMUEL 19

Making wounds (1–8). Joab had to hurt David to help him: "Faithful are the wounds of a friend" (Prov. 27:6). David's sorrow over his dead son almost cost him the kingdom. It is right to mourn, but not to the point that we lose touch with reality.

Healing wounds (9–15). It was time for the whole nation to affirm loyalty to God's chosen king, and David declared an amnesty except in certain cases. The tribes brought him back; he forgave Shimei and Mephibosheth; he rewarded Barzillai.

Opening wounds (40–43). Intertribal jealousy appeared again (Judg. 8:1; 12:1), and David faced a new rebellion (Prov. 13:10). Instead of using the soft answer (Prov. 15:1), the men of Judah held to their rights and made the situation worse. Romans 12:10 and Philippians 2:1–4 give the counsel we need.

2 SAMUEL 20

Events create opportunities, and people use opportunities in different ways.

Sheba saw the tribal conflict as an opportunity for promoting himself. Because he was a Benjamite, he hoped to get broad support from Saul's friends and David's enemies, and he almost succeeded. Once again, the people deserted God's chosen king for an opportunist.

Amasa was chosen to lead David's army to victory (2 Sam. 19:13), but he delayed and lost his opportunity for greatness. However, Joab seized the opportunity, removed his replacement, won the battle and got his job back. Joab had murdered Abner, Absalom, and Amasa; yet David apparently did nothing to discipline him. Perhaps Joab knew too much about David (2 Sam. 11:6ff.).

The wise woman saw an opportunity to end the war and prevent many innocent people from being killed. Blessed are the peacemakers!

Opportunities will come your way today. How will you use them?

2 SAMUEL 21

Promises are not to be made carelessly or broken with impunity.

God kept His promise. If the nation obeyed God's law, He promised to bless them with rain and plenty, but if they disobeyed, He would discipline them. God often sent famines to discipline His people (Deut. 28:23–24).

Saul broke a promise. Israel's covenant with Gibeon (Josh. 9) had been honored for centuries, and then Saul violated it. Old sins can create new problems long after the sinners are dead.

David kept a promise. The law demanded fair and equal punishment for each crime (Exod. 21:23–25). Saul had killed innocent people, so his family had to pay the price to purge the innocent blood from the land (Deut. 19:11–13). David kept his promise to Mephibosheth (2 Sam. 9:7) and to Jonathan (1 Sam. 20:15–16) by sparing Mephibosheth's life. David also saw to it that the dead in Saul's family had decent burial.

David made a promise. Giants have a way of multiplying, and David discovered that he was not the giant killer he had been in his youth. There comes a time when we must give up some lesser things to protect the things that are more important. It was difficult for David to lay aside his armor and weapons, but it was a wise thing to do.

2 SAMUEL 22

This psalm of victory is almost identical to Psalm 18. Note that David did not list Saul as one of his enemies (v. 1). What grace!

David did not take credit for any of his victories; he gave the glory to God. Nor was he ashamed to admit that he had cried out to God for deliverance and strength. His words should encourage us when we experience times of trial and testing.

Verses 21–24 are not a declaration of sinless perfection, for David was a sinner like any other man. They describe David's integrity of heart (Ps. 78:70–72). David obeyed the Word of God and trusted God to keep His promise and put him on the throne of Israel.

As he looked back on those years of danger and difficulty, David did not see the hardness of life; he saw the gentleness of God (v. 36). David affirmed that the yoke was easy and the burden was light (Matt. 11:28–30). Your life today may seem hard, but keep trusting and obeying. One of these days, God will give you your own victory song, and you will experience greatness from the gentle hand of God.

2 SAMUEL 23

Leaders (1–7). Earlier in his reign, David wrote a long psalm about victory (2 Sam. 22), but when he closed his life, he wrote a beautiful brief song about leadership. Leaders must be called of God and empowered by Him (v. 1). They must be taught the Word of God by the Spirit of God (v. 2). They must be men and women of character who fear God (vv. 3–4). They are ruling for God, not for self.

A Cup of Water

David's hands accomplished many things as he held a sword, a spear and a harp. The finest thing he ever did was with a cup of water, for in making it a drink offering to the Lord, he revealed true character. "We can do no great things," said Mother Teresa, "only small things with great love."

Two metaphors describe leadership that is spiritual: the dawning of a new day, and the springing up of grass after the rain (v. 4). Saul brought darkness to the land, but David brought light. Saul caused storms, but David brought calm after the storm and caused the storms to produce fruit. That is leadership!

Followers (8–39). True leaders are not afraid to surround themselves with people of ability and then give them opportunities for greatness. Those men were so close to David that his whispered desires became their marching orders (vv. 15–17). David loved them so much that he would not selfishly enjoy what had cost them dearly. What an example those men are to us who follow Jesus Christ!

2 SAMUEL 24

A stubborn heart (1–9). There are sins of the spirit as well as sins of the flesh (2 Cor. 7:1). In his pride, David numbered the people, but he did not connect the census with the redemption money (Exod. 30:11–16) and seek to honor God. The Lord gave David nine months to change his mind, just long enough for the "pregnancy of sin" to give birth to death (James 1:13–15).

A smitten heart (10–14). David's sin was a sin of the will, so God asked him to make some decisions. He confessed his sin ("I have sinned *greatly*") and was forgiven, but he still had to suffer the consequences of sin.

A suffering heart (15–17). David had a shepherd's heart and longed to deliver his people. It is more difficult to watch those you love suffer than to endure it yourself.

A sacrificing heart (18–25). David did not take the easy way out. His repentance was sincere, and he paid the full price to prove it. Who pays for your sacrifices? Amazing grace! Solomon built the temple on the property that David purchased for his altar. Solomon was the son of Bathsheba. What amazing grace that God could take David's two great sins and build a temple out of them! (See Rom. 5:20.)

1 and 2 KINGS

---◆---

As the name indicates, these books record the history of the Jewish kings, from Solomon to Zedekiah. When the account begins, the nation is one (1 Kings 1—11). After Solomon's death, it divided (1 Kings 12—22); then both kingdoms went into captivity (2 Kings). The northern tribes were taken by Assyria (2 Kings 1—17), and the southern kingdom was taken by Babylon (2 Kings 18—25).

Israel was a nation greatly blessed by God, and yet it ended in disgrace and defeat. The cause was sin. Solomon worshiped the idols of the foreign nations, and the nation followed him. It took only one generation for the nation to decay and divide, as the false prophets and the worldly priests led the people astray. The leaders and the people would not listen to God's prophets and return to the true worship of Jehovah, so there was nothing left for God to do but discipline His people as He had warned (Deut. 28).

1 KINGS

--- ✦ ---

1 KINGS 1

Some people are gullible and unwilling to learn from the past. Like Absalom, Adonijah was handsome, popular, and proud. His "I will be king!" sounds like another boast that ended in judgment (Isa. 14:12-15). Foolishly, Joab and Abiathar joined Adonijah and opposed God's man, Solomon, and they paid for it. They should have paid more attention to this pronouncement: "You shall not follow a crowd to do evil" (Exod. 23:2).

Sometimes leaders must be led, and Nathan and Bathsheba did it wisely. David had given up the sword (2 Sam. 21:15-17), and now he must give up the scepter. Wise is the leader who knows when to step aside. Solomon was God's choice for the throne (2 Sam. 12:24-25).

Adonijah fled to the altar for safety, not for sanctity. Religion was something he used only for personal profit, but some insincere people today do the same thing.

1 KINGS 2

The king died. Death is an appointment we all must keep (Heb. 9:27), unless the Lord comes to take us home (1 Cor. 15:51ff.). Before he died, David gave Solomon wise counsel about the men who were a threat to the throne. It is good to know where the enemy is hiding. David had served his generation well (Acts 13:36).

The usurper died. Adonijah still wanted the throne and almost tricked Bathsheba into helping him. Since Abishag was one of David's concubines, claiming her would be the same as claiming the throne. Adonijah had planned a wedding, but he ended up at a funeral.

The murderer died. Abiathar and Joab were both traitors, but Abiathar was spared because he was a priest. However, the exile removed the descendants of Eli from office as had been predicted years before (1 Sam. 2:30–35). Joab paid for murdering three men and also for his treachery to David. Benaiah was a priest (1 Chron. 27:5), but he was one of David's mighty men and Joab's successor as head of the army.

The accuser died. (See 2 Sam. 16:5–14; 19:18–23.) Had Shimei obeyed orders, he would have lived, but he defied the king and lost his life.

How true is the declaration: "Righteousness and justice are the foundation of His throne" (Ps. 97:2).

1 KINGS 3

Politics. The Jews were not forbidden to marry Egyptians, but Solomon's marriage to Pharaoh's daughter was the first step toward his breaking the law of God and bringing tragic consequences to himself and the people (1 Kings 11:1–8; see also Deut. 7:1–4). It was purely a political move designed to bring peace to the land, and it worked.

Prayer. How would you answer God's question: "What shall I give you?" Your answer reveals what you believe about yourself and the work God has called you to do. Solomon knew that he needed wisdom more than anything else, and God gave him that and much more (Matt. 6:33; Eph. 3:20–21). Prayer is not simply getting things from God. It is getting so that we might be able to give to others. Solomon's concern was ability to serve his people well.

Perception. Prostitutes had access to the king (Matt. 9:10–11)! The wisdom God gives is practical and helps us in the decisions of life (Prov. 1:1–7; James 1:5).

1 KINGS 4

Samuel's dire prediction came true (1 Sam. 8:10–18), for Solomon did a great deal of "taking." He divided the nation into twelve districts, each with a governor, and required each district to supply provisions for the royal household once a year. When you read the daily menu, you can see how difficult meeting those requirements must have been for the people (1 Kings 12:4).

Verse 20 describes a prosperous people but not a spiritual people. Peace and prosperity do not always breed nobility of character, and rejoicing without responsibility is the way to ruin. As for Solomon's horses, read Deuteronomy 17:17.

Jesus Christ is "greater than Solomon" (Matt. 12:42) in wisdom (Col. 2:3), wealth (Col. 1:19; 2:9), and the bounty He shares with His people (Eph. 3:20–21). He does not promise you a life of "eat, drink, and be merry" (v. 20), but He does promise to meet all your needs (Phil. 4:19) and never forsake you (Matt. 28:19–20; Heb. 13:5). One day you shall share His heavenly home and live with Him forever (John 14:1–6)!

1 KINGS 5—7

Cooperation. God gave David the design for the temple (1 Chron. 28:11–19), and David and the people provided most of the materials (1 Chron. 29). A gentile king, Hiram, supplied the timber, and a Canaanite work force (1 Kings 9:20–22) assisted the Jewish workers. It was a cooperative effort supervised by King Solomon. God is building His "holy temple" today (Eph. 2:19–22), and He uses the service of all kinds of people. Are you helping to build His church?

Pillars

The two pillars were called Jachin ("He will establish") and Boaz ("In Him is strength").

God provides stability and strength for His people because they worship Him. God's house was costly and beautiful, but it also needed stability and strength (Ps. 96:6).

Construction. They built with gold, silver, and costly stones (1 Chron. 28:14—29:9), the same materials God wants in His church (1 Cor. 3:10–23; see also Prov. 2:1–9; 3:13–15; 8:10–11). Every detail was spelled out, and Solomon saw to it that the design was followed perfectly.

Concern. Wealth beyond measure went into the building of the temple, but the important thing was *obedience to the Lord* (1 Kings 6:11–13). God is not impressed with our buildings, for He provides everything we put into them (Isa. 66:1–2). He wants our loving obedience, and then He can make the buildings a blessing.

1 KINGS 8

Solomon's temple was a place of glory (vv. 1–12). However, despite its extraordinary beauty, it was just another building until God moved in and consecrated it (Exod. 40:34–38). So it is with our lives (1 Cor. 6:19–20; Eph. 5:18) and our assemblies (1 Cor. 14:23–25). The presence of God is the important thing. A. W. Tozer aptly stated, "If God were to take the Holy Spirit out of this world, much of what the church is doing would go right on, *and nobody would know the difference.*"

The temple was a place of testimony (vv. 14–21, 56), bearing witness that God keeps His word. It was to be a place of prayer (vv. 22–53). Solomon was especially concerned that God hear the prayers of His own people as well as those of the stranger and foreigner. In later years, the religious leaders would turn the house of prayer into a den of thieves (Matt. 21:12–13).

Who Is Justified?

Solomon prayed that God would condemn the wicked and justify the righteous (1 Kings 8:32). But through Jesus Christ, God justifies (declares righteous) the wicked (Rom. 4:5), and He does it on the basis of grace, not works. God cannot justify the righteous because there are none (Rom. 3:10).

It was a place of blessing (vv. 54–61) and sacrifice (vv. 62–66). The two go together: we give our best to the Lord, and then we share our best with others. It is unfortunate that Solomon failed in the very thing he exhorted his people to remember—loyalty of heart (v. 61).

Finally, the temple was a place of witness to the world (vv. 41–43, 60), for Solomon had a "missionary vision" for the gentile nations. What an opportunity Israel had to win the lost people around them!

The Heart of the Matter

Solomon's emphasis was on the heart: each one knows his own heart (1 Kings 8:38); God knows the heart (v. 39); we return to God with all our hearts (v. 48); God must incline our hearts to obedience (v. 58); God wants each of us to have a loyal heart (v. 61).

1 KINGS 9

Assurance. We dedicate, but only God can consecrate (sanctify) what we give Him. It is important to hear from God when a task has been completed, lest there be a letdown that can lead to discouragement (1 Kings 19). The phrases "My name . . . My eyes . . . My heart" (v. 3) indicate God's nearness to His people. He is identified with us; He watches over us; He loves us.

Admonition. Because He loves us, God warns us not to disobey Him. Solomon did not heed this warning, and God kept His promise and sent discipline. God would rather destroy His holy temple than permit His people to pollute it with their sin.

Agreement. Solomon was a successful maker of treaties with the gentiles, and that ability helped to keep Israel out of war. However, there was a price to pay and a constant danger to avoid. Ultimately, Solomon was controlled by the gods of those nations (1 Kings 11).

Achievement. But everything looked grand as Solomon

built buildings, walls, and ships and increased the wealth of the nation. They needed the warning of Revelation 3:17–18. The spiritual life of the nation was gradually decaying behind the veneer of prosperity.

1 KINGS 10

Our fame and God's name must go together (v. 1). If God magnifies your name (Josh. 3:7; 6:27), be sure He gets the glory (Ps. 135:13). Fame is a heavy burden to bear, and only God can help us do it wisely.

The queen traveled twelve hundred miles to see and hear Solomon. Her reasons were both personal and political, for she wanted to enter into trade agreements with the king. The people of Jesus' day rejected a "greater than Solomon" who was there among them (Matt. 12:42), and they were judged for it.

Do we take our blessings for granted? In spite of the queen's enthusiasm, perhaps even Solomon's servants got accustomed to hearing his wise words and beholding his great wealth (v. 8). Israel grew accustomed to the miracle of the manna (Num. 11), and the church at Ephesus grew accustomed to Christ's love (Rev. 2:1–7).

Chariots and horses (vv. 26–29) were another indication of decay (Deut. 17:17). And don't forget what Jesus said about all of Solomon's glory (Matt. 6:29).

1 KINGS 11

Apostasy. Solomon had wisdom for everybody else but would not apply it to himself (Rom. 2:21–24). The man who wrote Proverbs 4:23 did not obey it (v. 4; 1 Kings 8:61). The king was required to write a personal copy of Deuteronomy and study it (Deut. 17:18–20), so surely Solomon knew Deuteronomy 7:1–11; 17:17. It is one thing to know the Word but quite another thing to do it (James 1:22–25).

Anger. God's blessings are given by grace, but they are enjoyed by obedience. Solomon was disobedient, and yet surely he knew that the covenant included warnings about disobedience (2 Sam. 7:14; 1 Kings 3:14; 9:4–9).

Adversaries. God had a special love for Solomon (2 Sam.

12:24–25); therefore, He had to chasten him (Prov. 3:11–12). Hadad, Rezon, and Jeroboam all created problems for the king as the flimsy tissue of Israel's "peace" began to fall apart. Solomon even planned to murder his rival, Jeroboam! God was kind to Solomon only for the sake of David (v. 32), but how long can a nation (or a church or a family) live on the spiritual dividends of their ancestors' sacrifice and obedience?

1 KINGS 12

Rehoboam did not seek God's wisdom, as had his father before him (1 Kings 3). Instead, he turned to men for guidance and even then did not heed the right advice. Like some people who seek counsel today, he wanted somebody to tell him to do what he already decided to do. The new king grew up in luxury. What did he know about the burdens of the common people?

We lead by serving (Matt. 20:20–28), and a true leader seeks to lighten the loads people carry. (Compare Matt. 11:28–30 and 23:4.) The king used the people to build his authority instead of using his authority to build the people. The result was a divided nation as Ahijah predicted (1 Kings 11:29ff.). As much as we love unity, we must accept the fact that some divisions are of God.

Afraid that his people would return to Jerusalem to worship, Jeroboam established a "religion of convenience" (v. 28) and made it easy for the nation to sin. Abandoning the true worship of Jehovah, he repeated the sin of Aaron (Exod. 32). Patterned after the Mosaic system, his religion was popular, but it did not have God's approval (Hos. 13:2).

1 KINGS 13

Courage. The anonymous prophet received his message from God and delivered it to the king. It was fulfilled nearly three hundred years later by King Josiah (2 Kings 23:15–20). The prophet did not fear the king's threats or succumb to the king's bribes, both of which would have invalidated his ministry.

Compromise. Had the prophet continued to obey God's directions, he would not have been killed, but gradually he got out of the will of God. Instead of hurrying home, he sat down (v. 14). Instead of obeying his original commission from God, he believed the lies of the old prophet. The prophet ended up eating and drinking with an enemy who pretended to be a friend.

Unless they can back it up from the Word, beware when others know God's will for your life. The sign found on some traffic lights preaches a good sermon: OBEY YOUR OWN SIGNAL.

1 KINGS 14

Disguise. Why did the king not consult one of the false gods he worshiped? And why not go to the Lord's prophet *personally* and *openly*? Because Jeroboam was a coward and did not want to weaken his "religious establishment." He did not dare identify himself publicly with the true worship of Jehovah, even though he knew that his own religious leaders could not help him.

Death. Abijah had good news about the son but bad news about everybody else in the royal family. God saw true devotion in the son and would not permit him to grow up in such an evil home. The boy was the only male to have a decent burial and be mourned. See verse 18 and 1 Kings 15:25–30 for the fulfillment.

Decay. Under King Rehoboam, Solomon's great kingdom lost both quantity (the tribes) and quality (the treasures). The costly golden shields (1 Kings 10:16–17) were replaced by bronze shields, but the guards and the king went through the same ceremony. What a picture of some lives and ministries today: everything looks the same, but the value has vanished. All we do is keep up appearances (Matt. 23).

1 KINGS 15

A flickering lamp. God blessed Judah for David's sake, just as He blesses us for the sake of His beloved Son (Eph. 1:3) and because of the faithfulness of those who have gone before us. "Except in the matter of Uriah the Hittite"—and what a costly exception that was! Even a man who sinned greatly can be restored and become a blessing to others. But the lamp of truth was flickering, and Judah's sins would one day be judged.

An inconsistent ruler. Asa had a wonderful beginning to his reign but a disappointing ending. He was courageous enough to cleanse the temple of religious prostitutes and purge the land of idols, and he even dethroned his own grandmother. But instead of trusting the Lord for victory, he robbed the temple and bribed a pagan king to assist him in a war.

A certain judgment. God had promised that the house of Jeroboam would be destroyed, and Baasha was the instrument of that judgment. But Baasha repeated the sins of Jeroboam! Did he think that *he* would escape punishment? F. von Logau commented, "Though the mills of God grind slowly, yet they grind exceeding small."

1 KINGS 16

Whenever the kings or priests led the people into sin, God sent faithful prophets to warn them and to call them back to the true worship of Jehovah. Jehu was such a prophet; he was not afraid to give God's message of judgment to evil King Baasha. Are we today willing to take our stand against evil, or do we just drift with the crowd?

Baasha had imitated Jeroboam's sins, so he would suffer Jeroboam's judgment (1 Kings 14:7–11). God used Zimri to fulfill His word against Baasha. If we do not heed what God says, we must suffer His judgment.

Zimri's reign was brief. Rather than fall into the hands of Omri and his faction, Zimri committed suicide. Omri, too, chose to disobey God and "did worse than all who were before him" (v. 25). And one of the worst things he did was to leave his son Ahab to reign over Israel.

Ahab married a heathen princess, worshiped a heathen god, and provoked the Lord greatly. He made Baal worship a popular religion in Israel. Baal was the Canaanite storm god, and his worship was attractive to a nation that depended so much on rain. Besides, the rituals involved temple prostitutes, and that appealed to the baser appetites of the people.

1 KINGS 17

Samuel grew up being recognized as God's prophet (1 Sam. 3:19–21), but Elijah *suddenly* appeared before Ahab declaring God's message. The drought, for which he had prayed (James 5:17), was Elijah's declaration of war against Ahab, Jezebel, and the storm god Baal. If the king and the people had humbled themselves before the Lord, He would have sent rain to the land (Deut. 11:13–17; 2 Chron. 7:12–15), but most of the nation trusted Baal, not Jehovah.

The drought had three more years to go (1 Kings 18:1; Luke 4:25), and God took care of His faithful servant (Ps. 37:3–6). During that time of "retirement," God led him, fed him, and enabled him to help others, including a *gentile* widow (Luke 4:25–26). When we walk by faith, God supplies our needs and opens doors of opportunity for us.

Be sure to trust the Provider and not the provision. Brooks dry up, but God never fails.

1 KINGS 18

Searching for water. Ahab's capital city suffered severely, but the godless rulers did not repent. It takes more than suffering to break a proud heart; it takes hearing and yielding to the word of God. But Ahab and Jezebel tried to silence God's word by killing God's prophets. They showed more concern for their animals than for their people. When a nation's leaders have their priorities confused, the nation will suffer greatly.

Searching for Elijah. Ahab wanted to kill Elijah (v. 10), but God protected His servant. To Ahab, Elijah was an enemy (1 Kings 21:20), but Ahab was his own worst enemy. We commend Obadiah for protecting the prophets, but that was not the final solution. Israel had to make a decision between Baal and Jehovah (Josh. 24:14–21).

Searching for God. Baal was the storm god, so he should have been able to send rain, but he failed. Elijah rebuked the people (v. 21), repaired the altar (v. 30), and relied on the Lord (vv. 36–37), and God revealed Himself by sending fire (v. 38). In response to Elijah's prayer, God sent rain. Elijah was the man of the hour: he honored God, and God honored him.

Some may ask, "Where is the LORD God of Elijah?"

(2 Kings 2:14). Perhaps the better question is, *Where are the Elijahs?*

1 KINGS 19

The "Elijah complex" can rob you of power and joy, so beware! Elijah went from victory to defeat because he started walking by sight and not by faith (v. 3). He believed the queen's words but not God's word, and he forgot how God had cared for him for three and a half years. Fear replaced faith, and he ran for his life.

He became concerned about saving himself rather than giving himself (Mark 8:34–38; John 12:23–28). Note the sequence: "your life" (v. 2), "his life" (v. 3), "my life" (v. 4). If he had said, "Take my life," as an act of surrender to God, the Lord would have worked in power; but his "Take my life" was a confession of pride and defeat. Beware when you think you are the only faithful one left!

They Wanted to Die!

Sometimes we feel so depressed about our work and ourselves that we wish God would call us home. Of course, had Elijah really wanted to die, Jezebel would have gladly accommodated him. But Elijah was not the only one to feel that way. Moses wanted to die (Num. 11:15), and so did Job (Job 3:20–21), Jeremiah (Jer. 8:3), and Jonah (Jon. 4:3). Of course, this is not the answer to despair because it is selfish and does not glorify God. The real answer is to die to self and trust God to work things out. "The future is your friend when Jesus is your Lord."

God taught Elijah that He does not always work in the dramatic big events, such as the contest on Mount Carmel, but that He works by means of a "still small voice," ministries that are neither big nor loud. Elijah was not forsaken, for God was with him. He was not alone, for seven thousand people had not bowed to Baal. His work would go on, for God had a young man ready to take his place.

We need to obey these words: "Do not be afraid; only believe" (Mark 5:36).

1 KINGS 20

Victory. In His grace, God gave wicked King Ahab two victories over the enemy. The first victory was to teach Ahab that the Lord was the true God (v. 13), and the second was to show the enemy that Jehovah was not weak and limited like the heathen idols (v. 28). We must never think that we receive blessings because we deserve them.

Compromise. Instead of claiming complete victory and destroying Ben-Hadad (v. 42), Ahab entered into a treaty with him! King Saul made the same mistake with the king of the Amalekites (1 Sam. 15:8–9), and both kings lost their kingdoms because of their disobedience. When you think the battle is over, you may face your greatest danger and experience your greatest defeat.

Defeat. The Lord had given the king ample evidence that He was God, but Ahab persisted in hardening his heart. Too spiritually blind to know who the prophet was or what he was talking about, Ahab pronounced his own death sentence (v. 40). His pouting did not change anything (Prov. 19:3), but he refused to turn to the Lord.

1 KINGS 21

Covetousness. Ahab asked Naboth to break the law, but Naboth refused (Num. 36:7). The king thought that every man had his price, but Naboth was not for sale. "You shall not covet" is the last of the Ten Commandments (Exod. 20:17), but in breaking it, Ahab broke several of the other nine. Ahab and Jezebel put things ahead of God; they lied, murdered, and stole a man's property; and they tried to cover it up. How many commandments do we have to break to be guilty before God?

Conspiracy. Evil leaders could never succeed were it not for weak people who obey their orders. Jezebel did not fear God's name or believe in fasting, but she knew how to use both to get what she wanted. An innocent man died, but God saw it happen. Elijah found Ahab, Ahab's sin found Ahab (Num. 32:23), and the word of judgment was pronounced.

Clemency. Ahab humbled himself before God, not because he felt the burden of his sins but because he faced the terror of death. God delayed the execution of the sentence, but it came just the same. Ahab had sold himself to do evil, and his master—sin—finally paid the wages (Rom. 6:23).

1 KINGS 22

Fight your own battles. Jehoshaphat had no reason to meddle in Ahab's wars. He made the mistake of marrying Ahab's daughter (2 Chron. 18:1; 2 Cor. 6:14–18), so there were family obligations to fulfill.

Deliver your own message. False prophets usually agree in their messages of success and glory. The messenger tried to get Micaiah to imitate them, but he gave the true message of the Lord. It was not easy to be a prophet in Israel in that day, but Micaiah was faithful.

Know your own enemy. Ahab cleverly tried to make Jehoshaphat a decoy and get him killed (Luke 16:8), but God overruled and Ahab was slain instead. The prophecy of 1 Kings 21:19 was fulfilled (v. 38). Paul may have had verse 31 in mind when he wrote Ephesians 6:12ff. Our real enemy is the god of this age and the prince of darkness, so let's not waste time and ammunition on lesser foes.

Learn from your own mistakes. When the new king of Israel, Jehoshaphat's brother-in-law, asked for a new alliance, Jehoshaphat refused. He had learned his lesson the hard way, but at least he had learned it and profited from his mistakes. He was a great and godly man, and we must not allow one event to discredit his service for the Lord.

2 KINGS

◆

This book records the collapse and captivity of the kingdom of Israel (chaps. 1—17) and the kingdom of Judah (chaps. 18—25). Spiritual decay led to political and social deterioration. In spite of the ministries of the prophets and the frequent chastenings God sent, Israel and Judah rebelled against the Lord and had to be judged. This is a warning to individuals (Prov. 29:1) and nations (Prov. 14:34) to listen to God's Word and obey it.

2 KINGS 1

"What kind of man was it?" (v. 7) is a key question. The messengers described Elijah's physical appearance, but they left out the most important thing. Elijah was "a man with a nature like ours" (James 5:17), but he was also a "man of God" (vv. 9–13). The physical description in verse 8 is incidental, yet that is what most people emphasize in their lives.

He was guided by the Lord. Elijah knew what was happening because he listened to God's voice (Ps. 25:4–5, 14). We today do not hear an audible voice, but we have His Spirit within us and His Word before us.

He glorified the Lord. The very idea of the king going to a false god for help! Elijah wanted Ahaziah to know that Jehovah alone was the true God and that the king had better bow humbly before the Lord.

He trusted the Lord to care for him. Elijah was one man against fifty-one soldiers, but the Lord protected him. Had the soldiers completely forgotten the fire that came down on Mount Carmel? The third captain humbled himself, and God spared him and his company.

He did the Lord's will. He delivered the message to the king as he was commanded to do.

Can God's people today be men and women of God? Certainly! Ponder 1 Timothy 6:10–12 and 2 Timothy 3:14–17.

The Man of God

The title "man of God" was given first to Moses (Deut. 33:1), then to Samuel (1 Sam. 9:6–7), Elijah (1 Kings 1:9–13), Elisha (2 Kings 4:9), David (2 Chron. 8:14), and Timothy (1 Tim. 6:11). You need not be a prophet to be a godly person, nor do you display your godliness by calling down fire from heaven (Luke 9:51–56). God wants us to use "coals of fire" and turn enemies into friends (Rom. 12:14–21).

---

2 KINGS 2

Companions. Elisha's ministry began with Elijah saying, "Go back!" (1 Kings 19:20). Now Elijah is saying, "Stay here!" Elisha did not go back but faithfully served Elijah about ten years. And Elisha did not linger at Bethel or Jericho but walked with Elijah to the very end. Think of what Elisha would have missed had he tarried!

Spectators. The students had knowledge without experience. They were just spectators, yet they tried to tell the prophet what was going on! Elisha was not a spectator; he was right in the middle of what God was doing. What good is our knowledge of spiritual things if it does not make a difference in our lives?

Doers. Elisha did not build a monument to Elijah. Instead, he trusted Elijah's God and did miracles. We cannot live *in* the past, *on* the past, or *for* the past. We must accept the heritage of the past and trust the living God for power today. There were problems to solve and needs to meet, and Elisha trusted God to help him. God's servants may leave us, but God's Spirit goes on working.

Mockers. They were not little children; the youths were old enough to know better. They mocked Elijah's going to heaven ("Go up!") and Elisha's personal appearance, and God rightly judged them for it. Today, God is patient with the mockers (2 Pet. 3), but one day, His judgment will fall on them.

2 KINGS 3

King Jehoshaphat was wrong to ally himself with the king of Israel (1 Kings 22), but Elisha did not withdraw from him because of that. The presence of the king of Judah was the only thing that motivated Elisha to help the kings in their plight. God still had a lamp in Judah for the sake of David.

The lack of water reminded all three kings that God was in control and their combined power meant nothing without Him. Samson had a similar experience (Judg. 15:18-20). The same water that meant salvation to the three armies brought defeat to overconfident Moab. (See Exod. 10:21-23; 2 Cor. 2:14-16.)

Hoping to get some good out of the war, the king of Moab attacked Edom alone, but he failed to conquer. In desperation, he even sacrificed the crown prince. The deed was so repulsive to Judah and Moab that they left the field in great anger against Israel for ever getting them involved. When you join forces with those who do not love God, you never know what will happen to embarrass or offend you or to disgrace the Lord's name.

2 KINGS 4

Elisha ministered to individuals and accepted the hospitality of friends. He was like Jesus Christ in that respect, while Elijah was more like John the Baptist: alone, rugged, a preacher to the nation. Although God equips different people to work in different ways, He is Lord of all (1 Cor. 12:1-11). It is too bad people do not recognize this fact and receive the ministry no matter who the minister is (Luke 7:31-35; 1 Cor. 1:10-17).

A husband died, yet God met the needs of the family (vv. 1-7). A son died, yet God raised him and restored the family (vv. 8-37). A group of prophets almost died because of poisoned stew, yet God removed the danger (vv. 38–41). A group of believers would have died from starvation, but God multiplied the bread and sustained them (vv. 42–44). All of these miracles remind you to *give God what you have and let Him do what He wills.*

Gehazi is declining spiritually, but the consequences will not appear until later. He was unkind to the Shunammite woman (v. 27; see also Matt. 15:23; Mark 10:13; Luke 9:49), and he had no power to help her. He went through the motions, but no life came. You can fellowship day after day with people of power, like the prophet Elisha, and still backslide. Beware!

Three Important Questions

What are your answers to the three questions the prophet asked the Shunammite woman? "Is it well with you? Is it well with your husband [or wife]? Is it well with the child?" (2 Kings 4:26).

---

2 KINGS 5

Servants. Servants played a major role in this miracle. The young Jewish girl gave a faithful witness for the Lord, and God used her testimony to get Naaman to visit Elisha. Naaman's servants encouraged him to obey the prophet, and his obedience led to his healing and his faith in Jehovah. No matter who or where you are, God can use your service. (See John 15:15.)

Suppositions. The king of Syria thought the king of Israel could perform the miracle, and the false assumption almost led to a war. Naaman supposed that Elisha would use some religious ritual to remove the leprosy, and the supposition almost led to his going home still a leper. Gehazi supposed that he could get away with sin, but God judged him.

Selfishness. Naaman was healed completely by God's grace, but Gehazi robbed God of glory by asking Naaman for gifts. The Syrians would think that they had to pay God to get His help. Gehazi lied to Naaman, to Elisha, and to himself, but he could not lie to God. Gehazi became poor by getting rich.

They Became Lepers

In the Bible, leprosy is used as a picture of sin (Lev. 13). Gehazi became a leper because of covetousness and deception. Miriam became a leper because of criticism and envy (Num. 12). King Uzziah became a leper because of pride (2 Chron. 26:16–23). If God did this to people today, would you be a leper? The hidden sins of the spirit are dangerous (2 Cor. 7:1)!

---

2 KINGS 6

Doing the impossible (1–7). All that we have is "borrowed," loaned to us by the Lord to get His work done (John 3:27). You can lose your cutting edge even while serving the Lord. But be honest about it, stop trying to chop without an ax head, and ask the Lord for help in recovering it. He alone can do the impossible if you trust Him.

Knowing the unknowable (8–12). Because Elisha knew what the enemy would do, Israel had the opportunity to escape surprise attacks. If you study God's Word, you can know the strategy of Satan and be able to defeat him.

Seeing the invisible (13–17). Many times we are afraid of the enemy because we walk by sight and not by faith. If God and His hosts are for us, who can be against us?

Accomplishing the unthinkable (18–23). Knowing that Elisha was his real enemy, the king of Syria tried to capture the prophet. *But Elisha captured them,* and he did it with prayer and kindness (Rom. 12:19–21; 2 Cor. 10:3–6). In the East, eating together is equivalent to making a covenant, so those soldiers could never attack Israel again.

2 KINGS 7

When times are tough, people may respond in the following ways:

Blaming. Like his evil father Ahab who blamed Elijah for his woes, King Joram blamed Elisha for the plight of the city (1 Kings 18:17; 2 Kings 6:31), when in reality it was his own fault. He tore his clothes and wore sackcloth, but the king's actions did not impress God as long as his heart was hardened (2 Kings 6:30; Joel 2:12–14).

Doubting (1–2). The officer did not believe the word of God, and his unbelief caused his death (vv. 17–20). God will open the windows when we obey Him (Mal. 3:10).

Reasoning (3–8). The four lepers were logical in their reasoning: "If we give up, we will die. If we give in to the enemy, we may die, or we may live. Let's surrender to the enemy." But there was no enemy! God scattered them with a noise!

Sharing (9–16). The lepers moved from giving up and giving in to giving out. Sharing the good news helped to save the city. We are living in a day of good news. Are you sharing it? We are here not to give in or give up but to give out.

2 KINGS 8

God knows the future. The Shunammite woman experienced three tragedies: the death of her son, the uprooting of her household, and the loss of her property. And yet she was faithful to the Lord and had been kind to God's servant (2 Kings 4:8ff.). God helped her escape the famine and then used the miracle of her son's resurrection to help her regain her property. Romans 8:28 certainly proved true in her life! You may wonder why God permits some of your trials, but wait and see how He will use them!

God sees the heart. When he was desperate, Ben-Hadad wanted Elisha's help, but he did not want Elisha's God. The prophet saw the murder in Hazael's heart, but Hazael denied it was there. We do not know how wicked our hearts really are (Jer. 17:9), and we must cry out to God for His help (Ps. 51:5–6, 10).

God keeps His promises. Jehoshaphat was a godly man,

but he had married a daughter of Ahab (2 Chron. 18:1); and his son followed his bad example. Jehoram also followed the bad example of his father-in-law Ahab and allowed his evil wife to lead him into great sin. But God kept His promise to David (v. 19) and did not destroy Judah. He had purposes to fulfill through the godly remnant, for Judah would bring the Savior into the world.

2 KINGS 9—10

It is not pleasant to read the events recorded in these chapters, but we need to hear their message: *eventually sin is judged, and God's word is fulfilled.* God had ordained the anointing of Jehu (1 Kings 19:16) and the end of Ahab's family (1 Kings 21:21–26), and He kept His word.

King Joram of Israel was slain and so was King Ahaziah of Judah. Jezebel, the queen mother, was killed just as the prophet had predicted. Then Jehu wiped out all of Ahab's family and Ahaziah's relatives (who were also relatives of Ahab) and the followers of Baal.

"*Sin is the only thing that God abhors. It brought Christ to the cross, it damns souls, it shuts heaven, it laid the foundations of hell.***"**

Thomas Brooks

Why was God so severe in His judgment? Because those leaders had turned the people away from the Lord and had polluted the nation. God had special work for His people to do (Gen. 12:1–3), and they could not do it if they were unfaithful to Him.

After displaying all that zeal, Jehu should have set the example in his devotion to Jehovah, but he did not. A nation does not become righteous simply by removing evil; it must also establish godliness. An empty house is an invitation to even worse tenants (Matt. 12:43–45), and they eventually came—and the nation had to be judged.

2 KINGS 11

The future of David's royal line was at stake when the queen mother slaughtered all the heirs, and her wicked deed also threatened the fulfillment of the promise of the Messiah. Satan's seed was at war with God's seed (Gen. 3:15), but God won the battle. The future rested in one little boy whom God protected in the temple.

Events around you may create doubts and fears in your heart, and you may wonder if God knows what is going on and if He cares. Rest assured that God not only knows and cares but that He is working out His purposes in spite of the evil deeds of wicked people. God does not need great armies to accomplish His plans. He can use a boy seven years old to change the course of a nation. Often when circumstances are the most difficult, God surprises you with a special victory. Trust Him!

2 KINGS 12

Young Jehoash was fortunate to have as his counselor Jehoiada the priest, husband of the woman who had saved the king's life (2 Chron. 22:11). Jehoiada gave the king God's Word (2 Kings 11:12) and taught him how to obey it. The secret of success in any venture for God is to honor His Word (Josh. 1:8). Do you let others strengthen you in the faith, and do you appreciate their ministry to you?

An idol-worshiping nation had allowed the temple to deteriorate. When we do not love God, we neglect the things important to God. A box by the altar was the ideal place for taking an offering. The sacrifices speak of our Lord's gracious work of redemption, and if that does not motivate us to give, nothing will (2 Cor. 8:9).

Jehoiada's death left Jehoash alone, and he led the nation back into sin (2 Chron. 24:15ff.). His religious zeal had not been very sincere. The king forgot the kindness of the high priest and even murdered his son. Jesus referred to this event in Matthew 23:34–35. It is not enough to promote religious works; we must have true devotion to God in our hearts. If your faith is "propped up" by others, what will you do when the "props" are gone?

2 KINGS 13

Hands of oppression. Jehoahaz followed the wrong example (v. 2) and brought Israel into bondage to foreign kings. Yet God was merciful to the disobedient king and His suffering people. As David wrote, "He has not dealt with us according to our sins, nor punished us according to our iniquities" (Ps. 103:10). Thank God for that!

Hands of power. Elisha was a dying man, yet he was able to communicate the power of God to the king. One man of God was equal in power to the whole army of Israel (v. 14)!

Hands of opportunity. Lacking spiritual discernment, the king did not understand the will of God as he followed the prophet's orders. Jehoash merely went through the motions, and as a result, he claimed only a limited victory over the enemy. He missed his opportunity and could never claim it again. What opportunity will God give you today that you may never have again?

"*The opportunity that God sends does not wake up him who is asleep.***"**

Sengalese Proverb

---

2 KINGS 14

King Amaziah made a fine beginning by following a good example, establishing justice in the land and obeying the Word of God (Deut. 24:16). But after he won a great victory over Edom, he became proud, and that led to his defeat.

Be content with your sphere of victory as the Lord gives you faith (Rom. 12:3). When you keep your eyes on the Lord, your victories will humble you, and God will get the glory. But when you forget the Lord, your victories will make you proud and lead you to defeat.

Beware the temptation to meddle. Learn to accept what God gives, stay at home, and do what He has called you to do. King Amaziah needed to heed Proverbs 16:18 and 26:17.

2 KINGS 15

As the time of reckoning drew near, the kingdoms of Israel and Judah suffered under the rule of men whose godless lives brought more and more trouble. Conspiracies abounded as God's law was ignored.

But there were two exceptions: Azariah (Uzziah) and his son Jotham, who followed his father's example. Unfortunately, Uzziah became proud and wanted to serve as a priest. The Lord punished him by making him a leper (2 Chron. 26:16ff.). It is the lesson of 2 Kings 14:10 all over again: accept the sphere of blessing God gives you and do not meddle with matters that are beyond you. (See Ps. 131.)

2 KINGS 16

Ahaz was a failure in his walk. He followed the wicked example of the kings of Israel. He was a descendant of David and should have obeyed the Word of God and trusted the God of the Word. Consciously or unconsciously, each of us follows various examples, and we must be sure they are the examples God wants us to follow.

Ahaz was a failure in his warfare. Because he had no faith in God, he was defeated by the enemy (1 John 5:4–5). He robbed God's temple to buy protection and he offered his son to a heathen god to secure help.

Ahaz also failed in his worship. Instead of following the divine pattern for the altar, he borrowed a pattern from a heathen temple (Exod. 25:40; 26:30). God's people do not need the novelties of the world (Rom. 12:2), no matter how attractive they may be. It is tragic when we try to worship God after the pattern of the world and not after the heavenly pattern. Building a different altar did not make Ahaz a better person. Are you looking for "religious novelties," or do you follow the pattern given by God in His Word?

2 KINGS 17

God's long-suffering ran out, and He called for Assyria to carry Israel away. What God did to Israel He can do to groups and individuals today. Consider some of their sins.

They forgot God's mercy (7) in saving them from Egyptian bondage. One of the best ways to remain true to the Lord is to remind yourself of all He has done for you (Ps. 103).

They imitated the ungodly (8) so that the true worship of Jehovah was corrupted by worldly practices. At first, they did those things secretly, but then the pagan practices were openly added to their worship of God.

They turned a deaf ear to the preaching of the prophets (13–18) and rejected the law of the Lord. When God disciplined them, they only hardened themselves more.

"They feared the LORD" but manufactured their own religion (25, 28, 32–34, 41)! Jehovah was "the God of the land" (v. 27) but not the only god. God rejected the religion of the Samaritans (John 4:19–24) as He rejects today all worship that is not "in spirit and truth."

2 KINGS 18—19

An idol within. Hezekiah removed all the idols from the land, including the brazen serpent that Moses had made (Num. 21:5–9). It is easy for God's people to make idols out of good things that outlive their usefulness.

An enemy without. Having conquered Israel, Assyria wanted to capture Judah. The nation was divided three ways: some wanted to give up to Assyria, others wanted to go to Egypt for help, and a minority wanted to trust the Lord for deliverance. Note the emphasis on the word *trust* in 18:19–25, and note that the enemy always has a bargain to offer (18:23). However, each bargain has a fatal "until" attached to it (18:31–32).

"*Prayer is not conquering God's reluctance, but taking hold of God's willingness.***"**

Phillips Brooks

An encouragement above. Hezekiah depended on the Word of God and prayer; he spread the matter before the Lord.

His only desire was to glorify the Lord before that heathen army (19:19). God gave him a message of peace and victory (19:6–7), and the enemy was defeated. God knows the battles you fight, and He will give you the help you need. Spread the matter before Him in faith, and seek to glorify His name.

2 KINGS 20

Verse 6 suggests that this event took place while Jerusalem was under siege by Assyria. It was bad enough that Judah was in danger, but the king was about to die. Sometimes it seems that troubles come in packs! Death is the last enemy we face (1 Cor. 15:26), and only God can give us victory over death.

Hezekiah was delivered because he prayed and used the means God provided for healing. Believing prayer can move God even to alter things in His universe just to meet our needs.

Hezekiah escaped the lion (1 Pet. 5:8) but succumbed to the serpent (vv. 12–19). He let the enemy know his secrets! Again, it was *pride:* "*my* house, *my* treasures, *my* days." His great victory over Assyria gave him false confidence as he entertained the Babylonians. He mortgaged his people's future by what he did and was thankful the defeat would not come in his own day.

Your decisions today will affect others tomorrow. Make the right decisions!

2 KINGS 21

Wicked King Ahaz fathered godly Hezekiah, and Hezekiah fathered evil King Manasseh whom the Lord allowed to reign for fifty-five years. King Manasseh was the father of godly King Josiah. Manasseh began his reign doing evil, but at the end of his life, he repented (2 Chron. 33:12). Josiah sought the Lord early in his life but closed his life disobeying God (2 Chron. 35:20ff.).

God's ways are not our ways; He is free to work as He chooses. People who claim to see clear patterns in history or who lock divine providence into a fixed formula must keep this in mind. God punishes the disobedient and vindicates His people but not always in the way or at the time that we expect. Ponder Psalm 73.

Sometimes God permits evil men to rule so that He may test His people or chasten them. We sometimes can do very little about world affairs, but we can pray for persons in authority (1 Tim. 2:1–8) and be faithful to obey God (Rom. 13).

2 KINGS 22

At the age of sixteen, Josiah began to seek the Lord and live for Him. Was his mother a special godly influence in his life? Her name means "beloved" and is very much like the Lord's "pet name" for Solomon (2 Sam. 12:25). Certainly Hilkiah the high priest saw to it that the young king honored the Lord. Never underestimate the power of godly influence.

Manasseh rebuilt everything that his father tore down (2 Kings 21:3), but Josiah tore down what Manasseh built up (2 Chron. 34:3–7). But reformation alone will not change people; there must be repentance and renewal within the heart. That came with the finding of the Law in the temple. (Imagine losing the Word of God in the house of God!)

It is good to *have* God's Word; it is even better to *hear* God's Word; but the greatest blessing of all is to *heed* God's Word (James 1:19–25). The king humbled himself before the Lord, and God spared the land.

Have you "lost" the Word of God somewhere, even in the midst of a religious life? Does God still speak to you, and do you obey?

2 KINGS 23

The temple was really in bad shape when Josiah began his reformation. The priests had lost the Word of God in the temple (22:8) and had permitted idolatrous things to accumulate there. When God's truth is neglected, it is easy for the false to move in and take over. Perhaps our lives and our churches could use a good "housecleaning" occasionally!

Josiah's work was the fulfillment of the prophecy that had been made years before (1 Kings 13:1–5). As he obeyed the Word of God, he removed what was evil and practiced what was good. The observance of Passover reminded the people that they belonged to the Lord and must put evil out of their lives.

It is sad that Josiah became proud and dared Pharaoh to fight him (2 Chron. 35:20–25). That led to his death and the ultimate downfall of the kingdom of Judah. Amaziah had made the same mistake (2 Kings 14:9–20).

2 KINGS 24—25

A series of weak and ungodly rulers led Judah into ruin as the sins of Manasseh came up for judgment. The consequences of decisions may not appear immediately, but they eventually come. Leaders may forget their decisions, but their decisions will not forget them. "Be sure your sin will find you out" is the sure word of God (Num. 32:23).

The nation had been rotting away at the center for years and was no match for the mighty Babylonian army. The king was captured, the city and temple were destroyed, and the people were taken into captivity. During the period of the judges, God had chastened them *in* the land; now He would chasten them *outside* their land. If they wanted to live like the idolaters, let them live *with* the idolaters.

As they were led off into captivity, do you think any of the people remembered Solomon's prayer to God (1 Kings 8:46–53) or God's message to Solomon (1 Kings 9:1–9)?

Submit to God

The governor urged the Jews to submit to God's chastening in Babylon and be good citizens (2 Kings 25:24). The prophet Jeremiah wrote them a letter saying the same thing (Jer. 29). When God chastens us, we only make matters worse when we resent it and resist it. We should yield to our Father's loving will and let Him work out His purposes (Heb. 12:1–11).

---

1 and 2 CHRONICLES

◆

The record in these books parallels that in Samuel and Kings. The focus is on David and the kingdom of Judah and the viewpoint is that of the priests. The opening genealogy takes you from Adam to Saul (1 Chron. 1—10), and that is followed by an account of David's reign (chaps. 11—29). Second Chronicles opens with the reign of Solomon (chaps. 1—9) and then describes the kings of Judah from the division of the kingdom to the captivity (chaps. 10—36).

These books were important to the Jews who returned to the land after the captivity. The genealogy established their tribal connections, something especially significant to the priests (Ezra 2:59–62). The people needed David's example of godliness, and the emphasis on the temple was needed at a time when it had to be rebuilt. The books of 1 and 2 Chronicles encourage people seeking to rebuild in a time of change and difficulty.

As you read 1 and 2 Chronicles, you will want to note the cross-references to Samuel and Kings and compare complementary passages.

1 CHRONICLES

$\blacklozenge$

1 CHRONICLES 1—9

You see nine chapters of unfamiliar names, many of them hard to pronounce, and you are tempted to skip them and get to the story. But stop to consider the importance of these chapters.

These names belonged to real people who once lived on this earth. Now most of them are forgotten, their names buried in an ancient list. One day *you* will be a name in a record file somewhere. History may forget you, but heaven never will. Are you living in the light of eternity (1 John 2:15 17)? Make your life count today.

These names were written on earth because these people were born on earth. The most vital listing is in heaven, the names of those who have been born again through faith in Jesus Christ (Luke 10:20; Phil. 4:3). Is your name written there?

These names belonged to what we would call "ordinary people." They were not all great men of faith like Abraham and David, but they all played a part in the working out of God's plan in this world. You may not consider yourself of consequence, but you are; every child of God has a place in God's heart and in His plan. Make yourself available to Him for the task He wants you to do, no matter how humble or unrecognized it may seem to you or to others.

These names belonged to Jews, one nation, called of God to witness for Him in a dark and wicked world. They were not always faithful, but through them, the world received witness of the one true and living God. They gave us the written Word of God, and in due time, they gave us the Savior. If nothing else, pause to give thanks for Israel, and "pray for the peace of Jerusalem" (Ps. 122:6).

For different reasons, some names stand out in this list. Abram had his name changed (1:27). Achan is identified as a troublemaker (2:7). Jabez had a sad name ("He will cause pain" [4:9–10]), but he overcame the stigma because he trusted the Lord. Reuben sinned away his birthright, which was given to the sons of Joseph (5:1). Joseph had refused to sin, so God honored him (Gen. 39). A father's sin can make a difference to the future of his family.

Read these chapters carefully. Here and there, you may meet some people who will warn you, challenge you, and even encourage you.

❝There is no such thing [as great people]! The greatest man or woman is 99 percent just like yourself.**❞**

G. B. Shaw

---

1 CHRONICLES 10

King Saul's life is ignored as the writer focuses on his death. He was a man with a good beginning and a tragic ending, and the reason is given in verses 13–14: he was unfaithful to the Lord and disobeyed His Word.

First Samuel 13—31 records Saul's gradual decline. He ran ahead of the Lord and offered a sacrifice. He spared King Agag and then lied to the Lord about it. He wanted recognition from Samuel and the people even though God had deserted him. He envied David and tried to destroy him. He wasted God-given opportunities for repentance. Finally, he turned to Satan for help and ended up committing suicide.

Not belonging to the tribe of Judah, Saul was never meant to establish the dynasty (Gen. 49:10), but that was not the cause of his sin. He could have been a godly leader and prepared the way for David, but Saul would not obey. Alexander Whyte quoted a relevant comment by Thomas Shepard: "Oh, the grievous shipwrecks of some great ships! We see some boards and planks lying in the mud at low water, but that is all!"

1 CHRONICLES 11

Some people become leaders because God chooses them in a special way and anoints them for a special work. That is how David came to the throne. In contrast to Saul, David was faithful to the Lord.

Others become leaders because people like David challenge them to do their best. Joab became head of the army because he conquered a stronghold, and all of David's "mighty men" won their way into the inner circle of heroes. David was a mighty leader, but he could not accomplish anything alone. We all need one another.

Greatness is often shown more in little things than in big things. Real leaders see greatness in places where others may see little or nothing. David did not see water in the vessel; he saw the blood of the men who risked their lives to satisfy his desire. It is not what a thing *is* or *does* that impresses a leader, but what a thing *costs his people*. D. L. Moody observed, "There are many of us that are willing to do great things for the Lord; but few of us are willing to do little things." And only God can make the "little things" great!

1 CHRONICLES 12

Saul *drafted* men into his army (1 Sam. 14:52) while David *attracted* them because of his character and leadership. In fact, some of his best men came from Saul's tribe! Saul seemed to bring out the worst in people while David brought out the best.

If Jesus Christ were recruiting an army on earth today, how many of us would qualify? He seeks skilled people (v. 2), trained people (v. 8), people not afraid to get their feet wet (v. 15). He wants soldiers with loyal hearts (vv. 16–18) who know how to keep rank and face the enemy together (vv. 33, 38). He needs people who understand the times (v. 32).

Are you a volunteer? Are you willing for the Lord to make

you qualified? The only winning army is the Lord's army. "The real great man is the man who makes every man feel great," according to Gilbert K. Chesterton.

1 CHRONICLES 13

A unanimous decision is not always a right decision, and enthusiasm is not the best test of truth. Were David's motives mixed as he sought to bring the ark home? Was the king subtly promoting himself as well as glorifying the Lord (v. 3)? Perhaps.

One thing is sure: David did not pause to seek the Lord's direction in the venture. It was his habit to seek the will of God before he acted, but that time, he failed. Any Levite could have told him how to do the job!

The ark was God's throne (Ps. 99:1), and the throne of God does not depend on the hand of man for support or protection. Had the ark been where it belonged, on the shoulders of the Levites, Uzza would have lived. No matter how successful at the beginning, man's methods *without God* will ultimately fail. The time to find out how to do His work is before the job begins, not after the funeral.

1 CHRONICLES 14

David had his disappointments, but he did not allow them to keep him from getting things done. It has been said that the only people who never make mistakes are the people who never make anything. To permit past blunders to keep us from fulfilling present duties is to make those blunders even worse.

As you seek to serve the Lord, you will discover that friends will help you (v. 1), the Lord will establish you (v. 2), and the enemy will fight you (vv. 8-17). Building and battling are normal experiences in the life of faith (Luke 14:25-33). Be like Nehemiah's workers on the wall, and have a tool in one hand and a ready weapon in the other (Neh. 4:17).

Twice David sought the mind of the Lord as he confronted his old enemies. Unlike Joshua at Ai, he did not assume that what worked once would work again (Josh. 7). Depending on past victories is a good way to guarantee future defeats. Ponder Judges 16:20-22.

1 CHRONICLES 15

Do God's work biblically (1–15). David turned the work over to the Levites, and 870 of them united to bring the ark to Jerusalem. They had no problems because they did it God's way.

Do God's work joyfully (16–24). They served "the LORD with gladness" (Ps. 100:2). Singers and musicians joined their talents in praising the Lord joyfully (vv. 16, 24). Harps, horns, trumpets, and even cymbals accompanied the singers' hymns of thanksgiving and praise.

Do God's work sacrificially (25–26). If they are to be acceptable to the Lord, our worship and service must come from the altar where a price has been paid. Cheap ministry is powerless ministry that cannot bless people or glorify the Lord.

Do God's work fervently (27–29). It was an enthusiastic procession with the Levites singing and playing instruments, the people shouting, and David leading them in praising the Lord. There are times when you should be silent before the Lord, but there are times when He wants to hear your praise. Vance Havner noted, "Too many church services start at eleven o'clock sharp and end at twelve o'clock dull."

1 CHRONICLES 16

Special times of praise and celebration are good to have, but you cannot live on these experiences. A satisfying walk with the Lord depends on daily worship of the Lord. That is why David assigned Asaph and the Levites their work in the ministry of worship "as every day's work required" (v. 37). Sacrifice and praise were parts of their daily service, as they should be in your life.

The main thing is to focus on the Lord, and David did just that in the special psalm he wrote. (For parallels, see Pss. 96; 105.) "The LORD" is named fourteen times as David reminds the people of God's works (vv. 8–13), God's words (vv. 14–22) and God's wonder (vv. 23–36)—His glory, greatness, and goodness. The excitement of the day would disappear, but the inspired song of praise would remain for all generations to use in worshiping God.

But after you have worshiped, remember to witness to the

lost (v. 23) and to do your part in getting the Gospel out to the nations of the world (vv. 24, 31). Archbishop William Temple pointed out the essential nature of worship: "For to worship is to quicken the conscience by the holiness of God, to feed the mind with the truth of God, to purge the imagination by the beauty of God, to open the heart to the love of God, to devote the will to the purpose of God."

1 CHRONICLES 17

Nathan was too quick to encourage David in the noble enterprise of building a house for the Lord (Josh. 9:14). How did Nathan know that was God's will for David? But the prophet's ear was ever open to God's voice (Amos 3:7), and he received from God the words that he delivered to David the next day.

Ten times in this chapter David is called "servant." The servant does not command the master; the master commands the servant. And what a wonderful Master the Lord is! Whether we look at the past ("I took you" [v. 7]; "I have been with you" [v. 8]), or the future (God says "I will" ten times), we see the grace and goodness of the Lord. How David was humbled by the goodness of the Lord!

It is one thing to *know* God's promises and quite something else to *claim them by faith*. Like a little child, David went in and "sat before the LORD." He thanked God for the mercies He had promised, and then he said, "Lord, do it!" Faith turns God's promises into reality, but before praying, take time to praise Him.

1 CHRONICLES 18

David defeated four great enemies because the Lord was with him. But David saw them as more than wars: they were opportunities to claim more territory for the Lord and gather more wealth for His treasury. He looked beyond the battle to the temple.

David reasoned, "If I cannot build the Lord's temple, at least I can help my son do it." One generation's victories can help build the next generation's temples. David dedicated to the Lord the spoils he won and the gifts and tribute he received. (See 1 Chron. 28.)

Each enemy can give you something to help build God's work on earth. Temptation is the opportunity to get the treasure without first winning the battle. Faith overcomes the enemy and claims the spoils for the Lord.

Benaiah

In the Old Testament record, the name Benaiah belongs to at least a dozen men, but the most fascinating of all is the man mentioned in 1 Chronicles 18:17. He was born a priest (1 Chron. 27:5) but became a soldier. He began his military career as one of David's mighty men (2 Sam. 23: 20–23) and was put over David's personal bodyguard. Eventually, Benaiah became head of Solomon's army (1 Kings 2:35). He could have enjoyed a relatively safe and easy life as a priest, but he chose the dangerous life of a soldier to serve his king. He "killed a lion in the midst of a pit on a snowy day" (2 Sam. 23:20). Frank Boreham wrote, "He met the worst of enemies, in the worst of places, under the worst of conditions; and he won." What a man!

1 CHRONICLES 19

If you fear a person and consider him or her your enemy, nothing that person does will please you. Instead of taking his or her words and actions at face value, you get suspicious. Malice poisons us to the point that our ears hear nothing good and our eyes see nothing good, no matter what that person may say or do. (See 1 Pet. 2:1–3.)

Hanun's actions were a public offense against David, so he

had to act, especially when he saw the Ammonites getting ready for war. But what should Christians do when they are handed evil in return for good?

Consider these verses when deciding what action to take: "Love . . . does not seek its own, is not provoked, thinks no evil" (1 Cor. 13:5); "In return for my love they are my accusers, but I give myself to prayer" (Ps. 109:4); "Father, forgive them, for they do not know what they do" (Luke 23:34). Ponder Matthew 5:10-12, 43-48, and then ask God to help you practice it. Francis Bacon commented on the situation: "In taking revenge, a man is but even with his enemy; but in passing it over, he is superior."

1 CHRONICLES 20

Not a word is offered here about David's tarrying in Jerusalem and committing adultery with the wife of Uriah, one of his mighty men. But the story had already been written in 2 Samuel, and there was no need to repeat it. However, the writer gave an account of David's sin of numbering the people (chap. 21). Sins of the spirit can be more insidious than sins of the flesh (2 Cor. 7:1). You may be tempted more often by pride than by the lusts of the flesh.

Joab and the army won the war, but David came to the battlefield in time to direct the final victory and then claim the crown. It was a heavy one: seventy-five pounds of gold! But all crowns are heavy, for it is not an easy thing to be a leader.

Giants have a way of multiplying! David had killed Goliath, but other giants remained; and God had His servants ready to defeat them. We remember David and Goliath and tend to forget these other heroes, but God remembers them.

1 CHRONICLES 21

Pride: David and Joab (1-6). Satan attacks leaders and it behooves us to pray for them. He appealed to David's pride by encouraging him to find out the size of his kingdom. David was stubborn as well as proud, and his attitude got Israel into real trouble.

Humility: David and the Lord (7-17). When David realized his sins, he confessed to the Lord and was forgiven, but he still had to bear the consequences (Gal. 6:7-8). Dressed in sackcloth, David publicly begged God to stop the plague. What a picture of humility!

Obedience: David and Ornan (18–30). In the hour of penitence and prayer, we will hear a word from God. Gad brought that word to David. David could have claimed the property and sacrifices, but the Lord would not have been pleased. David said "I will not take what is yours for the LORD, nor offer burnt offerings with that which costs me nothing" (v. 24). Do you look for the easy way out when sin catches up with you? Our Savior did not have it easy when He paid for our sins on the cross.

1 CHRONICLES 22

Preparation. So David made "abundant preparations before his death" (v. 5). He was making preparations not for dying but for building the temple. (The idea of *preparation* is found five times in this chapter.) For years, David had been preparing for this great project and gathering materials (vv. 3–4). He had risked his life in battle and claimed the spoils for the Lord. His reputation was that of a soldier, but his heart was that of a builder.

Promise. David claimed God's promise and used it to encourage his son, a young man with little practical experience. The work we do is for God, and it must be our best.

Prosperity. You cannot escape the basic principle stated in Joshua 1:8 (vv. 11–13): if we obey God's Word, He will prosper our work. David had collected over forty million tons of gold and silver, but all that wealth was of no value apart from the blessing of God.

Partners. We cannot do God's work alone; we need helpers (vv. 2, 15, 17–19). Leaders, stonemasons, timber cutters—all were a part of the work, and each worker was important.

1 CHRONICLES 23—27

A beautiful and costly temple is a waste of money unless ministry is going on for the good of God's people and the glory of God. So, before he died, David organized the temple workers and put them under proper leadership: "Let all things be done decently and in order" (1 Cor. 14:40).

The work of the Lord called for dedicated service from

many kinds of people: priests, Levites, musicians, treasurers, gatekeepers, soldiers, and state officers. Each of us has a calling from the Lord and we must be faithful to take our place and do our job. We are helping to build the church, and we must give God our best (Matt. 16:18; Eph. 2:19–22).

Being a musician himself, David was no doubt especially concerned that the music in the temple be the finest available. God gave him people who were skillful and trained (25:7), but their task was not to magnify their talents: they were to glorify their Lord (25:3). Do you open and close each day with praise to the Lord (23:30)?

1 CHRONICLES 28—29

A disappointed heart (28:2). Instead of complaining because he could not build God's house, David began preparing to help Solomon do the job. David served his own generation and generations to come because he unselfishly served the Lord. When disappointments come into your life, how do you handle them?

A loyal heart (28:9). Solomon had all that he needed for building the temple, but the most important thing only he could supply: a heart loyal to God. His motives had to be right, or his work would not be blessed.

A generous heart (29:9, 17). The people joined their king in generously giving to the Lord. Of course, whatever we give Him, He has first given us (29:11–15). There were even gifts from the past, from Samuel, Saul, and Abner (26:28).

A devoted heart (29:17–18). "Fix their heart toward You" means "Keep them loyal and devoted to You." In his latter years, Solomon's heart turned away from the Lord (1 Kings 11:3). That can happen to any of us, so we must heed Proverbs 4:23. Why should we generously give to the Lord? David's song of praise in 29:10–15 presents some reasons: God is great (vv. 10–12); God deserves glory (v. 13); God has given so much to us (v. 14); life is short and we must make it count (v. 15). Take comfort in this truth: "He who does the will of God abides forever" (1 John 2:17).

2 CHRONICLES

2 CHRONICLES 1

The ruler. God "exalted him exceedingly" (v. 1). Solomon could strengthen his kingdom, but only God could exalt his name. If Solomon had tried to exalt himself, God would have disciplined him (1 Pet.5:5).

The worshiper. Solomon's hands were filled with sacrifices for the Lord; his ears were open to the word of the Lord; his heart was devoted to the service of the Lord. His great desire was to be capable of serving his people with wisdom, and God granted that desire. Have you asked God for wisdom (James 1:5)?

The trader. King Solomon had a flair for foreign trade. In spite of the admonition in Deuteronomy 17:16–17, he amassed silver and gold and multiplied horses. David had only 100 chariots (1 Chron. 18:4), but his son added 1,300 more. Trade brought wealth to the nation, but it may have been the beginning of Solomon's downfall (1 Kings 11). Oliver Goldsmith wrote, "Ill fares the land, to hastening ills a prey,/Where wealth accumulates and men decay."

2 CHRONICLES 2—4

The plans for both the temple and the tabernacle were given by God; in both projects, the people were permitted to share their gifts. There was one difference: God's Spirit equipped two Jewish men to make the tabernacle and its furnishings (Exod. 31), but an artisan from outside Israel supervised the construction of the temple. Had God's Spirit failed to equip anybody for the task? Or was that another one of Solomon's ways to build strong bonds with his neighbors?

At least his motives were pure: he built the house "for the name of the LORD" (2:1). He used the best materials ("pure gold," "fine gold"), and he laid a good foundation (3:3). The apostle Paul surely had Solomon's temple in mind when he wrote 1 Corinthians 3:10–17.

The pillars (3:17) in God's spiritual temple, the church, are dedicated people who serve Him devotedly (Gal. 2:9). Are you a pillar, or must you lean on others?

2 CHRONICLES 5

The beautiful temple was empty until God's throne was put in place (vv. 2–10) and God's glory filled the house (vv. 13–14). When Moses dedicated the tabernacle, the glory came in when the work was finished (Exod. 40:33–38). It was the song of praise that brought the glory into the temple. When you worship with God's people, does your praise increase His glory in the assembly?

The tables of the Law were still in the ark (v. 10), but the pot of manna and Aaron's rod were no longer there (Heb. 9:4). Some things God does are temporary, and we must not make permanent institutions out of them.

David had carefully organized the priests and Levites, but that order was forgotten as they led the worship on that holy day (v. 11). There are times when the Spirit of God ignores our plans and procedures and reveals God's glory in a new way. Let Him do it! We are not to worship organization; we are to worship God.

2 CHRONICLES 6

In his dedication address and prayer, King Solomon looked in five different directions.

He looked back (1–11). He recalled how God chose him to build the temple.

He looked up (12–21). He asked God to fulfill the covenant promises He had made with David. The covenant included the coming into this world of the Son of David, Jesus Christ, who was born of the house of David.

He looked ahead (22–31). Solomon asked God to help His

people in various trials of life, particularly to forgive them when they sinned. Coming to the temple, or looking toward the temple, and praying to God would bring them forgiveness. In this chapter, there are numerous references to prayer.

He looked around (32–35). The king called on God to help the Gentiles. The temple was to be "a house of prayer for all nations" (Isa. 56:7); God's desire was that Israel bring blessing to all the world (Gen. 12:1–3).

He looked within (36–40). He ended his prayer by pleading for forgiveness for sinning Israel. His words must have been very meaningful to the Jews taken captive to Babylon four centuries later.

The temple is gone, but the record of that great day of dedication remains to encourage and bless God's people. Read the chapter again, and note the promises you can claim today. In his closing prayer (vv. 41–42), Solomon asked God to bless everybody present: the priests, the people, and himself as God's anointed king. But any blessing that came would result from God's mercy and His promises to David. David could not build the temple or attend the dedication service, but he was there just the same!

2 CHRONICLES 7

Fire and glory. The fire came to devour, and the glory came to dwell. There was glory at the start of the service (2 Chron. 5:14) and glory at the close! But there could be no glory apart from the sacrifices that took care of the sins of the people. Isaiah saw God's glory, but before he was ready for service, he had to feel the fire (Isa. 6:1–8). Most of us want the glory, but we resist the fire.

Falling and feasting. This demonstration of God's power and glory brought the people to their knees, but when the service ended, they rejoiced with feasting. Contradictory? Not in the least. We are to "serve the LORD with fear, and rejoice with trembling" (Ps. 2:11). It was said of Moses and some others: "So they saw God, and they ate and drank" (Exod. 24:11).

Promise and warning. What an encouragement to know that God hears our prayers! God graciously granted what the king asked for, but He added a word of caution: "These blessings are given when My children obey." Disobedience brings discipline, not because God hates us but because He loves us and wants to bless us even more.

Prayer went up, fire came down, and glory moved in. Could you ask for more?

2 CHRONICLES 8

David was known for his battles, Solomon for his buildings. It was a time of peace, so the opportunities and resources for building were available.

It is disappointing that Solomon married a foreign woman who could not be identified with the Lord's throne. God wants each home to be a tabernacle (Isa. 4:5–6); He wants His children to enjoy His presence (2 Cor. 6:14—7:1). Apparently in this decision, Solomon was concerned more about politics than about piety.

Solomon was faithful in his public worship despite these inconsistencies in his life, and he continued to increase the wealth of the nation. But the people were not growing in the things of the Lord. Alexander Whyte wrote that "the secret worm . . . was gnawing all the time in the royal staff upon which Solomon leaned."

The most important part of your life is the part that only God sees. Are you concerned about character—or reputation?

2 CHRONICLES 9

Wealth and wisdom are the central themes of this chapter; gold is mentioned sixteen times and wisdom six times. According to King Solomon, wisdom is better than wealth (Prov. 3:13–15; 8:10–11), although most people today would probably rather have money. They measure life by prices, not values.

If you want gold, silver, and jewels, you must dig for them. Very little treasure lies on the ground, convenient to pick up. If you want wisdom, you must "seek her as silver, and search for her as for hidden treasures" (Prov. 2:4). That means work! It means taking time to read, meditate, pray, and put truth into practice.

The only convenient materials you will find are wood, hay,

and straw, but they will not last (1 Cor. 3:10–15). To sacrifice the permanent for the immediate is folly, not wisdom.

2 CHRONICLES 10—11

The chronicler does not mention Solomon's apostasy or God's warning (1 Kings 11—13), but he does record Rehoboam's folly. You would think *younger* men would recommend easier lives for the people, for youth is generally a carefree time. But the king's friends did not have to bear any of the burdens, and their decision made them appear strong. They used the people to advance their authority instead of using their authority to help the people. (See Matt. 23:4; Gal. 6:2.)

Some divisions are of God (11:4), even though they create problems and cause hurts. For one thing, divisions force people to make decisions, and the decisions they make reveal the kind of people they are. The priests and Levites left Israel and came to Judah because they wanted to serve in the true temple and be ruled by a king from David's line.

God's program for this world is to bring things together in Christ (Eph. 1:10), and He will succeed despite man's rebellion. The devil's program is to tear things apart. Which side are you helping?

2 CHRONICLES 12

Rehoboam refused to serve the Lord or the people, so he ended up serving Egypt. God wanted him to learn the difference between His easy yoke and the heavy yoke of sin (v. 8; Deut. 28:47–48). Some people must learn the hard way. Are you one of them?

No matter how strong you think you are, your strength becomes weakness if you forsake the Lord. Rehoboam relied on his fortified cities for protection, and the Egyptians took every one of them. His son Abijah would rely on the Lord and win a great victory (2 Chron. 13:18). Where is your faith today?

Solomon's treasures became Egypt's spoils because the king turned away from God. The king and the elders humbled themselves before God, but they could not escape the consequences of their sin. God spared them from wrath, but He permitted them to suffer. Alexander Maclaren stated, "Every sin is a mistake, as well as a wrong; and the epitaph for the sinner is, 'Thou fool!'"

2 CHRONICLES 13

The army of Israel had strategy and great numbers, but it did not have God. It was twice as big as Judah's army (Luke 14:31–32), but by the time the battle was over, Israel had lost 500,000 soldiers.

"God Himself is with us as our head," King Abijah announced (v. 12). He obviously believed that "If God is for us, who can be against us?" (Rom. 8:31). Abijah had his faith in the God of the covenant who always keeps His promises (v. 5). He was living by faith and not by sight.

For a brief moment, it looked like Israel would win, but God gave Judah the victory. Their "secret weapon" was back in Jerusalem: their faithful worship of the Lord (vv. 8–11). They kept the commandments of the Lord, and He kept His promises to them. Public victories are the result of private ministries to the Lord. Those who rejoice before the Lord can rely on the Lord.

2 CHRONICLES 14—16

Asa is another sad example of a man who made a splendid beginning but had a tragic ending. Early in his reign, he relied on the Lord, and God gave him a great victory. Then he believed the prophet's message and removed the idols from the land and called the people to reaffirm their allegiance to the Lord. He even deposed the queen mother for her idolatry!

But when he had been king thirty-six years, he stopped relying on the Lord. He took the Lord's treasures and bought protection from a heathen king! The prophet Hanani told the king what was wrong: his heart was not loyal to the Lord (16:9). Instead of humbling himself and obeying, as he had done before, in anger Asa resisted the Word and God's servant (James 1:19). When we are wrong, we should admit it instead of trying to resist God. God is much stronger than our stubbornness.

God is with us—seek Him (15:2). God answers prayer—trust Him (15:4). God rewards faithfulness—obey Him (15:7). You never outgrow the ability to sin. Noah was a mature man when he got drunk (Gen. 9:20–23), and so was Abraham when he lied about his wife (Gen. 12:10ff.). Moses was a seasoned leader when he lost his temper (Num. 20), and so was David when he committed adultery and murder. Asa's corpse lay on a bed of fragrant spices, but his name was not as fragrant as it had been. Ponder Proverbs 10:7, Ecclesiastes 7:1 and 1 Corinthians 10:12.

2 CHRONICLES 17—18

Jehoshaphat's life is described in Psalm 1:1-3. He walked in the right counsel (17:3), he delighted in God's ways (17:6), and he was fruitful in his service, sharing the Word with the people (17:7-9). He practiced the fear of the Lord, so he was protected by the fear of the Lord. When you fear God, you need fear nothing else (Ps. 112).

But Jehoshaphat married the wrong wife, joined the wrong allies, fought the wrong war, and almost came to the wrong end. By walking "in the counsel of the ungodly" and sitting with the scornful (18:9; Ps. 1:1), the king found himself in serious trouble. He had to listen to false prophets and go to battle with a king depending on false confidence.

The pressure to conform is greater today than in that day. Are you resisting it? Can you detect the false prophet and his message, or are you impressed with his "visual aids" and pleasing message (18:10)? Read the last three verses of Psalm 1 and beware!

2 CHRONICLES 19

Jehoshaphat returned home safely only because God was gracious to him and protected him in the battle. When we are out of the will of God and get into places of danger, we tempt God, and it is a sin to tempt God and force Him to work miracles on our behalf. That is the way Satan tempted the Lord Jesus (Matt. 4:5-7).

He submitted to God's Word and went back to ministering to his people. While he was away fighting somebody else's battle, his own people were being neglected (Song of Sol. 1:6). Like a good shepherd, he sought the lost and brought them back to the Lord (Ezek. 34:1–10), and he saw to it that the people were protected by honest judges and served by godly priests.

Note the emphasis on the fear of the Lord (vv. 7, 9). Jehoshaphat had sinned, but God forgave him. The result of forgiveness should be the fear of the Lord (Ps. 130:4). John Calvin wrote, "True piety consists . . . in a pure and true zeal which loves God altogether, and reveres Him truly as Lord, embraces his justice and dreads to offend Him more than to die."

2 CHRONICLES 20

Seek the Lord. When you see big problems on the horizon, seek the Lord before you do anything else. What does that mean? It means to do what Jehoshaphat and Judah did. They remembered who God is (v. 6), what He did in the past (v. 7) and what He said He would do in the future (vv. 8–9). It means to trust Him and keep your eyes on Him by faith (v. 12).

Hear the Lord. God always has a special word for those who turn to Him for help. When you face a battle, spend much time in His Word and in prayer, for then He will give you that needed word of encouragement.

Praise the Lord. The battle was won by the singers, standing in the most dangerous place of all—between two armies. But they sang the Lord's praises and routed the enemy. The choir praised God after God gave the word (v. 19), before the battle (v. 21), and after the victory (vv. 26–28), a good pattern for us to follow in our praise.

In Hebrew, *Berachah* means "blessing" (v. 26). Even a valley can become a place of blessing if we learn how to praise the Lord. "Prayer changes things" is a familiar saying that is certainly true. But it is also true that "praise changes things." Why? Because true praise changes people, and God can work in and through people who praise Him. True praise involves faith, hope, and love, the strongest weapons in the Christian armory.

2 CHRONICLES 21

God kept His promise to maintain David's descendants on the throne of Judah, but He also kept His promise to chasten them if they disobeyed Him (2 Sam. 7:12–17). He disciplined Jehoram in several ways.

To begin with, Jehoram's rule began to disintegrate as the Edomites revolted and the Philistines invaded. Even the Levitical city of Libnah revolted (v. 10; Josh. 21:13). Life starts to fall apart when you stop obeying the Lord.

Elijah's letter warned the king and gave him opportunity to repent, but Jehoram went his own way. What a privilege to get a letter from a famous prophet! And what a tragedy to treat it with disdain. The king died in severe pain, and nobody regretted it. Yet he was the son of the great Jehoshaphat.

If you received a loving letter of warning today, how would you respond to it?

2 CHRONICLES 22—23

Corruption. The British poet Samuel Taylor Coleridge called mothers "the holiest thing alive," but you could not apply those words to Athaliah. Imagine a mother teaching her son how to sin! She was the Old Testament version of Herodias (Matt. 14:1–12), just the opposite of godly Hannah (1 Sam. 1—2). But what else would you expect from the daughter of Jezebel and Ahab? Athaliah was the only woman to rule over the kingdom of Judah, and it was a rule of evil.

Coronation. But God had another woman on the scene, the godly wife of the high priest, and she did the will of God in saving the infant Joash. At the right time, her husband orchestrated the coronation of Joash and the condemnation of Athaliah. Note the three covenants involved: with the army (23:1), with the king (23:3), and with the Lord (23:16).

Contribution. We cannot escape David! He provided the king (23:3), the weapons (23:9), and the temple organization and music (23:18). But how long can Judah live on the dividends of the spiritual investments made by godly men and women of previous generations? *How long can God's church today?*

2 CHRONICLES 24

Joash did many fine things, but he was a "leaner." As long as godly Jehoiada was on the scene, the king obeyed the Lord, and the temple prospered. But after the high priest died, the king began listening to other counselors; soon he led the nation into sin.

When you truly obey God's Word, you do it regardless of the messenger. If you lean on others and fail to develop spiritual depth, your spiritual life will be gone when those people are gone. Joash would not listen to the prophets and he even killed one of them (vv. 19–21). God abandoned the people, the army was defeated (v. 24; see also Deut. 32:30), and the king was assassinated.

The godly priest was buried with the kings (v. 16), but the ungodly king was not (v. 25). Joash was untrue to his friends and treated them like enemies (Prov. 27:6, 10, 17). He refused to listen to God and became another example of a man who made a good beginning but came to a tragic ending. Henry Ford commented, "My best friend is the one who brings out the best in me.".

2 CHRONICLES 25

Amaziah was halfhearted in his religious life and was not loyal to the Lord. Instead of trusting God for victory, he hired men from Israel; then he worried about the money he would lose if he obeyed the Lord! Once you start measuring obedience by profit and loss, you are not living by faith (Matt. 6:33). When you start asking yourself, "Is it profitable?" instead of "Is it right?" you had better read Philippians 2:1–11 and Hebrews 11:24–26 .

Amaziah argued with God's will but finally obeyed it; then the army became angry with him and declared war! They had been paid, so they should have gone home rejoicing, but they wanted a chance to fight and get spoils of war. Such is the wickedness of the human heart. Amaziah lost money and was upset; the soldiers made money and were angry. Money does not satisfy the heart.

The king refused to hear God's servant and threatened to kill him (vv. 15–16), but in the end, Amaziah died. He lived for the wrong values and by the wrong counsel, and he died a failure. God is seeking disciples who are wholehearted (Matt. 6:19–24).

2 CHRONICLES 26

The *starting point* in Uzziah's success was his seeking God and wanting to do His will (v. 5). Unlike his father, Uzziah was a man wholly given to the Lord. He believed and practiced Joshua 1:8 and Psalm 1:1–3.

The *turning point* was his pride (v. 16). He became famous (vv. 8, 15) and strong, and God helped him wonderfully (vv. 7, 15); but he could not handle success. If God's blessings do not humble us, they will eventually destroy us. It is true that "a man's pride will bring him low" (Prov. 29:23; see also Prov. 11:2; 16:18).

The *finishing point* was his isolation as a leper (vv. 19–21). Not content to be a king, he also wanted to be a priest. He did not respect the boundaries God had established, so God shut him in a narrow place as a leper. God gives the wide places to those He can trust with freedom (Ps. 18:16–19).

Uzziah did not commit a gross sin of the flesh. *He sinned in the realm of spiritual things.* It is possible to disobey God in the temple with a censer in your hand, but if you do, expect God to deal with you drastically.

The Peril of Pride

In his pride, Moses lost his temper and was kept out of the Promised Land (Num. 20:1–13). Pride kept Joshua from seeking God's will at Ai, and he lost the battle (Josh. 7). King Nebuchadnezzar's pride turned him into an animal (Dan. 4), and Peter's pride led to his denial of Christ (Luke 22:31–34). "No matter how dear you are to God," said Charles Haddon Spurgeon, "if pride is harbored in your spirit, He will whip it out of you. They that go up in their own estimation must come down again by His discipline."

2 CHRONICLES 27

Uzziah sinned and was disciplined by the Lord, but that one event did not destroy his godly influence. His son Jotham followed his father's example but avoided his father's sin, and the Lord honored him.

Jotham lived a brief life and had a short reign, but he was faithful to the Lord. It is not how long we live that counts but *how* we live. Although Jotham's chapter in Chronicles is short, 1 John 2:17 is still true.

2 CHRONICLES 28

The spiritual leadership that began with Uzziah and continued with Jotham disappeared with Ahaz. We wonder why the godly examples of his father and grandfather did Ahaz no good. Historians tell us that Ahaz was coregent with his father for four years, which means he started when he was sixteen. Did Ahaz become proud? Did he listen to wrong counsel?

The Ammonite god Molech was worshiped in the Valley of the Son of Hinnom. The king even put his children on the heathen altar. When a father is disobedient to God, often the children suffer most. King Josiah defiled the place (2 Kings 23:10) and made it a garbage dump. The word *gehenna* came to refer to the place of eternal judgment, hell.

Judah experienced a humiliating defeat from Israel, but God mercifully overruled and rescued the people. It was a prophet, not a king or general, who saved the day.

Instead of repenting and returning to the God of his father and grandfather, Ahaz adopted the gods of the victorious enemy. It seemed logical to him because the enemy was winning! Instead of going by the Word of God, he took the pragmatic approach (Prov. 3:5–6). Have you ever done that? It is dangerous!

2 CHRONICLES 29

When Hezekiah became king, the situation at the temple was not unlike the condition of some churches today (v. 7). Closed doors speak of no access to God and no service for

God. He has set before us an open door (Rev. 3:8), and we close it.

The lamps were out, which indicates no witness (Matt. 5:16), and the incense altar was cold, which signifies that no prayer was going up to God (Ps. 141:2). There were no sacrifices on the altar (Rom. 12:1-2), but there was plenty of rubbish in the temple. No wonder the nation was experiencing the wrath of God instead of the blessing of God.

Hezekiah's formula for revival was simple: sanctification, sacrifice, and song. He started with the priests and Levites, for if God's servants are not clean, God cannot bless their work. Then the priests sanctified the temple, offered the sacrifices, and sang the song of the Lord.

It all happened suddenly (v. 36), but what happened was not new or novel. It was simply a return to the ways of the Lord (Jer. 6:16).

2 CHRONICLES 30

When God's Spirit is at work, Jesus Christ will be glorified, and God's people will be unified. Hezekiah called the whole nation back to the celebration of the Passover, the feast that depicts Jesus Christ, the Lamb of God, and many participated with oneness of heart (v. 12). What an occasion of blessing it was!

How tragic that the spiritual leaders were to blame for delaying the event (v. 3). How tragic that some of the people laughed at the invitation (v. 10; Matt. 22:1-14). But how wonderful that God blessed abundantly, healed the people and sent them home rejoicing (vv. 21, 23, 25, 26). The people who turned down the invitation missed a special opportunity.

God looks at the heart and does not permit ceremonial matters to get in the way of His grace (1 Sam. 15:22; Ps. 50:7-15; 51:16-17; Hos. 6:6). Hezekiah saw to it that the people were taught the Word (v. 22) because the Word nourishes the heart and cleanses the life, long after the memories of great events have faded away. The people experienced great joy as a result of sharing in the Passover feast (v. 26). The Jews would have great joy at the dedication of the walls of Jerusalem (Neh. 12:43). Other people who experienced great joy from the Lord are the wise men (Matt. 2:10), the apostles (Luke 24:52), and the new believers in Samaria (Acts 8:8). The message of the gospel is good news of great joy (Luke 2:10). Are you sharing it with others?

2 CHRONICLES 31

When you come back to walk with the Lord, the evidences of the new life are there to see.

Cleansing. For too long, the worship of Jehovah had taken place alongside the worship of the heathen gods; that would now end. The people assisted the king in destroying the obscene images and pagan altars. After all, the nation had just celebrated Passover, and the week following Passover was to be a time of "housecleaning" (Exod. 12:15–20).

Serving. It is not enough to get rid of the bad; we must also establish and strengthen the good. The king made certain the priests obeyed God's law and ministered at the temple. Had the priests been ministering faithfully to begin with, the nation would not have gone into apostasy.

Giving. If the priests are to serve, the people must support them. One of the first signs of spiritual awakening is the generosity of those whose hearts God has touched. Nobody had to plead or urge; the giving came from the hearts of people who were right with God.

2 CHRONICLES 32

Testings usually come after times of great blessing, and Hezekiah faced three of them.

War. After other times of awakening, the nation was given protection and rest from enemies (2 Chron. 15:15; 20:29–30), but this time, God allowed the enemy to come in. God was testing the faith of the king and the people to see how deep it really was. It is one thing to participate in a huge religious meeting, but quite something else to have your land invaded and your capital city threatened.

Sickness. Hezekiah's illness was both a national and a personal crisis, for he did not have any sons to take the throne. God had promised that David's family would never lack for a man on the throne, so Hezekiah prayed that he might be able to live and have a son.

Honor. Hezekiah weathered the invasion and the illness, but he capitulated to pride. It began when he failed to thank God for sparing his life, and apparently even God's chastening did not cure him. The extent of his wealth and the praises of the visiting dignitaries made Hezekiah proud, and God had to deal with him.

We have learned that if Satan cannot conquer us when he comes as the lion (1 Pet. 5:8), he will come again as the serpent (2 Cor. 11:1–3). You may be in greater danger when things are going well than when you are fighting a battle, so keep alert.

2 CHRONICLES 33

Manasseh rebuilt what his father had torn down and then tore it down again so he could rebuild. (Compare Gen. 26:18.) He did not learn from the past or listen to the prophets, so he had to live with the punishment God sent him. Some people only learn the hard way.

How gracious of God to see Manasseh's repentance, hear his prayer, and restore him to Jerusalem. But even God's forgiveness could not automatically nullify the king's bad example or undo the terrible damage he had done in the land. Sin has consequences long after sinners are forgiven (2 Kings 23:26; 24:3).

God is ready and willing to forgive, and we should seek that forgiveness early. The longer we wait, the more damage we do; the more damage we do, the more we and others will suffer because of our sins.

2 CHRONICLES 34

Find the Book. The greatest treasure you have is not money but the Word of God, which too often is "lost" amid the "rubbish" you can easily accumulate. Do you treasure God's Word? (See Ps. 119:14, 72, 127, 162.) Is it "buried" somewhere?

Read the Book. God's Word is not a relic to admire in a religious museum. They did not put the Book back in its niche in the temple. Rather, they read it publicly and honored it as the living Word of God.

Obey the Book. The king trembled at God's Word (Isa. 66:2) and immediately sent for God's message. There is always a fresh word from the Lord as you read the Bible and seek His will.

Share the Book. The king gathered the people to the temple to hear God's Word (vv. 29-30). It is good to be a receiver of the Word, but it is also good to be a transmitter and share it with others (1 Thess. 1:6-10).

Stand for the Word. The king and the people made a covenant with the Lord and took their stand publicly. After all, the result of Bible knowledge ought to be obedience and service, a living commitment to the God of the Word.

2 CHRONICLES 35

Remembering the past (1-19). Passover is the great feast of Jewish liberation, when the nation recalls its deliverance from Egypt (Exod. 13:1-10). Following the example of godly Hezekiah (2 Chron. 30), Josiah held a feast and called the people to praise God. As in the days of Hezekiah, the spiritual leaders had to be encouraged to do their jobs. Too often those who should be leading are standing in the way.

Mortgaging the future (20-27). If God defeated Egypt in the days of Moses, surely He could do it again for Josiah! Without seeking the mind of the Lord, Josiah meddled in a war that had nothing to do with Judah, and it led to his death. A disguise is no protection if we have disobeyed God (v. 22; 2 Chron. 18:29). Judah was back in bondage to Egypt!

We wonder what the future of Judah might have been had Josiah heeded the warning God gave him. Strange as it seems, God can speak through messengers who may not even know Him (John 11:49-52).

2 CHRONICLES 36

Second Chronicles opens telling how the temple was built. It closes telling how and why the temple of God was destroyed.

First the enemy *robbed the temple* (vv. 7, 19), taking the treasures of the Lord to their pagan temple in Babylon. You expect an enemy to do this, but you do not expect the priests and people to *defile* their own temple (v. 14)! While Nebuchadnezzar was taking Jerusalem to Babylon, the Jewish leaders were bringing Babylon to Jerusalem! Do we ever learn?

The next step was *death in the temple* (v. 17). God had shown compassion to His people (v. 15), but the enemy showed no compassion at all. The people fled to the temple, hoping for God's protection, but it was too late. The house of prayer had become a den of thieves.

Finally, the temple was *destroyed,* just as Jeremiah had warned (Jer. 25–26). The nation had disobeyed the Word of God in many ways, including ignoring the Sabbatical Years (Lev. 25:1–7; 26:27–35). The only thing left was judgment.

But the book closes with an announcement of the *rebuilding* of the temple, something that Jeremiah also prophesied (29:10). Even in wrath, God remembers mercy (Hab. 3:2).

EZRA and NEHEMIAH

◆

In 606–605 B.C., the Babylonians began their conquest of Jerusalem, deporting many of the people and finally destroying the city and the temple in 587–586 B.C. In 538, Cyrus issued a proclamation allowing the Jews to return to their land and rebuild their temple, and nearly fifty thousand returned under the leadership of Zerubbabel (Ezra 1—6). The seventy years of captivity were ended. In spite of difficulty and delay, the temple was completed in 515.

Ezra the scribe went to Jerusalem in 458 with about two thousand Jews, including some Levites to help in the temple ministry (Ezra 7—10). In 444, Nehemiah, a layman, went to rebuild the walls (Neh. 1—6) and rededicate the people (Neh. 7—13).

Following their restoration to the land, the Jewish nation experienced times of trial and reproach, but the Lord saw them through. The emphasis in Ezra and Nehemiah is on trusting God for a new beginning and doing His work—no matter what obstacles and opposition are encountered. Although the days may be dark, God is there to guide us, protect us, and help us.

EZRA

$\blacklozenge$

EZRA 1—2

The book opens with the closing words of 2 Chronicles, for God's plan was not finished. Judah had rejected Jeremiah's warning, but the prophet's words came true. God is at work in human history. His purposes will be accomplished, regardless of the nations' activities. Jeremiah warned of coming judgment, but he also promised restoration; and the promise was fulfilled (Jer. 29:10).

From God's Word to the king's word! Cyrus fulfilled a prophecy given a century and a half before (Isa. 44:28). God can use even a pagan ruler to accomplish His divine purposes. When the words and actions of world leaders disturb you, just remember that God is still on the throne and has things in control.

Not all the Jews of the captivity wanted to return to a desolate land. Some of those who did not go at least encouraged the others and helped with the expenses, as did some of their Babylonian neighbors (1:4, 6).

The trip was difficult, and life in the land was demanding; however, the courageous Jews paid the price to do God's will. No matter how you may have failed in the past, God gives you an opportunity for a new beginning.

EZRA 3

How do you go about restoring things after God's chastening hand has been removed?

Put worship first. There was no temple as yet, but that did not hinder them from setting up an altar and sacrificing to God. This is an illustration of Matthew 6:33. They needed to worship God for their own sake as well for a witness to the people around them.

Celebrate God's goodness. It was time for the Feast of Tabernacles, a joyful feast of thanksgiving. Times were tough, but the people obeyed the Word and praised the Lord. This in itself would be a testimony to the Gentiles, and it would do their own hearts good. It is always the right time to praise the Lord.

Establish the foundations. The Scriptures told them all they needed to know to rebuild the temple, and they followed God's plan. The foundation is the most important part of the building, for it determines the size, shape, and strength of the structure. Do you have the right foundations for your life?

Look to the future. The old people looked back and wept while the young people looked ahead and rejoiced. Tears and cheers, not too different from what is happening in families and churches today. The men were able to work together but not praise God together. If you concentrate on your past, you are sure to rob yourself of a glorious future (Phil. 3:12–14).

The Future   *You cannot change the past, but the past can change you, either for better or for worse. It all depends on how you look at it. The past can be a rudder that guides you or an anchor that hinders you. Leave your past mistakes with God, and look to the future by faith.*

EZRA 4

As soon as God starts to bless, the enemy starts to battle. Satan is a destroyer, and he gets angry when God's people unite to build. He has three favorite weapons.

Cooperation (1–3). The people were descendants of the Jews who intermarried with the Gentiles the Assyrians brought to the land (2 Kings 17:24ff.). The "mixed multitude" would have corrupted the Jews and interfered with the work (Exod. 12:38; Num. 11:4). Beware volunteers; they may be working for the enemy!

Intimidation (4–5). Discouragement and fear are effective weapons, especially when the work is already difficult. When you start to experience fear, lean on Isaiah 12:2.

Legislation (6–24). The people of the world will use "official influence" to hinder God's work. From their viewpoint, Jerusalem had been a rebellious city, and the king would certainly be concerned about taxes. The tactic worked, and the construction had to stop.

But God was still at work!

"*There is no need to fear; if we keep within the moral frontiers of God, we can say boldly, 'The Lord is my helper.'***"**

Oswald Chambers

EZRA 5—6

About fifteen years elapse between 4:24 and 5:1. During that time, God prepared two prophets to renew and strengthen the work. After all, God's Word commenced the project (Ezra 1:1), so only God's Word could continue it and complete it (Gal. 3:3). When God wants to get something done, He sends His servants with His Word, for nothing but our unbelief can hinder the power of the Word. Even the pagan king had to bow before the Word of God!

When God's Word is with you and God's eye is upon you (5:5), your work will prosper (6:14; see also Josh. 1:8; Ps. 1:1–3). Revival comes when God's people heed God's Word and do what God tells them to do. Read Haggai's four sermons of encouragement and rebuke and see what true "revival preaching" is like. Do those messages speak to you now?

The project began with mingled joy and tears (3:8–13), but

it ended with all the people rejoicing (6:16–22). The traditional feast took on new joy because of what God had done for His people.

EZRA 7—8

There is a gap of fifty-seven years between the completion of the temple and the arrival of Ezra. Unfortunately, the people had lapsed into sin; and it was Ezra's task to bring them back to the Lord. One of the emphases in these chapters is *hands.*

God's hand. Ezra was a gifted man (7:10), but he could do nothing unless God's hand was upon him and the people traveling with him. God's hand is a *providing* hand (7:6; 8:18), a *protecting* hand (8:22, 31), an *encouraging* hand (7:28), and a *guiding* hand (7:9).

Ezra's hand (7:14). God's Word was in Ezra's heart as well as his hand (7:10), and it was the Word that the people needed. There can be no cleansing or reviving apart from the Word of God.

A Balanced Life	*According to Ezra 7:10, Ezra studied God's Word, obeyed God's Word, and taught God's Word. He was like the person Jesus spoke about in Matthew 13:52: a student (learning) who was a disciple (living) and a householder (sharing). Having a balanced life is most important.*

The Jews' hands (8:26, 33). The hands of the people carried the treasures of the Lord, faithfully delivered to the temple at the end of the journey. When you meet the Lord, you will "weigh in" and find out how faithful you have been with what He has given you. Heed the words of 8:29: "Watch and keep!"

EZRA 9

Astonished (1–4). For at least three reasons, the Jewish remnant should have obeyed God's Word about marriage. To begin with, God had been good to bring them back to the land. He had also chastened them in Babylon, and they knew from their own past the consequences of compromise. No wonder Ezra was astonished.

Ashamed (5–9). Ezra used several images to show their plight. They were like drowning men because of their sins (v. 6), and yet they sinned more. They were a little peg on which so much future was hanging (v. 8), a remnant that had to serve as a wall against the awful encroachments of sin (v. 9). If the nation was polluted, how could Messiah be born (v. 2)?

Alarmed (10–15). God had revealed His Word, and they did not obey it. God had shown them grace (v. 8), and they did not appreciate it. God had held back punishment (v. 13; Ps. 103:10), and they took advantage of it. All God could do now was punish them even more.

As he prayed, Ezra trembled (v. 4), knelt (v. 5), and bowed down (v. 6) because nobody could stand before God (v. 15; Ps. 130:3).

EZRA 10

When things look dark, there is always a ray of hope. Shechaniah encouraged the people to confess their sins and obey the Word. He may have been thinking of God's promises in Exodus 34:6–7, Isaiah 55:6–7, and Jeremiah 3:11–13. Believers today turn to 1 John 1:9.

But confession must not be a routine thing that comes only from the lips. We must tremble at God's Word (Ezra 9:4; 10:3; Isa. 66:2) and truly bring Him a broken heart (Ps. 51:16–17). That explains why Ezra fasted and prayed, for he identified himself with the people in their sins. Note the pronouns in Ezra 9:6–15.

Not everybody agreed to obey (v. 15), but those who did submit to Ezra confessed their sins publicly, offered a sacrifice, and put away their pagan wives and children. The experience was painful for them, but it was the only way to keep the nation pure (Matt. 18:7–9). There is no easy way to deal with sin.

Our Hope   *God's people have hope because of salvation (Rom. 5:1–2), suffering (Rom. 5:3), the Word of God (Rom. 15:4), and the Spirit of God (Rom. 15:13). Of course, there could be no hope were it not for the resurrection of Jesus Christ (1 Pet. 1:3). He is our Hope (1 Tim. 1:1).*

NEHEMIAH

NEHEMIAH 1

Great distress (1–3). Nehemiah enjoyed security and prestige as the king's cupbearer, so there was no reason for him to ask about the needs of people hundreds of miles away. But he loved Jerusalem and was concerned about the welfare of his people (Jer. 15:5). How do you respond when you learn that others are hurting?

A great God (4–9). Nehemiah was a man of prayer; you will find ten of his prayers in this book (1:4ff.; 2:4; 4:4; 5:19; 6:9, 14; 13:14, 22, 29, 31). He believed in a great God (1:5; 4:14; 8:6; 9:32) who kept His promises, forgave sin, and helped His people when they called on Him. Like Ezra before him, Nehemiah identified himself with the sins and sorrows of the nation (Ezra 9:5ff.).

You Can Make the Difference

It was a day of reproach for the people of God (Neh. 1:3; 2:17; 5:9; 6:13). The great city of Jerusalem was no longer beautiful (Ps. 50:2), and the Jews were no longer powerful. But one man made the difference! Nehemiah led the Jews from great reproach (1:3) to great rejoicing (12:43). God is still seeking men and women willing to sacrifice to do His work. Are you available?

Great power (10–11). Nehemiah did more than weep and pray; he made himself available to the Lord to get the job done. He depended on God's great power to work in and through him (Eph. 3:20–21). He was not content merely to *get* answers to prayer: he wanted to *be* an answer to prayer. Has God used you lately to be an answer to somebody's prayers?

NEHEMIAH 2

Waiting. Nehemiah did not suddenly quit his job and hurry to Jerusalem. He prayed and faithfully worked for four months, waiting to approach the king in the Lord's time. Waiting may be much harder than working, but it is dangerous to rush ahead of the Lord.

Praying. Nehemiah's "telegraph prayers" were effective because he spent much time alone with God. The throne of grace in heaven has greater authority than any throne on earth (Eph. 1:15–23). Are you in the habit of talking to God during your daily activities?

Explaining. Nehemiah had been planning his work carefully, so he was able to give the king satisfactory answers. Prayer and concern are not substitutes for clear thinking and adequate organization.

Preparing. Nehemiah paid attention to this advice: "Whoever believes will not act hastily" (Isa. 28:16). Before enlisting the leaders, Nehemiah became personally acquainted with the needs (v. 11; Ezra 8:32). Dedicated leaders are awake when others are asleep, but they see more in the darkness than others do in the light (Prov. 20:18).

NEHEMIAH 3

The workers were involved in building, repairing (the word is used forty times) and fortifying (v. 8), ministries needed in the church today. The walls and gates were important for the protection of the people and the beauty of the city.

There is a place of ministry for everybody who has a mind to work: priests (v. 1), rulers (vv. 12–19), craftsmen (v. 8), and dedicated women (v. 12). God sometimes brings outsiders to help us (vv. 2, 5, 7), and some people are willing to do extra work (vv. 11, 19, 21). The significant thing is that they cooperated as they served the Lord. But don't be surprised if some people do nothing (v. 5), including some leaders. Just keep on working!

The best place to start working is at your own house (vv. 10, 23, 28). If each of us served the Lord first at home, what a difference it would make in the work of the Lord!

Who Does the Work?

Some people are constructionists, *helping to get the job done. Others are* destructionists, *busy tearing things down. A third group is made up of* obstructionists *who create problems for the people doing the work. In which group are you?*

NEHEMIAH 4

The enemy knows what we are doing and will be quick to fight us. Expect opposition, and be ready for it. Note the different weapons that the enemy used then and still uses today.

Mockery (1–6). The enemy wants you to think that your work is not important, that you are too weak to do it, and that if you finish it, it will not last. In other words, he wants you to believe that it is not worth it all, so you might as well quit. Just keep in mind that it is God's work and therefore a great work (v. 19; 6:3). Keep the greatness of God before your eyes (v. 14; 1:5, 10).

Threats (7–9). If your enemy cannot fool you, he will try to frighten you. The people practiced Ephesians 6:10–18; they armed themselves, prayed, and kept working.

Fear (10–23). The Jews living outside the city came to work with frightening tales about the enemy's plans. Again, the greatness of God helps us overcome the fear of man (v. 14), plus our willingness to stay on the job despite the sacrifices that may be required.

> *"Watch and Pray!"*
>
> *This means trusting God while at the same time being alert to what the enemy is doing. It is the way to be ready for Christ's return (Mark 13:33) and to be victorious over temptation (Mark 14:38) and Satan (Eph. 6:18). It is also the way to have open doors for ministry and make the most of them (Col. 4:2–6).*

NEHEMIAH 5

Now the enemy attacks from inside the nation, and Nehemiah must deal with selfishness and greed among his people. The wealthier Jews took advantage of the famine and economic crisis to exploit their own people (Hag. 1:7–11). How did Nehemiah respond?

Anger (6). There is a righteous anger against sin that itself is not sinful (Eph. 4:26). Although it is difficult not to get angry with people, we must try to focus on what they do rather than who they are. (See Exod. 32:19; Mark 3:5.) A person who lacks anger may also lack conviction and courage.

❝It is easy to fly into a passion—anybody can do that— but to be angry with the right person to the right extent and at the right time and with the right object and in the right way—that is not easy, and it is not everyone who can do it.**❞**

Aristotle

Deliberation (7). It was not Nehemiah's practice to exercise leadership without first thinking things through (Prov. 18:13; 29:22). No doubt he also prayed for God's wisdom.

Resolution (7-13). Once he decided what to do, he did it! He appealed to their love ("brother" in v. 7) and their devotion to the Word of God (Exod. 22:25). He reminded them of the fear of God and their witness to the enemy (v. 9).

Example (14-19). Had Nehemiah not been an unselfish and sacrificing man, he could not have appealed as he did (Matt. 7:1-5). He had helped the people generously and did not take advantage of his position as governor. A clear conscience is a mighty weapon in God's hands.

NEHEMIAH 6

As long as God's people sin against one another, the enemy can rest, but as soon as sin has been dealt with, the enemy must attack once more. Here are some more weapons he uses.

Guile (1-4). Beware when the enemy is smiling and holding out his arms to hug you! We must say no to invitations that compromise our witness (2 Cor. 6:14—7:1) and take us away from the great work God has called us to do.

> ### Keep on Course
>
> *A true leader will not desert his or her post, but a hireling flees when the going is tough (Prov. 28:1). The enemy tried to get Jesus to flee, but He refused to alter His course (Luke 13:31–33). Paul continued on his course even though he knew that suffering lay before him (Acts 20:22–24; 21:13). We must always flee sin and temptation (Gen. 39:12; 1 Cor. 6:18; 1 Tim. 6:11; 2 Tim. 2:22), but we must not flee the place of duty.*

Accusation (5-9). Satan is both a liar and an accuser (Rev. 12:10); he seeks to slander God's servants (Job 1:6ff.). When you have a clear conscience (Acts 24:16) and you know how to pray, this weapon will fail to frighten you or stop your work.

Fear (10-19). Jesus had His Judas and Nehemiah had his Shemaiah, an informer who tried to frighten Nehemiah. There were also "family informers" opposing the work (vv. 17-19). But Nehemiah was a true shepherd and not a hireling (v. 13; John 10:11-15). He was not going to flee. The work was completed in a record fifty-two days, and God was glorified.

NEHEMIAH 7—8

The city of God. Every ministry and home needs gatekeepers and guards, for after a work is finished, it must be protected from the enemy (2 John 8). We also need leaders with courage and integrity. After all, there is a battle going on!

The people of God. The record of the original returnees helped Nehemiah determine who should become a citizen of Jerusalem, for he did not want any of the "mixed multitude" to come in and cause more trouble. One of the most difficult things in the Christian life is maintaining the purity of the faith and of the fellowship.

The Word of God. When Nehemiah arrived in Jerusalem in 444 B.C., Ezra was already there, instructing the people in God's law. When the work of rebuilding was completed, Ezra held a great "Bible conference" during the Feast of Tabernacles. The emphasis in chapter 8 is on "the Book" (vv. 1, 3, 5, 8, 18). They honored God's Word by standing when it was opened (v. 5), listening when it was read, and seeking to understand it when it was explained (vv. 2-3, 7-8, 12-13). They rejoiced at understanding the Word (v. 12) and at obeying the Word (v. 17; James 1:25).

NEHEMIAH 9

The Feast of Tabernacles was a time of joy, but when it ended, the people took an extra day for hearing the Word, confessing sin, and worshiping the Lord. This is a balanced ministry: the Word reveals our sin and God's forgiveness;

confession brings forgiveness; and forgiveness should lead to praise.

The people stood up to hear the Word (8:5), and the choir encouraged them to stand up and praise the Lord (v. 5)! He is the God of creation (v. 6), the God of the covenant (vv. 7–8), and the God of redemption (vv. 9–15). He is long-suffering with His people and meets their needs even when they do not obey His commands (vv. 16–31). The song ended with the people entering into a covenant with the Lord (vv. 32–38).

It is a beautiful summary of God's ministry to Israel. He brought them out (v. 7), brought them through (v. 11), brought them in (v. 23), and saved them from their enemies (v. 27). But what a record of Israel's sins! However, God invites His people to make new beginnings and to let Him bury the past.

NEHEMIAH 10—11

It is one thing to attend a feast, sing praises to God, and hear the Bible read and explained, and quite something else to commit yourself to obey the will of God. The eighty-four men who put their seal to the covenant wanted God and the people to know that they were serious about obedience. These names represented whole families (10:28), so that more people were involved in this solemn commitment than are named in chapter 10.

"Most church members live so far below the standard, you'd have to backslide to be in fellowship. We are so subnormal that if we were to become normal, people would think we were abnormal.**"**

Vance Havner

Their dedication was public, and it was also specific and included obedience with regard to marriage (10:30), the Sabbath and the Sabbatical year (10:31), their support of the temple (10:32) and their gifts and sacrifices for the temple ministry (10:33–39). Their dedication was costly, but it was worthy of all that God had done for them. When we are right with God, we will support His work and His house: "We will not neglect the house of our God" (10:39).

NEHEMIAH 12

Completion. Any work that we do for God succeeds only because of His working in us (Phil. 2:12–13). Therefore, that work must be dedicated to Him for His glory. Otherwise, we may become proud, and the work then becomes an idol that takes God's rightful place in our lives (Deut. 8:11–20).

Celebration. The emphasis is on joy and thanksgiving to God. The work was finished, the enemy was humiliated, and the Lord was glorified; so why not rejoice? Nehemiah and Ezra each led one of the two choirs as they sang their way around the city walls and met at the temple area. The sound of the joy "was heard afar off" (v. 43; Ezra 3:12–13).

Cleansing. Of what value is a dedicated wall without dedicated people? Verse 30 parallels Isaiah 1:16 and 2 Corinthians 7:1. A singing people should be a sanctified people.

NEHEMIAH 13

After the big celebration, then what? The work of a spiritual leader is never finished, for the enemy never quits. How sad it is to read that during Nehemiah's absence from the city, the Jews gradually stopped keeping the covenant they had made with God (10:28–39). By the time Nehemiah returned, the people were terribly backslidden.

Separation. The people had mixed with the pagans, the priest had let the enemy into the temple, and Jewish parents were allowing their children to marry pagan mates (vv. 23–27). The walls of the city were still strong, but the spiritual walls of separation were crumbling.

Stewardship. The people had promised to support the temple ministry but had not been faithful to bring the required tithes and offerings. Decreased giving is often a sign of diminished spiritual vitality.

Sacrifice. God gave them six days for work and business

and asked for only one day for Himself, but some people robbed Him of that (vv. 15–22). They were actually robbing themselves of blessing and of the opportunity to witness to the pagans around them.

Nehemiah was resolute, and the secret of his courage was prayer (vv. 14, 22, 29, 31). Are you willing to be different from others to the glory of God?

A Worthy Role Model *Nehemiah was a layman who loved Jerusalem and the temple and wanted the city to glorify God. He is a good example for all of us to follow in his devotion to duty, his discipline in planning and doing his work, his dedication to the Word of God, and his dependence on prayer. He did not use his authority selfishly but humbly and sacrificially served God and the people. He did not run from difficulties or dangers but trusted God to help him face them honestly and solve them successfully.*

ESTHER

---◆---

Esther and Ruth are the only books in the Bible named after women. Ruth was a Gentile who married a Jew, while Esther was a Jewess who married a Gentile. Both were women of faith and courage; both helped to save the nation of Israel, Ruth by the birth of a son and Esther by the death of an enemy.

The Persians conquered Babylon in 539 B.C. The events in the book of Esther occurred at Susa (Shushan; Esther 1:2; see also Neh. 1:1), where the king's winter palace was located, and they belong between chapters 6 and 7 of Ezra. The king who married Esther was Xerxes I (the name Ahasuerus was a title, like Pharaoh); the events in the book cover about ten years, from his third year (1:3) to his twelfth year (3:7).

The name of God is not mentioned in this book, but the hand of God is seen throughout the account. A primary lesson is that God is sovereign in the nations of the world, and His people must surrender and do His will. The Jews who were struggling in Jerusalem and Judah needed the encouragement of this book and the reminder that God keeps His covenant promises (Gen. 12:1–3).

ESTHER 1

A man is very poor if he can show *all* his glory and wealth in six months! It will take eternal ages for us to begin to fathom the riches of God's grace and glory (Eph. 1:18). Where is the glory of Xerxes today?

A man is poor if he must entertain his guests with "wine in abundance" (v. 7). What began as a royal banquet degenerated into a drunken party (Prov. 20:1; 23:29–31). Queen Vashti was wise to refuse to attend such a feast (Prov. 23:20). She lost her crown, but she kept her integrity.

A man is poor if he lets his temper get the best of him (Prov. 14:17; 16:32). Xerxes made some foolish decisions, which is what usually happens when anger takes over. But God was in control, working out His plan even through a proud pagan monarch (Prov. 21:1).

ESTHER 2

The selection of Esther (vv. 1–18) and the detection of the plotters (vv. 19–23) may seem to be events that do not belong together, but they were both part of God's plan to save His people. Esther's coronation was a grand public affair, while Mordecai's service to the king was rather private. But God would use Esther's position and Mordecai's service to fulfill His purposes.

You may be prone to believe that God works only in the "important events" of life. All events are important if you are living in the will of God. Mordecai was not immediately rewarded for saving the king's life, but God would take care of it at the right time (chap. 6). Do your duty today, and let God take care of the consequences.

ESTHER 3

The king promoted an evil man and approved a wicked project. No doubt many of the Jews were asking, "Why has God permitted such a thing?" The fact that God permits evil in this world does not mean that evil is good or that God is unconcerned or unable to help. When men do not allow Him to rule, He overrules, and He always accomplishes His purposes.

No matter how you examine Haman, he is a wicked man. Promote him and he gets proud. Ignore him and he becomes angry and takes out his anger on a whole race. (Prejudice usually works that way.) Make him rich and he uses his money to destroy and not to build.

Everything about Haman was hateful to the Lord (Prov. 6:16–19), but He did not interfere with Haman's evil deeds. Haman's sins would ultimately destroy him and be used by God for the good of Israel.

Prejudice

"Prejudice is the dislike for all that is unlike," said Israel Zangwill, author and Zionist leader. When Haman said that the Jews were a different people (3:8), he was right, and that difference meant salvation for the world. Mark Twain called anti-Semitism "the swollen envy of pigmy minds." From Pharaoh to Hitler, every leader who has tried to destroy the Jews has tasted the wrath of God. No race is perfect, including the Jews, but no race should be singled out for oppression as they have been. God's covenant with Abraham still stands (Gen. 12:1–3).

ESTHER 4

An irrepressible grief. A crisis does not make a person; it shows what a person is made of. In spite of the danger involved, Mordecai publicly displayed his grief and let people know his position. He would not stand by and do nothing when the authorities were about to slaughter innocent people, including children.

An inaccessible king. Oriental monarchs were supposed to hear only good news; they reigned in a world of illusion, sheltered from reality. Even the queen had to have permission to talk to him! How different it is with the King of kings. He has worn the sackcloth of sorrow, He knows how we feel, and He gives us free access to His throne (Heb. 10:19–22).

An incomparable opportunity. God uses people to accomplish His purposes, and Esther was God's prepared servant for that hour (v. 14; Eph. 2:10). God accomplishes His purposes even if we disobey His call, *but we are the losers*. Mordecai did not want Esther's gifts; he wanted her life surrendered to the Lord. She became a living sacrifice to accomplish the work of God (Rom. 12:1).

ESTHER 5

Sometimes it takes a crisis to remind us that we never serve the Lord alone. Esther enjoyed comfort and ease in the palace, but now she had a difficult task to perform. Her people were fasting and seeking God's help for her; she could not have succeeded alone.

Poor Haman was basking in false glory, boasting about false wealth, enjoying false happiness, and resting on false confidence. He did not realize that the shadow of death was over him. But is he much different from the proud unbelievers of this day who build their lives on illusions?

Esther sensed that this was not the right time to reveal her nationality. The delay of one day gave Haman opportunity to have the gallows built on which he would be hanged. Promoted by the king, honored by the queen, and advised by his wife, Haman appears to have all his problems solved! But read Psalm 37.

ESTHER 6

Providence. If any chapter in the book of Esther reveals the providence of God, it is this one. (*Providence* [pro, "before"; *video*, "to see"] means "to see beforehand.") God kept the king awake, led the reader to the record about Mordecai, and had Haman arrive at just the right time. All of that happened behind the scenes, so Esther, Mordecai, and the Jews did not know about it. God is working on your behalf today, so trust Him (Rom. 8:28).

Conceit. Haman hated Mordecai so much that he got up very early to ask for his enemy's death. And Haman loved Haman so much that he could not imagine the king honoring anyone but himself! The proud man has a mirror in which he sees himself; the humble man has a window through which he sees others (Rom. 12:10; Phil. 2:3–4). Haman's pride destroyed him (Prov. 16:18; 18:12).

Disgrace. What a humiliating experience! Haman had to dress Mordecai in the robes he wanted to wear, put him on the horse he wanted to ride, and then lead him—a Jew—through the busiest part of the city! That should have been a warning to Haman that his plot would fail, and his wife's words only confirmed it. Had he heeded the warning and humbled himself, his life would have been spared, but pride does not easily give in to truth.

"*Humility is the source of all true greatness: pride is ever impatient, ready to be offended. He who thinks nothing is due to him, never thinks himself ill-treated.***"**

Fenelon

ESTHER 7

The wise person knows *what* to say and *how* and *when* to say it (Prov. 15:28; 16:23). In her brief reply to the king's question, Esther revealed her nationality (Esther 2:10, 20), her danger, and the presence of an enemy in the palace. She gave no names but waited to see the reaction of the king. God gives us the wisdom we need when we need it (James 1:5).

What a blow to the king's pride to learn that the man he had promoted and honored was only a self-seeking traitor. "As messengers of death is the king's wrath" (Prov. 16:14). Haman took Mordecai's place on the gallows, and the king's anger was appeased: "The righteous is delivered from trouble, and it comes to the wicked instead" (Prov. 11:8).

Beware if you are digging a pit for an enemy; you may fall in it yourself (Ps. 7:14–16). An enemy is a costly thing, a luxury that is too expensive to maintain.

The Prosperity of the Wicked	*Today it seems that the wicked are prospering and the righteous are suffering, but one day that will change (Prov. 11:8). Pharaoh had the Jewish boy babies drowned and God drowned his army in the Red Sea (Exod. 14:19ff.). Daniel was delivered from the lions' den, and the people who falsely accused him took his place and were slain (Dan. 6). Peter was delivered from prison, and his guards were executed (Acts 12). King Herod killed James and was slain by God (Acts 12). Read and ponder Psalm 73.*

ESTHER 8

Esther had exposed the enemy and saved her own life, but what about her people? The king himself could not revoke his edict, but he could issue another edict. He gave the Jews the right to arm and protect themselves and gave them nine months to get ready. The people of the land got the message: the king did not want the Jews to be harmed.

Can you see here an illustration of how God solved the sinner's plight? You were under condemnation because of the law of sin and death (Rom. 3:23; 6:23). God did not revoke that law—He *obeyed* it! He sent His Son to die for our sins and to bring in "the law of the Spirit of life" (Rom. 8:2). Any sinner who believes the message and trusts the Savior will receive everlasting life (John 3:15–16).

But that is not the end. We are the King's couriers, sent into the world by His authority to share the good news that *condemned sinners need not die!* Just as those couriers "hastened and pressed on by the king's command" (v. 14), so we must get the gospel to the ends of the earth as quickly as possible. After all, people will perish unless we tell them the good news!

ESTHER 9—10

We discover that the Jews had many enemies throughout the king's provinces. Had Haman's plan succeeded, the nation would have been annihilated. We are not told how these enemies had been persecuting God's people, but their day of reckoning finally came. God kept His covenant promise to Abraham (Gen. 12:1–3).

It is a good thing to set aside days for special remembrance and celebration. We need to remind ourselves of what the Lord has done and show our gratitude to Him. The Feast of Purim (*pur* means "lots" [3:7; 9:26]) is a time of great gladness and feasting. (See Ps. 30.)

God turned defeat into victory (9:1–3) and sorrow into joy (9:22). Of course, God does not write a "happy ending" *on earth* for every life story. Some of God's choicest saints have had to suffer and even die for the faith (Heb. 11:36–40). But God still writes that last chapter, even if it looks to us like failure. Ponder Paul's words in 2 Corinthians 4:7–18, and look forward with joy to the future God has planned for you (1 Cor. 2:9–10).

Trust in Him

"Never be afraid to trust an unknown future to a known God," said Corrie ten Boom. And Dr. Bob Jones, Sr., advised, *"Never doubt in the darkness what God has told you in the light."*

JOB

---◆---

Most of this book is poetry, but it is not fiction. Job was a real person in a real place who suffered real trials (Ezek. 14:14–20). James points to Job as an example of endurance, which means faithfulness under trial (James 5:11). Job did get impatient with himself, his circumstances, and his friends, but he did not turn away from his faith in God.

The book describes three encounters: Job and Satan (chaps. 1–2), Job and his friends (chaps. 3–37), and Job and the Lord (chaps. 38–42). His friends did their best to convince Job he was suffering because he was a sinner, but Job refused to compromise his integrity. In spite of some rash statements, Job spoke the truth, but his friends did not (Job 42:7).

It is usually said that the book of Job deals with this question: "Why do the godly suffer?" Actually, the theme goes deeper than that. Satan accused Job of serving God *only because God blessed him*. Unfortunately, there are still people like that, people with "commercial faith" who say to God, "If you bless me, I will serve You!" (See Satan's temptation of Christ in Matt. 4:8–10.)

The basic question is not "Why do the righteous suffer?" (there are many answers to that question) but "Is our God worthy of our worship and service, or must He 'buy' us with His blessings?" Satan was not only slandering Job; he was also slandering the Lord! He was saying, "God would not have any followers if He did not reward them!"

As you read, note the many images used by the speakers. These similes and metaphors help us see ourselves, the world of nature, life and death and, most of all, almighty God. (God is called "Almighty" thirty-one times in Job.) Job suffered so that you and I might learn some valuable lessons about what it really means to trust the Lord.

JOB 1

Job knew nothing about Satan's challenge to God and had no idea that the enemy was using him as a reason for slandering the Lord. Neither did Job know that God would use his sufferings to defeat Satan. God's people are soldiers on the battlefield, but there are times when they *are* the battlefield!

If you obey God only because He blesses you, the shallowness of your faith will show up in the testing time (Matt. 7:24–27; 13:20–21). Faith that cannot be tested cannot be trusted (James 1:1–8; 1 Pet. 1:3–9).

When Satan accuses you before God (or to yourself), remember that Jesus Christ is your defending Advocate in heaven; turn your case over to Him (Zech. 3; Rom. 8:31–39; 1 John 2:1–2; Rev. 12:10).

Satan

Origin. *Satan is a rebellious angel who was judged by God and fell from holiness to wickedness (Isa. 14:12–15). The angels who fell with him make up his army of spirits opposed to God and God's people (Eph. 6:10–13; Luke 11:18). Because Satan is a created being, he is not equal to God; though he possesses tremendous wisdom and power, Satan is always subject to God's will.*

Nature. *He is a liar and murderer (John 8:44); an adversary (1 Pet. 5:8–9); the god of this age (2 Cor. 4:4); the ruler of this world (John 12:31; 14:30; 16:11; 1 John 5:19); a deceiver (2 Cor. 11:3); a destroyer (Rev. 9:11; Abaddon means "destruction"); and a counterfeiter of God (Matt. 13:24–30, 36–43; 2 Cor. 11:13–*

15). The word Satan means "adversary," and devil means "slanderer, accuser" (Zech. 3:1–5).

Works. Satan can seek to deceive your mind (Gen. 3:1ff.; Matt. 16:21–23; 2 Cor. 11:3); snatch away God's Word (Matt. 13:19); attack your body (Job 2: 4–7; 2 Cor. 12:7); control your will (1 Chron. 21:1ff.; 2 Tim. 2:26); destroy your possessions (Job 1:13ff.); hinder your work for the Lord (1 Thess. 2:18); make you proud (1 Tim. 3:6–7); cause persecution (Rev. 2:10); and tempt you to sin (Matt. 4:1ff.). When you have sinned, he can accuse you and discourage you (2 Cor. 2:6–11). You must claim God's forgiveness by faith (1 John 1:9).

Defeat. In His life, death, resurrection, and ascension, Christ defeated Satan and his evil hosts (John 12:31–33; Eph. 1: 15—2:10; Col. 2:13–15). God's people must recognize the devil and know when he is at work (2 Cor. 2:11); respect him, because he is powerful and subtle (1 Pet. 5:8); and resist him with the Word of God and prayer (Matt. 4:1–11; James 4:7; Eph. 6:17–18). The believer must wear the whole armor of God (Eph. 6:10ff.) and use the spiritual equipment. There is overcoming power in the blood of Christ (Rev. 12:11) and the power of the Spirit (1 John 4:4).

"Nor give place to the devil" (Eph.
4:27). In Ephesians 4:17–32, Paul names
some sins that can give Satan a foothold
in your life: lust, lying, anger, stealing,
corrupt speech, evil speaking, an unforgiving spirit, bitterness, malice, and so
forth. Any sinful thing that belonged to
your old life can be used by the devil to
ruin your new life, so be sure to keep
your heart clean before the Lord.

Future. Satan still has access to heaven
(Job 1—2; Zech. 3) but one day will be
thrown out (Rev. 12:7–12). When the
Lord Jesus comes to establish His kingdom, He will cast Satan into hell, the lake
of fire, where he will be tormented forever
(Rev. 19:11—20:3). Hell was prepared for
Satan and his angels, but people who reject Christ and believe Satan's lies will
suffer in hell with him (Matt. 25:41; Rev.
20:11–15).

JOB 2

Satan's prediction about Job was wrong, which shows that
he cannot foresee the future as God can. Instead of hearing
Job say, "Cursed be the name of the Lord!" Satan heard,
"Blessed be the name of the Lord!" Job had lost his wealth and
his children, yet he did not blame God. (See James 1:2–12;
1 Pet. 1:3–9.)

Satan never gives up (Luke 4:13). He suggested to God a
new test for Job: personal physical suffering (2 Cor. 12:1–10).
Pain can weaken our resistance and make everything feel
and look worse than it really is. More than one person who

has victoriously survived tragedy has fallen apart under the onslaughts of pain.

God Will Provide

Are health and wealth necessarily marks of God's blessing? Are sickness and poverty proof that we are out of God's will? To the Old Testament Jew, the answer would be yes to both questions. God promised to bless Israel physically and materially if they obeyed His law (Deut. 28). The nation of Israel was like a little child that had to be taught by means of rewards and punishments. But these old covenant blessings are not guaranteed to God's people under the new covenant today. With the coming of Jesus Christ to earth, the "childhood" period of Israel's history ended (Gal. 4:1–7). Our Lord was poor, and so were the apostles and many of the great men and women of faith (2 Cor. 8:9; 6:4–10; Heb. 11:36–40). Paul lived with a physical affliction (2 Cor. 12:7–10), and one of his most beloved workers almost died from illness (Phil. 2:25–30; see also 2 Tim. 4:20). It is the wicked who seem to be prospering today, not the righteous, but one day, God will turn things around (Ps. 73). God has promised to meet your needs (Matt. 6:25–34; Phil. 4:19), so stop fretting and trust Him to provide.

What kept Job going? His faith in God and his personal integrity. God had no cause to inflict pain on Job (v. 3), and Job knew that he was right in his relationship with God (Job 23:10–12; 27:1–6). God would use Job to refute the explanation of his friends, to silence the accusation of the devil, and to strengthen the determination of all who will suffer in the will of God. If today you are perplexed about something in your life, wait on the Lord and let Him work out His hidden purposes.

JOB 3

Job did not curse God, but he did curse the night of his conception and the day of his birth. The prophet Jeremiah did the same thing one dismal day (Jer. 20:14–18). When you hurt, physically and emotionally, you are prone to lose perspective and forget the joys of the past. Times of suffering can be times of remembering God's goodness and thanking Him for all you have received from His hand. Ponder Psalm 77.

Job asks the question "Why?" seven times in this monologue (vv. 11, 12, 16, 20, 23). "Why?" is an easy question to ask but a very difficult one to answer. Suppose God had told Job the reasons behind his troubles. Would that have solved his problems? After all, God's people live on promises, not on explanations.

A Spiritual Diet

According to Job 3:24, Job was "feeding" on his grief and could not eat. Some people feed on their tears (Ps. 42:3), and others feed on their sins (Job 20:12–19). How much better to feed on God's Word (Jer. 15:16; Matt. 4:4), His will (John 4:34), and His faithfulness (Ps. 37:3).

It is too bad that Job's three friends listened to Job's *words* instead of to his *feelings*. They decided to tell Job why he was suffering, but they only made his situation worse. Suffering people need love, acceptance, and patient encouragement, not arguments and accusations.

JOB 4—5

The three friends sincerely meant to console Job, but they ended up condemning him and taking Satan's place! Why? Because each of them saw Job's plight from his own narrow perspective and failed to identify with Job's perplexity and pain. We all need to obey Romans 12:9–16.

Eliphaz asked Job why he did not practice what he preached (4:1–6), a fine way to start encouraging a hurting friend! He told Job that sinners always reap what they sow (4:7–11), suggesting that it was Job's fault that he was now poor and sick instead of being rich and healthy. What encouragement!

Then Eliphaz shared his "experience with God" (4:12–21) on which he based his whole interpretation of life. Avoid those who make *their* experience the only test of truth. The Word of God does not change, but experiences do. We are all different, and God deals with each of us in ways suitable to our needs, our natures and our level of maturity.

Eliphaz closed his speech by telling Job to seek God and submit (5:8), and to accept His correction (5:17); then God would bless him again. But his suggestion played right into Satan's hands: "Does Job fear God for nothing?" (1:9). Eliphaz had the same theology as the devil and did not know it!

If you want to help others, listen with your heart as well as your ears; try not to make your experience the only test of truth. We all "know in part" (1 Cor. 13:9).

JOB 6—7

Job admits that his words were rash (6:3), and he explains why: his grief was a burden that his friends did not feel or try to help him carry. God was shooting poisoned arrows at Job, and his friends were not applying medicine to his painful wounds. One day God will change our burdens into glory (2 Cor. 4:16–18), but until then, we must bear one another's burdens (Gal. 6:2) and relieve one another's wounds (Luke 10:25–37; Acts 16:33).

The friends were like desert brooks that dry up when they are most needed. The thirsty travelers hope for refreshment, but they are disappointed (6:14-23). Do you disappoint hurting people by being critical and failing to care?

In chapter 7, Job talks to God about the seeming futility of his life. Why should God keep him alive? What is all this suffering accomplishing? Job is like a weary hired man who gets no wages (7:1-5). His life rushes by like the shuttle on a loom; it is like a breath and a cloud (7:6-10; James 4:13-17). Job is a target (6:4; 7:20), but what is God aiming at?

"If I am a great sinner," says Job, "then either pardon my sins or take my life. Either way, I will find some peace." (See 6:9-10; 7:15, 20-21.) It seems a logical argument, but God's thoughts are not our thoughts; what seems meaningless to us is reasonable to God (Isa. 55:8-9). We must walk by faith.

Hurting people need encouragement, not argument. Ask God to make your words like healing medicine (Prov. 12:18) and refreshing water (Prov. 18:4). Start the day praying for wisdom to say the right things at the right times (Isa. 50:4).

JOB 8

Theology (1-7). Eliphaz emphasized the sinfulness of man, and Bildad majored on the justice of God. Both men were right in their doctrine but wrong in their conclusion. They locked God into a formula and refused to let Him exercise His freedom to do what He wants to do. Before the book ends, Job and his friends will discover that God is much greater than the words they used in speaking about Him. Have you limited God? Do you know the living God or only theological words?

History (8-10). Bildad was a devoted traditionalist who called his witnesses from the past. There is nothing wrong with our learning from the past, provided it does not turn the present into a museum and the future into a cemetery. Someone has said, "Tradition is the living face of dead people, while traditionalism is the dead face of living people." Is the past encouraging you or embalming you?

Science (11-22). Bildad argues from nature: for every effect, there is a cause. If Job is suffering, there must be a cause, and since God is just, that cause has to be Job's sin. But God's dealings with His people cannot be studied in a laboratory.

Science has its place, but it cannot explain God. He is too great for man's feeble instruments.

JOB 9—10

Job accepted Bildad's affirmation that God is just, but doing that did not solve his problem. "I am blameless," he said (9:21); "therefore, why should God condemn me?" Job then shared three complaints.

"I cannot contend with Him" (9:1–13). God is so much greater and stronger than we are, who would dare to declare war on Him? God is wise and powerful; we are ignorant and weak.

"I cannot answer Him" (9:14–35). If God and Job went to court, Job would not have an argument to present. God is the Judge, He has all power, and nobody can contend with Him. Meanwhile, life goes by swiftly, like a fast runner, a ship and an eagle. For Job to put on a smiling face (v. 27) will not change his circumstances. It would be hypocrisy.

"I cannot understand Him" (10:1–22). God made Job, and He seems to be destroying His own work. Why was Job born to begin with? God could have saved Himself a lot of trouble!

The answer to these complaints is in 9:33—a mediator, someone who could bring Job and God together. You have that Mediator in Jesus Christ, God's Son (1 Tim. 2:5; Heb. 12:24). As both God and man, Jesus understands your needs and can do something about them. Are you complaining—or trusting Him?

JOB 11

Job has heard two points of the sermon from his friends: man is sinful (Eliphaz), and God is just (Bildad). Zophar now finishes the sermon with the third point: God punishes sin and gives less than we really deserve (v. 6). "Things could be worse!" is a cruel statement to make to somebody who has lost everything.

People in pain think that their suffering is worse than anybody else's, so do not argue with them. Zophar responded to Job's words, not his feelings, and that was a mistake. He told Job to repent and seek God, promising that God would hear him. He warned Job that if he did not repent, he would die (v. 20).

You cannot measure pain or the greatness of God (vv. 7–9). These are dead-end streets. Instead, *lose yourself in the measureless love and power of God* (Eph. 3:14–21). God is not found at the end of an argument, but He is near to those who call on Him.

JOB 12—14

"My life" (12). Job replied to all three friends and reminded them that *he* had wisdom as well as they. In fact, all creation knew the things that they said to him. God is great: His hand made everything (v. 6), and His hand keeps everything alive (v. 10). Job wanted to die and escape his suffering, but God held his life in His hand (Acts 17:24–28; Col. 1:16–17). If your life is in God's hand, have you anything to fear?

What About Suicide?	*The life of every living thing is in God's hand (Job 12:10). He has numbered our days (Job 14:5) and set a limit beyond which we cannot go (Ps. 139:16). But can we determine a limit* sooner *than* He planned? *Is suicide permissible? Job's wife counseled her husband to curse God and thereby invite His judgment, but Job rejected that suggestion as foolish (Job 2:9–10). Job wanted to die (Job 6:8–10; 7:15–16) but did not assume that he had the right to take his own life. Our lives are in God's hand, and our times are in His hand (Ps. 31:15). There is no incident in the Bible of a godly person committing suicide. Saul had rebelled against God (1 Sam. 31:3–5); Ahithophel had*

turned against the king (2 Sam. 17:23); Zimri was a rebel and a conspirator (1 Kings 16:8–20); and Judas betrayed the Lord (Matt. 27:4–5). Samson's death (Judg. 16:23ff.) appears to be more martyrdom than suicide. The sixth commandment forbids murder (Exod. 20:13). Man is made in the image of God, and we have no right to attack that image, even if we are suffering greatly. In the Bible, men like Moses, Elijah, and Jonah became discouraged and wanted to die, but they did not attempt to take their own lives. "To run away from trouble is a form of cowardice," wrote Aristotle, "and while it is true that the suicide braves death, he does it not for some noble object but to escape some ill." Ponder 2 Timothy 4:6–8.

"My faith" (13). In the previous chapter, Job saw God as Creator, but now he sees Him as Judge. "I desire to reason with God" (v. 3) means "I want to meet Him in court." Job would rather meet a just God than "worthless physicians" like his friends. When you seek to help others, keep in mind that you are a witness and not a prosecuting attorney. Even if God did condemn him, Job would still trust Him (v. 15). What faith!

"My hope" (14). Like a flower, man is born to die. He disappears like a shadow (v. 2) or like evaporating water (v. 11). Man's days are numbered (vv. 5–6), but does he have a future? Even a tree will grow again after it is cut down (v. 7), but what about man? The truth about resurrection was not fully revealed in Old Testament days, but Job still rested his hope on God. God has revealed the blessed hope that His people have because of faith in Jesus Christ (John 11:25–26; 1 Cor. 15; 2 Tim. 1:9–10).

"In spite of my sufferings," said Job, "my life, my faith, and my hope are in God." Is that your testimony?

JOB 15

The wise man (1–13). Eliphaz thought himself a wise man, so he rebuked Job for his sins. For one thing, Job's words were so much "hot air" and revealed that he had no fear of God. Job claimed to be wise but was really surpassed in that virtue by his three friends, all of whom were older than he. (Is age a guarantee of wisdom?) Most of all, Job had refused the "consolations" God had sent him through his friends (v. 11). If the words of the three men were "gentle," what would their harsh words be like! How difficult it is for us accurately to hear ourselves or see ourselves.

The wicked man (14–35). Eliphaz painted this picture of Job. All of us are born in sin (vv. 14–16; Rom. 3:9–23), but some sinners are worse than others. Eliphaz described the fate of the wicked: pain, fear, dreadful noises, hunger, poverty, darkness, and then death. Eliphaz did not explain why the ungodly seem to prosper in this world while the godly often suffer. His theology was "cut and dried." He had an answer for everything, but he had no help for Job.

JOB 16—17

No comfort (16:1–8). Job's three friends were indeed "miserable comforters." They only added to his pain. If the situation were reversed, Job would have spoken words of strength and help to them in their suffering. Their words wore him out and made him shrivel up, as when a desert wind blows. Does God use your words to bring new life to others (Prov. 15:4)?

No defense (16:9–22). Job told what God did to him. God was an adversary against whom Job had no defense. God permitted the people in Job's life to gape at him, shoot at him, and scorn him. Job was in a battle! If only he had a mediator who could represent him in heaven and bring justice (vv. 18–22)! (See Job 9:33.)

No hope (17:1–16). Job had expressed hope that God would vindicate him even after death (14:14), but his hope was almost gone (v. 15; 6:11; 7:6; 14:19). All he saw in his future was a decaying body, death, and the grave (vv. 1, 13). Once again, Job cried out for a representative before God (v. 3), somebody who would put up security for him ("shake hands") and get his case settled.

Jesus Christ is Advocate and Mediator for His people and their hope (1 Tim. 1:1). He gave His own blood as security (Heb. 9:12ff.), and those who trust Him always have living hope (1 Pet. 1:3ff.).

JOB 18

Since Job brought up the matter of death and the grave, Bildad decided to elaborate on the subject. He painted some vivid pictures of the death of the wicked.

It is like a light put out (5–6). For the lost sinner, death does indeed mean darkness, but not for those who have faith in Christ (Prov. 4:18). Believers go to heaven where there is no darkness (Rev. 21:25); unbelievers go to hell where there is no light (Matt. 22:13).

It is like an animal trapped (7–10). The wicked man tries to run away, but the path is filled with devices to catch him. Bildad named six different kinds of traps—but it takes only one. There is no escape when your time comes.

It is like a criminal pursued (11–14). As he tries to escape "the king of terrors," the criminal runs, falls down, gets weary, and finally is caught. (See Heb. 9:27.)

It is like a tree rooted up (15–21). The tree seemed strong and solid, but the roots were already dry and death could easily pull the tree up. People even forget that the tree was once there!

This is the death of the wicked, not the death of the righteous. For those who trust Jesus Christ, death means "to be absent from the body and to be present with the Lord" (2 Cor. 5:1–8). Is that your confidence?

JOB 19

Wronged by his comforters (1–4). Their harsh words tormented him, broke him, and reproached him. Why should they go on? After all, it was not *their* sin that God was punishing, but *his* sin, and they were only making matters worse.

Wronged by God (5–12). Why should one sinner receive so much punishment? Bildad's description of death (chap. 18) was Job's description of his life (vv. 7–12)! He was a "living dead man," and his hope was gone.

Wronged by his family and friends (13–22). Those closest to him stayed farthest from him, and those who should have shown him respect only mocked him. Job was a lonely man crying out for pity, but nobody answered. Ask God to help you be sensitive to the cries of those who hurt, no matter what others may do.

Job still had faith in God (vv. 25–27)! If he died, he would see God, and one day, he would have a new body from God. This promise gives great confidence to God's people (John 11:25–26; 1 Cor. 15:50–58).

They Had Faith	*Job 19:25–27 is one of the great declarations of faith found in the Bible. Other important statements of faith were made by Ruth (Ruth 1:16–17), Jeremiah (Lam. 3:22–24), the three Hebrew men (Dan. 3:16–18), Habakkuk (Hab. 3:17–19), a Roman centurion (Matt. 8:5–13), a Canaanite mother (Matt. 15:21–28), Peter (Matt. 16:13–20), and Paul (Acts 20:24).*

JOB 20

Zophar's speech is an echo of Bildad's (chap. 18) as he describes the fate of the wicked man. The speech did not apply to Job, but it should be taken to heart by self-confident, successful people who leave God out of their lives.

Success is temporary (1–11). No matter how rich, famous,

or secure he may be, the wicked person will eventually perish. Zophar used graphic images: he will go away like refuse (v. 7, human excrement) or like a dream or night vision (v. 8). Here today, gone tomorrow! Ponder James 4:13–17 and 1 John 2:17.

Life is bitter (12–19). Dainty food becomes poison and wealth makes him sick. The things he thought he would enjoy only bring pain to him. Riches without God can never give anyone true enjoyment (1 Tim. 6:1–10).

Life is painful (20–29). He has no peace because everybody has declared war on him, including God, who rains judgment on him. Arrows (note 6:4), terrors, darkness, and fire are his lot, and then—the end.

Zophar tried to frighten Job into confessing his sins and "getting right with God," but his approach did not work. The fear of God is a legitimate motive for obedience (Matt. 10:28), but it is not the only motive and it must be tempered by love (2 Cor. 5:10–11, 14).

JOB 21

Bildad and Zophar tried to use logic to silence Job, and their reasoning went like this: (a) God blesses the righteous but makes the wicked suffer; (b) Job is suffering; (c) therefore, Job is wicked. How reasonable!

But Job questioned their basic premise. He had often seen the wicked enjoying great blessing: long life, many descendants, peace and safety, riches, success, and days filled with joy. Yes, the wicked die, but even their death is often quick and easy (Ps. 73:1–14).

Job's friends were looking at the *outside* of things and ignoring the heart (John 7:24). The test of godly character is not success but *what people think about God* (vv. 14–15). The ungodly ask, "What will we get out of it if we obey God?" But that is Satan's approach (Job 1:6–11) *and the three friends agreed with him!*

If comfort and wealth are evidences of holiness, our Lord was not holy, for He had little earthly comfort and wealth, and He died a terrible death on the cross. Perhaps you need to examine your own "logic" and see if you are thinking like God or like the devil (Ps. 1:1; Matt. 16:21–28).

It's an Illusion

Now we can better understand why the three friends were so hard on Job: they were afraid that trials might come to them as they did to Job. *They protected themselves with a false theology that was born in the pit of hell: "If we obey God, He will bless us and protect us from suffering." Job detected their fear (6:21) and refuted their reasoning, which made them angry. The three friends had a very shallow view of God and of faith and life, while Job penetrated the deep things of God. People who trust a false theology are living a life of illusion that one day will vanish.*

JOB 22

Satan and Job's friends all agreed that Job was a sinner at heart and that he obeyed God only because God blessed him. The fact that Job still trusted God after losing his children and his wealth should have proved to them that his faith was not "commercial."

Eliphaz then took a new approach, asking whether Job's righteousness *did God any good.* (Compare v. 2 with Job 21:15.) God is just and does what is right; therefore, He is not influenced by man's good deeds. Eliphaz then named sins that Job must have committed (vv. 4-11), sins Job thought God could not see (vv. 12-20), sins God would forgive if Job would only repent (vv. 21-30). It was the same argument in a new dress, and Satan could not have done better.

Like any loving parent, our heavenly Father delights in the obedience of His children and finds pleasure in their worship, service, and growth. Whether you are rich or poor, healthy or sick, your highest joy ought to be to please Him (Ps. 40:8; John 8:29).

	We please the Lord by living holy lives (Col. 1:10; 1 Thess. 4:1ff.), being devoted fully to Him as soldiers (2 Tim. 2:4), living by faith (Heb. 11:5–6), giving generously (Phil. 4:18), obeying parents (Col. 3:20), and accepting and using our spiritual gifts (1 Cor. 12:18). The Father is well pleased with His Son (Matt. 3:17; 17:5), and when we seek to honor Him, we please the Father. God takes delight in the way of the believer who obeys His will (Ps. 37:23).
Pleasing God	

JOB 23—24

In the courtroom (23:1–9). Job still wanted to meet God and get a fair trial, but he did not know where to find Him. In the end, when God showed up and asked Job to present his case, Job was speechless. Why? Because beholding the majesty of God made all his arguments useless. He had seen God, and that was all that mattered!

In the furnace (23:10–17). The important thing is not to win an argument with God but to become more like God. For that to happen, you often need the furnace of affliction (1 Pet. 1:6–9), which separates the dross from the pure gold and leaves you a better person. You cannot control the temperature of the furnace or the duration of the testing time, but you can obey Him (23:11) and feed on His Word (23:12).

On the watchtower (24:1–25). Job again presented proof that all sinners are not immediately judged by God. As it were, he took his friends into the watchtower and pointed out various kinds of sinners who seemed to be getting away with their evil deeds. Job did not deny the fact of God's judgment (vv. 22–24), but he did affirm that man could not fully explain how He worked.

When there are more questions in your life than answers, and when the furnace is hot, remember Abraham's great statement of faith: "Shall not the Judge of all the earth do right?" (Gen. 18:25; see also 2 Tim. 4:8).

JOB 25—26

Bildad's brief speech (the shortest in the book) emphasized the greatness of God (25:1–3) and the nothingness of man (25:4–6). God finds no righteousness in any part of His creation, including the angels, so how could He find it in Job? Again, Bildad was trying to get Job to confess, but he failed. It is too bad Bildad did not encourage Job with the other attributes of God, such as His love, mercy, and grace.

Job's reply (chaps. 26—31) is almost like the "summing up" argument of an attorney. In 26:1–4, he rebuked Bildad for giving him no help at all. These verses suggest ways by which we can help others today, so let us not fail as Bildad did. Your words can bring help and hope to people who desperately need them.

Nobody can escape the eye of God, not even the dead (26:5–6). No matter where you are in creation, He sees you: in the heavens (26:7–9, 13), on the earth (26:10–11), and on the seas (26:12). But the voice of God in creation is only a whisper and we see only the "fringes" of His ways (26:14). Creation clearly reveals the power and wisdom of God, but the grace and mercy of God are seen but dimly.

As you try to help others, keep in mind that "we know in part" (1 Cor. 13:9). It will keep you humble and make you more useful.

JOB 27—28

Justice (27). Job still wanted to take God to court and get his case settled. He was bitter (v. 2; 3:20) because God would not solve his problems *on his terms*. Trials can make you bitter or better, depending on how you relate to God. If you see Him as an unkind Judge, you will be bitter; if you see Him as a loving Father, you will be better.

Job was right in holding to his integrity (2:9-10). His friends urged him to admit his sins, even if he had not committed them, because that would gain him the favor of God. (Satan's philosophy again!) Job described the judgment of the wicked man, but he did not say that he qualified.

Wisdom (28). "Where is wisdom found?" is Job's key question (vv. 12, 20). Does it have to be mined like silver and gold (Prov. 2:1-9)? In one sense, yes, for wisdom is not found on the surface of things. You must dig into the Word of God and into life if you would have the wisdom of God (Prov. 8:10-11). True wisdom begins with the fear of the Lord (v. 28; Prov. 1:7; 9:10; 15:33; 19:23). When we reverence Him and seek to please Him, He teaches us His wisdom and His way (Isa. 33:6; James 1:5).

"Knowledge is proud that he has learned so much; wisdom is humble that he knows no more.**"**

William Cowper

JOB 29—30

Longing for the past (29). When life is difficult, it is normal to look back to "the good old days" and want to turn back the clock. But that approach is selfish (note how many times Job says "I" and "my") and only adds to your pain. It makes enjoying happiness more important than experiencing holiness. Job listed some of the blessings he had enjoyed and some of the services he had performed for others, and all of that should have prepared him to face his trials with confidence.

The past must be more than a memory; it must be a ministry. Today will soon be a yesterday. Are you using today to grow in the Lord so you are prepared for tomorrow? Is life an investment or just enjoyment?

Lamenting the present (30). "But now," says Job (vv. 1, 16), and he launches into his complaint about his sufferings. His friends mock him (vv. 1–15), his body hurts him (vv. 16–19), his God has deserted him (vv. 20–23), and his hope has fled from him (vv. 24–31). He cannot return to the past, endure the present, or face the future!

Whenever your circumstances lead you to join Job in the "dust and ashes" (v. 19), remember that the Lord Jesus once was there (Ps. 22:15) and knows how you feel. He is adequate for your yesterdays and tomorrows as well as your todays (Heb. 13:8). Do not just remember your past enjoyments; also remember God's past mercies (Ps. 77:1–12), and trust Him for the future.

> **"** *The good old days are often a combination of a bad memory and a good imagination.* **"**

JOB 31

As he concluded his final defense, Job named specific sins and denied that he had committed them. He knew that God watched him (v. 4) and weighed him (v. 6), and he was not afraid to speak. He wanted more than anything else for God to speak and either accuse him or defend him (v. 35).

This chapter helps you take inventory of your spiritual life. Do you have eyes that wander lustfully (vv. 1–4) or feet that move deceitfully (vv. 5–8)? Has lust been fulfilled in overt sin (vv. 9–12)? Have you treated others as God wants them treated (vv. 13–23)? Have you coveted wealth or been proud of what you possess (vv. 24–28)? How do you respond to the suffering of an enemy (vv. 29–30) or the needs of a stranger (vv. 31–34)? Are you a faithful steward of the natural resources God gives (vv. 38–40)?

Job has seen himself and is satisfied, but he has not yet seen God. When he does, he will change his opinion of himself and get started on the road to victory.

JOB 32—33

Anger. Elihu was polite in his waiting and kind in his speaking, but he was an angry young man (32:1-5). He was angry with Job for accusing God and with the three friends for failing to convince Job of his sins. Elihu agreed with their view that Job was a sinner, but he disagreed with their arguments. We must beware when our speech is motivated by self-righteous anger.

Pride. As the youngest man in the group, Elihu knew his place, but he was still quite sure of himself. The discussion needed *his* opinion (32:6, 10, 17) because everybody else was wrong. He was bursting with words (32:18-20) and could not hold them in. That is the time to ask God for self-control and wisdom, lest your words do more harm than good.

Knowledge. Elihu was sure he was right and challenged Job to refute him (33:1-8). He had not yet learned that Job needed understanding and love and not accusations and arguments. Like the three friends, Elihu had a great many facts in his mind but very little truth in his heart.

He quoted Job's own words (33:9-11) and explained that God owed him no explanation of what He was doing (33:13). God may speak in dreams (33:14-18), in trials (33:19-30), and through people (33:31-33). God had used all three in Job's life, and Job had rejected them! No wonder Job was miserable!

God may indeed teach us valuable lessons at night, in times of pain. Are we listening?

JOB 34—35

God is just (34). Elihu must have been a good listener because he was able to quote Job's words. However, Elihu listened with his ears and not with his heart, which made his speeches harsh and unkind. He was too sure of himself and kept reminding Job and his friends to listen to him (vv. 2, 10, 16, 34). Were their minds wandering?

It was the same old argument: God is just and therefore cannot be accused of sin or partiality. God sees all we do and judges sin righteously. Job has rebelled against God and ought to confess and get right with God!

God is great (35). How important did Job think he was in God's sight? Can his sin or his righteousness affect God? That was only pride on Job's part (vv. 12–13). But Job *was* important to God, so much so that God and Satan had a discussion in heaven about him!

The greatness of God does not mean that He is far from us and unconcerned about us. He is great in His love (Eph. 2:4), mercy (Ps. 86:13), and kindness (Ps. 117:2). He may not immediately take away your trials, but He can give you a song in the night (v. 10; Ps. 42:8; 77:6; 119:62).

❝ *Any man can sing in the day. . . . It is easy to sing when we can read the notes by daylight; but he is the skillful singer who can sing when there is not a ray of light by which to read. . . . Songs in the night come only from God; they are not in the power of man.* **❞**

Charles Haddon Spurgeon

JOB 36—37

Elihu criticized Job for questioning God, but he did not judge himself for speaking "on God's behalf." What pride that any man should claim to have "perfect knowledge" and be able to serve as God's spokesman and defender! The apostle Paul had been to heaven and back, and had learned great mysteries, yet he never made claims like that (Rom. 11:33–36). No matter how smart you think you are, you never know enough to "play God" in somebody's life.

"Behold, God is mighty" (36:5–21) in power and understanding. He blesses the obedient but judges the ungodly and the hypocrite. (We have heard that someplace before.)

"Behold, God is exalted" (36:22–25), and no one can teach Him what is right or accuse Him of doing what is wrong. He is sovereign in all that He does.

"Behold, God is great" (36:26—37:24), and we cannot know

Him. (But Elihu claimed to be the spokesman for God!) A storm may have been brewing about that time, and Elihu used it as an example of God's greatness: the water cycle (36:27–28), the clouds, the thunder and lightning. The thunder is God's voice (37:2–5), and the weather is His servant.

How should we respond to the evidences of God's greatness in nature? We should see the majesty of God, thank Him for His provision, and obey and fear Him. But Job knew all this before Elihu was born! Nature does reveal the greatness of God; but it is in Jesus Christ that we see the grace of God, and grace meets our needs.

The Creator and His Creation

When Jesus spoke about nature, He usually emphasized the nearness of God and His care for His people. The Father knows the price of the sparrows, and He observes when they fall to the earth (Matt. 10:29–30). He feeds the birds, even though they never sow or reap (Matt. 6:25–27), and He makes the flowers beautiful, even though they last such a short time (Matt. 6:28–34). We are more valuable to God than the sparrows are, and we live much longer than the flowers, so surely the Father will care for us. Today, God's creation is in travail because of sin (Rom. 8:22); but the Creator is our Father, and we can trust Him to care for us.

JOB 38—39

The storm finally broke on the five men seated on the ash heap, and God spoke to Job out of the storm. We do not enjoy it when the storm comes, but if we listen for His voice, the storm will accomplish good things in our lives. When the storm was over, Job was ready to meet God and help his friends.

God's Word is light (Ps. 119:105, 130), but too often our words bring darkness. Words without knowledge are like lamps that shed darkness instead of light and only make the situation worse. Elihu recognized this in Job's speeches (34:35; 35:16), but Job did not recognize it. Be sure your words are true; otherwise, you will find yourself in the darkness. (See 1 John 1:5-10 and note the repeated phrase "if we say.")

Job claimed to know a great deal about God (27:11), so God examined him on several subjects: creation (38:4-11), the regulating of nature (38:12-30), the stars and clouds in the heavens (38:31-38), and the ways of the animals and birds (38:39—39:30). Needless to say, Job failed the examination—and so would you and I.

The problems of life are solved not by *reasons* but by *relationships*. Job wanted to reason with God, but what he really needed was to rest in God. Job saw God's greatness and his own littleness, and that was the turning point. However, the smaller we are in our own eyes, the greater God makes us in His sight.

"*I had a million questions to ask God: but when I met Him, they all fled my mind; and it didn't seem to matter.***"**

Christopher Morley

JOB 40—41

God finally gave Job the one thing he wanted most, the opportunity to meet Him in court and defend his case. Suppose God gave you the same opportunity. What would you say to Him? Would you rather meet God in court or at the throne of grace? The more you meet Him at the throne of grace, the less interested you will be to meet Him in court.

But Job had nothing much to say! He saw himself as insignificant and ignorant and totally unable to face God. The revelation of God completely stopped his mouth. But when we are silent, we can hear God's voice better, even if we are in a storm.

God asked Job many humbling questions, but they can be summarized in these three: (1) "Are you My equal?" (40:6–14); (2) "Can you explain the behemoth?" (40:15–24); (3) "Can you control Leviathan?" (chap. 41). The behemoth was probably the hippopotamus and the Leviathan the crocodile. Job certainly would be afraid to fight these two creatures, *but he was not afraid to challenge God, their Creator!* Job could not control them, but he wanted to tell God what to do!

God made each living thing, including man, suited to its environment and task. But man is not content to be the creature: he wants to be the Creator (Rom. 1:25); and that is Satan's promise to him if he will disobey God (Gen. 3:5). The next time you hear that invitation from Satan, look at God's creation and remember that you are not God.

The Value of Silence

God cannot do much for us as long as we are busy telling Him what to do. He must shut our mouths, as He did with Job (40:4), Moses (Deut. 3:26), and David (Ps. 39:9). The lost sinner's mouth must be stopped (Matt. 22:12; Rom. 3:19). One day, the whole earth will be silent before the glory of the Lord (Hab. 2:20).

JOB 42

Job the sinner. Job had said some rash things during this discussion, but unlike his friends, he had spoken the truth about God (v. 7). Job had a new understanding of God's power and purpose (v. 2), and he realized that he had to repent. Job's sufferings gave him a new vision of himself and of the glory and greatness of God (Heb. 12:11).

Job the servant. Four times in verses 7–8, God called Job "My servant." Although he had weaknesses and failures, *Job served God during his time of suffering.* By maintaining his faith in God in spite of trials, Job unknowingly silenced the devil and revealed to the world that God is worthy of our trust and worship, no matter how much He allows us to suffer. In the will of God, trials work *for* us, not *against* us (Rom. 8:28; 2 Cor. 4:16–18); therefore, we can work for God as we suffer. Suffering can be a ministry.

Job the intercessor. The friends had said some unkind things *to* Job and some terrible things *about* Job, *yet he forgave them and prayed for them.* The friends had to do what they admonished Job to do: confess their sins and repent. Do you pray for people who have wronged you (Matt. 5:43–48)? Do you pray for condemnation or restoration?

Job the receiver. Job had wanted to go to court and argue law, but instead he went to the altar and experienced grace. He received forgiveness, friends, family, wealth and honor, twice as much as he had before. God does not guarantee this kind of happy ending *in this life* to everybody who goes through trials (Heb. 11:36–40), but He does promise to reward all who are true to Him (Rev. 2:10). Job came out of the furnace a better person (Job 23:10), and so can you if you will trust God and let Him have His way.

The Trials of Job

If you feel your sufferings are beyond what anybody else has experienced, consider Job's trials. He was shot at like an enemy (6:4; 16:12–13), hunted like a wild animal (10:16), covered by darkness (19:8), uprooted like a tree (19:10), and put into a furnace (23:10). His wife discouraged him, his three friends attacked him and the Lord seemed to abandon him. However, the greatest example of endurance in suffering is the Lord Jesus (Heb. 12:1–3). He was forsaken even by the Father and suffered the shameful death of the cross. He was made sin for us, yet He was sinless. There was no cause of suffering or death in Him, yet He willingly yielded to the Father's will. He endured, He conquered, and we can conquer in and through Him. Job's suffering makes it clear that God is worthy of our obedience—no matter what "profit" or "loss" may come from obeying Him. God is not obligated to make the righteous healthy and rich or the wicked sick and poor. Our Lord's death and resurrection make it possible for God to transform our suffering into glory, not simply replace it with glory. Job's suffering was replaced with earthly glory, but the believer's suffering will be transformed into heavenly glory. Therefore, our sufferings are not in vain, for the Lord is working out His glorious purposes.

PSALMS

◆

This book is the hymnal of the Bible. The word *psalm* comes from a Greek word that means "a poem sung to musical accompaniment." Many psalms were sung in the Jewish temple, and the New Testament church also used psalms in worship (1 Cor. 14:26; Eph. 5:19; Col. 3:16). Some of the church's hymns and praise songs today are based on these inspired poems.

The psalms express man's praise to God for who He is and what He does. They also express man's need of God in times of trial and his confidence that God will help. You will find in the psalms a full range of human emotions, from ecstatic joy to despair and contrition. You will also find a revelation of God that brings comfort and encouragement when you trust Him.

That explains why the book of Psalms is so greatly beloved by God's people, for each of us can identify with the writers as they found God's grace sufficient in the experiences of life. No matter what your circumstances or feelings may be, there is a psalm that perfectly fits your situation.

The book is divided into five sections, each one ending with a doxology: (1) Psalms 1—41; (2) Psalms 42—72; (3) Psalms 73—89; (4) Psalms 90—106; and (5) Psalms 107—50.

Where to Look in the Psalms

When you cannot sleep	*Pss. 3—4*
When you have sinned	*Pss. 32; 51*
When you are ill	*Ps. 31*
When you need God's guidance	*Ps. 25*
When you are traveling	*Ps. 121*

When people create problems	Ps. 37
When you are downcast	Pss. 42—43
When sinners seem to succeed	Ps. 73
When you are afraid	Pss. 27; 91
When you "feel old"	Ps. 102
When you worry about the future	Ps. 34
When you think about death	Ps. 116
When you are in deep waters	Pss. 124; 130
When problems seem bigger than God	Ps. 139
When you just want to praise Him	Ps. 103

Jesus Christ in the Psalms (Luke 24:44)

The King	Ps. 2 with Acts 4:25–26; 13:33; Ps.118:26 with Matt. 21:9
The Son of man	Ps. 8; Heb. 2:6–11
The Resurrection	Ps. 16 with Acts 2:25–31; Ps. 22:21–31 with Heb. 2:12
The Crucifixion	Ps. 22:1–21; Matt. 27:35–46
The Shepherd	Ps. 23; John 10
The sacrifice for our sins	Ps. 40:6–8; Heb. 10:1–10
Judas's betrayal	Ps. 41:9; John 13:18–19
The royal Bridegroom	Ps. 45; Heb. 1:8–9
The Ascension	Ps. 68:18; Eph. 4:7–16
The rejection	Ps. 69:4 with John 15:25; Ps. 69:8 with John 7:3–5; Ps. 69:9 with John 2:17 and Rom. 15:3

The eternal Son	Ps. 102:25–27; Heb. 1:10–12
The divine King-Priest	Ps. 110; Matt. 22:41–45; Acts 2:34–35; Heb. 1:13; 7:17–21; 10:12–13
The Stone	Ps. 118:22–23 with Matt. 21:42

PSALM 1

Blessing (vv. 1–3). God enjoys blessing your life, but you must be "blessable." That means having *discernment* (v. 1), avoiding the steps that lead to sin: considering sin (walking), contemplating sin (standing), being comfortable in sin (sitting). Watch that first step!

Blessing involves *delight* (v. 2). The Word guides your walk and rejoices your heart (Jer. 15:16). Meditation is to your inner person what digestion is to your body: you make the Word a part of your life and you grow.

Blessing involves *dependence* (v. 3). Your spiritual roots go deep into the resources of God's grace, and you bear fruit because His life is at work in you.

Perishing (4–6). How tragic that anyone is perishing when Jesus offers abundant life! Contrast *tree* and *chaff* if you want to see the difference between the godly and the ungodly. The godly receive blessing but the ungodly receive judgment.

The psalm starts with "blessed" and ends with "perish." The choice is yours.

Psalms and Hymns

Some of our best-loved songs are based on psalms.

TITLE	COMPOSER	PSALM
"A Mighty Fortress"	Luther	Ps. 46
"O God, Our Help in Ages Past"	Watts	Ps. 90

TITLE	COMPOSER	PSALM
"The King of Love My Shepherd Is"	Baker	Ps. 23
"Joy to the World"	Watts	Ps. 98
"Ivory Palaces"	Barraclough	Ps. 45
"O Worship the King"	Grant	Ps. 104
"All People That on Earth Do Dwell"	Kethe	Ps. 100
"Praise, My Soul, the King of Heaven"	Lyte	Ps. 103
"Glorious Things of Thee Are Spoken"	Newton	Ps. 87
"Under His Wings"	Cushing	Ps. 91

PSALM 2

God hears (1–3). He hears the raging of the nations and the plots of the rulers. What do they want? *Freedom from God!* But the way to real freedom is by submission and not by rebellion. To throw off God's will is to invite bondage and destruction.

God laughs (4). Puny man does not worry God with all his noise and threats. God is on His throne and has everything in control. When the world's noise frightens you, turn to the Lord and let Him take over (Acts 4:23–31).

God speaks (5–12). God the Father announces that His King is enthroned in the heavenly Zion where the nations cannot touch Him. God the Son announces that the nations are His, so their rebellion is futile (vv. 7–9). Finally, God the Spirit invites the rebels to submit and be blessed instead of destroyed (vv. 10–12).

Over the noise of the nations, listen for the assuring voice of God.

PSALM 3

If worry keeps you from getting a good night's sleep, Psalms 3 and 4 are what you need. Both psalms were probably written when David was exiled from Jerusalem because his son Absalom had stolen the kingdom (2 Sam. 15—18). Psalm 3 is a morning psalm (v. 5), and Psalm 4 is an evening psalm (v. 8).

How was David able to sleep when he was in such danger? The enemy was against him (vv. 1, 6) but David knew that God was for him. God surrounds you (v. 3), sustains you (v. 5), and saves you (v. 7). When people discourage you (v. 2), God lifts up your head and keeps you going (v. 3).

God never sleeps (Ps. 121:3-4), so why should you stay awake and worry?

> **❝**If you can't sleep, don't count sheep—talk to the Shepherd!**❞**

PSALM 4

David wrote this psalm as he was about to retire for the night (v. 8). He could not do much about the war around him, but he could do something about the war within him. He did not want to lie in bed and worry, so he committed himself and his situation to the Lord.

He asked (1-3). Asking the Lord for help is still a good way to deal with inner turmoil (Phil. 4:6-7).

He believed (4-5). He faced his anger honestly and gave it to the Lord (Eph. 4:26). Instead of lying in bed and thinking about your problems, meditate on the Lord and offer Him sacrifices of praise.

He received (6-8). In the darkness, he saw the face of God and received light. In his sorrow, he discovered the gift of gladness. In the time of battle, he received peace. God did not immediately change the situation, but He did change David; He can do the same for you.

PSALM 5

When he served in King Saul's court, David was often attacked by some of Saul's officers who flattered the king and lied about David (vv. 4–6, 9). King Saul actually believed that David was trying to steal the throne. When people lie about you, follow David's example and pray about the matter. Note his requests.

Hear me (1–6). David began the day with his heart lifted up to God. God knew the sinful words of the liars, but He also heard the believing prayers of His servant.

Lead me (7–8). David had to be careful because Saul and his leaders were watching him and his life was in danger. He worshiped God and asked for God's daily direction.

Protect me (9–10). David did not fight Saul or Saul's men; he left those battles to the Lord. He trusted God to care for him, and God did not fail.

Bless me (11–12). Protection is the last thing named (v. 12). Beyond that, David was blessed with joy, confidence, and a deeper love for the Lord. Times of suffering can be times of growing if we let the Lord have His way.

PSALM 6

This psalm grew out of an experience of sickness and pain, when David thought he was going to die. Besides that, he had to put up with the attacks of his enemies who *wanted* him to die. It was a time of deep discouragement for David, but he did not waver in his faith.

The Penitential Psalms

Psalms 6, 32, 38, 51, 102, 130, and 143 are known as "The Penitential Psalms." You may use these psalms as your own prayers when you want to confess sin and ask for God's forgiveness (1 John 1:9).

As he prayed, he asked for mercy for his body (vv. 1–2) and his soul (vv. 3–5). Mercy means that God does not give us what we deserve, and grace means that He gives us what we do not deserve. What a loving God He is!

David reminded God of his tears of repentance and confession (vv. 6–7). His bed should have been a place of rest, but it had become a place of trial as God chastened him.

But there is a happy ending: David was assured and his enemies were ashamed (vv. 8–10)! God heard and answered his prayers! When the night is dark and long, keep on trusting, and the dawn will come in God's good time.

PSALM 7

We do not know what Cush said about David, but apparently he was one of the "court liars" who flattered Saul and made life difficult for David (1 Sam. 24:9). When you have a "Cush" in your life, do what David did.

Be honest with God (1–5). David did not say that the enemy was telling the truth, but he was willing for God to examine him and punish him. He had nothing to hide.

Let God be the judge (6–13). It is wise to let God be the judge because His judgment is always right (1 Cor. 4:3–5). We do not see ourselves and others as He sees, so it is best to turn the matter over to Him. David was careful to maintain his integrity (v. 8) and let God be his defense (v. 10).

Wait on the Lord (14–16). Sin has a way of bringing its own punishment if we wait long enough. It is like giving birth to pain and trouble (v. 14; James 1:14–15), falling into a pit (v. 15), or getting back the trouble that they tried to impose on others (v. 16).

Give God thanks (v. 17). What does it matter that men slander us, so long as the righteousness of God prevails and the name of the Lord is glorified!

PSALM 8

The universe is vast and full of grandeur, so why should God pay any attention to weak and insignificant men and women? *But He does!* He can use the weakness of babes to reveal His great strength (Matt. 21:16) and to defeat the enemy (the way David defeated Goliath [1 Sam. 17]). If He can use infants, surely He can use anybody.

You are important because God made you in His image (v. 5; Gen. 1:26–28). Sin has marred that image, but in Jesus Christ, that image can be restored (2 Cor. 3:18; Col. 3:10).

You are important because God has shared His dominion with you (vv. 6–8). Man lost that dominion when he sinned, but Jesus Christ has regained it (Heb. 2:6–8). Can you think of occasions when Jesus Christ proved that He had dominion over beasts, birds, and fish?

Yes, you are important to God, and He has a purpose for you to fulfill. He wants you to "reign in life" through His Son (Rom. 5:17), for you are enthroned in the heavenlies with Him (Eph. 2:6). Why live like a slave when you can live like a sovereign?

PSALM 9

Praise (1–6). God had won a victory for David, so he sang a song of praise to the Lord. It was not a personal battle. Because David was doing *God's* will, the Lord maintained his cause. Take time to praise the Lord for the victories He graciously gives you.

Promise (7–12). David looked ahead to the time when God would finally judge sin and establish His righteous kingdom. His people do not need to worry: He is their Refuge and will never forsake them (Heb. 13:5). The Father forsook His Son on the cross, but He will not forsake you.

Prayer (13–20). From considering the past and the future, David turned to his present need as he prayed for God's help. His need was for mercy; his motive was that he might praise the Lord and tell others of His salvation. Why? Because there is a place called hell (v. 17) and God's salvation is the only escape from that terrible place.

Paul advised, "Knowing, therefore, the terror of the Lord, we persuade men" (2 Cor. 5:11).

❝*The safest road to hell is the gradual one—the gentle slope, soft underfoot, without sudden turnings, without milestones, without signposts.*❞

C. S. Lewis

PSALM 10

Does God hide (1–4)? "Why do the wicked prosper?" is a perennial question God's people ask. As they consider the suffering of the godly and the security of the ungodly, they feel that God has forgotten and forsaken His people. He is hiding.

Does God hear (5–13)? Note the repetition of "He has said in his heart" (vv. 6, 11, 13). God hears what the ungodly say and does not approve of their pride and rebellion. The ungodly announces, "I shall not be moved! God does not see what I do! Even if He does, He will never judge me!" What arrogance!

Does God help (14–18)? Of course He does! He sees the trouble of His people, feels their grief, and helps them in the right way at the right time. After all, the Lord is King! It may look as though the ungodly are winning the day, but the Lord will triumph in the end.

PSALM 11

David was in great difficulty. Around him, the archers were getting ready to shoot. Under him, the foundations of society were shaking. What should he do? What would you do?

When you are in that kind of situation, your first thought may be to get away as fast as you can. Even David's friends advised him to act like the bird and fly away. It is right to flee from temptation (Gen. 39:11–13) but not from duty (Neh. 6:10–11; Luke 13:31; John 10:12–13). Instead of flying away like a frightened bird, you should trust God and "mount up with wings like eagles" (Isa. 40:31).

If the foundations are destroyed, *lay the foundations again.* That is what Ezra did (Ezra 3:8ff.) and what each new generation may have to do. David became king of Israel and laid the foundations for a godly society. After all, God is still on His throne (v. 4) and will one day judge the wicked (vv. 5–6). If you love righteousness, God is on your side (v. 7).

"*It is always too soon to quit.***"**

V. Raymond Edman

PSALM 12

David's words (1–2). In the previous psalm, David saw the *foundations* failing; in this one, the *faithful* were vanishing from the earth (v. 1). The godly remnant was getting smaller and smaller, and David was feeling very much alone. No wonder he cried out, "Help, Lord!"

Man's words (3–5). What made David conclude that godliness was on the decline? *The way people spoke.* David heard flattering words, proud words, and oppressive words, and he knew that God was displeased. In our "age of communication," are you able to discern what is true and right? When you speak, is it communication or manipulation?

God's words (6–8). God's Word is pure, proved, and preserved, and you can depend on it. So much of what man says is cheap and temporary, but God's Word is like pure silver that is valuable and lasting. Let your words be controlled by His Word and God will make your words valuable (Prov. 10:20; 25:11).

PSALM 13

Asking (1–2). Four times David asked, "How long?" He had prayed, but God had hidden Himself and not answered. David had examined his heart and knew of no reason why God should abandon him. The longer God waited, the more the enemy would succeed. When you have this same feeling, do what David did and talk to God with an honest and humble heart.

❝It is faith's work to claim and challenge lovingkindness out of all the roughest strokes of God.**❞**

Samuel Rutherford

Arguing (3–4). Would God be glorified by David's defeat? Would God's cause be helped by David's death? Should the enemy rejoice while God's people suffer? David reasoned with God but did not try to tell God what to do. Sometimes prayer means wrestling.

Affirming (5–6). Faith does not always give answers, but it does give encouragement. No matter how successful the enemy appears to be, you can trust the Lord, rejoice in the Lord, sing to the Lord and know that He will always deal bountifully with you.

Don't Despair

"How long?" is a question frequently asked in the Psalms: 6:3; 35:17; 74:10; 79:5; 80:4; 82:2; 89:46; 90:13; and 94:3. Time seems to rush by when we are enjoying life but to linger when we are suffering. God knows how long our trials should last because He knows exactly what we need (1 Pet. 1:6–8).

PSALM 14

The contrast is between the generation of the wicked and the generation of the righteous (v. 5). The latter group is made up of those who have trusted the Lord and seek Him and His will (Ps. 24:6).

The generation of the wicked is composed of people who are "practical atheists": God is not in their hearts, no matter what they may say and do outwardly. They can live without God! They disobey God and exploit people made in the image of God. They are corrupt (v. 1), and so they do corrupt things.

The generation of the righteous calls on the Lord and He answers (v. 4). God dwells with these people (v. 5), protects them (v. 6), and gives them joyful hope (v. 7). The group may not be large, but it is precious to God; and the future of God's program rests with it.

Of which group are you a member? Have you made your allegiance known?

PSALM 15

David loved God's house and longed to dwell there and fellowship with God (Ps. 27:4–5). He yearned to be like the priests who lived in the tabernacle and had constant access to holy things. David wished he could even be a guest and pay God a visit, but did he qualify? Does anybody qualify?

God's children have open access into His presence through the work of Jesus Christ (Heb. 10:19–25). He is our High Priest and Advocate in heaven, and He welcomes us. We come on the basis of His righteousness, not our own. But we had better be sure we have experienced the cleansing of Hebrews 10:22 before we rush into His presence.

This psalm helps us examine our walk, our works, and our words (v. 2). The inventory includes our relationship with others (vv. 3–4), how we keep our promises, and how we use our money (v. 5). Meditating on this psalm and pondering these "qualifications" could help us deepen our relationship with God.

PSALM 16

You have taken a giant step toward true Christian maturity when you can say to the Lord *and mean it,* "My goodness is nothing apart from You" (v. 2).

Good fellowship (3–4). God's people are not perfect, but we should delight in their fellowship and not in the fellowship of the world's crowd (2 Cor. 6:14–18). The world needs our witness, but we must take care not to start loving the world (1 John 2:15–17).

Good heritage (5–6). Not just God's gifts, but God Himself! What a joy it is to let God choose your inheritance for you instead of acting like the world and fighting for your "place in the sun."

Good counsel (7–8). God gives wisdom if you will ask Him (James 1:5). God teaches you in the darkness as well as in the light. These verses are summarized in Matthew 6:33.

Good hope (9–11). This passage is one of the few in the Old Testament dealing with resurrection. It refers to the resurrection of Christ (Acts 2:22–32), and that is what gives us our hope (1 Pet. 1:3).

PSALM 17

"God is Spirit" (John 4:24) and therefore does not have a body. Sometimes Scripture uses the parts of the human body to describe God's activities with respect to His people. He does not have eyes, but He sees us; He does not have ears, but He hears our cries. David referred to four of these in this psalm.

God's ears (1–2). The enemy opposed David's just cause, so he cried out to God for vindication. David's prayer was sincere, and he wanted God to judge righteously.

God's eyes (3–5). David had nothing to hide. His heart was right and his walk was righteous. You must be able to say the same of your heart and walk if you expect God to answer your prayers (Ps. 66:18).

God's hand (6–14). David trusted not his own hand but the hand of God to protect him and to defeat the enemy. The pride of the enemy grieved David because he wanted God alone to be glorified.

God's likeness (15). God has in mind this goal when He permits you to go through trials: He wants to make you more like His Son (Rom. 8:29; 2 Cor. 3:18). Although this verse may refer to future resurrection (1 John 3:1–3; see also 1 Cor. 15:49), it can be applied to life today. Our Lord goes with us into the furnace so that we may be more like Him when we come out of it (Dan. 3:19–25).

PSALM 18

David sang this song after God delivered him from his enemies and established him as the king of Israel. (See the comments on 2 Sam. 22.) But keep in mind that he often sang to God in the midst of his trials. It is easier to sing after the victory; it takes faith to sing *during* the battle. As David looked back on those difficult years, what did he see?

God's faithfulness (1–3). God saved David, protected him, and strengthened him when Saul and his men were out to kill him. Is God your refuge and your strength (Ps. 46:1)?

God's righteousness (4–27). Those had been stormy years for David, yet God rescued him and upheld His dedicated servant. David had obeyed God's Word and accomplished God's will, so God rewarded him. When the storms come, remember that God is greater than the storms and will help you see the rainbow.

God's gentleness (28–36). God did many things to make David a great soldier, but His gentleness made David what he was (v. 35). God was doing more than winning wars; He was building character. It humbled David to think that God would condescend to call him, equip him, and help him (Ps. 8:3–5). (See Ps. 113:6; Isa. 57:15–16.)

God's exaltedness (37–50). David did not take credit for his victories; he gave all the glory to the Lord. Whatever David had, God gave it to him; whatever he was, God made him; whatever he did, God enabled him. Blessed be the name of the Lord!

PSALM 19

God reveals Himself in creation (vv. 1–6), in the Scriptures (vv. 7–11), and in your heart as you worship Him (vv. 12–14). To be properly "educated" in spiritual things, you must seek to master three books: the book of nature, the Bible, and the book of humanity. A scientist studies the book of nature and a psychologist the book of human nature, but if they ignore God's Book, their conclusions may be wrong. Keep balanced. All truth is God's truth.

The goal of all study is a knowledge of Jesus Christ and of yourself. Verses 7–11 tell you what the Bible can do for you if only you will read it, meditate on it, and obey it. The better you understand your Bible and obey it, the more you will appreciate God's creation and the better you will understand yourself and others. God's Word is the basic book.

Open each day beholding God's glory in Jesus Christ (v. 1). Enter each day with the devotion of a bridegroom and the determination of an athlete (vv. 4–5). At the end of the day, what you have done will please Him (v. 14).

PSALM 20

A day of trouble (1–3). David was going out to battle, and he and his people gathered to pray. His secret of victory was the name of the Lord (v. 1), the Lord he worshiped sincerely and sacrificially.

A day of triumph (4–6). Again, it is in the name of the Lord that you fight the forces of evil (v. 5). God hears and answers prayer and sends you the help you need.

A day of trust (7–9). David had a great name, but the name of the Lord is much greater. Some people have names that cannot be trusted, but God's name has never failed. Your days of trouble can become days of triumph if you trust in the name of the Lord.

What's in a Name?

In the Bible, names are important because the name represents the person. When somebody had a life-changing experience, the name was often changed. For example, Abram became Abraham and Sarai became Sarah (Gen. 17), and Simon was given the name Peter (John 1:42). The Bible records many names of God, and all of them can be trusted. (See Pss. 9:10; 33:21; 44:5.)

PSALM 21

If Psalm 20 is a prayer before the battle, Psalm 21 is the praise after the victory. Too often we forget to praise God when He answers prayer and gives us what we requested. (See Luke 17:11–19.)

God and the king (1–7). God gave David strength to win the battle and then gave him honor and majesty from the victory. Before the battle, David asked God to spare his life, and God gave him his request. God responded to David's faith by protecting him, and David responded to God's blessings by praising Him. David rejoiced in God's strength and salvation (v. 1) and in His presence with him (v. 6).

God and the enemy (8–12). These were the enemies of God

because they wanted to destroy His people Israel. David fought the Lord's battles, and the Lord gave victory. God kept His promise to Abraham (Gen. 12:1–3).

God and the nation (13). Now the whole congregation praises the Lord. Individual praise in private is important, but we should share the joy with others and let them praise God with us. Praise Ye the Lord!

The Shepherd Psalms

Psalms 22, 23, and 24 are sometimes called the "Shepherd Psalms" because they speak of Jesus Christ in His shepherding ministry. In Psalm 22, the Good Shepherd dies for the sheep (John 10:11). In Psalm 23, the Great Shepherd lives and cares for the sheep (Heb. 13:20–21). In Psalm 24, the Chief Shepherd returns in glory for the sheep (1 Pet. 5:4). If you are one of His sheep, your every need is met as you trust Him and follow His leading.

PSALM 22

Crucifixion (1–21). Because he was a prophet (Acts 2:30), David was able to write about the Messiah centuries before He came. Crucifixion was not a Jewish form of capital punishment, yet David described it accurately. As you read, you see Jesus at Calvary: His cry to the Father (v. 1; Matt. 27:46); the period of darkness (v. 2; Matt. 27:45); the ridicule of the people (vv. 6–8; Matt. 27:39–44); His thirst and pain (vv. 14–15; John 19:28); His pierced hands and feet (v. 16; Luke 24:39); and the gambling for His clothes (v. 18; John 19:23–24). Remember, He endured all of these things for you.

Resurrection (22–26). The Savior is no longer on the cross but is alive and in the midst of His people, leading them in praise for the mighty victory God has won (Heb. 2:11–12). The first day of the week is the memorial to His resurrection, and we follow His example by meeting with God's people and praising the Lord. Resurrection day is victory day!

Coronation (27–31). Christ shares the blessings of Calvary with His church (v. 22), with Israel (v. 23), and with the whole world (vv. 27–31). We must get the message out to every nation that Jesus Christ is Savior and King (v. 27): "The Father has sent the Son as Savior of the world" (1 John 4:14).

PSALM 23

Though Psalm 23 is often read at funerals, its message applies to the days of your life right now (v. 6). The Savior who died for you also lives for you and cares for you, the way a shepherd cares for the sheep (John 10:1–18). If you can say, "The LORD is *my* Shepherd," you can also say, "I shall not want."

The Shepherd feeds us and leads us. Sheep must have grass and water to live, and the shepherd finds those essential elements for them. God meets the everyday needs of your life as you follow Him (Ps. 37:25; Phil. 4:18). Never worry!

If we wander, He seeks us and restores us, as He did with David, Jonah, and Peter. When we need to know which way to go, He shows us the right path and then goes before us to prepare the way. Even in the places of danger, we need not be afraid. (Note the change from "He" in vv. 1–3 to "You" in vv. 4–5.) He is with you!

At the end of the dark valley, He has a special blessing for you: you drink of the refreshing water of life, and you receive the Spirit's anointing. The Shepherd is there to care for every hurt and heal every bruise.

One day, you will look back at your life and see that it was only "goodness and mercy," and that includes the valley experiences. If life is difficult today, just keep following the Shepherd; He will never lead you where He cannot care for you.

PSALM 24

Psalm 22 points to our Lord's grace in dying for us, and Psalm 23 explains His goodness in caring for us. This psalm reveals His glory in coming for us.

Glory in creation (1–2). These verses remind you of Psalms 8 and 19. The world today is in travail because of sin, but the Creator will one day set His creation free (Rom. 8:18–23).

Glory in salvation (3–6). Psalm 15 is a parallel, and both passages emphasize the fact that nobody but the Lord Jesus Christ can meet God's qualifications to live in His holy place. We are all like Jacob, but He is "the God of Jacob" (Ps. 46:7) and will forgive us and let us live with Him forever!

Glory in the kingdom (7–10). These verses may originally have celebrated David's return to Jerusalem from a great victory, but they speak to us of our King of glory. When He rode into Jerusalem, Jesus came in humility and tears (Luke 19:29–44); but when He comes again, it will be in power and great glory (Matt. 24:29ff.).

Your Shepherd is the King of glory!

PSALM 25

This psalm is helpful when you are making decisions and seeking God's will. What kind of people does God guide?

Those who glorify Him (1–2). If you want His will for His glory, He will show you the right path. If you have selfish motives, He may let you have your way, and then you will regret it.

Those who wait (3). You are not wasting time when you wait on the Lord in prayer.

Those who ask (4–5). God wants to show you His ways, teach you His paths, and lead you in His truths. The Word of God and prayer always go together, so spend time in His Word. If you ask Him sincerely, He will answer you clearly.

Those who are clean (6–7, 16–22). Psalm 66:18 applies here, as does 1 John 1:9.

Those who submit (8–15). God does not guide rebels, but He joyfully leads those who fear Him and submit to His will (Ps. 32:8–9). Keep your eyes on the Lord and let Him have His way. He knows where He is going and what He is doing, so follow Him by faith.

The enemy was slandering David again, and he had no way to vindicate himself. Samuel Johnson called slander "the revenge of a coward," and it is. What should you do when people spread lies about you?

"On every level of life from housework to heights of
prayer, in all judgment and all efforts to get
things done, hurry and impatience are
sure marks of the amateur.**"**

Evelyn Underhill

PSALM 26

Examine yourself (1–5). Is your life what it ought to be? Let
God test your mind and heart (Ps. 139:23–24). In your walking,
standing (v. 12), and sitting, are you keeping yourself clean
(Ps. 1:1)? Sometimes God allows the enemy to attack us just to
make us take time for a personal inventory.

Focus on the Lord (6–10). If you look at others, you will be
upset, and if you look at yourself too long, you may get discouraged, *so focus your attention on the Lord*. Match your defects with His perfections and claim what you need from Him.

Keep serving the Lord (11–12). The enemy wants nothing
better than to upset you and get you on a detour (Neh. 6:1–14).
Continue to walk with the Lord and serve Him, come what
may. Bless the Lord and don't complain. God will vindicate
you in His time and in His own way.

"Look at others and be distressed; look at self and be
depressed; look at Jesus and you will be blessed.**"**

Anonymous

PSALM 27

What makes you afraid? Darkness? But the Lord is your
light. Danger? He is also your salvation. Deficiency? He is

your strength. Then why be afraid? See what He does for you.

God saves you (4–6). Because he was not a priest, David could not actually go into the tabernacle, but he could still rest in the Lord and trust Him as his refuge. The New Testament equivalent for this is "Abide in Me" (John 15:1–11). In Him is perfect safety.

God smiles on you (7–10). You must go beyond merely seeking God's help. *Seek His face* (Num. 6:22–27). The smile of God is all you need to overcome the scowls of men.

God shows you the way (11–13). Satan wants to trap you, but the Lord will show you the safe way. Believe His promise and walk by faith. His goodness will be with you.

God strengthens you (1, 14). We need strength for the battle and strength for the journey, and God abundantly provides. Be sure to take time to wait on the Lord (Isa. 40:31). If you run ahead of Him or lag behind, you will be a perfect target for the enemy.

PSALM 28

Requesting (1–5). David's enemies were undermining his reputation and his work, so he turned to the Lord with two special requests: that God would speak to him (vv. 1–2) and that God would save him (vv. 3–5). God speaks to us in answered prayer. "If You are silent," said David, "I might just as well be dead! And if You don't deliver me, You are treating me like the enemy!" Pretty powerful arguments!

Rejoicing (6–9). God heard him and helped him, and He does the same for you today as you trust Him. You can rejoice in the Lord even when you cannot rejoice in yourselves or your circumstances. Trust God to be your strength, your song, and your salvation (Isa. 12:2). He is the faithful Shepherd who can carry both you and your burdens.

PSALM 29

Praise before the storm (1–2). David called on the angels in heaven to ascribe praise to God. You never know when a storm is coming, so be sure you are worshiping Him and giving Him all the glory. The greatest beauty of all is the beauty of holiness, and it comes from worshiping the Lord.

Power in the storm (3–9). First the thunder rolled over the Mediterranean Sea. Then the storm broke and moved across the land. Seven times the storm is called "the voice of the LORD." (See Rev. 10:3–4.) What power there is in a storm! Even the angels shout, "Glory!" as they watch it!

Peace after the storm (10–11). David may have seen a rainbow and remembered God's promise given after the Flood (Gen. 9:8–17). God sat as King at the Flood, and He is still King! No storm is greater than God. If you trust Him, the storm will bring glory to God. If life is stormy just now, worship Him and wait on Him. The storm will pass, and He will give you peace.

"God Moves in a Mysterious Way"

God moves in a mysterious way, His wonders to perform;
He plants His footsteps in the sea, and rides upon the
*   storm.*
Ye fearful saints, fresh courage take; the clouds ye so much
*   dread*
Are big with mercy, and shall break
With blessing on your head.

William Cowper

PSALM 30

In this song of praise (vv. 1, 4, 11–12) David expressed his thanks to God for the changes God sent to his life.

From sickness to health (1–3). God had healed David and lifted him up from the grave. His sickness had been a discipline from God because of David's pride and self-sufficiency (vv. 6–7). Perhaps it was in connection with the sin of numbering the people (1 Chron. 21).

From weeping to joy (4–5). There is a contrast between God's momentary anger and His gift of lasting joy, between weeping and joy, and between the night and the morning. Things may seem dark to you now, but wait for His morning to dawn. He can change everything in a hurry!

From mourning to singing (8–12). David humbled himself before God and begged for help and mercy. When God saw that the discipline had done its work, He healed David and forgave his sins. David changed clothes, picked up his harp, and began to sing praises to the Lord.

No matter how dark the night, dawn will come. No matter how heavy your heart, one day there will be a song. Wait patiently and trust the Lord. "His favor is for life" (v. 5).

"Joys are always on the way to us. They are always traveling to us through the darkness of the night. There is never a night when they are not coming."

Amy Carmichael

PSALM 31

Foes. David's enemies persecuted him, lied about him, and spread a net to catch him. Where could he turn for help? Only to the Lord! If the hand of the enemy is against you (vv. 8, 15), find safety in the hand of the Lord (vv. 5, 15; John 10:27–29). Jesus quoted verse 5 when He was on the cross (Luke 23: 46).

Feelings. David was ill, possibly as the result of his own disobedience (vv. 9–13). God can use enemies and sickness to chasten us and bring us to a place of submission. David's enemies laughed at him and his friends ignored him. All David could do was turn to the Lord for help, and the Lord did not fail him.

Faith. The emphasis is on David's faith in the Lord. Because of his faith, David was not ashamed (v. 1) but rejoiced in God (vv. 6–7) and enjoyed the smile of God upon his life (vv. 14–16; Num. 6:22–27). He knew that God's goodness would carry him through (v. 19).

True faith is never alone, for it leads to love and hope (vv. 23–24), which give you the courage you need to win the battle, whether the foe is within or without.

PSALM 32

This penitential psalm grew out of David's experiences with the Lord after he had committed adultery and had tried to hide his sins (2 Sam. 11—12). When you refuse to confess your sins, the Lord must deal with you to bring you to repentance (Prov. 28:13). The longer you wait, the more miserable you will be, as you can see in David's experience. You must face the following:

The debt against you (1–2). God sees what you do and keeps a record of it. David had covered his sins on earth, but he could not cover the record in heaven. When we confess, God wipes the record clean (1 John 1:9).

The pain within you (3–5). Sin affects the body, and God's disciplines are painful but needful (Heb. 12:1–11). David became like an old man carrying a heavy burden.

The flood around you (6–7). God uses difficult circumstances to bring you back to Himself. In fact, because of his sins, David went through many deep waters with his family.

The road before you (8–9). David was like a stubborn animal that needed to be broken. When you are out of the will of God, your decisions will often create problems instead of solve them. The way gets harder.

David went from silence (v. 3) to singing (v. 7) because he finally was honest with God and confessed his sins (vv. 5–6).

PSALM 33

God's Word in worship (1–5). We dare not separate worship from the Word of God, for we must worship "in truth" (John 4:24). The better we know the Scriptures, the better we will be able to praise Him (Col. 3:16ff.).

God's Word in creation (6–9). God spoke the universe into existence (Gen. 1; John 1:1–3), and His Word controls it (Ps. 147:15–18). What a powerful Word it is!

God's Word in history (10–17). The nations may confederate and rebel against God, but His Word will prevail (Ps. 2).

Military strength is no guarantee of success. God has a plan for the nations, and He will fulfill it (Acts 17:24–28).

God's Word in your life (18–22). The Word that created and controls the universe can also control your life. When you trust His Word and obey it, all the universe works for you. When you abandon that Word, all the universe works against you (Jon. 1).

Never fear the will of God because it comes from the heart of God (v. 11).

" *Blessed are the single-hearted, for they shall enjoy much peace . . . If you refuse to be hurried and pressed, if you stay your soul on God, nothing can keep you from that clearness of spirit which is life and peace. In that stillness you will know what His will is.* **"**

Amy Carmichael

PSALM 34

Fearful that Saul would kill him, David fled to Gath and sought the protection of the enemy (1 Sam. 21:10—22:2). But you are never safe out of the will of God, and David had to lie to escape. This psalm is David's personal testimony of what God did for him.

"I will bless" (1–10). David had every reason to praise the Lord, for the Lord had rescued him from certain death. When you call on the Lord in faith, He saves (vv. 4–6), He keeps (v. 7), and He satisfies (vv. 8–10). Why run to the enemy when you can run to the Lord and be safe?

"I will teach" (11–22). David wanted the next generation to know the Lord and trust Him. He gave some wise counsel about how to have "good days" (vv. 12–14; 1 Pet. 3:8–12), and he urged them to call on the Lord in the time of trouble. God's eyes see your needs, God's ears hear your prayers, and God is near you when your heart is broken.

When God does something special for you, tell somebody else. The next generation needs to know that God is alive.

PSALM 35

Like David, you need God's deliverance from two different enemies.

Those who attack you (1–10). There are places in this world where it is a dangerous thing to be a Christian, and their number may increase. After all, Satan is a murderer (John 8:44) and would destroy all of God's people if he could. But the Lord fights for us. He has effective weapons (vv. 2–3) and knows the enemy's plots (v. 4). If you belong to the Lord, He is responsible to care for you.

Those who accuse you (11–28). Satan is an accuser as well as a murderer (Rev. 12:10), so David had to move from the battlefield to the courtroom where his enemies were lying about him. His prayer changed from "Fight for me!" to "Vindicate me!" (vv. 23–24). But his concern was that God's name, not his own, be magnified (v. 27). When the enemy slanders your name, he attacks the name of the Lord as well.

Note the results: "And my soul shall be joyful" (v. 9); "And my tongue shall speak of Your righteousness" (v. 28). Joy on the inside and witness on the outside!

PSALM 36

Man's wickedness (1–4). David had seen a good deal of life and knew what human nature was like. He knew his own heart as well! But in this psalm, he shared a special oracle that God gave him. The sinner flatters himself that he "gets away" with sin. He lives on lies as he plots against the godly. His words and his works are evil, but that does not bother him.

God's faithfulness (5–7). What a vivid contrast to the unfaithfulness of the sinner! God can be trusted always to do what is right, and the safest place in the world is under His shadow in the Holy of Holies (v. 7).

The believer's blessedness (8–12). God satisfies His people with the water of life and the light of life. He protects from the enemy and provides for every need. The word "pleasures" in verse 8 is *Eden* in the Hebrew. When you dwell in God, you are in Paradise!

PSALM 37

This psalm shares the wisdom of an old man who had walked with the Lord (v. 25). He had battled with evil men and knew the frustration of seeing the wicked prosper and the righteous suffer. As he reviewed the past, he gave some wise counsel to keep us from fretting against the Lord when things are not going the way we want them to go.

"Trust in the LORD" (3). If you walk by sight and not by faith, you will find it easy to fret. (See Ps. 73.) The wicked seem to be prospering, but they will not last (vv. 35–36). Believe what God says in His Word because that is where you find reality.

"Delight in the LORD" (4). Find all your joy and pleasure in His will. Make Him your delight, and your desires will be in His will. Living to please the Lord sets you free from fretting about what men are doing.

"Commit your way to the LORD" (5). When you trust Him and delight in Him, how could you do anything other than commit your way to Him? Let God guide your steps, choose your joys, protect your name, and bless your work.

❝'Rest in the Lord; wait patiently for Him.' In Hebrew, 'Be silent to God and let Him mold thee.' Keep still and He will mold thee to the right shape.**❞**

Martin Luther

"Rest in the LORD" (7). Restlessness is an evidence of unbelief. Faith rests in the Lord and enjoys "the peace of God, which surpasses all understanding" (Phil. 4:7). God sometimes waits in answering prayer so that He might strengthen our patience (James 1:2–8).

"Wait on the LORD" (34). For what are you waiting? *The inheritance God has for you* (vv. 11, 18, 22, 29, 34). The wicked

have only temporary pleasure on earth, but God's people have eternal treasure in heaven. You will one day receive your inheritance, so be patient.

PSALM 38

This is the third of the Penitential Psalms (cf. Ps. 6), and it reveals what happens to you when you sin.

What God does (1–2). God loves you too much to allow you to sin and get away with it. If you disobey, He will first rebuke you and then chasten you. He will shoot His arrows from a distance or come closer and put His hand on you, but He will let you know that He is displeased.

What sin does (3–10). David suffered from sickness because of his sin (Ps. 32:3–5). He carried a heavy burden and was crushed under it. He sighed and panted and was ready to quit. Sin comes as a friend to entice you and then becomes a master to enslave you.

What people do (11–14). Sin puts a wall between you and those who can help you, but it builds a bridge between you and those who want to exploit you and hurt you.

What Happens to Sins

When you trust Christ, what does God do with your sins? He takes them away (John 1:29); forgets them (Heb. 10:17); washes them away (Isa. 1:18); blots them out (Isa. 43:25); wipes them out like a cloud (Isa. 44:22); pardons them (Isa. 55:7); and buries them in the depths of the sea (Mic. 7:19).

What the sinner must do (15–22). The only hope is to confess sin and cry out to God for mercy. He promises to forgive, so claim His promise.

PSALM 39

God's silence to David. David had sinned, and God was correcting him. Chastening is a sign of God's love (Heb. 12:5–11), so submit to His will and let Him have His way. God had been silent to David (v. 12), and that worried him. Was he going to die (Ps. 28:1)?

David's silence to God. David was silent before the Lord and did not argue with Him (v. 9; see also Lev. 10:3; 1 Sam. 3:18). David accepted God's will and submitted meekly. He prayed that God would forgive him and help him, and God answered in His mercy.

David's silence before the wicked. When wicked men came to visit him in his sickness, David tried to be silent before them (Matt. 7:6). But he finally had to speak and remind himself and them that man was frail and life was short. Life is only a handbreadth long, a vapor that comes and goes (James 4:14) and a mere shadow. We are strangers and sojourners (v. 12), and the journey is not a long one. Why gather riches when you cannot take them with you when you go?

Silence sometimes is louder than speech. Know when to speak and when to be silent.

PSALM 40

Waiting (1–3). While experiencing trials at the hands of his enemies, David asked God for help, but the answer did not come immediately. He waited—and then God worked! What a change took place: David went from a pit to a highway, from miry clay to a rock, and from crying to singing!

Witnessing (4–10). When God does a great thing for you, share it with others. God's works and thoughts ought to be a part of your daily conversation. Share the good news by what you say and do. God can use your witness to bring others to Himself (v. 3).

Warring (11–15). So often David found himself surrounded by danger, and all he could do was turn to the Lord for help. You may not be battling against armies, but you are part of a spiritual warfare that demands diligence and devotion (Eph. 6:10ff.).

Worshiping (16–17). No matter what the problem, David took time to worship the Lord. When you do this, it helps to put things into perspective, and you see what God is doing for you. The important thing is that God is magnified. You may get impatient with Him, but He thinks about you and is working everything together for your good (Jer. 29:11).

The Ultimate Sacrifice

Psalm 40:6–8 is quoted in Hebrews 10:1–14 as referring to Jesus Christ. He came to hear God's will (the open ear [Isa. 50:4–6]) and to do God's work (the prepared body). His body was prepared in Mary's womb by the Holy Spirit (Luke 1:26–38; see also Isa. 7:14). Jesus delighted to do the Father's will because the Word was in His heart (John 4:34; 8:29). If you delight in God's Word, you will delight in God's will (Ps. 1:1–3). Jesus Christ is the sacrifice for sins that God has appointed, and in His death, He fulfilled the Old Testament sacrifices. His one sacrifice has settled the sin question once and for all—forever.

PSALM 41

As David lay sick, he *looked back* and recalled that he had been merciful to others and had helped the poor. This encouraged him, for he knew that God would help him (Deut. 15:1–11). God is merciful to those who show mercy to others (Matt. 5:7). When you are in pain, it is good to have a clear conscience to encourage you.

Then David *looked around* and saw that his enemies were gossiping about him and wishing he were dead. Even his close friend turned against him. If this happens to you, keep in mind that it also happened to Jesus (John 13:18). Greater than the pain of sickness is the pain of having a treacherous "friend."

Finally, David *looked up,* and that solved his problems. No matter what others might say, God was well pleased with David, and that was all that mattered. Let David's enemies spread their gossip. God would raise him up, hold him up, and brighten him up with the light of His countenance.

Sometimes, how you feel depends on where you look.

PSALMS 42—43

The refrain "Why are you cast down, O my soul?" ties these two psalms together (42:5, 11; 43:5). Why was the writer so depressed?

For one thing, God seemed far from him in his hour of need (42:1–3). He felt like a thirsty deer in the desert, searching for water. But the Lord is never far away; He is near even when you do not recognize Him (Isa. 41:10; Heb. 13:5; Ps. 46:7).

The writer's depression was aggravated because he looked back at "the good old days" (42:4–6). He longed to return to Jerusalem and minister in the temple. Sometimes retirement or a change of residence will make people depressed. The older we get, the less we enjoy change.

"When a man gets to despair he knows that all his thinking will never get him out. He will only get out by the sheer creative effort of God. Consequently he is in the right attitude to receive from God that which he cannot gain for himself."

Oswald Chambers

The discouraging talk of others was a third contributing factor (42:3, 9–10): "Has God forgotten you? Where is your

God?" The answer is in Psalm 115. Listen to God and not to the foolish talk of men.

What should you do when depression starts to control you? "Hope in God" (42:5, 11; 43:5). Look at the future and not at the past. If you feel drowned by circumstances, keep in mind that they are *His* waves and billows (42:7), and He knows what is best for you. Stop feeding on your feelings (42:3) and start feeding on His Word (43:3). God will guard you and guide you, no matter how miserable you may feel. God is greater than your feelings. Walk by faith and He will see you through.

PSALM 44

The nation was facing a crisis, and it seemed that God had forsaken His people and was helping the enemy (vv. 9–16). Israel was a scattered people, shamed and scorned. What do you do when it looks like God is on the side of the enemy?

You remember what God did (1–3). This does not mean living in the past but learning from the past. Your situation may be painful, but God has not changed. He can still work wonders and glorify His name.

You trust in Him (4–8). If you trust your own resources, you will fail. Sometimes God allows defeat just to remind you that you must trust Him and Him alone.

You remain faithful to Him, come what may (17–26). Remember Satan's lie about Job (Job 1:6–12)? Is yours a "commercial" faith? Are you faithful to God only because He does good things for you? God tests your faith to see if it is sincere (1 Pet. 1:6–9). Trust Him even though you may not fully understand what He is doing (Job 13:15).

PSALM 45

Written for a royal wedding, this psalm is messianic (vv. 6–7; Heb. 1:8–9) and shows us Christ the Royal Bridegroom.

His beauty (1–2). When He was here on earth, Jesus had no special beauty that would attract people (Isa. 53:2). It is the beauty of His character, His words, and His works that makes us love Him (1 Pet. 1:8).

His battles (3–5). He came a Savior, but He was also a warrior and defeated Satan (Matt. 12:25–29; Col. 2:15). He conquers today through His people as we yield to Him and practice truth, humility, and righteousness. One day He will come to conquer all the kingdoms of the world (Rev. 11:15; 19:11–21).

His bounties (6–9). Who else has an eternal throne, a righteous scepter, gladness, and the fragrance of grace and glory? If you know the King, you share all His bounties.

His bride (10–17). This is a picture of the church (Eph. 5:25ff.), all those who have been saved through faith in Christ. The Bridegroom is ready (v. 8), the attendants are ready (v. 9), and the bride is brought to the King with rejoicing. What a wedding that will be (Rev. 19:1–10)! Are you eagerly looking forward to being there?

PSALM 46

Some Bible students believe that this psalm was written in connection with the dramatic deliverance of Jerusalem from the Assyrians (2 Kings 18—20). This song was the inspiration for Martin Luther's "A Mighty Fortress Is Our God," and it can be an inspiration to you today.

When things are changing and threatening around you, focus your attention on God. He is with you (His presence); He is a refuge (His protection); He helps you (His power). Your world may be shaken with convulsions (vv. 2–3), but He has a river to give you peace (v. 4). You may be in the midst of battles, but He will end the war victoriously (vv. 8–9).

"Be still" (v. 10) means "take your hands off, relax." God knows what He is doing, and His timing is perfect (v. 5). When it is all over, He will be exalted (v. 10), and you will be blessed.

Wise Counsel

When you are nervous and fidgety, wanting to interfere with God's plans for your life, remember these three admonitions: "Be still!" (Ps. 46:10); "Stand still!" (Exod. 14:13); and "Sit still!" (Ruth 3:18).

PSALM 47

If you prefer quiet meditative worship, this psalm will challenge you, for it describes a praise celebration that involves hand-clapping, shouting, and loud singing. The cause of this excitement is the greatness of Christ our King. (If that does not excite you, what will? Get excited about these things:

His great victory (1–4). We do not know what military victory the psalmist was celebrating, but as believers today, we walk in Christ's spiritual victory (2 Cor. 2:14). Like Joshua, we submit to our Captain and trust Him to win the battle (Josh. 5:13–15). That is something to shout about!

His great throne (5–7). What a picture of the ascension of our Lord, returning to heaven and sitting at the right hand of God! Satan may be the god of this age, but Jesus is King of all the earth. That is something to shout about!

His great reign (8–9). His kingdom is a spiritual kingdom today, but He still rules in the affairs of men. One day, Christ will reign on earth, and His people shall reign with Him (Rev. 1:5–6; 5:9–10; 11:15–18). That is something to shout about!

PSALM 48

Like Psalm 46, this psalm celebrates God's deliverance of Jerusalem from an invading army (vv. 4–7). To Christian believers, Jerusalem and Mount Zion speak of "the Jerusalem above" (Gal. 4:26) and the heavenly Zion (Heb. 12:18–24) where their citizenship is recorded (Phil. 3:20).

Look at the city (1–8). It is the city of God, the Holy City, beautiful and joyful. But to the enemy who does not know the Lord, it is an awesome place that speaks of judgment. Ponder your heavenly destiny so that you may live a happier and holier life.

Enjoy the city (9–11). It is a place of God's loving-kindness and righteousness, where His name is praised and His people rejoice. You are not in the heavenly city yet, but you can still enjoy "the powers of the age to come" (Heb. 6:5). "Little faith will take your soul to heaven," said Charles Spurgeon, "but great faith will bring heaven to your soul."

Celebrate the city (12–14). Tell others what God has prepared for His people and invite them to become citizens of Zion by faith in Christ (Luke 10:20). To know the God of glory is to know a faithful Guide who will care for you in life and take you to Mount Zion when you die. What more could you want?

"If you read history you will find that the Christians who did most for the present world were precisely those who thought most of the next. It is since Christians have largely ceased to think of the other world that they have become so ineffective in this."

C. S. Lewis

PSALM 49

Whether you are rich or poor, this psalm is for you (v. 2) because it deals with two important subjects: death and money. "Do not boast in your wealth or trust in your wealth," wrote the psalmist, and he explained why.

Your wealth cannot prevent death (5–9). When Queen Elizabeth I was dying, she said, "All my possessions for one moment of time." Although money can buy medicine and professional help, it cannot buy God off when the death angel comes to claim you.

Your wealth cannot go with you (10–15). The dead bodies of both men and beasts turn to dust in the grave, and the rich are not exempt from this end. When a believer dies, the spirit goes to be with the Lord (2 Cor. 5:1–8), but you cannot take your wealth with you (v. 17). However, you can send it ahead as you share it with others in the name of the Lord (Matt. 6:19–34).

Your wealth cannot buy permanent fame (16–20). Men praise the rich while they live, honor them when they die (and perhaps hope to inherit something), and then forget them. The rich man can build himself a monument, but he cannot make people remember him.

Verse 15 reveals the believer's assurance of future resurrection (1 Thess. 4:13–18). That is what conquers death and makes life worth living (1 Cor. 15:58; 1 Pet. 1:3).

❝_There are no pockets in shrouds._**❞**

Jewish Proverb

PSALM 50

This psalm describes a courtroom scene. God is judge, witness and jury, and He brings an indictment against two kinds of "religious sinners."

Insincere worshipers (1–15). He calls the court to order, not with the rap of a gavel but with the revelation of His glory (vv. 1–3). He indicts His people who offer sacrifices insincerely—their worship is just empty routine—and hope to "earn" God's blessing. God does not need the things we give Him (Acts 17:24–25), but we need to give Him spiritual sacrifices of thanksgiving, praise, and obedience (vv. 14–15, 23).

❝_For to worship is to quicken the conscience by the holiness of God, to feed the mind with the truth of God, to purge the imagination by the beauty of God, to open the heart to the love of God, to devote the will to the purpose of God._**❞**

William Temple

Hypocritical worshipers (16–22). Here the issue is not sacrifices but the covenant they made with God. They profess one thing and practice another (Titus 1:16); they are guilty of theft, adultery, deceit, and slander. They thought that God's silence meant escape from punishment, but they were wrong (Eccles. 8:11).

Judgment begins with God's people, not with the lost world (1 Pet. 4:17). Heed the warning of verse 22 and accept the admonition of verse 23.

PSALM 51

This is the fourth of the Penitential Psalms. Like Psalm 32, it came out of David's sin with Bathsheba (2 Sam. 11—12) and his futile attempt to cover it up. If any chapter in the Bible reveals the high cost of sinning, it is this one.

Sin hurts the sinner. David's whole being was affected by his sin: his eyes (v. 3), mind (v. 6), ears (v. 8), heart (v. 10), spirit (v. 10), and mouth (vv. 13–15). He lost fellowship with God (v. 11) and the joy of the Lord (v. 12). Are the pleasures of sin worth paying this great price?

Sin hurts others. Sin can bring tragic consequences to the lives of others (James 1:13–16), especially one's family. David's sin led to Uriah's death. Bathsheba's baby died. David's lovely daughter Tamar was violated by her brother Amnon, who was then killed by Absalom, who in turn was slain by Joab. Is a fleeting moment of sinful pleasure worth a lifetime of sorrow?

Sin hurts God. We hurt ourselves and others when we sin, but primarily, our sins are against God (v. 4). Sin makes us dirty (vv. 2, 7). Sin is rebellion against God's holy law. If you want to know how much sin hurts God, go to Calvary and see His Son dying for the sins of the world. God is love, and our selfish sins break His heart.

"How sad it is to have to live with the consequences of forgiven sin**"**

William Culbertson

God is merciful and gracious and forgives when we come in repentance and faith (1 John 1:9). David did not want "cheap" forgiveness; he came with a broken heart.

<table>
<tr><td>

David's Prayer

</td><td>

"Blot out my transgressions" was David's prayer (Ps. 51:1). To see how God answers, read Isaiah 43:25; 44:22; Micah 7:18–19; Acts 3:19; and Hebrews 10:14–18.

</td></tr>
</table>

PSALM 52

Doeg was an evil man who curried favor with King Saul by spying on David (1 Sam. 21—22). When David learned what Doeg had done, he turned to God for help, for God is the only One who can justly deal with our enemies.

The tongue can be a force for good or for evil. Doeg's tongue was boastful, deceitful, and destructive, like a sharp razor (vv. 1–4). David focused on the goodness of God, not the badness of men, because he knew that God's justice would ultimately prevail.

Doeg looked like a strong luxuriant tree, but he would be rooted up (vv. 5–7) while David would be fresh and fruitful (v. 8; Ps. 37:34–38). God protected David's name because David trusted God's name (v. 9). More people call their sons "David" than "Doeg."

PSALM 53

In this adaptation of Psalm 14, "God" (Elohim) is used instead of "Lord" (Jehovah); verse 5 has more words; and verse 6 has fewer words. Some psalms were adapted by the musicians for various uses in the temple worship. One of the wonders of Scripture is that it can be applied to every situation.

What you think concerning God helps to determine your character and conduct. The fool ignores God and exploits people made in the image of God. Many people are "practical atheists"; they may claim to believe there is a God, but they live as though He did not exist. Are you guilty of this?

God will have the last word!

PSALM 54

David had not bothered the Ziphites, yet they turned against him to win favor with King Saul (1 Sam. 23:15–23). The world does not love God's people and even strangers will create problems for you while you seek to serve the Lord.

Do what David did: pray for God to take charge, protect you and vindicate you against your enemies. God hears (v. 2) and God helps (v. 4). When the answer comes, be sure you take time to praise the Lord (v. 6).

PSALM 55

Troubles around him (vv. 1–3), terrors within him (vv. 4–5), and treachery next to him (vv. 12–15, 21) combined to make David wish he could get away from it all (v. 6). It was not easy being God's anointed king, for with the privileges came great burdens and responsibilities, and God's enemies became David's enemies. Leadership is not easy.

David wanted wings like a dove so he could fly *away from* the storm. What he really needed were wings like an eagle so he could fly *above* the storm (Isa. 40:31). How do you get them? By going into the Holy of Holies, under the shadow of His wings (Pss. 57:1; 91:1–4). When you call on the Lord (v. 16) and cast your burdens on Him (v. 22), He enables you to overcome.

You cannot fly beyond the storm because you will find problems everywhere, but you can fly above the storm. God permits the burdens you face today to help you "win your wings." Claim verse 22 and 1 Peter 5:7.

PSALM 56

David prayed this prayer while he was in danger in enemy country (1 Sam. 21:10–15). After God delivered him, he wrote Psalm 34 as an expression of praise. When you are in the midst of trouble, remember these truths about God.

God sees where you are (8a). David should not have been in Gath to begin with, but the Lord was gracious to go with him and help him. God understands your situation far better than you do!

God knows how you feel (8b). He not only knows your tears, but He records them and retains them! Why? So that one day He may transform them into gems of joy and glory. No tears are ever wasted when you follow Him.

God hears when you call (9). Terrors and tears must be handled with trust (vv. 3–4, 10–11). But be sure your motive is not just deliverance. He delivers us that we might delight in Him and serve Him (vv. 12–13). The highest purpose of prayer is the glory of God.

PSALM 57

This psalm and Psalm 142 are "cave" psalms that can give you great encouragement. Your own "cave" may be a sickroom, a difficult place of ministry, or even a home where there is tension or trouble. If you do what David did, you will experience peace and victory even in the cave.

David's faith transformed his cave into a Holy of Holies (v. 1)! His confidence was not in the rocks but "under His wings." (See Ruth 2:12.) In spite of sharp teeth (v. 4), nets and pits (v. 6), David was sure of God's help.

His desire was not just to escape but to exalt the Lord (vv. 5, 11). In fact, when he awakened the next morning, he picked up his harp and sang praises to God!

Trust Him; exalt Him; sing praises to Him. This approach worked for David in his cave, and it will work for you in your cave.

PSALM 58

In words that may seem unchristian to us, David denounced the unjust rulers of his day, people who promoted evil by condemning the righteous and defending the wicked. In a prayer that would probably not be "Amened" in churches today, he asked God to judge sinners and establish righteousness on the earth.

David used many images as he prayed for their judgment: "Make them toothless lions! Let them disappear like water on the sand or like the slime of a snail! Make them broken arrows! Let them be like stillborn children! Let them burn up like fuel under a pot! Let them be taken away in a whirlwind!"

You will find similar passages in other Psalms, such as 35:1–8, 26; 59:11–15; 69:22–28; 109:6–20; and 139:19–22. These verses seem to contradict the admonition of Matthew 5:43–48 and the examples of Luke 23:34 and Acts 7:60. How should today's Christian respond?

Because he was God's chosen king, David's enemies were God's enemies (Ps. 139:21–22). No doubt his personal feelings were involved in these prayers, but his great concern was the righteousness of God and the good of God's people. David had the authority to denounce *national* enemies; we have the privilege of forgiving *personal* enemies.

But you cannot forgive enemies until you realize how wicked their words and deeds are. A holy anger against sin, and a forgiving spirit toward sinners, is the mark of a true child of God. The person who has no concern to oppose wickedness in this world does not know the sinfulness of sin or the holiness of God. That believer needs some backbone!

❝If the Jews cursed more bitterly than the pagans this was, I think, at least in part because they took right and wrong more seriously. For if we look at their railings we find that they are usually angry not simply because these things have been done to them but because these things are manifestly wrong, are hateful to God as well as to the victim.**❞**

C. S. Lewis

One day, God will judge the wicked. When you pray the first three petitions of the Lord's Prayer, you are expressing briefly what David wrote in vivid detail. David left all judgment to the Lord but did his part to further God's holy will on the earth. If more saints today felt a holy anger against sin

(Ps. 4:4; Eph. 4:26), the church might have a more effective ministry as the salt of the earth and the light of the world.

PSALM 59

I will pray (1–7). David compared his enemies to dogs prowling the city streets and growling over the garbage. Saul was after him again (1 Sam. 19:1–11), and only the Lord could deliver David.

I will wait (8–15). David's wife helped him escape that time, but David faced several years of danger and exile before he received his rightful throne. Twice he could have killed Saul, but he refused to do so. He knew that God would deal with his enemies in His way and in His time (1 Sam. 26:8–11).

I will sing (16–17). David had a song in the morning because God gave him joy in the morning (Ps. 30:5). Things often look worse at night, so wait for the morning; God will give you your song of praise.

PSALM 60

Broken (1–3). David and Joab were leading the armies of Israel against two enemies in the north when a third enemy invaded in the south. When you get one problem solved, another one comes along! It seemed that God had abandoned His people and that the end was near.

Bold (4). But David did not run away. Instead, he boldly lifted God's banner of truth and listened for God's word of assurance (vv. 4–8). The Lord is our banner (Exod. 17:8–16), and we can trust Him to give the victory.

Beloved (5). His banner over us is love (Song of Sol. 2:4; Rom. 8:37). The name *David* means "beloved." God's people are beloved not in themselves but in Jesus Christ, the Beloved One (Matt. 3:17; Eph. 1:6). In the midst of life's battles, remember that God loves you.

Believing (6–12). God assured David that He was in control of the nations, so David and Joab stepped out by faith and won both battles. When you feel broken, you are still His beloved. If you believe, you can boldly win the battle. March under God's banner of truth!

PSALM 61

Distance. No matter how far away you go, God hears your prayers, for His ears are open to the cries of His children (Ps. 34:15). David was far from the house of God, yet the Lord heard his prayer and answered.

Depth. No matter how far down you sink, God can lift you up. When life overwhelms you, take time to pray. Let God lift you up and put you on the Rock that will never sink.

Danger. Prayer brings you into the Holy of Holies, under the shadow of His wings (Exod. 25:20), where God's glory dwells. God preserves and protects His own until that hour when He calls them to Himself.

Delight. Do you find delight in prayer, or is prayer only an "emergency exercise" to get you out of trouble? David ended the psalm with an expression of praise and an affirmation of obedience. Prayer changes things, but prayer also changes people, starting with the one who does the praying!

Daily Benefits

When daily we obey God (Ps. 61:8), praise His name (Ps. 72:15), and pray (Ps. 88:9), then daily He shares His benefits (Ps. 88:9).

PSALM 62

Waiting on the Lord (vv. 1, 5) does not mean being idle or indifferent because sometimes waiting is harder than working. For your waiting to be meaningful and spiritually productive, do what David did.

Wait silently (1, 5). This means not telling your trials to everybody who will listen or even telling them repeatedly to the Lord. When a child rests in the arms of the mother or father, there is no need to make noise. Much talk is sometimes evidence of little faith.

Wait expectantly (5). God will work as you trust Him and

let Him have His way. Your hope is not in human or material resources (vv. 9–10) but in the power of God (v. 11).

Wait continually (8). It is not easy to wait "at all times," especially when you feel that God is not following your schedule. If your times are in His hands (Ps. 31:15), you will have perfect peace as you wait for Him to work (Isa. 26:3).

PSALM 63

This psalm probably grew out of David's painful experience during the rebellion led by his son Absalom (2 Sam. 15:13–23). Imagine the king having to leave his comfortable palace and flee to the wilderness to hide! When you find yourself in a "wilderness" situation, take inventory of the things that really are important. David said:

"I still have God" (1–2). The God you worship in the sanctuary is with you in your difficulty. If you hunger and thirst after Him, He will satisfy you (Matt. 5:6).

"I still have a song" (3–4). David could not go to the altar and offer sacrifices to God, but he could lift his hands and his voice as "spiritual sacrifices" (Heb. 13:15). When you praise God, your inner person is nourished (v. 5), and you are satisfied.

"I still have joy in the Lord" (vv. 6–11). If you cannot rejoice in your situation, you can always rejoice in your Savior: His past help (v. 6), His present protection (v. 7), and His future guidance (v. 8). He hides you and holds you, so you have nothing to fear.

PSALM 64

David's fear of the enemy. The king asked to be preserved not from the enemy but from the *fear* of the enemy. Fear and faith cannot live in the same heart (Mark 4:40). If the enemy can make you afraid, he has almost won the battle. A calm heart makes a confident soldier.

The enemy's fear of nothing. They "do not fear" (v. 4) to form secret plans or lead open insurrections. (Absalom's rebellion, perhaps?) Their words are like swords and arrows, and they set hidden traps. It looks like David is defeated!

The fear of the Lord. "But God" is the turning point in the story. When the enemy least expects it, God shoots at them, and they fall into their own traps. "All men shall fear" (v. 9), and the righteous shall be glad.

Conquering Fear

On March 4, 1933, during the dark days of the depression, President Franklin D. Roosevelt said in a radio speech, "The only thing we have to fear is fear itself." On September 7, 1851, the naturalist Henry David Thoreau wrote in his journal, "Nothing is so much to be feared as fear." Three centuries before that, the French essayist Montaigne wrote, "The thing of which I have most fear is fear." People in all ages of history have fought their fears in one way or another, but the only thing that really conquers fear is faith in the Lord: "I will trust and not be afraid" (Isa. 12:2).

PSALM 65

The worship goes up (1–4). This is a harvest psalm for believers who want to thank God for His goodness and care during another year. Praise and prayer go up to the Lord from the hearts of grateful people. We are told that "in everything [we are to] give thanks" (1 Thess. 5:18).

The witness reaches out (5–8). The ends of the earth need to hear about the God of grace and glory. He reveals Himself to them in creation, but they must be told the good news of salvation: God has provided atonement (v. 3). God blesses you that you in turn might be a blessing to others.

The wealth comes down (9–13). How good He is to send the rain, fill the rivers, and water the fields! The fields provide food for the flocks, and they rejoice at His kindness. We take the rain for granted until it does not fall, and then we learn how much we need it.

You can find joy in God's goodness at the beginning and ending of each day (v. 8), so do not wait until the "crowning" of the year to praise Him (v. 11).

PSALM 66

Come and praise (1–4). He invites the whole world to praise the Lord because God loves the world and sent His Son to be the Savior of the world. When you know Jesus as your Savior, you have something to sing about, but do not do it alone. Share the praise!

Come and see (5–12). This brief review of Israel's history mentions the Exodus (v. 6), the conquest of Canaan (v. 7), and the nation's times of trial (vv. 10–12). When you go through testing in the will of God, keep in mind that the same God who brings you in will see you through and make you better for having been in the furnace.

Come and sacrifice (13–15). Have you ever made promises to God when you have been in the furnace of suffering? Did you keep those promises? When the test was over, did you praise God for what you learned?

Come and hear (16–20). David wanted to tell others that God answers prayer. Worship should lead to witness to the glory of God.

The Lord and David say, "Come!"

PSALM 67

This missionary psalm exhorts us to get the message out to all the nations of the world. Why?

Because they need *light* (vv. 1–2). The lost walk in darkness and need the light of God's face to shine upon them (2 Cor. 4:3–6). They have lost their way and are headed for eternal darkness. Does that burden you?

Because they need *joy* (vv. 3–4a). Sin gives pleasure for only a short time, but in Christ there are "pleasures forevermore" (Ps. 16:11). How can we keep to ourselves the joy that Jesus gives?

Because they need *righteousness* (v. 4b), which can come only through faith in Jesus Christ (Rom. 3:21–31). Man's righteousness can never satisfy the demands of God's holy law.

Because they need *life* (vv. 5–7). "The field is the world" (Matt. 13:38), but that field is not producing fruit to the glory of God. Only with God's life and blessing can the harvest of righteousness come.

If every believer did what you do about missions, would *all* the people of the earth be praising the Lord?

PSALM 68

This victory psalm celebrated how God blew the enemy away like smoke and melted them like wax (v. 2). It pictures three triumphal processions.

The victorious nation (1–16). Great victories were nothing new to Israel, for God had been with them from the beginning. He had delivered them from Egypt and led them through the wilderness into the Promised Land. He gave them Mount Zion and dwelt with them there. What a history of victory! Have you reviewed lately all that God has done for you?

The victorious Savior (17–18). Paul quoted verse 18 in Ephesians 4:8 and applied it to the ascension of Jesus Christ. Believers today are part of a spiritual army, marching in a triumphal procession (2 Cor. 2:14; Col. 2:15) and claiming their inheritance. They are seated with Christ in the heavenlies (Eph. 2:4–6) using their spiritual gifts to serve Him on earth. What a victory!

The victorious singers (19–35). The happy procession reached the sanctuary where they lifted their praises to God and asked for His continued strength as new enemies attacked (vv. 28, 34–35). The God of past victories would not forsake them as they trusted Him and obeyed His will (2 Cor. 1:8–11).

Are you marching like a conqueror in a victory celebration or like a mourner in a funeral procession?

PSALM 69

Psalm 69 begins with sinking (vv. 1–3, 14–15) but ends with singing (vv. 30–36). It goes from prayer to praise, from reproach (vv. 7, 9, 10, 19, 20) to rejoicing, because David poured out his heart to the Lord. No matter how painful your situation may be, tell God exactly how you feel.

This is a messianic psalm. Out of David's sufferings, the Lord revealed His Son. (Compare v. 4 with John 15:25, v. 8 with John 7:3–5, v. 9 with John 2:17, v. 21 with Matt. 27:48, and v. 25 with Acts 1:20.) One purpose God has in allowing His people to suffer is that they might become more like Jesus Christ. That makes it worth it all!

This is also an imprecatory psalm (vv. 22–28; review the comments on Ps. 58). Paul quoted these words in Romans 11:9–10, applying them to unbelieving Israel. In attacking King David, the enemy were also rebelling against God and inviting their own judgment.

It is not easy to bear reproach because we want to be accepted and approved by others. But in the battle against sin, God's soldiers are often falsely accused and lied about. When this happens to you, remember that it also happened to David and to Jesus. You are in good company! Meditate on Isaiah 54:17.

❝I would rather play with forked lightning, or take in my hand living wires with their fiery current, than speak a reckless word against any servant of Christ, or idly repeat the slanderous darts which thousands of Christians are hurling on others, to the hurt of their own souls and bodies.**❞**

A. B. Simpson

PSALM 70

David was in a hurry when he wrote this brief psalm because God was *not* in a hurry! Three times he cried, "Make haste!" and he ended with, "Do not delay!" Like Peter sinking into the water, he did not have time for a long prayer. All he could cry was, "Lord, save me!" (See Matt. 14:30.)

Why does God delay answering your prayers? Surely He can see your desperate situation. He promises to give "grace to help in time of need" (Heb. 4:16), which can be translated "grace for well-timed help." *Your Father's timing is never wrong.*

When God waits, He may have a better gift for you than what you are asking Him for (Isa. 30:18). His delays are neither denials nor defeats, so put your times in His hands and wait on the Lord (Ps. 31:15).

God's Perfect Timing

Joseph in prison had to wait for God to free him and then to reconcile him to his brothers. Israel had to wait for deliverance from Egypt, and Moses had to wait through ten difficult plagues before Pharaoh would let the people go. Joshua and Caleb had to wait forty years before claiming their inheritance, and the delay was not their fault. David had to wait to receive his throne. Mary and Martha had to wait for Jesus to come to Bethany, and while they waited, their brother died (John 11). God is not in a hurry even when we are, and His schedule is better than ours.

PSALM 71

The psalmist reviews a life of dependence on God. The Lord cared for him at birth, and he trusted the Lord as a youth (vv. 5–6). God taught him when he was young (v. 17) and was with him during his mature years. Now he is old, and he prays that God will not abandon him (vv. 9, 18).

As you read this psalm, you discover the ideal way to spend old age as a Christian. Devote time to prayer and trust the Lord to help you. Instead of complaining about what is wrong, praise God for His righteousness and goodness. Practice continual prayer (v. 3), continual praise (vv. 6, 8), and continual hope (v. 14).

Depend on His strength and use every opportunity to witness for Him (vv. 15–16). Ask God to make you a walking wonder (v. 7) who will point people to Christ. Keep a song on your lips and in your heart. After all, the best is yet to come!

PSALM 72

Solomon prayed for blessing on his reign when he followed David. A young man, Solomon knew he could not succeed without the help of the Lord. The psalm also pictures our Lord Jesus when He reigns as King of kings and Lord of lords.

Solomon asked for wisdom to administer justice to his people (vv. 1–7), and God granted his request (1 Kings 3). His reign was like a refreshing shower that made the earth fruitful and beautiful (2 Sam. 23:1–7). God can give you wisdom for your tasks (James 1:5) and make you a blessing to others. Do you bring refreshing showers or storms?

Glory Overcomes Gloom

When things around you look dark, just remind yourself that God will one day fill the earth with His glory (Num. 14:21; Pss. 22:27–28; 86:9; Isa. 6:3; Hab. 2:14). Trust Him to see you through (Jude 24–25).

Peace and security prospered while Solomon was on the throne, and Israel's domain was extended. Of course, verses 8–11 especially apply to the Lord Jesus and His glorious reign yet to come, but He can give you peace and safety today as you yield to Him. He wants you to "reign in life" right now (Rom. 5:17).

God's purpose is to fill the whole earth with His glory (v. 19) as He unites all things in Christ (Eph. 1:10). Are you helping to extend His glory on the earth?

PSALM 73

The psalm begins with "God is good" and ends with "It is good" (v. 28), but between those statements, things are not so good!

The philosopher. Asaph's basic premise was correct: God is good. But when he pondered the success of the wicked and the sorrows of the righteous, he began to falter in his faith. It seemed that he was wasting his time and energy being faithful to God because the unfaithful received all the blessings. *He did not realize that what he called "good" was not what God would call "good."* He was walking by sight and not by faith.

The worshiper. The turning point came when he went into the sanctuary and started looking at things from God's viewpoint. *The important thing is not so much what you own or enjoy but where you are going.* What good is an easy death (v. 4) if it ushers you into pain? When life seems unfair, take time to worship and get your spiritual vision properly focused.

The friend. Asaph realized that because he had God as his Friend, he needed nothing else. He had more than the wicked, and what he had would last forever. God would hold him, guide him, strengthen him, satisfy his spiritual desires—and one day, take him to heaven!

We are not philosophers, living on man's explanations. We are pilgrims, living on God's promises, *and His promises never fail.*

PSALM 74

What we see (1–8). Written probably after the destruction of the temple, this psalm reveals the anguish of one who deeply loved God and could not understand why He permitted such desecration. Israel was His flock and His inheritance, and Mount Zion was His dwelling-place; yet He allowed evil men to destroy His people and His house. Why, O Lord?

What we do not see (9–17). God is King, but we do not see His hand working as in past centuries. We see no signs, and we have no prophet to interpret the times and give us God's message. One of God's judgments is to leave His people without a word of guidance because they have refused to obey His will.

What we want to see (18–23). Surely Asaph knew that the sins of the nation caused the invasion of the enemy and the destruction of the temple. As a faithful Jew, he wanted to see the city and the people delivered and the enemy defeated. That would happen in due time, when God's discipline of His people was ended and their rebellion conquered (Heb. 12:9–11). Meanwhile, all he could do was weep, pray, trust God, and wait.

PSALM 75

God is the Judge; His people are only His witnesses. We can tell others about His great works (v. 1) and His gracious warnings (vv. 4–5), but we cannot tell them when His judgment will fall. God will choose the proper time, and His judgment will be just.

The proud rulers of the nations think they are secure, but the God who set them up can also pull them down (1 Sam. 2:7–8; Dan. 4:25). The wicked think they are getting away with their evil deeds, but one day they must drink the wine of God's wrath.

Meanwhile, God's children continue to sing His praises because they are sure God knows what He is doing. The world needs our witness, and worship is the greatest witness of all. The next time you are disturbed by the evil in the world, pause and praise the Lord.

PSALM 76

God is to be praised (1–6). We do not know what military victory is celebrated here, but it brought great glory to the Lord. The enemy's fortresses (v. 4), soldiers (v. 5), and equipment (v. 6) were unable to stand before the Lord of hosts. It is encouraging to know that God is for us in the battles of life.

God is to be feared (7–12). Man's fury does not frighten God (Ps. 2:1–4). In fact, He uses it to bring Himself glory, like a woman wearing a special garment (v. 10). God is long-suffering, but one day He will arise to judge the wicked. Meanwhile, His people must also fear Him and be faithful to keep their vows to Him (v. 11). Never trifle with God.

"Judgment for an evil thing is many times delayed some day or two, some century or two, but it is sure as life, it is sure as death."

Thomas Carlyle

PSALM 77

Joyless days of trouble and sleepless nights of despair plagued the psalmist. Why? Not because of unbelief but because of faith. Because he believed in the Lord, he wrestled with himself and with God. He could not understand why the Lord did not keep His promises and deliver His people from bondage. What do you do in a situation like that?

Of course, you pray (v. 1) and tell God just how you feel. Reach out to Him in the night seasons (v. 2), *but do not refuse the comfort that He sends*. He will remind you of His past works and wonders, and the more you meditate on them, the better you will feel.

Asaph meditated on Israel's exodus from Egypt and recalled that God kept the people waiting by the Red Sea, that it was night, and that deliverance came just in the nick of time. The people were afraid and certain that God had forgotten them, but He showed His power and humiliated the enemy.

His way is a holy way (v. 13) and a hidden way (v. 19). You need not understand it; just follow as He leads you.

PSALM 78

This long psalm reviews the history of Israel: the Exodus (vv. 12–16, 42–53); their wilderness journey (vv. 17–41); the conquest of Canaan (vv. 54–55); and disciplines God sent them there (vv. 56–64). A nation's true history is a record not only of how the people treated one another but of how they treated God.

But why the long history lesson? For the sake of the generations to follow (vv. 1-8). The Jews were commanded to teach their children the works and ways of the Lord so that each generation would know the Lord and trust Him (Deut. 6:1-9). We have the same obligation today. When Israel stopped doing this, the nation forsook the Lord and God had to chasten them (Judg. 2:7-10).

Israel was a rebellious nation, but God was gracious and gave the people opportunities to start again. This is not an excuse for us to sin and tempt God, but it is an encouragement to repent when we do sin.

God's answer to Israel's needs was to give them a spiritual leader, David, the shepherd. He had both integrity (the heart) and ability (the hands), and he sought to serve the Lord and love the flock of Israel. People have not changed; they still rebel against God. There is still a need for faithful instructors in the home (vv. 1-8) and leaders in the nation (vv. 70-72). Do all you can to help the next generation serve the Lord acceptably.

❝What are all histories but God manifesting Himself?**❞**

Oliver Cromwell

PSALM 79

Once again Asaph is lamenting the invasion of the enemy (cf. Ps. 74). He had several concerns.

God's inheritance. The temple was defiled, the city destroyed, and the people slain. God permitted these things to happen to His inheritance! But God would rather destroy His inheritance than allow His people to sin and rebel.

God's name. What will the heathen nations say about Israel and Israel's God? The corpses and ruins bore witness to something that the world needed to know: *God is holy and does not tolerate disobedience.* Asaph confessed the sins of the nation and asked God to honor His name before the nations (vv. 8–10, 13).

God's wrath. Asaph asserted, "Pour out Your wrath" (v. 6)! "Avenge our blood" (v. 10)! Years later, that prayer was answered, and God punished Babylon for the way she treated Israel.

God's people. They are "Your servants" and "Your saints" (v. 2), "the sheep of Your pasture" (v. 13). Care for them, Lord! Deliver them! God did care for them, but He also chastened them so that they might learn to obey His will.

When you want God to be harder on others than He is on you, it is time to start seeing your sins the way God sees them.

PSALM 80

Asaph prayed for the restoration and illumination of God's people by the shining of God's face (vv. 3, 7, 19; Num. 6:22–27). He gave two pictures of the nation.

A flock (1–7). Israel was like a flock of sheep led by God (Pss. 77:20; 78:52): "We are His people and the sheep of His pasture" (Ps. 100:3). But they were *wayward* sheep who would not follow the Shepherd. So, instead of enjoying green pastures and still waters (Ps. 23:2), they were enduring tears and the reproach of the enemy (v. 5).

A vine (8–19). This picture parallels Isaiah 5 and our Lord's parables in Matthew 21:28–46. Israel was a fruitful vineyard until she turned from the Lord and began to worship the gods of the nations. God used those very nations to discipline His people and destroy the vineyard. The prayer in verses 17–18 was partially answered when some of the people returned to the land after the captivity, but it is fully realized in Jesus Christ.

God's people today are sheep in the flock (John 10) and branches in the Vine (John 15). Do not take your blessings for granted. He is seeking faithfulness and fruitfulness.

PSALM 81

The things that were (vv. 1–10). This section is an invitation for the people to participate in a joyful celebration, probably

Passover. Asaph gave them two reasons for sharing: obedience (it was God's ordinance) and gratitude (all God had done for them). It is good to set aside special times to meditate on the work of the Lord in your life.

The things that are (11–12). In spite of all that God did for His people, they would not listen to His Word or do His will. One of God's most painful judgments is to permit you to have your own way. For a time, you enjoy it; then you learn how much you have missed.

The things that might have been (13–16). Had they obeyed, they would have experienced victory instead of defeat, fullness instead of emptiness, and the best instead of the worst. They could have looked back with rejoicing, but instead they had to remember with regret.

The things that might have been *will be* if *today* you let the Master have His way.

PSALM 82

The throne in heaven (1–4). The Lord stands as Judge and indicts the human judges for their failure to defend the poor and needy and condemn the wicked. Their partiality made a farce out of the legal system God ordained for Israel (Lev. 19:15; Prov. 24:23–25). What does He think of our judicial system today?

The foundations on earth (5). The foundations for peace and order in society are righteousness and justice (Pss. 89:14; 97:2). Whether in the home, church, or government, abandoning righteousness and justice makes the very foundations tremble (Ps. 11:3) and brings darkness where there should be light.

The graves under the earth (6–8). The human judges are called "gods" because the Hebrew word *elohim* means "mighty ones." (It is also one of the names for God.) Leadership is a serious thing, for leaders stand in the place of God and will one day answer to Him. The selfish judges may have their days of pleasure, but one day they will die, and then what? The judges will be judged righteously by the Judge of all the earth, and there will be no escape.

PSALM 83

Asaph was perplexed (vv. 1–8). Israel was in danger, but God was silent and inactive. The nations were noisily forming a military confederacy against the Jews, but God was speechless and seemingly doing nothing. The enemy wanted to destroy the nation (v. 4) and take the land (v. 12), and apparently God was going to let them do it.

So, Asaph prayed (vv. 9–18) and reminded God of what He did to Israel's enemies during the days of the judges (vv. 9–12). Then he shifted from history to nature and asked God to send a storm to wipe them out (vv. 13–15).

Asaph had a purpose in mind—not just the safety of Israel but the glory of the Lord (vv. 16–18). Some of the enemy soldiers might even trust in the God of Israel! It was not important that Israel's name be preserved (v. 4), but it was important that God's name be glorified.

When it seems that God is saying and doing nothing, rest assured that He is working on your behalf. He is not as noisy as the enemy, but He is more powerful; *and He will win.*

PSALM 84

The Jews were required to go to Jerusalem three times each year, to celebrate Passover, Pentecost, and the Feast of Tabernacles. The author of this psalm was unable to join the pilgrimage, even though his soul yearned to be there. Life has its disappointments, but the three beatitudes in this psalm tell you how to handle them.

The blessing of dwelling (4). Perhaps the priests and Levites took for granted their privilege of dwelling in the courts of the Lord, but the psalmist did not. God's altars were to him what a nest was to a bird, a place of safety and satisfaction. Abiding in the Lord is not a matter of geography, for you can worship Him and love Him wherever you are. When life disappoints you, abide in Him.

The blessing of desiring (5). What is in your heart is what counts. He would rather serve in the temple than be served anywhere else. When your desires are godly, the Lord will give you all you need. When life disappoints you, be sure your heart's desires are pleasing to God.

The blessing of depending (12). God's pilgrims go "from strength to strength" and "from faith to faith" (Rom. 1:17). As you trust the Lord, He gives "grace and glory," for He is your sun (provision) and shield (protection). He gives you all you need on the pilgrimage of life. When life disappoints you, depend on the Lord for what you really need.

PSALM 85

Restoration (1–3). We do not know from what crisis the Lord had delivered His people; perhaps it was the captivity in Babylon. His wrath had ended, their sins were forgiven, and they had come home again. In times of divine chastening, rest on Psalm 30:5.

Revival (4–7). When the refugees got back to the land, life was difficult, and they were ready to give up. God had forgiven their sins, but that did not make life a paradise. They wanted new life from God so they could rejoice in Him. New beginnings should lead to experiences of new life.

❝*It is no use to pray for the old days; stand square where you are and make the present better than any past has been. Base all on your relationship to God and go forward, and presently you will find that what is emerging is infinitely better than the past ever was.***❞**

Oswald Chambers

Responsibility (8–13). God forgives us that we might fear and serve Him (Ps. 130:4). You must hear and obey His Word and trust Him to send the needed increase. Mercy and truth met in His passion when Jesus died for the sin of the world. Righteousness and peace meet in His person: King of righteousness and King of peace (Heb. 7:1–3).

God's chastening is for your good, and He is with you when it is ended. He will help you make a fresh new start for His glory.

PSALM 86

"Preserve my life" (1–10). David was in trouble again. As he always did, he turned to the Lord for help, and he presented some reasons why God should answer him. God was *his* God, and he was God's servant. God was merciful, and he needed mercy. He wanted God alone to be glorified in the victory. God is good and great and ready to help.

"Unite my heart" (11–13). A divided heart leads only to instability (James 1:5–8), because you cannot serve two masters (Matt. 6:22–24). With a single heart, fear the Lord, learn from the Lord, obey the Lord, and praise His name.

"Strengthen my hand" (14–17). David's strength and experience were inadequate to face the foe; he needed the strength of the Lord. David knew his theology (v. 15; Exod. 34:6; Neh. 9:17), and that helped him in his praying. The better you know God, the better you can approach Him with your needs.

PSALM 87

The earthly Mount Zion is a figure of the heavenly Zion, the city of God and God's redeemed people (Gal. 4:21–31; Heb. 12:18–24). As you ponder this psalm, take inventory of your spiritual life.

On what are you building (1–3)? Are you building your life on God's foundation (1 Cor. 3:11)? "Salvation is of the Jews" (John 4:22), for God's gracious work in this world came through Israel (Gen. 12:1–3). Your Bible is a Jewish book, and the Savior came from the tribe of Judah. When the church was born, the Holy Spirit came on Jewish believers in the temple in Jerusalem. To obey Him is to build on an unfailing foundation (Matt. 7:21–29).

Where is your citizenship (4–6)? Some people like to boast about the place of their birth, but the "once-born" do not have the blessings of the "twice-born." Through faith in Christ, God's children are enrolled in the heavenly Zion (Luke 10:20; Phil. 3:20; 4:3)—and will live with the Father forever.

What are your joys (7)? Jerusalem is one of the few ancient cities that is not built by a river. The psalmist found all his joys in Jerusalem, and he wanted nothing more. By faith, you can drink of the river of His pleasures (Pss. 36:8; 46:4) and be satisfied.

"What man needs is not a boost from below but a birth from above."

Vance Havner

PSALM 88

This is one of the few psalms that does not end on a note of glorious victory. When Heman wrote it, he was suffering greatly, and God had not given him relief. *But he kept on praying and trusting God* (vv. 1–2, 9, 13).

The next time you want to say, "Nobody knows how I feel!" take time to read this psalm. How did Heman feel? Like a dead man buried in a dark pit. Like a drowning man sinking under cold waves and billows. Like a defiled man watching everybody run away and leave him alone. Most of all, he felt like a doomed man whom God had forsaken.

But Heman did not give up. Instead, he looked by faith to God, the God of wonders, loving-kindness, and faithfulness (vv. 10–12). He cried out to God and told Him just how he felt. Your feelings may change, but God never changes. You can trust Him even in the dark, even when you seem to be drowning.

God knows how you feel (Heb. 4:14–16) and is working out His purposes for you. The final verses of your "psalm" have not been written yet, but God knows what they are, so wait for Him. They are worth waiting for!

PSALM 89

God made a covenant with David that he would always have a descendant on his throne and that the Davidic line would rule forever (2 Sam. 7). But Ethan the Ezrahite had a problem. One of the Davidic kings had been defeated in war and had lost his throne (vv. 38–45). It seemed to Ethan that God had broken His covenant (vv. 3, 28, 34, 39) and that God was not faithful to His people.

Faithfulness is a key word in this psalm (vv. 1, 2, 5, 8, 24, 33). God's faithfulness is seen from generation to generation (vv. 1–4), among His people (vv. 5–10), in creation (vv. 11–13), among the nations (vv. 14–18), and toward David and his family (vv. 19–37). Ethan knew all of this because he knew the Scriptures, but recent events seemed to deny the truthfulness of the covenant and the faithfulness of the Lord.

Ethan's problem was caused by spiritual shortsightedness. The ultimate fulfillment of the Davidic covenant is in Jesus Christ, the Son of David (Matt. 1:1), and He will reign forever (Luke 1:26–33). God's faithfulness does not fail!

When Jeremiah viewed the destruction of Jerusalem, he may have felt as Ethan did when the king was defeated and dethroned. Instead of questioning God's faithfulness, Jeremiah reaffirmed it: "Great is Your faithfulness" (Lam. 3:23). Never judge God's faithfulness on the basis of what you see or how you feel. His promises do not fail (2 Cor. 1:18–20).

PSALM 90

The somber tone of this psalm suggests that Moses may have written it when the nation rebelled in unbelief at Kadesh Barnea (Num. 13–14). God announced that everybody twenty years old and older would die within the next forty years. No wonder Moses prayed, "So teach us to number our days" (v. 12).

We number our years, but it is wiser to number our days, for we live a day at a time. Life is brief, like the changing of the guard, or taking a nap, or mowing the lawn (vv. 3–6). In the camp of Israel, a twenty-year-old would not live beyond sixty, and the older people would never make it to eighty (v. 10). It was a funeral march for forty long years!

In the light of eternity (vv. 1–4), life is brief—no matter how long you live. You need God's help to use your days wisely (v. 12) and joyfully (vv. 14–15). There is real satisfaction in doing God's will (v. 14; 1 John 2:17), revealing God's glory (v. 16) and growing in God's beauty (v. 17). In spite of the burdens of life and the brevity of life, *life is worth living when you trust the Lord.*

The Land of the Living

Charles Spurgeon told about a man who said to a dying believer, "Farewell, friend! I shall never see you again in the land of the living!" The dying Christian replied, "I shall see you again in the land of the living where I am going. This is the land of the dying!"

PSALM 91

What a relief to turn to this psalm and move out of the shadows into the sunshine! In light of the sobering admonitions of Psalm 90, we appreciate even more the sublime assurances of Psalm 91.

The theme is *security:* God preserves those who abide in Him and love Him. These promises are not for people who run to the Lord only in times of danger but for those who *dwell* in His presence (v. 1) and make the Holy of Holies their *habitation* (v. 9).

What are the dangers we face? Snares and pestilences (v. 3), arrows (v. 5), plagues (v. 10), stones (vv. 11–12), and lions and snakes (v. 13; perhaps referring to Satan). You can easily give the modern equivalents for these ancient perils that Jewish travelers faced.

The abiding life (vv. 1–4) produces the assuring life (vv. 5–13), the life without fear, which leads to the abounding life (vv. 14–16), the life of victory and peace. The safest place in the world is under the shadow of the Almighty.

PSALM 92

It is good to thank the Lord *for every day He gives you* (vv. 1–4). As the day begins, you can look ahead by faith and praise Him for His loving-kindness. As the day ends, you can look back and praise Him for His faithfulness.

It is good to thank the Lord *that you are part of what is eternal* (vv. 5–9). You cannot understand eternity, but you can have eternal life through faith in Christ; and you can live for what is eternal (1 John 2:17). Ponder 1 Corinthians 15:58.

It is even good to thank the Lord *for old age* (vv. 10–15). In old age, those who live for Christ become fresh (v. 10), flourishing (vv. 12–13), fruitful (v. 14), and faithful (v. 15). Instead of complaining, they are praising the Lord and witnessing for Him.

"*It does not pay to get sour as you get old. I pity a man who lives in the past. He lives on stale manna. He gets stunted.***"**

D. L. Moody

PSALM 93

When the floods are rising (v. 3), lay hold of three anchors that will steady you.

God's throne (1–4). No matter what may come to you today, "the LORD reigns!" God is sovereign and everything is under control. His majestic throne is strong, established, and everlasting. His throne is above the floods, but He is with you in your trials and will see you through (Isa. 43:1–2).

God's testimonies (5a). You can trust the Word of God because it never fails (Josh. 21:45; 23:14). Cling to His testimonies (Ps. 119:31) and withstand the floods by faith.

God's temple (5b). God's throne was the mercy seat in the Holy of Holies (Ps. 99:1), and there His glory rested. Satan himself cannot dethrone our Lord, and the men who attempt it are attempting vanity (Ps. 2:1–3). When the storms come and the floods rise, you can experience peace, for "the LORD is in His holy temple. Let all the earth keep silence before Him" (Hab. 2:20).

PSALM 94

God alone can judge and punish the wicked (vv. 1–3), but God's people must stand up and be counted in the battle for truth (v. 16). It is easier to be a spectator or an advisor than to be a soldier. When you enter the battle against evil, rely on God.

God knows all about the enemy (1–11). He hears their insolent speech, He sees their wicked deeds, and He will eventually bring them to judgment. The Captain of your salvation will not be caught off guard!

God will teach you what to do (12–15). The basic "Handbook for Battle" is the Word of God, and God will teach you what you need to know. Gideon was an ordinary farmer when God called him, and yet he became a mighty warrior because he let God teach him (Judg. 6—7). Even though he was hiding from the enemy, God called him a "mighty man of valor" (Judg. 6:11–12).

God will help you fight (16–23). God is for you if you are against what He is against. When you fight, He will help you. If you slip, He will hold you. If you worry, He will comfort you, and if you are attacked, He will defend you.

Who is on the Lord's side? Are you?

PSALM 95

God is great (1–7a)! This is a call to jubilant worship, not just participation in services as usual. He invites us to "shout joyfully" and to "kneel before the LORD." Why? Because God is great! He is a great Creator and a great King, and we are privileged to be His people.

God is grieved (7b–11). The opposite of a worshiping heart that pleases the Lord is a hard heart that grieves the Lord. Imagine seeing God's wonders and not submitting gladly to Him! The unbelieving Jews paid a high price for their sin: they died in the wilderness and never entered the Promised Land (Heb. 3—4).

Do you want to enjoy your life of faith? Then take time to see the greatness of God and to praise Him. Do you want to inherit all that God has planned for you in this life? Then give yourself to worship and praise. A hard heart leads to a hard life, so keep your heart tender before God.

PSALM 96

In this invitation to worship the Lord, you are given three admonitions.

Sing to the Lord (1-6). Sing a *new song* because you have had a new experience with Him. Sing a *worship hymn* because God is glorious (v. 3) and great (vv. 4-5). Sing a *gospel song* because the nations need to hear the good news of salvation. Sing a *song of victory* and reveal the strength of the Lord. Sing a *song of devotion* and reveal the beauty of the Lord.

Give to the Lord (7-10). Give Him glory with your lips and heart, and give Him offerings with your hands. God does not need your gifts (Acts 17:24-25), but you need to bring your gifts to God. He deserves the best (Mal. 1:6-14).

Look for the Lord (11-13). All nature is eagerly anticipating the Lord's return, for then creation will be set free (Rom. 8:18-25). The oppressed people will be vindicated, and sinners will be judged when Jesus Christ comes to reign. God's people shall reign with Christ and then worship Him perfectly. Hallelujah!

PSALM 97

"The Lord reigns!" Not "the Lord *will* reign," but "the Lord reigns!" Right now! In another psalm the Lord declared, "I have set My King on My holy hill of Zion" (Ps. 2:6). We are children of the King.

Let the earth be glad (1-6). You may not see much righteousness and justice in the world today, but that does not mean God has been dethroned. For reasons we do not fully understand, God permits evil men to exploit the earth and its people, but one day He will come in power and glory and set things right.

Let Israel be glad (7-9). Israel has played the key part in God's gracious plan of salvation, witnessing the true God, passing the Bible on to us, and giving us the Savior. The nation has suffered much, but one day her Messiah King will come in glory and fulfill the promises made to the patriarchs.

Let the righteous be glad (10–12). This group includes all of God's people, sinners declared righteous through faith in Jesus Christ (Rom. 3:21—4:8). They love the Lord and rejoice in the Lord. If you are yielded to the King, you have good reason to be glad, so joyfully tell the world, "The Lord reigns!"

"Rejoice, the Lord Is King!"

Rejoice, the Lord is King!
Your Lord and King adore;
Mortals, give thanks and sing,
And triumph evermore.

Jesus the Saviour reigns,
The God of truth and love;
When He had purged our stains
He took His seat above.

He sits at God's right hand
Till all His foes submit,
And bow to His command,
And fall beneath His feet.

Rejoice in glorious hope;
Jesus the Judge shall come,
And take His servants up
To their eternal home.

Lift up your heart, lift up your voice,
Rejoice, again I say, rejoice!

Charles Wesley

PSALM 98

Why should we praise the Lord? Because of His redemption (v. 1), the revelation of His righteousness (v. 2), and the remembrance of His mercy (v. 3). That should keep you busy singing His praises for a long time!

How should we praise the Lord? With a joyful shout and song (v. 4), and with musical instruments skillfully played to please Him (vv. 5–6). Let voices and instruments join in praising the Lord! Not religious entertainment but the joyful expression of praise to God.

Who should praise the Lord? Everybody in the world—and all the world of nature (vv. 7–9). The anticipation of His coming excites creation, and you should be a part of their excitement.

Joy to the world—the Lord has come!

A New Song — The psalmist often exhorts us to "sing a new song" (Pss. 33:3; 40:3; 96:1; 98:1; 144:9; 149:1). The word translated "new" means "fresh, new in quality." The song may be an old one, but our growth in the Lord and our new experiences of His grace enable us to sing an old song with fresh new meaning and blessing. This explains why the Lord allows us to go through trials. He is tuning us up to praise Him in a new way!

PSALM 99

"He is holy" (vv. 3, 5, 9), and He is high (v. 2); therefore, give God the honor due Him.

Fear Him (1–3). The greatness of God makes the earth

shake, and it should make the people tremble (Isa. 64:1–5). Even the demons tremble when they think of God (James 2:19). It is frightening to hear how carelessly many people speak *about* God or *to* God. It is even more frightening to see how carelessly people live, as though God will never require an accounting from them.

Exalt Him (4–5). The Lord is exalted in strength, righteousness, and holiness. One way to exalt Him is by your worship, but you must back that up by a consistent walk. Christ should be magnified in your body so that the lost around you may realize how great He is (1 Cor. 6:19–20; Phil. 1:19–26).

Call on Him (6–9). Three great men of prayer are mentioned to encourage you in your praying. They were not perfect, but they heard God's word, obeyed it, and God answered when they called. The Word of God and prayer must always go together (John 15:7; Acts 6:4), and so must prayer and obedience (Ps. 66:18).

PSALM 100

The hymn "Old Hundredth" ("All People That on Earth Do Dwell") is based on this psalm, as is the familiar "Doxology." Thanking the Lord is something we must do with our lives as well as with our lips. How shall we do it?

By serving (2). "Enter to worship—depart to serve" should be written clearly above the door to the church sanctuary. Too many people serve themselves and not the Lord, and too often we do not serve the Lord "with gladness." The Lord loves a cheerful servant.

By submitting (3). As creatures, we submit to the Creator who made us. As sheep, we submit to the Shepherd who died for us and now leads us in His paths. He not only made us, but *He is making us* as we yield to Him (Eph. 2:10). Submission means fulfillment.

By sacrificing (4–5). As priests, we are privileged to offer spiritual sacrifices to the Lord (1 Pet. 2:5). They include our songs of praise (Heb. 13:15), good works (Heb. 13:16), and material gifts (Phil. 4:15–18). Because of who He is (v. 5) and what He does for us, He is certainly worthy of our joyful thanks.

"Old Hundredth"

All people that on earth do dwell,
Sing to the Lord with cheerful voice;
Him serve with mirth, His praise forth tell;
Come ye before Him and rejoice.

Know that the Lord is God indeed;
Without our aid He did us make;
We are His folk, He does us feed;
And for His sheep He doth us take.

O enter then His gates with praise,
Approach with joy His courts unto;
Praise, laud and bless His name always,
For it is seemly so to do.

For why? The Lord our God is good,
His mercy is forever sure;
His truth at all times firmly stood,
And shall from age to age endure.

William Kethe
(Published 1560–61)

PSALM 101

Determination and dedication characterize this psalm as David says "I will" nine times and "shall" six times. He wanted a perfect (blameless) heart (v. 2), not a perverse (twisted) heart (v. 4) or a proud heart (v. 5). To be "perfect" before the Lord does not mean to be sinless; it means to be sincere and without pretense. John called it "walking in the light" (1 John 1:5–10).

David wanted justice in the land and the city (v. 8), just as we do today. But civic righteousness must begin in the heart and in the home (vv. 2, 7). Yes, we need honest people enforcing just laws, but we also need godly people living holy lives, starting at home.

We must be careful what we look at (v. 3) and listen to (v. 5), and with whom we fellowship (vv. 6–7). In a world full of illusion, we must avoid lies and must walk in God's wisdom (vv. 7, 2). Unlike David, we do not have authority to execute judgment on the wicked. But if our hearts and homes are what God wants them to be, our influence will be felt in the city and the nation.

“*Strength of character may be acquired at work, but beauty of character is learned at home. There the affections are trained. There the gentle life reaches us, the true heaven life. In one word, the family circle is the supreme conductor of Christianity.*”

Phillips Brooks

PSALM 102

God enjoys endless years, but we endure shortened days (vv. 23–24), troubled days (v. 2), days that disappear like smoke, grass, and a shadow (vv. 3, 4, 11). We sit alone like birds in a desert and dying patients in a hospital (vv. 5–9). How depressing!

Do you ever have days like that? If you do, beware. Looking at yourself and your feelings will only make things worse. Do what the writer of this penitential psalm did: look by faith to the Lord. Things will be different when you look from yourself to God and say, "But You."

"But You shall endure" (12–22). If you know Jesus Christ by faith, you possess eternal life (1 John 5:11–13). So, living in a

world of death and decay need not be a threat to you because you will live forever with the Lord (1 Thess. 4:13–18).

"But You are the same" (25–28). As you grow older, you may find yourself resisting change. Loved ones move away or die, your body weakens, the world changes, and it is easy to become bitter and afraid. But God does not change (Heb. 13:5–8), and He is your Friend and Guide to the very end (Ps. 73:24).

The temporary things will change, but the things eternal will last (2 Cor. 4:11–18).

"Abide with Me"

Swift to its close ebbs out life's little day;
Earth's joys grow dim, its glories pass away;
Change and decay in all around I see;
O Thou who changest not, abide with me.

I fear no foe, with Thee at hand to bless;
Ills have no weight, and tears no bitterness.
Where is death's sting? where, grave, thy victory?
I triumph still, if Thou abide with me.

Henry Francis Lyte

PSALM 103

David makes no requests in this psalm. All he does is praise the Lord for three wonderful blessings, which he names in verses 3–5 and then explains in the rest of the psalm.

Forgiveness (3, 10–14). Forgiveness is like healing when you are sick (1 Pet. 2:24), relief when you are burdened (vv. 11–12; Lev. 16:20–22; John 1:29), and reconciliation when you have hurt someone (vv. 13–14). All of this comes because Jesus died for your sins on the cross and you have trusted Him.

Redemption (4, 6–9). God redeemed the nation from bondage and from difficulties they faced on their journey to Canaan. He frees us that He might be our Master and care for us forever. When He crowns us, He transforms slaves into kings (Rom. 5:17). What grace!

Satisfaction (5, 15–18). Man is frail and temporary, but believers enjoy "eternal youth" and spiritual renewal. David compares it to the eagle that looks old but still soars upward with new strength (Isa. 40:31).

You belong to the King who rules over everything (v. 19)! The angels praise Him (vv. 20–22), so why not join in their worship?

Renewal   *Just as God renews the face of the earth and brings it new life and beauty (Ps. 104:30), so He can renew your life if you will let Him. It begins with a renewed mind (Rom. 12:1–2) as you permit the Spirit to teach you God's Word (Eph. 4:23; Col. 3:10). Wait before the Lord in worship, and He will renew strength (Isa. 40:31). When you walk by faith, you have a constant experience of renewal in spite of the changes of life (2 Cor. 4:16–18). There is always something new to enjoy when you "walk in newness of life" (Rom. 6:4).*

PSALM 104

Psalm 104 praises God for His fullness as Creator, Psalm 105 for His faithfulness as Redeemer, and Psalm 106 for His forgiveness as Savior of His people. How easy it is to take for granted the world that God created! We see the blemishes but not the blessings, and we forget what kind of world God gave us.

It is a place of *greatness* (vv. 1–9), not the greatness of man but the greatness of God. The psalmist compared creation to the building of a house: laying the foundations, putting up the beams, hanging the curtains, and taking care of the water system. Only a great and wise God could make this kind of world.

It is a place of *goodness* (vv. 10–30). He provides life, water, food and homes for man and beast and also the birds, and He sees to it they are cared for. Everything in creation is God's gift to us to enjoy (1 Tim. 6:17).

It is a place of *gladness* (vv. 31–35). God rejoices over creation (v. 31), and we should be "glad in the LORD" (v. 34). Creation is a window through which we see God, not a mirror in which we see ourselves; and the more we see Him, the happier we should be. Only this will make us good stewards of God's creation.

"This Is My Father's World"

This is my Father's world,
Oh, let me ne'er forget
That though the wrong seems oft so strong,
God is the ruler yet.
This is my Father's world;
Why should my heart be sad?
The Lord is king; let the heavens ring.
God reigns; let the earth be glad.

Maltbie D. Babcock

PSALM 105

The previous psalm extols the Creator, while this one exalts the Redeemer and His providential care for His people, Israel.

His deeds (1–6). When you read the history of Israel, you are encouraged by God's mighty and marvelous deeds wrought for His needy people (Rom. 15:4). You want to praise Him, rejoice in Him, seek Him, and tell others about Him.

His covenant (7-15). God bound Himself by an oath to only one nation, Israel. He gave His promise to Abraham (Gen. 12:1-3) and then reaffirmed it to his descendants. The covenant was their assurance that they would inherit the land. God's new covenant people have the assurance that their future inheritance is secure (Matt. 26:26-29; Heb. 8:6-13).

His servants (16-45). God sent Joseph to Egypt to preserve Jacob's family so they could become a nation. He sent Moses to Egypt to deliver His people. He sent Aaron to assist Moses and serve as high priest for a sinful people. God always has a man or woman ready to send when a job must be done. He waits to hear you say, "Here am I! Send me!" (Isa. 6:8).

PSALM 106

In light of God's goodness to Israel, you would have expected the nation to submit to Him and serve Him gratefully. Instead, they sinned and had to be disciplined many times. Before you judge them, however, consider whether you may be guilty of some of the same sins they committed.

God delivered Israel from Egypt, but they soon forgot His mercy and ignored His counsel (vv. 6-23). He gave them manna, and they lusted for meat. They criticized their leaders. They worshiped a golden idol and would have been destroyed had Moses not interceded for them.

They came to the border of the Promised Land and refused to go in (vv. 24-27). While wandering in the wilderness, they compromised with the heathen nations (vv. 28-31). Their stubborn attitude even made Moses sin (vv. 32-33). Once in the land, they compromised with the wicked nations, and God had to chasten them repeatedly (vv. 34-43).

Were it not for His covenant, God would have destroyed them. But He forgave them and allowed them to have many new beginnings. Finally He had to disperse them among the Gentiles (v. 47).

Paul gives you most of the story in 1 Corinthians 10:1-13. Take it to heart!

PSALM 107

How easy it is to take God's mercy for granted! Ingratitude seems to be natural to the sinful human heart (vv. 8, 15, 21, 31; Rom. 1:21ff.). Here are four pictures of God's mercy toward sinners and how they responded.

Travelers (4–9). Being lost in the wilderness without food or drink would be a frightful experience. God not only saved them but led them to the safety of the city. Did they take time to thank Him?

Prisoners (10–16). They were in prison because they had rebelled against God's will, so they deserved to suffer. But when they cried out to God, He heard them and set them free. Did they take time to thank Him?

Sufferers (17–22). We move from the prison to the hospital where people were dying because of their foolish way of life. They had "made their own bed" and should lie in it, but God mercifully healed them. Did they take time to show their appreciation?

Sailors (23–32). Dangers on the water usually exceed dangers on the land, for where can you go for help in the midst of a violent storm? You can only look up, which is what they did, and the Lord rescued them. He calmed the storm, and He brought them to their desired destination (John 6:15–21).

Farmers (33–38). Only God can send the rain that turns the wilderness into a garden, and only God can make the cattle multiply. We eat and are full, but do we take time to thank the Lord for giving us food (Deut. 6:10–13)? Be wise and understand the loving-kindness of the Lord.

PSALM 108

This psalm is adapted from Psalm 57:7–11 (vv. 1–5) and Psalm 60:5–12 (vv. 6–13). It is the song of a warrior, and in it, David makes three affirmations.

"I will praise" (1–6). A steadfast heart is a singing heart because confidence in God gives you something to sing about. David arose early in the morning to sing to the Lord. Worship is good preparation for warfare.

"I will listen" (7–9). God heard the voice of David, and then

David listened to the voice of God. It was a word of assurance as the king went out to battle: "All nations are mine, and I can do with them as I please."

"I will conquer" (10–13). God leads us into the battle, helps us capture the enemy's strongholds, and gives us the victory. Verse 13 is David's version of Philippians 4:13. It was true for him, and it is true for you today.

PSALM 109

When people have lied about you, spoken hatefully to you, and rewarded you evil for good, you would benefit from reading this psalm. When your heart is wounded within (v. 22) and there is no way to set the record straight, take it to the Lord and tell Him how you feel.

Verses 5–20 record another of King David's "imprecatory prayers." (See the comments on Ps. 58.) He asks God to judge the man who lied about him (vv. 6–8) and also to judge the man's children (vv. 9–13). He even asks that the man's ancestors' sins come up before God for judgment (vv. 14–16), and that the liar reap just what he has sown (vv. 18–20).

When you feel that way, give the Lord the opportunity to heal your wounded heart (Ps. 147:3). No matter how God deals with your enemies, be sure you praise Him. And remember, He is long-suffering with sinners—including you! The best way to get rid of an enemy is to leave him or her with the Lord.

PSALM 110

This psalm is quoted in the New Testament more than any other one. It was quoted by Jesus (Matt. 22:41–46) and Peter (Acts 2:32–36), and the writer of Hebrews quoted it (or alluded to it) many times.

The Lord (1). Jesus focused on the real issue when He asked, "If Messiah is David's Son, how can Messiah be David's Lord?" There is only one answer: Messiah must come as a man *through the family of David*. Messiah is both eternal God and man, divine and human. He is seated in the place of glory and authority.

The King (2–3). This is a picture of victory over Messiah's enemies. The final victory has not yet been won, but He still rules in the midst of His enemies. Are you one of His volunteers in the battle against sin?

The Priest (4). Hebrews 7—10 expounds this verse, and the background for it is in Genesis 14. Melchizedek and Jesus Christ are the only king-priests God has accepted. As King, Jesus can deal with the circumstances around you; as Priest, He can help with the feelings and weaknesses within you.

The Judge (5–7). A day of wrath is coming when the Lord Jesus will deal with His enemies once and for all (Rev. 19:11—20:15). He will be victorious and His head lifted up in exaltation.

If you know Him as God's Son and your High Priest, obey Him as your King, and seek to win others before He comes as Judge.

PSALM 111

Psalm 111 is for people who study. It explains how to be a student who pleases the Lord and grows in understanding of truth.

Start with worship (1). The lower you bow before the Lord, the more He will instruct you. Go right to the Source!

See God in His works (2–6). Whether it is science or history, you are examining God's works in this world. His works are great and glorious, revealing His power and wisdom. To see the creation but ignore the Creator is to move into idolatry and sin (Rom. 1:18ff.).

> **"**All men naturally desire to know, but what does knowledge avail without the fear of God?**"**
>
> Thomas à Kempis

See God in His Word (7–9). The Word of God and the book of nature do not contradict each other, for the same Author wrote them. The theories of scholars come and go, but God's Word stands forever.

Obey what God teaches you (10). The search into truth is not simply an academic endeavor of the mind; it must involve your whole person. If you are willing to *do* God's truth, He will teach you (John 7:17). F. W. Robertson said, "Obedience is the organ of spiritual knowledge."

All truth is God's truth. If you love truth, learn truth, and live truth, the truth will set you free (John 8:31–32).

PSALM 112

"Blessed is the man who fears the LORD," says verse 1; and verses 7–8 declare, "He will not be afraid." When you fear the Lord, you need not fear anything else. The fear of God is the fear that conquers fear.

This applies to fears about your family (v. 2) and your finances (v. 3), and even fear of the dark (v. 4). If you dread making decisions, the Lord will help you (vv. 5–6). When you fear the Lord, you need not fear bad news (vv. 7–8) because you know He is in control of all things (Rom. 8:28).

You need not be afraid to give because God will use your gifts and reward you (v. 9). And do not be alarmed at your enemies; God will take care of them as well (v. 10).

Isaiah proclaimed, "The LORD of hosts. . . . Let Him be your fear, and let Him be your dread" (Isa. 8:13).

PSALM 113

A concise manual of worship is presented here.

Who should worship (1). "Servants of the LORD" includes all of God's people, for those who have trusted Him surely would want to live for Him.

When we worship (2). Start right now and keep on going! It is always time to praise the Lord. Make every breath a hymn of worship.

Where we worship (3). His name should be praised from east to west, all day long, no matter where we are. If you find yourself in a place where you cannot praise the Lord, maybe you do not belong there.

Why we worship (4–9). Because of who God is (vv. 4–6) and what God does (vv. 7–9). The better you know God, the more you will worship Him. The more you experience His grace in daily life, the more praise you will bring to Him.

If you have a problem praising the Lord from sunup to sundown, what will you do for all eternity?

Praise the Lord!

Mary's joyful song of praise (Luke 1:46–55) echoes Psalm 113:7–9. God's grace makes kings out of beggars and joyful mothers out of the barren. Praise the Lord!

PSALM 114

This beautiful poem celebrates the exodus of Israel from Egypt. The sea, the river, the mountains, and the hills all made way for the people of God as they marched in triumph. Even the rocks became Israel's servants and gave them water to drink.

God brings us out (v. 1), takes us through (v. 3), and leads us over (v. 4). When you are following Him, no obstacle can keep you from the goal He has set for you, except your sin and unbelief.

When you are in the will of God, all of creation works for you to accomplish God's purposes. You are God's sanctuary (1 Cor. 6:19–20); let Him have dominion in your life (v. 2).

PSALM 115

The message of this psalm raises some important questions for you to answer.

"Where is your God?" Gentiles visiting Jerusalem would notice the absence of idols. Back home, they could point to their gods and introduce you to the craftsman who made them. Is your God in heaven, ruling over all? Are you trusting something less than God?

"What is your God like?" Be careful! You become like the god you worship (v. 8). The living God can see you, hear your prayers, walk with you and help you. He can speak to you from His Word.

"Do you praise your God?" He has blessed you; have you blessed Him? He has given you promises; do you trust Him? He is the *living* God; does your life glorify Him?

The Living God

The Bible uses human illustrations to explain divine attributes. God is spirit and does not have a body, but He can see you, hear you, and walk with you. After all, we can do those things, and we are made in the image of God. If we fail to trust the Lord and worship Him, we might just as well worship a dead idol! Do you have living faith in the living God?

The Good Hand of Our God

When God wanted to create a world, He merely had to use His fingers (Ps. 8:3). To save lost sinners, He had to bare His arm (Isa. 53:1). When He wants to accomplish a task, He uses His mighty hand (Ezra 7:6, 9, 28; Neh. 2:8).

PSALM 116

From danger to deliverance. The psalmist almost died (v. 3), possibly because people lied to him (v. 11). But when he cried out to the Lord, the Lord saved him (v. 8). The death of a believer is precious to the Lord; He will not permit it to be merely an accident (v. 15). This does not mean that God *enjoys* the death of one of His own. Rather, it means that He values His own so much that He makes death an appointment. It is a part of a loving plan (Pss. 31:15; 139:16).

From agitation to rest. He was surrounded by the pains of death and was worried about his future, but the Lord gave him rest (v. 7).

From prayer to praise. Praise is the logical response when God has answered prayer and seen you through your difficulties. Note these assertions: "I will walk" (v. 9); "I will offer . . . the sacrifice of thanksgiving" (v. 17); "I will pay my vows" (v. 18); and "I will call upon Him as long as I live" (v. 2).

PSALM 117

This short psalm is about a big subject: helping all the nations to praise the Lord. God called Israel to be a blessing to all the nations of the world (Gen. 12:1–3), just as He has called His church to take the gospel to the whole world (Matt. 28:18–20).

The nations are worshiping false gods, so what do we tell them about the true God? That His mercy is great and His truth is enduring. What He does is merciful and what He says is dependable.

God blesses you so that you might be a blessing to others, not only the people you see every day but people you will never see until you get to heaven. Are you helping the peoples of the world learn about Jesus?

" *The Spirit of Christ is the spirit of missions, and the nearer we get to Him the more intensely missionary we must become.* **"**

Henry Martyn

PSALM 118

The Jewish people sing Psalms 113 to 118 at Passover, so this is one of the songs that Jesus sang before He went to the Garden to pray (Matt. 26:30). If you knew you were going to be executed unjustly, would you be able to sing praises to the Lord?

This is also a messianic psalm. The crowds shouted verses 25–26 as Jesus rode into Jerusalem on Palm Sunday (Matt. 21:9), and Jesus quoted verses 22–23 in His debate with the religious leaders (Matt. 21:33–46).

But it is also a song of praise, thanking God for deliverance from a difficult situation (vv. 10–14). The name of the Lord (vv. 10–12) and the hand of the Lord (vv. 15–16) can give you the victory you need. When you are hemmed in by the enemy (vv. 10–12), cry out to God and He will put you into "a broad place" (v. 5). He will open the gates for you and give you new freedom (vv. 19–20).

Claim verse 24 for every day that you live.

A Song of Faith

"The LORD is my strength and song, and He has become my salvation" (Ps. 118:14)—Israel sang those words when they were delivered from the Egyptian army at the Red Sea (Exod. 15:2). They will sing those words again when God gathers them from the nations and restores them to their land (Isa. 11:10— 12:2). It is a song you may sing today by faith.

PSALM 119

The theme of this unique psalm is the Word of God. Every verse except five (84, 90, 121, 122, 132) refers to God's Word, what it is and what it can do in your life if you let it. The arrangement is also unique. There are twenty-two sections of eight lines each, and the lines in each individual section begin with the same letter of the Hebrew alphabet. The first eight lines begin with *Aleph,* the next eight with *Beth,* and so on through all twenty-two letters. This may have been a device to help people memorize the psalm.

The writer had a great love for the Word of God and was

persecuted because he obeyed God and opposed sin. Most of the verses are either prayers for God's help or affirmations of the writer's faith in God's truth despite his difficulties. Meditating on this psalm ought to make you love and treasure the Word of God more and obey it more willingly.

Our approach will be to emphasize in each section one special ministry of the Word to your life.

The Word of God — *Psalm 119 contains ten different names for the Word of God: word, law, saying, statutes, way, commandments, path, testimonies, precepts, and judgments. Each name indicates what the Word is and how we should respond to it. The writer pictured the Word of God as water (v. 9), treasure (vv. 14, 72, 127, 162), a companion and counselor (v. 24), a song (v. 54), honey (v. 103), light (vv. 105, 130), and a heritage (v. 111). Meditate on these pictures and see what they mean to your personal life of faith.*

PSALM 119:1–8

Knowing and obeying God's Word will bring blessings to your life, some of which are given in the following sections. But if God is to bless you, you must sincerely seek the Lord and not just study the Bible. It is not facts in the head but truth in the heart that makes you grow in the Lord. Review Psalm 1.

PSALM 119:9–16

Here is the first blessing: God's Word can keep you clean. You must heed God's Word (v. 9) and hide God's Word in your heart (v. 11). Campbell Morgan explained verse 11: "The best book, in the best place, for the best purpose." You must also rejoice in God's Word, delight in it and meditate on it. Meditation is to your inner person what digestion is to your body.

Heavenly
Meditation

When you truly delight in the Word, you will have a desire to meditate on it and make it a part of your life. In Psalm 119, the writer connects "delight" and "meditation" (vv. 15–16, 23–24, 47–48, 77–78). Cultivate an appetite for the Word of God.

PSALM 119:17–24

God's Word will guide you on the pilgrim path of life. You are a stranger on the earth (v. 19; 1 Pet. 2:11), and you need a "road map" to help you know the way. That road map is the Bible. Ask God to open your eyes to the Word (v. 18) and keep your eyes on the way (v. 21; Prov. 3:1–6; 4:25–27). Let your Bible be your trusted counselor (v. 24).

PSALM 119:25–32

The Word of God brings you the blessing of life (v. 25) because it *has* life (Heb. 4:12), *imparts* life (1 Pet. 1:23–25), and *nourishes* life (1 Pet. 2:1–3). God's Word can revive and strengthen you (v. 28), even when you are in the dust. Nine times in this psalm the writer prayed for new life from the Lord (vv. 25, 37, 40, 88, 107, 149, 154, 156, 159). No need to stay in the dust when there is life for you in the Word of God!

PSALM 119:33–40

If you want real values, get them from the Word of God (v. 37). How tragic that so many people waste time, energy, and money on things that amount to little or nothing (Isa. 55:2). The Hebrew word translated "worthless things" means "that which is nothing (vanity) because it is false." The word was used of idols. What your heart covets (v. 36), your eyes will see, and then you will make wrong decisions. This is what happened to Lot (Gen. 13).

Proper Values   *The psalmist had the right values. He would rather have God's Word than food (v. 103), sleep (vv. 55, 62, 147–48), or money (vv. 14, 72, 127, 162).*

PSALM 119:41–48

Freedom is another blessing God will give you if you love and obey His Word (v. 45). His Word is truth (v. 43), and the truth sets you free (John 8:32). Disobedience may seem like freedom, but it is really bondage (2 Pet. 2:19). When you obey God's Word, you enjoy true freedom because His Word is "the law of liberty" (James 2:12). Law and liberty are not enemies; they are coworkers in your life in building character and bringing joy.

PSALM 119:49–56

The Word of God will bring *comfort* to your life if you will let it. The writer suffered affliction and persecution because of his faith, but the Word gave him comfort and hope. When the days are difficult and the nights are long, remember God's promises and God's name, and He will comfort you. (See also vv. 76, 82, 92.)

PSALM 119:57–64

If you are true to God's Word, you will have friends who are worth having (v. 63). Solomon taught this same lesson in Proverbs 2 (see also Prov. 13:20). If you walk with the wicked, they will bind you (v. 61), but if you walk with God's people, they will help you to enjoy life and liberty. People who love the Word will be glad to see you (v. 74) and will turn to you and help you (v. 79).

PSALM 119:65–72

The Word of God can encourage you in times of affliction (vv. 67, 71; see also vv. 50, 92). What life does to you depends upon what life finds in you. If the Word is in your mind and heart, affliction can bring out the best in you. If not, it may bring out the worst in you. The school of suffering never graduates any students, so ask God to teach you the lessons He wants you to learn.

PSALM 119:73–80

God made you and knows best how you should manage your life. The Bible is His how-to-do-it manual for making life work successfully (v. 73). It tells you how to use your body and mind, how to handle your time and money, and how to make right decisions. Obeying it can keep you from getting into trouble and hurting yourself and others. Do not wait until "all else fails" before you read the instructions! It may be too late!

PSALM 119:81–88

The Word of God will help you get victory over your enemies (vv. 84–87). When your eyes are failing and your soul is fainting, the Word will give you strength and comfort. When it looks like the end has come, God's Word helps you make a new beginning. Your worst enemy is on the inside, so let the Word work in your heart.

PSALM 119:89–96

If you trust God's Word, you will have a solid foundation in a world that offers you no stability. The Word of God is settled; nothing can change it or destroy it (v. 152; Matt. 24:35). God is faithful and His Word can be trusted. The same Word that created the world (v. 90) and runs the world (v. 91) will also govern your life and make it secure.

PSALM 119:97–104

Those who love God's Word and obey it develop a practical wisdom for guiding their lives. It is dangerous to learn from your enemies (v. 98), and both your teachers and your elderly friends may not know what you need to know (vv. 99–100). Learn all you can from every good source, but let God, not man, be your teacher (John 14:26; 16:13–15).

❝ *Everywhere among Conservatives we find persons who are Bible-taught but not Spirit-taught. They conceive truth to be something which they can grasp with the mind. If a man holds to the fundamentals of the Christian faith he is thought to possess divine truth. But it does not follow. There is no truth apart from the Spirit.* **❞**

A. W. Tozer

PSALM 119:105–12

In a dark world, God's Word can be your light (v. 105) to keep you from the traps and detours of the enemy (v. 110). God gives you the light you need a step at a time. If you want more light, you must obey what He says; then more light will come (John 7:17). God sends the light into your heart (v. 130) and gives you the wisdom you need.

PSALM 119:113–20

Doubleminded people are unstable people (James 1:8), and unstable people eventually fall. If you put God's Word first in your life, it will hold you up and you will not fall (vv. 116-17; 2 Pet. 3:17-18; Jude 20-25). Cultivate a holy fear of the Lord and His Word (v. 120) and you will not be ashamed of your hope (v. 116).

PSALM 119:121-28

God's Word will assure you and enable you when you feel the oppression of the enemy (vv. 121-22). God's people are aliens in enemy territory, and only the Word can protect them from the lies of the oppressor. But you must accept *all* that God's Word says about *all things;* if you love the truth, you must also hate the false (v. 128).

PSALM 119:129-36

When you live by the Word of God, your life becomes wonderful because the Word of God is wonderful (v. 129). The Spirit shows you wonderful things in the Word (v. 18) and enables you to meditate on His wonderful works (v. 27). God transforms your mind and enables you to escape the dull conformity of the world (Rom. 12:1-2). His light shines within you (v. 130) and His face shines upon you (v. 135), so that you become a light in a dark world (Phil. 2:14-16).

PSALM 119:137-44

A key word of this section is *righteousness.* No matter how zealous we may be for God's truth (v. 139), we must also have His righteousness if we are going to succeed. The Word helps us practice righteousness in a sinful world. There is no substitute for integrity, which comes from loving the Word and obeying it.

PSALM 119:145-52

In this section, the psalmist is crying out to God in prayer and reminding us that the Word of God helps us to pray in the will of God. The Word of God and prayer must never be separated (Acts 6:4); if they are, we will get out of balance. The better we know the Word, the more effectively we will pray (John

15:7), and the more effectively we pray, the better we will learn the Word.

PSALM 119:153-60

One of the most difficult things in the life of faith is to be accused by Satan and ungodly people. "Plead my cause," prayed the psalmist (v. 154), and God defended him. When the enemy accuses you, let the Word of God assure you (Zech. 3), for the Word is truth (v. 160; John 17:17). If Satan tries to drag you into his court, read Romans 8:31-39.

PSALM 119:161-68

Knowing the Word of God and obeying it will bring joy to your heart, the kind of joy you would have if you found a buried treasure (v. 162) or inherited a fortune (v. 111). If material wealth is your goal, God's Word will not be a joy to you; but if you love the Word more than money (v. 127), you will have eternal spiritual treasures. Along with joy, you will experience love (vv. 163, 167), peace (v. 165), and hope (v. 166)—treasures money cannot buy.

PSALM 119:169-76

If you put the Word of God first in your life, you will have something to sing about (vv. 171, 172, 175). Spontaneously, you will find yourself *singing God's Word* and turning statutes into songs (v. 54)! When your heart delights in God's law (v. 174), your lips must declare God's praise (Matt. 12:34). After all, you talk about the things that you love. When God's Word fills your heart, the right words will come out of your mouth (Col. 3:16; 4:6).

"THE SONGS OF ASCENTS"

The next fifteen psalms are known as "the Songs of Ascents." They are thought to be the songs the Jewish pilgrims sang when they went up to Jerusalem for the feasts three times each year. Whoever made this selection chose four psalms by David and one by Solomon; the other ten are anonymous.

Honor His Word

You have been thinking about what the Word of God will do for you if you allow it to work in your life. Now it is time to discover what you must do with God's Word. You must do more than simply read it, although that is necessary. You should also love it (v. 97), treasure it (v. 72), learn it (vv. 26–27), memorize it (v. 11), meditate on it (v. 15), believe it (v. 42), and practice it (vv. 1–4). The way you treat your Bible is the way you treat your Lord, for it is His Word to your heart.

The Hebrew word translated "ascents" also means "degrees," and for this reason some scholars relate this special collection to King Hezekiah and his experience related in Isaiah 38. The fifteen psalms mark the fifteen years added to his life, and the ten anonymous psalms are a reminder of the shadow going back ten degrees.

The emphasis in this "hymnal within the hymnal" is on trusting the God of Mount Zion, even in the midst of suffering and trial. The writers describe both the trials and the triumphs of the people of God and reveal that God is with His people—no matter what the difficulty.

PSALM 120

Deliverance (1–4). The familiar rhyme "Sticks and stones will break my bones, but names will never hurt me" is not always true. Words *can* hurt us, and the psalmist felt them keenly. Only God can deliver you from lies and their destructive power, and only God can judge the liars. Just be sure you are "valiant for the truth" in your own life (Jer. 9:3).

Endurance (5–7). God did not change the psalmist's circumstances; he had to remain among people who hated him

and lied about him. But God gave him the endurance he
needed to be faithful under pressure. God can easily change
your circumstances, but He needs your help if He is to change
you. Before God gives deliverance, He first must give endurance.

PSALM 121

God is your Helper (1–2). The God who made the hills is the
God who gives you help. He is a God of the hills and the valleys (1 Kings 20:23–30), and His help is available to all who will
call upon Him.

God is your Keeper (3–8). The pilgrims traveled together for
fellowship and safety because the roads were dangerous. The
dangers in modern society are just as great, if not greater. But
God goes *before you* (vv. 3–4) and stays awake to guide you and
guard your path. He is *next to you* (v. 5) and *over you* (v. 6), and
He will take you safely to Zion (vv. 7–8).

See His Greatness	*Be sure you lift your eyes high enough so that you see by faith the great God who cares for you. The ten spies in Canaan did not look high enough: they saw the giants and the walls but not the Lord far above all (Num. 13:28–33). When things on earth seem too big for you to handle, lift your eyes to God by meditating on Isaiah 40 (note v. 26). He is able!*

PSALM 122

"Let us go" (1). Do you really rejoice when you have opportunity to go to God's house and worship Him? We today can
travel easily to a place of worship, but the ancient Jews had to
walk a long distance. Yet the pilgrim was happy to go to God's
house.

"Let us praise" (2–5). How the people loved Jerusalem! It was a holy place because the temple was there, an honored place because David's throne was there, and a happy place because the tribes were there to celebrate the greatness and goodness of God.

"Let us pray" (6–9). Do you pray for the peace and prosperity of the people in your local "house of God"? Do you pray for God's people Israel? There can be no peace in our world until the Prince of Peace rules His people and there is peace in Jerusalem.

PSALM 123

Throughout their history, the Jews have often had to endure the scorn and contempt of their enemies. The world does not love God's people. As we make our way on the narrow road that leads to Zion, we run up against the crowd going in the other direction.

Look to God's heaven (1). If you look at the enemy, you will get discouraged, so look by faith to the God of the universe who reigns in heaven. Psalm 121 shows you how.

Look to God's hand (2). He is the Master, we are the servants, and He tenderly cares for His own. Just be sure your ears are open to whatever orders your Master wants to give you.

Look for His help (3–4). Adequate mercy is available for you when your heart is filled with pain. Let God's words of strength drown out the enemy's words of scorn.

PSALM 124

The Lord is on your side when people want to *devour you* (vv. 1–3), when circumstances seem to *drown you* (vv. 4–5), and when Satan tries to *deceive you* (vv. 6–8).

You can usually detect man's anger, and you can feel it when circumstances overwhelm you. But Satan's traps might catch you if you are not careful. In His death, resurrection, and ascension, Jesus Christ has not only set you free from the snares, but *He has broken the snares and they can never trap you again unless you let them.*

You are free as a bird, so use your wings of faith and live in the heavenlies!

PSALM 125

Trusting the Lord means *security and stability* (vv. 1–2). Built on Mount Zion and surrounded by the mountains, Jerusalem was an impregnable fortress. The pilgrims felt safe when they arrived there after their dangerous journey. As a citizen of the heavenly Zion, you are safe in the Lord's care.

Trusting the Lord also means *sovereignty* (v. 3), bowing down to the God who holds the righteous scepter. Wickedness in our world is a temptation even to the righteous, so keep submitted to Him.

Sanctity (vv. 4–5) is a third result of trusting the Lord. When you walk by faith, you avoid the dangerous detours that lead you away from the path of righteousness. God has made you safe that you might be submitted, and your submission should lead to separated living: "Faith without works is dead" (James 2:20).

PSALM 126

This song probably celebrates Jerusalem's deliverance from the Assyrian army in the days of Hezekiah (2 Kings 18–19). It all happened so quickly that the people thought they were dreaming, and even the other nations had to admit the greatness of God.

But deliverance is just the beginning; God always wants to do something more. He wants to make us rivers of blessing (v. 4), like the dry wadis in the desert that become rushing torrents in the rainy season. If God sends you "showers of blessing," share the blessing with others.

He also wants you to get to work in the harvest (vv. 5–6). Whether it is plowing the field (Luke 9:62), sowing the seed, or reaping the sheaves, God has a place for you. If you water the seed with your tears, you will one day rejoice as you bring in the sheaves. This is the formula for a harvest: going, weeping, sowing, reaping.

> *His*
> *Grace*
>
> *"Great things He has done!" is the theme of many people who have experienced God's grace. Samuel preached about it (1 Sam. 12:24); David thanked the Lord for it (2 Sam. 7:21, 23); Mary sang about it (Luke 1:49); and the healed demoniac told everybody about it (Luke 8:39).*

PSALM 127

Do not forget the Lord (1–2). Jesus warned, "Without Me you can do nothing" (John 15:5), and that truth is illustrated in this psalm. What good is all your working, watching, and waking if the Lord is not with you? Long hours and sleepless nights are a waste apart from the blessing of the Lord. This psalm is not a plea for idleness, for God expects you to work and watch. But He wants to work in you and to accomplish His will (Phil. 2:12–13).

Do not neglect your family (3–5). What good are a lovely house and a big income if the people in your life are robbed of the joys of a happy home? Children are a gift and a heritage, so appreciate them and guard them. They are like fruit, so lovingly cultivate them. They can be arrows for fighting the Lord's battles, so keep them polished and sharp and aimed in the right direction. Give yourself to building a *home*, not just a house, and building for the *future*, not just the present.

PSALM 128

This song parallels Psalm 112 and reminds you of the blessings God sends when you fear the Lord and walk in obedience to His Word.

God will bring you enjoyment in employment (v. 2) so that your work will be a blessing and not a curse. Your work will be a ministry for the Lord.

God will bless you at home, beginning at the heart of the home (your spouse) and touching everybody else around the table. Your home will be a fruitful garden, not an ugly desert.

The blessing will then spread to the city and the nation, and it will go from generation to generation (vv. 5 6).

"*The beauty of the house is order; The blessing of the house is contentment; The glory of the house is hospitality; The crown of the house is godliness.***"**

An old motto often placed

above fireplaces

PSALM 129

Israel's afflictions are compared to the plowing of a field. Think of what it would feel like to be face down in the dirt while a plow goes down your back! How do you handle a situation like that?

First, you accept it from the Lord. *If the Lord is allowing people to plow your back, it is happening because He has planned a harvest.* Just be sure you plant the right kind of seed. If you plant anger and malice, you will not reap the blessings of the Lord.

Second, you trust the Lord to help you. In His own time, He will stop the plows *and cut the cords so they cannot plow anymore*. All their efforts will be useless.

Third, you wait for the Lord to judge your enemies. He will put them to shame and make them wither like grass on a sod roof. On the other hand, God's people will hear God's blessing in their ears and have God's blessing in their hands.

Plowing times can be productive times.

PSALM 130

As you ponder this psalm, see yourself in four different situations, and learn what it means to trust the mercy of the Lord.

In the depths (1–2). The depths of despair overwhelm you. You are drowning, and all you can do is cry out to God. He hears—and He rescues you!

In the court (3–4). You are on trial, facing your sins, and you have no defense. The Judge pays the penalty, and *you are forgiven!*

In the dark (5–6). You are waiting patiently, yet it seems morning will never come. But the sun rises, and God gives you the dawning of a new day!

On the block (7–8). You are a slave, bound by your own sins, and you are about to sell yourself to a terrible master. But the Savior comes and purchases you and sets you free!

What a wonderful salvation you have!

PSALM 131

Most children naturally resist weaning because they want to continue enjoying the special attention of mother and the security it brings. Children do not realize that the traumatic experience of weaning is the first step toward maturity and freedom.

From birth to death, life is a series of weanings, and God never takes anything from you without giving you something better. You may weep and try to hold on to the past, but God tenderly leads you toward the future.

Weaned children discover who they are and what they can do. They have quiet hearts and no desire to go back to babyhood. They live for the future and watch for the special things that come to children growing up. They learn to obey, for only then can they fully experience all that the Father has for them.

As you mature in the Lord, you must "put away childish things" (1 Cor. 13:11). When God weans you away from something, do not fret; He has something better to take its place.

PSALM 132

Some students believe that this psalm was written when the Jewish exiles returned to their land from Babylon. This theory explains why David is mentioned. It was a difficult time as the Jews tried to rebuild their temple, their city, and their nation, and their beloved King David had been involved in these endeavors. The returned exiles wanted God to remember His covenant with David and restore their land.

The temple (1–9). David yearned to build the temple, but the Lord chose his son Solomon instead. However, David provided the plans for the temple (1 Chron. 28:11–19) and much of the wealth needed. Would God desert His people as they tried to rebuild the temple that meant so much to David?

The throne (10–12). God promised that David's line would continue on the throne (2 Sam. 7), but now Israel was without a king. In fact, there would be no king until Jesus came, and they would reject Him. One day, He will return and restore David's throne (Luke 1:30–33; Acts 15:14–18).

The city (13–18). Jerusalem was in ruins, but it was the City of David and would not be forgotten by the Lord. He would dwell there, bless the people, and give them joy. He would restore power (the horn) and light (the lamp) and make the city a testimony to the nations.

When the going is tough, remember those feeble Jews who sacrificed to restore what sin had destroyed. They prepared the way for the Son of God who came to their city and temple and gave His life for the sins of the world.

PSALM 133

It is one thing for a group of people to *journey together* to Jerusalem for a feast and quite something else for them to *live together* day after day. Abraham and Lot, Isaac and his family, Jacob and Laban, and Joseph's brothers remind us that brethren do not always dwell together in unity.

Unity must come down from above, like the oil running down Aaron's beard and bathing the twelve jewels on the breastplate (Exod. 29:5–7), or like the dew descending on the mountains. You can manufacture uniformity by manipulating people and exerting pressure, but true unity can come only from God by His Spirit.

Unity is good like the dew and produces fruitfulness. It is pleasant like the oil and produces a lovely fragrance. Divisions among God's people produce opposite results. Have you heeded the admonition of Ephesians 4:1–6?

PSALM 134

Have you ever given thanks for the people who work the night shift? Were it not for them, you would have no electricity or water at night, no fire or police protection, or no emergency service at the hospital. While you are asleep, others are serving. Be grateful!

But do the people on the night shift give thanks? Perhaps not. The psalmist admonished the priests in the temple to give thanks as they served God and the people at night. It may have been a lonely ministry, but it was an important ministry.

Your High Priest in heaven intercedes for you day and night. He never grows weary or impatient. Have you told Him you are thankful for His faithful ministry? Are you willing to be like Him and serve others, even on the night shift?

PSALM 135

The psalmist opened his song praising the Lord four times (vv. 1–3), and he ended it blessing the Lord four times (vv. 19–21). In between, he gave four excellent reasons why the Lord deserves your heartfelt praise.

To begin with, He is the God of *salvation* (v. 4). In His grace, He chose you; in His mercy, He made you His special treasure. You belong to Him. He values you and He loves you.

He is the God of *creation* (vv. 5–7), which means He provides for you day after day and gives you the things you need. He is in charge of the storms and uses them to accomplish His perfect will.

He is the God of *history* (vv. 8–14). The Jews prided themselves in the fact that God worked especially on behalf of their nation. He worked for Israel and through Israel to bring about His great plan of salvation.

He is the God of *celebration* (vv. 15–18). These verses parallel Psalm 115 and show the greatness of the living God in contrast to the dead idols of the nations. Celebrate the Lord today! Bless His holy name!

PSALM 136

Two choirs sang this psalm. One choir sang the first line of each verse, and the other choir answered, "For His mercy endures forever." This was not vain repetition (Matt. 6:7), for the second choir was offering inspired praise to the Lord. You can never say too much about the mercy of God!

God reveals His mercy by giving you a wonderful creation to use and to enjoy (vv. 4–9). Just think, He had everything ready for our first parents when He made them! It is too bad that many people are such poor stewards of God's creation gifts. Never take for granted the wonderful world you live in.

He reveals His mercy in His care for you, helping you fight your battles and defeat your enemies (vv. 10–25). Israel was not always faithful to God, but that is where His mercy comes in! He was faithful to them.

The God of heaven is caring for you on earth! His mercy endures forever!

PSALM 137

This psalm came out of Israel's exile in Babylon, and it can serve as an inventory of your spiritual life today.

What makes you weep (1)? The Jews wept as they remembered the past, but they did not weep over their sins. They wept because their sins caught up with them, not because they had sinned.

What makes you sing (2–4)? They lost their song, so they hung up their harps. David had a similar experience (Ps. 32:1–7). Can you sing praises to God in a difficult place (Acts 16:25)? Can you praise the Lord at all times?

What makes you yearn (5–6)? What is the ache in your heart? What do you long for more than anything else? Is it in God's will?

What makes you angry (7–9)? God had promised to judge Babylon (Isa. 13; note v. 16), so they were praying in His will; but the note of anguish is missing. (See the entry on Ps. 58 for comments on the "imprecatory psalms.") If you love the Lord, you must hate evil (Ps. 97:10; Rom. 12:9) but leave the judgment to the Lord (Rom. 12:17–21).

PSALM 138

Walking "in the midst of trouble" did not hinder the psalmist's *worship* (vv. 1–3). If anything, it helped him to pray and to praise the Lord even more. David could not go to the temple, so he worshiped "toward the temple"; and God helped him.

His troubles did not hinder his *witness* (vv. 4–6). David may have been among the Gentiles when he wrote this psalm, but he was careful to share the Word and instruct them on singing God's praises. Trouble can be God's way to open doors for you to share the gospel.

His troubles did not hinder his *walk* (vv. 7–8). God revived David and enabled him to defeat his foes. Best of all, God perfected His plan for David and made him a better man (Eph. 2:10; Phil. 2:12–13).

You may think that your troubles give you an excuse to stop living for the Lord. This psalm says that just the opposite is true! Read it again and follow David's example.

PSALM 139

If you are faithful to the Lord, this psalm will encourage you. If you are trying to hide from the Lord, this psalm will make you realize you are fighting a losing battle.

He knows what you do (1–6). He knows you personally and intimately, so do not try to fool Him. Be open and honest with God, and rest in His love (1 John 4:18). His eye is upon you, and you have nothing to fear.

He knows where you go (7–12). What a comfort to know that God is with you and cares for you! Whether you go up or down, east or west, He is there (Heb. 13:5). Sinners try to hide *from* God, but believers hide *in* God.

He knows what you are (13–16). After all, He made you, planned your potential, and ordered your days. This is not some kind of blind fatalism that paralyzes you. It is the wise plan of a loving Father who knows what is best for you. Accept what you are as His gift to you, and then use it wisely as your gift to Him. You are *unique;* God made you that way.

He knows what you think (17–18). The psalmist pondered the thoughts of God and in this way cultivated the presence of God in his life. "You are to meditate on these things" (Phil. 4:8).

He knows what you love (19–22). Take these words to heart: "You who love the LORD, hate evil" (Ps. 97:10); "Love not the world" (1 John 2:15–17).

He knows what you desire (23-24). You do not know your own heart as well as you may think you do (Jer. 17:9-10). Let God search you and deal with the things that make you anxious. Let Him lead you. He knows where you ought to go.

PSALM 140

Satan fights anyone who is doing the will of God, and David was no exception. You must pray for Christian leaders especially, for they are prime targets for the evil one. The enemy has two favorite weapons: poisonous tongues (vv. 1-3) and hidden traps (vv. 4-5). He slanders God's leaders (sometimes using the lips of professed Christians), and he sets traps for them, hoping to trip them up.

David depended on prayer (vv. 6-11), God's promise (v. 12), and praise (v. 13). God hates a lying tongue (Prov. 6:17) and will one day judge slanderers. Meanwhile, maintain your character before God and let Him take care of your reputation. So live that when people hear lies about you, they will not believe them.

PSALM 141

"My voice . . . my hands" (1-2). David was away from God's house, but he knew he could worship the Lord even without a priest or an altar. His prayer would be like the incense on the golden altar (Exod. 30:1-10), and the lifting of his hands in praise like the burnt offering on the brazen altar (Exod. 29:38-41; Heb. 13:15). No matter where you are, worship the Lord!

"My mouth . . . my lips" (3-4). When evil is near you, and evil people tempt you, it is easy to say the wrong thing. It is the heart that needs protection (Matt. 12:34-37).

"My head" (5-7). "Faithful are the wounds of a friend" (Prov. 27:6): they may hurt, but like oil, they heal. Watch out for the kisses—and delicacies (v. 4)—of the enemy.

"My eyes" (8-10). Keep your eyes of faith on the Lord, and He will direct and protect your steps.

David gave *himself* to the Lord as the evening sacrifice, every part of his being (Rom. 12:1-2). This is the highest kind of worship and the greatest privilege.

PSALM 142

Another of David's "cave" psalms (Ps. 57; see also 1 Sam. 22:1-2, 24:1ff.), Psalm 142 is filled with assurances you can claim when you find yourself in a difficult place.

God hears your prayers (1-2). There are times when prayer is worship (Ps. 141:1), and there are times when prayer is warfare. In the heat of the battle, pour out your heart to the Lord and tell Him how you feel and what you need. Turn the cave into a Holy of Holies.

God knows your path (3). David walked in God's will, but the enemy lied about him and set traps to catch him. Walk with the Lord a step at a time and He will see you through (Ps. 16:11; Prov. 3:5-6).

God feels your pain (4). David felt completely abandoned, but he knew the Lord was with him (2 Tim. 4:16-18). When you feel like nobody cares, remember that *He cares for you* (1 Pet. 5:7).

God is your portion (5). If you have God, what more do you need? One with God is a majority, so be wholly satisfied with Him.

God will be praised (6-7). It may not look like it now, but one day your trials will turn out for your good and God's glory. Start praising Him now—by faith—and you will be "tuned up" when the answer comes.

PSALM 143

Unless you have been engaged in the Lord's battles, you may not understand this prayer, for it is the cry of a soldier in combat. It is also a penitential prayer.

"Hear me" (1-6). Depend on God's grace and faithfulness, not on your righteousness. Tell God what is happening in your life. David was in the dust and in the darkness. He felt like a thirsty man dying in a desert.

"Answer me" (7-9). When God does not answer prayer, it is as though His face turns away from us and we sink into the grave. Do you find strength and joy in answered prayer?

"Teach me" (10). David met with the Lord each morning and got his orders for the day. Without those orders, he did not

know how to walk. Trust God's Spirit to lead you as you yield yourself to Him.

"Revive me" (11–12). David was in the dust (v. 3), and only God could raise him up. David wanted to fight the Lord's battles and establish righteousness in the land. True prayer means that we serve God, not that God serves us (v. 12).

PSALM 144

This is another battle song to help you in your spiritual warfare.

Let God train you *before the battle* (vv. 1–4). In yourself, you are nothing, but God loves you and equips you for what lies ahead. God does not always explain how He prepares you, so accept His disciplines by faith. David fought a lion and a bear before God let him fight a giant. Each morning, put on the whole armor of God and be ready for the trumpet call (Eph. 6:10–18).

Let God help you *in the battle* (vv. 5–8). God's hand is there to strengthen and deliver you, so do not be afraid to engage the enemy. You are fighting the Lord's battles; He will not abandon you (2 Chron. 20:14–19).

Sing God's praises *after the battle* (vv. 9–15). Thank Him for all He has done for you personally (vv. 9–11), for your family (v. 12), and for your nation (vv. 13–15).

PSALM 145

David extols the Lord for His greatness (v. 3), grace (vv. 8, 17), goodness (v. 9), glory (vv. 11–12), and generosity (vv. 15–16). If you are having a hard time praising the Lord today, that should help get you started! God's people will praise Him forever, so we had better learn to do it day by day (v. 2).

David extols the Lord as an encouragement to others. Members of each generation need to learn to praise the Lord (vv. 4–7), so your praise is an example and witness to them. Are others growing in their worship because of you?

David hears all God's works praising Him (v. 10). Nature takes on new meaning and new beauty when you realize this (Ps. 19:1–6).

When you live a life of praise, you have the Lord's help in every situation. If you stumble, He helps you up (v. 14). If you are hungry, He feeds you (vv. 15–16). If you call, He draws near (v. 18). No wonder David blessed the Lord so much!

PSALM 146

Praise is an evidence of *life* (vv. 1–2), not just physical life, but the life of God in the heart. In heaven, it is all praise; in hell, there is no praise; here on earth, you must make a choice.

Praise is an encouragement to *faith* (vv. 3–4). When you have faith in somebody—your doctor, for instance—you praise that person to others. When your faith is low, your praise will gradually subside, but when you major on praise, your faith will grow.

Praise is an encouragement to *hope* (vv. 5–7). When your hope is in the Lord, you can praise Him no matter what the circumstances may be. Faith is the upward look, and hope is the forward look.

Praise is an encouragement to *love* (vv. 8–10), your love for God and others, and God's love for you. When you love someone, you trust that person, and greater trust brings greater love.

Life, faith, hope, and love—all are bound up in the experience of praise.

PSALM 147

Praising the Lord is the highest exercise of your faculties. He is worthy of praise, and you should praise Him whether or not you think your praise is accomplishing anything in your life. However, there are some blessings that come to those who worship Him in truth.

Praise brings spiritual beauty to God's people (v. 1; Pss. 27:4, 29:2; 149:4). It builds His work and unifies His people (v. 2). It heals the inner person (v. 3) and lifts the fallen (v. 6). Praise is good medicine!

Praise makes God's world real and personal to you (vv. 7–9, 15–18), even the storms; and it is great protection against the enemy (vv. 12–14). Praise pleases the Lord and enables Him to work in your life (vv. 10–11).

Praise must never become a pragmatic device for getting blessing from God. When you sincerely praise Him, the blessing will come. Praise changes things—and people.

How Do You Mend a Broken Heart?	*The God who numbers and names the stars knows about your broken heart and can heal it—if you give all the pieces to Him (Ps. 147:3–4).*

PSALM 148

When it comes to praising the Lord, the psalmist will not permit anyone or anything in all creation to escape.

The heavens (1–6). He starts with the angels, then summons the heavenly bodies, and even includes the clouds! God created them, established them, and controls them. They should praise Him—and they do!

The earth (7–10). Whether the depths of the sea or the heights of the mountains, the winds or the fruitful trees, all should praise the Lord—and they do! When the weather is bad, it is good to know that even the storms fulfill God's Word (v. 8).

Mankind (11–14). Made in God's image, men and women have more reason to praise God than does any other thing in creation. And when you have been saved by God's grace, your motive is even greater. Praise the Lord!

PSALM 149

God's people should be a singing people. They should sing *in the sanctuary* (vv. 1–4) because God is their Savior (v. 1), their Maker, and their King (v. 2). You are reminded again that praise pleases God and beautifies God's people (v. 4; Ps. 147:1, 11).

You should sing *at home* (v. 5), even when in bed! Sing when you wake up in the morning, when you take a nap, when you go to bed at night. If it is a bed of illness, sing to the Lord even more.

Sing to the Lord *on the battlefield* (vv. 6–9). God's Word is your sword (Eph. 6:17; Heb. 4:12), and it should be on your lips as well as in your hand. Praise is a wonderful weapon for defeating the enemy.

PSALM 150

It is only right that the closing song in the Hebrew hymnal be an invitation to praise the Lord. The word *praise* is used thirteen times here.

Where should we praise Him? Locally and universally, in the temple and in the vast heavens (v. 1). In other words, wherever you are, praise the Lord!

Why should we praise Him? Because of what He does and who He is (v. 2). The better you know God's character and works, the more you will praise Him and the more you will enjoy praising Him.

How should we praise Him? With voices and instruments, including the cymbals, and with our bodies expressing the joy we feel within (vv. 3–5). The whole person should be one living sacrifice that praises the Lord.

Who should praise Him? "Everything that has breath" (v. 6). But things that do not have breath praise Him (Ps. 148:7–9), so we have even more reason to do so! Our breath comes from Him (Acts 17:25), so we ought to use it to praise His name. Breath is the weakest thing we have, but we can devote it to the highest service, praising the Lord.

PROVERBS

—————————— ◆ ——————————

A *proverb* has been defined as a "short statement based on
long experience." The Hebrew word translated "proverb"
means "to be like," and many of the proverbs are contrasts or
comparisons. The proverbs deal with the ethical and moral
aspects of life. They are practical, not theoretical, and point
the way to godly character and a fulfilled life.

The theme of Proverbs is wisdom, the right use of knowledge. This wisdom is more than an intellectual pursuit; it also
involves devotion to the Lord. The wise person fears the Lord,
trusts Him, and seeks to obey His will. The wisdom described
in Proverbs is like a spiritual "sixth sense." It enables you to
evaluate circumstances and people and make the right decisions in life.

Since a proverb is only the statement of a general truth, it
must not be taken for a divine promise. David and Jesus both
pleased the Lord, but they still had enemies (Prov. 16:7); and
more than one obedient child of God has died young (Prov.
10:27). Not all godly people have houses full of money (Prov.
15:6), and many godless people eat well (Prov. 13:25). In the
light of eternity, the wicked are the losers—no matter how successful they may be—but Proverbs focuses primarily on this
life, not the next.

These wise sayings are "distilled truth" made practical for
daily living. You find in them principles, warnings, and coun-
sels that really work *when you fear the Lord and want to please
Him*. The book of Proverbs is not a do-it-yourself success kit
for the greedy but a guidebook for the godly.

Most of the book was written by Solomon (1:1; see also
1 Kings 4:32), with contributions from other writers (22:17;
24:23; 30:1; 31:1). "The men of Hezekiah" (25:1) probably edited
the book to its present form.

Proverbs covers a wide range of subjects, and the verses are not arranged in topical order. In our meditations, we will concentrate on a major emphasis in each chapter, and from time to time, we will bring together verses that relate to a common theme.

PROVERBS 1

The importance of wisdom (1–6). All you need for success is yours when you receive God's wisdom. "Success" means much more than making a living. It means making a life that honors God and serves others. Wisdom is more important than riches and power (Prov. 8:12–21) because wisdom helps you build for all eternity.

The instruction of wisdom (7–19). "The fear of the LORD" means reverence for God and respect for His Word, a willingness to listen and a promptness to obey. God uses different people to teach you wisdom, and you must be alert to each lesson. Note the warnings: "Do not forsake! Do not consent! Do not walk!" God says no that He might say yes.

Who Is Wise?

The truly wise person will hear the Word of God (Prov. 1:5) and obey it (Prov. 12:15); store up what is learned (Prov. 9:9; 10:14); win the lost (Prov. 11:30); turn from sin (Prov. 14:16); control the tongue (Prov. 10:19; 16:23); and be diligent (Prov. 10:5). The wise person will inherit glory (Prov. 3:35); bring joy to others (Prov. 10:1; 15:20); have his or her needs met (Prov. 21:20); and have strength for war (Prov. 24:5–6).

The invitation of wisdom (20–33). Wisdom is like a lovely woman inviting hungry people to a great feast (Prov. 1:20–33;

8:1ff.; 9:1ff.). Folly is like an evil woman seducing the ignorant into sin (5:1ff.; 6:20ff.; 7:1ff.). Accept wisdom's call and you will be blessed; accept folly's call and you will destroyed.

PROVERBS 2

Wisdom is not only a person to know (chap. 1) but also a path to walk. The word *path* is used seven times in this chapter. It suggests to us that life involves direction, decision, and determination, just like walking a path. God will do His part (vv. 6–9) if you do your part (vv. 1–5).

The Path of the Unwise

Wisdom addresses three kinds of people: the simple, the scorner, and the fool. The simple are people who believe everything (Prov. 14:15). They have no understanding (Prov. 7:7; 9:4) and cannot see the road ahead (Prov. 22:3; 27:12). Scorners think they know everything (Prov. 21:24), so they never attain wisdom (Prov. 14:6) or even profit from rebuke (Prov. 9:7–8; 13:1; 15:12). They are great troublemakers (Prov. 22:10) who ought to be punished (Prov. 19:29; 21:11). Fools are self-confident (Prov. 12:15; 28:26) and hate instruction (Prov. 1:7, 22; 23:9). They speak proudly (Prov. 10:18; 14:3), love to fight (Prov. 18:6–7; 27:3), meddle (Prov. 20:3), speak without thinking (Prov. 18:13; 19:11), and mock at sin (Prov. 14:9). They are not helped by discipline (Prov. 17:10; 27:22) and will finally fall (Prov. 10:8, 10, 14).

The path of wisdom is a guarded path (v. 8) and a good path (v. 9) that leads to life (v. 19) and righteousness (v. 20). The path of folly is a dark (v. 13) and devious (v. 15) path that leads to death (v. 18).

If you want to walk on the path of God's wisdom, heed the admonitions in verses 1–5.

PROVERBS 3

Your heart (1–8). What you do with your heart determines what you do with your life (Prov. 4:23). Cultivate an obedient heart (v. 1) that receives God's Word (v. 3; 2 Cor. 3:1–3) and a trusting heart that obeys (vv. 5–6). Verse 5 does not suggest that you ignore your mind or common sense, but that you not lean only on them and reject God's way.

Your possessions (9–20). Put God first in the way you use His wealth (Matt. 6:33) and major on the things that money cannot buy (vv. 13–18). When God corrects you, accept it as an evidence of His love (Heb. 12:5–6).

Your conduct (21–26). Let every part of your body be controlled by God's wisdom (Rom. 12:1–2). Sleep is one of the tests of faith and true surrender to God (Ps. 4).

Your neighbors (27–35). If you want God's blessing on your home, be a blessing to those around you. Share what you have and never plan evil against others (Rom. 12:9–21).

PROVERBS 4

The wise person encourages others to hear the Word and find wisdom. The father received wisdom when he was a boy, and he admonished his children to do the same. Live today so that your counsel and example will influence others and help them live wisely.

When you have wisdom, you have protection (v. 6) and promotion (vv. 8–9) and you will have the freedom to make progress (v. 12). As you obey His Word, the light will get brighter on the path of life (v. 18). But this is not true if you are on the path of the wicked.

Again, Solomon emphasized having your whole person controlled by God's Word (vv. 20–27; Col. 3:16). This will guide you on the right path and keep you from detours.

Samson on the Wrong Path

Samson was a gifted man who ignored many of the instructions given in Proverbs 1—4. Read Judges 13—16 and note that he did not seek God's wisdom but went his own rebellious way. He took his eyes off the right path and ended up on the path of darkness and death. He chose the wrong friends and followed folly instead of wisdom. Had he allowed the Word to control his whole person, Samson would have brought blessing to himself and glory to God.

PROVERBS 5

In a world that has commercialized sex and turned adultery into entertainment, this warning is desperately needed. Few people believe that there are tragic consequences to sexual sin, but Solomon names some of them.

Sexual Sin

Sexual immorality is like walking a path that leads to death (Prov. 2:16–22) and hell (Prov. 5:5); like deliberately burning and wounding yourself (Prov. 6:20–35); like being slaughtered as an animal (Prov. 7:6–27); like closing your eyes and falling into a pit (Prov. 22:14; 23:26–28). Ponder Hebrews 13:4.

What begins as something "sweet" gradually turns into something bitter; what is "life" becomes death; and the end is hell (vv. 4–5). You lose honor, years of life, wealth, and joy (vv. 7–14), and what you think is freedom is really the worst kind of bondage (vv. 21–23). The physical consequences alone ought to make a person want to obey God (v. 11).

Sex in marriage should be like drinking refreshing water from a clean fountain, while illicit sex is like drinking at a sewer (vv. 15–20). The Hebrew word translated "enraptured" in verse 19 means "intoxicated." When husband and wife love each other as God wants them to, the water turns into wine! (See John 2:1–11.)

PROVERBS 6

Deliver yourself (1–5). Wicked works will ensnare you (Prov. 5:22), but so will reckless words. You must be careful when you make promises. If you do not learn to say no, you will end up in bondage, and the price will be very high. Better to humble yourself and get free than to let your pride ruin you.

Teach yourself (6–11). Learn from the world of nature (Prov. 30:15–31). The ant makes good use of opportunities to prepare for the future, but the sluggard is aimless and lazy and ends up in poverty. The preacher who used this text was correct when he titled his sermon "Rock-A-Bye, Lullaby, Bye-Bye."

Guard yourself (12–35). Watch out for the wicked man (vv. 12–19) and the evil woman (vv. 20–35). Hate what God hates and love what God loves and you will enjoy what God enjoys.

The Sluggard

The sluggard likes to sleep (Prov. 6:6–11; 24:30–34) and expects everybody else to serve him (Prov. 12:27; 19:24). He dreams of wealth but ends up poor (Prov. 13:4; 21:25–26). He is good at excuses (Prov. 20:4; 22:13; 26:13–16) but poor at performance (Prov. 10:26). He is not a builder but a destroyer (Prov. 18:9).

PROVERBS 7

When wisdom is your sister, you will not be seduced by the temptress (vv. 1–5; Ps. 119:11). Your feet will not go near her house. And if she should come after you, your heart will see through all her enticements and have no desire for her.

Expensive tapestries cannot cover the ugliness of sin, and the most aromatic spices cannot turn the stench of sin into fragrant perfume (vv. 16–17). No matter what temptation is offered you, look beyond the externals and see it as it really is.

You are made in the image of God, but sin drags you down to the level of a beast (vv. 22–23) and eventually to the level of Satan himself (v. 27)! Is it worth it?

PROVERBS 8

Listen! Wisdom's first call was from the crowded city square (1:20ff.), but now she is "where the paths meet" (v. 2). When you are confronted with truth, you are at a place of decision, and the decision you make will have inevitable consequences. Keep your ears open and listen to God's wisdom (vv. 6, 32, 34).

Love! Wisdom says, "I love those who love me" (v. 17). Love wisdom rather than wealth (vv. 10–11, 18–21), for wisdom enriches you for eternity. Verses 22–31 make you think of Jesus Christ, who is the Wisdom of God (1 Cor. 1:30; Col. 2:3). To love wisdom is to love Christ, and when you love Christ, you live for Him.

Linger! Spend time daily at wisdom's door as you read God's Word and meditate on His truth. According to verse 14, God will give you counsel (what to do), wisdom (how to do it), understanding (why you do it), and strength (the ability to do it). Instead of serving as a slave, you will reign as a king (vv. 15–16).

PROVERBS 9

Come and dine! You see two houses and hear two invitations. Wisdom offers you a banquet of bread, meat, and wine; folly offers you stolen bread and water. Wisdom promises you life, but if you eat at folly's table, you will die. Which house will you enter?

Come and learn! Scoffers know so much that nobody can teach them anything, but the wise learn from rebuke. You may not enjoy it when somebody reproves you, but it will do you good. (See Ps. 141:5.)

Come and live! Wisdom multiplies days (v. 11). Those who abuse their bodies with sin usually cut their lives short, but when you follow wisdom, you can add years to your life—and life to your years! God gives a fullness of experience to those who obey Him.

Rebuke *The way you respond to criticism and rebuke reveals the kind of person you are (Prov. 9:7–9). Scoffers will not listen to rebuke (Prov. 13:1) or love those who rebuke them (Prov. 15:12). The wise person knows that rebuke is evidence of love (Prov. 27:5) and will value it (Prov. 25:12) and gain understanding from it (Prov. 19:25). Ponder Proverbs 27:6.*

PROVERBS 10

Wise and *righteous* are key words in this chapter, and they go together, for the wise practice righteousness and the righteous grow in wisdom.

The wise bring joy and not grief to their parents (v. 1). They will take advantage of God-given opportunities (v. 5) and will obey orders (v. 8). Wise people gather knowledge (v. 14) and share it with others (vv. 13, 21, 31). They also know when to be quiet (v. 19). They do not jest about sin (v. 23) but are serious about obeying the Lord.

The righteous have God's protection and provision (vv. 2–3, 24–25), and He blesses them in life (v. 6) and after death (v. 7). Their words give life (vv. 11, 20–21, 31–32), and their works prosper (v. 16). Their future is secure (v. 30) and joyful (v. 28).

If you are wise and righteous, those traits will be revealed by your words (vv. 6, 11, 14, 20–21, 31–32) as well as by your works.

> **The Tongue of the Righteous**
>
> *The wise person's words are like silver (Prov. 10:20), a tree of life (Prov. 15:4), food (Prov. 10:21), refreshing water (Prov. 10:11; 18:4), and medicine (Prov. 12:18). They should be seasoned with salt (Col. 4:6) and must not become destructive (James 3:1–12).*

PROVERBS 11

The contrast is between the righteous and the wicked. God delights in the righteous (v. 20) and delivers them from lust (v. 6), death (v. 4), trouble (v. 8), and gossip (v. 9). God also delivers their families (v. 21).

God guides the upright in their integrity (v. 3) because they desire what God desires (v. 23). They sow righteousness (v. 18) and flourish like a healthy tree (vv. 28, 30). The upright are a blessing to others (vv. 10–11), and they gain a sure reward (v. 18).

Reread the chapter and discover what happens to the wicked.

PROVERBS 12

God uses the mouth of the righteous to bring deliverance (v. 6), but the mouth of the wicked brings bondage (v. 13). Right words must begin with right thoughts (v. 5) and a love for learning (v. 1), and this is where the ungodly person fails.

Right words bring good to others (Prov. 10:21) and also to those who speak them (v. 14; Prov. 13:2). With your words, you can help to heal those who have been hurt (v. 18) and who have suffered because of lies (vv. 19–22). You can bring joy to those who are depressed and worried (v. 25).

Be alert today for God-given opportunities to speak healing words to hurting people.

Liars

Because He is a God of truth, the Lord hates a lying tongue (Prov. 6:17; 12:22). With lies, people cover their true feelings (Prov. 10:18) and promote hypocrisy (Prov. 26:23–26). Liars do not last (Prov. 12:19), but lies can go on for years and do great damage. Wealth gained by lies is fleeting (Prov. 21:6), and all liars will one day be punished (Prov. 19:5, 9). If God hates lies, we must hate them, too (Prov. 13:5). Ponder Ephesians 4:17–32.

PROVERBS 13

This chapter gives some practical counsel on how to be wise. First, listen to rebuke and instruction (v. 1) and learn to take advice (v. 10) and discipline (v. 24). Walk with the wise (v. 20) and listen to their conversation (v. 14), and you will become more like them. As you meditate on the Word of God, you walk with the wisest of the wise, so do not neglect the Scriptures (v. 13).

The chapter also offers counsel concerning wealth. Diligent people will work and gain wealth (v. 4) and not get it dishonestly (v. 11). Verse 7 cautions you not to be rich in the things money can buy while you ignore the things money cannot buy. The rich are often poorer than the poor when it comes to what really counts!

Discipline "Spare the rod and spoil the child" is an old English proverb that was probably based on a similar Latin proverb. The Bible's version is Proverbs 13:24. When parents discipline their children in love, they follow the example of the Lord Himself (Prov. 3:11–12; Heb. 12:5–6; Rev. 3:19). The purpose is improvement (Prov. 22:15), not the venting of anger, and their only desire must be the welfare of the child (Prov. 19:18; 23:13–14; 29:15, 17).

PROVERBS 14

Watch out for fools (v. 7)! Wisdom builds but folly destroys (v. 1), and the tent of the godly is stronger than the house of the wicked (v. 11). When you obey the Word of God, you build on a solid foundation (Matt. 7:21–27).

Watch out for fools! Their speech can tear you down (v. 7), for their words are like a rod that hurts (v. 3). You cannot trust what they say (v. 8); they mock at sin (v. 9); and they rage in their self-confidence (v. 16). Be sure to watch out for their temper (vv. 17, 29); it can get you and them into trouble.

When you fear the Lord, your walk will be marked by uprightness (vv. 2, 16), confidence (v. 26), and protection (v. 27). The fear of the Lord is better than the folly of fools.

PROVERBS 15

When you open your mouth, you let people know whether you are foolish or wise. The wise share knowledge and are like fruitful trees that feed many (v. 4). Fools pour out words that accomplish nothing (v. 2).

The wise know how to control anger (v. 18) and respond to anger (v. 1). The "soft answer" is neither deception nor flattery, but saying the right thing (v. 28) at the right time (v. 23) in the right spirit (v. 1).

What comes out of the mouth begins in the heart (Matt. 12:35), so maintain a joyful heart before the Lord (vv. 13, 15) and fill your heart with His truth (v. 14). God sees your heart; do not try to hide anything from Him (v. 11).

Most of all, ask God for help in saying the right thing (vv. 8, 29). David's prayer in Psalm 141:3–4 is a good place to start.

PROVERBS 16

A prepared heart (1–3, 23) is a heart that receives God's truth and submits to God's will. Since the mouth speaks what the heart has treasured up, the Lord can guide your words when your heart is prepared (Matt. 10:19–20).

A proud heart (5, 18–19). Pride is one sin that God especially hates. It leads to all kinds of trouble and robs you of the blessing of the Lord.

A purposeful heart (7, 9, 25). If your heart is not devoted to God's purposes, then it will lead you astray. Take time to think and pray, meditate on the Word, and make your plans; and then trust the Lord to guide you.

A prudent heart (20–24). When wisdom is your food and drink, then you will be able to make prudent decisions. A prudent heart is revealed by lips that speak sweet words of wisdom.

A perverse heart (27–30). What is in the heart eventually comes out in the life, and the life described here is anything but beautiful or useful. No wonder Proverbs 4:23 is in God's Word! Are you heeding it?

PROVERBS 17

Use this chapter as the basis for a spiritual inventory. God has many ways of testing your heart (v. 3).

What do you listen to (4)? Your ears will hear what your heart loves, so guard your inner affections.

What do you rejoice in (5)? Are you glad when others suffer? Do you use the plight of others to promote yourself?

What do you talk about (9)? Do morsels of gossip bring delight to your heart, and do you enjoy sharing them with others? The best thing is to cover sin and let God deal with it.

What do you get angry at (10, 13-14)? Do you accept criticism or respond with anger? Do you think of ways to retaliate, or do you try to stop disagreements at the beginning?

What do you give in to (23)? "Every man has his price," claims the world, but it must not be true of believers. Is your conscience for sale?

PROVERBS 18

Friends. Friendship has its risks (v. 19), but the isolated person is not wise (v. 1). We belong to each other, and we need each other (v. 14). We may have many acquaintances, but we have few real friends. The person with too many friends may end up in trouble (v. 24 margin). Be a true friend and God will give you true friends who will stick close to you throughout life.

True Friends

A real friend can be trusted (Prov. 11:13; 17:9) and will stay with you when you are in trouble (Prov. 17:17; 25:19). Friends love you too much to pamper you (Prov. 27:6, 17), and their counsel helps you (Prov. 27:9). A real friend is good for generations (Prov. 27:10)! Some people do not make good friends: those who tempt you to sin (Prov. 1:10ff.); gluttons (Prov. 28:7); drunkards (Prov. 23:20-21); gossips (Prov. 20:19); the violent and angry (Prov. 16:29; 22:24-25); and flatterers (Prov. 27:14). Your best friends are those who have Jesus Christ as their Friend and seek to be like Him (John 15:12-15).

Fools. Fools do not make good friends for many reasons. For one thing, they like to talk so much that they do not hear what others say (v. 2). Their foolish words cause fights (vv. 6–7) and inward pain (v. 8). Their impatience to speak makes them jump to conclusions (vv. 13, 17), and that creates problems (v. 5). The only hope for fools is that they will stop talking and start to listen to wisdom (v. 15).

❝No one can develop freely in this world and find a full life without feeling understood by at least one person.**❞**

Paul Tournier

PROVERBS 19

Rich and poor. It is better to be rich in character and poor in wealth, especially when that wealth is acquired by deception (vv. 1, 22). If friendship is based on wealth, it is not friendship at all (vv. 4, 6–7). True friendship goes much deeper. Be careful how you treat the poor because God is concerned about them (v. 17).

Wise and foolish. Wise people submit to the Lord and walk a straight way, but fools argue with the Lord and twist their way (v. 3). Wealth is no evidence of wisdom (v. 10); in fact, a fool only wastes wealth.

The Poor   Some people become poor because of having wrong values (Prov. 16:16), being lazy (Prov. 10:4; 14:23), following sinful pleasures (Prov. 21:17; 23:21), refusing good counsel (Prov. 13:18), and not planning carefully (Prov. 21:5). But some are poor because they cannot help it. They may be the victims of injustice (Prov.

22:22–23) or have such heavy debts they cannot succeed (Prov. 22:7). You should show mercy to the poor (Prov. 14:21, 31; 19:17; 21:13), for the same Lord made us all (Prov. 22:2).

Fathers and sons. Every father wants wise sons who will use their inheritance wisely (vv. 13–14). Lazy sons only bring poverty (v. 15). The father who chastens his son will help him build character (v. 18), but the son who chases his father away will bring shame and reproach (v. 26). Sons who listen to their fathers (and their Father in heaven) will stay on the right path (v. 27). (This paragraph can also be applied to mothers and daughters.)

PROVERBS 20

If you are wise, you will consider the consequences of your decisions and actions. You will ask, "What about *afterward?*"

The afterward of strong drink (v. 1) is not pleasant, and the afterward of starting trouble (v. 2) could be dangerous. Better to stop the trouble at the beginning (v. 3).

Lazy People

The book of Proverbs has nothing good to say about laziness. Even the feeble ants are more diligent than the sluggard (6:6–11)! It is shameful to sleep when there is work to do (10:4–5; 24:30–34). One of these days, the lazy person will be forced to work (10:24) to get something to eat (19:15). Lazy people can think up many excuses not to work (20:4; 22:13; 26:13–16), and nothing anybody says will do them any good.

Sleep is essential to good health, but the afterward of too much sleep is poverty (vv. 4, 13). A crooked business deal may be profitable financially, but you will not enjoy the aftertaste (v. 17). You may enjoy getting your inheritance now, but afterward it may do you more harm than good (v. 21). Remember what happened to the prodigal son (Luke 15:11ff.).

Rash promises have an afterward of regret (verse 25; Eccles. 5:1–7), but loving discipline has an afterward of reform. Ponder Hebrews 12:3–11, and especially note v. 11.

PROVERBS 21

God can turn hearts (v. 1) and accomplish His purposes. He can also test hearts to see what we are really like (v. 2). He wants both righteousness and justice in our lives, not simply empty religious ceremonies (v. 3; 1 Sam. 15:22; Mark 12:38–44). Note the emphasis on justice (vv. 3, 7, and 15).

God sees the wicked—their pride (v. 4), violence (v. 7), evil desires (v. 10), false confidence (v. 12), sinful sacrifices (v. 27), and hardness of heart (v. 29)—and He will judge them in due time.

The wicked may try to outmaneuver God, but God will have His way (v. 30; Prov. 19:21). No matter what resources men may lean on, only God can give success (v. 31). Use whatever means God provides, but put your faith in God alone.

PROVERBS 22

If you measure life by riches, you will be disappointed. God made both the rich and the poor (v. 2), and both are important to Him. (See Luke 6:20–26; James 2:1–13.)

Major on character—a good name—and not on great wealth (v. 1). Money can buy fame but not a good name. If you are proud, all you may get is money, but if you are humble, God will give honor and life along with the wealth He wants you to have (v. 4).

Do not allow debt to put you into bondage (v. 7) or the love of money to cause you to oppress others (vv. 16, 22–23). If you give gifts to the rich just to get their favor, you will end up poor.

No matter how rich or poor you may be, it is integrity that really counts. Even the king, probably the richest person in the land, pays attention to people of character (vv. 11, 29). And do not forget the King of kings before whom you will one day stand.

Properly View Wealth

The book of Proverbs issues a number of stern warnings about wealth. Wealth cannot give you peace (15:16) or wisdom (16:16), but it can create pride (18:11, 23) and trouble (15:6, 27) and friends who will not last (14:20). You should fear God (22:4) and share with others what God gives to you (11:24–25; 19:17). Watch out when somebody promises to make you rich in a hurry because those schemes backfire and leave you poor (20:21; 28:20, 22). The way to gain wealth is through hard work (10:4, 22) and faithfulness to the Lord.

PROVERBS 23

The repeated "do not" reminds you that there are some things God does not want His children to do.

Do not desire luxuries (vv. 1–3), even when the rich offer them to you. You may get an appetite for such things and start living to get rich (vv. 4–5). But riches fly away, while character remains for eternity. At the same time, do not get friendly with miserly people (vv. 6–8). No matter how much they offer you, their hearts are not with you. It is not the food on the table but the love in the heart that makes fellowship real and lasting.

Do not speak carelessly around fools (v. 9), for they will misunderstand and misquote you and get you into trouble. Do not change the boundaries that men and God have made (vv. 10–11; 22:28; Deut. 19:14). This is robbery and oppression, and God will judge it.

Respect the Truth

"Buy the truth, and do not sell it" is the advice of Proverbs 23:23. Lot sold the truth for a home in the city (Gen. 13:1–13), and Esau sold the truth for a mess of pottage (Gen. 25:29–34). King Saul sold the truth for the support of the people (1 Sam. 15:24–35). Judas sold the truth for thirty pieces of silver (Matt. 26:14–16), and Pilate sold the truth for the approval of the crowd (Mark 15:15). It is not worth it!

Beware Strong Drink!

The Bible does not demand total abstinence, but it does magnify it and warn against the sin of drunkenness. Strong drink is a mocker (Prov. 20:1): it promises one thing but gives another. Instead of wealth, it gives poverty (Prov. 21:17; 23:20–21); instead of pleasure, it gives misery (Prov. 23:29–35). For a short time, the drinker feels good, but then things start to change. Alcoholics can be saved and changed by the grace of God (1 Cor. 6:9–11). You must be careful not to cause others to stumble because of the things you do (Rom. 14:14–23).

Do not fail to discipline your child (vv. 13–14), so that he or she might have wisdom and bring you joy (vv. 15–16). No matter what other families may do, do not envy sinners (vv. 17–18), but trust the Lord and obey Him. Set a good example by respecting your parents (v. 22).

Do not mix with drunkards and gluttons lest you become like them (vv. 19–21). Do not even look at the wine (vv. 29–35) lest you end up embarrassed and bruised.

Do not sell the truth at any price (v. 23)! It costs something to live by the truth, but it costs even more to abandon the truth.

PROVERBS 24

The wise person builds while others tear down (vv. 1–4) and is strong for the battles of life (vv. 5–6). There is no need to faint (v. 10); and if you fall, you need not stay down (vv. 15–16). (See Ps. 37:23–24.)

Honey

Honey was one of the sweetest things in the Jewish diet, and Solomon used it to teach some important lessons. He warned about the sweet words of the harlot (Prov. 5:3) that would lead only to bitterness. Studying may not be easy for you, but knowledge is like honey, so learn to enjoy it (Prov. 24:13–14). When people praise you, they are feeding you honey (Prov. 25:27), so do not eat too much of it! If you take too much, it will make you sick (Prov. 25:16), so learn to be satisfied without it (Prov. 27:7). You cannot live on honey, and you cannot live on praise.

The wise person seeks to deliver people who have been unjustly condemned (vv. 11–12). If you hide your head and fail to help when you can, God will judge you (James 4:17). At the same time, be careful not to rejoice when an enemy falls (vv. 17–18), fret when the wicked prosper (vv. 19–20), or pay back those who may have hurt you (vv. 28–29).

The wise person labors while there is opportunity (v. 27) and does not live for ease and pleasure (vv. 30–34; 6:6–11). Follow the example of your Master (John 9:4).

PROVERBS 25

Leaders (1–7). People in authority must know what is going on. God has the right to conceal things, but nobody should hide things from the leader. However, a wise leader knows how to keep his counsel (v. 3) and share his plans at the right time. The wise leader gets rid of evil associates and does what is right. Verses 6–7 remind us of our Lord's parable in Luke 14:7–8. Humility leads to honor, but self-promotion leads to shame.

Neighbors (8–19). Keep problems between you and your neighbor and try to settle them out of court (Matt. 5:21–26). Let your words be appropriate (vv. 11–12) and helpful (v. 13), and keep your promises (v. 14). Do not be a neighborhood pest (v. 17) or troublemaker (v. 18). Be dependable (v. 19)!

Enemies (21–22). Paul quoted these words in Romans 12:20, and Elisha practiced them (2 Kings 6:8–23) and so did Jesus and the early believers (Luke 22:49–51; Acts 7:59–60).

Handling Disputes

The time to stop a dispute is when it begins (Prov. 17:14; 30:32–33). As much as possible, do not let arguments get started (Prov. 20:3). Some people contribute to peace (Prov. 12:20); others contribute to war (Prov. 22:10; 26:21); and there are some people that nobody can get along with (Prov. 29:9). God blesses the peacemakers (Matt. 5:9), so let God's wisdom direct you and use you to make peace (James 3:13–18).

PROVERBS 26

Solomon names some people you should avoid, and the first is the *fool* (vv. 1–12). You cannot change him by promotion (vv. 1, 8), correction (v. 3), or admonition (vv. 4–5). If you answer a fool, do not stoop to his level of folly or you will make him think you have elevated him to wisdom. No matter how much you correct him, he goes right back into folly (v. 11; 2 Pet. 2:22).

The second is the *sluggard* (vv. 13–16) who has excuses for everything. He has motion but no progress (v. 14) and is even too lazy to feed himself (v. 15)! You are wasting your time trying to help him (v. 16; 27:22).

The *troublemaker* (vv. 17–28) is the third problem person. This category includes meddlers (v. 17), pranksters (vv. 18–19), talebearers (vv. 20–22), and deceivers (vv. 23–28).

Are you anywhere in this chapter?

PROVERBS 27

True friendship will occasionally involve wounds (vv. 5 6) as you speak the truth in love (Eph. 4:15) because friendship cannot be built on deception or envy (v. 4).

Don't Fall for Flattery

Sincere praise can be an encouragement, but flattery only does harm (Prov. 26:28). Beware the kisses of an enemy (Prov. 27:6; 2 Sam. 20:9–10; Matt. 26:48–50)! There are times when flattery may seem the only way to save a friendship, but afterward, you will regret it (Prov. 28:23). The flatterer is like a hunter who spreads his net (Prov. 29:5), so be on your guard.

Friends should encourage each other with loving counsel (v. 9) and honest praise (v. 2). But beware flattery (v. 14)! The way you respond to praise reveals your character, just as a jeweler's furnace reveals the nature of the precious metal

(v. 21). Praise brought out the best in David but the worst in Saul (1 Sam. 18:1–16). What does it do to you?

Friends should be faithful to each other (v. 10; 17:17), but you also need to be loyal to family and neighbors (v. 10). You never can tell when you may need them or they may need you! Not everybody will become a close friend, so do not get so exclusive that you neglect other people.

❝ *Flattery is not communication; it is manipulation.* **❞**

PROVERBS 28

As crime increases, the government must pass more laws and hire more people to enforce them (v. 2). When you break God's law, you promote the wicked; when you obey His law, you promote righteousness (v. 4) and enable God to answer your prayers (v. 9). Read Romans 13 and see what God says about Christian citizens.

Wicked rulers are like fierce animals (v. 15) who drive the righteous into hiding (vv. 12, 28). This includes ignorant leaders and those grasping after money (v. 16). The people in that day could not vote to replace leaders or correct laws, so all they could do was protect themselves.

When laws and leaders are unjust, usually the poor suffer and the rich profit. But even a poor person can have integrity (v. 6) and understanding (v. 11) and faith that God will meet his needs (v. 27).

Is there someone you should help today?

PROVERBS 29

When honest people enforce the law, there is joy (v. 2), and society is established with security and order (v. 4). A few leaders who scoff at the law can endanger things, so the wise must be ready to act (v. 8). Of course, even a wise leader cannot change some people (v. 9).

Leaders must act on the basis of truth and not lies (vv. 12, 14). The foundation for law is God's truth, and where that is preached and obeyed, there will be happiness (v. 18). If leaders try to please people, or if they fear people, they will get into trouble; but if they obey the Lord, He will bless them (vv. 25–27).

Everybody must practice self-control in feelings (vv. 11, 22) and words (v. 20). We may not be able to run the government, but we can manage the kingdom within our own hearts (Prov. 16:32; 25:28).

Bribery   *Bribery erodes the very foundation of the law and of the land (Prov. 29:4) and must be hated as an enemy (Prov. 15:27). It perverts justice (Prov. 17:23), provides offices for dishonest people (Prov. 18:16), purchases favors (Prov. 19:6), and pacifies people without solving problems (Prov. 21:14). The person whose integrity is for sale is not fit to govern.*

PROVERBS 30

Agur's reverence for God (vv. 2–4) and His Word (vv. 5–6) proves that he was a wise man worth listening to. He had the right attitude toward wealth (vv. 7–9; Phil. 4:10) and the family (v. 17), and he was concerned about a generation that had turned away from God (vv. 11–14). He shares some lessons with you.

Some things are never satisfied (15–16). The leech wants more blood, the grave wants more dead, the barren mother yearns for children, the earth thirsts for more water, and the fire wants more fuel (Prov. 26:20–21). Dissatisfaction creates many problems in our world.

Some things must never lose their wonder (18–19). Science may explain the flight of birds, the movements of snakes, the currents of the ocean, and human sexuality, but that does not take away their wonder. Life and love are not explained by laboratory experiments or the convenient formulas of the experts. As you go through life, do not lose your sense of wonder.

Some things always seem to cause trouble (21–23). Servants do not always know how to handle the luxury and authority of the throne (Prov. 19:10), so they create problems instead of solve them. Folly and hatred are not changed by food and marriage; if anything, they become worse. Genesis 16 illustrates what happens when a maidservant gets promoted.

Some small things are very big in wisdom (24–28). The ants are wise to prepare, the badgers to protect, the locusts to cooperate, and the spiders to get into the best places and hold on. Good examples for you to follow!

Some things are made for honor (29–33). The lion, greyhound, and male goat are regal because God made them that way. The dog is not a lion and the goat is not a beautiful dog, but each has its own kind of honor. The king is regal because of his office and his official trappings (such as an army). If you exalt yourself (v. 32), you will have only artificial honor. If you let God fulfill in you the purpose for which He made you, you will have true honor.

Respect in the Home

Proverbs has much to say about the home. When children walk in wisdom, they bring joy to their parents (10:1; 15:20; 17:21, 25; 19:26; 23:24–25). It is tragic when children do not respect their parents (23:22; 30:17), when they speak evil of them (20:20), waste their money with the wrong friends (28:7; 29:3), and rob their parents (28:24). Early discipline helps a child learn to respect parental authority and appreciate parental love (13:24; 19:18; 22:15).

PROVERBS 31

The book of Proverbs opens with warnings about evil women but closes with a description of a godly woman. Everything about this woman is praiseworthy.

Look at *her hands*. She is a willing worker (vv. 13, 19), and her work is fruitful (v. 31). She cooks, sews, manages real estate, and even plants a garden. Her family needs nothing, and she is generous to the poor (v. 20).

Her mouth speaks wisdom (v. 26), and she gives wise counsel to her family and friends. *Her eyes* are alert to opportunities (vv. 13, 16) and to the needs of the home (v. 27).

Most important, *her heart* is faithful to the Lord and to her husband (vv. 11–12, 30). It is no surprise that she is praised, by her children and husband (vv. 28–29) and by her works (v. 31).

Compare verse 30 with 1 Peter 3:1–6 and find out what kind of beauty really lasts.

ECCLESIASTES

◆————————————◆

His name is not mentioned in the book, but King Solomon probably wrote it. He calls himself "the Preacher," which means "one who calls an assembly and discusses a topic." The Greek word for "assembly" is *ekklesia* (the New Testament word for "church"), and the book's title comes from this word. As the wisest, wealthiest, and most powerful man of his day, Solomon certainly had the opportunity and resources to do the things mentioned in Ecclesiastes.

In this book, Solomon seeks to answer the question, "Is life worth living?" First, he states the problem and argues for the negative (chaps. 1—2). Then he examines the problem from many different angles (chaps. 3—10) and argues for the positive. He concludes that life is worth living if you put God first and obey His Word (chaps. 11—12).

Called a pessimistic book, Ecclesiastes is actually realistic. Solomon looked at life and death, success and failure, time and events, and wrote some wise counsel about how to live a meaningful life in a world of contradictions and seeming futility. When viewed apart from God ("under the sun"), life is indeed "vanity" (futility); but when you live for Christ, life is never "in vain" (1 Cor. 15:58).

Six times Solomon advises you to enjoy life *now* and be grateful for God's gifts (2:24; 3:12–15, 22; 5:18–20; 8:15; 9:7–10; 11:9–10). This is not the pleasure-seeking philosophy of the epicurean ("eat, drink, and be merry, for tomorrow we die") but the joyful outlook of the believer who accepts life as God's gift to enjoy and employ for His glory (1 Tim. 6:17–19).

ECCLESIASTES 1

When Solomon began his discussion, he was convinced that life was meaningless. Perhaps you feel the same way at times and for the same reasons. When you look around, you see nature functioning as it has since creation (vv. 1–8). When you look back, you see history only repeating itself (vv. 9–11). When you look within, you find (as Solomon did) that your wisdom and experience cannot explain the mysteries of life or solve life's problems (vv. 12–18). Vanity of vanities!

Solomon's big mistake was to leave God out of the picture and forget that God has broken into creation and done new things. He stopped the sun for Joshua (Josh. 10:12) and moved it back for Hezekiah (Isa. 38:8). He opened both the sea (Exod. 14) and the river (Josh. 3) for His people. God is in charge of the world and human history, and what He does is not "vain."

Knowledge can increase sorrow *if you leave out the God of wisdom and the wisdom of God*. Satan promises knowledge apart from God (Gen. 2:17; 3:1–5), but it leads only to sin and death. Be sure to grow in grace as you grow in knowledge (2 Pet. 3:17–18), or knowledge will make you critical and cynical.

❝Nine-tenths of our unhappiness is selfishness and is an insult cast in the face of God.**❞**

G. H. Morrison

ECCLESIASTES 2

God made life for enjoyment and investment (1 Tim. 6:17–19), but Solomon decided to turn it into experiment. He tested his heart with pleasure (vv. 1–3), works (vv. 4–6), and the acquisition of wealth (vv. 7–9), and he discovered that they did not satisfy. These things can bring a certain amount of enjoyment while you are doing them, but when it is all over, you feel empty (vv. 10–11). *Enjoyment without God is only entertainment, not enrichment;* you cannot live on entertainment.

At that point Solomon became cynical and hated life (vv. 12–23; see also Ps. 34:11–14; 1 Pet. 3:10–12). "Why bother to do all these things," he asked, "when I am going to die anyway? Who will remember me?" Paul's answer is found in 1 Corinthians 15:58 and John's in 1 John 2:17.

Instead of complaining about what you do not have, thank God for what you do have *and enjoy it* (vv. 24–26).

The Cynic   Henry Ward Beecher described a cynic as a person who "never sees a good quality in a man, and never fails to see a bad one. He is the human owl, vigilant in darkness, and blind to light, mousing for vermin, and never seeing noble game."

ECCLESIASTES 3

Balance (1–8). When life is especially difficult, we are prone to see only one side of the situation. In these statements, Solomon reminds you that God is in control of life and keeps everything balanced. You feel pain when there is bereavement, but you feel joy when there is birth. You are not always weeping, but neither are you always laughing. Job knew this principle, and it gave him strength in his trials (Job 1:21).

Beauty (9–17). It may not look like it now, but God will bring beauty out of all that happens (Rom. 8:28; Isa. 61:1–7). No matter what the seed looks like, the flower will be beautiful, so give God time to work. You were made for the eternal; in Christ, you now share eternal life, the life of God (1 John 5:9–13).

Burial (18–22). Again, Solomon faces the fact of death, as he will several times in this book. Both people and animals die and are buried, and their bodies go to the same place: the dust. The spirit of man goes to meet God (v. 21). One day, God will bring beauty even out of the dust (1 Cor. 15:35–58)! Enjoy today and thank God for all He gives you.

ECCLESIASTES 4

Have you ever wished you could just get away from it all? People get on your nerves, circumstances ruin your plans, and the best solution to the problem seems to be to "go it alone." But is it the best solution?

As Solomon looked at the problems of life, he saw adversity and inequality (vv. 1–6), but he realized that *nobody can make it alone*. The solitary worker may get all the profits, but he is so busy making money that he has no time to enjoy it (vv. 7–8). And how rich will he be in the grave?

There are risks in society as well as rewards, but the rewards are greater. If you fall and break a leg, or if you are in danger, you are thankful to have a friend at your side to help you (vv. 9–12). We all need times of solitude, but nobody can be independent. Life is tough enough even when we have friends to encourage us. What would it be like if we had to do it alone?

"*Loneliness is the first thing which God's eye named not good.***"** *(See Gen. 2:18.)*

John Milton

ECCLESIASTES 5

Do not speak rashly (1–7). Your mouth can cause you to sin, especially when you pray hypocritically or make rash promises to God. Hasty words and lying words do not please God, nor will He accept excuses when you fail to keep your vow. Do not live in a dream world of religious fantasy, expressed by words alone. Be honest with God (1 John 1:5–10).

Do not marvel at wrongs (8–9). This does not mean that you should *approve* them, but do not be surprised when they happen. The poor Jews in Solomon's day had to put up with selfish bureaucrats who had to be paid off before they would help. (Have times changed?) Certainly you should work to see that justice is done, but do not be disappointed if many of your efforts fail.

Do not covet wealth (10–20). The poor think all their problems will be solved with more money, and the rich have problems because of their money! Money does not satisfy (v. 10) or guarantee peace (v. 12). You can buy sleep, but you cannot buy peace. Be thankful that God not only shares His gifts with you but also enables you to enjoy them. Not everybody can do that.

❝ *O God, give us serenity to accept what cannot be changed, courage to change what should be changed, and wisdom to distinguish the one from the other.* **❞**

Reinhold Niebuhr

ECCLESIASTES 6

Accept what you have. Instead of looking around for something different (v. 9), accept what you now have as God's gift. This does not suggest laziness or resignation because God expects you to make good use of what He gives you (Matt. 25:14–30).

Enjoy what you have. How tragic to have riches and a long life but not be able to enjoy them! The poor man wishes for more while the rich man wishes he could enjoy even a part of what he has (Prov. 15:16–17).

Enjoy what you have TODAY. Life passes by like a shadow, and you do not know the future (v. 12). In the will of God, make the most of today's opportunities and blessings, and you will be ready for what lies ahead.

❝ *A man is rich in proportion to the number of things he can afford to let alone.* **❞**

Henry David Thoreau

ECCLESIASTES 7

The better life (1–12). The better life involves some "bitter things," such as sorrow and rebuke, but the bitter things can make life better. On the day of your birth, you were given a name. On the day of your death, that name will be either putrid or fragrant, depending on how you lived. If you have a good name, your death will be better than your birth *because nothing will be able to hurt your name.* In that sense, the end is better than the beginning (v. 8). Sorrow and rebuke can teach you lessons that will not be learned any other way (Prov. 27:5–6, 12).

The balanced life (13–24). God gives both prosperity and adversity, and He knows how much and how long. Instead of peering into the future (v. 14b), live in the present and learn to profit from both pain and pleasure (Phil. 4:10–13). In verses 16–17, Solomon did not suggest that you play it safe and get the best of both worlds. The tenses of the verbs in Hebrew give the meaning, "Do not claim to be righteous and wise." You are still on the way and have not arrived yet (Phil. 3:12–16). That is why God balances your life with trials and triumphs: to keep you from getting proud and set in your ways.

How Do You React? Solomon recommends that you "do not take to heart everything people say" (Eccles. 7:21). Proud people are alert to what others say about them and quick to react and retaliate. This keeps the fires burning and robs everybody of peace and joy. Charles Spurgeon advises, "You cannot stop people's tongues, and therefore the best thing to do is to stop your own ears and never mind what is spoken."

ECCLESIASTES 8

You will not always get things your way, so learn to deal wisely with disagreements. A shining face is better than a stern (impudent) face, and it is wisdom that makes the face shine. Learn to smile—and to laugh!

As much as possible, submit to authority, do what you are told, and keep your promises. Do not get angry and resign, but do not be a partner in anything wrong: "We ought to obey God rather than men" (Acts 5:29). Wise people have discernment and know the right time to speak and to act (v. 6; James 1:5).

There are many injustices (vv. 10–13) and mysteries (vv. 14–17) in this life. Leave them with God and do what He calls you to do. There are still many enjoyable things in life *if* you do not make yourself the most important person to be pleased. Put God first and serve others, and life will become meaningful and joyful.

"To consider persons and events and situations only in the light of their effect upon myself is to live on the doorstep of hell."

Thomas Merton

ECCLESIASTES 9

Death is a fact of life. You can avoid thinking about it, but you cannot avoid the appointment (Heb. 9:27). The only way to be prepared for death is to receive God's gift of eternal life through faith in Jesus Christ (John 3:16; Rom. 6:23; 1 John 5:9–13), and then obey God's will until He calls you.

The reality of death need not rob you of the enjoyments of life. God wants you to enjoy feasts (vv. 7–8) and family (v. 9) and the work He has called you to do (v. 10). Life is unpredictable (v. 11), but it need not be irrational. Let God give you wisdom to use each day profitably for His glory (vv. 16–18). The thought of death should energize you, not paralyze you (Phil. 1:19–26; 2 Tim. 4:6–8).

ECCLESIASTES 10

The wiser you are, the more damage even a little folly can do to both your character and your reputation. The world seems to honor the fool and humiliate the honorable (vv. 5–7), but that is no reason for you to permit even a little folly in your life.

In Bible times, the right hand stood for honor and the left hand for dishonor (Matt. 25:33, 41). Verse 2 is another way of saying what Solomon wrote in Proverbs 4:23. If you guard your heart, you will avoid folly in your work (vv. 8–10) and your words (vv. 11–14). Verse 10 is Solomon's version of, "Don't work harder, work smarter!" Don't lose your cutting edge!

Leaders who live for themselves are only wasting time, resources, and opportunities for service, and that is folly (vv. 16–19). Yes, they have a good time at the expense of the citizens, but eventually, their folly will catch up with them.

Are there any "dead flies" that need to be taken out of the perfume of your life?

ECCLESIASTES 11

Live by faith (1–2). Solomon owned a fleet of merchant ships (1 Kings 9:26–28) that helped add to his great wealth. Life is like that: you have to launch out by faith if you hope to get anywhere. Limiting yourself to one ship may lead to disaster, so trust God to guide you in several endeavors.

Avoid excuses (3–5). The weather is rarely right for what the farmer wants to do, but he does it anyway. You cannot explain the growth of the unborn child, but that does not stop people from having families!

Work hard (6–8). Get started early in the morning, and keep in mind that night is coming "when no one can work" (John 9:4). You will get older and one day not be able to work as much, so use your opportunities while you can. If dawn is sweet to you, your sleep at night will be sweet (Eccles. 5:12).

❝One must wait until the evening to see how splendid the day has been.**❞**

Sophocles

Please God (9–10). The best way to remove sorrow is to avoid evil and walk in the fear of the Lord. The sooner you start, the happier your life will be. Childhood and youth are transient; you have but a short time to lay those important foundations. But it is never too late to make a new beginning and do it right.

ECCLESIASTES 12

What are your days like at this stage in life?

Days of decline (1–8). Solomon makes one last plea: make use of your opportunities while you can, before you get old and the storms come (v. 2). This poetic description of old age is quite graphic: trembling limbs and poor vision (v. 3); deafness and nervousness (v. 4); fear, gray hair, loss of appetite and then—death (vv. 5–7; 2 Cor. 4:16–18).

Days of learning (9–12). Listen to what God says and be admonished, no matter how old you are. You are never too old to get wiser—or to act like a fool! You can read many books about many subjects, but major on understanding God's Word and living a life of wisdom. His words are like nails: you can depend on them. They are goads: they prod you to do His will.

Days of obedience (13–14). If you fear God, you need fear nothing else; you are safe in the Father's will. So live that God could publish a book about you and you would not be ashamed for the whole world to read it. Live with eternity in view, and the ravages of time will not distress you.

THE SONG OF SOLOMON

---◆---

Jewish tradition sees this book picturing Jehovah's love for Israel, and Christians see it illustrating Christ's love for the church (Eph. 5:23–33) as well as the individual believer (John 14:21–24).

The "plot" centers on King Solomon's love for a humble maiden. Courtship (1:1—3:5) leads to marriage (3:6—5:1) and then to the joys and trials of married love (5:2—8:14). The book is indeed a beautiful presentation of the love of husband and wife, for the Jews accepted sexuality as a precious gift from God, a holy expression of true commitment in marriage.

The Song of Solomon is also an expression of the love relationship of the believer and the Savior. Christ calls us away from the trivial things of life that we might enjoy a deeper communion with Him. This communion is not without difficulties and disciplines, but it leads to a happier and holier life.

"The historical books I may compare to the outer courts of the temple; the gospels, the epistles and the psalms bring us into the holy place, or the court of the priests; but the Song of Solomon is the most holy place—the holy of holies, before which the veil still hangs to many an untaught believer."

Charles Haddon Spurgeon

As you read the Song of Solomon, be sure to distinguish the various people speaking. Many recent translations of the Bible, such as the New King James Version, will identify them for you. Also keep in mind that this is a poem for mature people. It is rich in Oriental imagery and must be "felt" as well as read. Solomon wrote Ecclesiastes for the inquiring mind, Proverbs for the obedient will, and the Song of Solomon for the loving heart. It takes all three for a balanced life.

SONG OF SOLOMON 1

Christ loves you, no matter what you may see in yourself (vv. 5–6, 8, 15). Be sure that your love for Him is expressed in both words (vv. 2–3, 16) and deeds (John 14:21–24). Spend time with Him and enjoy His love as you would food and drink (vv. 2, 12) and the fragrance of sweet perfume (vv. 3, 12–13; John 12:1–8).

Your love relationship must never become stagnant because He wants to lead you into deeper experiences in His chambers (v. 4) and His banquet hall (2:4). Never be afraid to follow Him, for His love will never lead you astray. Enjoyment and enrichment will be yours as you commune with Him.

At the same time, never neglect your work (v. 6); faithful service is one way you show Him your love. You do not choose between Mary and Martha (Luke 10:38–42), for both service and devotion belong to the balanced Christian life. Also, do not allow yourself to become isolated from others. Follow His flock and His footsteps and you will walk in paths of loving fellowship (John 21:15–25).

❝Love is the greatest thing that God can give us; for Himself is love: and it is the greatest thing we can give to God.**❞**

Jeremy Taylor

SONG OF SOLOMON 2

As you grow in your love for Christ, you must expect a variety of experiences, both pleasant and painful. You will enjoy His shade (v. 3), His banquets (vv. 4–5), and His tender expressions of love (v. 6). But you must also expect mountains (v. 8), walls (v. 9), winter seasons (v. 11), and enemies that creep in and try to destroy your work (v. 15).

You never know when your Lord will come to you for a time of communion, so be ever alert. When you least expect it, He will come (v. 8), stand (v. 9), look (v. 9), and speak (v. 10). No obstacle stands between Him and you *except the ones you put up yourself.* He leaps over the mountains because He yearns to be with you and lift you higher (v. 14).

When you spend time in loving communion with Christ, it is like springtime after the winter (vv. 10–13) and the dawning of a new day (v. 17).

"Jesus, the Very Thought of Thee"

Jesus, the very thought of Thee
With sweetness fills my breast;
But sweeter far Thy face to see,
And in Thy bosom rest.

When once Thou visitest the heart
Then truth begins to shine,
Then earthly vanities depart,
Then kindles love divine.

Twelfth-century Latin hymn,
attributed to Bernard of
Clairvaux; translated by
Edward Caswall

SONG OF SOLOMON 3

Seeking (1-3). There are times when the Lord comes to you (2:8), but there are also times when you should seek Him. It was not easy for her to leave the comfort and security of the bed for the danger of the street, but love cannot rest until it finds its beloved. Do you have that kind of love?

Finding (4-5). She was not satisfied with information from the watchmen; she wanted personal communion with her beloved. It is not enough merely to listen to what others say about Jesus, as helpful as that may be. Press on until you enjoy Him personally.

Enjoying (6-11). In a triumphant and beautiful wedding procession, Solomon claims his bride and takes her home. The church is awaiting the Lord's glorious coming, but as we wait, we experience His love and joy (vv. 10-11; John 15:9-11). Find your delight in Him today and the joys of heaven will be greater.

SONG OF SOLOMON 4

Do you want to experience His love?

Listen to His words (1-8). He wants to tell you how fair you are in His sight because of His grace (Eph. 1:6). If you listen to what others say about you, you may be led astray, and if you listen to yourself, you may become discouraged. Believe His Word and rest in His love. Let your heart listen for His voice.

Look to Him in love (9-11). You cannot see Him physically, but you can still love Him (1 Pet. 1:8). See Him in His Word, in the world He has made, and in His providential care for you each day. Tell Him that you love Him!

Live to please Him (12-16). A garden, spring, and fountain are not useful if they are shut up, so open your life to Him and let Him bring out of you all that will delight Him and help others. Sometimes He must send trials to bring out the best blessings (v. 16). You are His unique garden and He is the loving Gardener (John 20:15), and He will cultivate your life and make it fruitful as you commune with Him (John 15:1-8).

When the Lord comes to your garden, let Him enjoy your love (5:1; John 20:11-18).

SONG OF SOLOMON 5

No matter where you are or what you are doing, fix your heart on the Lord and keep alert to His voice. You never know when He may come to have fellowship with you.

When He comes, He will speak and knock, *and you must respond to Him immediately*. No excuses! She heard his knock and his voice, and she saw his hand, but she did not yield to his call. When finally she opened the door, he was gone, even though he left a token blessing behind (v. 5). Better to have your beloved than any blessing he might give.

A loving heart will seek the Lord, no matter what the cost (vv. 6–8). How much better it would have been for her to respond to Him when she first heard His call. But she does not blame her Beloved; she gladly tells others how wonderful He is (vv. 10–16).

An affectionate heart is an alert heart, quick to respond to the Beloved's calls.

SONG OF SOLOMON 6

The friends of the bride noticed that her Beloved was missing, and they asked about Him (v. 1). Often others can tell when we are out of fellowship with the Lord. Of course, we know where He is (v. 2) and what we must do to be reconciled to Him (1 John 1:9). We know that we belong to Him (v. 3) and that He still loves us and sees beauty in us (vv. 4–10) in spite of our lack of loving response. Contrast verse 3 with 2:16 and 7:10.

The bride went where her beloved was (v. 11) that she might be forgiven and restored. If we are to be reconciled to him and enjoy his communion once more, we must go back to the place where we left him (Gen. 13:3). Instead of being beaten (5:7), she is now in his glorious triumphal procession (vv. 10–12; 2 Cor. 2:14), sitting regally in the lead chariot!

Her friends begged her to remain that they might enjoy her beauty (v. 13). Do God's people today impress the world with their beauty and Christlikeness? Perhaps we need to meet the Beloved in His garden.

SONG OF SOLOMON 7

He admires you (1–5). Once more, the Beloved tells His wife how attractive she is to Him. This reminds us that husbands and wives need to express their love to each other often and find their joy freely in each other. Perhaps we would use different similes today, but each of these descriptions was meaningful in that day.

66*I ask you, Lord Jesus, to develop in me, your lover, an immeasurable urge towards you, an affection that is unbounded, a longing that is unrestrained, a fervor that throws discretion to the winds! . . . There is no one more blessed than he who dies because he loves so much. No creature can love God too much.*99

Richard Rolle

Lovely Feet

We do not usually think of feet as attractive parts of the body (Song of Sol. 7:1), but our Lord wants us to have beautiful feet, spiritually speaking. Our feet should be clean (John 13:1–11) and shod (Luke 15:22; Eph. 6:15) and busy carrying the good news of salvation (Isa. 52:7; Rom. 10:15). Defiled feet and disobedient feet will grieve His heart and make it difficult for Him to fellowship with us as He desires.

He desires you (6–13). What incredible love that He should want to share His life with sinners such as we are (1 John 3:1)! Verse 10 is an improvement over 2:16 and 6:3, for it focuses on His desire for us and not just on our relationship with Him. Ask Him to go with you to some special place where you can give Him your love (vv. 11–13). There are times when He invites you (2:10ff.), but He enjoys it when you invite Him.

SONG OF SOLOMON 8

Imagining love (1–2). When you love someone, you think about that person and imagine all kinds of wonderful experiences together. But true love cannot remain only in the mind; it has to be fulfilled in life. An imaginary love for Christ is fatal to a vital Christian life.

Experiencing love (3–5). Your love for Him must be a living and growing experience, not something you manufacture yourself. You can commune with Him in private worship, lean on Him in the wilderness, and enjoy Him in the field. Everywhere, He awaits your affection.

Cherishing love (6–7). Solomon used three images to illustrate true love. The seal speaks of ownership, two lovers belonging only to each other until separated by death. This is the permanence of love. The fire reminds us of the power of love—nothing can quench it. And the wealth illustrates the preciousness of love.

Protecting love (8–11). The picture is that of a family, protecting a young daughter until she is old enough to marry. If she is a "door" (open to everybody), she must be protected, but if she is a "wall," she has the integrity to protect herself.

Listening for love (12–14). The Savior listens for your voice (v. 13; 2:14), and you must listen for His voice (2:8; 5:2). He will speak to you through His Word and by His Holy Spirit, so be attentive.

ISAIAH

$\blacklozenge$

The book of Isaiah may be compared to the whole Bible because it has two parts, like the two testaments. In the Old Testament section (chaps. 1—39), the prophet condemns the sins of Judah and warns of coming judgment. In the New Testament section (chaps. 40—66), he prophesies Judah's deliverance from Babylonian captivity. Throughout both sections, he announces the establishment of God's glorious kingdom. The first section primarily highlights law and condemnation, while the second emphasizes grace and glorious redemption. "The Holy One of Israel" is one of Isaiah's favorite names for the Lord.

The name *Isaiah* means "the salvation of Jehovah," and the prophet deals with four different kinds of salvation: (1) Judah's national salvation from the attacks of other nations; (2) Judah's salvation from the Babylonian captivity; (3) the future salvation of the Jews when their kingdom is established; and (4) the personal salvation of the sinner who puts his faith in the Redeemer.

Isaiah prophesied seven hundred years before Christ, in a period of international tension. Egypt, Syria, Israel (the northern kingdom), Babylon, and Assyria had their eyes on Judah, and the leaders of Judah tried to play one nation against another in their attempt to avoid war. Isaiah warned them not to trust in politics but to trust the Lord and obey His Word. The leaders did not listen, and Judah was eventually taken captive by Babylon. Isaiah's book guided and comforted the exiles both during and after their captivity.

As you read this book, you will see how believers should respond to international conflicts, political decay in the nation, and religious decay among the people, including the religious leaders. Isaiah ministered at a time when "religion" was popular but not spiritual, and the ministry at the temple was only a formality. The nation as a whole was corrupt, but God had His faithful remnant just as He does today.

Tradition says that the prophet Isaiah was sawed in half by King Manasseh. Hebrews 11:37 is said to refer to his death.

ISAIAH 1

Isaiah had access to four different kings, but his great concern was the spiritual state of the nation and not the political success of the leaders. There is a place for diplomacy and political action, for God established human government; but the leaders' faith must be in God's truth and not in man's schemes.

Outwardly, the nation seemed prosperous and even religious, but God saw a different picture. His people were rebellious children, lower than animals (vv. 1–3). They were sick with sin, like lepers (vv. 4–6), and their "garden city" had become another Sodom and Gomorrah (vv. 7–9).

Their popular religious meetings were futile and a grief to the Lord (vv. 10–15). In fact, their religious activities defiled the people instead of making them clean (vv. 16–20; Matt. 23:25–28). The wife of Jehovah was now a harlot (v. 21); their treasures were now cheap (vv. 22–26); and their garden was destined to be destroyed by fire (vv. 27–31).

Sin breaks God's heart, cheapens a nation or an individual, and invites the judgment of God. God graciously offers His forgiveness if we will repent (vv. 18–20).

The Virtue of Cleanliness

It is good to pray, "Wash me" (Ps. 51:7), but keep in mind that God says, "Wash yourselves" (Isa. 1:16). Paul wrote, "Let us cleanse ourselves" (2 Cor. 7:1). Follow that advice and keep yourself clean!

ISAIAH 2

The house of the Lord (1–4). In the previous chapter, Isaiah looked *within* the heart of the nation; now he looks *ahead* to the future glorious kingdom God promised His people. Instead of being a place for corrupt worship, the temple will be a center of truth and blessing for Jews and Gentiles. Instead of international conflict, there will be peace. When world conditions distress you, remember that things will not always be like this.

The light of the Lord (5–9). Judah was borrowing new religious ideas from the gentile nations and not walking in God's truth. Their faith was in material progress and not in the Lord. How they needed to get back to the light of God's Word! In our own day, astrology and Eastern religions have replaced the Bible, and making money is more important than serving the Lord.

The day of the Lord (10–22). This is a time of judgment from the Lord that can apply locally, as with Judah, or worldwide, as in the end times. Man's pride will be brought low, and all that man lives for will be destroyed. God patiently waits as people rebel against the truth, but in the end, sin will be judged and the Lord will be exalted (vv. 11, 17). God will protect His believing remnant when that day of judgment comes (1 Thess. 1:10; 5:9–10).

ISAIAH 3

The leaders of Judah trusted substitutes that would not help them in the coming day of judgment: natural resources, material wealth, military might, political experience, and even "religion" (vv. 1–3). God would take away in His wrath everything that dethroned Him in the hearts of the people.

But that was not all. God would replace their proud leaders with weaklings, nobodies without ability, who would oppress the people (vv. 4–8). Why? Because the nation not only sinned but boasted about it openly!

Isaiah was especially grieved because the women of the land had become addicted to wealth and fashion and were more interested in social status than spiritual character. The day would come when their artificial glamour would be gone and they would be sitting in the dust. (See 1 Pet. 3:1–6.) So many men would die in the coming war that the women would do anything to get a husband (Isa. 4:1).

Beware living on substitutes!

ISAIAH 4

"In that day" refers to the coming kingdom when the Lord will be exalted (Isa. 2:11, 17). Isaiah looked beyond the impending crisis to the glory that one day would come to Israel.

It will be a day of glory and not shame as Jesus Christ (the "Branch of the LORD" [Isa. 11:1; Jer. 33:15]) reigns on earth (v. 2). It will be a time when the nation will be washed and sanctified (vv. 5–6) and *every home* on Mount Zion will become a "tabernacle of God" with the distinctive pillar of glory above it (Exod. 40:34ff.).

But why should we wait for these blessings when God can give them to us now? He will wash us clean (Isa. 1:18), set us apart for Himself, and bless us in our homes with His presence. Perhaps it is time we followed Vance Havner's advice and started living "in kingdom come."

ISAIAH 5

This chapter contains a song (vv. 1–7), a lament (vv. 8–23), and a judgment (vv. 24–30).

The nation of Israel is the vineyard for which God did so much (Matt. 21:33–46). The people's sin was ingratitude, taking their blessings for granted and using them selfishly. Instead of serving the Lord, they served themselves, and the result was a corrupted nation.

The lament names some specific sins of the nation ("wild grapes" [v. 2]), sins that people still commit today. The rich stole from the poor (vv. 8–10), and people lived for sensual pleasure rather than godly enrichment (vv. 11–17). Confident of their own wisdom (v. 21), they questioned God's counsel (vv. 18–19) and for a price changed His words (vv. 20–23). There was no justice in the land because evil leaders turned from the truth of God's Word.

God was angry; His hand of judgment was stretched out against His people (v. 25; 9:12, 17, 21; 10:4; 14:27). Judgment comes like a prairie fire (v. 24) when the invading army conquers the land (vv. 26–30).

Today, He stretches out His hands in love, inviting sinners to repent (Isa. 65:2; Rom. 10:21); but tomorrow, He will stretch them out in wrath.

ISAIAH 6

Sight: he saw the Lord (1–4). Isaiah had a life-changing vision of Jesus Christ (John 12:38–41). The throne of Judah had changed occupants, but God was still on His throne and in perfect control of everything. When you worship, focus on God's holiness, sovereignty, and glory. When things on earth are discouraging, start looking at things from heaven's point of view.

Insight: he saw himself (5–7). Isaiah had pronounced woes on other people, but now he cried, "Woe is me!" He admitted that he was a sinner, he confessed his sin, and the Lord cleansed him. Were it not for the sacrifice on the altar, we could never approach the Sovereign on the throne.

Vision: he saw the need (8–13). True worship leads to service. You hear God's call, and you respond with obedience. God did not send Isaiah to a receptive people or give him an easy message to preach. But when you have seen the Lord and felt His touch, you can obey His will without fear.

He Shall Be Immanuel

Isaiah 7—12 is sometimes called the "Book of Immanuel" (Isa. 7:14; 8:8, 10). Immanuel *means "God with us." God gave this prophecy to the whole "house of David" (Isa. 7:13) and not just to King Ahaz; it refers ultimately to the Lord Jesus Christ (Matt. 1:18–25). He is God, and He is "God with us."*

ISAIAH 7

Fear. King Ahaz was frightened (vv. 2, 4, 16) because Syria and Israel united to depose him and crown a new king in Judah. Assyria and Egypt were also on the move, so it was not an encouraging time. When circumstances threaten you, what do you do? Alas, Ahaz trusted in his own wisdom and made a treaty with the king of Assyria, only to see him break it.

Faith. Isaiah's word to the king was from God and could be trusted. Ahaz pretended to be very spiritual when he refused to ask a sign, but his rejection of the sign was actually a rejection of the Lord and His messenger. God's Word goes to work when we believe it and act on it. Ahaz only talked about it!

Fulfillment. Both Syria and Israel were eventually out of the picture as Isaiah had promised, but Assyria became the new threat. Israel was invaded by Assyria in 722 B.C., and the nation came to an end. The Assyrians invaded Judah in the days of King Hezekiah, but God defeated them. However, Assyria humbled Judah because God's people would not trust God's Word. It is *faith* in God, not faith in man's treaties, that brings the victory.

Isaiah the Evangelical

Isaiah is called "the evangelical prophet" because he says so much about Jesus Christ. Isaiah writes about His birth (7:14; Matt. 1:23); the ministry of John the Baptist (40:1–6; Matt. 3); His own ministry in the Spirit (61:1–2; Luke 4:17–19); His rejection by the nation (6:9–13; Matt. 13:10–15; John 12:38); the Stone of stumbling (8:14; 28:16; Matt. 21:42; Rom. 9:32–33; 1 Pet. 2:6); His ministry to the Gentiles (49:6; Luke 2:32; Acts 13:47); His future kingdom (11:1–9; Rev. 12:10); and His atoning death on the cross (53:1ff.; Mark 10:25).

Jesus' Birth

The virgin birth of Jesus Christ is a basic doctrine of the Christian faith, for the Son of God could never be born as you were born. Every baby is a new creation, but Jesus Christ existed from eternity. He was not only born, but He "came into the world" (John 3:17; 10:36; 16:28). According to Isaiah 9:6, the Child was born (His human nature) and the Son was given (His divine nature). The holy Son of God could not partake of sinful human nature. His body was miraculously conceived by the Holy Spirit in Mary's womb (Luke 1:26–38; Heb. 10:5). He did no sin (1 Pet. 2:22); "in Him there is no sin" (1 John 3:5); He knew no sin (2 Cor. 5:21). Hallelujah, what a Savior!

ISAIAH 8

Two rivers (1–10). The lengthy name in verse 1 means "Speed to the spoil! Hasten to the booty!" It refers to the victory Assyria would win over Syria (Damascus) and Israel (Samaria). This would give Assyria a clear path to Judah, so Ahaz's treaty did not work. He rejected the quiet waters of Shiloah (a reference to a spring in Jerusalem) for the flood waters of the Euphrates (a reference to Assyria). God's wisdom brings peace, but man's wisdom brings confusion (James 3:13–18).

Two fears (11–15). If you fear God, you need not fear the threats of men. Make Jesus Lord in your life, and He will take care of your fears (1 Pet. 3:13–17). Christ is the Stone of refuge for His people but a snare to those who reject Him.

Two authorities (16–22). The Word of God is the only authority for the believer, even if circumstances seem to challenge it. In Isaiah's day, the leaders were even consulting mediums (Deut. 18:10–12)! Let the Word be your light in this dark world (Ps. 119:105).

ISAIAH 9

What a difference it makes in our lives that Jesus Christ came and died for our sins! And what a difference it will make in this world when He comes to sit on David's throne and rule righteously!

Jesus is the difference between light and darkness, life and death (v. 2). He is also the difference between joy and sorrow, freedom and bondage (vv. 3–4). As you wait for His return, be sure the government of your life is on His shoulders. Let Him be to you all that His names proclaim, for every name that He bears is a blessing that He shares.

The proud will be judged (vv. 8–21), as was Israel (the northern kingdom) when Assyria took the nation captive. First, God chastened them in love; and when they would not submit, He judged them (vv. 13–14). They were led astray by the very people who should have led them in the right way (v. 16; Lam. 4:13).

Our God is a God of grace and truth (John 1:17). If you acknowledge His truth, you can receive His grace (Ps. 51:3–4); but if you reject His truth, His hand of judgment must be stretched out to you. Which will it be?

ISAIAH 10

Greed (1–4). The leaders in Israel were greedy for gain. They used unjust laws to support their selfish practices as they robbed the poor and needy. Just before God's judgment fell on the nation, the rich were prospering and the poor languishing. "What will you do in the day of punishment?" (v. 3) is a question we all must answer. What good is all your wealth if you are not prepared to meet God?

Pride (5–19). Assyria was God's tool for punishing Israel (vv. 5, 15), but the tool cannot boast about what it does. Assyria was proud of its conquests, so God had to humble its people and judge them for their evil deeds. The army would vanish like trees in a forest fire. Nineveh, the capital of Assyria, was conquered by Babylon in 612 B.C. Nations may boast, but God has the last word.

Hope (20–34). In His grace, God saved a remnant and permitted them to return to the land. God also promised Judah that Assyria would not capture Jerusalem (vv. 24–27; Isa. 37). The tall proud tree (Assyria) would be cut down to size (vv. 33–34)! Even in the midst of wrath, God gives His people hope.

ISAIAH 11—12

Reign (11:1–10). God cuts down the tall trees (Isa. 10:33–34), but He builds a great kingdom from a tiny shoot (v. 1). Our Savior had a humble beginning at a time when David's family was in dishonor; but in the end, His kingdom will prevail over all earthly powers. He will bring peace on earth and the glory of God will cover the earth. Are you praying, "Thy kingdom come"?

Return (11:11–16). The humble Root is now the leader of an army! He defeats the enemy and gathers His people to their land, and He also rallies the Gentiles who seek Him. It is the picture of another "exodus" as God dries up the waters and makes a highway for His people. But this time there will be no wilderness wandering!

Rejoicing (12:1–6). Worshiping people give thanks to the Lord for saving them and bringing them home again. Witnessing people tell all the nations of the greatness of God. Compare verse 2 with Exodus 15:2 and Psalm 118:14, and be sure to believe this "song" for yourself.

ISAIAH 13

In chapters 13—23, Isaiah announces God's judgment on ten gentile peoples as well as on His own people in Judah and Israel. He begins with Babylon, which would one day swallow up the Assyrians, take Judah captive and then itself be defeated by the Medes and Persians (vv. 17–22). The rise and the fall of nations are in the hands of God (Dan. 4:25, 32; Acts 17:26). God can even use heathen soldiers to do His work and can call them "My sanctified ones" (v. 3). He is sovereign.

In the defeat of Babylon, Isaiah saw a picture of the final "day of the Lord" when the world will taste the judgment of God. God is long-suffering with sinners, but there comes a time when His judgment must fall. Isaiah's message against Babylon was fulfilled, and the city and empire are no more.

In Scripture, Babylon symbolizes the world system confederated against God (Gen. 11). Like Babylon in Isaiah's day, the world today seems so successful and invincible; but one day, the whole system will fall (Rev. 17—18). That is why God calls His people to separate themselves from it (2 Cor. 6:14–18).

ISAIAH 14

There is more to the fall of Babylon than the deposing of a proud king (vv. 3–11, 16–21) or the destroying of a great city (vv. 22–23). Behind the evil Babylonian system was Lucifer ("Day Star"), the enemy of God (vv. 12–15). As God taunts the king of Babylon, He also speaks to Satan who motivated and energized him.

It appears that Lucifer was an angel who rebelled against God and wanted to take to himself the worship that belonged only to God. "I will be like the Most High" (v. 14) is the ambition of the evil one and the temptation he puts before man (Gen. 3:5). The world today worships and serves "the creature rather than the Creator" (Rom. 1:25). Man is his own god; in worshiping and serving only himself, he plays right into the hands of the evil one.

The Christian's ambition is to be like Jesus Christ in all things, "conformed to the image of His Son" (Rom. 8:29). Contrast Isaiah 14:12–15 with Philippians 2:1–11 if you want to see the difference between Satan's approach and our Lord's approach.

ISAIAH 15—16

The nation of Moab was born out of Lot's incestuous union with one of his daughters (Gen. 19:30–38). It was a proud nation that would not honor the God of Israel but trusted in its fortifications. Pride is a sin that God hates (Prov. 6:16–17), whether in nations or in individuals, and it leads to judgment.

When the Assyrians invaded, the Moabites turned from boasting to weeping (15:1–4) and fleeing (15:5–9). They had faith in their fortifications, but everything failed them. Contrast this with Isaiah 2:10–11. They should have made peace with Judah (16:1–2) and gone to Jerusalem for asylum. God had promised to protect Judah from the Assyrian army (10:24ff.) because that was where David's throne was (16:5).

The prophet looked beyond this event to the time when the Son of God would sit on David's throne and bring in righteousness and justice (16:5). God could do without Moab; but He had a covenant with David (2 Sam. 7), and He would be faithful to His promises. Judah was safe because the people trusted the Lord.

ISAIAH 17

The northern kingdom of Israel had allied with Syria (Damascus), and both would fall to the Assyrians. If the people you trust do not trust the Lord, their judgment may become your judgment.

God's judgment on Israel is pictured by a sunset and a heavy person losing weight (v. 4), as well as a field that has no fruit for the gleaners (vv. 5–6). Israel had decayed beyond hope, and all her efforts at recovery were wasted (vv. 10–11).

If only they had turned to God before the sun set or the disease wasted away the body or the blight destroyed the harvest! But they trusted their own idols and not the true God (vv. 7–8). How easy it is to put confidence in the work of your own hands and not in the God who made those hands!

The judgment carried them off, like houses before a flood (vv. 12–13a) or chaff and tumbleweeds before the wind (v. 13b). Israel could have had the quiet waters of Shiloah (8:6), but they chose the turbulent waters of Assyria.

The will of God is your greatest security.

ISAIAH 18

The people of Ethiopia (ancient Cush) sent ambassadors to Israel, hoping to form a strong alliance against Assyria, but the venture was doomed to fail. God was not in it, because all of man's clever ideas are worthless if they run contrary to the will of God (1 Cor. 3:18–20). First find His will, then do it!

The Assyrian invasion was God's plan, and He would not intervene until He accomplished His divine purposes. He would hover over the scene like summer heat or the morning dew (vv. 3–4). When the time was right, He would reap the harvest (v. 5) and leave the corpses to the scavengers (v. 6). It is not a very pretty scene, but that is the way civilization is moving today (Matt. 24:28; Rev. 19:17–21).

Those clean-shaven ambassadors should have gone to Jerusalem with a gift for the Lord. They should have been humble worshipers, not haughty negotiators (v. 7), and trusted the God of Israel, not their armies or treaties (Ps. 20:7).

ISAIAH 19

A strong faction in Judah advised the king to get help from Egypt (Isa. 31), but Isaiah warned that Egypt could not help them. Why? Because the Lord had discouraged and divided the Egyptians (vv. 1–2), their counsel was from the devil (v. 3), and they were heading for bondage themselves (v. 4). Furthermore, their economy was about to fail (vv. 5–10). How could they help?

The counselors in Egypt were supposed to be very wise, but God said they were deluded fools (vv. 11–13). God's people get their wisdom from God, not from the world (James 1:5). The wisdom of Egypt would lead them into staggering and humiliating defeat (vv. 14–15).

In verses 16–25, the prophet sees the future of both the Jews and the Egyptians, when the Lord will establish His kingdom. The situation will be reversed, with Egypt turning to Israel for help (vv. 16–17)! In fact, the Egyptians will worship the God of Israel (vv. 18–21)! The nations will no longer battle but will visit one another on God's highway.

Going Down to Egypt

When Abraham faced a famine in Canaan, he went down to Egypt for help, and he almost lost his wife (Gen. 12:10—13:4). After the Exodus, God led His people so they would not want to go back to Egypt (Exod. 13:17–22). During their wilderness wanderings, the people wanted to go back (Num. 11; 14), but God would not permit it. Isaiah warned against it (32:1ff.), and so did Jeremiah (42—43). The book of Hebrews uses this image to warn believers not to go back in unbelief but to go forward in faith (3:7–19; 6:1).

ISAIAH 20

This brief chapter records two object lessons that the Lord used to try to convince the people not to form unholy alliances.

The first was the defeat of Ashdod by the Assyrians. The people of this Philistine city had depended on Egypt and Ethiopia to help them, but their help failed. Why then should God's people trust Egypt and Ethiopia? Remember, the one thing we learn from history is that we do not learn from history. "It can't happen here!"

The second object lesson was personified by Isaiah the prophet who for three years did not wear his prophetic garb or his sandals. He looked like a prisoner of war, which is what the Egyptians and Ethiopians eventually became (vv. 3–4). God's people did not take it to heart, and eventually they were led off to Babylon.

God uses things we see and hear to help us make the right decisions. Do we really pay attention?

ISAIAH 21

Three pictures help us better understand what is involved in faithful ministry.

The woman in travail (1–4). If you are faithful to your calling, your ministry will not be easy. Isaiah was distressed as he saw what God was doing in the world. He felt like a woman in travail (v. 3); it was very painful for him to "give birth" to his message.

The threshing floor (10). Why would Isaiah be distressed at the fall of the city of Babylon? (This was not the destruction of the city but a temporary takeover by a rival power.) Isaiah had hoped Babylon would stop the advances of Assyria and thus save the Jews from suffering. He saw them being winnowed and crushed by the enemy. He longed for a calm evening of his life (v. 4); instead, he had to carry distressing burdens to the end.

The watchman (5–9, 11–17). While the prophet was anxiously watching so he could warn the people, the nation's leaders were carelessly feasting and thinking only of themselves (v. 5). The watchman sees both night (trouble) and morning (blessing), and that is how it will be until Jesus comes. The most important thing is that the watchman be faithful to warn when danger is coming (Ezek. 25:12–14).

"Preaching that costs nothing accomplishes nothing.**"**

John Henry Jowett

ISAIAH 22

Isaiah's vision was probably of the Assyrian attack on Jerusalem (chaps. 36–37), and one of the messages of the chapter is this: when a crisis occurs, different people respond in different ways.

The prophet saw events from a spiritual viewpoint and was burdened (vv. 1–4). The city leaders depended on their defenses (vv. 8–11) and did not call for fasting and prayer. The people feasted and expected the worst. They had no faith in God (vv. 12–14; 1 Cor. 15:32).

Shebna used his office for personal gain (vv. 15–19), and the crisis brought him only shame. In taking inventory of the city's resources, somebody uncovered his deceit and exposed him. Instead of enjoying retirement, security, and a fine burial, he experienced captivity, exile, and a lonely death.

The crisis brought out the best in Eliakim (vv. 20–25). He was a servant who was a father to the people, a person who could be trusted with authority (the keys), and a strong peg on which the nation could put their burdens. He is the kind of leader needed today.

ISAIAH 23

Tyre and Sidon were Phoenician cities that brought great wealth to the nation by shipping and trading. It seemed incredible that such a successful economy would be wiped out, but it happened just as the prophet warned. Some of the people were stunned into silence (v. 2), while others openly expressed their grief by wailing (vv. 1, 6, 14). It seems that people who rarely weep over anything else will weep when they have money problems. The joy left the city (v. 7).

Assyria put Tyre and Sidon out of business for seventy years, and then they were restored.

God considered the business of Tyre and Sidon as nothing but fornication (v. 17; Rev. 17:1–2). They were harlots promoting themselves and ready to sell themselves at the highest price (v. 16). But some of their goods would be used to help rebuild the temple of the Lord (v. 18; Ezra 3:7).

Men may think they control the economy and what they do with their profits, but God makes the final decision.

ISAIAH 24

The whole earth is now the focus of attention and not just individual nations and cities. The Lord made the earth and is King over all the earth (Ps. 47:2), so He has a right to do what He pleases. He will punish sinners because they have not respected His covenant (v. 5; Gen. 9:8–17) or cared for the earth as faithful stewards of His gifts. They have disobeyed His will, claimed the earth for themselves, and abused it selfishly.

When that time of judgment comes, God will pay no attention to anyone's economic or social status (vv. 2–3). The joyful feast will become a funeral (vv. 7–13); those who try to escape will be trapped (vv. 17–18); and proud leaders will become prisoners (vv. 21–23). The Lord will humble the "haughty people" (v. 4) and the "exalted ones" (v. 21).

But Isaiah ends on a note of triumph: the Lord will reign gloriously (v. 23)! Will you be reigning with Him?

ISAIAH 25

The prophet now addresses God instead of the people and praises Him for who He is and what He has done. Isaiah's knowledge of God's truth did not make him proud; it humbled him and moved him to worship the Lord.

God is Judge (1–3, 10–12). "The city" ultimately refers to Babylon (Rev. 18:1—19:5), but it applies to anything man makes and uses to defy God. It does not take God long to wipe out a nation or destroy a city.

God is Refuge (4–5). Tribulation is like a storm, but He is the Refuge; it is like desert heat, but He is the Cloud that blots out the hot rays. God silences the noise of the enemy and brings peace.

God is Host (6–9). The Jews pictured the future kingdom as a great feast with God as the Host (Matt. 8:10–12; Rev. 19:6–9). But the feast will do more than sustain life; it will give life, for death will be destroyed forever (Rev. 20:11–15; 21:4).

Can you join the praise expressed in verse 9?

ISAIAH 26—27

The phrase "in that day" links these two chapters (26:1; 27:1, 2, 12, 13) and focuses attention on the glory of God in the promised kingdom (26:15). Knowing that the future is secure in the Lord is an encouragement when you suffer (Rom. 8:18–25; 2 Cor. 5:1–8).

Israel sings to the Lord (26). The proud enemy has been brought down (vv. 5–6), and God has given peace to His people (vv. 3, 12). The city of Jerusalem, where the Redeemer will reign, is strong and righteous after having been weak and defiled; and the nation's time of tribulation will be ended. This is not something the Jews will do for themselves, for they will be like women in travail who give birth only to wind (vv. 16–18). God will do it, and His people will praise Him for His mercy.

The Lord sings about Israel (27:1–5). In chapter 5, God

sang about the failure of the vineyard, Israel. But here the theme is the fruitfulness of the nation and God's care over it. In that day, the enemy will be defeated (v. 1), and God will gather His people back to their land (vv. 12–13). From Israel, blessings shall flow to the whole world (v. 6).

The Peace of God

When you trust Jesus Christ to save you, your sins are forgiven (Col. 2:13), and you have peace with God (Rom. 5:1). He will never call you into judgment for them (John 5:24; Rom. 8:1). You may also enjoy "the peace of God" in your heart and mind as you pray (Phil. 4:6–7) and fix your mind on Him (Isa. 26:3; Phil. 4:8–9; Col. 3:1ff.). "The peace of God" is not the absence of problems; it is the presence of divine sufficiency in the midst of problems (Isa. 26:4; Phil. 4:13, 19). George Morrison said, "Peace is the possession of adequate resources"; and those resources come from the Lord when you yield heart and mind to Him.

ISAIAH 28

In verses 1–13, the prophet addressed the northern tribes (Ephraim) and indicted them for drunkenness (vv. 1–8) and an unteachable spirit (vv. 9–13). The religious leaders told Isaiah not to talk to them like children (vv. 9–10); after all, they knew the Law! But God would talk to them through the Assyrians whose tongue Israel would not understand. If God's people will not listen to His voice from the Word, they may have to listen to foreign voices that speak no peace and show no love.

It was a confident time in Israel, but their prosperity would fade like a trampled flower (vv. 1, 3–4), be carried away in a storm and flood (v. 2), and be swallowed like fruit (v. 4). Judgment was at the gate (v. 6).

Then Isaiah denounced the sin of Judah (vv. 14–29), which was trusting false gods (vv. 14–15). Jesus Christ is God's Stone and He alone is a sure Refuge from the storm (Isa. 8:14; Matt. 21:42–44; Eph. 2:20). You have as much protection from lies as you do from a blanket that is too short! God is seeking a harvest and knows exactly how to handle the soil and the seeds (vv. 23–29). God's people may not enjoy the plowing and threshing, but the results are worth it.

ISAIAH 29

The prophet presented three descriptions of Ariel ("lion of God"), the city of Jerusalem.

A besieged city (1–8). The immediate reference is to God's victory over Assyria (Isa. 36—37), but the final application is to His defeat of the armies that will surround Jerusalem in the last days (Zech. 14:1–3). The enemy will be like dust and chaff. They will wake up and discover their dreams of success have become nightmares of defeat. God knows how and when to deliver His people.

A blind city (9–16). God's people were like drunken sleeping blind men trying to read a sealed book! They had no understanding of spiritual things nor did they worship God in the Spirit (Matt. 15:8–9). Even more, they made their own plans (political alliances) and thought God did not know (vv. 15–16)! Does the clay know more than the Potter (Rom. 9:20)? Can the thing made fool the Maker?

A blessed city (17–24). When the Lord returns and establishes His kingdom, things will change! God's people will hear and see His truth, rejoice in it, and honor the Holy One of Israel. But you need not wait to have Him change your life. Give Him an honest heart, and let the Potter have His way in your life.

ISAIAH 30—31

When Assyria threatened Judah, the leaders did not immediately turn to God for help but trusted in diplomacy. Their ambassadors went through dangerous territory (30:6–7) to go to Egypt, *but Egypt could not help Judah*. Egypt was as helpful as a shadow (30:1–5), a wall about to fall down (30:12–13), or a broken clay vessel (30:14). The Egyptians were only men, not God (31:1–3). Are you trusting things that cannot help you while the Lord waits for you to come to Him for help (30:15, 18)?

Those who wait on the Lord for help will experience blessings, such as answered prayer (30:18–19), God's guidance (30:20–21), cleansing (30:22), fruitfulness (30:23–26), victory (30:27–33; 31:4–9), and a song (30:29).

The horses of Egypt can never take the place of the chariots of God (Ps. 20:7–8).

ISAIAH 32

Dependable people (1–2). Although our Lord fits this description (Isa. 25:4), the prophet is speaking primarily about leaders in the kingdom. They should be both *rocks* and *rivers*, providing *security* and *sufficiency*. Rocks do not move or change, while rivers are ever moving and changing. Leaders must be both consistent and adaptable, combining the faithfulness of the rock with the fruitfulness of the river.

Wise people (3–8). Fools, scoundrels, and schemers abounded in Isaiah's day and made the nation weak. But God wants people whose eyes, ears, and hearts are open to spiritual truth, people who are able to share that truth clearly with others.

Concerned people (9–15). Isaiah had a special burden for the careless women of the land (Isa. 3:16ff.; see also Amos 6:1ff.), for wives and mothers can have great influence for good or for evil. They were living at ease as God's judgment was about to fall. Their happy homes were about to be destroyed, but they did not seem to care.

Peaceful people (16–20). The prophet ends on a happy note, describing the peace and prosperity of the future kingdom. There can be no lasting peace without righteousness, and Jesus Christ is our "King of righteousness" and "King of peace" (Heb. 7:1–3).

ISAIAH 33

The prophet looked out at the horizon and saw the plunderer coming to conquer the land. Then he looked around at some of the people in the nation who helped cause this judgment: the traitors who sold out to the enemy (v. 1); the ambassadors who sought help from Egypt (v. 7); and the religious hypocrites who pretended to serve God (v. 14; 1:10–20; 29:13). All of this was discouraging, but one thing encouraged Isaiah: a godly remnant that trusted the Lord and interceded for the land (vv. 2–4, 14–15). When you pray, you see the Lord exalted (vv. 5–6), you hear His words of encouragement (vv. 10–13), and you view your King in glory and power (vv. 17–24). Are you looking in the right direction? Are you a part of the godly remnant of intercessors?

> ### It's a Promise
>
> *All the plunderers will be plundered, and all the traitors will themselves be betrayed (Isa. 33:1). We reap what we sow (Gal. 6:7–8).*

ISAIAH 34

From judgment upon His people, God turns to warn about judgment upon the whole world. It will be like slaughtering whole armies (v. 3), shaking heaven (v. 4), and sacrificing people like animals (vv. 5–7).

God will also judge the land (vv. 8–17) and make it a wilderness. When you read the judgments described in Revelation 6–19, you see what ruin will come to the earth. Isaiah specifically names Edom, one of Israel's longtime enemies; but no nation will escape.

Why this indignation? "For the cause of Zion" (v. 8). God fights *against* His people if they disobey Him, but He fights *for* them when His chastening has accomplished its purposes. He will keep His covenant with Abraham and Abraham's descendants (Gen. 12:1–3).

ISAIAH 35

Once again, God balances the announcement of judgment with the assurance of glory. He wants sinners to repent and believers to be encouraged. When Jesus Christ comes to reign, marvelous changes will take place.

The desolate wilderness will become a beautiful garden (vv. 1–2, 7). Human history began in a garden, but man's sin turned the garden into a desert. God's creation will rejoice when it is set free from the bondage of sin (Isa. 55:12–13; Rom. 8:18–25).

The weak will be strong, and the disabled will be handicapped no longer (vv. 3–6). The wanderers will never lose their way as they walk safely on God's Highway of Holiness (vv. 8–9), and the weepers will have their sorrows turned into joy (v. 10).

As you wait for these physical blessings, you can enjoy them in a spiritual way. God can give you deliverance, fruitfulness, strength, holiness, and joy as you yield to Him.

"O For a Thousand Tongues to Sing"

Hear Him, ye deaf;
His praise, ye dumb, Your loosened tongues employ;
Ye blind, behold your Saviour come;
And leap, ye lame, for joy!

Charles Wesley

The Desert Will Bloom

Eighty-nine workers were accidentally killed during the building of Boulder (Hoover) Dam. The memorial plaque reads: "For those who died that the desert might bloom." One day, the desert will bloom to the glory of God because Jesus Christ died on the cross for the sins of the world.

ISAIAH 36

Chapters 36—39 are historical and describe three special tests that King Hezekiah faced: enemy invasion (chaps. 36—37), sickness (chap. 38), and flattery (chap. 39). See 2 Kings 18—19 and 2 Chronicles 32 for additional data.

The prophet warned that the Assyrian army was coming, and now it surrounded Jerusalem.

Assyria conquered Israel and then moved into Judah where it captured every fortified city. From the words of the Rabshakeh (army field commander), you can learn much about warfare against your own spiritual enemy, the devil.

Satan is proud and confident of victory. He tries to frighten you into surrendering. He knows that the most important thing is *where you put your faith* (v. 4). Are you trusting the world, yourself or the Lord (vv. 6—7)?

The enemy offers to give you something in return for your obedience (vv. 8, 16), *but there is always an "until" involved* (v. 17)! He wants you to think that his gifts are as good as the Lord's gifts and that the Lord cannot be trusted to help you (vv. 14—15, 18).

Use the shield of faith to quench those fiery darts (Eph. 6:16) *and never negotiate with Satan* (v. 21). Do what Hezekiah did: ask the Lord for help and believe His Word.

ISAIAH 37

Not all victories are as dramatic as this one, but Hezekiah's experience shows you what to do when you are attacked by the enemy.

Take your burdens to the Lord. It is good to talk things over with others, but only the Lord can work in your heart and turn fear into faith. God knows everything the enemy says and writes, and He has a perfect plan. By faith, take everything to Him in prayer.

Listen for God's message. The words of the enemy will discourage you, but God's Word will encourage you. In every battle, His word to you is, "Do not be afraid" (v. 6). After all, He has everything under control.

Seek to glorify God alone. More than anything else, Hezekiah was concerned for the glory of God (vv. 4, 16—20). "Hallowed be Thy name" must be your primary prayer.

Trust God to work. Sennacherib defied the God of Israel, and yet he died in the house of his god *who could not protect him*. God can handle the enemy far better than you can.

Trust God after the victory. The Assyrians had devastated the land, but God promised to feed His people and give them a harvest. Your future is in God's hands.

❝The future is as bright as the promises of God.**❞**

William Carey

ISAIAH 38

In the prime of life (v. 10), Hezekiah contracted a boil (v. 21) that so infected his body that he was told he would die (v. 1). All this happened before the events of chapters 36 and 37 (v. 6), but Hezekiah knew Assyria was coming. What a predicament to be in!

The king's prayer was certainly a normal response. After all, most believers want to go on living and serving God. He was concerned, too, about the future of the nation in view of the Assyrian advance. At any rate, God not only answered his prayer but even gave him a special sign to encourage his faith.

❝If you are swept off your feet, it is time to get
on your knees.**❞**

Frederick Beck

Hezekiah pictured death as going through a gate (v. 10), taking down a tent (v. 12), being cut from a loom and rolled up (v. 12), and being attacked by a beast (v. 13). But he clung to the Word of God (v. 17) and gave praise to God for all He did (vv. 16–20).

Difficult experiences should give us a new appreciation for life and a new desire to live for the Lord.

ISAIAH 39

This was the third test (2 Chron. 32:31), and the king failed miserably. What could not be accomplished through an army or an illness was accomplished through flattery. If Satan cannot succeed as a lion, then he comes as a serpent: "Faithful are the wounds of a friend, but the kisses of an enemy are deceitful" (Prov. 27:6).

The kisses. The king of Babylon wanted one thing: Judah's cooperation in opposing the Assyrians. The enemy is a liar and uses every excuse to get entry into your life. It was foolish for Hezekiah to welcome them and show them the royal treasures, but pride took over and discernment disappeared. Ephesians 4:17–32 lists some "footholds" you can give Satan in your life.

The wounds. Isaiah did not fear the king but told him truthfully that Babylon was the real enemy *and one day would conquer Judah.* However, instead of repenting, Hezekiah felt relieved that the judgment would not come in his day. How shortsighted can a man of faith become! Had he no concern for the future of his people?

Wound with Truth

It is not always easy to deliver God's message to those who need it. It takes courage to wound a friend. Nathan faced King David with the truth (2 Sam. 12), and Isaiah confronted both Ahaz (Isa. 7) and Hezekiah (Isa. 39). The apostle Paul fearlessly confronted Peter (Gal. 2:11ff.). One writer observed, "A lying tongue hates those who are crushed by it, and a flattering mouth works ruin" (Prov. 26:28). Speak the truth in love (Eph. 4:15) and give wounds that heal.

ISAIAH 40

Voices (1–11). Though Isaiah wrote a century before the fall of Judah, his words greatly encouraged the exiles when they read them in Babylon. The voice of *comfort* (vv. 1–5) tells you that God knows how to measure your chastening and that He forgives and gives you a new beginning. The voice of *confidence* (vv. 6–8) assures you that His Word stands in spite of the frailty of man. The voice of *conquest* (vv. 9–11) is *your* voice as you share the good news with others. Shout it aloud!

Vision (12–24). Returning to the land and rebuilding the nation seemed impossible tasks to the exiles, so Isaiah invited them to behold the greatness of God. God is greater than every burden you bear and every challenge you face. Babylon was but a drop in the bucket to God! The world's false gods can do nothing to hinder the working of your great God, so trust Him to see you through.

Victory (25–31). You may be weak like grass (vv. 6–8), sheep (v. 11), dust (v. 15), grasshoppers (v. 22), and even worms (41:14); but if you trust the power of God, you can be like an eagle, a runner, and a patient pilgrim (vv. 28–31). In the emergencies of life, God helps you soar; in the daily routine of life, He helps you patiently walk. Both are the working of His mighty power (Eph. 3:20–21).

Servanthood

"Servant" is a key concept in the second half of Isaiah's prophecy. It refers to the nation of Israel (41:8–9); to Cyrus, king of Persia, who defeated Babylon (41:2; 44:28—45:1); and to the Lord Jesus Christ, God's "Suffering Servant," who died for the sins of the world (52:13—53:12).

ISAIAH 41

As the exiles prepared to return to their land, they looked around, saw other nations, and were afraid (vv. 1–7). But God was (and is) in control of the nations, and He raised up Cyrus to do His bidding (vv. 2, 25). The false gods of the nations are no match for the true God of Israel.

Then the exiles looked at one another and asked, "Are we able to travel to our land and rebuild our nation?" (vv. 8–20). But God gave them assurance: "You are My servant! Fear not, for I am with you! I will help you!" He can make a toothless worm into a sharp threshing instrument (v. 15)! He can transform the arid desert into a garden (vv. 17–20).

Finally, they looked ahead and wondered about the future (vv. 21–29). God knows the future (the idols do not!) and has everything under control, so there is no need to worry.

As you contemplate your situation and face an unknown future, are you trusting Him? God's promise is still "I will help you" (vv. 10, 13, 14), and He will keep it!

Fear Not

The admonition "fear not" is often repeated in Isaiah, backed up by various reasons why God's people need not be afraid. God is with us no matter what the circumstances, and He strengthens us and helps us no matter what the task (41:10). He holds us as He helps us (41:13–14). He will not forsake us because He made us and redeemed us, and we belong to Him (43:1, 5) He was with us before we were born, and He has a purpose for us to fulfill in this world today (44:2). How can we be afraid when God's words are sure and He is the Rock of our salvation (44:8)?

ISAIAH 42

God helped His Servant, Jesus Christ (1–13). Matthew 12:18–21 applies this to our Lord in His earthly ministry to the needy. He was chosen by God and empowered by God, so He did not get discouraged and quit. Jesus Christ lived and served by faith, trusting His Father to meet His needs, and that is the way you must live today. His power is available to you.

God helped His servant, Israel (14–25). Weak as they were, the nation returned to the land after their years of captivity. They were spiritually blind and obstinate, but God led them and worked on their behalf.

God helps His servants today. When you belong to God's family, your Father is ready to forgive and restore you. Putting life back together again may appear impossible, but the Lord will work for you if you let Him. He can do new things (v. 9), guide you on new paths (v. 16), and give you a new song (v. 10).

ISAIAH 43

There is no reason to be afraid when you realize what God has done for you. He formed you (v. 1) and made you for Himself (v. 21) and for His glory (v. 7). When you trusted Jesus Christ, God redeemed you (v. 1) and blotted out all your sins (v. 25). He is "the LORD, your Holy One, the Creator of Israel, your King" (v. 15). He loves you (v. 4) and knows your name (v. 1). What a privilege to belong to such a great and gracious God!

Even more, God promises to be with you (v. 5) and take you through the water and the fire (v. 2). At the Exodus, He took Israel through the Red Sea and defeated the Egyptian army (vv. 16–17). Perhaps the three Hebrew heroes claimed this promise when they faced the fiery furnace (Dan. 3).

In spite of all the ministry He shares with us, God does not get weary as we do (40:28); but we can weary Him with our empty religious ritual and our sins (vv. 22–24). You are precious in His sight (v. 4), so do not cheapen yourself by disobeying Him.

ISAIAH 44

The faithfulness of God (1–8). Once again, God reminds His people that He formed them, chose them, and would help them. There is no need to be afraid, for God meets every need

(vv. 2–5) and keeps every promise (vv. 6–8). He knows what lies ahead and helps you prepare yourself to meet it.

The folly of idolatry (9–20). Israel learned in Babylon the futility and folly of idolatry. How easy it is to trust something other than the Lord, including the things we manufacture. Those who trust false gods will be afraid (v. 11) and become like the gods they worship (v. 18; Ps. 115:1–8). Their bodies may feast on excellent food (v. 19), but their souls feed on ashes (v. 20). They live on substitutes.

The future of Israel (21–28). Just like the exodus from Egypt (Exod. 14–15), the nation's exodus from Babylon would be a time of redemption and rejoicing, and God would confirm His Word to His people. Jerusalem would be restored and the temple rebuilt, and God would even use a pagan ruler to accomplish His purposes! He is the God of the impossible, so do what He commands.

Even a Pagan Ruler

The gods of the nations could not predict the future, but the Lord told Isaiah what would happen. A ruler named Cyrus would conquer Babylon and allow the Jews to return to their land (44:28; 45:1). Cyrus founded the Persian Empire, which defeated Babylon in 539 B.C. (Dan. 5:30). The next year, he issued the famous decree that permitted the Jews to go back to their land and rebuild their temple (Ezra 1:1–6). If God can use a pagan ruler to serve His people and fulfill His Word, you have no reason to be afraid of what people may say or do. The predictions of astrologers and other "prophets" are ashes. God's Word is the true light in the darkness (2 Pet. 1:19–21).

ISAIAH 45

God makes declarations to Cyrus (vv. 1–7), to the Jews (vv. 8–19), and to the gentile nations (vv. 20–25); and in these messages, He speaks to His people today.

His message to Cyrus was one of *sovereignty*, focusing on His uniqueness: Jehovah is the Creator and the Lord of history. Cyrus did not even know the Lord; yet the Lord called him by name and used him to accomplish His purposes. When life seems to be tumbling in, remember that God is on the throne and is sovereign.

Look Now!

> The famous British preacher Charles Haddon Spurgeon (1834–92) was converted to Christ when he heard a layman preach a sermon based on Isaiah 45:22. "He was an ignorant man," said Spurgeon in later years. "He could not say much; he was obliged to keep to his text. Thank God for that." The preacher looked at young Spurgeon and said, "Young man, you are very miserable. Young man, look! In God's name, look, and look now!" Spurgeon said, "I did look, blessed be God! I know I looked then and there, and he who but that minute before had been near despair had the fullness of joy and hope." Have you looked to Christ by faith and received His gift of salvation?"

His message to Israel emphasized *submission*. God can tell the rain clouds what to do, but His own people resist Him. This is like the clay telling the potter what to do (Jer. 18) or the child scolding the parents. If Israel would trust Him, they could share in the great things He was doing. Cyrus would cooperate with the Lord, and he did not even know Him!

The message to the Gentiles was one of *salvation*. God's purpose through Israel was that all nations be blessed (Gen. 12:1–3). One day God will gather His people and establish His kingdom, and then the nations will know the true God and trust the Savior. Meanwhile, we must get the message of salvation to every tribe and nation.

ISAIAH 46—47

The prophet speaks to the Babylonians and warns them that judgment is coming because of their many sins.

He begins with their idolatry (chap. 46) and contrasts Jehovah and the gods of Babylon. The idols must be carried, but Jehovah is a God who carries His people. The false gods cannot predict the future or control history, but Jehovah does both. The idols are all alike, but Jehovah is the only true God and there is none like Him. Rejoice that you can worship the true and living God (Ps. 115)!

There Is No Substitute

An idol is a substitute for God, something that we value and serve other than God. We trust it and sacrifice for it; but in the end, it can do us no good. Isaiah mocked the idols of the nations and affirmed repeatedly that Jehovah was the only true and living God (40:18–20; 41:5–7; 44:9–20; 45:15–21; 46:1–7). Martin Luther said that "all such as rely and depend upon their art, wisdom, strength, sanctity, riches, honor, power, or anything else" are guilty of worshiping idols.

God then accused them of being proud (47:1–3), having no humanity (47:4–7), living for pleasure (47:8–9), and depending on occult practices (47:10–15), sins that are prevalent today. The "Lady of Kingdoms" would sit in the dust like a barren widow, and the astrologers and stargazers would be burned to stubble. Why did they not see the fire coming?

Nations and kingdoms have their day, but God reigns as King. Just be sure you are not learning the practices of Babylon.

ISAIAH 48

Rebuke. When you end up in trouble because you did not listen to sound advice, the last thing you want to hear is somebody saying, "I told you so!" But that is just what God says to Israel in this chapter. He had warned them that their sins would bring judgment, but they hardened their necks and closed their ears. It was time to repent and seek forgiveness.

Refining. The captivity was about to end. It had been a time of refining for the nation (v. 10; Job 23:10; 1 Pet. 1:7), but they had learned to turn from idols and trust Jehovah alone. If you resist, the fire will burn you and make you hard; if you submit, the fire will purify you and make you tender.

Renewing. God declares new things (Isa. 42:9) and does new things (Isa. 43:19), and His people can hear new things (v. 6). Verse 20 has its parallel in 2 Corinthians 6:14–18. As you obey God, He leads you (v. 17), gives you peace (v. 18), and meets your needs (v. 21). No matter how weak you are, you can lean on Him (v. 2).

ISAIAH 49

The Servant is the Lord Jesus Christ, to whom several meaningful names are given.

He is God's *weapon* to conquer the enemy (vv. 1–2; Heb. 4:12; Rev. 1:16; 19:15) and to bring salvation to the nations. He is God's *Israel* (v. 3), accomplishing what the nation failed to accomplish, namely, bringing God's salvation to the Gentiles.

He is a *light* (v. 6) to guide the Gentiles to God (Luke 1:79; Acts 13:47); and He is the *covenant of God* (v. 8), fulfilling all the promises God made to the fathers (Isa. 42:6; Rom. 15:8–13; 2 Cor. 1:20). The nation's return to the land was a picture of their final return when Messiah comes (vv. 8–13).

There are times when you wonder if God really cares about you (v. 14), but He assures you that you are not forgotten. You are His beloved child (v. 15; Ps. 27:10), and He will never forget your name (v. 16). He will gather His family and bring them home (vv. 19–23).

ISAIAH 50

The unfaithful wife (1–3). Israel was "married to Jehovah" when she accepted His covenant at Sinai. But the nation eventually turned to idols, committed spiritual adultery, and sold herself into slavery; and God had to put her away (Hos. 1–4). God will restore His chosen people one day just as He forgives and restores believers today who turn from sin and obey Him (James 4:1–10).

The faithful Servant (4–9). This is our Lord Jesus Christ with a ready-tongue and an open ear (vv. 4–5), a set face (v. 7; Luke 9:51), and a body surrendered to suffering (v. 6). What an example for us to follow as we seek to serve the Lord (Rom. 12:1–12).

The perplexed disciple (10–11). People who fear God and obey Him can still end up in the darkness of perplexity. Then they are tempted to light their own fires and try to find their way out by themselves. Instead, trust the Lord, wait on Him, and He will give you the light you need when you need it.

ISAIAH 51

As the nation prepared to leave Babylon and return home, they needed to strengthen their faith in Jehovah God. God told them to do the following:

Look back! God urged His people to recall their spiritual roots: the call of Abraham (vv. 1–2) and the exodus from Egypt (vv. 9–10, 15). They are a covenant people, and God will not break His promises. They are a redeemed people, and God will care for them. Take time to remember your spiritual roots; you will be encouraged in your faith.

Look up! He said, "Lift up your eyes" (v. 6; Gen. 15:1–6). Again, Isaiah tells the people to consider God's creation and remember what a great God He is and how lasting is His Word (40:6–8, 12–14). When you are prone to fret, remember that the Creator is your Father, and you have nothing to fear.

Look ahead! The wilderness will become a Garden of Eden (v. 3), and the people will "exodus" from Babylon and return joyfully to Zion (v. 11). The ultimate fulfillment will be when the kingdom is established and all of Israel's enemies will be defeated.

ISAIAH 52

It is a new day and time for God's people to *wake up* (v. 1; 51:9, 17; Rom. 13:11–14). The night of trial is over, and God will do a new thing for them. This is a new day for you, so wake up to God's blessing (Lam. 3:22–23).

It is also time to *dress up* (v. 1), for the feast is about to begin. God has forgiven His people and brought them home, and it is time to rejoice (v. 9; Luke 15:22–24).

It is time to *speak up* (vv. 7–10) and tell the world what God has done for His people. Paul applies this to the sharing of the gospel with the lost (Rom. 10:15).

It is time to *clean up* (vv. 11–12). As the exiles left Babylon, they were not to defile themselves but be clean and carry the holy vessels back to Zion. There is always a new "Babylon" for God's people to flee if they would keep themselves clean (Rev. 18:1–8). As you obey, God goes before you and behind you, so you need not be afraid of the enemy.

ISAIAH 53

This chapter is about Jesus Christ, God's perfect sacrifice for the sins of the world (Acts 8:26–40). It actually begins in 52:13 where the prophet tells us that the Servant suffered for doing God's will and yet was highly exalted by the Lord. Humiliation and exaltation, suffering and glory, are key themes in this prophecy.

Consider the humiliation of His birth and life (vv. 1–3) as well as the humiliation of His trial and His sufferings and death (vv. 4–9). Consider the glory of the salvation He purchased for you on the cross (vv. 10–12). The Father was pleased, not that His Son suffered, but that His sacrifice accomplished eternal salvation. God's justice was satisfied, and believing sinners can be justified (v. 11; Rom. 3:21–31).

Consider the pictures of the Savior: a beaten servant (52:13–14), a root (53:2), an innocent lamb (53:7), an offering for sin (53:10), a woman in travail giving birth to spiritual "seed" (53:10–11), and a victorious general (53:12). Hallelujah, what a Savior!

Yet people still do not believe in Him (v. 1). Instead, they despise and reject Him (v. 2) and laugh at the message of the Cross (1 Cor. 1:18–25). But heaven praises the Lamb of God (Rev. 5), and His people on earth glory in His cross (Gal. 6:14). Are you among them?

He Paid the Price

Isaiah 53 is cited or alluded to frequently in the New Testament. (Along with the passages in the Gospels that describe Christ's sufferings, death, and burial, see John 1:29; 12:38; Acts 8:26–40; Rom. 10:16; Heb. 9:28; 1 Pet. 2:21–25; Rev. 5.) The chapter teaches substitutionary atonement, that the innocent Son of God died in the place of guilty sinners and paid the price for sin. We do not understand all that was involved in that "holy transaction" on the cross, but we do know that it accomplished salvation for a lost world.

ISAIAH 54

The future regathering and restoring of Israel is a picture of the wonderful changes God makes when trials and sufferings end.

The barren woman gives birth to so many children that the family tent must be enlarged (vv. 1–3). The widow loses her shame and is wed once again, this time to Jehovah (vv. 4–6). The storm is over and God gives peace (vv. 7–15), and the covenant sign of the rainbow is in the sky (v. 10).

Times of chastening or suffering may seem spiritually barren to you, but God uses them to give birth to blessings. Times of sorrow and reproach are painful, but they can lead to greater joys. Storms are frightening, but they polish God's jewels (vv. 11–12) and bring Him glory. It is painful to go through the furnace (vv. 16–17), but God uses the experience to make you a stronger and better tool.

The best is yet to come!

❝We say, 'sorrow, disaster, calamity'; God says, 'chastening,' and it sounds sweet to Him though it is a discord to our ears. Don't faint when you are rebuked, and don't despise the chastenings of the Lord. 'In your patience possess ye your souls.'**❞**

Oswald Chambers

ISAIAH 55

Again, the prophet depicts the changes God makes in the lives of those who turn from their sins and trust the Savior.

From substitutes to reality (1–2). The lost sinner is bankrupt because he spends all he has for what cannot satisfy. When you hear God's Word and obey, you start to enjoy the water of life and the bread of life, found in Jesus Christ (John 4; 6).

From death to life (3–5). Compare verse 3 with John 5:24. Jesus is the fulfillment of the covenant God made with David (2 Sam. 7; Acts 13:34). When you trust Him, you share in His life and His victories.

From guilt to pardon (6–7). When the sinner repents and turns to Christ by faith, God shows mercy and grants pardon. But do not delay (Prov. 1:20–33)!

From fear to certainty (8–11). God's ways are beyond man's comprehension, but you can be sure He is accomplishing His purposes in His times. Like the rain and snow that seem to be wasted, God's Word accomplishes His will on the earth.

From wilderness to paradise (12–13). Sin turns the garden into a desert (Isa. 5:3–6; 32:12–15), but grace transforms the desert into a joyful and fruitful garden. Abundant satisfaction, pardon, and joy are available to all who accept God's gracious invitation.

ISAIAH 56

It was God's purpose that through Israel the Gentiles might come to know the true God and His salvation (Gen. 12:1–3). But instead, Israel adopted the false gods of the Gentiles! Their leaders were like blind watchmen, greedy watchdogs that could not bark, and shepherds concerned only for themselves (vv. 9–12). No wonder the nation went into captivity! And what a warning to spiritual leaders today!

But God did not abandon the Gentiles. The "outcast" foreigner is accepted (vv. 6–8), and the eunuch is welcomed (vv. 3–5; Deut. 23:1). In Jesus Christ, the wall between Jews and Gentiles is broken down; and any sinner can come to the Savior and find forgiveness and acceptance (Eph. 2).

Jesus quoted from verse 7 when He cleansed the temple in Jerusalem (Matt. 21:13). How tragic that the religious leaders had turned a place of worship and witness into a den of thieves. Would any Gentile want to know the God of Israel after seeing the Court of the Gentiles made into a marketplace? But what do outsiders see when they attend our church services today (1 Cor. 14:23–25)?

ISAIAH 57

Deterioration (1–2). When God wants to judge His people, He sometimes takes the godly leaders away; and they are spared the pain of seeing their nation deteriorate and then go into judgment (vv. 1–2; 3:1–5). Do you appreciate the men and women God has given to provide spiritual leadership, and do you encourage them?

Denunciation (3–13). This description of the godless society in Judah seems quite contemporary. God denounced them for lying, worshiping idols, indulging in sexual sins, sacrificing their children, and mocking the godly. These people had no fear of God because He did not immediately send judgment, but their day was coming.

Dedication (14–21). Even in a godless society, here and there are dedicated people who have fellowship with God. God longs to dwell with His people (John 14:21–24), and He will if they are humble and contrite (Ps. 51:17; Isa. 66:2). Does God "feel at home" in your heart (Eph. 3:14–21)?

ISAIAH 58

When you strive to be a spiritual person, you fight the constant battle of "ritual versus reality." It is much easier to go through the external activities of religion than it is to love God from your heart and let that love touch the lives of others. It is a matter not of either/or but of both/and: worshiping God from the heart and serving others in love. James stated, "Faith without works is dead" (2:20).

The orthodox faith was popular in Judah at that time, and people enjoyed learning the Word and even participating in fasts (vv. 2–3). But when the services were over, the worshipers went back to exploiting people and pleasing themselves.

What a difference it makes when we repent and return to the Lord (vv. 8–12)! We have light instead of darkness, healing instead of disease, righteousness instead of defilement, glory instead of disgrace; and life becomes a watered garden, not a dismal swamp.

ISAIAH 59

The images in this chapter teach important spiritual truths.

Hands (1–3). God's hand is unable to work when our hands are defiled with sin. Our prayers accomplish nothing (Ps. 66:18), and His power is absent from our lives and ministries.

Poison (4–5). A lie is not just a sound in the air or a sentence on paper. It has a life of its own and gives birth to all kinds of trouble. Try to live on lies, and they will poison you. When lies finally "hatch," they will bite you and may kill you (James 1:13–16).

Spiders' webs (6–8). Trying to hide behind lies and hypocritical religious works is like clothing yourself with a spider's web. The sins described here were committed by *religious* people. No wonder God withheld His blessings! Is He doing that today?

Traffic jam (9–15). It is dark. The pedestrians on the streets are blind and are acting like beasts. Truth has fallen in the street and progress has ceased. The "traffic officers" (justice and righteousness) are standing far off because the people will not let them exercise authority.

Manhunt (16–21). God searched for one person to intercede for His people, but He found none, so He did the work Himself. Are you an intercessor? Are you concerned about the "traffic jam" that hinders God's work and robs God of glory?

❝God will bless Elijah and send rain on Israel, but Elijah must pray for it. If the chosen nation is to prosper, Samuel must plead for it. If the Jews are to be delivered, Daniel must intercede. God will bless Paul, and the nations shall be converted, but Paul must pray. . . . Let me have your prayers, and I can do anything! Let me be without my people's prayers, and I can do nothing!**❞**

Charles Haddon Spurgeon

ISAIAH 60

Light (1–3, 19–22; Rev. 21—22). As Isaiah looked ahead to the redeemed people and the restored city of Zion, the thing that impressed him most was *glory* (vv. 1, 2, 7, 9, 13, 19, 21). It would be the dawning of a new day for the nation. Ponder John 17:22–24; Romans 8:18; and 1 Peter 5:10.

Unity (4–9). The nations will stream to the light of Israel, and Jews and Gentiles will unite in worshiping and serving God. Our world is plagued by division and conflict, but one day God will give peace.

Joy (10–18). God's favor and mercy will enrich His people as He surrounds them with beauty and joy. Zion's citizens will know the Lord and give Him praise.

ISAIAH 61

Release (1–3). Jesus took these verses as His text when He preached in Nazareth (Luke 4:16ff.) and announced that He was ushering in the Year of Jubilee (Lev. 25). It is a time of releasing the slaves, canceling all debts, and making a new beginning. Today, those who trust Christ begin to enjoy their Jubilee; those who reject Him face judgment.

Renewal (4–6). The land of Judah was in ruins after the Babylonian captivity, but God would help the people repair and rebuild. The whole nation would become priests of the Lord (1 Pet. 2:5, 9) and servants of God.

Rejoicing (7–11). Instead of shame, there would be rejoicing and everlasting joy. It would be like going from a funeral to a wedding (Luke 5:27–39) and from a desert to a beautiful garden!

Have you entered your Jubilee?

ISAIAH 62

God's promises should become our prayers. Isaiah prayed that Jerusalem might be restored (v. 1), and he urged the watchmen and all of God's people to pray as well (vv. 6–7). The psalmist also prayed "for the peace of Jerusalem" (Ps. 122:6). When there is peace in Jerusalem, there will be peace in the world.

The nation's restoration will be as joyful as a wedding (vv. 4–5; 61:10). *Beulah* means "married," and *Hephzibah* means "My delight is in her." The people were "divorced" from God because of their unfaithfulness, and He was not delighted in them; but that will change when God cleanses their sins.

Now is the time to make ready, for the King is coming to Zion (vv. 10–12; Matt. 21:5; Rev. 22:12)!

ISAIAH 63

Indignation (1–6). When Jesus Christ returns to establish His kingdom, He will come as a conquering warrior (Rev. 19:11–21). When He came the first time, He was a servant who shed His blood for sinners; but the next time, the sinners will shed their blood in a futile defense against the Lord. The Year of Jubilee will become the "day of vengeance" (Isa. 61:1–2).

Compassion (7–14). Jesus will defeat His enemies, but He will save His own people (v. 8). The emphasis is on loving-kindness, goodness, mercy, and love. God cares for His children and promises them glory (1 Thess. 5:9–10). Just as He saved them in the days of Moses, so He will save them in the latter days.

Intercession (15–19). Isaiah continues to pray for his people (62:1). As a child pleading with a father, he begs God to return and overcome the enemy. He longs to see the temple restored and the people obeying their Lord. Have you joined in that prayer?

Are Your Trials Overwhelming?

Isaiah said, "In all their affliction He was afflicted" (63:9). God not only goes with you in the difficulties of life (Isa. 43:2), but He knows how you feel. Your High Priest in heaven is able to sympathize with you because He has experienced the trials and temptations of life (Heb. 2:17–18; 4:14–16). You should cast "all your care upon Him, for He cares for you" (1 Pet. 5:7).

ISAIAH 64

The missing demonstration (1–4). When the enemy attacked Jerusalem, the Lord held His peace and did not intervene. The Jews were both defeated and disgraced before their foes. Is this somewhat parallel to the situation of God's people today? Demonstrations of divine power are easily found in history books but not readily found among God's people today. Why?

The missing intercession (5–7). Isaiah once again emphasizes the importance of prayer (62:1, 6–7; 63:15–19). God wonders that there is no intercessor (Isa. 59:16), nobody who will get stirred up about the need for confessing sin and seeking

God's face. Until we pray and get right with God, He will not reveal His power (2 Chron. 7:14).

The missing submission (8–12). The clay should yield to the Potter, and the children should obey the Father (Isa. 29:16; 45:9–10; Jer. 18; Rom. 9:20–21). No wonder the temple, the city, and the land were desolate, for God cannot bless those who rebel against Him. If God is going to "come down" with His power, we must fall down in surrender to Him.

Riches Beyond Compare

Paul quoted Isaiah 64:4 in 1 Corinthians 2:9. Some people think this refers to heaven, but Paul applied it to the Christian life here and now (1 Cor. 2:10). When you read the Word of God and let the Spirit teach you, you can find out the wonderful things God has done for you and will do for you as you trust and obey. Your Bible is your "passbook" to the Bank of Heaven; it tells you how rich you are in Jesus Christ (Eph. 1:3, 7, 18; 2:7; 3:8, 16).

ISAIAH 65

The rebels (1–7). God pleaded with His people to turn from their sins and come back to Him, but they refused. They acted so pious and yet were guilty of many sins: worshiping idols, following occult practices, violating dietary laws, and blaspheming God. But if the Jews rejected God's call, the Gentiles responded in their stead (Rom. 10:20–21; Matt. 21:43).

The remnant (8–16). God always has His faithful remnant, like a few grapes after the harvest (Deut. 24:21); and He uses them as the nucleus of a new beginning. The rebels will be judged, but the remnant ("My servants") will be blessed.

The regeneration (17–25). That is what Jesus called the kingdom God has prepared for His people (Matt. 19:28). The blessings named are in contrast to the judgments listed in Deuteronomy 28:15ff. It will be a time of joy and fulfillment when the blessing of the Lord flows without interference from man.

> **"**We should all be concerned about the future because we will have to spend the rest of our lives there.**"**
>
> Charles F. Kettering

ISAIAH 66

Trembling (1–6). How can anyone build a house for the Lord when He made everything (Isa. 40:25–26)? He is so great that He uses the earth for His footstool (v. 1)! But with all of His greatness, God deigns to dwell with the humble (v. 2; 57:15), those who tremble at His word and seek to glorify Him (v. 5).

Tremble at His Word

To "tremble at God's word" (Isa. 66:2, 5) means to respect what God says and fear to disobey it (Ps. 119:120). The Jews experienced this when Ezra exposed their sins (Ezra 9:4; 10:3), and the prophet Habakkuk experienced it when he saw the vision of God's judgment (Hab. 3:16). Saul of Tarsus trembled when he met the Lord (Acts 9:6). However, King Jehoiakim did not tremble at the Word; he tried to destroy it (Jer. 36), and that led to his destruction (Prov. 13:13). Paul urged, "Work out your own salvation [Christian life] with fear and trembling" (Phil. 2:12).

Travailing (7–13). The restoration of Israel's kingdom will be as sudden and joyful as the birth of a baby. The travail of their tribulation will give birth to glory, and God will love them just like a mother (v. 13). It will be a time of peace and joy.

Triumphing (14–24). God will defeat His enemies (vv. 14–17), summon the gentile nations to share the glory (vv. 18–19), and make Israel a holy offering to the Lord (vv. 20–24). Isaiah opened his prophecy indicting Israel for her religious hypocrisy (chap. 1), but he ended it promising that her worship will be acceptable to the Lord.

JEREMIAH

◆

The prophet Jeremiah ministered in Judah during the last forty years of the nation's history, from 627 to perhaps 582 B.C. In spite of his faithful preaching of the Word, Jeremiah watched the nation decline until Judah was taken captive by the Babylonians and Jerusalem and the temple were destroyed. He expressed his grief vividly in the book of Lamentations.

He was a priest called to be a prophet, a sensitive man called to confront kings, false prophets, and hypocritical priests. He was bold before men but broken before God, and we call him "the weeping prophet." When Jesus was here on earth, the people identified Him with the prophet Jeremiah (Matt. 16:14). Jeremiah's life was not easy, and his ministry did not appear successful. But he was faithful to the Lord and accomplished God's will.

66Jeremiah lived about sixty years. Across that life span there is no sign of decay or shriveling. Always he was pushing out the borders of reality, exploring new territory. And always he was vigorous in battle, challenging and contesting the shoddy, the false, the vile.99

Eugene H. Peterson

After describing his call to ministry (chap. 1), Jeremiah records his messages to Judah, pleading with the people to repent (chaps. 2—33). He shares some of his personal sufferings (chaps. 34—45) and sermons to the gentile nations (chaps. 46—51). The last chapter reviews the fall of the city and the nation (chap. 52).

Jeremiah is a master of imagery who creates many word pictures to give his message. As you read his prophecy, use your imagination and "see" what Jeremiah is saying. Also, note the occasional personal disclosures in the book, particularly the honest expressions of the prophet's feelings. Jeremiah reveals his own heart as he preaches about the broken heart of God.

JEREMIAH 1

Kings and rulers come and go, but the Word of God remains and accomplishes God's work in the world. Yet God needs a voice to herald the Word, and nobody feels adequate for the task.

Hearing (1–10). God's word to Jeremiah was, "You will be what I want you to be, go where I want you to go, and say what I want you to say. I supervised your conception, I consecrated you, and now I am ordaining you." If God calls you, believe what He says and obey Him. You may not feel up to it, but your adequacy comes from God, not from yourself.

Are You Available?

Moses did not feel adequate for the task when God called him, but the Lord reassured him (Exod. 3—4). "And who is sufficient for these things?" asked Paul (2 Cor. 2:16); and his answer was, "Our sufficiency is from God" (2 Cor. 4:5–6). When God calls you to do a task for Him, He does not ask you to be adequate; He only asks you to be available.

Seeing (11–16). God's servants must have open eyes as well as open ears, for God can "speak" through what they see. In Hebrew, the words *almond* and *watch* are similar. God watches over His Word to perform what He says. Our job is proclamation; His job is performance. Babylon came from the north and destroyed Judah and Jerusalem.

Doing (17–19). It was difficult for youthful Jeremiah to confront his elders with a message of denunciation, but *God made him* and *God was with him*. God's messengers must be walls and not shifting sand.

God's Touch	*The touch of God makes the difference between success and failure. God touched Isaiah's lips to give him purity (Isa. 6:1–7) and Jeremiah's lips to give him power (Jer. 1:9–10; Luke 21:15). He touched Jacob's hip and gave him a limp (Gen. 32:25), thus helping him to become a "prince with God." God touched Daniel and set him on his feet (Dan. 8:18), gave him strength (Dan. 10:18), and opened his mouth for ministry (Dan. 10:15–16). The call of God and the touch of God must go together or we fail.*

JEREMIAH 2

Why was judgment coming to the nation of Judah? Because the people were unfaithful to God and had mixed the worship of Jehovah with the worship of heathen idols. Religion was very popular in Judah, but it was not very spiritual.

Judah was *an unfaithful wife* who had not maintained her "honeymoon love" (vv. 2, 32; Rev. 2:4). The people were *a wasted harvest* devoured by the enemy (v. 3). They forgot what God did for them and turned to false gods (vv. 4–8). It was like exchanging a pure artesian well for a dirty, leaky cistern (vv. 9–13).

They were *stubborn animals* that hated the yoke (v. 20) and *a degenerate vine* that bore no fruit (v. 21; Isa. 5). Their sins were so deep that they could not be washed away (v. 22). Like *wild animals in heat* (vv. 23–25), they lusted after sin; yet they denied that they had sinned (vv. 33–36)!

The last picture is that of *prisoners of war*, marching away with their hands on their heads (v. 37). What the people thought was freedom turned out to be slavery.

JEREMIAH 3

The word *backsliding* is used seven times in this chapter. Judah was gradually sliding away from the Lord and ignoring His loving pleas. What is *backsliding* like?

Backsliding

Backsliding is an Old Testament word used only by Isaiah (57:17), Jeremiah, and Hosea (11:7; 14:4). It means "disloyalty," "faithlessness." Most Christians do not jump into sin and get away from God's will. They gradually decline spiritually, then find themselves in trouble and wonder how it happened. They leave their first love (Rev. 2:4) and start living for the flesh and not the Spirit (Gal. 3:1–3). That is why our Lord admonished us to watch and pray (Matt. 26:41). When we least expect it, the germ of sin can enter the system.

Backsliding is like harlotry. The nation was "married" to Jehovah at Sinai when God gave her His covenant. But Judah became an unfaithful wife whose love was growing cold (Jer. 2:2) and whose "lovers" were many. God could "divorce" His defiled wife; but if He did, *she could not return to Him* (Deut. 24:1–4). So, instead of divorcing her, God warned her (vv. 3, 6–

10). However, she would not listen. He begged her to return, for returning is the only remedy for backsliding; but she refused.

Backsliding is like sickness (22). It begins with a secret "infection" of sin, which leads to loss of spiritual appetite, gradual decline and, if not attended to, death. God heals our backsliding if we honestly accept His diagnosis and humbly return to Him.

JEREMIAH 4

Over forty times in his book, Jeremiah calls for God's people to return to the Lord. To describe what that is like, he uses several images.

It is like *plowing* (vv. 1–3). Hard hearts need plowing up so they can receive the seed of the Word and bear fruit.

It is like *performing surgery* (v. 4). The Jews put their confidence in external religious ritual and did not let God operate on their hearts (Deut. 10:12–16; 30:6; Rom. 2:28–29). He wants truth deep within the heart (Ps. 51:6).

It is like *joining the army* (vv. 5–6, 19–21). The backslider is serving the enemy; but then he hears the trumpet call, realizes he is a traitor, and returns to obey his commander.

It is like *taking a bath* (v. 14). When we confess our sins, God cleanses us (1 John 1:9) and gives us a new beginning (Ps. 51:1–2, 10–11).

It is like *growing up* (v. 22). Believers should be childlike but not childish (Matt. 11:16–17). Backsliders are foolish, like disobedient children who are only hurting themselves.

No wonder God repeatedly calls to His backslidden people, "Return! Return!"

JEREMIAH 5

Looking for a man (1–9). God would have spared Sodom had He found ten righteous men (Gen. 18:26–32); but to spare Jerusalem, He would have settled for *one!* Yet Jeremiah could not find one, not even among the "great men" who were spiritual leaders in the city. Never underestimate the importance of one person living wholly for the Lord. Perhaps you can be that "righteous one" in your home or place of employment.

Looking for truth (3). The eyes of the Lord search for people who are faithful to Him and His Word. They may be in the minority and they may be persecuted, but they are God's own people and He will bless them.

Looking but not seeing (20–25). The eyes of the spiritual leaders were blind to God and what God was doing (Isa. 6:10; Matt. 13:15). They were also blind to the judgment about to fall on the nation. The waves of the sea know where to stop, but Judah's leaders went beyond the limits God had set. They might be popular and prosperous, but their prosperity would destroy them.

A Righteous Man

Henry Varley said to evangelist D. L. Moody, "The world has yet to see what God can do with and for and through and in a man who is fully and wholly consecrated to Him." Moody asked God to make him that man, and the Lord gave him his request. God used Moody in a marvelous way, and his work is still being blessed around the world.

JEREMIAH 6

The watchman. The prophet saw the invasion coming and warned the people, but they would not listen to him (v. 10). The delicate woman (Jerusalem) would be ruined (v. 2); the sun was going down (vv. 4–5); and the harvest of sin would be reaped (v. 9).

The physician. Jeremiah saw the sickness and wounds of the nation and pointed to God as the only source of healing (3:22). The false prophets gave a superficial diagnosis and a false remedy (v. 14), which led the nation into judgment (Lam. 2:14). Beware of religious teachers who look only at the surface and never get to the heart of the problem.

The guide (16). Jeremiah saw the people wondering which way to go. The "new religions" confused them, so he called them back to God's Word. Seek "the old paths" of the Word, not to try to repeat "the good old days," but to go forward to do God's will in your day.

The assayer (27–30). Jeremiah's words were like a fire (23:29) that separated the precious metal from the dross. But the people chose to be cheap alloy instead of precious gold and silver: all God's judgments were in vain.

Heart Trouble

The false prophets in Judah, like the false teachers today, dealt superficially with the problems in society, but Jeremiah dealt with the heart. *The word* heart *appears more than sixty times in his prophecy, and one of his favorite phrases is "the imagination of his heart." The heart is deceitful and wicked (Jer. 17:9), and only God can change it (Jer. 31:31–34). Honest diagnosis by a faithful physician is the first step toward recovery, but too many people prefer the superficial encouragement that says "Peace, peace!"*

JEREMIAH 7

God told Jeremiah to preach a sermon at the gate of the temple and tell the people that their confidence was unfounded because they were trusting the wrong things. The false prophets were saying, "Nothing can happen to Jerusalem because the temple is here" (v. 4); "We are safe because we offer sacrifices to the Lord" (v. 21); "We have the ark of God's covenant, the throne of the Lord" (3:16); and "We have the law of God" (8:8).

The temple, the sacrifices, the ark, and the Law were indeed precious things, but they could not be used to please God apart from the sincere devotion of the people to the Lord. The people were hiding their sins behind religion (vv. 8–15, 21–27). The so-called revival under King Josiah (2 Kings 22—23) was merely a surface reformation; it did not change the hearts of the people.

Never be satisfied with surface religion; be sure that God ministers to your heart and that you obey Him from the heart (Eph. 6:6). The only way to have confidence is to build on the Rock (Matt. 7:21–29), and the only way to build on the Rock is to obey what He says.

The True Source of Confidence

In what do you put your confidence? In lying words from optimistic false teachers (Jer. 7:4, 8)? In riches (Ps. 52:7)? In important people (Ps. 146:3–4; Amos 6:1)? In the intuitions of your own heart (Prov. 28:26)? In excellent equipment (Isa. 31:1)? In your own experience and expertise (Ps. 44:6)? Or in the living God (Ps. 118:8–9; Prov. 3:21–26)?

JEREMIAH 8

Four times in this chapter, Jeremiah asks and answers the question, "Why?"

Why are they backsliding (1–12)? The answer is plain: they believe lies and will not heed the truth of God's Word. They will not admit their sins or repent of their sins. They are happy with the superficial ministry of the false prophets (v. 11) and the right it gives them to be religious and still live in sin.

Why are they sitting still (13–17)? Because they do not really believe the enemy is coming! They have false confidence based on lying words, so they are at peace.

Why did they provoke God (18–19)? Because they believed they could serve both the Lord and their idols. They did not abandon the Lord; they just made Him one of their many gods. But the Lord will not accept equality with any other god, for He is God alone. Just as an unfaithful husband or wife provokes a spouse, so the unfaithful child of God grieves the heart of the Lord.

Why is there no recovery (20–22)? Because the people did not heed God's warning and His long-suffering reached its limit. Had they plowed their hearts (4:3), there could have been a harvest of repentance; but it was too late. The sickness was too far gone, and no medicine was available.

When God calls you to return, do not wait too long. Seek the Lord while He may be found (Isa. 55:6–7).

JEREMIAH 9

Most people want to stop their weeping, but Jeremiah wanted to weep more, so burdened was he for his people. The easiest thing for him would have been escape (Ps. 55:6–7). However, like a true shepherd, he stayed with the people and sought to minister to them.

He would not be the only one weeping, for he saw the day coming when the wailing women would lament the death of the nation (vv. 17–21). The people used their tongues like bows (v. 3) to shoot the arrows of deceit (v. 8), and they went from evil to evil.

Are you among those who are valiant for the truth (v. 3)? If you are, you know that the only thing to glory in is the Lord of glory (v. 24). It is not our minds, our might, or our money that wins the day (v. 23) but our faith in God and our desire to glorify Him.

Pilgrim's Progress

Life never stands still and Judah was going "from evil to evil" (Jer. 9:3). Those who know Jesus Christ can go "from faith to faith" (Rom. 1:17), "from strength to strength" (Ps. 84:7), and "from glory to glory" (2 Cor. 3:18). That is the kind of progress God's pilgrims should make!

JEREMIAH 10

Jeremiah spoke to both Israel (already in exile) and Judah and reminded them that they belonged to the true God, the living God, the everlasting King (v. 10) about whom they could say, "There is none like You" (vv. 6–7). He is the Creator of everything (vv. 11–13).

Then why should they fear the idols of the nations or seek their help? The idols have no breath, so they are dead. They cannot speak. They must be propped up or carried because they have no strength. (See Ps. 115; Isa. 40:18–20.) They are indeed futile!

Today's idols are much more subtle, but they are just as worthless when it comes to a life that is real: money and the things money can buy, position, authority, fame, and so forth. When we trust and serve anything other than God, we practice idolatry.

We have been told, "Little children, keep yourselves from idols" (1 John 5:21).

JEREMIAH 11

Deliverance (1–5). Jehovah repeatedly reminded His people of their deliverance from Egypt and the covenant He made with them at Sinai. He reminded them of His grace in giving them the Promised Land. Why turn to idols when all their blessings came from the Lord?

Disobedience (6–8). Israel accepted the covenant (Exod. 19:8) but then disobeyed the law of God. The new generation accepted the covenant as found in Deuteronomy, entered the land, and eventually turned to idols.

Disaster (9–17). The Babylonians would come, capture the nation, and destroy Jerusalem and the temple. God *would not* defend His people and their false gods *could not,* and He would not even answer the prayers of His servant.

Defense (18–23). The prophet's own friends and relatives tried to silence him and then slay him, but God defended His servant. Jeremiah took his life in his hands when he preached, but nothing stopped him. He was bold before men because he was broken before God.

Docile Lambs

Both Jeremiah and Jesus were like sheep led to the slaughter (Jer. 11:19; Isa. 53:7). They did not fight back but committed themselves to God and trusted Him to work (1 Pet. 2:18–24).

JEREMIAH 12

Perplexity (1–4). "Why do the wicked prosper?" is asked not only by Jeremiah, Job (21:7), and Asaph (Ps. 73), but also by many believers who suffer because of their faithfulness to God. The wicked treated Jeremiah like a sacrificial lamb (11:19), but he wanted God to slaughter them (v. 3)! Would that have solved the problem?

Perspective (5–6). God's answer helped to prepare His servant for the trials ahead. Serving God is a blessed privilege, but it is also a difficult task; *and it gets more and more difficult.* Jeremiah would go from racing with men to racing with horses, from a land of peace to the thickets of the Jordan. This is the only way we can mature in life and service.

> **"**His promises are checks to be cashed, not mere mottoes to hang on the wall.**"**
>
> Vance Havner

Plunder (7–13). The people depended on the temple (7:4), but God had forsaken it. The enemy was about to come like vultures eating a corpse (v. 9) or strangers tramping down a vineyard or a garden (vv. 10–13).

Promise (14–17). God chastens, but His compassions do not fail (Lam. 3:22–24). He promised to judge the invading nations and one day free Judah from her exile and bring her back to her land, and He kept His promise.

The prophet asked for *explanations,* but God met his need by giving him *promises.* When you cannot explain God's ways, you can still trust His promises.

JEREMIAH 13

Jeremiah sometimes preached object lesson sermons, parables in action using familiar things. Like our Lord's parables, they got the attention of the people and awakened the interest of the indifferent.

The sash (1–11) was probably part of the priestly garments, which would make it especially holy. As long as the people clung to God in humble obedience, He was glorified. When they defiled themselves in pride, they became ruined and useless like the sash under the rock. Too proud to repent, Judah ended up in the darkness (vv. 15–17).

The bottles (12–14) represented the leaders and the people who were all empty of spiritual life. God would fill them with drunkenness, which symbolizes judgment (25:15–25). Then He would smash the bottles and show no pity.

The flock (15–22) is a familiar picture of God's people (Ps. 100:3). Their leaders were to be like loving shepherds; instead, they were selfish hirelings. The sheep would be taken to slaughter by the invaders.

The Ethiopian and the leopard (23) were reminders that Judah's sin was deeper than the skin and could not easily be removed by some superficial means. Disobedience was such a habit with the people that it was part of their very nature.

Useless, broken, and slaughtered because of sin too deep to be removed: those are the sad consequences of pride and disobedience.

JEREMIAH 14

No hope (1–6). God sent a drought to Judah to bring His people to repentance, but the chastening did no good. The people mourned for the land but not for their sins. They were sorry for their plight but not for their evil ways.

Hope (7–9). Their only hope was in the Lord, but He would

not do anything for them as long as they refused to return to Him. Instead of being King in residence, God was a tourist passing through the land and a warrior unable to help. If God is not with us, everything will be against us.

False hope (10–22). Their religious activities could not save them because their hearts were far from God. The messages of the false prophets gave the people only a false hope for peace and healing that never came (v. 19). They prayed to the idols, but the idols could not send rain.

Sometimes all you can do when God is a stranger in the land is to imitate Jeremiah and get alone and weep. Wait on the Lord with a broken heart (vv. 17, 22).

"Now may the God of hope fill you with all joy and peace in believing, that you may abound in hope by the power of the Holy Spirit."

Paul (Rom. 15:13)

JEREMIAH 15

The chapter presents Jeremiah in several different roles in his spiritual ministry.

The mourner (1–9). Jeremiah did not rejoice that the people were facing either captivity or death. He was a man with a broken heart. He knew that the nation deserved their fate, but it pained him just the same. Jesus felt that pain when He wept over Jerusalem in His day (Luke 19:41–44). Does the wickedness of today's world break your heart?

The troublemaker (10–14). Jeremiah did not preach "smooth words" as the false prophets did (12:6), and his messages made people curse him. Sometimes you must cause problems before you can solve problems.

The sufferer (15–18). The prophet experienced the loneliness of leadership and the anguish of ministry, but God encouraged him as he fed on the Word. God may not take away the pain in your heart, but He can balance it with His joy.

The separator (19–21). The prophet had to be careful to preach only the true Word of God and not mix it with lies as the false prophets did. As a wall, he brought division; but God would defend him from the attacks of the people. God did not keep him out of the battle, but He did bring Jeremiah through.

> *To be a true minister to men is always to accept new happiness and new distress, both of them forever deepening and entering into closer and more inseparable union with each other the more profound and spiritual the ministry becomes. The man who gives himself to other men can never be a wholly sad man; but no more can he be a man of unclouded gladness.*

Phillips Brooks

JEREMIAH 16

God gave His servant four prohibitions.

Do not take a wife. A godly wife can be a great encouragement to a minister, but Jeremiah had to serve alone. His singleness was a witness to the nation that homes would be destroyed. (See 1 Cor. 7:25–33.)

Do not mourn. People were dying because of the drought, but Jeremiah was not to join in mourning. Why? Because the dead were better off than those who would perish in the siege. The prophet was a living witness that God's comfort was taken from His people.

Do not celebrate. There were weddings as well as funerals, but what joy could they bring knowing that death was imminent? When people asked Jeremiah about his strange behavior, he would have opportunity to declare the Word of God.

Do not look back. He ended with a message of hope: the future restoration of the nation will be greater than the exodus from Egypt. In the discouraging hours of life, God is working out His purposes, so take refuge in Him.

JEREMIAH 17

The engraver (1–4). When we sin, we write it on our hearts, and only God can erase it when we repent and trust Him. He writes His Word on our hearts so we will get victory over sin (Ps. 119:11; 2 Cor. 3:1–3). The altar was to be a place of remitting sin, not recording sin; but their sins were engraved even there.

The farmer (5–8). Faith in the Lord makes you a deeply rooted tree that survives the drought. Faith in man makes you a shrub in the desert.

The doctor (9–11). The heart is "sick," and only the Great Physician can diagnose its problems and bring the necessary healing. Think of Jeremiah 17:9 the next time you say, "If I know my own heart!" You may be surprised what God sees there!

The worshiper (12–18). The throne of Judah had decayed, but because the prophet saw God's glorious throne on high, he had hope. God's throne room is our sanctuary, and He welcomes us to come to get the help we need.

Where Are You Written?

Those who will not trust the Lord have neither salvation nor security and are "written in the earth" (Jer. 17:13). Those who trust the Lord are written in heaven (Luke 10:20) in the Lamb's Book of Life (Rev. 21:27). When our Lord wrote on the ground (John 8:6, 8), was He perhaps referring to Jeremiah 17:13?

JEREMIAH 18—19

Mending the vessel (18:1–11). Individual believers are God's vessels (Acts 9:15; 2 Cor. 4:7), but the reference here is to the nation of Israel, a chosen vessel to bring God's blessing to the world. Romans 9:1–5 tells you what God put into the vessel. Many times in her history, when the nation would not yield to God, He made her again. She was marred but still in His hands. She was marred but had potential. She was marred and He made her again; and He will do the same for anyone who yields to His will (Rom. 9:19–21).

Breaking the vessel (19:1–13). However, if the vessel becomes hardened, it cannot be made again. All God can do is break it, and that is what He did when Babylon captured Judah. The nation was beyond repair. The Valley of the Son of Hinnom was a site for pagan worship, but Josiah turned it into a garbage dump (2 Kings 23:10). In the Greek it is *Gehenna,* the New Testament word for "hell." *Tophet* (vv. 12–13) means "burning." Jeremiah gave a new name to the place: "the Valley of Slaughter" (v. 6).

People with hard hearts and stiff necks (19:15) may be easily broken.

Earthen Vessels

We have the spiritual treasure in earthen vessels (2 Cor. 4:7) so that we might share it with others. A vessel does not manufacture; it only contains and shares. All God asks is that we are clean, empty, and available. He will do the rest.

JEREMIAH 20

Jeremiah went from joy (v. 13) to despair (vv. 14–18), from bold proclamation (vv. 1–6) to burdened prayer (vv. 7–12). God's servants are human and have changes in their feelings. If we were in danger as he was, we might feel and act as he did.

As officer second to the high priest, Pashhur had a job of punishing persons who committed offenses against the temple, and his main target was Jeremiah. Religious people who have no saving faith in the Lord oppose those who have a true experience and message. Jesus was crucified by the Pharisees, who were certainly religious, and the disciples were scourged in the synagogues (Matt. 10:17).

Jeremiah gave Pashhur a new name: "Fear on every side." He was successful in the temple, but his success would vanish when the enemy appeared. Let God take care of the people who create problems for you.

Once again, the prophet was bold before men but broken before God. Always tell the Lord just how you feel and let Him apply the medicine to your heart. When He answers your prayers, sing His praises! The enemy waits for you to stumble (vv. 10-11), but the Lord can hold you up (Jude 24–25).

A Personal Lament

"I wish I had never been born!" Job felt that way when he was suffering (Job 3), and now Jeremiah takes up the lament (Jer. 20:14–18; see also 15:10). But when we speak that way, we seem to forget all the wonderful blessings we have enjoyed throughout life. Suffering has a way of erasing the happy memories and putting sad memories in their place. Remembering His mercies helps encourage us in times of trial.

When Upon Life's Billows

When upon life's billows you are tempest-tossed,
When you are discouraged, thinking all is lost,
Count your many blessings, name them one by one,
And it will surprise you what the Lord has done.

Johnson Oatman, Jr.

JEREMIAH 21

The prophet delivered three messages, and the first was *to the king* (vv. 1–7). Zedekiah, the last king of Judah, rebelled against Babylon and ended up being captured and seeing his sons slain (2 Kings 24—25). Although he was not a man of faith, he wanted God's help. Jeremiah told him, "Babylon is not fighting against you, *God is!*" People ignore the Lord until they desperately need His help, and then they discover He is their enemy.

The second message was *to the people* (vv. 8–10), giving them the choice between life or death. Because of this counsel, Jeremiah was considered a traitor; but it was God's word to the people, and those who obeyed it lived.

The recipients of the third message were *members of the house of David,* Judah's kings (vv. 11–14). Josiah was Judah's last good king; the four kings who followed him were evil men whose doom Jeremiah announced. Had the kings led the nation in repentance, God would have shown mercy, but they persisted in their sins.

Jeremiah was not a popular preacher, but his message was faithful. Those who heeded him lived; those who resisted the Word died.

JEREMIAH 22

The prophet addressed four kings of Judah, beginning with Zedekiah, the last king, and then taking the preceding kings in the order of their reign.

He reminded Zedekiah (vv. 1–9) that he sat on the throne of *David* but was not ruling as David ruled. Not only would Zedekiah's palace be ruined, but the house (dynasty) of David would have no king until the Messiah would come.

He reminded Shallum (Jehoahaz [vv. 10–17]) that his father Josiah had been a godly man but Shallum was not following his example. His besetting sin was covetousness (v. 17). He reigned only three months before being taken to Egypt where he died.

Jehoiakim (vv. 18–23) would not listen to the voice of God. Even the animals know and obey their Creator (Isa. 1:2–3), but the heir to David's throne would not hear David's God. Instead of having the usual state funeral, the king was buried in disgrace.

Coniah (Jeconiah; Jehoiachin [vv. 24–30]) was apparently very popular, but the idol would fall and be smashed. He had several children, but none of them would inherit the throne of David. Coniah was a castaway (vv. 26, 28) who by his sins jeopardized his future and the future of his family and the nation.

When we do not learn from the past or hear God and obey Him in the present, we destroy our future.

JEREMIAH 23

God expects the leaders of His people to be shepherds who love, guide, and care for them. But the shepherds in Judah at that time were selfish and disloyal to God's covenant.

The kings (1–8) scattered the people and did not protect them or provide for them. But one day God's King will gather them and establish His kingdom in righteousness. The more we are like Jesus Christ today, the better we will serve others in love.

The prophets and priests (9–40) did not give the people spiritual direction, nor were they examples of godliness. People who lack spiritual direction will lack spiritual discernment and believe anything. The false prophets invented their visions and passed them off as oracles from God. They did not get their messages from God. What they said was chaff compared to the wheat (v. 28).

No wonder false teachers are so popular! The sinful human heart does not want to be burned and broken by the fire and hammer of the Word of God. It prefers the chaff, even though chaff gives no nourishment.

Be sure that the people who give you spiritual counsel are called by God, walk with God, and obey God's Word. The false prophets' dreams eventually become nightmares.

JEREMIAH 24

The firstfruits were to be offered to the Lord as a sacrifice of thanksgiving for His goodness. Israel was to be like firstfruits to the Lord (Jer. 2:3), but the nation was not wholly devoted to God. Like the two baskets of figs, most of the people were bad, and only a remnant were good because they obeyed God.

What life does to us depends on what life finds in us. The godly remnant experienced good things from God during the exile, but the ungodly citizens were consumed by trouble. The godly remnant made the best of a bad situation because they trusted the Lord (Rom. 8:28).

The important thing is a heart that knows the Lord and is wholly devoted to Him (v. 7). You may not be able to control the situation, but you can control how you respond to it and to God. You are to "keep your heart with all diligence, for out of it spring the issues of life" (Prov. 4:23). Believers today are to be "a kind of firstfruits of His creatures" (James 1:18), and we want to give Him the best.

JEREMIAH 25

Imagine preaching for twenty-three years and seeing no visible results! Jeremiah was faithful to his calling even though the people opposed him and would not hear God's Word. We are judged by God according to our faithfulness, not our outward success. By men's standards, Jeremiah would be considered a failure (1 Cor. 4:1–5).

Judah's Punishment

According to 2 Chronicles 36:20–21, the Lord punished Judah for seventy years because that was the number of Sabbatical Years they had not observed (Lev. 25:1–7). The people did not rest on the weekly Sabbath (Jer. 17:19–27), and they did not give the land its rest every seven years (Lev. 26:27–35). When we keep to ourselves what belongs to God, we eventually lose it and suffer in the process.

The Babylonian captivity was God's way of punishing the rebels and purifying the godly remnant of the nation. The nation was deaf to God's Word (vv. 4, 7, 8), but that Word would be fulfilled, not only to Israel, but to all the nations to which God sent it by His prophet.

God is long-suffering toward disobedient people and gives them many opportunities for repentance, but eventually He must act. He will be like a host who makes his guests drunk (vv. 15–29), a lion that attacks the flock (vv. 30–31, 34–38), a whirlwind that sweeps across the nation and destroys it (vv. 32–33).

JEREMIAH 26

How patient the Lord is with us! He keeps speaking to us and pleading with us to listen. "Listen and turn—hear and heed!" is His loving message to us. Will we obey?

How prone human nature is to resist the Word! The leaders should have called for a time of fasting and prayer, but instead they called for the execution of God's prophet! Are we "swift to hear, slow to speak, slow to wrath" (James 1:19)? Do we want what is right for us and the nation, or what is popular?

A Special Family

God used Ahikam, the son of Shaphan, to rescue Jeremiah. Shaphan was the man who found the Book of the Law when Josiah was restoring the temple (2 Kings 22:3–13). His son Gemariah begged King Jehoiakim not to destroy the book Jeremiah had written (Jer. 36:25). The whole family was devoted to God's Word, and God used it to help His servants.

How wise are those who learn from the past! The elders knew the Word of God and the history of the nation, and they were able to guide the mob toward sanity and justice.

How safe are those who are faithful to God when everything seems against them! Jeremiah stood his ground, and God protected him. Urijah ran away and was captured and killed. The safest place in the world is in the will of God, for there you are ready to live or die.

JEREMIAH 27—28

Jeremiah wore a yoke (28:10) to convey his message that Judah must surrender to Babylon. He delivered his "yoke sermon" three times: first to some ambassadors who had come to form an alliance (27:1–11); next to King Zedekiah (27:12–15); and then publicly to the priests and people (27:16–22).

The false prophets were giving the nation false hopes, but Jeremiah told them the truth. Nebuchadnezzar was God's servant, doing God's will; and all nations should submit to him. If they accepted his yoke, they would live; if they rejected it, they would die.

God is in charge of yokes. The yoke He gives you is the right one for you, no matter who may put it on your shoulders. God can even use unsaved people to help you do His will. Accept every yoke as the yoke of God and He will transform it from bondage to blessing. Break the light yoke and the next yoke will be heavier. Everyone must wear a yoke.

Yokes

The nation broke God's yoke by her sins (Jer. 2:20; 5:5), and those sins became a heavy yoke (Lam. 1:14). This led to the even heavier yoke of Babylonian captivity. But God promised to remove the heavy yoke and give His people a new beginning (Jer. 30:8–11). Your youth is the best time to learn to wear the yoke (Lam. 3:27). Let God "break you" and control you now, and the future will be bright. Jesus said, "My yoke is easy and My burden is light" (Matt. 11:28–30).

JEREMIAH 29

In 597 B.C., the Babylonians began to deport the Jews to Babylon. Jeremiah's letter to the exiles helps us understand how we can make the best of a difficult situation.

Accept it. Live as normal a life as you can and put up with inconveniences without complaining. Try to be a blessing to others. Be a peacemaker, not a troublemaker.

Be patient. God has the timing all worked out, and His plans never fail. He knows how long and how much.

Trust God. Verse 11 is a powerful promise to claim when you are "in exile." God thinks about you personally and is planning for you. His plans are for peace, not war, so you need not fear the future. His plans are purposeful, so let Him work out His will. No matter how difficult your situation may be, do not waste your suffering by resisting God.

Avoid false hopes. It is human to indulge in false hopes and grasp at every straw, but this approach leads to despair. Avoid the subtle voices of the false teachers with their false hopes. The Word of God will tell you what to do.

Far From Home

God's people in the world today are somewhat like the Jewish exiles in Babylon, for we are away from our heavenly home and living among those who do not accept our way of life. "Seek the peace of the city" (Jer. 29:7) is good counsel for us to follow as strangers on this earth. Peter explains how we should do this in 1 Peter 2:11— 3:19.

JEREMIAH 30

Jeremiah saw in Judah's exile a picture of the future day of national suffering ("the time of Jacob's trouble" [v. 7]), when the Jews will go through tribulation. He also saw in their restoration from exile a promise of the regathering of Israel in the latter days.

Judah had sinned, so God had to correct them in love; but He would not permit their enemies to take advantage of them. God is faithful to His people even when they are not faithful to Him (2 Tim. 2:12–13).

He chastens us so that He might heal us (vv. 12–17). The trials that He sends may be like bitter medicine, but they have a way of healing the sinful heart: "Now no chastening seems to be joyful for the present, but grievous; nevertheless, afterward it yields the peaceable fruit of righteousness to those who have been trained by it" (Heb. 12:11).

In times of suffering, live for the joys of "afterward."

JEREMIAH 31

The tragedy of sin is that it keeps God from being to us all that He wants to be.

He is our Lover (1–6). The image of marriage is frequently found in both Jeremiah and Hosea. When we disobey God, we sin not only against His law but also against His love. We break the heart of God when we give our love to what He hates.

He is our Father (7–9). Israel is His firstborn; He redeemed the people in Egypt (Exod. 4:22). God wants to be a Father to us (2 Cor. 6:14–16), but our sins stand in the way.

He is our Shepherd (10–14). The flock of Israel was smitten and scattered, but the Lord was caring for it just the same. No matter how dark the day, the Shepherd will find you, lead you, and give you a song.

He is our Comforter (15–40). What lamentation there was when homes were broken up and people were carried off to a foreign land! But God gave the word of comfort: they will come home again. He promised them a new covenant that would change their hearts, and we have that covenant in Jesus Christ (Heb. 8; 10:1–25).

JEREMIAH 32

"Put your money where your mouth is!" is an American saying that means "Practice what you preach!" Jeremiah had been preaching that the Jews would one day return from exile, so God made him prove that he really believed God's promise. Whenever you share the Word with people, expect to be tested. This is the only way they can tell the reality of your faith.

How foolish to purchase property in a town occupied by the enemy! But if you believe that there is a future for that land, you will not hesitate to buy it. God's people live in the future tense and measure today's decisions in the light of tomorrow's certainties.

You may feel let down after you have made a great step of faith, and that is the time to pray and let the Lord speak to you and assure you. People may laugh at you, but rest in the Lord and allow Him to encourage you.

JEREMIAH 33

Men may shut up God's servant, but they cannot shut out God's Word (2 Tim. 2:9). The Word comes to you—no matter where you are—if your heart is open to the Lord. God sometimes has a "second" message for you, so be alert.

God sent his imprisoned prophet a message of encouragement. The "sick" nation would one day have health; the defiled nation would be cleansed; war would give way to peace; and the truth of God would conquer the lies of the false prophets. There would be wedding songs, not funeral dirges; and righteousness would reign from the throne of David.

When will this occur? When Jesus Christ, the Son of David, reigns on earth (23:5–6) and makes Jerusalem a city of righteousness. Meanwhile, as He reigns in our lives, we can be His servants and minister to those who need these same blessings. Through us, the Lord can bring to others the life-changing message of spiritual health, cleansing, and peace, and they can start rebuilding what sin has torn down.

JEREMIAH 34

Bondage to the enemy (1–7). When the enemy finally broke through the city wall, King Zedekiah would try to escape but would fail (2 Kings 25:1-7). Jeremiah told the king to submit to Babylon, but he would not obey. Therefore, the king would be captured, bound and blinded, and taken to Babylon where he would die. His bondage to sin led to bondage to the enemy. He destroyed himself.

Bondage to the brethren (8-22). The Jews were not to enslave their brethren; and every seven years, their servants were to be set free (Exod. 21:1-11; Deut. 15:12-18). The people in Jerusalem obeyed this law during the siege; but when the Babylonian army retreated because of the Egyptian army (v. 21; 37:5-10), the people took their slaves back again! The owners had obeyed when things were difficult, hoping to appease the Lord; but when things got better, they changed their minds (Ps. 66:13-14).

Obedience must come from devotion within us (Eph. 6:6) and not depend on circumstances around us. These masters were in greater slavery than their servants because they did not seek to please the Lord.

JEREMIAH 35

The founder of the Rechabite family had assisted Jehu in removing Baal worship from the land (2 Kings 10:15-17), so they had a godly heritage. When the Babylonian army moved in, the Rechabites had to abandon their nomadic way of life and enter Jerusalem for safety.

They abandoned their tents, but they did not abandon their standards. Even though they were in the house of the Lord with a prophet of the Lord, they refused to drink wine. The Rechabites did not ask others to agree with their tradition, but they would not violate it themselves. They were a loyal clan.

Man's tradition is not necessarily bad, unless it is contradicted by or substituted for God's truth (Matt. 15:1-20). You may not agree with the traditions of others, but are you as devoted to God's Word as they are to their traditions? The Jews refused to obey *the very law of God,* but the Rechabites obeyed *human traditions.* What an indictment against the Jews who claimed to know the true God! Is it an indictment against us today?

JEREMIAH 36

God's Word written (1–4). Unlike any other book, the Bible is God's Word, inspired by the Spirit of God (2 Tim. 3:13–17; 2 Pet. 1:19–21). Therefore, it can be trusted, and it must be obeyed.

God's Word announced (5–10). God uses human instruments to declare His divine Word to men: "And how shall they hear without a preacher?" (Rom. 10:14).

God's Word destroyed (11–26). The king should have been copying the Law for himself (Deut. 17:18–20) and heeding its message. Instead, he destroyed what Jeremiah had spoken and Baruch had written. You can try to destroy the Bible, but you will fail.

God's Word preserved (27–32). The king and his family are gone and would be forgotten were it not for the Book he tried to destroy! God's Word will endure: "Forever, O LORD, Your word is settled in heaven" (Ps. 119:89); "Heaven and earth will pass away, but My words will by no means pass away" (Matt. 24:35).

> **"**The deathless Book has survived three great dangers: the negligence of its friends; the false systems built upon it; the warfare of those who have hated it.**"**
>
> Isaac Taylor

JEREMIAH 37

Expect to be "used" (1–10). Zedekiah wanted the intercession of the man of God but not the instruction of the Word of God. He never should have separated the two (John 15:7; Acts 6:4). He wanted God to be his servant and deliver the city, but he was not willing to be God's servant and obey the Word. Do you ask God for help only in emergencies, or do you seek His direction each day?

Expect to be misunderstood (11–15). While going on an innocent trip, Jeremiah was arrested, beaten, and put into prison! (See Acts 16:16–24.) The ungodly look for every opportunity to persecute the godly.

Expect to be ignored (16–17). It did not worry the king that God's servant was in prison illegally and suffering miserably. The king would not be seen with Jeremiah, but he still wanted Jeremiah's help.

Expect to be cared for by God (18–21). The Lord had promised Jeremiah years before that He would care for him (1:8, 19), and He kept His promise. Jeremiah did not have an easy life, but he had a good conscience, for he knew he had been faithful to God.

JEREMIAH 38

Zedekiah was a weak king who was more interested in being popular with his friends than in being right with God. Since he was a doubleminded man, he was "unstable in all his ways" (James 1:8).

First, he allowed some of his friends to arrest Jeremiah and put him in a dungeon. Next, he let Ebed-Melech and thirty guards rescue Jeremiah and take him to a safe place. Then, Zedekiah had a private meeting with Jeremiah to ask for help! If the king had accepted God's message and obeyed it, he would have had the courage to stand up to his unbelieving friends and do what was right.

Jeremiah sank in the mire (v. 6), but the king was sinking even deeper (v. 22). His fear (v. 19) and unbelief ruined him. He could have saved himself and his people had he submitted to the Lord. Instead, he trusted his friends, and they dragged him down into the mire of disgrace and defeat.

JEREMIAH 39

God rewarded Zedekiah for his wickedness (vv. 1–10). The king thought he could escape, but the enemy caught up with him. The last thing Zedekiah saw was the execution of his own sons; then he was blinded. He walked by sight and ended up in darkness. He lived to serve himself and lost everything. He learned the truth of these words: "Be sure your sin will find you out" (Num. 32:23).

God rewarded Jeremiah for his faithfulness (vv. 11–14). For forty difficult years, he courageously proclaimed God's Word, even though the people refused to obey it. If you measure ministry by "results," Jeremiah was a failure. Given his freedom, he chose to remain with his people and minister to them. He had a shepherd's heart.

God rewarded Ebed-Melech for his kindness (vv. 15–18; 38:7–13). Now we know why this foreigner rescued Jeremiah: he had put his faith in the God of Israel (v. 18). It must have been Jeremiah's witness that won him. An outsider trusted the God of Israel, but the Jews would not trust Him!

JEREMIAH 40—41

Liberty (40:1–6). God has a word for you in the crisis hours of life, so take time to listen. In this case, it came from the mouth of a Babylonian officer who knew Jeremiah's prophecies. If you could go where you wanted, where would it be? Jeremiah chose to remain with the hurting people of the land. What an encouragement he must have been to them!

Authority (40:7–12). God has ordained that men live under authority (Rom. 13); otherwise, there is chaos. Gedaliah told the people exactly what Jeremiah had counseled: submit to the enemy and seek to live normal lives. Are you praying for those in authority (1 Tim. 2:1–3)? Their job is not easy, and they need God's help.

Treachery (40:13–16). Was Gedaliah a bit naive? Did he have too much faith in human nature? Perhaps, but he should at least have taken precautions to protect his life. Ishmael was loyal to Zedekiah (41:1) and rejected the rule of the governor. His love for the fallen king was greater than his love for God, others, and the nation. He was more concerned about revenge than righteousness. What could have been a peaceful transition became a civil war—all because of one man's wickedness.

JEREMIAH 42

"Back to Egypt!" was Israel's cry whenever they found themselves in trouble. It was true in the days of Moses (Exod. 16:3; 17:3; Num. 11:4–6; 14:1–5) and Isaiah (Isa. 30:1–5; 31:1–3), and now in the trying days after the Babylonian conquest (41:17). God had told them to stay in the land, but they were afraid to obey.

They had already made up their minds to go, but they thought it would be good to ask the prophet to pray for them: "Pray for us! We will obey!" How pious their words sounded! (See Matt. 15:7–9.) Have you ever tried to fool God's servants with pious prayers and promises?

Jeremiah prayed and waited for God's word for that hour. Perhaps God did have another plan for the people. No, God's plan had not been changed. God told them not to be afraid; He told them to stay in the land and trust His care. But God also told His servant that the leaders were hypocrites and not to be trusted.

Faith and patience go together (Heb. 6:12; 10:36): "Whosoever believes will not act hastily" (Isa. 28:16).

"Solemn prayers, rapturous devotions, are but repeated hypocrisies unless the heart and mind be conformable to them."

William Law

JEREMIAH 43

Everything Jeremiah had predicted had come true, but they called him a false prophet! Once you have decided to disobey the Lord, you can always find excuses for rejecting God's truth. It must have been painful for Baruch and Jeremiah to endure the slander of those arrogant men, people they had helped for many years. But Jesus was treated the same way, so Jeremiah was experiencing "the fellowship of His sufferings" (Phil. 3:10).

God had the last word: their trip to Egypt would be a death march. *The only safe place is in the will of God*. The army from which the Jews fled in Judah would come to Egypt and judge them because no one can run away from problems.

JEREMIAH 44

How shall God bring His people to the place where He can bless and enjoy them? He sent His servants with the Word, but people would not listen. He chastened them with drought, but they did not repent. Then He allowed the enemy to humiliate them, but the people still would not obey the will of God.

Perhaps it would be different in Egypt. No, the change in geography did not change their hearts. They practiced their idolatry in Egypt, they even defended it! Before King Josiah's reform, when they bowed down to idols, "they had plenty of food, were well-off, and saw no trouble" (v. 17)—as if those things are tests of truth! The wicked may prosper, but that is no excuse to sin.

In His mercy, God would rescue a small remnant of His people. The rest would be slain in the land they thought was so safe. Was God watching over them? Yes, but not for blessing (v. 27).

JEREMIAH 45

This brief chapter focuses on Jeremiah's faithful secretary, Baruch, who shared the prophet's trials and sorrows. It records an event that occurred after Baruch wrote a second copy of the prophecy because Jehoiakim had burned the original (chap. 36).

God sees your work. What a disappointment it was when Baruch heard that everything he had written had gone up in smoke. When it seems like your work and witness are useless, remember for whom you are doing them.

God knows your trials. Baruch could have had an easier life, but he chose to identify himself with the most unpopular man in the land. Why? Because he believed in the Lord and relied on His Word.

God hears your words. Like any servant of God, Baruch had his difficult days when he felt everything was falling apart. God heard in Baruch's cry a dangerous desire for "great things." If he had not identified with the prophet, how great Baruch might have been!

God meets your needs. Suppose Baruch had become a great man in the kingdom? Where was the kingdom then?

Baruch was alive and cared for because he was associated with Jeremiah. If you are going to seek great things, seek them for God, not for yourself.

Baruch, An Honorable Servant

Baruch's brother Seraiah was an officer in the king's court (Jer. 32:12; 51:59), so he might have gotten an appointment for Baruch; but God chose Baruch to be His servant and His servant's servant. Beware selfish ambitions that run contrary to the will of God; God may let you succeed! (See Matt. 20:20–28.)

JEREMIAH 46

Jeremiah was a prophet to the nations as well as to Judah (1:5), and his book closes with prophecies concerning the nations, beginning with Egypt.

Josiah, Judah's last good king, was slain at Carchemish when he fought Egypt (2 Chron. 35:20–27); but now Egypt would be defeated at Carchemish by the Babylonians. The Egyptians thought they were like the Nile, rising up to flood the enemy, but they would fail (vv. 7–10).

When God looked at the Egyptians, He did not see a mighty river. He saw a heifer that would be bitten by the Babylonian fly (v. 20), and her allies were fat bulls heading for the slaughter (v. 21; see also v. 10). The army of Babylon was like grasshoppers in number (vv. 23–24), and Egypt would flee like a frightened serpent (v. 22). God had spoken!

God gave a message of peace to His people in captivity: they would return to their land and be established again (vv. 27–28). They had to be corrected in love, but they would not be destroyed: "I will save you . . . I am with you." What words of encouragement! Claim them today!

JEREMIAH 47—48

The Egyptians had defeated Philistia, but the Babylonians would destroy both Philistia (chap. 47) and Moab (chap. 48). The Babylonian army would be like a rising river (47:2) and a sword in the hands of the Lord (47:6).

Moab was known for its pride (48:29, 42), so the Lord brought those people low. They relied on a false god and trusted material wealth (48:7), so their god was captured and their wealth was plundered. They lost all their defenses!

Moab was also known for its wine. But the vessels would be emptied and broken, and the people would become drunk with God's wrath (48:12, 26, 38). The Babylonians were God's "wine-workers" to give Moab a "new taste" they had never had before (48:11). Sometimes God has to pour us "from vessel to vessel" to make us what He wants us to be.

The bottles were broken (48:12), the staff was broken (48:17), and their arm was broken (48:25): "How she is broken down!" (48:39). Had Moab been broken *before* the Lord, she would not have been broken *by* the Lord.

JEREMIAH 49

The Ammonites and Moabites were descended from Lot (Gen. 19:30–38) and were enemies of the Jews. Milcom (Molech) was the god of the Ammonites, worshiped in terrible orgies that involved the sacrificing of children. His name means "the reigning one," but he would reign no more. He would go into captivity and not be able to rescue himself, which is what happens to all false gods.

The Edomites were the descendants of Esau, brother of Jacob (Gen. 36), and they, too, hated the Jews. They were recognized for their great wisdom (Obad. 8), but they would not be wise enough to stop the Babylonian invasion.

Their judgment would be like the stripping of a vineyard (v. 9), getting drunk (v. 12), the destroying of Sodom and Gomorrah (v. 18), the attacking of a lion from the Jordan thicket (v. 19), and the sudden swooping down of an eagle (v. 22). There was no escape!

Damascus would be feeble and fearful, like a woman in labor (v. 24); and Kedar, Hazor, and Elam would be scattered to the wind like chaff (vv. 32, 36). All these proud kingdoms felt secure in resisting the Lord, and He bore with them in His long-suffering. But their day of opportunity ran out, and all God could do was judge them.

> *Our Merciful God*
>
> *In His wrath, God remembers mercy (Hab. 3:2). He gave promises to the Jews (46:27–28), the Moabites (48:47), the Ammonites (49:6), and the people of Elam (49:39). These nations did not re-appear on the scene when the Jews went back to their land, but they will be in-cluded when the Lord restores His people at the return of Christ and the establish-ment of His kingdom.*

JEREMIAH 50—51

This prophecy was given in the fourth year of Zedekiah's reign, and Jeremiah sent it with Baruch's brother, Seraiah, to be read publicly in Babylon (51:59–64). In Scripture, Babylon symbolizes man's worldly system organized in opposition to God (Gen. 11:1–9; Rev. 17—18).

The Persians would come out of the north, defeat Babylon, and leave it desolate (50:3). Babylon had been God's hammer (50:23), cup (51:7), and "battle-ax" (51:20–23) to bring His judg-ment to the sinful nations; but now her sins would be judged, particularly her brutal treatment of Israel (51:34–35).

Throughout this prophecy, God gives words of hope to His people still in captivity. Both Israel and Judah will be reunited and restored to their land (50:4–5). The scattered flock will be gathered (50:6–7, 17) and the sinful nation forgiven (50:19–20). They are guilty of sin, but God the Judge will plead their case (50:33–34). The forsaken wife will be reunited to her Husband (51:5), and the nation will be vindicated (51:10).

How will all of this happen? By the power of the God of Israel who is not like the dead idols of the heathen (51:15–19). His people must flee this evil system (51:6, 45–48) and separate themselves wholly to the Lord (2 Cor. 6:14—7:1; Rev. 18:4).

Babylon is still a desolation, and that ruin is a reminder that God is Governor of the nations and Judge of all the earth. Israel is still among the nations because her God is the Maker of all things (51:19).

JEREMIAH 52

Jeremiah's prophecy opens with God saying, "I am ready to perform My word" (1:12); and it closes with evidence that God did what He said He would do. This chapter parallels 2 Kings 24—25 and also Jeremiah 39; and it sets the stage for your reading of Lamentations.

Zedekiah was a rebel, not only against the king of Babylon but also against the Lord; and he lost both battles. He led his sons and his leaders into death and himself into darkness and bondage (Judg. 16:20–21). The religious leaders who had persecuted Jeremiah were slain by the enemy (vv. 24–27).

The temple was plundered despite the promises given by the false prophets (27:19—28:4). The walls were broken down, and the city and the temple were burned. God would rather destroy His city and His house than permit His people to sin successfully. If they will not glorify Him in obedience, they must honor Him in judgment.

The people were deported to remain in captivity for seventy years (25:1–14). The words of Jeremiah were precious to them during those difficult years, just as God's Word should be precious to His people "in exile" in this world today. Follow Jeremiah's good example and joyfully feed on His Word (15:16).

LAMENTATIONS

◆

As the name indicates, this is a book of "funeral dirges," written by Jeremiah after the destruction of Jerusalem in 586 B.C. His heart was broken, and his grief reveals the broken heart of God. God had to chasten His people, and it grieved Him to do it.

The verses in chapters 1—2 and 4—5 follow the successive letters of the Hebrew alphabet. Chapter 3 has sixty-six verses, and each triad of verses begins with a successive letter. The turning point in Jeremiah's grief is found in chapter 3, although he gives expressions of faith and hope here and there in his lament.

Sin is costly, God must punish sin, but God's mercy never fails: these are the key lessons of Lamentations.

LAMENTATIONS 1

Is sin worth it? Sin promises to enrich you, but in the end it robs you of the good things God has given you. Jerusalem had been a popular princess; now she had become a lonely widow who was a slave (vv. 1–2). Once she had enjoyed splendor, but now her glory was gone (v. 6). All she had left were memories (v. 7), and remembering only made the pain greater. She had refused the yoke of submission to the Lord (Jer. 27—28), but now she had to wear the yoke of the enemy (v. 14; Jer. 5:5).

Does anybody care? There was no one to comfort the people (vv. 2, 9, 16–17, 21). Even those who beheld the ruins showed no concern (v. 12). Former friends who praised her were now enemies who despised her (vv. 2, 8). Even the Lord was like an enemy to His people. The people who encourage you in your sin will discourage you in your suffering.

Can anybody question God? "The LORD is righteous," but

His people had been rebellious (vv. 18, 20). Read the chapter again and note the words used to describe their sin. Jeremiah had warned them, but they listened instead to the false prophets (2:14; 4:13). God is holy, and sin must be judged.

Those Who Pass By

Lamentations 1:12 is sometimes applied to our Lord Jesus Christ when He hung on the cross. Except for a small group of followers who stayed at the cross, nobody else offered Him any sympathy. They mocked Him and added to His pain. Yet, He did it for you and me! *He felt the anger of God against* our *sins.* Do we have compassion on those who suffer, or do we pass by "on the other side" (Luke 10:25–37)?

LAMENTATIONS 2

Sin brings destruction (5–6, 8–9, 11, 22; Jer. 5:6, 10, 17). History records that Babylon was the enemy, but Jeremiah said that God was the enemy (vv. 4–5). He supervised the destruction of the walls and defenses (vv. 5, 8–9), the temple (vv. 6–7), and the people (vv. 10–12); Babylon was just His battle ax (Jer. 51:20–23).

Sin brings disgrace (15–16). The passersby not only offer no comfort (1:12) but contribute to Jerusalem's shame (v. 15). The enemy boasts of a great victory but does not give glory to God. All the faithful remnant could do was trust the purposes of God (v. 17) and cry out to Him for mercy (vv. 18–20).

LAMENTATIONS 3

This central chapter marks the turning point in Jeremiah's experience of grief and prayer. As he *looked at himself* (vv. 1–18), he saw an aged man on a winding path in the dark, being pursued by lions. The more he considered his feelings, the more hopeless he felt.

Then he looked away from himself and by faith *looked to the Lord* (vv. 19–39). Now he can say, "I have hope" (v. 21). Why? Because of God's mercies, compassions, and faithfulness: "For He does not afflict willingly" (v. 33; Hos. 11:8–9), and He "will not cast off forever" (v. 31). God does not enjoy having to chasten His people; but as a loving Father, He must do it (Prov. 3:11–12).

Finally, Jeremiah *looked to the people* (vv. 40–66) and called for a time of prayer and confession of sin. The "weeping prophet" (vv. 48–49) pleaded with the people to lift their hearts and hands to the Lord and ask Him for forgiveness and mercy.

What did God do for His suffering servant? "You drew near on the day I called on You, and said, 'Do not fear!'" (v. 57). Wait before the Lord (vv. 25–26), and He will speak to you from His Word.

A New Day   *If God's compassions are "new every morning" (Lam. 3:23), you have the right to claim them daily. Let each morning be for you the dawn of a new day. Start over again, no matter how many times you failed the day before. If God's mercies never fail, depend on them during the day. He is faithful, and His faithfulness will not fail.*

LAMENTATIONS 4

The greatest destruction from sin is not to buildings but to people. In God's sight, His people had been like gold and precious gems (Exod. 19:5), but now they were only cheap clay pots. People accustomed to luxuries could not find the necessities of life (v. 5). The healthy young men were but walking corpses and would be better off dead (vv. 7–9). If you want to cheapen yourself and others, sin will help you do it.

The children suffered the most (vv. 4, 10; 2:20) as children often do when parents sin. And it all came about because the leaders of the land would not obey the Word of God but listened to false teachers (v. 13; 2:14). God's Word to Joshua is still true (Josh. 1:8), and the Lord still keeps His promises.

❝I'm against sin. I'll kick it as long as I've got a foot, and I'll fight it as long as I've got a fist. I'll butt it as long as I've got a head. I'll bite it as long as I've got a tooth. When I'm old and fistless and footless and toothless, I'll gum it till I go home to Glory and it goes home to perdition.**❞**

Billy Sunday

LAMENTATIONS 5

Remember. There is no prayer in chapter 4, but now the people pray to God and describe their reproach. They have lost their freedom, their joy, and their inheritance, and they are paying dearly just to stay alive—all because of the sins of their fathers. God knows your needs and will not forget you (Isa. 49:14–18).

Rule. They had lost their crown (v. 16), but God was still on His throne (v. 19). The defeat of Judah was not the victory of the false gods of Babylon! No matter how hopeless you feel, no matter how difficult the present situation may be, God is still ruling in this universe, and He will not forsake you.

Renew and restore. God's chastening is proof that He loves you and has not forsaken you (Heb. 12:5–11). One day, He will take you out of the furnace and give you a new start. You will be a new and better person if you let Him have His way.

EZEKIEL

◆

While Jeremiah was ministering to the people in Judah, Ezekiel was ministering to the exiles in Babylon. He was taken to Babylon in 597 B.C. with the second deportation; and five years later, he received his call to ministry (592 B.C.). Like Jeremiah, he was a priest who was called to be a prophet; and also like Jeremiah, he preached action sermons that caught the attention of the people.

There are four sections to the book: (1) God's call of Ezekiel (chaps. 1–3); (2) God's judgment on Jerusalem (chaps. 4–24); (3) God's judgment on the nations (chaps. 25–32); and (4) God's restoration of His people (chaps. 33–48).

Ezekiel's prophecy emphasizes the glory of God and the honor of God's name. Sixty-seven times the statement "I am the LORD" is found in this book, and several times God is said to act "for [His] name's sake" so that His holy name would "not be profaned." Had the people of Judah been concerned for the honor of the Lord, He would not have dishonored them before their enemies.

EZEKIEL 1

At the age of thirty, when he could have started serving in the temple (Num. 4:3), Ezekiel was called to serve as God's prophet in Babylon. He was in captivity, but that did not keep the heavens from opening so that he could see the glory of God (Rev. 1:9ff.).

He saw God's providence (1–21). The vision shows how God is working in His world. What looks like a storm to us is the tool of His providence, the wheels spinning within the wheels and the living creatures going back and forth like lightning. It is all too much for us to understand but not for God to control. Romans 8:28 still stands!

He saw God's throne (22-27). Far above the storm, the wheels, the living creatures, and the firmament is God's throne ruling over all. It looked as though Nebuchadnezzar was ruling everything, but God was still on His throne: "The LORD sits as King forever" (Ps. 29:10). The next time you face a storm, look high enough to see God's exalted throne.

He saw the rainbow (28). Usually you see the rainbow when the storm is over (Gen. 9:8-17), and only an arc at that. Ezekiel saw the rainbow during the storm, and it completely encircled the throne! A symbol of God's grace, the rainbow assures us that the Lord is with us and will not forsake us, especially when we are going through a storm.

EZEKIEL 2—3

After the vision came the voice, which is as it ought to be. God's Word endures after the memory of visions fades (2 Pet. 1:16-21). Ezekiel had all the qualities that make for success in serving the Lord.

He saw God's glory and fell on his face in humble worship (1:28). Only a vision of the glorious throne of God can sustain you when the way grows difficult.

Faithful Watchmen

It is a serious thing to be a watchman, for the destiny of precious souls is at stake (Ezek. 3:16–21; 33:1–9). The watchman must be alert to every opportunity and must not be afraid to sound the alarm. False watchmen are not faithful (Isa. 56: 10–12) and will have much to answer for at the Judgment. Paul was a faithful watchman who was able to say, "I am innocent of the blood of all men. For I have not shunned to declare to you the whole counsel of God" (Acts 20:26–27).

He stood on his feet, was filled with the Spirit, and listened to the Word of God (2:1-5). He fed on the Word, which gave him what he needed to speak God's Word (2:6—3:3). In this, he was like Jeremiah (Jer. 15:16), John (Rev. 10:9), and Jesus (Matt. 4:4).

He set his face to do God's will (3:4-11; Isa. 50:7; Luke 9:51). Several times in the book God tells him to "set his face" against something. Ezekiel depended on the hand of God to strengthen him (3:12-14). He sat with the people and identified with their pain (3:15), and he waited patiently for God's word to come to him (3:16-23).

When God spoke, He made Ezekiel a watchman and told him to stay home and be quiet until he received the message to speak. His solitude and silence were signs to the people that God was angry with them for rejecting His Word.

Ezekiel knew that he had been called at a difficult time to do a difficult work with a difficult people, and yet he obeyed the Lord. Little did he know the price he would have to pay to be a watchman, but he was faithful.

EZEKIEL 4—5

Ezekiel began his public ministry with four action sermons that declared God's judgment against Jerusalem. First, he "played war" to demonstrate the siege of the city (4:1-3). The iron plate represented the barrier between God and His people (Lam. 3:43-44). Nothing could stop Babylon from capturing the city.

Then, he lay bound for part of each day, 390 days on left side and then 40 days on the right, to show how many years both Israel and Judah had sinned. How long-suffering God was during those years and how they broke His heart (6:9)!

During those fourteen months and ten days, Ezekiel had to ration his food and water as the people in Jerusalem would do. Compare 4:14 with Acts 10:14. Though he was not serving as a priest, Ezekiel still obeyed the priestly code. No doubt the people watched him day after day and told others about his bizarre behavior, and that helped to spread the message.

His fourth sign involved shaving his head and face, a real sacrifice for a Jew. The hair represented the people in Jerusalem who faced three destinies: death by famine, death by the sword, and dispersion among the nations (Deut. 28:47-57). But a believing remnant would be protected and saved by the Lord.

Why was God angry with His people? Because they rebelled against His law (5:6), defiled His temple (5:11), and did more abominations than the heathen nations around them (5:6–7). They did not glorify the Lord but used all His blessings to promote their sin.

Three hundred and ninety years is a long time to continue in sin! We can only marvel at the long-suffering of the Lord (2 Pet. 3:1–9).

EZEKIEL 6—7

Ruin (6:1–7, 11–14). The signs were over; now the prophet gave two sermons. Judgment was coming to the mountains and valleys where the people carried on their idolatrous worship. The whole system would be destroyed and the people with it. It was the end!

Repentance (6:8–10). In grace, God would spare a remnant that would remember Him and repent of their sins. The sin that breaks the heart of God should break our hearts as well.

Repayment (7:1–27). Four times God says, "I will repay" (7:3–4, 8–9; See also Gal. 6:6–8). All the things Judah trusted will not help them, not money (7:19), idols (7:20–22), or their leaders (7:23–27).

It was the end: "The end has come!" (7:2, 3, 6); "Then they shall know that I am the LORD" (7:27).

EZEKIEL 8

Chapters 8—11 constitute a vision God gave to Ezekiel of the defilement of the temple (chap. 8), the destruction of the people (chap. 9), and the departure of God's glory from His house (chaps. 10—11). The vision burdened Ezekiel to pray (9:8) and prepared him to preach the Word (11:25). God will one day judge our evil world. Knowing this, what does it motivate you to do?

What happened in the temple was indicative of what was happening in the nation: it was given over to the worship of idols. There was an image at the door, and there were idolatrous pictures in the inner chamber. Men and women worshiped idols openly, and others did it "in the dark" (v. 12); but all were guilty. When sin comes in at the door of a person's life, it eventually moves to the inner chambers and takes over. Ponder Proverbs 4:23.

This sin brought violence to the land (v. 17) and removed God's glory from His house (v. 6). What a price to pay for sin!

EZEKIEL 9

The glory of God moved from the Holy of Holies and began to depart from the temple: "Ichabod—the glory has departed" (1 Sam. 4:19–22; Jer. 7:1–15). Without the glory of God, the temple was just another building; and without the presence of God, we are just like other people (Exod. 33:12–16).

God's judgment begins with His people (v. 6; 1 Pet. 4:17), for greater privileges bring greater responsibilities. Either we judge our sins, or God will judge them (1 Cor. 11:31).

Even in His wrath, God is merciful and saves a believing remnant, those who "sigh and cry" over the sins of God's people. Are you among "the sighers and criers"? Like Ezekiel, are you interceding and asking for mercy?

EZEKIEL 10

The throne (1). If all you do is look at the sins of the land, you will end up very discouraged. Do as the prophet did: lift your eyes higher and get a new vision of the throne of God (Jer. 17:12).

The fire (2–17). Coals from the altar brought cleansing to Isaiah (Isa. 6:6–7), but they brought judgment to Jerusalem. The altar is the place where sin is atoned for because sin is judged. Had the nation sought God's mercy and obeyed His Word, the coals would have brought cleansing. Yet even in the midst of terrible judgment, God's "wheels" were still turning and His purposes being worked out in the world.

The glory (18–22). God will not share His glory with idols (Isa. 42:8); therefore, He had to abandon His house. His glory moved to the door of the east gate, poised to move again (11:22–23). If the nation would not glorify God in their obedience, they would glorify Him in judgment.

The Fullness of the Spirit

In Old Testament times, the Spirit came upon people temporarily for special reasons, but Jesus promised that the Holy Spirit would stay with His church forever (John 14:16). God took His Spirit from King Saul (1 Sam. 16:14), and David prayed that the Spirit would not depart from him (Ps. 51:11). Our prayer must be that we not grieve the Spirit (Eph. 4:30), lie to the Spirit (Acts 5), or quench the Spirit (1 Thess. 5:19) but have the Spirit's fullness for life and service each day (Eph. 5:18ff.).

EZEKIEL 11

The caldron (1–13). The leaders in Jerusalem committed two errors. First, they rested on a false confidence that since the deportation was ended, nothing terrible could happen to them. Jerusalem was safe. The second error was that they were the "choice meat" and the people they had slain (the "sighers and criers" of 9:4) were only "scraps." Pride and false confidence made them arrogant.

But God saw things differently. The slain people were the "choice meat," and the leaders of the city were the "scraps." The evil men would try to flee the sword, but God would meet them "at the border." They would *almost* make it! Then the city would indeed be a caldron where God would pour out His anger (chap. 24).

The sanctuary (14–21). The remnant might be taken from their city and temple, but they could not lose the presence of their God. They would one day be regathered, renewed, and restored to their land. There is always hope.

The glory (22–25). Judgment cannot fall as long as God's

glory dwells in the city, so the glory moved out to the Mount of Olives. This parallels Matthew 23:38—24:3.

If in your character and conduct you major on the glory of God, you need not fear the judgment of God.

EZEKIEL 12

When people become spiritually blind and deaf, God uses unusual means to get His Word across to them. Ezekiel preached two more action sermons to warn them that judgment was at hand. The prophet lived the message he was declaring.

His actions in the morning portrayed the people who were packing to go into captivity, while his actions in the evening portrayed the futile attempt of King Zedekiah to escape. God knew what would occur, and nobody could alter His plans.

Ezekiel's actions at his meals portrayed the terror the people would experience in spite of their believing that the worst was past. The false prophets said that people like Ezekiel and Jeremiah were "doomsayers" and their dire predictions would not occur. But God's Word never fails, and it is always fulfilled on time.

God does not ask you to do bizarre things as He did Ezekiel, but can others tell by your life-style that you believe Jesus is coming and that He will one day judge the world (2 Pet. 3:10–18)? Is your life an action sermon that catches the attention of people who are blind and deaf to God's truth?

EZEKIEL 13

False prophets. Imagine being called to preach against the preachers! Why were those prophets so dangerous? Because they invented their messages and did not get them from the mouth of God. Instead of being shepherds who faithfully led the flock, they were foxes living on refuse. Spiritually speaking, the false prophets were religious scavengers, living among ruins they had made themselves.

False peace. This was also Jeremiah's word of warning (Jer. 6:14; 8:11), and yet the people rejected it. Even though he was running away from God, Jonah was able to sleep in a storm

(Jon. 1:5). Having confidence in our feelings is not the same as having confidence from God.

False protection. No matter how strong the wall looked, it would not survive the storm. God wanted to wash things white (Isa. 1:18), but the false prophets whitewashed things. The common people rejoiced at the comforting words of the false prophets, but the "sighers and criers" were saddened by them (v. 22).

John asserted, "I have no greater joy than to hear that my children walk in truth" (3 John 4).

EZEKIEL 14

The prophet had seen idols in the temple in Jerusalem (chap. 8), but now he saw idols in the hearts of the elders in Babylon (vv. 3, 4, 7). God had disciplined those men by taking them from Judah to Babylon, and He had been merciful to them in sparing their lives; yet nothing brought them to repentance. They pretended to be spiritual by inquiring of Ezekiel, but God saw their hearts and told His servant the truth (Heb. 4:13).

Jesus' Righteousness

Sinners are saved from God's eternal wrath not by their righteousness (Titus 3:4–7) but the righteousness of Jesus Christ, the Son of God and the Savior of the world (Isa. 53:6; 2 Cor. 5:21). Not only that, but He is in heaven today, interceding for His people at the right hand of God (Heb. 4:14–16; 1 John 2:1–2). This is not an excuse for us to sin, *but it is an encouragement to know that our future is secure because of what He did for us on the cross and what He is now doing for us in heaven.*

> *Depth of mercy,*
> *Can there be Mercy still reserved for*
> *me?*
> *Can my God His wrath forbear,*
> *Me, the chief of sinners, spare?*
>
> *There for me the Saviour stands,*
> *Holding forth His wounded hands;*
> *God is love! I know, I feel,*
> *Jesus weeps and loves me still.*
>
> —Charles Wesley

Judgment was inevitable: famine, hungry beasts, war, and pestilence (Rev. 6:1–8). Noah saved his family (Heb. 11:7), Daniel rescued his friends (Dan. 2), and Job prayed for his three friends and delivered them (Job 42:7–10); but *nobody's intercession would save Jerusalem or anybody in it.* A person's righteousness could save only himself or herself; it could not save another.

Cherishing sin in the heart will lead to practicing sin in the life: "For as he thinks in his heart, so is he" (Prov. 23:7). A good prayer for all of us is Psalm 139:23–24.

EZEKIEL 15—16

Unfruitfulness (15). The vine was a familiar emblem of Israel (Ps. 80:8–13; Isa. 5:1–7). Vines are good for only two things: bearing or burning. You do not build with wood from the vine because it does not lend itself to being cut and shaped. If the vine does not bear fruit, it is useless, and that was the condition of God's people in Ezekiel's day. If you share the life of God through faith in Jesus Christ, let that life reveal itself in the fruit you bear for His glory.

Unfaithfulness (16). Israel was the wife of Jehovah only because of His grace and love. She was in wretched shape when He called her and saved her. He showered her with gifts, which she used to commit spiritual adultery as she worshiped the idols of the other nations. She was both an adulterous wife who broke the marriage covenant and a harlot who paid others to sin with her. God judged Sodom and Israel (Samaria, the northern kingdom), but that did not deter Judah; she went right on sinning. No wonder God became angry and judged the people.

In Romans 7:4, Paul applies these two images to believers: we are "married to another—to Him who was raised from the dead, that we should bear fruit to God." Jesus Christ wants our single-hearted devotion as we share our love with Him (2 Cor. 11:2-3).

" *Lord, let me not live to be useless.* **"**

John Wesley

EZEKIEL 17

God used allegories to arouse interest and capture attention. Jesus used parables for the same purpose (Matt. 13:10-17).

The great eagle (Nebuchadnezzar) came to Jerusalem (Lebanon) and took to Babylon the top branch of the cedar (King Jehoiachin). He left some of the seed (King Zedekiah), which grew into a low vine. Zedekiah made a covenant to be loyal to Babylon, but then he broke it (vv. 15, 16, 18) and turned to Egypt for help (vv. 7-8; Jer. 37). The result? The king of Babylon will come back and destroy the lowly vine of Judah (vv. 9-10).

The cedar represents the Davidic dynasty. One day God will take a lowly young twig from David's line (Jesus Christ) and will establish His glorious kingdom (Isa. 11:1-9). But before He can enter into that glory, He must suffer for the sins of the world.

"O come, let us adore Him, Christ, the Lord!"

EZEKIEL 18

Have you ever accused God of not being fair? The Jews were doing that (vv. 25, 29-30) and quoting a familiar proverb to argue their case (v. 2; Jer. 31:29–30). If the fathers did the sinning, why should their children do the suffering? Is not God unjust when He punishes the children for the fathers' sins?

But God does not do that, nor does He take pleasure in sending judgment (vv. 23, 32). He would gladly forgive sinners if they would only repent. God judges *individuals*—regardless of what their fathers have done (vv. 4, 20). You cannot claim your father's righteousness, nor can you be punished for your father's sin. You might be punished *by* your father's sin, but that is another matter (Deut. 5:9).

The supreme need is for a "new heart and a new spirit" (v. 31), which can come only through faith in Christ. "Turn and live!" is God's loving call to sinners today. It is a matter not of fairness but of grace.

Punishment for Sins

God does not punish the innocent for the guilty except in the case of His Son. On the cross, Jesus took the punishment for your sins. God has no pleasure in the death of the wicked, "yet it pleased the LORD to bruise Him" (Isa. 53:10), "for Christ also suffered once for sins, the just for the unjust, that He might bring us to God" (1 Pet. 3:18).

EZEKIEL 19

Jeremiah was not the only prophet to write funeral dirges. Ezekiel wrote this one five years before Jerusalem fell. He used two familiar images of the nation in speaking about the fate of their kings.

The lioness (1–9). The lion is the royal animal, and Ezekiel was speaking about the rulers of the land: Jehoahaz (vv. 2–4; Jer. 22:11–12), who died in Egypt; and the present king, Zedekiah (vv. 5–9), who was blinded and taken to Babylon (Jer. 39).

None of Judah's "cubs" succeeded in saving the land because they resisted the Word of God.

The vine (10–14). We have met this image of Israel several times already. The prophet had spoken *about* Zedekiah, but now he speaks *to* Zedekiah and tells him that the beautiful, luxuriant vine would be withered by the east wind (v. 12; 17:10), plucked up, and planted in Babylon. That would be the end of David's line; there would be no strong branch out of which to make a scepter—until the birth of Jesus Christ, the Son of David (Matt. 1:1; Luke 1:30–33)! Judah will supply the scepter (Gen. 49:8–10).

When it looks like man has done his worst and everything is at an end, remember that God always has the last word— and His "Last Word" is His Son, Jesus Christ (Heb. 1:1–2).

EZEKIEL 20

History (1–32). In his message to the Jewish elders, Ezekiel reviewed the nation's history: the Exodus (vv. 1–9), the wilderness journey (vv. 10–17), and the conquest of their land (vv. 18–32). He pointed out two facts: (1) the nation was guilty of repeated rebellion against the Lord (vv. 8, 13, 21), and (2) the Lord acted as He did for His name's sake (vv. 9, 14, 22). He could easily have destroyed the nation, but what would the Gentiles have said about Israel's God?

Honor God's Name	*For His name's sake, the Lord forgives our sins (1 John 2:12), guides us (Pss. 23:3; 31:3), deals with us (Ps. 109:21), and revives us (Ps. 143:11). For His name's sake, we ought to serve Him (3 John 7; Rev. 2:3), sacrifice for Him (Matt. 19:29), and be willing to suffer reproach (Matt. 10:22; 24:9). All that we do should be for the honor and glory of God's name (1 Cor. 10:31).*

Repeated rebellion against God's will is serious. The Lord is long-suffering, but we must never take this for granted. Eventually He must chasten His rebellious children for His name's sake. If we do not glorify Him by obeying His commandments, we must glorify Him by submitting to His chastening (Heb. 12).

Hope (33–49). God chastens us that He might restore us, and there is always hope. The repeated "I will" statements assure us that God is working for us and not against us: "I will bring you out! I will plead! I will bring you in! I will accept you!" Why does He do it? "For [His] name's sake" (v. 44).

EZEKIEL 21

Jeremiah called Babylon God's battle-ax (Jer. 51:20–23), and Ezekiel called Babylon God's sword. (The word *sword* is used more than a dozen times in this chapter.) God pulled His sword out of the scabbard (vv. 1–7), prepared it for use (vv. 8–17), and then pointed it toward Jerusalem (vv. 18–27) and Ammon (vv. 28–32). The Ammonites had united with Judah against Babylon but had escaped invasion. However, their judgment eventually came.

God uses unbelievers to accomplish His purposes and can even overrule their pagan methods of making decisions (vv. 18–23; Prov. 16:33). God's people did not obey the declared will of God, but the pagan nations obeyed God and did not know it. What a paradox!

The prophet's responses to this message attracted the attention of the people, for he sighed (vv. 6–7) and wailed (v. 12). What is your response to the message of the coming judgment of God (2 Pet. 3:10–18)?

EZEKIEL 22

Four images stand out in this chapter.

The court (1–16). The prophet became a prosecuting attorney as he indicted Judah for her sins, proving that the leaders and the common people alike were guilty of breaking the law of God.

The furnace (17–22). Jerusalem would indeed become like a furnace when the army of Babylon encamped around it. But there was no good metal left in the city; all was dross. The nation had been cheapened by sin.

The jungle (23–27). The prophets were like lions and the princes like wolves, all fighting to get what they could from the people. Like animals, the priests did not make a difference between what was holy and what was unclean (Matt. 7:6).

The wall (28–31). With their false visions and messages, the prophets whitewashed the nation's sins and covered its weaknesses. (See Ezek. 13.) God is still looking for people who will not only build strong walls but *become walls* by standing in the gap in the hour of danger.

People in the Breach

In the history of Israel, God raised up "gap people" to stand in the breach and stay off the judgment. Moses and Phinehas were such men (Ps. 106:23, 30), as were Joseph (Ps. 105:17) and Samuel (1 Sam. 3). Had the people heeded the messages of Jeremiah, God would have spared them, but they refused to obey. Today, God needs "gap people" with the courage to stand for what is right, even if they must stand alone.

EZEKIEL 23

Because the Jewish nation was wedded to Jehovah, idolatry was the same as infidelity. They were giving themselves to foreign gods and committing harlotry and adultery. That is why God brought judgment on His people.

Oholah ("her tent") represents Samaria, the northern kingdom; and Oholibah ("My tent is in her") represents the southern kingdom of Judah. The Samaritans had devised their own religion, but God dwelt in Judah because of His covenant with David. What they did in His temple grieved Him greatly

(vv. 36–39; 1 Cor. 6:19–20). God judged Samaria in 722 B.C. when He permitted Assyria to take them captive, but Judah did not profit from that lesson. Judah persisted in sin, so God had to judge them.

When God judges sin in others, never say, "That will never happen to me! I can get away with my sin!" God waits for us to repent, and we must not try His patience (Eccles. 8:11). In the end, our sins punish us, and we learn afresh that He is the Lord (v. 49). God wants single-hearted devotion from His bride (2 Cor. 11:1–4; James 4:1–10).

EZEKIEL 24

The death of a city. Ezekiel was far away in Babylon, yet he knew what was happening in Jerusalem (Amos 3:7; John 15:15). The parable of the pot (11:3) revealed the city's wickedness. As the fire of judgment grew hotter, only the scum appeared, and then the pot and everything in it were destroyed. The date was January 15, 588 B.C., when Nebuchadnezzar began the siege of Jerusalem.

The death of a wife. During his years of ministry, Ezekiel had paid a price to "act out" some of his sermons (chap. 12), but none was as costly as this one. The life you live is the greatest sermon you can ever preach. The city of Jerusalem was the delight of the Jews, but she would be buried—*and that was what the nation deserved.* Ezekiel told the people in the morning that his wife would die, just as he had told them for years that their beloved city would be destroyed; in the evening, his words came true.

If the people wanted to mourn at all, they should have mourned over their sins and not over the loss of their city and temple. But it was too late. They should have heeded this advice: "Seek the Lord while He may be found" (Isa. 55:6).

EZEKIEL 25

God's judgment begins with God's people (Ezek. 9:6). If *they* are judged for their sins, what will happen to those who do not know the Lord (1 Pet. 4:17–18)?

In chapters 25—32, Ezekiel described God's judgment of the gentile nations surrounding Judah. The Jews had sinned against God's love and law, but the gentile nations had sinned against God's people. Note the repetition of "because"; God's judgments are reasonable.

The Ammonites rejoiced at the fall of Judah and the captivity of the people (vv. 1-7), so God promised to destroy them. Moab (vv. 8-11) said that the Jews were like any other nation (20:32), which meant that Ammon had no reverence for Jehovah. He was just like the idols of the other nations! (See Ps. 115.)

The Edomites (vv. 12-14) actually helped the Babylonians instead of assisting the Jews, who were their relatives (Ps. 137:7; Obad. 11-14). The Philistines saw an opportunity to pay back an old debt and vent their hatred of God's people.

Although Judah sinned, they were still the people of God. God will not defend our sins, *but He will defend His people and allow no outsiders to touch us without His permission.* God's chastening is born out of His love, while man's revenge is born out of hatred. That is why David prayed as he did in 2 Samuel 24:14.

"Restore Such a One"

When other believers are experiencing God's chastening or are suffering the consequences of their sins, what is your attitude toward them? Do you pray for them and encourage them to seek the Lord and yield to His will, or do you add to their trials? Ponder Galatians 6:1–5, Hebrews 12:12–17, and Matthew 7:12.

EZEKIEL 26—28

The judgment of the proud and wealthy cities of Tyre and Sidon is the theme of these chapters, described in three vivid pictures.

The scraping of a rock (26). The city of Tyre seemed impregnable, but Nebuchadnezzar would besiege it and Alexander the Great would wipe it off the face of the earth in 332 B.C. Tyre would become a bare rock, a place only for drying fishing nets (vv. 4, 14). What a rebuke to civic pride!

The sinking of a ship (27). Ezekiel described Tyre as a beautiful and costly ship, loaded with riches and growing wealthy as it did business with all the nations. But the ship would be broken and would sink, and all the merchants would lament the loss of their great wealth. What a rebuke to covetousness!

The dethroning of a king (28). The king of Tyre thought he was God, and his heart was lifted up with pride. Surely Satan was the cause of this (Gen. 3:5). In fact, God may have been addressing Satan in verses 11–19, for the description surely fits. Pride lifted him up, but God cast him down. What a rebuke to his feeble attempt to take the place of God!

EZEKIEL 29—32

These chapters focus on Egypt, the nation that the Jews trusted instead of trusting the Lord (Isa. 30:1–7; 31:1–3). Ezekiel detailed four illustrations of the coming judgment of Egypt.

The capturing of a monster (29). The king of Egypt thought he was a great monster, guarding his royal river; but God said he was only a weak reed in the river (29:6–7). God would capture the monster and show Pharaoh that He owned the Nile River and could do with it what He pleased. The Babylonians would come and plunder Egypt, and Pharaoh would not be able to stop them.

The breaking of arms (30). God would break Pharaoh's arm and not allow it to heal, but He would strengthen Nebuchadnezzar's arms and give him victory over Egypt and her many allies. No more would God's people turn to Egypt for help.

The cutting down of a great tree (31). This message was for Pharaoh, who thought his nation was indestructible. Assyria once had the same idea, but look what God did to her. God would rebuke Pharaoh's pride, cut down his nation, and cast it into hell (vv. 15, 17).

The trapping of animals (32). Egypt was strong and active like a young lion, but the nation would be caught in God's net and go down into the Pit with all the other great nations of that era.

Remember that God is the King and rules among the nations as He pleases. What He does has one grand purpose: that the nations may know He is the Lord (29:6, 9; 30:8, 19, 26). When nations and rulers start to think they are gods, God has to remind them that He alone is the God of all the earth. Nebuchadnezzar himself had to learn that lesson (Dan. 4).

EZEKIEL 33

God warns (1–11). God had ordained Ezekiel to be a watchman (3:16ff.), but now the people were to ordain their own watchmen in each territory. The three key words are *sword, trumpet,* and *blood.* When you see the sword coming, blow the trumpet and warn the people; otherwise, their blood will be on your hands (Acts 20:26–27). (See Prov. 24:10–12.)

God is fair (12–20). Review chapter 18 where Ezekiel defended God's fairness in sending judgment to His people. This is a plea for repentance, for God wants each of us to have a broken and a contrite heart (Ps. 51:17). We should not judge God but allow Him to judge us. (See Mic. 7:18–19; Heb. 10:11–18.)

God judges (21–29). For seven years, the prophet had been silent except when delivering a message (3:26). His words about Jerusalem had been fulfilled, and he could engage in normal conversation again. But his first words had to do with the nation's sins! How could the people call God unfair when they were so guilty before the law of God?

God sees the heart (30–33). Imagine calling a watchman's warnings "a very lovely song"! They did not take God's Word seriously; if they had, they would have obeyed it (James 1:21–27). Complimenting the preacher is not the same as obeying the Master. (See Isa. 29:13; Matt. 15:8–9.)

EZEKIEL 34

The watchman serves the people in times of danger, but the shepherd cares for them day after day; and we need both. The civil and religious leaders were expected to shepherd the nation by feeding them, uniting them, and protecting them from enemies. But Israel's leaders exploited the flock in order to feed themselves, scattered the flock, and failed to protect the flock from danger. See Acts 20 for Paul's example of faithful shepherding.

One day God will seek His people and bring them back to their land, and He will be their shepherd. Note the "I will" statements in this message, and see what assurance they bring to hearts even today.

Today, Jesus Christ is the Great Shepherd of the sheep (Heb. 13:20–21), and He cares for His own. He sends "showers of blessing" on the dry land and makes it into a garden (vv. 26, 29). What a difference it makes when the Lord is in control!

EZEKIEL 35

God announced blessing for Jacob, but He pronounced judgment on Edom, the descendants of Jacob's brother Esau (25:12–14). The Edomites were guilty of sins that are still practiced today.

Hatred (5). Their grudge went all the way back to Genesis 27, and they would not forgive and forget. How tragic that brothers could not dwell together in unity (Ps. 133)!

Grudges

Some people nurse a grudge the way a mother nurses a child: they love it, cherish it, and cannot live without it. But they forget that the child is growing and may one day turn on them and destroy them. A grudge against an enemy is a very expensive thing, no matter how much enjoyment you may get nursing it. Ponder Matthew 5:21–26, 43–48.

Anger and envy (11). When you hate others, you are envious of their blessings and angry when they succeed. The Edomites revealed their anger when they helped the Babylonians ravage Jerusalem (Obad. 10–14). Are you envious when others succeed and glad when they fail? Then you may be carrying a grudge. Beware! The judgment you want to fall on your enemy may fall on you (v. 15)!

Pride (12). The Edomites boasted of their great security in the rocks (Obad. 1–4), but God would bring them down in humiliation (Jer. 49). God still resists the proud—whether in nations or individuals—but gives grace to the humble (1 Pet. 5:5).

EZEKIEL 36

From this chapter on, the prophet focuses on reinhabiting the land, rebuilding the temple, and restoring the kingdom to the glory of God.

In His grace, God will bring the land from desolation to delight (vv. 33–36), and His people from dispersion to regathering (v. 24) and from defilement to cleansing (vv. 25–29). God will remove the disgrace of the people and bring great glory to His name (vv. 20–23). "I am for you!" says the Lord (v. 9); and "if God is for us, who can be against us?" (Rom. 8:31).

There is no future for those who persist in their sins, but those who confess and forsake their sins shall always find mercy with God (Prov. 28:13).

Confessing Sin

There is a difference between merely admitting sin and confessing sin. When we have confessed our sins sincerely to the Lord, we despise them and forsake them; even their very memory upsets us (Ezek. 36:31; see also 6:9). If the memory of your sin is pleasant to you and you enjoy "tasting it" from time to time (Ps. 10:7), you have not really confessed it to the Lord. A false confession is worse than no confession at all.

EZEKIEL 37

Resurrection (1–14). The nation seemed to be hopeless, like an army of skeletons in a desert. But God can give life through His Word (vv. 4, 7) and His Spirit (v. 14; the Hebrew word for "breath" also means "Spirit"). One day, the nation of Israel will be resurrected spiritually and will know their God.

Reconciliation (15–28). Not only will the dead nation receive life, but the divided nation will be united in a covenant of peace. There will be no more "Ephraim" and "Judah," but one nation with one king and one temple.

According to Ephesians 2, God is doing this today. He is raising lost sinners from the dead (Eph. 2:1–10) and reconciling Jews and Gentiles into one temple (Eph. 2:11–22). These spiritual miracles take place when you and I share the life-giving Word in the power of the Spirit of God.

The Breath of Life

The breath of God was breathed into man at creation (Gen. 2:7), into the Word when it was written (2 Tim. 3:16), and upon the disciples to empower them for ministry (John 20:22). It will one day sweep over God's chosen people and make them a new nation. Meanwhile, God longs to send the "wind of revival" to His church; and He will, if we honor His Word, pray, and depend on the Spirit of God.

EZEKIEL 38—39

God's people will have enemies until the very establishing of the kingdom. These two chapters describe a coalition of gentile nations in the latter days (38:16) as they attack Israel when she is at peace in her land (38:14). God will defeat the invaders with an earthquake (38:19–20), a storm (38:22), and the confusion of the enemy so they start to kill each other (38:21).

Why does God do this? So that the nations will know that He is the Lord (39:6) and that His name is holy (39:7), and so that Israel will know that He is their God (39:21ff.). In punishing them, God hid His face (vv. 23-24); but now He will reveal Himself to them and they will receive His Spirit (v. 29).

The day will come for God's people when every enemy will be defeated, every sin washed away, and every believer sharing in the glorious reign of the Son of God. What a day that will be!

EZEKIEL 40—43

The city of Jerusalem and the temple had been destroyed, the land had been taken over by the Babylonians, and the people had been scattered or exiled. It was not a time of good news. But Ezekiel did what God's people always must do in times of trial: he looked ahead to the glorious future God had planned. One day the scattered people would be regathered and the defiled people cleansed. The land would be restored to beauty and fruitfulness, and there would be a new city, a new temple, and a new priesthood serving the Lord in holiness.

This vision of a glorious land and temple was to be declared to the people (40:4) so that they would repent of their sins (43:10). We today do not understand the significance of all these details; however, Israel will understand them in that day, and their understanding will bring about a change in their lives.

The assurance of a glorious future helps to sustain God's people during the trials of life (John 17:22-24; 1 Pet. 1:1-9). It should also be a stimulus to holy living. (The word *holy* is used thirty-five times in chaps. 41—48.) For Christians, heaven is not simply a *destination;* it is a *motivation.* It should make a difference in your life today because you know you are going to heaven. Does it?

The temple will be a place of sacrifice and singing and a place where *God's glory will dwell* (43:1-5). Ezekiel had described how the glory left the old temple (11:22-23), and now he describes how the glory returns and fills the house (43:1-5;

44:4). The beauty and grandeur of the temple mean nothing if God is not present.

Today, the bodies of God's people are His temple (1 Cor. 6:19–20), and so is His church (Eph. 2:19–22). Just as God has a beautiful plan for His future temple in Jerusalem, so He has a plan for His people individually (Eph. 2:10) and His church collectively. We are to be a holy temple, dedicated to Him alone; we are to radiate the glory of God.

EZEKIEL 44—46

Somebody must serve in the new temple, so God gave Ezekiel instructions concerning the Levites and priests and the manner of worship He wanted. Note the emphasis on the word *My:* My sanctuary, My food, My covenant, My holy things, My table, and so on. One reason the temple was destroyed is that the priests and Levites forgot it was the house of God, and they did in it whatever they pleased.

Future Sacrifices

Since Jesus Christ has fulfilled all the Old Testament sacrifices in Himself (Heb. 10: 1–18), why will God reinstate them in the future temple worship? Certainly not for the purpose of dealing with sin, for Christ's sacrifice did that once and for all, and the blood of bulls and goats never did take away sin (Heb. 10:1–4). It seems that these future sacrifices, like the Lord's Supper today, will be memorials of what Jesus did. They will teach the Jews the meaning of their ancient religion in the light of the Cross.

What a privilege it is to minister for the Lord! You wonder why people would want to give their privileges to others, especially men who were not qualified (44:4–9). Never lose the wonder of belonging to God and being asked to serve Him (Mal. 1:6—2:9). Such an attitude always leads to sin.

Unfaithfulness in service can lead to loss of privileges (44:10–14), but faithfulness can mean being able to draw near to serve the Lord (44:15ff.). The priests had to be careful what they wore, what they ate and drank and how they looked. How could they teach the people to have discernment (44:23) if they did not practice discernment?

The prince will worship only at the threshold of the gate and the people only at the entrance (46:2–3), but we have the great privilege today of entering into the presence of God (Heb. 10:19–25). However, like the prince, we should not return from worship as we came; things should be different because we have met with the Lord (46:9). And we must not forget the daily burnt offering (46:13; Rom. 12:1–2).

EZEKIEL 47—48

Depths (47:1–12). This river speaks of the healing and life-giving power of the Holy Spirit of God (cf. John 7:37–39; Zech. 14:8). No matter how deep you want to go into the things of God, the opportunity is there. It's tragic that too many linger in the shallows when they could be enjoying the depths.

Dimensions (47:13—48:34). God assigns our inheritance (Ps. 47:4), and He will keep His promise to Abraham (Gen. 13:14–17; 15:17–21) and give Israel their land.

Jehovah   Jehovah-Shammah *is one of nine special names of God found in the Old Testament. The others are:* Jehovah-Jireh— *"the Lord will see to it" (Gen. 22:14);* Jehovah-Rophe—*"the Lord who heals" (Exod. 15:26);* Jehovah-Nissi—*"the Lord our Banner" (Exod. 17:15);* Jehovah-M'Kaddesh—*"the Lord who sanctifies" (Lev. 20:8);* Jehovah-Shalom—*"the Lord our peace" (Judg.*

> 6:24); Jehovah-Tsidkenu—*"the Lord*
> *our righteousness" (Jer. 23:6);* Jehovah-
> Rohi—*"the Lord my shepherd" (Ps.*
> *23:1); and* Jehovah-Sebaoth—*"the Lord*
> *of hosts [armies]" (Ps. 46:7). The Lord is*
> *to us all that we need, no matter what*
> *that need may be.*

Distinction (48:35). The important thing about the land is not the river or the borders but the glorious presence of God. The new name for the city of Jerusalem will be *Jehovah-Shammah*—"the Lord is there!" The Lord had departed from Jerusalem because of the sins of the people, but He will return to dwell with them and bless them. When you are discouraged about the way things are going on earth, lift your eyes to heaven by pondering Revelation 21:1–8.

Just think of it: we shall live forever *where the Lord is!* Are you looking by faith for that future city (Heb. 11:13–16)?

DANIEL

$\blacklozenge$

When Nebuchadnezzar began his conquest of Judah in 605 B.C., he deported a number of Jews to Babylon, including Daniel and his friends, who were probably teenagers at the time. God blessed Daniel and gave him important places of service under four different rulers who represented three different kingdoms. When you read about Daniel, you meet a man of God who was faithful to the Lord and glorified Him in the enemy's land.

The emphasis in Daniel is on the sovereign will of God in the affairs of nations (4:25). In a series of dreams and visions, God showed Daniel the course of gentile history until the establishing of the promised kingdom on earth.

Chapters 1 and 6 are historical and reveal Daniel's godly integrity. Chapters 2—5 record his interpretations of the dreams and visions of *others;* in chapters 7—12, he receives his own visions from God and shares with us their meanings.

With Babylon's taking of Jerusalem, the "times of the Gentiles" began (Luke 21:24) and will continue until Christ returns to set up His glorious kingdom. God is in control of history and will work out His perfect plan. God also wants to have control in your life, as He did in Daniel's life; and He will—if, like Daniel, you determine in your heart to serve Him faithfully. Daniel was a man of personal integrity who had nothing to fear because he feared the Lord and served Him.

DANIEL 1

The world always wants the best (vv. 3–4), but these young men determined to give their best to the Lord. It is possible to serve the Lord even in Babylon. Think of Joseph in Egypt and

Esther in Persia. Don't complain about the place where God puts you. Ask Him to use you while you are there.

The world wants to change you and make you a "conformer," but God can help you become a "transformer" (Rom. 12:1–2). Daniel and his friends had a new home, strange new names, new teachings, and were even offered a new diet; but they kept the same heart's dedication to the Lord (Prov. 4:23).

God can give us favor in difficult places (v. 9). Daniel was courteous to his guards and did not create problems for them. He was following the counsel of Jeremiah (Jer. 29) and the example of Joseph (Gen. 39:4).

When everything in your life is upset and you find yourself in new circumstances that you cannot control, let the Lord take over and work out the plan He has in mind. If your heart is right with Him, His hand will work for you.

Dare to Be a Daniel

> *Dare to be a Daniel,*
> *Dare to stand alone!*
> *Dare to have a purpose firm!*
> *Dare to make it known!*
>
> Philip P. Bliss

DANIEL 2

Nebuchadnezzar could conquer empires, but he could not conquer his own anger (v. 12; 3:13, 19; Prov. 16:32). He understood how to defeat the enemy, but he could not understand the message of God. Daniel had patience and self-control and could explain the mysteries of God. A pure heart is better than a powerful throne.

Daniel and his friends knew the "God of heaven" who is merciful (v. 18), answers prayer (vv. 19–23; James 1:5), reveals secrets (v. 28), establishes rulers (v. 37), and will one day set up His kingdom (v. 44). Because the four men could come to God's throne, they had no fear of Nebuchadnezzar's throne.

When he explained the dream, Daniel gave the glory to God and shared the credit with his three friends. He also saved the lives of the king's wise men (the Chaldeans) when he could have exposed them as frauds. The presence of a believer can mean deliverance for unbelievers (Job 42:7–10; Acts 27:21–25), and we must be forgiving to our enemies. After all, we want to win them to the Savior.

Progress?

From the human point of view, the kingdoms of the world look like metal; but from the divine point of view, they are like beasts (Dan. 7). Note that the value of the metal decreases as history unfolds, until the nations end up a weak mixture of iron and clay (Dan. 2:41–43). God does not see "progress" in what man does; He sees only increasing weakness.

DANIEL 3

This event involves three kinds of people, all of whom are still in our world.

Conformers (1–7). Nebuchadnezzar was not content to be the "head of gold" (2:38); he wanted to be represented by a whole image of gold! The people were happy to conform to his desires as long as he spared their lives and gave them what they needed.

Informers (8–12). These were some of the Chaldeans whose lives Daniel and his friends had saved. Unsaved people do not always appreciate what believers do for them. These men wanted only to win the king's favor and get the high offices he had given to the three Jews (2:49).

Transformers (13–30; Rom. 12:1–2). The three men did not know for sure that God would deliver them; but even if He did not, they would still obey the Lord and not worship the king and his idol. Were they trusting Isaiah 41:10 and 43:2? The fire brought them two blessings: the Lord came and walked with them, and they were set free from their bonds. Fellowship and freedom are often found in the midst of the furnace if you are committed to the Lord.

DANIEL 4

Nebuchadnezzar's second dream accomplished three things: it warned the king that his pride would lead to judgment (v. 37; Prov. 16:18); it exposed the incompetence of his magicians (vv. 6–7); and it gave Daniel another opportunity to glorify the God of heaven.

It was not easy for Daniel to give the king the message of the dream. Nebuchadnezzar had a short temper, and he might have ordered Daniel to be killed. Nathan had a similar situation when he had to confront David with his sins (2 Sam. 12). But when your ways please the Lord, you do not worry about your enemies (Prov. 16:7).

God gave the king a year's opportunity for repentance (v. 29), but he continued in his sins. Then God humbled him. The king learned his lesson, and when he was restored, he gave glory to God.

No matter what position we have in life, God gave it to us, and He is sovereign. When man tries to take the place of God, he becomes like a beast. God still resists the proud but gives grace to the humble (Prov. 3:34).

DANIEL 5

The events in this chapter occurred several years after those recorded in chapter 4. Belshazzar was coregent with his father Nabonidus, which explains why Daniel was named *third* ruler in the kingdom (v. 29).

The king may have been new, but the sin was old: pride and self-confidence. At that very hour, Darius was besieging the city; but so certain was Belshazzar of his defenses that he ridiculed Jehovah and praised the false gods of Babylon. It was Proverbs 16:7 over again.

God gave Nebuchadnezzar a year to repent, but He judged Belshazzar *that very night*. The king had not learned from those who had gone before, and Daniel told him so (vv. 17–23). But it was too late!

The self-confident sinner had better beware (Luke 11:16–21), and so should a proud world that says, "peace and safety!" (1 Thess. 5:1–11). In Noah's day and in Abraham's day, judgment came when people least expected it (Luke 17:26–32). It will happen again.

DANIEL 6

Daniel faced three crises, and the Lord gave him victory in each one.

The work crisis (1–5). When the other officers heard that Daniel might be promoted, they were envious and wanted to get rid of him. The unbelieving world does not want a believer in charge, even if he or she is gifted and efficient. The light always reveals what happens in the darkness (Eph. 5:8–13).

The prayer crisis (6–17). The officers lied when they used the word *all,* for that gave the king the idea that Daniel agreed with them. But no laws or threats could keep Daniel from his times of prayer. Is prayer to you a matter of life and death? It was to Daniel!

The faith crisis (18–28). God did not keep Daniel *out of* the den; He protected him *in* the den. Why? Because Daniel had faith in the Lord (v. 23; Heb. 11:33) and was faithful to the Lord (Ps. 18:17–24). Perhaps Daniel meditated on Psalm 37:1–15 and Proverbs 11:8.

When the lions are about to attack, trust the Lord and claim His promises.

DANIEL 7

A vision of world history (1–8). Man views human kingdoms as valuable metals (chap. 2), but God sees them as vicious animals that fight and devour each other. Human history will culminate in a worldwide kingdom under a satanic world ruler (Antichrist) who will defy God and eventually be defeated by God's Son.

A vision of heaven (9–14). While the beasts are fighting on earth, God is holding court in heaven, and everything is under

His control. Jesus Christ will one day establish a righteous kingdom that nobody will overthrow.

Daniel's Vision

Daniel's vision in chapter 7 parallels what Nebuchadnezzar saw in his dream (chap. 2). The lion (v. 4) is Babylon, the head of gold. The bear (v. 5) is Media-Persia, the arms and chest of silver. The leopard (v. 6) is Greece, the thigh of brass. The dreadful beast (v. 7) is Rome, the legs of iron. The little horn (v. 8) represents Antichrist and his kingdom, the toes of iron and clay. The Ancient of Days on the throne (vv. 9–14) parallels the smiting stone.

Bible Prophecy

How should believers respond when they get an understanding of God's prophetic Word? Daniel was affected physically by his visions and was left weak and prostrate (7:15, 28; 8:17–18, 27; 10:8). Those who are proud of a knowledge of Bible prophecy may have learned only what it says and not what it means. Revelation always brings responsibility with it. If we really believe these things, we will obey what God tells us to do.

A vision of saints on earth (15–28). These "saints" are believers during the end times, just before the Lord returns to set up His kingdom. But what Daniel says about them has spiritual application to believers today. They are involved in a war (v. 21) and suffer persecution (v. 25), but they will receive the kingdom (v. 18) and reign with Christ (v. 27).

When the course of world history depresses you, look at events from heaven's point of view.

DANIEL 8

Daniel saw himself in the Persian capital, for Persia would be the next world power after Babylon. In this vision, God pictured Persia as a ram and Greece (the next power) as a male goat (vv. 19–22). We have moved from wild beasts to beasts that have been domesticated.

The "notable horn" (v. 5) is Alexander the Great, who conquered many nations, including Persia, and built a great kingdom. After his death, his kingdom was divided into four parts by four of his generals (v. 8). The "little horn" (vv. 9–14) represents the evil general, Antiochus Epiphanes, who invaded Palestine, defiled the Jewish temple, and put the Jews under bondage. He is a picture of the world ruler to come, the Antichrist (vv. 15–26).

Daniel was so overwhelmed by the vision that he became ill and could not do his work! He could never be the same again, knowing what God had planned for his people in the latter days. How does Bible prophecy affect you?

DANIEL 9

Insight (1–2). Even though he received visions from God and could interpret dreams, Daniel still read the Scriptures and sought to understand them. While pondering Jeremiah 25, he understood that the seventy years of Jewish captivity would soon end. Not all world events have prophetic significance, but God's people should keep their eyes open.

Intercession (3–19). The Word of God and prayer go together (Acts 6:4), as do prayer and fasting (Acts 13:3). Compare this prayer with the prayers in Nehemiah 9 and Ezra 9. Daniel emphasized the sinfulness of himself and his people and the righteousness of God, and he asked for God's forgiveness. Note that he especially prayed for Jerusalem. Had he read Jeremiah 29:10–14 and 30:10–24?

The Seventy Weeks

The seventy weeks are in three periods: seven weeks (49 years), sixty-two weeks (434 years), and one week (7 years). The first period starts in 444 B.C. with the decree allowing the Jews to return to their land and rebuild the city. The next sixty-two weeks (434 years) take us up to the time of Christ (vv. 24, 26). The "missing" seventieth week is fulfilled in the end times and parallels Revelation 6—19. The "prince who is to come" (v. 26) is the Antichrist, who will make a covenant with the Jews to protect them for seven years. After three and one-half years, he will break the covenant and usher in a terrible time of trouble for the world. That final seven-year period climaxes with the return of Christ, the defeat of His enemies, and the establishment of His kingdom on earth (Matt. 24:29–31; Rev. 19). The New Testament declares, "Known to God from eternity are all His works" (Acts 15:18).

Instruction (20–27). God gave Daniel a preview of Jewish history. Jerusalem would be rebuilt and the temple restored. Messiah would come and die. An evil prince would break his covenant with the Jews and trigger desolation. But God would triumph, and Jerusalem would become truly a holy city. Men are free to make decisions and even rebel against God if they want to, but He will accomplish His purposes in the world. With confidence, you can pray, "Thy kingdom come!"

DANIEL 10

The Jewish exiles had returned to the land and were re-building the temple when Daniel had this experience. He had been fasting for three weeks, and the vision of the angel left him even more weakened. When you pray for deeper experiences with the Lord, expect to pay a price.

God assures us. Daniel was a man "greatly beloved" by the Lord (vv. 11, 19). The Father loves us as He loves His Son (John 17:23) and wants to share His love with us (John 14:21–23). God also said, "Fear not" (vv. 12, 19). You can rest today in the love of God and His promise that you need not be afraid.

God touches us. God's touch awakened and aroused Daniel (v. 10), enabled him to speak (v. 16), and gave him strength (vv. 18–19). By His Word, God gives us the peace and power that we need (v. 19).

God instructs us. Why did it take so long for the angel to come to Daniel? Because of a spiritual battle in the heavenlies (vv. 12–13, 20; Eph. 6:10ff.). When you pray, you become a part of spiritual warfare, so do not take lightly your times of prayer. The angel also instructed Daniel about the future of his people (v. 14), explained in chapters 11—12.

Daniel's companions did not see the vision or hear the voice, but in terror fled away. God still needs people like Daniel who see the glory of God, hear the Word of God, feel God's touch, and enter into the spiritual battle.

DANIEL 11

God revealed to Daniel a summary of what would happen to his people now that they were restored as a nation. They would not have an easy time of it! The chapter describes wars involving armies from the north (Syria) and south (Egypt) as well as from Greece (vv. 3–4). The words *forces [arms], army, anger,* and *intrigue* describe the course of history. Have things changed much in the world?

At verse 36, the angel shifts to the latter days and describes the program of Antichrist. Read 2 Thessalonians 2 and Revelation 13.

What should God's people do in such times of conflict and destruction? They should be strong in the Lord, carry out daring deeds of faith, and share the truth with others, despite persecution and possible death (vv. 32–33). Bad times challenge good people.

DANIEL 12

Keep in mind that this prophecy has to do with the Jewish people in the end times. But it gives encouragement to all of God's people in every generation to know that God is in control and will accomplish His purposes in spite of the forces of evil.

God assures His servant that the living believers will be delivered (v. 1) and the ones who die will be resurrected to shine in glory (v. 2; Matt. 13:43). No matter what kind of affliction or tribulation God permits you to experience, He is still in control.

What, then, are your responsibilities? To seek to win others to the Savior (v. 3), to leave the hidden things with the Lord (vv. 8–9), to grow in holiness (v. 10), and to wait on the Lord and rest in Him (vv. 12–13). This is the way Bible prophecy should affect us personally.

THE MINOR PROPHETS

◆

The prophets Jonah, Amos, and Hosea ministered in the northern kingdom (Israel, Ephraim) before it was taken by Assyria in 722 B.C. In the southern kingdom (Judah), Joel, Micah, Zephaniah, Nahum, Habakkuk, and Obadiah served prior to the Babylonian captivity. Ezekiel and Daniel, who are considered major prophets, ministered during the captivity; and Haggai, Zechariah, and Malachi ministered to the Jewish remnant after their return to the land from exile. Their messages are not "minor" as far as content is concerned; "minor" refers only to their size. Most of the minor prophets have a threefold message: the sin of the people; the coming judgment of God; and the future restoration of Israel. The promise of hope is present even in the message of judgment.

HOSEA

◆

Hosea preached in the northern kingdom when the nation was prospering outwardly but decaying inwardly and facing certain judgment. He is a master of imagery; as you read, notice the many comparisons he makes ("like a dry land," "like a morning cloud," etc.).

The overriding image in his book is that of *marriage*. Hosea married a woman who bore him three children and then deserted him and became a prostitute. He finally had to buy her back out of the slave market (3:1–2)! Hosea's painful experience was a sermon to the nation. Israel was married to Jehovah but committed "spiritual adultery" and turned to idols. That in turn led to moral decay in the nation. The nation would suffer for her sins, but the Lord would one day redeem her and restore her.

The development of the book is as follows: Hosea's marriage, (chaps. 1—3); Israel's sins, (chaps. 4—7); Israel's judgment (chaps. 8—10); and Israel's future restoration (chaps. 11—14).

It is easy for the church today to prostitute itself to the world and still claim to be faithful to the Lord (James 4:4–10). The warning of Revelation 2:4–5 must be heeded!

HOSEA 1

Gomer was not a harlot when Hosea married her, but God warned him that she would be unfaithful. Like Ezekiel, Hosea had to "live" his message before the people, and that was not an easy thing to do. Expect to pay a price if you want to have a ministry to others (2 Cor. 1:3–11).

The names of the three children summarize the spiritual history of Israel. *Jezreel* means "God will sow" (2:22–23) and refers to Jehu's slaughter of his enemies at Jezreel (2 Kings 9—10). He went too far in his zeal, and his descendants would suffer for it when Assyria would take the land. God's judgments come—no matter how long He seems to wait.

Lo-Ruhamah means "no mercy," which is the situation of Israel today (3:4). Although God is providentially guiding the Jewish nation, they are not enjoying God's mercies as before.

Lo-Ammi means "not my people" and speaks of God's temporary rejection of the nation because of their sins.

Jezreel

The Valley of Jezreel has been a battlefield for many different armies. Saul launched his last battle there (1 Sam. 29:1), and there Jehu destroyed the house of Ahab as well as some innocent people (2 Kings 9—10). When Assyria took Israel, they fought on the plain of Jezreel; and there God avenged the innocent blood shed by Jehu. But Hosea saw a new future for Jezreel (1:11—2:1). Israel and Judah would be united and restored to the land, and they would experience the blessing of God. God would "sow" them in the land (2:21–23) to bear fruit for the glory of God. Only God can give new meanings to old names and wipe out painful associations with old places. Even the Valley of Achor, where Achan died (Josh. 7:16–26), will become a door of hope (2:15).

Hosea closes with a great affirmation of hope (1:10—2:1)! God will gather His people, claim them once again, and show them mercy. The names of the children will be changed to "My People" and "Mercy." No matter how dark the day, God promises us hope if we will return to Him in sincere repentance.

HOSEA 2—3

God makes four declarations.

I will not have mercy (2:1–8). Israel accepted God's gifts but used them to worship idols. Do we ever use our God-given resources for things that grieve Him? God withheld His mercy and allowed the nation to sink deeper into sin. What a tragedy!

I will punish her (2:9–13). He did this by taking away His blessings, especially the land's fruitfulness. The people were still outwardly worshiping God (2:11), but their hearts were with the idols.

I will allure her (2:14–20; 3:1–5). Just as Hosea reclaimed his wife, so God will one day reclaim His people, renew His "marriage vows," and restore His people to blessing (Jer. 3:1–20). This will occur in the latter days after Israel has suffered greatly at the hands of the Gentiles. There is hope!

I will sow her (2:21–3:5). *Jezreel* means "God will sow" (1:4–5) and refers to God's planting His people again in their land where He will love them and bless them. The names will be changed (2:23)!

Note the declaration from the unfaithful wife: "I will go and return to my first husband" (2:7; Luke 15:18). When we return to our first love (Rev. 2:4–5), we can enjoy the first blessings.

HOSEA 4—5

Ignorance (4:1–10). What you don't know *can* hurt you! The priests and prophets did not teach the Word or help the people know God. The religious services were popular, but the people were being destroyed for lack of true spiritual knowledge. It was only a religious routine (Matt. 15:1–9).

Idolatry (4:11–19). The key word here is *harlotry,* which is what idolatry really is. Like Hosea's wife Gomer, Israel had forsaken the true God and gone after idols. What is God's response? "Let him alone!" (4:17).

Indignation (5:1–15). Any faithful husband would be indignant if his wife defiled herself by unfaithfulness (v. 3). Instead of pursuing Israel, God withdrew Himself and His blessings (5:6; 4:17) and let them reap what they had sown. But His judgment was at work: the water was gathering behind the dam (v. 10); the moth was silently destroying the fabric of society (v. 12); the rottenness in the bones would lead to death (vv. 12–13). Then the Assyrian lion would spring (v. 14) and the nation would be conquered.

God withdraws so that we may realize what we are missing and want Him to come back to us again (5:15). There is no reason to stumble (4:5; 5:5) or to be stubborn (4:16) when God will welcome us if we will sincerely seek Him.

HOSEA 6—7

Like the rain (6:1–3). When we come back to God, He brings the dawning of a new day with the refreshing showers. The God who chastens us also heals and revives us. Why do we delay? Because of what *we* are like!

Like a morning cloud and the dew (6:4–11). Israel's loyalty did not last but vanished like a cloud and evaporated like the dew. They brought sacrifices and engaged in religious services, but those activities made no difference in the way they lived. Their sacrifices were substitutes for obedience (1 Sam. 15:21–23; Amos 5:21–24).

Like an oven (7:1–7). The desire for sin can smolder like a fire in an oven and then blaze forth when the opportunity comes. If you have "burning desires," be sure that they are under God's control or they may destroy you.

Like a cake not turned (7:8–10). If the fire is not watched, it can burn the cake, and then the cake must be thrown away. The people were "half-baked": there was no depth to their religious experience. The nation was aging and did not realize it, and national death would come much sooner than the people realized.

Like a silly dove (7:11–12). In their foreign policy, the officials flitted between Egypt and Assyria, playing one against the other; eventually the nation was trapped. Instead of trusting the Lord and obeying His Word, they depended on politics and failed.

Like a deceitful bow (7:13–16). God could not depend on His people. They sinned against Him, lied to Him, and did not profit from His discipline. He tried to straighten them out, but they preferred to be substandard. In the battle against evil, are you a weapon that God can depend on?

HOSEA 8

The trumpet was blown in Israel to warn of impending battle (Num. 10:9). In this case, Assyria was coming, and there would be no escape. Israel claimed to know God (v. 2) and yet disobeyed Him (Titus 1:16). They made kings and rulers without seeking God's will, and they made idols in defiance of the Lord. The famous calf of Samaria would be destroyed (1 Kings 12:28–30) when the eagle swooped down (v. 1) and the whirlwind came (v. 7). What seems a lovely soft wind today can become a storm tomorrow (Acts 27:13–15).

Israel had become like a piece of junk pottery on the trash heap (v. 8). They trusted the gentile nations to protect them but left God out of their plans (vv. 9–10). Israel multiplied altars (v. 11; 10:1) and Judah multiplied fortifications (v. 14), but neither could deliver from judgment. Israel would be taken by Assyria and Judah by Babylon, and God's judgment would fall on a sinful people.

When God blows the trumpet, we had better wake up and listen!

HOSEA 9—10

The name *Ephraim* means "twice fruitful," and Hosea used that fact as the basis for his message in these chapters. There would be no fruitfulness *in the harvest* (9:1–9) because poverty was coming and God would judge the land (Deut. 28:38–42). That would be the end of harvest joy (9:1). Ephraim would no longer be known as the fruitful land.

There would also be no more fruitfulness *in the home* (9:10–17). Why allow them to bear children who would only worship idols and then be murdered by the Assyrian invaders? The fruitful womb was always a blessing to the Jewish people (Pss. 127:3–5; 128:3–4), but now the miscarrying womb would be a blessing.

What was wrong with Israel? They tried to serve two masters (10:1–2), they lied to God (10:4), they worshiped idols (10:5–

6), and their hearts were hard and needed plowing up (10:12). They sowed the wrong seed in the wrong kind of soil and yet expected to reap the right harvest!

Have you pondered Galatians 6:7-8 lately?

HOSEA 11—12

These chapters form a history lesson that reveals the sins of the people as Hosea reviews the history of Israel and of Jacob.

Ingratitude (11:1-4). Israel took for granted their covenant relationship with the Lord, forgetting that He chose them (Deut. 7:6-11). In love He delivered a child from Egypt, carried him, fed him, and taught him to walk and work; and that child abandoned Him for idols. What ingratitude!

Hardness of heart (11:5-11). They followed their own plans and gave no thought to the will of God. When God rebuked them, they did not repent. The soil of their hearts was hard (10:12), but God's heart was tender toward them. He could not destroy them as He did the cities of the plain (Gen. 14:2, 8). No, one day He will call for them with a lion's roar, and they will come with trembling hearts.

Deceitfulness (11:12—12:6). Both Israel and Judah (the southern kingdom) are included in this message. The prophet reviews the history of Jacob their founder and sees his deceit in his descendants. Jacob tried to trip up Esau at birth (Gen. 25:26); he fought with God (Gen. 32:22-32); but he returned to Bethel and found God's blessing again (Gen. 35). The time had come for Israel and Judah to return to God and repent of their sins (12:6).

Boasting (12:7-14). "I have become rich!" was their boast, but it was an empty boast and just a lot of wind (12:1). Why? Because they made their money deceitfully by cheating the poor, and such wealth can never last. Read and ponder Revelation 3:14-22.

HOSEA 13—14

Ephraim had been a great tribe in Israel (Gen. 48:10-20). Now it would become like the clouds, the dew, the chaff, and the smoke—*nothing* (13:3). But God would be to the people like a lion, a leopard, and a bear (13:7-8)!

God had saved them from Egypt and in the wilderness, and He could have saved them from Assyria; but they trusted their wealth, their kings, and their foreign policy. Now the east wind would dry them up (13:15), and the "twice fruitful" Ephraim would be fruitful no more.

But we can always heed God's loving call to repentance. If we return to Him, He will receive us (14:2-3), restore us (14:4), and revive us (14:5-9). The desert will become a fruitful garden where the roots go deep. Instead of ugliness, there will be beauty; instead of a stench, there will be fragrance. What a difference it makes when we obey Him!

God does not want our material sacrifices so much as the "sacrifices of our lips" (14:2; Heb. 13:15). He wants to hear words from our hearts that are honest and sincere, and He wants to see faith that depends on His mercy alone. Will you be a stumbling sinner (14:1, 9) or a forgiven sinner?

JOEL

The prophet Joel ministered in Judah at a time when drought and a plague of locusts had devastated the economy. He used the phrase "the day of the LORD" (1:15; 2:1, 11, 31; 3:14) to describe both their present calamity (1:1—2:27) and the future judgment that would come upon the whole world (2:28—3:21). God's "army" of locusts (2:11, 20, 25) was but a picture of a future army that would invade the land in the last days. Joel called the nation to repent (2:12-17) and promised that the Lord would forgive and bless them (2:18-27). He also promised blessings in the last days when Israel's tribulation would be ended (2:28-32; 3:18-21). God's message of judgment is not left without a promise of hope.

Campbell Morgan wrote, "It is always the day of the Lord." No matter what calamities may come to men and nations, He is always in control, and these calamities remind us of the greater judgment yet to come.

JOEL 1

The prophet gives us four instructions to follow when we find ourselves in difficult circumstances, instructions that should be heeded by individuals and nations.

Hear (1-4). Listen to God's Word and let Him interpret events for you. God raises up people to encourage us to turn to Him for help.

Awake (5-7). When Joel looked at the dying vines and trees, he addressed the drinkers and told them to wake up and weep. But they should shed tears not because the wine is gone but because their sins have brought judgment on the land.

Lament (8-18). The fields, orchards, vineyards, flocks, and herds were all ruined; and Joel called for the farmers to lament (v. 11) and for the priests to repent (vv. 13–14). It is time to seek the Lord!

Cry out (19–20). The prophet set the example by crying out to God for His mercy and help. Perhaps he claimed God's promise in 2 Chronicles 7:14. It is not enough for us to weep over the sad consequences of our sins; we must also weep over our sins.

JOEL 2

The trumpet of warning (1–11). The calamities that come to our lives should awaken us and remind us that the Lord is in control. The locusts were God's army (vv. 11, 20, 25), and the day was "the day of the LORD." This is a sobering truth, but it is also a comforting truth (2 Sam. 24:14). The Lord who wounds will also heal (Hos. 6:1).

Restoration

The Lord said, "So I will restore to you the years that the . . . locust has eaten" (Joel 2:25). God promised them bumper crops that would make up for all they had lost because of the drought and the locust plague. "Lost years can never be restored literally," said Charles Spurgeon. "Time once past is gone forever. . . . You cannot have back your time; but there is a strange and wonderful way in which God can give back to you the wasted blessings, the unripened fruits of years over which you mourned. The fruits of wasted years may yet be yours."

The trumpet of weeping (12–17). The prophet summoned the people to return to God with fasting and confession. Never be afraid to come to the Lord in honesty and humility because He is "gracious and merciful, slow to anger, and of great kindness" (v. 13). As you pray, think about magnifying the glory of God (v. 17) as well as escaping the suffering that sin causes.

The promise of blessing (18–32). God promised to remove their reproach and restore His blessings to the land. "Monstrous things" (v. 20) will be replaced by "marvelous things" from the Lord (v. 21), and joy will take the place of fear. Verses 28–32 refer especially to the future day of the Lord, but Peter's use of them at Pentecost (Acts 2:16–21) suggests that they have a spiritual application today.

JOEL 3

Four vivid pictures describe God's future dealings with His people and the nations.

The court (1–8). In the last days, God will summon the gentile nations to court and judge them for the sins they have committed against Israel: scattering them, dividing up their land, treating them like slaves, and robbing them of wealth. This judgment has been long in coming, but it will come.

The harvest (9–13). God will call the nations to conflict and reap a final harvest (Isa. 63:1–6; Rev. 14:14–20). But His people will be strong, and God will uphold their cause.

The storm (14–17). The nations will feel the wrath of God, but He will care for His people with shelter and with strength. (See Pss. 46; 91.)

The garden (18–21). The book opens with drought and famine but closes with a description of a land of milk and honey. God will forgive His people and graciously dwell with them. He will give them a new beginning.

War, Not Peace

Joel 3:10 expresses the opposite thought from Isaiah 2:4 and Micah 4:3. Isaiah and Micah describe the future glorious kingdom when the world will have peace instead of war. Joel's call was, "Prepare for war!" (3:9).

What the future holds for you depends on your relationship with the Lord. If you trust Jesus Christ as Savior, you will never be called into court (John 5:24; Rom. 8:1-4), and you never need fear the storm.

AMOS

The prophet Amos came from Judah, but his ministry was primarily to Israel, the northern kingdom. He was a herdsman/farmer (7:14–15), and his book contains many rural allusions. He did not have the formal training of a prophet but was called of God and effectively preached God's Word.

Under Jeroboam II, the northern kingdom was enjoying a time of peace and prosperity; interest in "religion" was high. But the "revival" was shallow and had little effect on the everyday life of the people. The rich were getting richer, and the poor had no one to defend them. Amos warned that God was sending judgment to Israel and the nations around her, and in 722 B.C., Assyria brought that judgment.

The book contains eight *accusations* against the nations (chaps. 1–2), three *messages* about the sins of Israel (chaps. 3–6), and five *visions* of future judgment (chaps. 7–9). The book ends with the promise of restoration for God's people (9:11–15; see also Acts 15:14–17).

The name *Amos* means "to be burdened" (2:13), and he certainly was burdened because of the sins of his people.

AMOS 1—2

Amos denounces the sins of six gentile nations before he pronounces judgment on Judah (2:4–5) and Israel (2:6–16). God did not give His law to the gentile nations, but He still held them accountable for their sins against humanity. Israel and Judah sinned against God's law (2:4) and God's love (2:9–12); but the Gentiles sinned against their "inner law," their conscience (Rom. 2:12–16).

The Gentiles sinned against their fellowman. Amos condemned their brutality, slavery, revenge, murder, and thievery. The nations seemed to get away with their sins but God eventually caught up with them. He is long-suffering, but He is also holy.

Being the chosen people of God, Israel and Judah had a greater responsibility before the Lord. In one way or another, they violated all the Ten Commandments; and that meant God would have to judge them (2:13–16).

If God judges *lost* people for their sins, what will He do to those who claim to know Him? Privilege brings responsibility (Luke 12:48), and where there is responsibility, there will be accountability. The people of Israel and Judah rejoiced when they heard Amos condemn their neighbors; but then he condemned *God's people* for their sins, and that was not acceptable to them.

Is God being long-suffering toward you? Is His judgment of others a warning to you? Are you heeding it?

AMOS 3

Past (1–2). This is another reminder that privilege brings responsibility. The Lord delivered the Jews from Egypt and called them to be His special people. *That was why He was punishing them.* God's gracious election of Israel did not give them the right to disobey Him, and the same truth applies to the church today. Election involves responsibility (John 15:16; Eph. 1:4; 1 Pet. 2:4–5, 9).

Present (3–10). What right did a common herdsman like Amos have to denounce his own people and warn of judgment? He and God were walking together because they agreed (v. 3). God was roaring like a lion (1:2; vv. 4, 8) and setting the trap for sinners (v. 5). Amos was blowing the trumpet to warn people (v. 6) because God had shared His secrets with him (v. 7; Ps. 25:14). In spite of his humble origins, Amos was God's servant.

Future (11–15). If a shepherd lost an animal, he had to pay for it, unless he could prove that a beast killed it. He did that by bringing home some of the parts that were not devoured. Israel could hear the lion roar, but the nation would not repent. Soon, only a remnant would be left.

"Religion"

The prophet Amos denounced luxury and urged the people to care for the poor of the land. He particularly condemned their expensive houses (3:15; 5:11), their drinking (4:1), their complacency (6:1), and their costly parties (6:3-6; 8:10). The rich got their money by exploiting the poor (5:11-15). Yet those wealthy people were "religious" and faithfully participated in the temple services (4:4-5; 5:21-27). Their "religion" was only a masquerade to cover their sins. Are professed believers guilty of any of these sins today?

AMOS 4

"Yet you have not returned to Me!" is the sad refrain of this chapter (vv. 6, 8, 9, 10, 11). God's disciplines are for the purpose of restoration, to bring people to true repentance.

God used several means of discipline—drought, famine, crop diseases, locusts, plagues, war, and local catastrophes (v. 11)—and yet the people did not get the message. They had met with God's disciplines, but the next step was to *meet God Himself* (v. 12). He was personally coming to judge them.

What a tragedy that the people kept living in luxury (vv. 1-3) and carrying out their religious duties (vv. 4-5) while ignoring the call of God. It took courage for Amos to call the wealthy women "cows" and to picture them being led away to slaughter. In their comfort and prosperity, the people thought they were immune from judgment, but it came just the same.

Are you prepared to meet your God?

AMOS 5

Lamentation (1–3). This is a funeral dirge for a nation that was dead and left unburied. The Assyrians would come, and Israel would be taken captive. Israel thought she was a lovely virgin, but she was only a fallen corpse, left to rot. No wonder Amos wept!

Invitation (4–15). But God still gives His gracious invitation: "Seek Me and live" (vv. 4, 6, 14). The people flocked to their holy places with their sacrifices, but that would not save them. The nation would not listen to the Lord's servants (v. 10), so the Lord told them to be quiet (v. 13). God knows our sins, and yet in mercy He calls us to come to Him for cleansing. What a gracious God!

Jesus' Coming

When you pray, "Thy kingdom come," be sure that you mean it. Do you really want the Lord Jesus to return today, or will His coming upset your plans? Some of God's people will be ashamed when they meet Him (1 John 2:28), while others will welcome Him with joy (1 Thess. 2:19–20).

The joyful anticipation of His coming is a great motivation for holy living (1 John 3:1–3) and faithful service (Luke 12:35–48).

Condemnation (16–27). Amos saw the day of the Lord approaching, a day of judgment, darkness, and despair. The people had a false confidence that "the day of the LORD" would bring blessing to the nation (vv. 18–20), not unlike some believers today who think of the return of Christ only as an escape to heaven. God would send judgment in spite of their religious activities and generous gifts of sacrifices (Isa. 1:12–23). God still wants obedience and not sacrifice.

Justice   *Amos 5:24 is a key verse in the book. There was gross injustice in the land as the rich exploited the poor and the religious leaders did nothing about it. God wants justice to be like a mighty river that cleanses society of evil and refreshes everything it touches.*

AMOS 6

The nation was guilty of complacency born of false confidence (vv. 1–2), trusting the military leaders and not the Lord. The people were also guilty of self-indulgence and unconcern for hurting persons of the land (vv. 3–8). After all, the day of judgment was far away! Or was it?

God appointed three judgments for them: death (vv. 9–10), destruction (vv. 11–13), and defeat (v. 14). The banqueters would become corpses, and the great houses would be left in ruins. The leaders boasted of their recent victories (v. 13), but Assyria would bring defeat.

Horses cannot safely run on the rocky cliffs, and oxen cannot plow there. But Israel was not as smart as the animals, for she was attempting the impossible: trying to escape judgment by disobeying the Lord. "We are an exception to the rule!" was the confident boast, but the people did not escape. Their sins found them out.

AMOS 7

Defending his people (1–9). The closing three chapters record five visions that describe the future of Israel. Eleven times the prophet refers to God as "the LORD God," the Sovereign Ruler over all things. After the first two visions, Amos interceded for the people, and the Lord relented. But Amos did not intercede after the third vision, for the nation had been measured and was found wanting. God weighs us (Prov. 21:2; Dan. 5:27) and measures us by His standards, and His examination is always accurate.

Defending his ministry (10–17). Here is a conflict between two ministries—priest and prophet, the institutional and the radical. The priest seeks to conserve the past while the prophet threatens the present because he wants to preserve the future. There is also a conflict between structure and ministry. Amaziah was a man of position while Amos was a humble farmer with a commission from the Lord. But Amos did not back down; he remained true to his calling and let God deal with Amaziah.

If you were to choose either Amaziah or Amos to be your spiritual leader, which would you select—and why?

Called of God

Amos is a good example of what Paul wrote in 1 Corinthians 1:26–29. God often bypasses the so-called great people and chooses to call and bless the humble and the weak. Yes, God can also use those who are gifted and who hold high positions in this world, but He is not limited to them. Both Moses (Acts 7:22) and Paul (Acts 26:24) were well-educated, but at least seven of our Lord's disciples were common fishermen (John 21:1–3). R. A. Torrey was a brilliant man and a gifted evangelist; he worked closely with evangelist Dwight L. Moody, who had very little education. God used both men in a remarkable way because both gave all they had to the Lord.

AMOS 8

Amos's fourth vision gave one clear message: "Israel is ripe for judgment!" As the farmer cuts off the ripe fruit, so God will cut off Israel. He had been long-suffering with them, but now the day of reckoning had come. The wealthy had sinned against both men and God. They were weary of their religious duties and only endured the Sabbath, waiting until they could start making money again. They changed God's standards so that they might exploit the poor, and they cheapened their products and then raised the prices. No wonder God was angry with them.

Amos told them to expect an earthquake (v. 8; 1:1), an eclipse (v. 9), a funeral (v. 10), and a famine (vv. 11–14). God's Word is our spiritual nourishment (Matt. 4:4; 1 Pet. 2:2), and there can be no substitute. When God's people reject His Word, He sometimes judges them by taking away His Word and leaving them to go hungry as they live on substitutes.

AMOS 9

Judging (1–4). Amos saw the Lord at the sanctuary at Bethel, where the people were carrying on their hypocritical worship. He was about to destroy the sanctuary and all the worshipers; nobody would escape. If anyone tried to escape, he would be tracked down and slain. It is a basic principle that judgment begins at the house of the Lord (1 Pet. 4:17; see also Ezek. 9:6).

Sifting (5–10). God would destroy the sanctuary at Bethel, but He would not utterly destroy His people. He would send them among the Gentiles and sift out the true from the false. In His grace, God spares a remnant so that the nation might continue.

Blessing (11–15). The royal dynasty of David was like a tent or booth that had fallen down, but God will raise it, repair it and restore it. His people will return to their land and enjoy once again the blessings of God (Isa. 11). Meanwhile, God is calling out His church from both Jews and Gentiles (Acts 15:6–21), and our task is to share the gospel with every creature.

OBADIAH

◆

When the Babylonians destroyed Jerusalem, the Edomites rejoiced and helped the enemy instead of helping their brethren (Gen. 25:21–26; Ps. 137:7–9). It was a repetition of the ancient conflict between Esau and Jacob, which symbolizes the battle between the flesh and the Spirit.

What were the sins of Edom? *Pride* stands at the top of the list, and God promised to bring them down (vv. 1–4). They were also guilty of *looting* (v. 13), and God said they would be looted (vv. 5–7). They were *violent* (v. 10) and *indifferent* (v. 11), and they *rejoiced* at the plight of the Jews (v. 12; Prov. 24:17–18); but God warned that they would one day be slaughtered (v. 8). What they had done to others would be done to them (v. 15), and there was no escape. (See Jer. 50:29, Matt. 7:12 and Gal. 6:7–8.)

But there is a bright future for Israel (vv. 17–21), for they shall "possess their possessions" (v. 17). Babylon burned the city of Jerusalem and the temple, but Israel will be a fire to burn the enemy: "And the kingdom shall be the LORD's" (v. 21)!

◆

"The Other Side"	*It is a cruel thing to stand "on the other side" when our brothers and sisters need our help. The priest and the Levite retreated to "the other side" instead of helping the wounded pilgrim (Luke 10:31–32). If it is in our power to help, we must do so (Prov. 24:11–12), and we must not substitute words for deeds (James 2:14–17; 1 John 3:16–19).*

◆

JONAH

◆————————————

The prophet Jonah was a real person and not just a character in a parable (2 Kings 14:25; Matt. 12:39–41). God sent him to Nineveh, the capital of the Assyrian Empire, to a people despised by the Jews. Jonah would rather that Nineveh be destroyed than that the city have an opportunity to repent and be spared. The Assyrians were a cruel people who showed no mercy to their enemies, and Jonah wanted them out of the way.

The book emphasizes God's grace both to Nineveh and to Jonah. Though Nineveh was a wicked city, God gave the inhabitants opportunity to be spared. Though Jonah was a rebellious servant, God forgave him, used him, and tenderly sought to help him overcome his anger. One outline of the book is the following: chapter 1—rebellion: Jonah goes down; chapter 2—repentance: Jonah goes up; chapter 3—restoration: Jonah goes to; and chapter 4—resentment: Jonah goes out.

The main character in this book is neither the prophet nor the great fish but *God,* who is mentioned thirty-eight times. The book deals with the important question, "How do you respond to the word and will of God?"

JONAH 1

Jonah thought he had a choice. He forgot that the will of God is not an option: it is an obligation and an opportunity. When we run from God's will, we always go down (vv. 3, 5, 15, 17; 2:6). We may end up sacrificing safety for danger and peace for a storm.

The "pagan" sailors reveal more character than does the prophet of God. While Jonah was sleeping, they were crying out to their gods, and they did their best to save him (v. 13).

Jonah was a Jew, and the Jews were to be a blessing to the whole world (Gen. 12:1–3). But the man who should have been saving the lost was being saved by the lost!

A believer out of fellowship with God can cause a great deal of trouble. Jonah put the crew in danger and left the Ninevites without a message of hope. God loves us too much to let us run away; therefore, He disciplines us (Heb. 12:1–11), and He keeps working on us until we submit to Him.

❝To fear God is to stand in awe of Him; to be afraid of God is to run away from Him.**❞**

Carroll E. Simcox

JONAH 2

When God first called him, Jonah should have prayed for divine help in carrying out his mission. Then he would have escaped discipline and the need for crying out to God for deliverance. When it was almost too late, the prophet prayed; and God graciously forgave him and rescued him.

The Old Testament Jew looked toward the temple in Jerusalem when he prayed (vv. 4, 7; Dan. 6:10). Perhaps Jonah claimed the promise of 1 Kings 8:46–53, just as today we claim the promise of 1 John 1:9. God is merciful toward His children and ready to forgive (Ps. 86:5).

How did Jonah get into all that trouble? He forgot God and neglected prayer (v. 7) and believed lies (v. 8). He learned the hard way that he could not escape God's will. But he was wise enough to run back to God and ask for forgiveness!

JONAH 3

How gracious God is to give us another opportunity after we have failed Him (Ps. 103:8–14)! God is as much concerned about the worker as He is the work. He could have sent somebody else to preach to Nineveh, but Jonah would have missed out on the lessons he needed to learn. God wants to work *in* us as well as *through* us.

How gracious God is to lost sinners! Why would a holy God give the vicious Ninevites an opportunity to repent? Because He is "not willing that any should perish" (2 Pet. 3:9) but "desires all men to be saved" (1 Tim. 2:4). Do you have a burden to share the gospel with a lost world that does not deserve to be saved? Remember, somebody shared it with you!

How gracious God is to bless the ministry of an imperfect servant! Jonah did not love the people he preached to, yet God used his message to bring the whole city to repentance. There is power in God's Word; it can convict and convert the greatest of sinners.

JONAH 4

If God wanted only to save the city of Nineveh, the book would have ended at chapter 3. But there was still more work to do, for God wanted to save His servant from himself. Jonah was an angry man (vv. 1, 2, 4, 9) who wanted to see Nineveh destroyed. Like the elder brother, he stayed outside and vented his bitterness (Luke 15:25–32).

The basic problem was that Jonah was not completely yielded to God. His mind knew God's truth, and his will obeyed God's orders; but he did not do the will of God "from the heart" (Eph. 6:6). He obeyed only because he was afraid of what God might do to him. His was not a ministry of love.

When we are angry with God, everything in life gets out of perspective, and we say and do selfish things. Things become more important than people, and comfort more important than ministry.

But God is long-suffering and tenderly deals with us to bring us to Himself. *It is essential in Christian service to be happy with the will of God*. Each of us should be able to say, "I delight to do Your will, O my God, and Your law is within my heart" (Ps. 40:8).

MICAH

◆

Micah was a contemporary of Isaiah (Isa. 1:1) and Hosea (Hos. 1:1) and prophesied concerning both Judah and Israel (Samaria). In this book, he gives us three messages, each introduced by a call to hear. He declared the coming judgment (chaps. 1–2), the future kingdom (chaps. 3–5), and God's invitation to the people to turn to the Lord (chaps. 6–7). He hoped that the people of Judah would learn from the sad experience of Israel, but they did not. His is a message of judgment mingled with mercy and hope. Micah's name means "who is like the Lord?" The prophet Jeremiah's life was saved by a quotation from Micah (Jer. 26:18; Mic. 3:12).

MICAH 1

The lawsuit (1–7). Micah convenes the court and announces Jehovah's verdict against Israel: judgment is coming! Assyria invaded the northern kingdom in 722 B.C. and made the capital city Samaria a heap of ruins. The nation's idolatry was but harlotry against the Lord, and unfaithfulness must be judged.

The lament (8–16). But the Assyrians would also invade Judah, which they did in 701 B.C., and would destroy nearly fifty villages. Although they tried, they could not conquer Jerusalem (Isa. 36–37), for the Lord spared it for David's sake (Isa. 37:35).

The prophet wept over the terrible things that would happen to the people. He did not say, "They are getting what they deserve!" Instead, he mourned like a man at a funeral. Does the certainty of coming judgment cause us to mourn over lost sinners and seek to win them to Christ?

MICAH 2

Hebrew Wordplay

In the Hebrew original of Micah 1:10–16, the prophet uses some clever wordplay to get his point across. Beth Aphrah means "house of dust." Shaphir means "beautiful." Zaanan means "going out," and Beth Ezel means "house of nearness." Maroth means "bitterness," Lachish sounds like the word for "a team of horses," Achzib means "a lie," and Mareshah means "an inheritance." Put these meanings with the prophet's statements about these towns and see what you discover.

MICAH 2

Micah names some of the sins of the people, beginning with *covetousness* (vv. 1–5), which is idolatry (Col. 3:5). The rich were exploiting the poor and getting away with it. But when the invader comes, nobody's boundary lines would be respected.

Another sin was *rejecting God's Word* (vv. 6–11). The false prophets tried to silence Micah because he was announcing doom. They wanted a pleasant message about security and strong drink. The "prosperity preachers" are usually popular while those who declare God's Word are often persecuted. But God's Word does good in the lives of those who want to do good and obey the Lord.

They had *defiled the land* with their idolatry and harlotry (Lev. 18:24–30), and now the land would destroy them. Personal sin will always affect society.

How gracious of God to end with a promise of hope (vv. 12–13)! He will spare a remnant (4:7; 5:7–8; 7:18) and gather them together for His future kingdom. Their King will be their Shepherd!

MICAH 3

"Hear now!" introduces Micah's second message, which was directed to the leaders. Because of *their* sins, the nation disobeyed God and eventually had to be judged (Lam. 2:14; 4:13). He used three pictures to describe their sins.

Hunters (1–4). Instead of caring for the people, the leaders treated them like animals and devoured them. But the day would come when those leaders would cry out to God and He would not answer them.

Shepherds (5–7). Instead of guiding the flock in God's paths, they led them astray with their message of false peace (v. 11; Jer. 6:14). Their deception would be followed by darkness, and they would have no hope.

Builders (8–12). Instead of building the city on the law of the Lord, they broke the law and built with bloodshed. Why? Because they wanted to get more money (1 Tim. 6:9–10). But everything they built would be torn down, and their money would be useless to them.

A true leader protects the people, guides them in God's will, and serves without thought of personal gain.

MICAH 4

In four pictures, Micah presents a vision of the judgment of Israel's enemies and the establishment of the future kingdom.

A city (1–5). Even though Jerusalem would be destroyed by Babylon, one day the city would become the capital of the kingdom. It will be a time of peace when all men will want to learn about the Lord and walk in His ways.

A flock (6–8). The Lord will gather His flock (the remnant) and care for the lame and the afflicted. Their Shepherd will be their King, and He will reign in righteousness.

A birth (9–10). As the pregnant woman must deliver the child, so Judah must be taken captive to Babylon. It would be a time of pain, but it would eventually bring blessing. God promised to deliver them and restore them.

A harvest (11–13). The day will come when God's people will defeat their enemies who seek to destroy them. It will be like the threshing of grain, and the harvest will be given to the Lord.

MICAH 5

The focus is on Israel's Deliverer, the Lord Jesus Christ.

Two cities (1–2). Micah contrasts great Jerusalem, experiencing the Babylonian siege, and humble Bethlehem, where the Eternal One will step into time to save His people. The future of God's plan of salvation lay in lowly Bethlehem (Luke 2:1–20; see also Isa. 9:6).

Two births (3–4). The birth of Messiah brought hope to Israel, but the nation would not receive Him. He had to give them up (Luke 13:34–35) until the day He returns to restore them (Rom. 9). Their salvation will be the birth of a nation (Isa. 66:8), and there will be peace to the ends of the earth.

Two victories (5–15). Messiah will win a victory over His enemies and will make His people victorious (the lion) and fruitful (the dew). But He will also win a victory over His own people and purge them of their sins (vv. 10–15). The things they trusted will then be removed—armaments, fortresses, sorceries, and idols—and they will learn to trust the Lord.

Perhaps God wants to remove some things from your life so you can enjoy His peace.

MICAH 6

We are once more in the courtroom.

The indictment (1–5). God called the mountains to witness His complaint against Israel. What had He done to His people that they should despise His Word and sin against Him? (See Isa. 5.) Had they forgotten all that He did for them? It is good for us to review God's gracious acts toward us and make sure we express gratitude to Him.

The confession (6–8). All that the people could say was, "Guilty!" The Judge did not want sacrifices; He wanted obedience (Isa. 1:10–18). Verse 8 tells us how we should live as God's forgiven people (Deut. 10:12).

The sentence (9–16). They would feel the rod of punishment because of their sins, and their efforts would be cursed. Omri and Ahab were two of the most wicked kings who ever ruled Israel (1 Kings 16:21—22:40), and the nation suffered because they followed their bad examples.

The Judge is the Savior, but He cannot save those who persist in disobeying Him.

"Sublime Revelation"

Micah 6:8 is not the gospel. We are not saved by obeying these words, but we cannot obey them unless we are saved. Our religious words and deeds (vv. 6–8) mean nothing to God if we lack character wrought by the Holy Spirit as we yield to Him. "All controversy, all resentful intellectualism, all selfish calculation, all vicious political Christianity, must fall before that sublime revelation," wrote Joseph Parker.

MICAH 7

A faithful God (1–7). The prophet was disgusted because the people were all given over to deception. He couldn't even find one faithful man (1 Kings 19:10; Ps. 12:1; Isa. 57:1). When people fail you, remember that the Lord is always faithful. Make the same three decisions that the prophet made: "I will look, I will wait, I will pray" (v. 7).

A righteous God (8–13). God lifts up those who fall and gives light to those who are in the darkness. Even when He must deal with us because of our sins, He does what is best. Be patient, for He will one day defeat your enemies and bring you into blessing.

A pardoning God (14–20). God delights in mercy! When we come to Him and confess our sins, He pardons us, puts our sins underfoot like defeated enemies, and hurls them into the depths of the sea and they are seen no more. (See Ps. 103:12; Isa. 38:17; Jer. 31:34; Acts 3:19.)

God's Pardon

In wonder lost, with trembling joy,
We take the pardon of our God,
Pardon for sins of deepest dye,
A pardon bought with Jesus' blood.
Who is a pardoning God like Thee?
Or who has grace so rich and free?

Samuel Davies

NAHUM

◆

Jonah was sent to Nineveh, the capital of the Assyrian Empire, to give the people an opportunity to repent. But Nahum was called to announce that their judgment was imminent. The city fell to the Medes and Babylonians in 612 B.C. The prophet Zephaniah also prophesied the fall of Nineveh (Zeph. 2:13–14).

Nahum means "comfort," and his message was certainly a comfort to the Jews who feared and hated the cruel Assyrians' threats to their security. The book focuses on the holy character of God who cannot allow sin to go unpunished. In chapter 1, Nahum *declares* Nineveh's fall; in chapter 2, he *describes* it; and in chapter 3, he *defends* it.

NAHUM 1

God is jealous (1–2). This means He deserves total obedience and will not permit any rivals. It is the jealousy of the husband over his wife or the mother over her child. He is jealous over His people and for His glory; therefore, He must punish sin.

God is long-suffering (3a). God does not have "temper tantrums." He patiently waits for sinners to hear His Word and repent. See Exodus 34:6, Numbers 14:18 and Romans 9:22.

God is sovereign (3b–6). He has His way because His way is best and He is totally in control. He commands the forces of nature, and no one can stand before His anger.

God is good (7–15). Nineveh will be destroyed by a flood (v. 8) and a fire (v. 10); but God's people will be safe in their refuge, Jehovah God (Ps. 46). Judah had been afflicted by Assyria, but that would now end and the yoke would be taken off (vv. 12–13). Judah would hear the good news from the courier that Nineveh had been destroyed! (See Isa. 40:9; 52:7; Rom. 10:15.)

NAHUM 2

What a dramatic picture of the invasion (vv. 1–4), the battle (vv. 5–7), the victory (vv. 8–10), and the humiliation of Nineveh before the Lord and her enemies (vv. 11–13)! It was not the Babylonians and the Medes who defeated Assyria; it was the Lord God of Israel (Isa. 10:5–19).

The watchmen on the walls see the enemy army approaching (v. 1) with their scarlet uniforms and shields and their swift chariots (vv. 3–4). The general puts his best troops on the wall, but they stumble over one another and cannot move fast enough (v. 5).

The invaders dam up a river and release the water, which destroys part of the city wall and the palace (v. 6; 1:8). The people start to flee, many are taken captive, and the city is pillaged (vv. 7–10).

Assyria was identified with the lion, an image in many of their sculptures (vv. 11–13). But the Assyrian lion would devour no longer, for it had been devoured! Assyria would roar no more and kill no more, but Judah would be restored and enjoy the blessing of God (v. 2).

NAHUM 3

The harlot (1–7). This image frequently occurs in Scripture for those who abandon truth and give themselves wholly to sin to gain wealth and pleasure. The Assyrian goddess of sex and war was Ishtar, a harlot. God would expose Assyria's shame and make her vile.

The drunkard (8–11). How could drunken soldiers hope to win a war! The nation had to drink God's cup of wrath (Jer. 25:15–29).

The fig tree (12–13). Ripe figs will fall easily when the tree is shaken, and these figs would fall right into the farmer's mouth! Nineveh's defenses were inadequate, and the city would fall right into the enemy's hands.

The locusts (14–17). Assyria had swarmed on other nations and stripped them, but now an army would swarm on them and empty the city of people and wealth. The great Assyrian leaders would be like cold locusts in a stupor; but when the heat came, they would wake up and try to escape. The mighty nation was just a swarm of weak insects!

The flock (18). The shepherds (leaders) were dead, and the sheep were scattered. Nobody would care for them or gather them.

The victim (19). Wounded and sick, the nation was about to die; there was no way to bring healing. Jeremiah used the same image concerning God's people, but he promised that God would heal them (Jer. 30:12–17). For Nineveh, there was no promise of hope.

HABAKKUK

◆

The name *Habakkuk* may come from a Hebrew word that means "to embrace." In his book, he comes to grips with some serious problems and lays hold of God by faith when everything in his life seems to be falling apart.

Habakkuk saw the impending Babylonian invasion, and he wondered that God would use a wicked nation to punish His chosen people. His book describes three stages in Habakkuk's experience—perplexity: faith wavers (chap. 1); perspective: faith watches (chap. 2); and perseverance: faith worships (chap. 3).

The key text is 2:4, "But the just shall live by his faith." It is quoted in Romans 1:17, Galatians 3:11, and Hebrews 10:38. The theme of Romans is "the just" and how to be justified before God. Galatians tells us how the just "shall live," and the emphasis in Hebrews is on living "by faith." It takes three New Testament epistles to explain one Old Testament text!

HABAKKUK 1

An unanswered prayer (1–4). Habakkuk saw the wickedness of God's people in Judah and prayed for God to work, but the Lord didn't seem to hear. The prophet longed to see God bring revival to the land, but his prayer went unanswered—or so he thought.

An unexpected plan (5–11). God told His servant that his prayers would be answered in a way he never expected. God was going to bring Babylon against Judah and chasten His people. From the human point of view, the invasion of the land and the captivity of the people would seem a tragedy, but it was God's work just the same.

An unsolved problem (12–17). Now the prophet has a greater problem: how can a holy God use a wicked nation to punish His chosen people? God seemed to hold His tongue as His servant cried out (v. 13), but soon the answer came. It was not the answer Habakkuk expected, but it finally brought him peace.

It is good to wrestle with God about the questions that perplex you—just be sure to stop talking long enough to listen.

"Do not rejoice in earthly reality, rejoice in Christ, rejoice in His word, rejoice in His law. . . . There will be peace and tranquillity in the Christian heart; but only as long as our faith is watchful; if, however, our faith sleeps, we are in danger."

St. Augustine

HABAKKUK 2

Habakkuk needed a right perspective on what God was doing in His world. Although it is good to pray about these things, it is also good to "be still and know that [He is] God" (Ps. 46:10). The Lord emphasized two truths about Himself.

God is just. The five "woes" made it clear that God knew the sins of His people and would deal with them in due time. He hates pride, greed, selfishness, murder, drunkenness, lust, and idolatry.

God is faithful. Three key verses (4, 14, 20) reveal this trait. You can trust Him because His character never changes and His Word never fails (v. 4). It may not seem that way now, but one day His glory will be revealed in all the earth (v. 14). Meanwhile, God is on His throne and has everything under control (v. 20). So, instead of looking around and asking God a lot of questions, *look up* and lay hold of His assurances.

HABAKKUK 3

Request (1–2). God said He was at work (1:5) so the prophet asked Him to keep on working (v. 2) but to be merciful to His sinful people. Prayer means reminding God of His promises and claiming them for ourselves.

Review (3–15). Habakkuk reviewed God's work in the past and recalled His greatness and power. In every era of Jewish history, God was there to work for His people; He would not fail them now. The Babylonian invasion and captivity would be painful experiences, but God would use them for His glory and the good of His people (Rom. 8:28).

Rejoicing (16–18). Habakkuk started in the deep valley (chap. 1), then went up to the watchtower (chap. 2), but now finds himself on the mountains! Faith always lifts us higher and makes us happier. Even when we cannot rejoice in the economy, we can rejoice in the Lord!

Divine Guide

Begone unbelief, my Saviour is near,
And for my relief will surely appear;
By prayer let me wrestle and He will perform;
With Christ in the vessel, I smile at the storm.

Though dark be my way, since He is my guide
'Tis mine to obey, 'tis His to provide;
Though cisterns be broken and creatures all fail,
The word He hath spoken shall surely prevail.

John Newton

Glorious Feet

God wants His people to have **bathed** *feet (John 13:1–11) so we can fellowship with Him;* **beautiful** *feet (Rom. 10:15) so we can share His gospel with others; and* **bounding** *feet (Hab. 3:19) so we can overcome the obstacles of life.*

ZEPHANIAH

━━━━━━━━━━ ◆ ━━━━━━━━━━

Zephaniah may be the only Old Testament prophet who had royal blood in his veins. But his kinship with King Josiah didn't prevent his preaching a message of judgment at a time when the king was leading the nation in a religious reformation (2 Kings 22—23). Both Jeremiah and Zephaniah saw that the "reform" was not true revival, for it never got to the hearts of the people. It was only a surface change because the king promoted it and the people went along with whatever was popular.

The prophet's emphasis is on "the day of the Lord," a phrase we have met in Joel and Amos. It applies historically to the invasion of Babylon in 606 B.C., but prophetically it speaks of a future day of wrath in the end times.

Like Habakkuk, Zephaniah saw both the wrath and the mercy of God. He announced that judgment would come to Jerusalem and Judah (chap. 1) and to the gentile nations (chap. 2), but that God would be merciful to a remnant (chap. 3). In wrath, He would remember mercy (Hab. 3:2).

ZEPHANIAH 1

Preaching a message of judgment at a time of national religious reformation would not be easy; but a true prophet not only sees *farther,* he also sees *deeper.*

I will consume (1–7). God's wrath will consume His creation (vv. 2–3) and the hypocrites in the land (vv. 4–6). It will be a sacrificial feast, prepared for Babylon (v. 7; Jer. 46:10; Rev. 19:17–21).

I will punish (8–11). Starting at the royal palace, the prophet walked through the city and invited the people to lament with him. The merchants would be especially grieved because their ill-gotten wealth would be seized.

I will search (12–13). The people of Jerusalem would try to hide, but the invading soldiers would find them and slay them. The complacent would discover that their theology was all wrong. What a rude awakening!

I will bring distress (14–18). Note the words that describe this day, among them: *bitter, trouble, devastation, darkness,* and *alarm*. People will be treated like refuse!

Behind the literal fire that destroyed Jerusalem was the fire of God's jealous love over His people (v. 18; Nah. 1:2). Because of that love, He accepts no rivals and permits no rebellion.

ZEPHANIAH 2

Because of their sins, the nations around Judah would also feel the wrath of God. The other prophets had warned them that judgment was coming (Isa. 14—20; Jer. 46—49; Amos 1—2), but the Gentiles did not repent. The prophet used several agricultural images to describe their coming judgment: like chaff (v. 2), like a tree uprooted (v. 4), "overrun with weeds" (v. 9), like a desert (v. 13).

God would punish their mistreatment of His people (v. 8; Gen. 12:1–3), their pride (v. 10), and their worship of false gods (v. 11). God still punishes these sins today.

In His mercy, God called the people to turn from their sins and seek the Lord (vv. 1–3). The meek ones (God's remnant; 3:12) would be hidden in God and cared for during the day of wrath (1 Thess. 1:10; 5:9–10; Rev. 3:10). Are you among the humble or the haughty (v. 10)?

ZEPHANIAH 3

The rebellious (1–7). The leaders in Jerusalem would not listen to God's servants or heed God's warnings. When God corrected them, they only committed greater sin. The time had come for God to judge them. It does not pay to test the long-suffering of God or tempt Him.

The restored (8–13). The prophet looked ahead to the last days when the people would be regathered and restored to their land. They would call on Him, serve Him, and have nothing to fear.

The rejoicing (14–20). The people will rejoice and sing because their discipline is ended, the enemy has been defeated, and the Lord is King over Israel. But the Lord will also sing (v. 17)! Like a loving Father, He takes His fearful children in His arms and quiets them with His love. Note the repeated "I will" promises that God gives.

If we delight in the Lord and obey Him, He delights in us and shares His best with us. If we sin, He will chasten us in love. If we turn to Him in repentance, He will forgive us and restore our joy and peace: "I will heal their backsliding, I will love them freely" (Hos. 14:4).

HAGGAI

◆

In 538 B.C., about fifty thousand Jews left Babylon and returned to their homeland to rebuild the temple and restore the nation. In 536, they laid the foundation of the temple; but the work was stopped by their enemies and was not resumed until 520 under the preaching of Haggai and Zechariah. (Review Ezra 1—6.)

The book is comprised of four messages that Haggai gave during a period of four months. His purpose was to get the workers back on the job and to keep them working until the temple was completed. His first message called them to *be honest* (1:1–15) and put God's house ahead of their own houses. Then he appealed to them to *be strong* (2:1–9), *be clean* (2:10–19), and *be encouraged* (2:20–23).

Whenever God's work is being neglected, the preaching of the Word gets things going again.

❝The test of a preacher is that his congregation goes away saying, not 'What a lovely sermon!' but, 'I will do something!'**❞**

Francis de Sales

HAGGAI 1

Priorities (1–4). If Haggai could have used a New Testament text for his sermon, it would have been Matthew 6:33. It is *never* time to sacrifice to do the Lord's work, but it is *always* time to do things for ourselves.

Adversities (5–11). When we put God first, we have the promise of His care. But when we put self first, we lose His blessing *and* whatever we spent on ourselves! The people knew God's covenant with Israel. He promised to bless them if they obeyed His Word and to discipline them if they disobeyed (Lev. 26). You never lose when you put God first in your life.

Ministries (12–15). God used the Word to arouse the leaders and the people, and they began to rebuild the temple. Accomplishing God's work takes leaders and workers, both stirred by the Lord and walking in the fear of the Lord.

David asked, "If the foundations are destroyed, what can the righteous do?" (Ps. 11:3). *Get to work and lay the foundations again!*

HAGGAI 2

Three messages are presented in this chapter.

Be strong! (1–9). The times were hard, the people were poor, and the leaders were discouraged. (Was there ever an *easy* building program?) The restored temple would be nothing like the temple of Solomon, and the people were wondering, "Is it really worth it all?" They did not realize that the Lord of glory Himself would minister in this temple! Beware that golden memories do not rob you of present opportunities.

Be clean! (10–19). The priests could not share holiness, but they could spread sin. The people had been defiled, and God could not bless them; but now they had returned to the Lord, and He promised them His blessing.

Be encouraged! (20–23). This was addressed to their governor who is a type of the Lord Jesus Christ. In the latter days, God will overthrow the gentile powers and restore David's line, to which Zerubbabel belonged (Matt. 1:12). Perhaps the governor thought his work was unimportant because the temple was so ordinary, or because the nation was so small and weak; but he was part of the plan that would lead one day to the coming of the Messiah.

Your part in God's kingdom today is not insignificant or

unimportant, no matter how it appears to you. Be encouraged and keep working!

"Whereas the house of God today is no longer material but spiritual, the material is still a very real symbol of the spiritual. When the Church of God in any place in any locality is careless about the material place of assembly, the place of its worship and its work, it is a sign and evidence that its life is at a low ebb."

G. Campbell Morgan

ZECHARIAH

◆————————

The prophet Zechariah ministered with Haggai as they encouraged the Jewish remnant to rebuild the temple. God gave Zechariah *eight visions* concerning Jerusalem and the Jews (chaps. 1—6) and *two burdens* (oracles) about the nation's future (chaps. 9—14). Chapters 7—8 deal with a question about fasting.

The focus is on Jerusalem, which is named over forty times in the book, and the key text is, "I am zealous for Jerusalem and for Zion with great zeal" (1:14). The city seemed to be forsaken, but God would remember His people and keep His promises. (*Zechariah* means "God remembers.") For God's people, the best is yet to come!

Haggai and Zechariah worked together, yet each ministry was unique. Haggai's book is brief and records no visions; Zechariah wrote a long book containing eight visions. Haggai focused on the present work of the people; Zechariah challenged them to look ahead. Both kinds of ministry were needed then to encourage God's people to work, and both are needed today. Like Ezekiel and Jeremiah, Zechariah was also a priest (1:1; Neh. 12:1–4, 16).

ZECHARIAH 1

God's anger was directed against three targets.

The previous generation (1–6). Their sins had helped to bring about the ruin of the nation, but the new generation was committing the same sins. Sin has a way of following us and finally overtaking us, like a wild beast let loose on our trail. It is always time to repent.

The present generation (12). During the seventy years of captivity, the nation felt God's anger; but now the time had come for God to show mercy. His discipline had accomplished His purposes; now He would begin to heal and restore His people.

The complacent nations (7–21). God's angels patrol His earth and work on behalf of His people (Heb. 1:14). The nations were at peace, but Israel was still in difficulty. When God used the other nations to punish Israel, they were excessively cruel; now God would repay them. Horns are a symbol of power, and God would break the power of the nations.

The feeble remnant, working on the temple, must have been greatly encouraged by God's promise of mercy and help (vv. 14–17). Are you claiming His promises today?

ZECHARIAH 2

Promise (1–5). The act of measuring was an indication that God owned the city and had plans for it. No matter how discouraged the people of the Jewish remnant were, they could be sure that their work was not in vain. There was a glorious future for Jerusalem.

Proclamation (6–7). Many Jews still in Babylon should have returned to their land. Babylon was destined to fall (Jer. 50—51), but Jerusalem would have a new beginning. Why stay in a condemned city? But some believers today still choose to stay in the world (2 Cor. 6:14–18; Rev. 18:1–8).

Being Silent God called the Jews to sing, but He told the nations to be silent (2:13). Why? Because He was about to pour out His wrath on them for their sins. It was the lull before the storm. (See Hab. 2:20; Zeph. 1:7.)

Protection (8–9). The Lord speaks and promises to care for His people. The pupil of the eye is vulnerable and feels pain keenly. God cares for us because we are dear to Him (Deut. 32:10; Ps. 17:8; Prov. 7:2).

Praise (10–12). Their sighing would be turned into singing, for the Lord was coming *to* them and would dwell *with* them. He will claim His inheritance (Exod. 19:5), and they will know Him and serve Him. The covenant with Abraham (Gen. 12:1–3) will be fulfilled as the gentile nations come to the Lord because of the glory of God in Israel.

ZECHARIAH 3

When we come to God to be forgiven, what does He do for us?

He rebukes the enemy (1–2). Satan is the accuser (Rev. 12:10), but Christ is the Advocate (1 John 1:9—2:2). We are chosen by God and belong to Him, and the enemy cannot condemn us (Rom. 8:31–39). The Spirit convicts in love to woo us back to God. Satan accuses us in hatred to make us despair of God's help. Be sure to distinguish these two voices.

He removes the iniquity (3–5). The dirty garments symbolized the sinfulness of the nation, for the high priest was to keep himself clean before the Lord. God removes our sin and clothes us anew because Jesus died for our sins and lives to intercede for us.

He restores the ministry (6–10). God did not set Joshua aside, for the purpose of restoration is ministry. God told him to go back and minister to the people and tell them about the coming Messiah, the BRANCH. Just as Joshua was cleansed and restored, so Israel will be cleansed and restored when Messiah comes to reign (vv. 9–10; 12:10—13:1).

In the Words of Zechariah

In the prophecy of Zechariah, the Lord Jesus Christ is presented as the BRANCH (3:8; 6:12; Isa. 11:1), the Stone (3:9; 10:4; Isa. 28:16), the King (9:9; 14:9, 16–17), and the rejected Shepherd (11:12; 13:7).

ZECHARIAH 4

Zechariah ministered to discouraged people attempting to accomplish a difficult task. If you find yourself ready to quit, consider the assurances God gives His workers.

God provides power (1–6, 11–14). Oil is symbolic of God's Holy Spirit, and He alone can give us the power to finish His work. Are you depending on Him or on your own strength and expertise? Ponder Ephesians 3:20–21.

God removes obstacles (7). Unbelief makes mountains out of molehills, but faith in God makes mountains into plains! The leaders faced all kinds of obstacles, but God would open the way for them. (See Isa. 41:15; Matt. 17:20.)

God gives promises (9). God finishes what He starts (Phil. 1:6; Heb. 12:1–2), so we can trust Him even in the midst of opposition. The temple project was delayed for many years, but God eventually helped them finish it.

God rejoices over our work (10). To the eyes of men, the temple project was but a small thing (Hag. 2:3); but to the eyes of God, it was a source of great joy. Do your work to please God and let Him be the final judge (1 Cor. 4:5).

Small Things

God delights in using small things: Moses' rod (Exod. 4:2), David's sling (1 Sam. 17), a jawbone (Judg. 15:15), a hammer and a tent peg (Judg. 4:17–24), a piece of rope (Josh. 2:15–21), a basket (Acts 9:23–25), loaves and fish (John 6:9), a cup of cold water (Matt. 10:42), and even mud (John 9:6–7).

ZECHARIAH 5—6

Wickedness condemned (5:1–4). The scroll was fifteen feet by thirty feet, so it could easily be seen and read. God condemned the thieves and the liars. (Satan is both; John 8:44.)

These sins are violations of the third and the eighth commandments and are still condemned by God (Eph. 4:25–28).

Wickedness confined (5:5–11). In the end times, there will be a concentration of evil at Babylon, that last expression of the evil world system (Rev. 17—18). The word *wickedness* is feminine in Hebrew, which explains why a woman was used as the illustration.

Wickedness controlled (6:1–8). The vision parallels Zechariah 1:7–11 and reminds us that God's angelic servants patrol the earth. The Jews frequently were invaded from the north, but God was keeping those nations at rest so the remnant could build the temple.

Messianic Titles

"The BRANCH" is an important messianic title, signifying our Lord's coming from the stock of David (Isa. 11:1). As Branch, He is King (Jer. 23:5; 33:15), God's Servant (Zech. 3:8), "the Man whose name is the BRANCH" (Zech. 6:12), and "the Branch of the LORD" (Isa. 4:2). Some see in these four titles a parallel to the four Gospels. Matthew presents the Branch of David, the King; Mark, the Servant; Luke, the Man; and John, "the Branch of the Lord" who is God come in human flesh (John 20:30–31).

Wickedness conquered (6:9–15). Three Jews from Babylon came to Jerusalem with gold and silver for the temple. But God told Zechariah to make a crown and put it on Joshua and make him a king-priest! No Jewish priest had ever reigned as king, and no king was permitted to serve as a priest (2 Chron. 26:16–21). All of this was symbolic of the coming Messiah, the King-Priest (Ps. 110:4; Heb. 7:1–3) who would reign from the future glorious temple (Ezek. 40ff.). Just as the three men brought gifts from afar, so the Gentiles would bring gifts to help build the future temple (Isa. 60:4–7).

As Haggai encouraged the people in their daily work, Zechariah urged them to live "in the future tense" and work because they were a part of God's glorious future. A "blessed hope" is a great motivation for service and faithfulness (Titus 2:11–15).

ZECHARIAH 7

While in Babylon, the Jews started a new tradition: fasting on the ninth day of the fifth month to commemorate the destruction of Jerusalem. But a remnant was now rebuilding the city and the temple, and the prophets said that an even greater city and temple were yet to come. Should this fast be continued?

There is nothing wrong with traditions that do not involve practices contrary to the Word of God. But it is good to examine these traditions from time to time just to make sure they are meaningful.

Are we doing this unto the Lord? Or is it just a ceremony that we endure regularly? If the Lord is left out, the tradition lacks both life and heart. (See Rom. 14:1–9.)

Does doing this help us serve others? The fast God wants is not an annual ceremony but a daily way of life. It means showing compassion and mercy and helping the poor and needy. God wants mercy, not sacrifice (Hos. 6:6; Amos 5:21–24; Mic. 6:8; Matt. 15:1–9).

Does doing this make us obedient to His Word? The previous generation carried out their traditions but hardened their hearts to the Word of God. Are we doing the same thing?

ZECHARIAH 8

Zechariah is still answering the question about the fast, but he uses this opportunity to encourage the Jews in their work. "Do not fear!" (vv. 13, 15) is the emphasis of this brief message, and he gave them three promises to encourage them.

God will restore Jerusalem (1–8). He looked beyond that present day to the day when Messiah would come, establish His kingdom, and make Jerusalem a city of truth and peace. The old would sit safely in the sunny streets, and the children would play without fear.

God will prosper your work (9–17). The people had not been faithful to God, so He had withheld His blessing (Hag. 1:1–11); but now He would prosper their labors, bless them, and make them a blessing (1 Cor. 15:58).

God will turn fasting into feasting (18–23). In the future kingdom, there will be no need for fasting. The events of the past will be forgotten in the glory of the worship of the Lord. Jesus came to bring us joy, not sorrow (Matt. 9:14–17).

Traditions — *The only fast God required of the Jews was on the annual Day of Atonement (Lev. 16:29). The four fasts mentioned in Zechariah 8:19 commemorated (in order) the breaching of Jerusalem's walls, the burning of the temple, the assassination of Gedaliah (Jer. 41), and the beginning of the siege of Jerusalem. The nation was adept at developing new religious traditions, but it was not good at obeying the Word of God.*

ZECHARIAH 9—14

Zechariah closes his book by giving two oracles (burdens) that focus on the future history of Israel.

Chapters 9—11 deal primarily with Christ's first coming when He presented Himself to His people (9:9) and was rejected (11:12). Events leading up to His coming include the conquests of Alexander the Great (9:1–8) and conflicts during the time of the Maccabees, 168–134 B.C. (9:14–17). Daniel 8:9–14 also touches on this latter period. Israel under Roman rule is seen in chapter 11.

Chapters 12—14 highlight Messiah's second coming and the establishing of His glorious kingdom on earth. The key phrase is "in that day." Zechariah describes the events that will take place "in that day" when Christ returns to earth. When the nations gather together against Jerusalem, He will come in power and deliver His people. The nation will recognize Him, repent, and be cleansed; and Jesus Christ will reign as King from Jerusalem.

Symbolism appears often in chapters 9—14, and at times the prophet refers to our Lord's first and second advents in succeeding verses; but this is not unusual in prophetic literature (Isa. 9:6, for example). As you read, see Christ in His grace and glory, and rejoice in His promised victory.

ZECHARIAH 9

The spread of Alexander's kingdom (vv. 1–8) helped to prepare the way for the birth of the Lord Jesus. God controls history and uses it to accomplish His purposes. Events in the news today, depressing as they may seem, are all in the hands of God.

Verse 9 was fulfilled when Jesus rode into Jerusalem (Matt. 21:1–11); verse 10 will not be fulfilled until He returns and sets up His kingdom. Israel rejected her own King and said (as people do today), "We have no king but Caesar!"

Verses 11–17 focus on the future deliverance of God's people. It will be like releasing prisoners from a pit (v. 11), gathering a scattered flock, putting jewels in a crown, and assembling a conquering army (vv. 16–17). What a glorious day that will be!

God appeals in verse 12 to the Jews still in Babylon, urging them to return to their people and their land. He promises twice as much blessing to those who will obey Him, so be sure you are in the place of His choosing.

ZECHARIAH 10—11

These two chapters portray Israel as God's flock and their leaders as shepherds.

The faithful Shepherd (chap. 10). The flock was in trouble because it had no shepherd care for it. But the Lord will return and be the Shepherd. He will rescue the people, strengthen them, and establish them in peace.

The false shepherds (11:1–14). The leaders were not true to God or their people, and God sent ruin (vv. 1–3). The flock was destined for slaughter (the Roman conquest in A.D. 70), division (the broken rod), and dispersion among the Gentiles. The prophet is a picture of the true Shepherd who cares for the flock, is rejected by the false shepherds, and is sold like a slave (vv. 12–13; Exod. 21:32; Matt. 26:14–16).

The foolish shepherd (11:15–17). This is the last world ruler, Antichrist, whom Israel will accept as their friend. He will agree to protect Israel but then will break his promise (Dan. 9:27). When you reject the true, it is much easier to accept the false (John 5:43). But God will strike the false shepherd and judge him (Rev. 19:11–21).

Jeremiah stated, "It is not in man who walks to direct his steps" (Jer. 10:23). We all need a shepherd, so be sure you follow the right one.

God's Strength	When God gives strength to His people, they become victorious. The sheep becomes a war horse (Zech. 10:3), and the worm becomes a threshing machine (Isa. 41:14–16). The feeblest person can be a hero like David (Zech. 12:8) when you go in the strength of the Lord.

ZECHARIAH 12

The phrase "in that day" used frequently in chapters 12—14 refers to the time of the end when "the day of the LORD" will climax with the return of Jesus Christ to the earth to defeat His enemies, deliver Israel, and establish His kingdom.

Jerusalem will be at the center of world attention. Note the images of Jerusalem that the prophet used: a cup of strong wine that will make the nations drunk (v. 2); a heavy stone that will crush the nations (v. 3); and a firepan and torch that will devour the nations (v. 6). Those who attack Israel will only defeat themselves, for God has covenanted to protect Israel (Gen. 12:1–3).

When the people of Israel see the Messiah (v. 10), they will recognize Him (Matt. 24:30; Rev. 1:7), repent, and be cleansed and forgiven. Their sorrow will exceed the sorrow displayed at the tragic death of godly King Josiah (v. 11; 2 Chron. 35:20–27).

Like God's people Israel, we experience many trials and testings; but the Lord will see us through and share His kingdom and glory with us (Acts 14:22).

ZECHARIAH 13

The fountain (1–6). The defiled will be cleansed of sin (Jer. 31:31–34), and the deceived will have all their idols and false prophets removed. Verse 6 refers not to Jesus Christ but to a false prophet who has wounded his body in some religious ritual (1 Kings 18:28). He tries to prove that he is not a prophet because he wants to escape judgment.

The flock (7). To save His flock, the Good Shepherd must be smitten, and that means suffering and death (Isa. 53:4, 10; Matt. 26:31). The next time you are smitten because of your faith, remember that your Shepherd felt it before you did (Matt. 5:38–42; 10:16–26).

The furnace (8–9). Israel's terrible suffering at the close of the age will be like a refining furnace, separating the true from the false (Isa. 48:10). Suffering in the will of God can be a time of purification when we can bring glory to God (Job 23:10).

ZECHARIAH 14

The prophet describes the great campaign that we call the Battle of Armageddon (Rev. 14:17–20; 16:14–16), when the nations of the world will gather against Jerusalem.

See the demonstrations of His power! He will make changes in the heavens (vv. 6–7) and the earth (vv. 3–5), and will send a plague that will frighten and destroy the enemy

(vv. 12–15). He will cause a river to flow that will restore and refresh the land (Ezek. 47).

Zechariah proclaimed, "And the LORD shall be King over all the earth" (v. 9)! Our prayer "Thy kingdom come" will be answered, and we shall reign with Him (Rev. 5:10; 20:6). The nations will "worship the King" (vv. 16–17), and even ordinary items like harnesses and kitchen pots will be holy to the Lord. No outsiders will be there to defile God's holy temple (v. 21).

The Feast of Tabernacles was Israel's most joyful celebration (Lev. 23:33–44), so the kingdom age will be a time of holiness and happiness in worshiping and serving the Lord.

MALACHI

$\blacklozenge$

Ministering about four centuries before Christ, Malachi encountered the same religious situation described in Ezra 9—10 and Nehemiah 8—13. The people were backslidden, the priests were worldly, and the nation was far from God. The name *Malachi* means "my messenger" (2:7; 3:1).

Because the promised kingdom did not come immediately, the Jews questioned God's love (1:2) and justice (2:17) and complained about the way He was treating His chosen people. It was not long before the priests grew careless in their ministry, and the people followed their bad example.

The book may be outlined as follows:

1. God questions their love (1:1–5)
2. God condemns their sins (1:6—2:17)
   a) Despising His name (1:6–14)
   b) Profaning His covenant (2:1–17)
3. God seeks their repentance (3:1—4:6)

We know nothing about Malachi the person; he does not even tell us his father's name as prophets usually do. But after all, he was a messenger; the important thing about a messenger is the message. Malachi was concerned about being faithful, not being famous.

MALACHI 1

Six times the Lord refers to *His name* (vv. 6, 11, 14), which means His character and His reputation. He wants His name to be magnified in all the earth (v. 5). The priests, however, despised His name, and He rebuked them for it. How do we despise the Lord's name?

We show disrespect to His name by questioning His love

(vv. 1–5). The times were tough, and the people blamed the situation on God. But their own sins had created their problems (Hag. 1), and God was willing to bless if they were willing to repent.

We despise His name by doing His work in a careless manner (vv. 7–11). They were bored with their blessings, and doing the work of the Lord wearied them.

Along with that, we despise the Lord's name when we offer Him less than our best (vv. 12–14). They offered defective sacrifices, animals that they would never give as gifts to their friends. They even brought sacrifices that were stolen! "I will not take what is yours for the LORD," said David, "nor offer burnt offerings with that which costs me nothing" (1 Chron. 21:24).

Beware when you get bored with your blessings and start taking for granted the privilege of ministry. God may take your privileges away from you.

MALACHI 2

The emphasis is on *covenants* (vv. 4, 5, 8, 10, 14); three are mentioned specifically.

The covenant with Levi (1–9). God gave the priesthood to the tribe of Levi and told them to teach and obey the law of the Lord. But they corrupted the covenant and disobeyed His Word, and God had to judge them by cursing their blessings. Their blessing of the people would turn out to be a curse (Num. 6:23–27), and Israel would bring trouble instead of blessing to the world (Deut. 28).

The covenant with Israel (10–12). This was made at Sinai when the nation was "married to Jehovah" (Exod. 19–20). But His bride was not faithful to Him because she committed adultery with false gods. Jeremiah warned about this (Jer. 2), and it is the underlying theme of the book of Hosea.

The covenant of marriage (13–17). The men were divorcing their wives and marrying foreign women (Exod. 34:10–17; Ezra 10), a sin that led even King Solomon into idolatry (1 Kings 11). The marriage covenant involves the husband and the wife *and God,* and He expects us to be faithful. The unfaithful husbands could weep and bring sacrifices (v. 13), but God would not accept them.

We expect God to be faithful to keep His word. Why do we think we have the privilege of not keeping our promises?

Blessings and Curses

God is able to turn curses into blessings (Neh. 13:2) and blessings into curses (Mal. 2:1–2). It is painful enough when God removes His blessings from us; but when He turns those blessings into curses, the pain is terrible.

The Extent of Sin

"Have we not all one Father?" (Mal. 2:10) does not mean that everybody is a child of God and therefore going to heaven. The context is Jewish: God created the nation and claimed Israel as His firstborn (Isa. 63:16; Exod. 4:22). When the Jewish men divorced their wives to marry heathen women, they were sinning not only against God but also against their brethren (1 Thess. 4:1–8).

MALACHI 3

Refining (1–5). As is often done in the prophetic Scriptures, events from our Lord's first advent (v. 1) are combined with events to take place at His second advent (vv. 2–5). The messenger was John the Baptist (Matt. 11:7–10) who prepared the way for the Lord (Isa. 40:3; John 1:23). When Christ comes as Judge, He will purify Israel, especially the priests, and will judge the sinners.

Returning (6–7). God does not change; therefore, He kept His covenant and did not destroy Israel, though she deserved it. The faithfulness of God sustains us (Lam. 3:22–24).

Robbing (8–15). Not only did the people bring the Lord defective sacrifices, but they failed to bring tithes and offerings commanded by the Law. Consequently, He cursed their blessings (2:2) and destroyed their crops. *When we rob God, we only rob ourselves.* We cannot keep anything that rightfully belongs to God.

Remembering (16–18). There is always a faithful remnant who fears the Lord, obeys Him, ponders His truth, and exercises spiritual discernment. God sees those people and keeps a record of their names. They are His jewels, and they will be spared in the coming day of judgment.

MALACHI 4

Burning (1). The day of the Lord will be a time of fierce judgment on the earth, and the wicked will be burned like stubble. The fire of God's jealousy will burn (Zeph. 1:18).

Fire

In Scripture, fire is often associated with judgment, for it is a symbol of the holy wrath of God. Fire consumed God's enemies (2 Kings 1) as well as His servants who disobeyed Him (Lev. 10:1–3). He has reserved the world for a judgment of fire (2 Pet. 3:10), and hell is compared to a lake of fire (Rev. 20:10, 14; 21:8) and a furnace of fire (Matt. 13:42, 50). Jesus often spoke of the fiery judgment that awaits those who do not trust Him (Matt. 5:22; 18:8–9; 25:41; Mark 9:44–48). When He returns to judge the world, He will come "in flaming fire" (2 Thess. 1:8). It behooves us to be ready and to share the Gospel with others.

Healing (2–3). "Sun of Righteousness" is a title for Jesus Christ (Ps. 84:11). He is to His people what the sun is to our galaxy: the center of all things and the source of life and light (John 1:4). The same Sun that brings burning to the lost will bring blessing to the saved.

Obeying (4–6). Malachi pointed back to the Law and commanded Israel to obey and be prepared for what God was going to do. Then he pointed ahead to the ministry of Elijah, which was fulfilled in a spiritual sense in John the Baptist (Luke 1:16–17; Matt. 17:10–13). It may be fulfilled literally if Elijah is one of the two witnesses described in Revelation 11:1–13.

The Old Testament ends with the awesome word *curse*. At the close of the New Testament, the promise is, "And there shall be no more curse" (Rev. 22:3). What made the difference? On the cross, Jesus Christ was made a curse for us (Gal. 3:13).

❝Men are not in hell because God is angry with them: they are in wrath and darkness because they have done to the light, which infinitely flows forth from God, as that man does to the light of the sun who puts out his own eyes.**❞**

William Law

THE FOUR GOSPELS

The word *gospel* means "good news." It is the message that Jesus Christ forgives the sins of all who trust in Him (1 Cor. 15:1–11; Gal. 1:6–9). *Gospel* also refers to the first four books of the New Testament, which present the life and teachings of the Savior. Apart from Jesus Christ—who He is, what He taught, and what He did—there can be no good news for lost sinners (Acts 4:12).

The four Gospels are not biographies in the modern sense of the word nor do they tell us everything about Jesus (John 20:30–31). Led by the Spirit, the authors selected material that helped them accomplish their purpose for writing.

Matthew wrote primarily for the Jews and explained that Jesus Christ is the Messiah who fulfills the Old Testament prophecies. Mark directed his book to the Romans and pictured Jesus as the active Servant of the Lord. Luke wrote for the Greeks and presented Jesus as the perfect and compassionate Son of man. John had the whole world in mind when he wrote and presented Jesus as Son of God and Savior of the world.

The first three Gospels give a somewhat parallel account of the life of Jesus and therefore are called "synoptic Gospels." (The word *synoptic* means "to see together.") John's gospel, written much later, contains material that supplements the accounts by the synoptic writers. Each gospel is unique, and all four are needed to provide a well-rounded view of the life, teachings, and works of Jesus Christ.

MATTHEW

$\blacklozenge$

Matthew ("gift of God") was a Jewish tax collector who obeyed Christ's call and became one of the original twelve apostles (Matt. 9:9–13). His given name was Levi (Luke 5:27).

Writing especially for the Jews, Matthew proves that Jesus Christ is the Son of David, the Messiah, the rightful heir to David's throne. At least 129 Old Testament quotations and allusions appear in his gospel, and the word *kingdom* is found over fifty times. Matthew's gospel stands first in the New Testament as the perfect bridge between the old covenant and the new, Israel and the church, prophecy and fulfillment.

The King presented Himself to His people (chaps. 1—10), but the religious leaders resisted Him (chaps. 11—13). The King therefore withdrew from the crowds with His disciples to prepare them for His coming arrest and crucifixion (chaps. 14—20). He was rejected and crucified (chaps. 21—27), but He arose from the dead and commissioned His disciples to take His message to the whole world (chap. 28).

As you read Matthew's gospel, you will be impressed with the authority of Jesus Christ over disease, demons, circumstances, and even death. He has authority over our lives, and we should follow Him in obedience.

MATTHEW 1

A special book (1). The Old Testament is "the book of the genealogy of Adam" (Gen. 5:1), but the New Testament is "the book of the genealogy of Jesus Christ." In fact, the genealogy of Jesus Christ is the last one given in the Bible, here and in Luke 3:23–28. The important thing is not your *first* birth but your *second* birth (John 3).

A special providence (2–17). What may be to some readers

a boring list of difficult names is actually the record of God's working throughout the ages to bring His Son to earth. God ruled and overruled and fulfilled His great promises. In the same way, He will keep His promises and send Jesus back again.

A special Child (18–25). The birth of Jesus was different from every other birth: He was conceived by the Spirit in Mary's womb and born with a sinless nature. He is "God with us," and He is also God *like us* because He took our nature and entered into human life and experience. What a wonderful Savior!

The Virgin Birth

The virgin birth of Jesus Christ is vital to the truth of the gospel (Isa. 7:14). Since Jesus Christ is God, He existed before Mary; therefore, He could not have been conceived as are other babies. He was not only born, but He "came into the world" (John 18:37). He is both God and man, the sinless Lamb of God (1 Pet. 1:19). Matthew opens and closes his book with "God with us" (1:23; 28:20).

MATTHEW 2

What were the responses to His birth?

Creation responded by putting a miraculous star in the heavens to tell the world a King had been born (Num. 24:17).

The Gentiles responded by worshiping Him and bringing Him gifts. Matthew shows early in his book that Jesus came to save Gentiles as well as Jews. The wise men were astrologer-scientists who studied the heavens. The star led them to the Scriptures, and the Scriptures led them to the Savior. (See Ps. 19.) God speaks to us in ways we can understand.

Herod responded with fear and deception. He wanted no new King to threaten his reign.

The chief priests and scribes gave the right information but the wrong response. They were only five miles away from the Messiah, yet they refused to go to see Him! What good is it to understand Bible prophecy if it doesn't make a difference in your life?

The Magi

The wise men (Magi) were scientists, yet they saw no conflict between science and Scripture or between searching for truth and worshiping the Savior. Devout Christians can worship the Lord with the mind as well as the heart (Matt. 22:37). "Science without religion is lame," said Albert Einstein. "Religion without science is blind."

MATTHEW 3

John the Baptist was a model preacher. He was a *road builder* who prepared the way for the Lord (v. 3; Isa. 40:3), and an *axman* who got to the root of sin and exposed it (v. 10). He was not intimidated by people, nor was he afraid to preach about judgment (v. 12). He was obedient to his Lord and magnified Him in all things (John 3:30).

Some people heard God's Word and confessed their sins (vv. 5–6), while others heard it and covered their sins (vv. 7–9; Prov. 28:13). The first group became children of God, but the second group were children of the devil (v. 7; John 8:44).

Jesus is the Son of God. The Scriptures (v. 3), John the Baptist (v. 11), the Holy Spirit (v. 16), and the Father (v. 17) attested to that truth.

Significance of Baptism

Jesus was not baptized to confess any sins (v. 5), since He was sinless. His baptism was His presentation to Israel (John 1:31) as well as a picture of His future baptism on the cross when "all the waves and billows" of judgment would go over Him (Matt. 20:22; Ps. 42:7). The baptism of John looked forward to the coming of Messiah (Acts 19:1–7). Christian baptism today looks back to the death, burial, and resurrection of Jesus Christ and witnesses of the believer's identification with Him (Col. 2:12; Acts 10:47–48).

MATTHEW 4

The Victor (1–11). Public ministry is built on private victory. Our Lord was not tempted so that God could examine Him, for the Father had already approved Him (3:17). He was tempted for our sake, that He might personally know temptation and be able to help us when we are tempted (Heb. 2:17–18; 4:15). He overcame the devil by using the same weapons available to us today: the Word of God ("It is written"), the power of the Spirit (v. 1; Luke 4:1), and prayer (Luke 3:21; 1 Cor. 10:13).

The Master (12–22). Having defeated "the strong man," Jesus now invaded his house and began to spoil his goods (12:24–30). He both obeyed the Word (vv. 15–16; Isa. 9:1–2) and preached it, calling men to become His disciples. Everyone must decide whether to follow Christ or make bargains with the devil (vv. 8–10). What is *your* decision?

The Healer (23–25). Our Lord's main ministry was teaching and preaching, but His compassion moved Him to minister to the physical needs of the people. How tragic that most of the people who followed Him wanted His services but not His salvation, the gifts but not the Giver; and these people are with us today.

> **"**Let no man think himself to be holy because he is not tempted, for the holiest and highest in life have the most temptations. How much higher the hill is, so much is the wind there greater; so, how much higher the life is, so much the stronger is the temptation of the enemy.**"**

John Wycliffe

THE SERMON ON THE MOUNT

The Sermon on the Mount was our Lord's "ordination sermon" for His apostles (Luke 6:12ff.). The theme is God's righteousness as contrasted with the hypocritical righteousness of the scribes and Pharisees (5:17-20; Matt. 23). The sermon is not a second Law with new commandments. It goes much deeper than the Law because it deals with internal attitudes as well as outward actions. It presents a picture of the truly righteous person and shows the spiritual principles that control his or her life.

Jesus opened the sermon with a description of the truly righteous person (5:1-16). Then He defined what sin is (5:21-48) and what real righteousness is in the areas of worship (6:1-18) and wealth (6:19-34). He concluded with warnings against making hypocritical judgments (7:1-12), following false prophets (7:13-20), and failing to obey God's will (7:21-29).

You are not saved by trying to obey the Sermon on the Mount any more than you are saved by trying to keep the Ten Commandments. Because they involve inner attitudes, the demands of the Sermon on the Mount are much more difficult than those found in the law of Moses. Only the true believer in Jesus Christ can put the Sermon on the Mount into practice (Rom. 8:1-4).

MATTHEW 5

Citizens (1–12). We enter the kingdom through the new birth (John 3:1–16), but we enjoy the kingdom by living for those things that please God the most (6:33). The world (and worldly believers) would disagree with Christ's description of a blessed (happy) person, but the description is true just the same. God majors on character, and so should we.

Salt and light (13–16). Tasteless salt and hidden light are good for nothing! Salt arrests decay in our world, and light banishes darkness. Salt is hidden, but light is visible. Both are needed in the world, and both must give of themselves in order to serve.

Worshipers (17–26). If you bring anger to the altar, you cannot worship God, so get rid of the anger quickly. Angry feelings lead to angry words and deeds, and the result could be murder. (See Eph. 4:25–32.)

Surgeons (27–32). Obviously Jesus is not suggesting literal surgery, for the real problem is in the heart (v. 28). This is a vivid reminder that sin is terrible, and we are better off "maimed" than whole and going to hell. Deal drastically with sin!

Children of the Father (33–48). "What do you do more than others?" (v. 47). We must measure ourselves not by others but by the Father (v. 48). This includes our words (vv. 33–37), our responses to injuries (vv. 38–42), and our dealings with our enemies (vv. 43–48).

❝In taking revenge, a man is but even with his enemy; but in passing it over, he is superior.**❞**

Francis Bacon

MATTHEW 6

Praise (1–4). We should give only to please God and receive His praise. If we give to win the praise of others, or to be able to compliment ourselves (v. 3), we get the *immediate* reward—

praise—but we lose the *eternal* reward. We cannot get our reward twice, so we must decide which one we want.

Prayer (5–15). Our public praying is only as good as our private praying, and our private praying should be secret (vv. 5–6), sincere (vv. 7–8), and systematic (vv. 9–13). The Lord's Prayer is a pattern for us to follow so that we will put God's concerns first and not forget to forgive others.

Possessions (16–34). We need *things* to live (v. 32), and God provides these things for us (v. 33); but acquiring things must not be the main goal of life. You are living for things when they capture your heart (vv. 19–21), divide your mind (vv. 22–23), and control your will (v. 24); and the result of this is *worry*. The solution is to put God first and start living with eternity's values in view.

Treasures in Heaven

We lay up treasures in heaven when we consider that all we have belongs to God and we use it to magnify His righteousness and advance His kingdom (Matt. 6:33). It means much more than merely giving offerings to God, although that is important. It means total stewardship of life so that God is in complete control and our one desire is to glorify Him. This is the secret of a unified life (Matt. 6:24) free of worry.

MATTHEW 7

Judges (1–12). One of the easiest ways to cover our sins is to judge others. It is not wrong to exercise discernment (v. 6), but we must start with ourselves. Often we are guilty of the sins we think we see in others (Rom. 2:1–3). We need prayer and love if we are to perform successful "eye surgery" on our brothers and sisters. We must treat them the way we want them to treat us.

Pilgrims (13–14). The gate into real life is narrow, and the way is difficult, so don't try to carry a lot of excess baggage. False teachers make the way easy and popular; if you truly follow Jesus, you pay a price and the way sometimes becomes lonely.

Trees (15–20). Life produces fruit, and good trees produce good fruit. There was a great deal of profession in the lives of the scribes and Pharisees, but no evidence of spiritual fruit.

Builders (21–29). To "build on the rock" means to obey the Word of God. *Saying* is not enough; there must be *doing* (James 1:22–25). If you claim to be a disciple of Jesus Christ, expect to have your profession tested in this life and the next. Fair-weather faith will not pass the test.

MATTHEW 8—9

In these two chapters, Matthew assembled several of our Lord's miracles and recorded them as proof that Jesus is the promised Messiah (1 Cor. 1:22; Isa. 35:4–6). In 8:17, he quoted Isaiah 53:4 and applied it to Christ's healing ministry while He was on earth. Some helpful lessons are evident in these miracles.

Growing in Your Faith

Some people have "no faith" (Mark 4:40), while others have "little faith" (Matt. 6:30). God wants us to have "great faith" (Matt. 8:10; 15:28). Faith is like a seed that grows if it is planted and cultivated in the heart (Matt. 17:20). The Word of God encourages faith (Rom. 10:17). As you exercise your faith in times of trial and testing, your faith grows and you glorify God (James 1:1–8; 1 Pet. 1:1–9). It is faith, not feeling, that gives the victory (1 John 5:1–5).

God is concerned with individuals. Jesus did not minister only to crowds (8:1; 9:36); He had time for individuals. He had compassion on people shunned by others. Peter and John had this same spirit: they ministered to thousands (Acts 2) and also took time for one beggar (Acts 3).

God can meet every need. Nothing is too hard for the Lord (Jer. 32:17). He can heal the sick and afflicted, calm the storm, cast out demons, and even raise the dead. Do you cast *every* care on Him (1 Pet. 5:7)?

Peter and Jesus

The healing of Peter's mother-in-law was the first of several miracles that Jesus performed especially for Peter. On two occasions, He enabled Peter to catch many fish (Luke 5:1–11; John 21:1–8), and He even helped him catch one fish with a coin in its mouth (Matt. 17:24–27). Jesus enabled Peter to walk on the water (Matt. 14:22–33). When Peter cut off the ear of Malchus, Jesus healed it (Luke 22:50–53); and He delivered Peter from prison and death (Acts 12). No wonder Peter wrote, "Casting all your care upon Him, for He cares for you" (1 Pet. 5:7).

God responds to faith. The centurion had *great* faith (8:10), while the disciples were guilty of *little* faith (8:26). The men who brought their friend exercised *cooperative* faith (9:2), while the sick woman had almost *superstitious* faith (9:21). Christ asks you the same question He asked the two blind men: "Do you believe that I am able to do this?" (9:28). What is your reply?

God's greatest concern is the salvation of sinners. The healing of the sick is a great miracle, and the raising of the dead an even greater one; but the salvation of the lost soul is the greatest miracle of all, Jesus is the Great Physician who came to heal sinners (9:12–13), the Bridegroom who invites sinners to the wedding feast (9:14–17), and the Good Shepherd who has compassion on the struggling sheep (9:35–36).

God calls us to help Him reach the lost. Peter opened his home and Jesus healed many there (8:14–16), and Matthew used his home to introduce his friends to Jesus (9:9–17). The blind men who were healed spread the news about Jesus to the whole country (9:31). Jesus is seeking disciples (8:18–22) and harvesters (9:37–38) to help Him get the job done.

MATTHEW 10

If you start to pray for laborers (9:38), beware: you may become an answer to your own prayer! You pray, and then you are sent out!

Some of these instructions applied mainly to the apostles (vv. 5–15) and some to those serving just before the Lord's return (vv. 16–23). However, spiritual principles are here for all God's servants.

Christ calls and equips. If the Lord calls you, He will equip you for the task He wants you to fulfill. It has well been said, "The will of God does not send you where the grace of God cannot keep you."

Christ does not promise an easy life. It is a wonderful privilege to be an ambassador for the King, but there is a price to pay. We are sheep among wolves (v. 16), sword-bearers (vv. 34–36), and cross-bearers (vv. 37–39). The world hates us because it hates Him (vv. 24–25; Phil. 3:10).

Christ wants us to give freely to others (8). The apostles had power to do miracles, but even giving a cup of cold water is service to the Lord (v. 42). Everything we have is a gift from God (John 3:27; 1 Cor. 4:7) and must be shared lovingly with others. We must live by faith and trust Him to provide.

Christ can take away all fear. If you fear God, you need fear nothing else (vv. 27–31; Ps. 112). You are precious to your Father, and He will care for you. God's servants are immortal until their work is done.

Review the chapter and mark the promises you need to claim today.

MATTHEW 11

John the Baptist was perplexed and perhaps discouraged. He had served God faithfully and yet was in prison. His work was ended, and he was not sure that Jesus was ministering in the right way. When you find yourself in a similar situation, do what John did: tell it to Jesus and wait for His word (vv. 4–6; Isa. 35:4–6). Isaiah 50:10 is a great promise to claim in dark days of disappointment.

John's disciples did not hear Jesus praise their leader. John was not a compromiser (a reed) or a celebrity; he was God's greatest prophet. John was in prison because of a cruel king and a crowd that was childish (vv. 16–19) instead of childlike (v. 25).

Leave the judgment to the Lord (vv. 20–24), and wait for Him to fulfill His perfect plan. You may think you have failed, but God will see to it that your work is blessed. In fact, John won people to Jesus long after he was dead and buried (John 10:40–42)! Surrender to Christ's loving yoke and you will experience His perfect rest (vv. 25–30).

MATTHEW 12

Hostility (1–8). The religious leaders were waiting for an opportunity to attack Jesus, and He deliberately gave it to them. What a tragedy to be burdened by legalism when you could enjoy the true Sabbath rest (11:28–30)! When Jesus is your Lord, all of life becomes a Sabbath and every place is God's temple, even a grain field.

Hypocrisy (9–14). The Pharisees were concerned about keeping the Sabbath but not about showing love to a man with a handicapping condition. Jesus wants mercy, not sacrifice (v. 7; Hos. 6:6; Mic. 6:6–8). Do you *use* people or *serve* them?

Victory (15–32). Jesus is the Stronger Man who has invaded Satan's house, overcome him, taken his weapons, and is now claiming his spoils (Eph. 1:15–23; Col. 2:15). Put on the armor and join Him in victory (Eph. 6:10ff.).

Neutrality (43–50). Beware an empty life! It is a standing invitation for Satan to go to work. In the spiritual war being waged today, you cannot be neutral. You are either for Him or against Him.

The Unpardonable Sin

The unpardonable sin is committed by people who resist the work of the Spirit and reject His witness concerning Jesus. It is a sin of the heart, not the lips, because what we say comes from the heart (Matt. 12:33–37). When the religious leaders allowed John the Baptist to be arrested and slain, they sinned against God the Father who sent him. When they crucified Christ, they sinned against God the Son. Jesus asked for their forgiveness (Luke 23:34), and God gave them another chance. When they persecuted the apostles and then killed Stephen, they sinned against the Holy Spirit who was working through them (Acts 7:51). That sin against the Spirit brought about the downfall of the nation. God can forgive all sins except the sin of rejecting His Son (John 3:36). God's children cannot commit an unpardonable sin, for all of their sins were forgiven when they trusted Jesus Christ (John 3:18; Rom. 8:1; Col. 2:13).

MATTHEW 13

These parables explain how God is at work in the world today. The kingdom of heaven is not the true church, for the kingdom of heaven contains both true and false, saved and lost. The kingdom of heaven is made up of all who profess any kind of allegiance to the King.

God is sowing His Word in human hearts and looking for fruit (vv. 1–9, 18–23). He is sowing His people in the world where they can produce a harvest (vv. 24–30, 36–43). At the end of the age, He will separate the true from the false and the good from the bad.

Is your profession of Christ authentic? Or will you be seen as a counterfeit at the end of the age? (See Matt. 7:21–29.)

Does your heart receive the Word? The seed has life and power and can produce a harvest of blessing in your life. Do you hear it?

Can God "plant you" where He wants you? You are a seed containing His divine life, but a seed must be planted to produce fruit (John 12:23–28).

Do you share with others what He teaches you (51–52)? Truth must not be hoarded; it must be shared so that others can be saved and built up in the faith.

Receive the Truth	*The word* parable *comes from a Greek word that means "to throw alongside." Jesus used the familiar to teach the unfamiliar ("things new and old" Matt. 13:52). He did that not to hide the truth but to arouse interest in the truth (Matt. 13:13–15). He wanted to get the people to open their eyes and ears and receive the truth into their sluggish hearts.*

MATTHEW 14

Tell it to Jesus (1–12). The disciples of John the Baptist were stunned, so they shared their grief with Jesus. Life will bring its disappointments, and you must learn how to handle them. Jesus will help you (Ps. 55:22; 1 Peter 5:7).

Bring it to Jesus (13–21). The Twelve said, "Send them

away!" But Jesus said, "Bring what you have to Me!" Give Him your all, and He will use it to meet the need. He can do the impossible with whatever is wholly given to Him. You can even bring to Him *people* who need His touch (v. 35).

Look to Jesus (22–33). Some storms come because of our disobedience, but this one came because they obeyed Jesus. Peter *did* walk on the water; but when distracted by dangers around him, he took his eyes off Jesus. We look to Jesus by faith when we trust His word (Heb. 12:1–3). Beware distractions!

"He is nigh when He seems absent. He is watching when He seems blind. He is active when He seems idle.**"**

G. Campbell Morgan

MATTHEW 15

Our Lord's disciples never knew what would happen next! You can check your own responses to life's challenges as you consider how they handled three different situations.

Offended people (1–20). Jesus rejected the man-made traditions of the scribes and Pharisees because they focused on the outside and ignored the inner person. These men were plants that God did not plant (13:24–30) and blind guides who were leading people astray. "Let them alone!" was our Lord's counsel.

Persistent people (21–31). Again, the disciples were wrong. Jesus seemed to ignore the woman, but He wanted only to increase her faith. His delays are not His denials. Jesus was ministering in gentile territory, and the people "glorified the God of Israel" (v. 31).

Hungry people (32–39). The disciples had already forgotten the miracle of feeding the five thousand! When you are faced with a crisis, take time to review His past mercies; remind yourself that He does not change.

Try to respond to people today the way Jesus responded. Ask Him for discernment.

MATTHEW 16

Are you guilty of these misunderstandings?

About the times (1–4). People believe the weather report but not God's Word! They fail to see what God is doing in His world. Keep your eyes open, and ask God for wisdom to understand His plan.

About false doctrine (5–12). Jesus compared false doctrine to *yeast*. It appears small and insignificant, but it grows secretly and soon permeates everything (Gal. 5:9). The only remedy is to remove it (1 Cor. 5:6–7).

About Jesus Christ (13–20). The crowd is confused about Jesus; do not follow it. Instead, let the Father reveal the Savior to you (11:25–27), and confess Him before others. He is the Son of God.

Peter

The name Peter means "a stone" (John 1:40–42). All of God's people are "living stones," but Jesus is the Rock (1 Pet. 2:4–8; Acts 4:11–12; Ps. 118:22), and His church is built on Him (1 Cor. 3:11). Whoever confesses faith in Christ becomes a living stone built into the spiritual temple (Eph. 2:19–22). Peter was given not the keys of heaven, for Jesus holds them (Rev. 1:18), but the "keys of the kingdom of heaven" (Matt. 16:19). He had the privilege of opening "the door of faith" (Acts 14:27) to the Jews at Pentecost (Acts 2), the Samaritans (Acts 8:14ff.), and the Gentiles (Acts 10).

About discipleship (21–28). In his misguided attempt to keep Jesus from suffering and dying, Peter the stone became Peter the stumbling block. Confessing Christ must lead to following Christ. The world encourages you to pamper yourself, but the Lord calls you to deny yourself. The only way to live is to die to self and follow Christ by faith.

MATTHEW 17

Listen to the King (1–13)! This event was a picture of the coming kingdom (16:27–28) and a proof that Jesus Christ is indeed the Son of the living God. The Law (Moses) and the prophets (Elijah) all converge in Him (Heb. 1:1–2). But the thing Peter remembered most was the emphasis on the unchanging Word of God (2 Pet. 1:16–21). The memory of visions will fade, but the Word endures forever. Hear Him!

Trust the King (14–21)! Jesus gave the disciples power to cast out demons (10:1, 8), but their unbelief and lack of prayer (vv. 20–21) robbed them of the power they needed. We cannot stay on the mountain of glory; there are needs to be met in the valley.

Obey the King (22–27)! The tax was an annual assessment of the Jewish men for the support of the temple (Exod. 30:11–16). Jesus affirmed His kingship by controlling a coin and a fish, but He affirmed His servanthood by submitting to their demands. "Lest we offend them" (v. 27) is a good principle when you lay aside your rights, but be careful not to set aside God's truth (15:12–14).

MATTHEW 18

Greatness (1–14). A child totally depends on others and must live by faith. An unspoiled child accepts his position in life, enjoys it, and does not try to act like someone older (Ps. 131). "He will be greatest who has the least idea he is great," wrote A. H. McNeile.

The way we treat children (including those who are "children in the faith") indicates how much humility we practice. Do we receive them (v. 5) or despise them (v. 10)? Do we imitate them (vv. 3–4) or cause them to stumble by our bad example (vv. 6–9)? It was a *sheep,* not a *lamb,* that went astray (vv. 10–14)!

Truthfulness (15–20). "Speaking the truth in love" (Eph. 4:15) is the secret of maintaining Christian fellowship. The longer we resist, the more people we involve in the problem (Matt. 5:21–26). Humility and honesty must work together in producing harmony.

Forgiveness (21–35). Peter wanted a rule to obey, which shows he was not in the spirit of what Jesus taught (Rom. 12:8–10). The parable is not about salvation but about forgiveness among God's people. We are to forgive others because God has forgiven us (Eph. 4:32; Col. 3:13), *and He has forgiven us at great cost to Himself!* It is possible to *receive* forgiveness but not truly *experience* forgiveness in our hearts; therefore, we have a hard time *sharing* forgiveness with others.

When you have an unforgiving spirit, you put yourself in prison spiritually and emotionally; you pay dearly for the luxury of carrying a grudge. Is it worth it?

> **"**He who cannot forgive breaks the bridge over which he himself must pass.**"**
>
> George Herbert

MATTHEW 19

Let Jesus heal your marriage (1–12). Some practices are lawful but not biblical, so follow the principles given in Scripture. God's original plan was one man for one woman for all of life (Gen. 2:18–25), but He made a concession for Israel and permitted divorce (Deut. 24:1–4). Divorce is not given as the solution to the problem. It takes a change of heart for two people to make a new beginning, and only Jesus can change hearts. Before you run away, run to God and seek His help.

Let Jesus bless your family (13–15). Children want to come to Jesus (v. 14), but too often adults get in the way. The best parents make it easy for their children to come to Christ, love Him, and receive His blessing.

Let Jesus have your all (16–30). The wealthy young man had much in his favor, but he thought too highly of himself and was not really honest before God. Money stood between him and salvation, and he would not repent and renounce his false god. You never lose when you give everything to Jesus. He blesses you in this life and in the life to come.

❝ *A good marriage is not a contract between two persons but a sacred covenant between three. Too often Christ is never invited to the wedding and finds no room in the home.* **❞**

Donald T. Kauffman

MATTHEW 20

What shall we have (19:27—20:16)? The parable is not about salvation, for we cannot work for salvation; nor is it about rewards, for we do not all receive the same reward. The story concerns the selfish attitude implicit in Peter's question. The key to the parable is that the first workers hired *demanded a contract and insisted on knowing how much they would get*. The other workers trusted the landowner. If you ask God for a contract, you will only rob yourself, for He is generous with His workers. Be faithful to do your job and avoid watching the other workers, and He will deal with you generously.

What do you wish (20:17–28)? Salome remembered His promise (19:28) and claimed it for her two sons. But she forgot what Jesus had just said about the cross (20:17–19). She should have known that the only way to glory is through suffering (1 Pet. 5:10). You do not *pray* for a throne; you *pay* for it. Beware selfish prayers: the Lord may answer them. James was the first apostle to be martyred (Acts 12:1–2), and John experienced great trial as a Roman prisoner (Rev. 1:9).

What do you want Me to do for you (20:29–34)? They knew what they wanted, and they trusted Him for it. Do you know what you want when you come to Him in prayer? Do you persist even if others try to discourage you? What a promise we have in Hebrews 4:16!

The Last Week

Traditionally, the events during our Lord's last week are as follows: Sunday—He entered Jerusalem as King. Monday—He cleansed the temple and cursed the fig tree. Tuesday—He debated with the Jewish leaders and gave the Olivet Discourse (Matt. 24—25). Wednesday—He rested. Thursday—He had the Last Supper; He was arrested in the Garden. Friday—He was crucified and buried. Saturday—He lay in the tomb. Sunday—He arose from the dead. Keep in mind that the Jewish day begins with sundown, so that their Friday begins Thursday evening.

MATTHEW 21:1—22:14

The King (21:1–11). The people were blind to their Scriptures (Zech. 9:9). They praised Him with Psalm 118:26 but overlooked verses 22–23, which Jesus quoted later (v. 42). Beware knowing the Bible but not knowing the Lord when He is at work in your midst.

The Judge (21:12–22). Jesus cleansed the temple and cursed the fig tree, two "unusual acts" for Him who came not to judge but to save (Isa. 28:21). Like the temple, Israel was corrupt within; and like the fig tree, it was fruitless without. A church can become a "den of thieves" if that is where we go to cover up our sins (Isa. 56:7; 1:10–20; Jer. 7:11). A person whose life is "nothing but leaves" is in danger of judgment, for Christ seeks fruit (Matt. 7:15–20).

The Son (21:23–41). Jesus has authority because He is the Son of God! The vineyard is Israel (Isa. 5) whose leaders did not respect the Son when He came. The nation rejected the Father when they refused the witness of John, and now they were about to reject the Son.

The Stone (21:42–46). The Jewish leaders pronounced their own sentence. Jesus quoted Psalm 118:22–23 to prove that their sins would not hinder His victory (Isa. 8:14–15; Dan. 2:34; Acts 4:11; 1 Pet. 2:9). If only they had become like the children and praised the Lord instead of fighting Him (Matt. 21:15–16; Ps. 8:2)!

The Bridegroom (22:1–14). The rejected Son is resurrected and reigns in glory. He is the Bridegroom who wants everybody to come to His feast. Israel's rejection of the invitation led to the destruction of Jerusalem (v. 7). But the invitation is still open today. Just be sure not to wear your self-righteousness (Isa. 64:6); let Him provide the garment of His righteousness (Isa. 61:10; 2 Cor. 5:21).

MATTHEW 22:15–46

His enemies questioned Jesus, hoping to get Him in trouble with Rome. After Passover, they could have Him arrested and tried. But how can mortal man question God and hope to win (Job 38:1–3)? What arrogance—and what ignorance!

Jesus asked the key question: "Who is your Lord?" (vv. 41–46; Ps. 110). If Jesus Christ is your Lord, the other questions pose no problem. You will be a good citizen (vv. 15–22; Rom. 13); you will not worry about the hereafter (vv. 23–33); and you will love God and your neighbor (vv. 34–40).

People who like to argue usually lack humility and need to submit to Christ (Phil. 2:1–11). Although it is good to ponder the great questions of life, it is also good to admit our ignorance and to worship Christ "in whom are hidden all the treasures of wisdom and knowledge" (Col. 2:3).

MATTHEW 23

The Word of God has authority even if the people who teach it lack integrity (vv. 1–3). Our Lord's standard is that we both *do* and *teach* His truth (5:17–20; 1 Thess. 2:10–12). Those who practice hypocrisy erode their character and do untold damage to others. The tragedy is that hypocrisy blinds people (vv. 16–19, 24, 26) so that they cannot see the Lord, themselves, or other people.

The God of the Pharisees is not the God of the Bible. He is a rigorous Law Giver who pays back those who pay Him. He is not "the God of all grace" (1 Pet. 5:10) or the loving Father who cares for His children (Ps. 103:1–14).

The Pharisees were blind to themselves. *They* were right, and everybody else was wrong. Because they majored on the externals, they never saw the rottenness in their hearts (vv. 25–28). Because they majored on the minor details, they ignored the great principles of the Word (v. 23).

Hypocrites never see the damage done to others: closing doors of blessing (v. 13); defiling those who touch them (v. 27); giving people a wrong sense of values (vv. 16–22). No wonder Jesus wept! These "woes" were born of anguish, not anger; and perhaps He is weeping over you and me.

Hypocrisy   *Failing to reach your goals or to be all that you want to be is not hypocrisy. Pretending that you have "arrived" is hypocrisy. The word* hypocrite *comes from the Greek word for the mask worn by an actor. Hypocrites deliberately play a part so people will think they are more spiritual than they really are. The remedy for hypocrisy is honesty with yourself and with God (1 John 1:5–10).*

THE OLIVET DISCOURSE

Our Lord's words about the desolation of the temple (23:37–39) prompted the disciples to ask Him about the future of the city, the temple, and the nation. In 24:1–35, the theme is the Tribulation ("day of the Lord") that will come upon the world in the last days. Jesus explained the events of the first half of the tribulation (24:1–14) and the last half (24:15–28); and then He announced His return to earth after the Tribulation (24:29–35).

In 24:1–35, the emphasis is on *the signs of His coming to the earth* and is directed primarily to Israel (vv. 15–28), telling the people to watch and be ready. But these words have a message for the church today, because "coming events cast their shadows before." We are looking for the Savior and not for signs (Phil. 3:20), because He can come at any time; but as we see these things developing in our world, we are encouraged to expect Him soon.

Matthew 24:36—25:46 focuses on the church rather than Israel. The emphasis is not on signs but on the fact that Jesus can return at any time (24:36, 44, 50). When He comes, He will reckon with His servants and reward those who have been faithful; it behooves us to be ready.

MATTHEW 24

When you listen to the news and see the tensions and troubles in today's world, keep in mind the warnings that the Lord gave.

Do not be deceived (4, 11). People will make grandiose claims and promises and will deceive many. You have the Word of God to enlighten you (Isa. 8:20) and the Holy Spirit to teach you (John 16:13–15), so you should not go astray (1 John 2:18–29).

Do not be discouraged (6). Political and natural disturbances have always been a part of world history, so do not allow them to discourage you. They are "the beginning of sorrows" (v. 8). The word translated "sorrows" means "birthpangs." The world's troubles are pregnant with possibilities! God is still on the throne!

Do not be defeated (13). This has to do with faithfulness under testing until the Lord returns. Do not let the lawlessness around you rob you of your fervor (v. 12). A lost world around you needs to hear the gospel (v. 14), so get busy!

Do not be doubtful (34–35). Religious leaders will come and go, stand and fall; but the Word will not change. Believe it, obey it, and hold to it—no matter what others may say or do. Your Bible is God's light in this dark world (2 Pet. 1:19–21).

Do not be distracted (42). We "watch" when we stay alert and remind ourselves that our Lord may come at any time. When in your heart you delay His coming (v. 48), you start to lose your effectiveness and witness. Keep watching and working!

MATTHEW 25

When Jesus Christ returns, it will be a time of *separation:* the wise will be separated from the foolish, the faithful servants from the unfaithful, the blessed (sheep) from the cursed (goats). The wise virgins had oil and were prepared to meet the Bridegroom. Many people profess to be Christians but do not have the Holy Spirit (Rom. 8:9) and are not born again. They may mingle with the saved, but they are not really one of them; and they will not enter into the marriage feast.

His coming also means *evaluation.* As we wait for the Lord to return, we must invest our lives and earn dividends for His glory. Christ gives us opportunities that match our abilities, and the one-talent servant is just as important as the five-talent servant. The key is *faithfulness* (1 Cor. 4:2), for God measures us against ourselves and not against the other servants. Are you afraid to step out by faith and take some risks for God?

When Christ returns, it will be a time of *commendation.* We will be surprised to learn about ministries we performed that we thought were insignificant but that He will reward. This parable is not teaching salvation by good works. Christ's sheep know that they are sheep (John 10:14, 27–30), but they do not always realize what their service means to Christ. We will experience some surprises in that day!

❝Great services reveal our possibilities; small services our consecration.**❞**

George Morrison

MATTHEW 26

Life presents us with many opportunities; how we respond to them depends on what we love and what we look for in life.

The Jewish leaders looked for opportunity to destroy Jesus, while at the same time Jesus was anticipating the opportunity to obey His Father and bring Him glory.

Mary used the opportunity she had for expressing her devotion to Christ, but Judas used that same opportunity to criticize her. Nothing given in love to Jesus is ever wasted. Judas was the one who ended up wasting his life!

Jesus eagerly anticipated the opportunity to be with His disciples, even though He knew one would betray Him, one would deny Him, and all would forsake Him. He sought to help them and prepare them for the trial before them.

Peter missed his opportunities to become strong and be a victor. He boasted when he should have listened (vv. 32–35), slept when he should have prayed (vv. 36–46), fought when he should have surrendered (vv. 47–56), and followed when he should have fled for safety (vv. 57–75; note v. 31). But when the opportunity came for him to repent, he wept.

No matter what others did, Jesus was in complete command and knew how to make the most of every opportunity. "Not as I will, but as You will" is the secret (v. 39). God will give you many opportunities today. Use them wisely!

God's best gifts are not things but opportunities. What we call adversity, God calls opportunity.

MATTHEW 27

Jesus is the example to follow when you suffer unjustly (1 Pet. 2:18–23).

He did not reply when accused (11–14). In this, He fulfilled Isaiah 53:7. There is a time to speak and a time to be silent (Eccles. 3:7), and we must exercise discernment. One thing is sure: no matter what He said, they would not have believed Him.

He did not retaliate when abused (15–31). He had the power to destroy those who mocked Him; in fact, legions of angels would have delivered Him. But it was the Father's will that He suffer as He did, and Jesus was obedient to His Father's will.

He did not accept the cup (32–38). The narcotic drink would have helped deaden the pain, but Jesus refused it. He drank the cup of suffering instead.

He did not come down from the cross (40–44). Had He come down from the cross, the people still would not have believed in Him. And if He saved Himself, He could not save others (John 12:23–28). First the suffering, then the glory; first the cross, then the crown. Remember that the next time you are tempted to take the easy way.

"Leave out the cross, and you have killed the religion of Jesus. Atonement by the blood of Jesus is not an arm of Christian truth; it is the heart of it."

Charles Haddon Spurgeon

MATTHEW 28

The message of the empty tomb is, "Do not be afraid!"

He overcomes His enemies (1–5). In His death and resurrection, our Lord defeated the world (John 16:33), the flesh (Rom. 6:1–7), the devil (John 12:31), and death itself (1 Cor. 15:50–58). You need not be afraid of life or death, time or eternity (Rev. 1:17–18).

He keeps His promises (6–7). Because His followers forgot His resurrection promise, they were sorrowing instead of rejoicing. The Lord always keeps His promises, no matter how dark the day may be.

He goes before you (7–10). When the women ran to share the message, they met the Lord; you always meet Him in the path of obedience. The Shepherd goes before the sheep and prepares the way for them (John 10:4). You have a living and victorious Savior who has everything under control. Trust Him!

He is our Lord (11–20). He has *all authority;* He commands us to take the gospel to *all nations;* and He promises to be with us *always*. What more assurance could we want? We are His ambassadors (2 Cor. 5:20) and should be faithful to Him in *all things*.

The Resurrection

The resurrection of Jesus Christ is a vital part of the gospel message, for a dead Christ can save nobody (1 Cor. 15:1–19). The empty tomb is proof that He is the Son of God (Rom. 1:4); that believers have a future inheritance (1 Pet. 1:3ff.); that we will once again meet Christians who have died (1 Thess. 4:14–18); that our Christian ministry is not in vain (1 Cor. 15:50–58); and that Jesus Christ will one day judge lost sinners (Acts 17:30–31). The early church bore witness of the resurrection of Jesus Christ (Acts 1:22; 4:2, 33), and so should we today.

MARK

◆————————————

John Mark was the cousin of Barnabas (Col. 4:10; Acts 4:36–37; 11:19–30) and the son of Mary, a leading woman in the Jerusalem church (Acts 12:12). He helped Paul and Barnabas on their first missionary journey (Acts 12:25—13:5) but for some reason did not remain with them (Acts 13:13). That failure caused Paul and Barnabas to separate, but Barnabas gave Mark another chance (Acts 15:36–41). In later years, Mark became one of Paul's associates (Philem. 24); and Paul commended him for his work (2 Tim. 4:11). It all ended well.

First Peter 5:13 suggests that John Mark was converted through Peter's ministry. Many Bible scholars believe that Mark's gospel is a record of Peter's reports of the ministry of Christ, presenting Jesus Christ as the Servant of God (Mark 10:45). Mark often used the word *immediately,* for he describes the work of a Servant who was busy obeying His Father and meeting the needs of people (1:10, 12, 20–21, etc.). Mark wrote with the Romans in mind, an active people who admired accomplishment.

After a brief introduction (1:1–13), the book tells of Christ's ministry in Galilee (1:14—9:50), His journey to Jerusalem (chap. 10), His ministry in Jerusalem, climaxing with His crucifixion (chaps. 11–15), and His resurrection and ascension (chap. 16).

MARK 1

Even a servant must have credentials, and our Lord has the very best. His coming was prophesied by Isaiah (40:3) and Malachi (3:1) and announced by John the Baptist. The Father and the Holy Spirit commended Him (vv. 9–11), and Satan could not defeat Him (vv. 12–13). He is a Servant you can trust.

But what can He do? What is His work? He can guide your life and make it a success (vv. 16–20). He can overcome Satan (vv. 21–28) and sickness (vv. 29–34, 40–45) and use you to bring the message of salvation to a lost and needy world (vv. 35–39). You can be a servant of the Servant and share in His wonderful work.

Where did the Servant get His power? He depended on the Holy Spirit (v. 12) and prayer (v. 35). He did not allow the demands of the work to rob Him of the time He needed to renew His strength. If the holy Son of God needed to pray, how much more do you need to pray! In the Lord's service, you cannot "run on empty." (See Isa. 40:28–31.)

MARK 2

Consider the unique ministries of God's Servant, Jesus Christ.

He forgives our sins (1–12). Imagine a servant having such authority! The healing of the body is a great miracle, but it does not last. The forgiveness of sin is God's greatest miracle, for it lasts forever and accomplishes the greatest good. The Servant forgives us *and pays the price for the miracle!*

Garments of New Life

Our first parents tried to cover their sins with garments they made (Gen. 3:7), but God would not accept them. Instead, He clothed them with skins (Gen. 3:21); blood had to be shed (Heb. 9:22). Jesus did not come to do a patchwork job on our lives; He came to make us whole. We have been raised from the dead (Eph. 2:1–10); and like Lazarus, we must take off the old garments of death and put on the garments of new life (John 11:44; Col. 3:1ff.).

He fellowships with "sinners" (13–22). Why? Because they are sick, and He is the only Physician who can heal them. They are hungry and lonely, and He is the Bridegroom who asks them to His wedding feast. Their lives are in tatters, and He wants to give them a new robe of righteousness. Others may be able to patch up life, but He alone can give new life.

He frees us from bondage (23–28). He is Lord of the Sabbath, the Giver of rest (Matt. 11:28–30). Man's religious traditions can be a terrible yoke of bondage; but when you follow the Lord, you experience freedom and rest.

MARK 3

Some resist the Servant (1–6, 20–30). The religious leaders were more concerned about protecting their tradition than helping a man with a handicapping condition. In spite of all that Jesus did and said, they hardened their hearts and resisted His ministry, even to the extent of accusing Him of being in league with Satan. In the end, *they* cooperated with the evil one!

Some assist the Servant (7–19). The crowds were so large that Jesus had to empower His disciples to help Him in ministry. There is a job for everyone, even if only giving Him a little boat to use (v. 9). If you want to assist Him, remember that the most important thing is *being with Him* (v. 14). As He said, "Without Me, you can do nothing" (John 15:5).

Some mistrust the Servant (vv. 31–35). Mary bore other children after the birth of Jesus, but they did not believe in Him (John 7:1–5). Even His mother seemed to have doubts about her "popular" Son who was arousing the anger of the leaders. But Jesus was doing the will of God, and so should we (v. 35).

MARK 4

Receiving God's Word (1–25). Even when we read the Bible, we should *hear* the voice of God speaking to our hearts. It must be personal. Never treat the Bible like any other book (1 Thess. 2:13). Jesus warns us to take heed *that* we hear (v. 9), *what* we hear (v. 24), and *how* we hear (Luke 8:18). The more of the Word we receive and share, the more God will give to us.

Reaping God's harvest (26–34). It is our job to sow the seed; we cannot make the seed germinate and produce a harvest. Even a busy farmer must sleep and let God work! However, when the harvest is ready, we must be alert and reap it, or the harvest may be lost (John 4:35–38).

Relying on God's power (35–41). Our faith in His Word is tested in the storms of life. If the disciples had really trusted His Word (v. 35), they would not have panicked and accused Him of not caring. You can trust His Word, for it will never fail.

MARK 5

The Servant comes to us (1–20). Jesus went through a storm to get to two demoniacs (Matt. 8:28) who needed his help. The demons begged not to be sent to the pit (v. 10), the citizens begged Jesus to leave (v. 17), and one healed man begged to be allowed to go with Jesus (v. 18). The citizens were concerned more with financial profit than with spiritual benefit. Imagine asking Jesus to leave you!

We can come to the Servant (21–34). All kinds of people came to the feet of Jesus. A well-known synagogue leader and an anonymous sick woman could find help there. Perhaps the woman's faith was a bit superstitious, but the Lord still honored it. If you cannot grasp His hand, touch the hem of His garment. The first step of faith, no matter how weak, will lead to greater blessings.

The Servant will go with us (35–43). No situation is so desperate that Jesus cannot work. Disease, delays, and even death are under His control. Jesus goes with you to the place of disappointment and sorrow and meets your needs. No matter how depressing your situation may appear, "Do not be afraid; only believe" (v. 36). The Servant is working for you.

MARK 6

The Servant cannot work (1–29). His neighbors were amazed at what Jesus said and did, but Jesus was amazed at their unbelief that would not let Him do more: "According to your faith let it be to you" (Matt. 9:29; Ps. 78:41). Ask God to strengthen your faith so that you can glorify Him (Rom. 4:20–

21). Our Lord's response to their unbelief was to send out His disciples to minister. Herod silenced one voice, but he could not silence the Word of God (Col. 4:2–4).

The Servant cannot rest (30–44). God's servants become weary as they work (John 4:6) and must care for the body. But when you have a compassionate heart, you will not have an idle hand. Our Lord interrupted His vacation to meet the needs of the people. He need not interrupt anything today, because caring for us is His constant ministry (Heb. 7:25).

The Servant cannot pray (45–56). After such a demanding time of ministry, Jesus had to go apart to pray (v. 46; 1:35). But once again, He was interrupted, this time by the plight of His disciples in the midst of the sea (v. 48). And it was the disciples who were amazed (v. 51)! Jesus intercedes for you and knows your situation. He will come to you, care for you, and lead you into His peace.

MARK 7

Defilement (1–23). Unless we are very careful, religious rituals can create serious problems. They may be given as much authority as God's Word (v. 7) and even replace God's Word (v. 9). They may give a false confidence that what you do on the outside will somehow change the inside. But the heart must be changed, and external rituals cannot do that. The heart can be purified only by faith (Acts 15:9).

Distance (24–30). Jesus healed both the centurion's servant (Matt. 8:1–13) and this woman's demonized daughter *from a distance*. Both were Gentiles, and the Gentiles were "at a distance" spiritually; but Jesus would erase that distance at the cross (Eph. 2:11–22). As you pray for those far from you, or far from the Lord, remember that He can send His Word and do mighty works (Ps. 107:20).

Deliverance (31–37). The miracles of healing this deaf man and healing a blind man (8:22–26) are recorded only by Mark. Both were in gentile territory, which would interest his Roman readers; both were performed away from the crowd; and both were performed despite difficulty. The Servant can work at a distance or when we bring people to Him, and He does not fail.

MARK 8

Defective faith (vv. 1–10). The disciples didn't know what to do with the hungry crowd, yet they had seen Jesus feed the five thousand (6:30–44). They apparently "soon forgot His works; they did not wait for His counsel" (Ps. 106:13). Each work that He does should encourage you to trust Him to help you solve the next problem. Keep a long memory for His mercies and a short one for your failures.

Defective understanding (11–21). The disciples did not perceive what He meant by the leaven (vv. 13–21). The blindness of the Pharisees does not surprise us (vv. 11–12), but why were His followers so blind? Like Israel of old, the disciples saw His acts but did not understand His ways (Ps. 103:7). Ask God to give you spiritual insight.

Defective sight (22–26). This is the only healing miracle recorded that took place in stages. Bethsaida was under judgment (Matt. 11:21–24), so Jesus took the man out of there and told him not to go back. Be careful where you send people whose eyes have been opened to Jesus and His mercy.

Defective devotion (27–38). One minute, Peter is inspired from heaven (Matt. 16:17); and the next minute, his tongue is ignited from hell (v. 33; James 3:6). Peter saw only shame in the Cross, but Jesus saw glory. Peter saw defeat, but Jesus saw great victory. Never be afraid or ashamed to be His disciple and bear your cross, for Jesus bore it first.

MARK 9

Consider some paradoxes of the Christian life.

Glory out of suffering (1–13). What happened on the Mount of Transfiguration was a confirmation of the testimony Peter gave. But it was also a revelation of the glory of the Cross (Gal. 6:14). First the suffering, then the glory. When you read 1 Peter, you discover that Peter learned his lesson well (1:6–8, 11; 4:12–16; 5:1, 10). Satan offers you glory without suffering (Matt. 4:8–10), but it ends up suffering without glory.

Victory out of defeat (14–29). Their failure to deliver the boy grieved the Lord, gave support to the enemy, and robbed God of glory. The nine disciples who were left behind had neglected their spiritual disciplines and lost their power (v. 29; 6:7). When you find yourself defeated, turn to Him for victory and discover where you went wrong.

Greatness out of service (30–41). This is a key passage in Mark's gospel because it emphasizes the importance of service. Do not aim for human greatness; aim to be more like Jesus Christ. Do not measure yourself by other servants (vv. 38–41); measure yourself by Him.

Gain out of loss (42–50). If you pamper sin in your life, you will lose your "salty" character and not be able to affect others for Christ. Deal drastically with sin as a surgeon does with a cancerous tumor. You gain by losing.

> **❝**One reason sin flourishes is that it is treated like a cream puff instead of a rattlesnake!**❞**
>
> Billy Sunday

MARK 10

How far can I go (1–16)? The rabbis didn't agree on their interpretation of the divorce law (Deut. 24:1–4), one school being lenient and the other strict. When you live "by permission," you are tempted to follow those who tell you what you want to hear. Our Lord led the Pharisees back to God's original plan and interpreted it for them.

How much can I keep (17–27)? The rich young man was looking for a bargain, the best of both worlds; but he was doomed to failure. Calculation and crucifixion do not agree. At Calvary, there was no bargaining—just Jesus giving His all.

How much will we get (28–45)? Jesus promises to reward all who faithfully follow Him, but He warns against having rewards as your only motive for service. If you are His disciple, expect a cross, a cup, and a baptism, for the servant is not greater than his Lord. The important question is, "How much can we give?"

> **"**Has He taken over in your heart? Perhaps He resides *there,* but does He preside *there?***"**
>
> Vance Havner

MARK 11

Honor (1–11). The donkey was a royal animal, and the event was a coronation celebration (1 Kings 1:32–40). It was the only time our Lord permitted a public demonstration in His honor, and He did it to fulfill prophecy (Zech. 9:9) and turn the people's hearts back to the Word of God. They did not listen. What changes would Jesus make if He entered our places of worship today?

Hunger (12–14, 20–26). The fig tree pictures Israel, taking up space but not producing fruit (Luke 13:6–9). When we stop bearing fruit, the problem always starts with the roots (v. 20; Matt. 3:10). Jesus reminds us that we must have faith and forgiveness when we pray, or God will not answer.

Holiness (15–19). The psalmist proclaimed, "Holiness adorns Your house" (Ps. 93:5). But unholiness made the temple a place for thieves to hide! The leaders were not *praying;* they were *preying* and using religion only to make money.

Honesty (27–33). The leaders had not been honest with John the Baptist, and now they refused to be honest with Jesus. When we obey, God teaches us more (John 7:17); if we disobey, we close the door on God's truth.

MARK 12

Each family chose its Passover lamb on the tenth day of the month and carefully examined it until the fourteenth day to be sure it had no defects (Exod. 12:1–6). During His last week of public ministry, God's Lamb (John 1:29) was examined in various ways, and He passed every test. No guile was found in His mouth (Isa. 53:9).

In His replies, Jesus revealed to them who He was; yet they

would not accept the truth. He is the Son sent by the Father (vv. 1–9) and the Stone rejected by the builders (vv. 10–11; Ps. 118:22–23; Acts 4:11). His enemies were so intent on destroying Jesus that they did not realize they were destroying only themselves.

All political questions (vv. 13–17) and hypothetical doctrinal questions (vv. 18–27) are chaff compared to the most important question of all: Is Jesus Christ your Lord (vv. 35–37) and do you love Him (vv. 28–34)?

If you were to point out the spiritual people in this chapter, would you indicate the pious scribes (vv. 38–40) or the poor widow (vv. 41–44)? Read Revelation 2:9 and 3:17.

On Giving   *The Lord watches how we give (Mark 12:41–44) and examines the motives of the heart (Matt. 6:1–4). He also sees how much we give and measures the proportion, not the portion (1 Cor. 16:2). An old epitaph reads, "What I gave, I have. What I spent, I had. What I kept, I lost."*

MARK 13

This is Mark's version of the Olivet Discourse (Matt. 24–25), written with gentile readers in mind (v. 14). If we are to be ready and faithful in these last days, we must heed the admonitions of Jesus.

Take heed that no one deceives you (5). Political and geological disruption will give false prophets and false Christs great opportunity to deceive people. Persecution against God's people will either strengthen us or weaken us.

Take heed to what Jesus taught (23). The Word of God is the only dependable light in this dark world (2 Pet. 1:19). Jesus has told us beforehand what to expect and what to avoid, and we must heed His words. His Word is dependable and durable, so trust it.

Take heed, watch, and pray (33). During the tribulation period, various signs will signal Christ's return to earth; but believers today are looking for the Savior and not for signs. "Be alert and keep praying!" is His admonition. "Do the work I have given you to do." You want to be found faithful when He comes, and He could come today.

MARK 14

Preparation for betrayal (1–2, 10–11). Judas solved the chief priests' problem by offering to lead them to Jesus. But how do you "conveniently" betray the Son of God? Is it not a *costly* endeavor in every way?

Preparation for burial (1–9). Mary's act of worship brought joy to the heart of Jesus and malice to the heart of Judas, who wanted the money she had spent (John 12:6). Other women came to anoint Him *after* His burial (16:1), but Mary did it when He could be encouraged by her love.

Preparation for fellowship (12–26). It meant much to Jesus to spend those hours with His disciples. He loved them (John 13:1), and their presence encouraged Him. He took the cup and the bread of the Passover and transformed them into memorials of His own blood and body, for He wanted the disciples to remember Him.

Preparation for danger (27–31, 66–72). The good fellowship in the Upper Room made the Twelve forget the danger outside, so Jesus gave them warning. Peter was not the only one who boasted and felt self-confident: "And they all said likewise" (v. 31). Heed His warnings; He knows what is coming.

Preparation for death (32–65). Jesus' prayers reveal the conflict in His holy soul as He faced bearing the sins of the world on the cross. When you have a Gethsemane experience, pray what He prayed: "Not what I will, but what You will" (v. 36). Peter had a sword, but Jesus took a cup. You need not fear the cup the Father has prepared for you. Jesus could submit to the abuse of men because He had already submitted to the will of God.

MARK 15

When you face the unjust assaults of an evil world, remember Jesus. The world says, "Defend yourself!" but Jesus was silent (vv. 1–5). The world says, "Pamper yourself!" but Jesus refused the drug (v. 23). The world says, "Save yourself!" but Jesus remained on the cross and finished the work the Father gave Him to do (v. 30).

Simon and the Cross

Simon of Cyrene had probably come to Jerusalem to celebrate Passover (Acts 2:10), and he met the Lamb of God! It seems certain that he was converted and went home to lead his two sons to faith in Christ. These men were known to Mark's Roman readers, so they must have become leaders in the church (Rom. 16:13). The next time your plans are interrupted and you have to carry another cross, remember what Simon did for Jesus—and what Jesus did for Simon.

Jesus Gave Himself

The devil told Jesus, "Serve Yourself!" (Matt. 4:3–4). Peter said, "Pity Yourself!" (Matt. 16:21–23). His unsaved relatives said, "Show Yourself!" (John 7:4). The crowd at Calvary said, "Save Yourself!" But Jesus was deaf to all those appeals and gave Himself.

The chief priests were guilty of *envy* (v. 10), and Pilate was guilty of *compromise* (v. 15). Their sins led to the release of an evil man (v. 15), the embarrassment of an innocent man (v. 21), and the death of a good Man (v. 25); yet envy and compromise are not looked upon as terrible sins today. Should they be?

Man was doing his worst, but God was doing His best and fulfilling His Word (vv. 28, 34): "But where sin abounded, grace abounded much more" (Rom. 5:20). And He did it for you and me!

MARK 16

He arose (1–8). Because they forgot His resurrection promises, the women were in sorrow and worrying about the future: "Who will roll away the stone?" When they learned that Jesus was alive, their first response was fear and not faith; but then they became the first heralds of the Resurrection. The angel had a special word for Peter (v. 7) who was no doubt still grieving his sins. The living Christ gives you something to rejoice in, something to talk about, and something to look forward to. He goes before you!

Saved Through Faith

Sinners are saved through faith in Christ (Eph. 2:8–9), and they bear witness of their faith through baptism (Mark 16:16; Acts 10:47). Some signs described in Mark 16:17–18 occurred during the apostolic period described in the book of Acts. They were the "credentials" of the apostles (Heb. 2:1–4; Rom. 15:19; 2 Cor. 12:12), so we must not assume that they belong to every believer today. It is foolish to tempt God by drinking poison or handling poisonous snakes, but it is not foolish to trust God when obedience to His will takes us into dangerous situations. Presumption can kill us, but faith can deliver us.

He appeared (9–18). This section summarizes the Lord's resurrection appearances. All to whom He appeared became witnesses of His resurrection (Acts 1:22), just as we should be today (Rom. 6:4; Phil. 3:10).

He ascended (19–20). The Servant is the Sovereign at the Father's right hand! He humbled Himself in obedience, and God exalted Him in glory (Phil. 2:5–11). But He is not idle, for He is working with His people as they take the gospel to every nation. What an encouragement to be a witness for your Lord!

LUKE

Luke was a physician, probably a Greek (Col. 4:10–11, 14), the companion of Paul on some of his journeys. (Note the pronouns "we" and "us" in Acts 16:10; 20:5; 21:1; 27:1.) He wrote the gospel of Luke and the book of Acts (Luke 1:1–4; Acts 1:1–3), both of which are records of journeys: Christ's journey to Jerusalem (Luke 9:51) and Paul's journey to Rome.

Dr. Luke wrote with the Greeks in mind and presented Jesus Christ as the perfect Son of man, the compassionate Savior (Luke 19:10). He mentions women, children, and the poor often in his gospel; and *joy* and *rejoicing* are repeated many times. There is also an emphasis on prayer and on God's love for the whole world. Luke addressed both books to Theophilus ("lover of God"), a Roman believer, possibly an official, who needed grounding in the faith.

Luke's approach is simple. He records our Lord's birth and early life (chaps. 1–2); His baptism and temptation (3:1—4:13); His ministry in Galilee (4:14—9:17); His ministry en route to Jerusalem (9:18—19:27); and His final week of ministry in Jerusalem (19:28—24:53).

As you read the gospel of Luke, you will come to love the compassionate Son of man who cares for those in need and wants His message of salvation to be taken to the whole world.

LUKE 1

Serving (1–25). His disappointment at not having a son did not keep Zacharias from serving the Lord. Be faithful; you never know when God's angel may arrive. Zacharias had the faith to keep on praying; but when the answer came, he did not have the faith to accept it. He looked at his limitations rather than God's great power. Unbelief produces silence (Ps.

116:10; 2 Cor. 4:13); faith opens your mouth in praise to God.

Submitting (26–38). What an honor to be chosen to be the mother of the Messiah! Mary humbly submitted to the Lord because she had faith that He would keep His promise. Her decision would bring her sorrow and suffering, but she willingly yielded it. She was "blessed among women" because of the grace of God given to her (vv. 28, 30). All who trust Christ as their Savior are highly graced by the Lord (Eph. 1:6).

Jesus' Greatness	*It was said of John the Baptist, "He will be great in the sight of the Lord" (Luke 1:15); but of Jesus it was said, "He will be great" (Luke 1:32). He is the great Prophet (Luke 7:16), the great God and Savior (Titus 2:13), the great High Priest (Heb. 4:14), and the great Shepherd of the sheep (Heb. 13:20).*

"Do Not Be Afraid"	*The encouraging phrase "Do not be afraid!" is found often in Luke's gospel, for the message of salvation replaces fear with joy. All kinds of people heard it: Zacharias (1:13), Mary (1:30), the shepherds (2:10), Peter (5:10), Jairus (8:50), and the disciples (12:7, 32).*

Singing (39–80). A pregnant Jewish girl from Nazareth, engaged to marry a poor carpenter, what did Mary have to sing about? She sang about the Lord, what He did for *her* (vv. 46–49), for *all who fear Him* (vv. 50–53), and for *His people Israel* (vv. 54–55). God gives power to the weak, thrones to the lowly, and food to the hungry; but the strong, the rich, and the mighty go away empty.

Zacharias praised God for what He would do for His people, Israel. It was the dawning of a new day (vv. 78–79) because the Messiah was about to be born. God keeps His promises and is faithful to His covenants.

LUKE 2

You cannot escape Jesus Christ.

His birth affected Caesar's politics (vv. 1–3), the ministry of the angels (vv. 8–15), and the activities of common men (vv. 15–20). In that day, shepherds were looked upon with disdain; but God singled them out to be the first human messengers of Messiah's birth. His coming touched worshipers (vv. 21–38) and even scholars (vv. 39–52).

The angels sang about Him, and He is still the theme of the greatest music. Luke wrote about Him, and He is still the subject of the greatest literature. The shepherds hastened to behold Him, and He is still at the center of the greatest art. Teachers listened to Him and marveled, and He is still the focal point for all truth and wisdom.

In His development, Jesus was perfectly balanced: intellectually (wisdom), physically (stature), spiritually (in favor with God), and socially (in favor with man); and He is still the greatest example for childhood and youth.

He alone is worthy of our worship!

Oh, come! Let us adore Him!

LUKE 3

Prophecy. God's message did not come to any of the "great leaders" of that day. It came to John the Baptist, the last and the greatest of God's prophets. John's ministry was foretold by the prophet Isaiah (vv. 4–6; Isa. 40:3–5). John was a prophet who was the subject of prophecy!

Ministry. John was privileged to prepare the nation for the Messiah and then present Him to them. John preached against sin and told the people to repent. He gave specific instructions to his converts on how to put their faith into practice. He was inspecting fruit (v. 8), getting to the root of sin (v. 9), and warning about wrath to come (vv. 7, 17). Would you accept that kind of ministry?

Mystery. The Son of God is baptized; the Spirit lights upon Him like a dove; and the Father speaks His approval from heaven. Never forget that all of the holy Trinity is involved in your salvation (Eph. 1:1–14).

History. The genealogy (vv. 23–38) is that of Mary whose father was Heli. Joseph was not the biological father of Jesus, though that was what people assumed (John 1:45; 6:42). The genealogy of Joseph is found in Matthew 1. It was unusual to pay attention to the genealogy of a woman, which shows Dr. Luke's concern for neglected people. Gentile history (v. 1) and Jewish history (vv. 23–38) are in the hands of almighty God, fulfilling His purposes.

LUKE 4

The Conqueror (1–13). You can be filled with the Spirit (v. 1) and obedient to God's will and still experience temptations and trials. Because He faced the enemy and conquered, Jesus can identify with you in your temptations and can help you win the victory (Heb. 2:17–18). It is not a sin to be tempted, for Jesus was tempted; but it is a sin to yield. Satan's promise is, "All will be yours" (v. 7); but in Jesus Christ, you already have all things (1 Cor. 3:21–23), and Satan can give you nothing.

The Preacher (14–30). The Spirit not only gives us victory, but He leads us (v. 14) and empowers us for service (v. 18). The text for our Lord's message was Isaiah 61:1–2. It describes what Jesus came to do and what He is still doing in lives today. The people in the synagogue wanted a comforting sermon, not a convicting sermon. When Jesus mentioned God's grace to the Gentiles (vv. 23–27), the people became angry and threw Him out! They forfeited His blessings because they rejected His word.

The Healer (31–44). Jesus fulfilled His commission (vv. 18–19) by bringing healing and deliverance to the poor and needy by the authority of His word. Had He not overcome the devil privately, Jesus could not have defeated him publicly. While the preaching of the Word was His major ministry (vv. 42–44), Jesus had compassion on the sick and healed them. We may not have the power to heal, but we can comfort and assist those who are needy; and we can do it in Jesus' name (Matt. 25:34–40).

LUKE 5

Jesus responds to submission (1–11). If you had fished all night and caught nothing, would you be getting ready to go out fishing again? One reason Jesus called several fishermen to be His disciples was that they never quit! Peter may have thought he knew more about fishing than Jesus did, but he did what Jesus commanded; and the Lord honored his obedient faith. No failure is final if you come to the Lord for a new start.

Jesus responds to sickness (12–14). Lepers were not to approach people; but the man came to Jesus in desperation, and Jesus healed him. The offering Jesus referred to is described in Leviticus 14 and pictures the salvation work of the Lord. Ponder it.

Jesus responds to success (15–16). The crowds sought Him, but Jesus withdrew to pray and commune with the Father. He did not allow popularity to detour Him from the Father's will. Vance Havner said, "Success can feather our nest so comfortably that we forget how to fly."

Jesus responds to sinners (17–39). He forgave the paralytic, Matthew the publican, and Matthew's friends who trusted Him because He is the "friend of sinners" (Matt. 11:19). He could not forgive the scribes and Pharisees because they would not admit they were sick and in need of new clothes!

"They Forsook All"

Peter and his associates had met the Lord earlier (John 1:35–42), had gone with Him on His ministry through Galilee (Mark 1:16–20), but had returned to their fishing business. They now had the call to leave everything and follow the Lord as His apostles (Luke 5:9–11).

LUKE 6

True liberty (1–11). People who live only by "Is it lawful?" cannot understand our Lord's principle, "Is it loving?" The scribes and Pharisees had transformed the Sabbath from a day of blessing into a day of bondage, and Jesus deliberately healed on the Sabbath so He could challenge them. It is always right to do good and to meet human need (Mic. 6:8), for love fulfills the law (Rom. 13:8–10).

True values (12–26). In His ordination sermon for the apostles, Jesus emphasized the true spiritual values of life in contrast to the false values of the Pharisees (Matt. 23). Comfortable living is not always Christian living.

True love (27–45). Yes, God's people have their enemies, even as Jesus did; and we must be Christlike in the way we treat them. We must be giving and forgiving; and we must pray for them, not that God would destroy them but that He would change them. The best way to conquer an enemy is to make him a friend. Keep your heart right with God (v. 45) and the Lord will produce the good fruit in your life.

True obedience (46–49). True obedience is not just words but deeds, and it involves hearing the Word and doing it (1 Thess. 2:13). Judas knew the vocabulary, but he did not do the will of God; and when the storm came, his house fell.

LUKE 7

He did not deserve it (1–10). "I am not worthy" was the centurion's confession of humility; and his confession of faith was, "Say the word!" It is great faith when we trust Christ to work just by speaking the Word. We can never deserve His blessings, but we can ask for them in faith.

True Rest

Christ's invitation to come to Him for rest (Matt. 11:28–30) precedes Luke 7:36–50. The sinful woman had heard that invitation and had come to Christ, and she found rest. She was ashamed of her past, but she was not ashamed of her Savior or of her tears.

She did not expect it (11–17). Nobody knew that Jesus would arrive and break up the funeral! Never despair, because your Lord may surprise you at the last minute and do the impossible for you.

He did not understand it (18–35). When the Lord is not doing what you expect Him to do, tell Him about it and listen to His Word. You may feel that your ministry has failed, but you are not the judge. Let Jesus have the final word.

She could not hide it (36–50). The sinful woman trusted Christ and He saved her; now she wanted to express her love to Him. True faith cannot be hidden, and true faith shows itself in love and worship. Simon the Pharisee was blind: he could not see himself, the Lord, or the woman. He did not know the debt he owed!

LUKE 8

A multitude hearing Him (1–25). Jesus was not impressed by the crowds that followed Him, for He knew the spiritual condition of their hearts. The parable of the sower helps us examine our hearts to see how we respond to the Word. But it is not enough to hear the Word (vv. 8, 18); we must also obey it (v. 21) and trust it when the time of testing comes (vv. 22–25).

A multitude rejecting Him (26–39). The healing of the Gadarene demoniacs (Matt. 8:28) should have endeared Jesus to the people, but the citizens were concerned more about pigs and money than about people and mercy. The man who begged to go with Jesus was the sanest one of all!

A multitude welcoming Him (40). This was on the other side of the Sea of Galilee, near Capernaum. Why did they welcome Him? Probably not because of their love for Him, but because they had seen many of His miracles and wanted Him to meet their needs. If Jesus were coming today, would you welcome Him? Why?

A multitude thronging Him (41–56). The people wanted to get next to Jesus so He could help them; but though they thronged Him, they did not have the touch of faith that the poor sick woman had. Being in the crowd is no assurance of receiving the blessing. Sometimes God has to get you away from the crowd before He can meet the need (v. 51).

LUKE 9

Christ equips us (1–6). He will never send us out to do a task without first giving us what we need. We are prone to trust what we have, but we should trust in Him alone. If we are in His will, we will have His supply.

Christ enables us (7–17). How could twelve men feed five thousand people? Only through the enabling of the Lord, for He did the miracle: they only distributed the blessing. Christ is looking for clean empty hands that He can fill.

Christ encourages us (18–36). If you confess Christ as Son of God and Savior, and take up your cross and follow Him, He will reveal to you His kingdom and His glory. When you experience the glory of God, the demands of discipleship become blessings that carry you along in joyful obedience.

Christ endures us (37–62). What strange words from the lips of Jesus: "How long shall I be with you and bear with you?" (v. 41). He must bear with our unbelief and failure (vv. 37–42), our spiritual blindness (vv. 43–45), our pride (vv. 46–48), our lack of love (vv. 49–56), and our lack of dedication (vv. 57–62). Is Jesus blessing you—or bearing with you?

LUKE 10

The chapter asks four questions by way of personal inventory.

What makes you serve (1–16)? Jesus was not limited to the Twelve; seventy others obeyed Him and helped to reap the harvest. But the laborers are still few, and Luke 9:57–62 tells why. The ministry is difficult and dangerous, but it is also very rewarding. Are you obedient to His call?

What makes you rejoice (17–24)? When the disciples rejoiced over their successful ministry, Jesus told them to rejoice because they were the citizens of heaven. After all, their work might not always be successful; but their salvation would never change. Jesus rejoiced because the Father's will was being accomplished in their lives. What brings joy to your heart?

What makes you pause (25–37)? It is not difficult to discuss neighborliness in the abstract, but it costs something to be a real neighbor. Do you pause to help when you see injustice and hurt, or like the priest and the Levite, do you look for an escape? You are never more Christlike than when you feel another's hurt and seek to help.

What makes you listen (38–42)? Here is the basis for all ministry, taking time to sit at the feet of Jesus and hear His Word. It is important to serve the Lord and serve others, but it is even more important to delight your Lord by spending time with Him. Are you so busy serving Him that you have no time to love Him and listen to Him?

Serving Him

Faithful to my Lord's commands,
I still would choose the better part;
Serve with careful Martha's hands
And loving Mary's heart.

Charles Wesley

❝Justice seeks out the merits of the case, but pity only regards the need.**❞**

Bernard of Clairvaux

LUKE 11

His generosity (1–13). If Jesus, John the Baptist, and the Twelve all needed to pray, how much more do *we* need to pray! We must put God's concerns first (vv. 2–4), because prayer is based on *sonship,* not friendship. God is a loving Father, not a grouchy neighbor; He gives us what we need. He neither slumbers nor sleeps; and He doesn't become irritated when we ask for help (James 1:5).

His authority (14–36). More dangerous than open hostility (vv. 14–22) is attempted neutrality (vv. 23–26), for an empty life is an opportunity for Satan to move in and take over. The only sign we need is the "sign of Jonah," our Lord's resurrection from the dead (Acts 2:22–36). Jesus has won the victory over the prince of darkness. Obey Satan and you let in darkness rather than light, and soon you will not be able to distinguish between them (Matt. 6:22–23).

His honesty (37–54). He was a guest in the home, but Jesus did not flatter His host or the other guests by avoiding the truth. He exposed their hypocrisy and condemned them for their sins (Matt. 23). They defiled people (v. 44), burdened them (v. 46), and locked the door on them (v. 52), all the while posing as holy men of God. Instead of taking the opportunity of repenting and being forgiven, they opposed Jesus and attacked Him. What fools!

"*Prayer is a mighty instrument, not for getting man's will done in Heaven, but for getting God's will done in earth.***"**

Robert Law

LUKE 12

A fearful heart (1–12). When you fear people, you start to hide things, and this leads to hypocrisy. You fail to confess Christ openly and depend on the Holy Spirit (vv. 8–12), and this silences your witness. When you fear God alone, you need fear no one else; and you can boldly witness for Christ. You are important to God and precious in His sight, so never fear what people can say or do.

A greedy heart (13–21). Imagine being so greedy that you would interrupt a sermon to ask for help to get more money! The weeds were certainly growing in that man's heart (Matt. 13:22). We all need a certain amount of money to live, but money is not a guarantee of security. If anything, it creates a *false* confidence that leads to foolishness.

A divided heart (22–34). The word translated "worry" (v. 22) means "to be pulled apart," and that is what worry does to you. If your heart is centered on Christ and trusting wholly in Him (v. 31), you will have a united heart that fears God alone (Ps. 86:11). If your treasures are heavenly, you need not worry; no enemy can take them!

A cold heart (35–59). We are God's servants, and He expects us to be faithfully doing our work when Jesus Christ returns. But when we stop looking for His coming, loving it (2 Tim. 4:8), and longing for it (Rev. 22:20), our hearts get cold, and we get worldly. The Lord will deal with careless servants when He returns, so we had better be ready.

LUKE 13

Tragedy (1–9). How easy it is to ask questions about others' tragedies and fail to learn the lessons they teach! The big question is not "Why do people die in tragic and seemingly meaningless ways?" but "Why does God keep me alive?" Am I really worth it? Am I bearing fruit or just taking up space?

Hypocrisy (10–17). The ruler of the synagogue was a hypocrite because he treated animals better than he treated people. Suppose the woman did come to the synagogue on another day. Could he have healed her? Of course not! We wonder how many needy people come to church meetings looking for love and help and go away disappointed.

"Yesterday is a canceled check. Tomorrow is a promissory note. Today is the only cash you have, so invest it wisely.**"**

Opportunity (18–35). God's kingdom is at work in this world, but many people fail to take advantage of their opportunities. Instead of entering the kingdom, some people only ask questions about it. Salvation is not a theory to discuss; it is a miracle to experience. No wonder Jesus wept when He saw sinners passing by their opportunities to be saved! Do not wait for opportunities to come; they are already here.

LUKE 14

Do I exploit people (1–14)? When we eat together, it should be a time of loving fellowship and joyful gratitude to God; but the Pharisees turned tables into traps and exploited people. They used a man with a handicapping condition in trying to catch Jesus; they went to feasts only to receive honors; and they invited to their feasts only people who would return the favor. Hospitality is ministry only if our motive is to help others and glorify God.

Do I invite people (15–24)? Salvation is a feast, not a funeral (5:33–39); and God wants His house filled. As His servants, we have the privilege to tell the world, "Come, for all things are now ready!" (v. 17). Even if some reject the invitation, keep sharing it. Those who think they are the least worthy are the ones He wants to have at His feast.

Do I follow people (25–35)? It is easy to be part of the crowd and follow a popular Jesus, but that is not true discipleship. He calls you away from the crowd to take up your cross and follow Him. When it comes to winning the lost, God wants His house filled; but when it comes to discipleship, Christ thins out the ranks and wants only those who will die to self and live for Him.

LUKE 15

These parables are Christ's defense of His ministry, explaining why He fellowshiped with sinners and even ate with them.

He saw what they were. They were sheep that had gone astray and needed a shepherd to bring them home. They were lost coins, stamped with the image of God, needing to get back into circulation again. They were disobedient sons who were wasting their inheritance and needed to come home to the Father.

He saw how they got that way. Sheep are foolish animals and naturally go astray, but the spiritual shepherds in Israel had not faithfully ministered to them (Jer. 23; Ezek. 34). The woman lost the coin because of carelessness, and the son was lost because of his willfulness. The father did not search for the boy but let him learn his lessons the hard way and discover how good it was back home. (See Rom. 2:4.)

He saw what they could be. Jesus always saw the potential in people. The sheep could be brought back to the flock and bring joy to the shepherd; the coin could be found; and the son could return home and lovingly serve his father. There is hope for every sinner because Jesus welcomes everyone.

LUKE 16

The subject is money, and the object is to teach us the proper place of money in life.

We can waste money (1). Stewards should use wealth for their masters' good and not for their own pleasure (1 Cor. 4:2). God wants us to *enjoy* His gifts (1 Tim. 6:17), but He also wants us to *employ* them wisely.

We can serve God with money (2–9). The man had a rude awakening: he had to give an account of his stewardship (Rom. 14:10–12; 2 Cor. 5:10). Then he learned to be wise and to invest wealth in people and in the future. We do not "buy" friends, but we can make friends for the Lord by the wise use of money. Will people welcome you to heaven because your stewardship made it possible for them to hear the gospel and be saved?

❝*Make all you can, save all you can, give all you can.***❞**

John Wesley

❝*Money is a wonderful servant, a terrible master,
and an abominable god.***❞**

We can try to serve God and money (10–18). The Pharisees tried it but it cannot be done. How can you serve both righteousness and unrighteousness, what is greatest and what is least, what God honors and what He abominates? The world measures people by how much they get, but God measures them by how much they give.

We can let money be our god (19–31). The rich man did not go to Hades because he was rich; he went there because riches were his god. Abraham was a wealthy man, and yet he was in paradise. Money can help send people to heaven (v. 9), or it can help send people to hell.

LUKE 17

Faith is like a seed: it seems small and weak, but it has life in it; and if it is cultivated, it will grow and release power. We need faith for many areas of life.

Faith to forgive (1–4). When people sin repeatedly, giving up on them is easy; but we must forgive them and trust God to work in their lives. We must be stepping stones and not stumbling blocks.

Faith to serve (5–10). It takes faith to do your duty, whether tending a field or a flock or preparing a meal. It takes faith to do the extraordinary, like moving a mountain.

Faith to pray (11–19). The ten men believed that Jesus could help them, and He did. The Samaritan not only brought joy to Christ's heart but received salvation from His hand: "Your faith has saved you!" When God answers your prayers, be sure to tell Him "thank You!"

Faith to be ready when He comes (20–37). The important thing is not to set dates but to be ready when He comes, for true faith leads to faithfulness. To *look around* at the increase in sin will discourage you, and to *look back* (as did Lot's wife) may destroy you, so *look up* and eagerly expect the Lord's return today!

LUKE 18

Confident prayer (1–8). If an unjust judge helps a poor widow, how much more will a loving Father meet the needs of His children? We have open access into His treasury (Rom.

5:2) and can claim His gracious promises (Luke 11:9–10), so we ought to pray with faith and confidence. No need to argue— just come!

Arrogant prayer (9–17). True prayer should humble us and make us love others more. We should be like children coming to a Father and not like attorneys bringing an indictment. If prayer doesn't bless the one praying, it isn't likely to help anybody else.

Ignorant prayer (18–34). Although the young man had many good qualities, one of them was not spiritual understanding. He did not really see himself, Jesus, or the peril he was in because of his riches. The publican went away justified (v. 14) while the young man went away sorrowful (v. 23). What happens at the close of your prayers?

Persistent prayer (35–43). The blind man was not to be stopped! He had his great opportunity, and he would not let it pass. Our Lord stopped, looked, listened—and healed! Jesus is not too busy to hear you. Just be sure you are in earnest when you pray.

66The revelation of our spiritual standing is what we ask in prayer; sometimes what we ask is an insult to God; we ask with our eyes on the possibilities or on ourselves, not on Jesus Christ.**99**

Oswald Chambers

LUKE 19

The day of salvation (1–10). Verse 10 is illustrated in the experience of Zacchaeus: Jesus *came* to him, *sought* him, and *saved* him. Though He was surrounded by a great crowd of people, Jesus took time for individuals, and He even saw a man in a tree! He is still the seeking Savior, but now He uses *your* eyes and lips.

The day of evaluation (11–27). There are three possible relationships with the King. You can reject His rule and be an enemy, but that leads to judgment. You can accept His rule and be unfaithful, but that leads to loss of reward. Or you can accept His rule, do His will faithfully, and receive His reward. You are not to *protect* what He gives you but to *invest* it for His glory.

The day of visitation (28–43). What a tragedy that the Jewish nation did not know their own King when He came to them! But when He comes again, "will He really find faith on the earth" (18:8)? Our Lord wept, for He saw the terrible judgment that was coming to the city and the people.

| *God Seeks . . .* | *What is God looking for? He is seeking the lost (Luke 19:10), worshipers (John 4:23), fruit in our lives (Luke 13:7), and faithful servants (Ezek. 22:30). Has He found you?* |

LUKE 20

In spite of their evasive and hypocritical reply, the leaders *could not escape the past* (vv. 1–8). They had rejected the ministry of John the Baptist, and that led to their refusal to trust Jesus Christ. You may forget your decisions, but they will not forget you. You may even try to bury them, but they will be resurrected to accuse you.

"*Truth is incontrovertible. Panic may resent it; ignorance may deride it; malice may distort it; but there it is.***"**

Sir Winston Churchill

Nor could they *escape future judgment* (vv. 9–19). They would reject the Son and the Stone, and that would bring about their ruin. Christ either saves you or judges you; there is no middle ground.

The leaders even failed to *escape present responsibility* (vv. 20–47). In asking Jesus trick questions, they hoped He would say something they could accuse; but His answers only exposed their folly and increased their guilt. They were fighting a losing battle and would not surrender.

LUKE 21

Maintaining the temple (1–4). Many of the religious leaders were corrupt, but the temple was still the place where God put His name and where sincere people could worship Him. Jesus did not criticize the people for supporting the temple ministry (Matt. 23:1–3), but He did notice *what* they gave. The *proportion,* not the portion, is important. Those who give "the widow's mite" give their all, not their least.

Destroying the temple (5–36). This is Luke's version of the Olivet Discourse found also in Matthew 24—25 and Mark 13. He is the only gospel writer who deals with our Lord's prediction of the fall of Jerusalem, which occurred in A.D. 70 (vv. 20–24). The rest of his report describes events in the last days before the return of Jesus Christ to earth. It will be a time of testing and testimony, oppression and opportunity, vengeance and victory.

Ministering in the temple (37–38). As a boy of twelve, Jesus discussed the Word in the temple (2:41–50); and He spent the last week before His death teaching the Word in His Father's house. He was hated by the religious leaders, and the temple was a den of thieves; but needy people were there, and Jesus taught them. He was quick to seize the opportunity, and the people were glad to hear Him.

LUKE 22

Satan in the temple (1–6). Judas was energized by Satan when he made his agreement with the religious leaders. Satan is a liar and murderer (John 8:44), and he helped Judas with his deception. But Satan deceived Judas as well, and the former disciple ended up a suicide. It is dangerous to make deals with the devil.

Satan in the Upper Room (7–38). Satan already controlled Judas, but he had to ask for permission to "sift" the disciples and to tempt Peter (Job 1:12; 2:6). Satan is not all-powerful and must obey the limits set by the Lord (1 Cor. 10:13). The apostles had experienced some great blessings that evening, but danger was very near. Be on your guard when you have had a rich spiritual experience, for Satan is about to attack. And especially beware when you are trying to decide who is the greatest!

Satan in the Garden (39–53). Jesus said to those who had come to arrest Him, "But this is your hour, and the power of darkness" (v. 53). Because He had prayed and was yielded to the Father's will, Jesus was prepared for the arrest, but the disciples were not. If ever the work of Christ appeared to be ruined, it was in the garden; *but that was when Jesus was doing His very best in the Father's will.*

Satan in the courts (54–71). Satan was in the courtyard to sift Peter and in the council chamber to lead the men astray. His victory over Peter was only temporary, for the apostle wept, repented, and was restored. His victory over the religious leaders was complete, for he blinded their eyes to the truth (2 Cor. 4:3–6) and they condemned their own Messiah.

LUKE 23

Pilate wanted to get rid of Jesus as quickly and as easily as possible, but you cannot avoid making serious decisions about Him. Pilate ended up condemning an innocent Man, releasing a guilty man, and making friends with a wicked man. What a record for a Roman ruler whose responsibility it was to uphold the law and give people justice!

Herod wanted to see Jesus do a miracle! The evil king would make the Son of God into a court entertainer. Jesus performed no miracle; He spoke no word. Herod had silenced God's voice, and there was nothing left for him but divine judgment.

Barabbas deserved to die but was set free because Jesus took his place. Did Barabbas go to Calvary and look at the Man who died for him? Probably not. He was glad to be free from the sentence of death so he could return to his old ways. He was free but still in the bondage of sin.

And for those people—and many more—Jesus prayed, "Father, forgive them, for they do not know what they do" (v. 34). What grace!

The thief exercised great faith when he asked Jesus to remember him, for Jesus did not look like He was able to save anybody.

Joseph exercised great courage when he openly took our Lord's body from the cross. He defiled himself for Passover week, but it made no difference: he had met the Lamb of God, and that was all that mattered.

LUKE 24

Forgetting His word (1–12). The stone was rolled away, the body of Jesus was gone, and the women were perplexed. Why? Because they had forgotten His word. Today, angels do not come to remind us of His word; the Holy Spirit has that ministry (John 14:26). Yield to the Spirit and let Him remind you of the promises that will encourage your heart.

Learning the Word (13–35). Those two men could have walked and talked for days and never gotten rid of their disappointment. Why? Because they lacked the key that unlocks the Old Testament: Messiah must suffer and die before entering His glory. Their hearts burned as they heard Him teach the Scriptures; and soon, the mourners became missionaries and shared the good news with others. Do you allow the Holy Spirit to teach you (John 16:13–15)?

Receiving the Word (36–45). Their hearts were troubled, frightened, and doubtful; yet the Lord lovingly reassured them with His word. We today cannot see or feel His body, but we have the Holy Spirit to make Him real to us from the Scriptures. When your heart is troubled or frightened, see Jesus in the Word (John 14:1–6). When your faith is weak, see Jesus in the Word (Rom. 10:17). The first step toward peace is receiving the Word.

Sharing the Word (46–53). God opens our eyes (v. 31) and opens our understanding (v. 45) so that when He opens the Scriptures to us (vv. 27, 32), we may open our mouths and tell others about Him (v. 48). Jesus gives us the commission, the power, and the message. There is no reason to be silent! When we experience joyful worship (vv. 52–53), we will have little problem giving the world a joyful witness.

JOHN

John had two purposes in mind when he wrote his gospel: to prove that Jesus Christ is the Son of God, and to invite people to believe in Him and be saved (20:30–31). His evidence for the deity of Jesus Christ is threefold: (1) the miracles He performed; (2) the words He spoke; and (3) the testimony of witnesses who knew Him.

As you read the gospel of John, you will hear Jesus speak (7:46), see Him act in power, and watch people respond to what He says and does. Seven witnesses declare that He is the Son of God: John the Baptist (1:34), Nathanael (1:49), Peter (6:69), a man who had been blind (9:35–38), Martha (11:27), Thomas (20:28), and the apostle John (20:31). Jesus also declared His deity (5:25; 10:36).

Matthew wrote for the Jews, Mark for the Romans, and Luke for the Greeks. However, John had the whole world in mind when he wrote and frequently used the word *world*. But he alludes to the Old Testament over one hundred times, showing that he was mindful of his Jewish readers.

The invitation in the synoptic Gospels is, "Come and hear!" But in the Gospel of John, the invitation is also, "Come and see!" There are sixty-seven references in the book to seeing and fifty-eight to hearing. His *works* and His *words* prove that Jesus is indeed the Son of God.

After the introduction (1:1–18), John describes the ministry of Christ to His people (1:19—12:50), to His disciples (chaps. 13—17), and then to the whole world (chaps. 18—21). In the first section, He is the Miracle Worker; in the second, the Teacher; and in the third, the Victor. Of course, throughout the book, Jesus is seen as Savior and Lord.

JOHN 1

The Creator came (1–14). Compare this passage with Genesis 1 and note the emphasis on *light* and *life*. Moses wrote about the old creation, but John wrote about the new creation (2 Cor. 5:17). Jesus is the creative Word and the living Word who reveals the Father to us. In His many miracles, Jesus showed His power as Creator. He is a faithful Creator, and you can trust your life to Him (1 Pet. 4:19).

The Savior came (15–34). He came with grace and truth, not law and judgment. He revealed the Father and gave the Holy Spirit to those who trusted Him. He is the Lamb of God who alone can take away sins. The blood of lambs *covered* the sins of *the Jews,* but the blood of Christ *takes away* the sins of *the whole world* (v. 29; 4:42).

The Master came (35–51). Jesus called a few men to follow Him, and He transformed their lives and used them to transform the lives of others. Simon's new name (Peter, meaning "a stone") symbolized a new beginning in his life. He became a part of the new creation, sharing in the fullness of grace (v. 16). Jesus calls each one individually and uses different approaches, but the same Master calls. Have you heeded His call?

Images of Jesus

John pictures our Lord's death as the slaying of the lamb (1:29), the destroying of a temple (2:19), the lifting up of a serpent (3:14), the voluntary death of a shepherd (10:11–18), and the planting of a seed (12:20–25).

The King came (49). Jesus came to His own creation and everything in creation obeyed Him; but His own people did not receive Him (v. 11; 12:37–41). During His trial before Pilate, His kingship was the paramount issue (18:33—19:22); and it is still the issue today. Who is the king of *your* life?

JOHN 2

Look at Jesus!

He is joyous (1–12). A Jewish wedding is a joyful event, and Jesus was very much at home there. He was "a man of sorrows" (Isa. 53:3), but He also experienced great joy (Luke 10:21); and He can share the joys and sorrows (chap. 11) of our lives. The joy the world offers will eventually fail, but the joy He supplies goes on forever. Be sure to invite Him, and be sure to obey what He says.

He is righteous (13–17). The other gospels record His cleansing of the temple at the close of His ministry, but John tells us He started His ministry by cleansing the temple. Judgment begins at the house of God (1 Pet. 4:17). The temple was then "a house of merchandise" (v. 16); three years later, it was a "den of thieves" (Matt. 21:13). Outward reformation without inward renewal is a temporary thing.

He is victorious (18–25). The Jews repeatedly asked Him for a sign (1 Cor. 1:22) and then rejected the evidence He provided (12:37–41). His resurrection was the greatest proof of His deity (Matt. 12:38–40), but the Jews did not understand what He was talking about (8:42–45). They would destroy the temple by crucifying Him, but He would triumph over them in His resurrection.

Understanding Divine Truths

In his gospel, John points out that unsaved people did not understand what Jesus taught. When He used symbolic language to illustrate a spiritual truth, they took it literally. That was true when He spoke about the temple (2:18–22), the new birth (3:1–9), living water (4:7–15), and eating His flesh and drinking His blood (6:51–52). Apart from the Spirit, you cannot understand His Word (1 Cor. 2:6–16).

Miraculous Works

Out of the many miracles Jesus performed, John selected seven to reveal His glory and prove His deity: turning water into wine (2:1–11); healing the nobleman's son (4:46–54); healing the man sick for thirty-eight years (chap. 5); feeding the five thousand (6:1–14); walking on the stormy sea (6:15–21); restoring sight to a man born blind (chap. 9); and raising Lazarus from the dead (chap. 11). The catch of fish (chap. 21), was performed after His resurrection.

JOHN 3

A birth from above (1–9). In our first birth, we are "born of the flesh" and "born of water"; but in our second birth, we are "born from above [again]" and "born of the Spirit." Our first birth leads to death, but our second birth brings eternal life. The new birth is a new beginning that results in "newness of life" (Rom. 6:4).

A Savior from above (10–21). Jesus is the Son of God come down from heaven. He is the serpent Moses wrote about (Num. 21:4-9); He is the Father's love gift (v. 16); He is the Light in a dark world (v. 19). Like the serpent, He was lifted up, and He died on a cross for the sins of the world. All who look to Him by faith receive eternal life.

A witness from above (22–36). John's ministry was given to him from heaven (v. 27). His task was to bear witness to Jesus (1:6-8). Jesus is the Word, and John was only a voice proclaiming the Word (1:23). Jesus is the Bridegroom, but John was only the best man. John did no miracles, but his witness was used to win people to Christ, even after he was dead (10:40–42). Can you honestly say, "He must increase, but I must decrease" (v. 30)?

Nicodemus

Nicodemus came to Jesus by night, but he finally came out into the light and identified with the Lord Jesus (19:38–42). Nicodemus gave Jesus an honest hearing (7:45–52), examined the Word, and became a believer.

JOHN 4

Thirst (1–26). Because Jesus was truly human, He experienced weariness, hunger, and thirst, but His deepest desire was for the salvation of the sinful woman. He forgot His physical needs and concentrated on her spiritual needs. Patiently He revealed Himself to her: "a Jew" (v. 9), "greater than Jacob" (v. 12), "a prophet" (v. 19), "Messiah" (vv. 25, 29). She believed in Him, and her life was so changed that she immediately shared the good news with others (20:30–31).

Hunger (27–42). The will of God should be food that nourishes us, not medicine that upsets us. The disciples were satisfied with material food, but Jesus wanted the satisfying spiritual food from God. The will of God gives us the strength we need to do our job in the great harvest all around us.

Health (43–54). Salvation is to the inner person what health is to the body. The boy would have died had Jesus not intervened and given him health. The father *heard* (v. 47), *believed* (v. 50), and *knew* (v. 53), which is a normal Christian experience.

Jesus won the woman; the woman won many Samaritans; and the father won his whole household. Are you busy in the harvest?

JOHN 5

Works (vv. 1–21). The Father "broke" His Sabbath rest to help two sinners (Gen. 3:8ff.), and Jesus followed His example. In the world of nature, the Father is healing bodies, multiplying food, turning water into wine, and so forth; but He takes longer to do those things. Our Lord's miracles are the Father's works done instantly. Whether instantly or gradually, they are wonderful works of God.

Wrath (22, 24–30). Today, Jesus is the Savior; tomorrow, He will be the Judge (Rev. 20:11–15). Even death cannot keep lost sinners from the judgment, for He will raise them from the dead. There is no escape, except faith in Jesus Christ (5:24).

Worship (23). If you worship God the Father, you must also worship the Son; and if you dishonor the Son, you dishonor the Father. Those who claim to worship God but ignore the Son are not even worshiping God! They are only fooling themselves.

Witness (31–47). How can anyone deny that Jesus is the Son of God when so many witnesses affirm that He is: John the Baptist (vv. 31–35), the miracles (v. 36), the Father (v. 37; Mark 1:11), and the Scriptures (vv. 38–39)? But when people believe on Him, they have the witness within themselves (vv. 39–47; 1 John 5:9–13).

JOHN 6

The disciples faced three tests because of the great crowds that followed Jesus.

Feeding the multitude (1–14). Philip thought the answer was money, but Andrew saw the answer in a lad with a lunch. When you face a seemingly unsolvable problem, claim the promise of verse 6, give what you have to Jesus, and let Him tell you what to do.

Leaving the multitude (15–21). This incident occurred at the high point of our Lord's popularity. The disciples (especially Judas) would have welcomed a kingdom, so Jesus sent them away into a storm. They went from popularity to peril, but they were safer in the storm than with the multitude; and Jesus came to them and met their needs (Isa. 43:2). Can you obey His will even when you disagree with Him?

Losing the multitude (22–71). People want the Lord to meet their physical needs but not their spiritual needs. The manna (Exod. 16) came only to the Jews and *sustained* physical life, but Jesus came for the whole world and *gives* eternal life. Just as you take food into your body, so you take Christ into your life; and He becomes one with you. The disciples had opportunity to follow the crowd, but they remained with Jesus.

JOHN 7

How the world thinks (1–9). Because He was doing the Father's will, Jesus lived on a divine timetable (v. 30; 2:4; 8:20; 13:1), and so should we (Ps. 31:14–15). The world does not understand this and will give you advice contrary to God's will. Live on God's schedule and you will always have God's help.

How the world decides (10–36). This discussion reveals the confusion and unbelief of the people. Some were for Him because of His miracles, while others opposed Him because He broke the Sabbath laws. Some waited to see what their leaders would do (v. 26), and their leaders wanted to kill Him. They were judging by appearances (v. 24) and going astray.

What the world needs (37–53). One ritual during the Feast of Tabernacles was the pouring out of water in the temple. It was a reminder that God gave Israel water in the wilderness. Water for drinking pictures the Holy Spirit who is given to those who trust Christ. The world is thirsty and can find its thirst quenched only by coming to Christ.

Life
Life *is a key theme in John's gospel; he uses the word nearly fifty times. Jesus is the life (14:6), the light of life (1:4; 8:12), and the bread of life (6:48); and He gives the water of life (7:37–39). Jesus laid down His life so that we might have life (10:14–18, 27–30).*

JOHN 8

Condemnation (1–11). The woman was guilty, but where was the man? Both of them deserved to die (Lev. 20:10). It was a trap and Jesus knew it, but He ended up trapping the trappers. Did He write on the ground to remind them that He had written the Law (Exod. 31:18) or to refer them to Jeremiah 17:13 (see Luke 10:20)? Here is our wonderful assurance: "There is therefore now no condemnation to those who are in Christ Jesus" (Rom. 8:1).

Illumination (12–29). The religious leaders did not know where they were going or where He was going because they were in the dark spiritually. They had the light of the Law (v. 5; Prov. 6:23) and of conscience (v. 9), but they did not have the light of life. Consequently, they did not know the Father or understand what Jesus taught them.

Liberation (30–59). The people were in bondage to Rome and to the Law of Moses, yet they said they were free! In verse 35, Jesus may have been referring to Isaac and Ishmael (Gen. 21:8–21), since the Jews had mentioned Abraham (v. 33). The Son makes you free (v. 36), so trust Him and follow Him. His truth makes you free (v. 32), so study it, believe it, and obey it. Satan imposes slavery that seems like freedom (2 Pet. 2:19); Jesus gives you a yoke that sets you free (Matt. 11:28–30).

Whose Child Are You?

There is no record that Jesus ever called the publicans and sinners "children of the devil." He reserved that title for the hypocritical Pharisees. By nature, we are all "children of wrath"; and by choice, we become "children of disobedience" (Eph. 2:1–3). When you receive Jesus Christ, you become a child of God (John 1:12–13). But if you reject Christ and have a false righteousness (Rom. 9:30—10:13), you are in danger of becoming a "child of the devil," for Satan is an imitator (2 Cor. 11:13–15). If Satan becomes your father, hell will be your home.

JOHN 9

Irritation (1–12). By putting clay on the man's eyes, Jesus encouraged him to obey and wash on the Sabbath. Sometimes the Lord irritates us before He illuminates us. His power is so great that He can use common things like dirt and water to produce a miracle. The man could hear but not see, and the Word produced faith (Rom. 10:17).

Interrogation (13–34). The man was questioned by the neighbors (v. 10) and by the Pharisees (vv. 15, 19, 26). Instead of seeking the truth and the freedom it brings (8:32), the Pharisees denied the truth and ended up in worse bondage. If we ask questions sincerely, with a willingness to obey, the Lord will lead us to the truth (7:17). If we are not honest with God, He will never show us His light.

Identification (35–41). The Pharisees were false shepherds who threw the man out, but Jesus the Good Shepherd took him in! The man knew that He was "a Man called Jesus" (v. 11), "a prophet" (v. 17), and "a Man of God" (v. 33); but he needed to learn that He is "the Son of God" (v. 35). He believed and was saved. Beware a spiritual experience that comes short of true salvation.

JOHN 10

God's people are His flock (Ps. 100:3; Acts 20:28), and they must beware strangers (v. 5), thieves (vv. 1, 10), and hirelings (v. 12). Jesus is the Good Shepherd who knows His sheep (vv. 14–15) and speaks to them (v. 27), so He is not like the strangers. He protects the sheep (vv. 28–29), so He is not like the thieves; and He gives His life for the sheep, so He is not like the hirelings who run away from danger (vv. 11–13).

When you trust the Good Shepherd, He leads you out of the wrong fold and into the right flock (vv. 3–4, 16). He goes before you and leads you by His Word (v. 4), and He leads you in and out to find spiritual nourishment (v. 9).

There are many churches but only "one flock and one shepherd" (v. 16). Is the Lord using you to bring the "other sheep" to Him?

<blockquote>

In the Good Shepherd's Flock

Why does the Lord compare His people to sheep? They are prone to wander (Isa. 53:6) and need a shepherd to guide them. Sheep are clean animals (1 Pet. 2:25; 2 Pet. 2:20–22) and were used for sacrifices (Rom. 8:36; 12:1). They flock together (Acts 4:32) and are useful because they produce milk, lambs, and wool. The Good Shepherd knows His sheep intimately and calls them by name. He protects them and provides for them (Ps. 23). How wonderful to be one of His sheep!

</blockquote>

JOHN 11

This experience was difficult for the Bethany family, but look at it in the light of God's love (vv. 3, 5, 36).

Love hears (1–3). The sisters sent their message to the Lord because they knew He was concerned about them. God's love keeps His ears open to our cries (Ps. 34:12–16).

Love waits (4–6). We think that love must act immediately, but sometimes delay brings a greater blessing. "God's delays are not God's denials." Jesus gave them a promise to encourage them while they waited (v. 4). The promise seemed to have failed, but Jesus knew what He was doing.

Love risks (7–16). It was dangerous for Jesus to return to Judea, but He went just the same. The raising of Lazarus helped to precipitate the plans that led to His death (vv. 45–57).

Love comforts (17–32). Jesus came to the sisters, listened to them, and assured them with His word. He cannot really help us until we move from "Lord, if . . ." (vv. 21, 32) to "Yes, Lord, I believe" (v. 27).

Love weeps (33–37). Jesus identifies with our sorrows (Heb.

4:15–16). He knew He would raise Lazarus from the dead, but He still wept with the sisters and their friends.

Love serves (38–44). We today are not able to raise the dead, but we can serve others as they go through the valley (Rom. 12:15). A loving heart will always find a way to bear others' burdens (Gal. 6:2).

---

66 *If God is at work week by week raising men from the dead, there will always be people coming to see how it is done. You cannot find an empty church that has conversion for its leading feature. Do you want to know how to fill empty chapels? Here is the answer: Get your Lazarus.* **99**

Samuel Chadwick, Methodist evangelist and educator (1860–1932)

JOHN 12

Fragrance (1–11). What would your plans be if you knew you had only six days to live? Jesus took time to visit dear friends and fellowship with them. Mary's adoration not only revealed her love, but it brought joy to His heart, exposed Judas's sin, and gave the church an example to follow. Are the places where you go filled with Christ's fragrance because of you (2 Cor. 2:15–16)?

Festival (12–19). Jesus took advantage of the large Passover crowd to present Himself as King (Zech. 9:9). He was forcing the Jewish leaders to act, for it was the Father's will that Jesus die on Passover. The crowd did not stay with Him. It is easier to shout in a parade than stand at a cross.

Fruitfulness (20–36). Jesus looked upon His death as an opportunity to glorify God (vv. 23, 28). Do you take that attitude when you face a time of trial? He saw Himself as a seed that would die and produce fruit and as a conqueror who would defeat Satan (v. 31; Col. 2:14–15). The Cross would open the way of salvation for both Jews and Gentiles (v. 32).

Faithlessness (37–50). In His words and works, Jesus showed Israel the light, but they chose to walk in darkness. The praise of men meant more to them than the praise of God (5:44). Be careful what you do with His words because you will hear them again when you see the Savior (v. 48).

JOHN 13

What Jesus knew (1–11). Because of what Jesus knew, He did what He did: He washed the disciples' feet. Jesus knew where He came from and where He was going. He knew that the Father had given Him all things (3:35). If you have all things in your hand, you will have no problem picking up a towel (1 Cor. 3:21–23). Jesus taught them a lesson in fellowship and in keeping themselves clean before the Lord (1 John 1:5–2:1).

What the disciples knew (12–20). Jesus taught them a second lesson: true happiness comes from humble service. Jesus gave them an example that we must follow today (Phil. 2:1–11). Alas, soon after this lesson, the disciples began to argue over who was the greatest (Luke 22:24–30).

The Holy Spirit

The Holy Spirit is the Father's gift to you, a gift that will never be taken back (John 14:16). The Spirit is a person, like the Father and the Son, and is God; and He dwells in God's people (14:17). He enables you to witness for Christ (15:26–27; Acts 1:8) and through your witness convicts the lost (16:7–11). He will teach you the Word (14:26) and use it in your life to glorify Christ (16:12–15).

What Judas knew (21–30). Jesus did not reveal Judas's secret; in fact, He treated him just like the others and they detected nothing amiss. What love that Jesus should not only protect the man who betrayed Him but even wash his feet! Jesus with the towel is the perfect example of humility; Judas with the bread is a perfect example of hypocrisy and treachery.

What the world must know (31–38). The distinguishing mark of true disciples is their love for one another (1 John 2:7–11), and it is the kind of love that the world can see. He commands us to love, and He gives us the power to obey (Rom. 5:5).

JOHN 14

No wonder the disciples were troubled (vv. 1, 27): Jesus was going to leave them, one of them would betray Him, and Peter would deny Him. Jesus encouraged them by telling them about Himself and the Father.

Jesus takes us to the Father (1–6). We have a home in heaven when life is over, and we shall meet Jesus and the Father. James M. Gray wrote, "Who could mind the journey when the road leads home?" Blessed assurance!

Jesus reveals the Father (7–11). In what He said (7:16) and did (5:19) during His earthly ministry, Jesus revealed the Father: "I and My Father are one" (10:30). How can we not love the Father when He is like Jesus?

Jesus glorifies the Father (12–18). He does it through His people as they do God's works and keep His commandments. Apart from the power of the Holy Spirit and prayer, we could never glorify the Lord.

Jesus and the Father dwell with us (19–31). It is one thing for us to go to heaven and quite something else for heaven to come to us! There is a deeper fellowship with the Son and the Father for those who love Him, seek Him, and obey Him. We experience His peace as we commune with the Father and the Son in love.

Jesus is the way to the Father; He reveals the truth about the Father; and He shares the life of the Father with us. Why should our hearts be troubled?

JOHN 15

His life (1–8). A branch is good for only one thing—bearing fruit. It may be weak in itself, but it has a living relationship with the vine and can be productive. To abide in Christ means to be in communion with Him so that our lives please Him. We know that we are abiding when the Father prunes us, cutting away the good so that we can produce the best. We glorify God with fruit, more fruit, much fruit.

His love (9–17). Abiding depends on obeying, and obeying depends on loving. Love and joy go together and make it easy for us to obey His will. We should love Him, love His will, and love one another. Note the "fruit of the Spirit": love (v. 10), joy (v. 11), and peace (14:27; Gal. 5:22).

His name (18–27). We enjoy the love of Christ and of the brethren, but we also must endure the hatred of the world for His name's sake. The more we are like Christ, the more the world system will oppose us. Depend on the Spirit's power and you will be a fruitful, faithful Christian (vv. 26–27).

JOHN 16

The world's opposition (1–15). The Lord warned them about the opposition that would come. Do not be surprised when you are persecuted by religious people (v. 2), for this has been going on ever since Cain killed Abel (Gen. 4; Luke 11:47–51). The Spirit helps us witness to the world and glorify Christ before the world (Acts 4:8ff.), so depend on Him.

The world's joy (16–24). When Jesus was arrested, crucified, and buried, the world system rejoiced because their Enemy was out of the way. But today He is alive, and we have every reason to rejoice! The Lord does not *replace* our sorrow with joy; He *transforms* our sorrow into joy. The same baby that gives the mother pain also gives her joy. The world's joy does not last, but the believer's joy is forever (Ps. 16:11).

The world's defeat (25–33). In the next few hours, the disciples would watch their world fall apart; and yet Jesus assured them that He was the winner. "I have overcome the world" is a fact, not a promise, and it applies to us today. We are overcomers through Him (1 John 5:1–5).

JOHN 17

In this, his high priestly prayer, Jesus prayed for Himself (vv. 1–5), His disciples (vv. 6–19), and all of His church (vv. 20–26).

The prayer reveals our Lord's spiritual priorities: glorifying the Father (v. 1), the unity of the church (vv. 21–23), the sanctity of the church (v. 17), and the winning of a lost world (vv. 18–19). Are these priorities in your life?

It also reveals the gifts He has given His people: eternal life (vv. 2–3), the Word (vv. 8, 14), and His glory (v. 22). But note that believers are the Father's gift to Him (vv. 2, 6, 9, 11–12), just as Jesus is the Father's love gift to us (3:16). It is all of grace!

The word *world* appears nineteen times in this prayer, for this prayer tells us how to "overcome the world" (16:33). We must seek God's glory first (vv. 1–5), experience His joy (v. 13), be sanctified by the Word (v. 17), seek to win the lost (vv. 18–19), and encourage the unity of God's people (vv. 20–23).

Judas the Lost	*Judas was not a saved man, even though he was one of the Twelve. He never believed in Jesus (6:66–71) and therefore was never washed from his sins (13:11). He was not chosen by Christ (13:18) and therefore not kept (17:12). Judas is a frightening example of how near one can get to the kingdom and still be lost.*

Glory is another key word. Christ laid aside His glory to come to earth (v. 5b), glorified God on earth (v. 4), and was glorified when He returned to heaven (v. 5a). Christ is glorified in His church (v. 10) and has shared His glory with the church (vv. 22, 24). We already have the glory; we are just waiting for it to be fully revealed (Rom. 8:18–21, 30).

The Scottish Reformer John Knox had this prayer read to him daily during his last illness. But you would benefit by starting now to read it and meditate on it. What a treasury of truth it is!

JOHN 18

Judas depended on the strength of numbers, Peter on the strength of his arm, Annas and Caiaphas on the strength of their position, but Jesus on the strength of love and devotion to the Father. Jesus had a cup in His hand, not a sword, but that cup was His scepter. He was in complete control.

On the other hand, Peter fought when he should have yielded and followed when he should have fled. Yielding and fleeing looked like defeat, but they were the Father's will; and Peter should have obeyed. While Jesus was giving His witness to the high priest, Peter was denying the Lord. Which was the successful witness, Peter or Jesus?

As a Roman governor, Pilate was worried about the threat of another kingdom. Verse 36 is certainly a rebuke to believers who follow the example of Peter. At Pentecost, Peter wielded the sword of the Spirit and won a victory.

JOHN 19

The crown (1–16). Jesus and Pilate had been talking about a kingdom, so it was only right that the King have a crown. It was meant for mockery, but it preached a message, for Jesus was wearing the consequences of Adam's sins (Gen. 3:17–19). But a crown is a sign of victory. He has overcome!

The cross (17–27). Jesus started out bearing His own cross, but then Simon was drafted to carry it for Him (Mark 15:21). We are not told why, although tradition says that Jesus fell and could not carry it. Considering all He had been through, that is not difficult to believe. Criminals carried the cross as a sign of guilt, *and Jesus was not guilty!*

The conquest (28–42). "It is finished!" was the cry of a conqueror. Jesus accomplished what all of the old covenant sacrifices could not do (Heb. 10:1–18). The prophecies and types were fulfilled and the sacrifice for sins made once and for all forever. It was not a martyr that Joseph and Nicodemus put into the tomb; it was a victor.

Our Final Payment

The Greek word translated "It is finished!" was a familiar word in that day. Bankers used it when the final payment had been made on a debt. Jesus completely paid the debt we owed, and it will be remembered against us no more forever. Hallelujah, what a Savior!

JOHN 20

Confusion (1–10). Mary jumped to conclusions and soon had Peter and John on the run. They were busy, but they had nothing to say and were accomplishing little. They saw the evidence for the Resurrection, but it did not change their lives. They needed a meeting with the living Christ.

Love (11–18). Unbelief blinds our eyes to the Lord's presence. When He speaks His word to us, faith and love are rekindled. Mary was changed from a mourner to a missionary when she met the living Lord.

Peace (19–23). Locked doors will not give you peace, nor will they keep out your loving Savior. He comes with the message of peace based on His sacrifice on the cross (v. 20; Rom. 5:1).

Faith (24–31). The Lord tenderly deals with our doubts and unbelief. We today cannot see Him or feel His wounds, but we have the Word of God to assure us (vv. 9, 30–31). When your faith falters, do not ask for signs. Open His Word and let Him reassure you.

JOHN 21

Jesus the Stranger (1–4). When Peter returned to the old life, he took six other men with him. Their work was in vain (15:5) because the Lord was not with them. How kind He is to come to us when we have disobeyed Him and have failed in our work!

Jesus the Master (5–8). When Jesus takes charge, failure is turned into success; and the difference was only the width of the ship! You never know how close you are to victory, so admit your failure and obey what He tells you to do. He never fails.

Jesus the Host (9–14). It took six men to drag the net (v. 8), but Peter did it alone when Jesus gave the orders (v. 11). We should always remember that "God's commandment is God's enablement." Did the fire of coals remind Peter of his denials (18:18ff.)? Did the miraculous catch of fish remind him of his call to service (Luke 5:1–11)? How kind of Jesus to feed Peter before dealing with him about his sins!

Jesus the Shepherd (15–17). The most important thing in ministry is loving Christ, for all ministry flows from that. Peter the fisherman was also to be a shepherd and care for the lambs and sheep.

Jesus the Lord (18–25). By saying, "Follow Me," Jesus reinstated Peter as an apostle. But Peter turned around and took his eyes off the Lord (Matt. 14:30), and Jesus had to rebuke him. The next time you are tempted to meddle in somebody else's ministry, ponder Christ's words: "What is that to you? You follow Me!" (v. 22).

Peter followed the Lord right into the excitement of the book of Acts!

ACTS

◆

Perhaps a better title is "The Acts of the Holy Spirit through the Church." This story tells how God's people obeyed the Lord's commission to take the gospel to the whole world. Luke wrote it as a companion volume to his gospel (1:1–3; Luke 1:1–4), and it describes what Jesus *continued to do and teach* after He returned to heaven.

Peter's ministry dominates the first part of the book (chaps. 1–12), and then Luke focuses on Paul's ministry (chaps. 13–28). These two men had parallel experiences of both trial and ministry. Peter used the "keys" (Matt. 16:19) to open the door of faith to the Jews (chap. 2), the Samaritans (chap. 8), and the Gentiles (chap. 10); Paul took the good news to the Gentiles in the Roman Empire.

Acts 1:8 outlines the book, for the gospel went from Jerusalem (chaps. 1–7) to Judea and Samaria (chaps. 8–9) and then to the ends of the earth (chaps. 10–28). The book of Acts describes a transition from ministry to Jews to ministry to the Gentiles and explains how the gospel got from Jerusalem to Rome.

This book is for every Christian who wants to experience the power of the Holy Spirit and be a witness for Jesus Christ "to the end of the earth" (1:8). Ask God what part He wants you to play in taking the gospel to the whole world, starting right where you are. "Lord, what do You want me to do?" (9:6).

ACTS 1

One hundred and twenty ordinary people hardly constitute an imposing army; but in a few days, they would make an impact that is being felt even today. The same resources God gave them are still available to us.

A living Lord (1–3). Christ is the Head of the church (Eph. 1:22; 4:15) and supplies life to His body, giving dynamic and direction to His people. What He began to do and teach, the church continues as He guides and empowers through His Spirit.

The power of the Spirit (4–8). God's power is available to God's people who want to do His will and be His witnesses. You do not have to be an apostle to have the power of the Spirit in your life (Eph. 5:18).

The promise of His return (9–11). He is the Lord of history, working out His purposes in this world. The church may lose some battles, but we will win the war!

Trust God's Guidance

If we are faithful to read God's Word, study it, meditate on it, and obey it, God will guide us when we have decisions to make. The Holy Spirit teaches us (John 14:26; 16:13–14) and directs us when we pray and seek the Lord's will. The Holy Spirit uses truth, not ignorance; so the more facts we have, the better. We should use our common sense but not lean on it (Prov. 3:5–6), for we walk by faith and not by sight. If we sincerely move in the wrong direction, the Lord will show us (Acts 16:6–10; Phil. 3:15), so we need not fear. It is good for believers to read the Word and pray together as they seek the mind of the Lord.

The power of prayer (12–14, 24–26). God shares His power with us as we pray and ask Him for His help. Throughout Acts, notice Luke's emphasis on prayer. The first church was a praying church.

The guidance of Scripture (15–23). His Word is still our lamp and light (Ps. 119:105), and we must obey what it says. God guides His people when they are willing to follow.

ACTS 2

The Spirit came, not because the believers prayed but because the day of Pentecost had come, the day appointed for the "birthday of the church" (Lev. 23:15–21). He baptized the believers into one body (1 Cor. 12:13) so that they had a living connection with their Head exalted in heaven. Luke 2 describes the birth of the Lord's *physical* body and Acts 2 the birth of His *spiritual* body.

The Spirit also filled the believers and empowered them for witness. He gave Peter insight into the Word and the ability to show men Christ in the Word. The Spirit used the witness of the church to convict the lost, just as Jesus said He would do (16:7–10).

The Gift of Tongues

The believers praised God in "other tongues," that is, known languages understood by the people present (Acts 2:6–11). The apostles worshiped and praised God in tongues (v. 11) but preached the gospel in Aramaic, a tongue the Jews could understand. During the transition in ministry from Jews to Gentiles, each time Peter used the "keys," the gift of tongues was evident: among the Jews (2:1–4), the Samaritans (8:14ff.), and the Gentiles (10:44–48). Not all believers speak in tongues (1 Cor. 12:30), and it is not identified as one of the most important gifts (1 Cor. 12:7–11).

But the same Holy Spirit assisted the believers in their church fellowship (vv. 40–47). The original group was outnumbered by the new believers, but there was still harmony in the church family. They worshiped daily and witnessed daily, and "the Lord added to the church daily" (v. 47). Is your experience with the Lord a *daily* one?

ACTS 3

Priorities. Peter and John were not so caught up with large crowds that they had no time for individuals. Nor were they so busy in ministry that they could not pray. They had learned their lessons well from the Lord Jesus (Mark 1:35; Luke 8:40ff.).

Power. The emphasis in chapters 3—4 is on the name of Jesus (3:6, 13, 16, 20, 26; 4:2, 7, 10, 12, 17–18), the name above every name (Phil. 2:9–11). Faith in the name of Jesus releases power so that lives are changed. To pray or minister in His name means to ask or act on His authority (Matt. 28:18–20) so that He alone gets the glory.

Proclamation. At Pentecost, the sound of a rushing wind drew the crowd (2:2, 6); but here the witness of a changed life brought the people together. Thus, Peter had the opportunity to preach, and two thousand people were converted. Reach out to the individual (v. 7) and God will give you opportunities for a bigger harvest (John 4:28ff.).

"*It's the individual touch that tells. He [Jesus] doesn't love in the mass, but in ones.***"**

Amy Carmichael

ACTS 4

In his sermon at Pentecost, Peter proved from the Scriptures that Jesus was alive; but now he proved it by the miraculous change in the beggar's life. The man was healed through the power of the name of Jesus. The Sadducees did not believe in resurrection (23:6–8), so they wanted to put a stop to the ministry of the apostles. This was the beginning of the official persecution of Christians.

What do you do when they tell you to stop sharing the gospel? What did the apostles do? Certainly they recalled the words of Jesus Christ (Matt. 10:16–26) and depended on the Holy Spirit to help them. Furthermore, they were so filled with their message and with love for Christ that they could not stop telling people about Him!

They depended on prayer (vv. 23–31) and directed their prayer to a sovereign God who made everything and can do anything. They based their petitions on Psalm 2, a marvelous psalm to read when you are being attacked.

When you are "let go," where do you go (v. 23)? When you are in trouble, to whom do you turn?

ACTS 5

Pretending (1–11). Barnabas's gift (4:36–37) exposed the sin of Ananias and Sapphira, just as Mary's gift exposed Judas's sin (John 12). The couple lied to the Spirit, to the church, and to Peter; and it cost them their lives. Their sin was not in taking money from God but in pretending to be something they were not.

Obeying (12–16). Dealing with sin in the church often results in new power for the church. Can you imagine a church so spiritual that people were afraid to join with them? Even Peter's shadow had power!

"We make our decisions, and then our decisions turn around and make us.**"**

F. W. Boreham

Opposing (17–32). Because the Sadducees could not tolerate evidences of resurrection power, they arrested the apostles again and told them to be quiet. "We ought to obey God rather than men" (v. 29) is the only position to hold when you have the Word of God on your side. Be sure it is conviction and not just opinion.

Hesitating (33–42). Gamaliel advised neutrality, which means avoiding the truth and letting Satan move in (Matt. 12:30, 43–45). With all the evidence they had seen, the council's neutrality was actually dishonesty. If you followed Gamaliel's advice in any area of life—science, cooking, finance—it would lead to paralysis and then death.

> **"** *There is no more miserable human being than one in whom nothing is habitual but indecision.* **"**
>
> William James

ACTS 6

When you yield yourself to do God's will, you never know what challenges you will face.

Serving tables (1–7). No ministry is unimportant for a Christlike servant, for Jesus said, "I am among you as the One who serves" (Luke 22:27). In serving tables, the men released the apostles for their ministry of prayer and the Word; and the result was an increase in conversions (v. 7). People filled with the Spirit see no small jobs or big places. They see only their Master and the opportunity to glorify Him.

Doing wonders (8). From serving tables to doing miracles! Stephen reached out to the lost and sought to win them to Christ. If you are faithful with a few things, the Lord may give you many things (Matt. 25:21).

Facing enemies (9–15). The unbelievers treated Stephen the way the Sanhedrin treated Jesus: they arrested him on trumped-up charges and hired false witnesses to testify. Stephen experienced "the fellowship of His sufferings" (Phil. 3:10), and so will you if your witness hits home (Matt. 5:11–12). They said Stephen was opposing Moses, but he had a shining face just like Moses (Exod. 34)!

<table>
<tr><td>

Tradition or Truth?

</td><td>

They accused Stephen of being unorthodox in his beliefs (Acts 6:13); but yesterday's orthodoxy had become today's heresy, and the council was behind the times! The Law had been nailed to the cross (Col. 2:14), and the veil of the temple had been torn in two. Within a few years, both the city and the temple would be gone, and Hosea 3:4 would be fulfilled. Are you following man's tradition or God's truth?

</td></tr>
</table>

❝There are many of us that are willing to do great things for the Lord; but few of us are willing to do little things.**❞**

D. L. Moody

ACTS 7

The main thrust of Stephen's message is that Israel always resisted the truth and rejected the deliverers God sent to them. They opposed Moses and repeatedly wanted to return to Egypt. They opposed Joseph, and he later became their redeemer! They rejected the many prophets God sent to warn them and call them back to His way. Finally, they rejected their own Messiah and crucified Him.

Israel's history reveals the patience of God and the hardness of man's heart. But it also reveals a ray of hope: Israel rejected their deliverers the first time *but accepted them the second time*. That was true of Moses and Joseph, and it will be true of Jesus when He returns (Zech. 12:10).

Stephen's death was the third murder in Israel's history and a turning point in God's dealings with the nation. They had rejected the Father when they allowed John the Baptist to be slain; they had rejected the Son when they asked for Jesus to be crucified; and now they had rejected the Holy Spirit. There could be no more forgiveness (Matt. 12:31–32). The line had been crossed, and the gospel moved out to Judea and Samaria.

Stephen *The name* Stephen *means "a crown," and he won the crown of life because he was faithful unto death (Rev. 2:10).*

ACTS 8

The death of Stephen seemed to be a defeat for the church, but it resulted in some great victories for the Lord. Wherever the believers went, they shared the gospel and many trusted the Savior (vv. 1–7; 11:19). Stephen's witness made a tremendous impression on Saul and was instrumental in his conversion (22:20). Never give up when the enemy seems to be winning. It may be your finest hour of victory.

> **❝**I live for souls and for eternity, I want to win some soul to Christ. If you want this and work for it, eternity alone can tell the result.**❞**
>
> D. L. Moody

Like Stephen, Philip was a deacon who was also an evangelist; and God led him to witness in Samaria to people hostile to the Jews (John 4:9). The coming of Peter and John and the giving of the Holy Spirit linked the Samaritan believers to the saints in Jerusalem and the ancient division was healed. The way to turn enemies into friends is to make them brothers and sisters in Christ.

In times of great blessing, wherever God sows true seed, the devil sows a counterfeit (Matt. 13:24-30, 36-43). Like Peter, we must be alert and exercise discernment.

Philip left a great harvest to talk to one man, but that is the mark of a true servant of the Lord. We must go where God sends us, do what God tells us, and leave the results with Him.

ACTS 9

The conversion of Saul of Tarsus was a turning point in the church's history, and God used several people to touch his life. We remember Paul and are prone to forget the people who helped him get started.

The witness of Stephen was significant (22:20) as were the testimonies and prayers of persons Saul persecuted (Matt. 5:44). Ananias baptized him and encouraged him, and the disciples at Damascus saved his life. When the church in Jerusalem feared to welcome Saul into their fellowship, Barnabas ("son of encouragement") built the bridge. Barnabas later enlisted Saul to serve in the Antioch church (11:25-26) and traveled with him in evangelistic ministry among the Gentiles (13:1-3).

You may not be called to a prominent work as Saul was, but you can do the job God has called you to do and be an encouragement to others. We do not know the names of the brave men who smuggled Saul out of Damascus (v. 25), but holding the ropes was an important job!

ACTS 10

Peter uses the "keys" for the third and last time as he opens the door of faith to the Gentiles. How wonderful is the providence of God! Paul, the apostle to the Gentiles, was being prepared for his life's work; and Peter was about to break down the ancient barriers between Jews and Gentiles: "Known to God from eternity are all His works" (15:18).

But God had to prepare both Peter and Cornelius. He

spoke to Cornelius while he was praying and to Peter while he was relaxing. Be alert to the voice of God; you never know when He may have a word for you.

"Not so, Lord! For I have never . . ." (v. 14) is the response that leads to defeat. God was about to do a new thing, and Peter wanted to hold on to the old. He calls Him Lord but refuses to obey Him! Yet God tenderly instructed Peter, and the apostle surrendered to His will.

Peter did not get to finish his sermon. When he said, "Whosoever believes in Him will receive remission of sins" (v. 43), they believed and were saved. What a great way to stop a sermon!

❝You can say 'Lord,' and you can say 'Not so,'
but you cannot say, 'Not so, Lord.'**❞**

W. Graham Scroggie

ACTS 11

Some people make things happen. Peter was available to the Lord, and God used him to officially bring gentile believers into the church. The wall between Jews and Gentiles had been broken down (Eph. 2:11ff.)! The news was astounding to the Jewish believers, for they thought the Gentiles must first become Jewish proselytes before they could become Christians. Thank God that Peter was the kind of person who makes things happen!

Some people hear that things happen. This category may include most of us, but how do you respond when you hear that God has done something new? Do you sincerely try to get the facts, or do you depend on hearsay? We are to "test all things; hold fast what is good" (1 Thess. 5:22).

Some people oppose things happening. The legalistic members of the Jerusalem assembly attacked Peter for eating with the Gentiles, so he explained how God had led. He proved from Scripture (v. 16; 1:5) that what happened was the will of God, and his explanation silenced his critics for the time. However, the legalistic element in the church would rise again (chap. 15) and seek to limit the freedom of the gospel.

Some people help other people make things happen. Barnabas enlisted Saul (vv. 25–26) and put him to work in the Antioch church, which led to their going together to the Gentiles with the message of salvation. Barnabas lived up to his name of "son of encouragement."

He Worked for the Great Physician

John Calvin's physician told him to stop working or he would die, and Calvin replied, "Would you have my Master come and find me loitering?"

ACTS 12

The will of the Lord is always wise and good, but it is not always predictable. God spared Peter but allowed James to be killed. He did not deliver Peter from prison until the last minute. He allowed Herod to slay James, but He did not permit the king to act like a god. Is that how *you* would have done it?

Some Christians are like Job's friends: they think they always know exactly what God is doing, will do, and wants done; but they may be wrong. Whenever you are tempted to "play God" in somebody's life, ponder Isaiah 55:8–9.

It is always right to pray, even if your faith is so weak you are surprised when the answer comes! Keep knocking—God opens doors.

ACTS 13

Opportunities come to people busy serving the Lord. God calls people who take time to worship and minister to the Lord. If you want God's guidance, get busy where you are, and He will show you the next step.

Opportunities usually produce opposition (1 Cor. 16:9).

Here is another example of the parable of the tares (Matt. 13:24–30, 36–43): God sowed the good seed (Paul and Barnabas), and Satan sowed a counterfeit.

Opportunities reveal character. Paul and Barnabas kept going, but John Mark returned home. We do not know why, nor should we pass judgment (1 Cor. 10:12). Barnabas reclaimed John Mark (15:36–41) and Paul eventually accepted him (2 Tim. 4:11).

Opportunities develop leadership. The trip began with "Barnabas and Saul" (v. 2), but it became "Paul and his party" (v. 13). Barnabas rejoiced to see Paul being used so mightily of God (Rom. 12:9–11). It was a team effort, and the vital thing was the glory of God.

His Word Endures Forever

Note the emphasis in Acts 13 on the Word of God (vv. 5, 7, 15, 26, 44, 46, 48–49). In his preaching, Paul quoted from 1 Samuel, Isaiah, Habakkuk, and Psalms. He preached salvation by faith in Jesus Christ whom God raised from the dead (vv. 38–39). Our words do not last, but the Word of the Lord endures forever.

ACTS 14

Paul was a man on the move but not a man easily moved because of difficulties. "But none of these things move me" was his testimony of faith (20:24), and he lived it.

When he and Barnabas were expelled from Antioch in Pisidia, they shook off the dust of their feet and went to Iconium (13:50–52; Luke 10:11). When the people there tried to stone them, they went to Lystra where they were treated like gods! (That was a greater danger than persecution.) Crowds are fickle: they changed their minds and stoned Paul, but he just got up and went to Derbe.

That was not all. Paul and Barnabas had the courage to retrace their steps so they could help and encourage the new Christians! And when they returned home, they told the church what the Lord had done, not what they had suffered.

Paul and Barnabas put Christ first, others second, and themselves last. They had a job to do, and they were determined by God's grace to do it. How much does it take to move you out of the will of God?

> **"The will to persevere is often the difference between failure and success."**
>
> David Sarnoff

ACTS 15

When God opens a door (14:27), the enemy has somebody handy to try to close it. In this case, the legalists from Judea visited the Antioch church and taught that Gentiles must become Jews before they can be Christians. Their teaching was a denial of salvation by grace through faith (10:43; Eph. 2:8–9).

It was difficult for the orthodox Jews to see that their glorious religious system, given by God, had been fulfilled in Christ and was now out-of-date. (That is why the book of Hebrews was written.) Rather than abandon it, they tried to blend the old religion with the new (Matt. 9:14–17).

When sincere Christians disagree, they must get together, see what God is doing in His church, and find out what the Word has to say about it. Peter, Paul, and Barnabas told what God was doing among the Gentiles, and James related it to the Word (Amos 9:11–12).

In the decision, there was no compromise doctrinally, but there was consideration practically. In the decree, the church asked the Gentiles not to deliberately offend the Jews. You will find the expansion of this principle, the basic principle of love, in Romans 14—15 and 1 Corinthians 8—10.

ACTS 16

Paul wrote, "But in all things we commend ourselves as ministers of God: in much patience" (2 Cor. 6:4). See the patience of Paul . . .

In waiting for a helper (1-5). Timothy replaced John Mark and became a true son in the faith to Paul. God has the right person ready at the right time, so be patient.

In seeking God's will (6-10). He was an apostle, yet he did not always know the direction God wanted him to take. He took steps, God closed doors, so he waited; and then God showed him the way.

In ministering the Word (11-15). They waited "some days" before seeking a place to witness, and God had hearts all prepared.

In bearing annoyance (16-18). Paul put up with the demonic promotion as long as he could and then cast out the demon. Paul knew that his action would create problems for him, and it did.

In enduring suffering (19-25). Paul did not use his Roman citizenship to protect himself from pain (22:22-29), but later he used it to protect the new church (vv. 35-40). When you hurt, ask God to give you songs in the night (Ps. 42:8).

In winning a lost soul (26-34). Paul had his eyes on the keeper of the prison and in kindness won him to Christ. How much are we willing to suffer to win someone to the Lord, especially someone who has hurt us?

❝Patience is power. With time and patience, the mulberry leaf becomes silk.**❞**

Chinese Proverb

ACTS 17

Rejecting the new (1-9). The Jews in Thessalonica were not interested in the new faith or the "new king" that Paul preached, but the Gentile "God seekers" accepted the gospel and were saved. Read 1 Thessalonians 1 to see the change they experienced.

Investigating the new (10–15). The next town was just the opposite! The Jews in Berea took time to examine the evidence and study the Scriptures. There are fair-minded people in every nation, and God knows who they are.

Looking for the new (16–34). The people in Athens "spent their time in nothing else but either to tell or to hear some new thing" (v. 21). How like our world today! The quest for novelty overshadows the search for reality. Paul's sermon was a masterpiece of tact and teaching, and a few people were converted. Paul offered them "newness of life" through the Resurrection (Rom. 6:4), and most of the listeners rejected it.

ACTS 18

The tentmaker (1–3). All Jewish rabbis had a trade because they did not charge their pupils for their lessons. Paul worked hard to support himself and his associates in their ministry. He also worked so that the unsaved could not accuse him of preaching the gospel just to make money (1 Cor. 9). What sacrifices do we make today to further the gospel?

The watchman (4–6). The image is from Ezekiel 3:16–21. As a faithful watchman, Paul warned sinners of the wrath to come, so his hands were free from their blood.

He Is with Us

"I am with you" is a promise God gave to Isaac (Gen. 26:24), Jacob (Gen. 28:15), the Jewish remnant returning from Babylon (Isa. 41:10; 43:5), Jeremiah (Jer. 1:8, 19; 15:20), and the Jews rebuilding the temple (Hag. 1:13; 2:4); and Jesus gave it to us (Matt. 28:20). He said, "I will never leave you nor forsake you" (Heb. 13:5).

The evangelist (7–10). Paul moved next door to the synagogue and kept witnessing! He was not one to run away from either the battlefield or the harvestfield. The Lord promised, "I am with you" (v. 10), a promise He gave to many people and still gives to us today (Isa. 41:10; Matt. 28:20).

A Godly Couple

Aquila and Priscilla, husband and wife, appear several times in apostolic history and were important workers in the early church. They are always mentioned together because they were a team. Being Jews, they were expelled from Rome; as a result, they met Paul in Corinth and opened their home to him. Paul left them in Ephesus where they helped Apollos better understand the gospel (Acts 18:18–28). They returned to Rome where they had a church in their home (Rom. 16:3–5). We do not know how they risked their lives for Paul; but their actions show how much they loved him. They were with Paul in Ephesus when he wrote 1 Corinthians (1 Cor. 16:8, 19), so perhaps it had something to do with the riot described in Acts 19. In his last epistle, Paul sent loving greetings to them (2 Tim. 4:19). Every pastor is grateful to God for couples like Priscilla and Aquila whose hearts, hands, and homes are completely given to the Lord.

The builder (11–28). Paul did not just win souls; he also built a local church by teaching the converts the Word of God

(1 Cor. 3:9–23). In fact, he followed the commission of Matthew 28:18–20. After reporting to his home base in Antioch, Paul revisited some churches to build them up in the faith.

ACTS 19

We read in this chapter that "the word of the Lord grew mightily and prevailed" (v. 20). When does this happen?

When we confirm our faith (1–10). When you believe in Jesus Christ, you receive the gift of the Holy Spirit (Acts 10:43–48; Rom. 8:9). Many people think they are converted but do not have the Spirit's witness within (1 John 5:9–13). Paul could not build a church on men with an inadequate spiritual experience, nor can we today. We must be honest with God.

When we confess our sins (11–20). The devil is a great imitator, but in this case, his attempt was a humiliating failure. The Lord used it for good, because the believers became convicted about their secret sins and confessed them. Then the Spirit could work in mighty power, and the Word increased!

When we confront the enemy (21–41). Paul did not openly attack their idolatry by picketing the temple of Diana or petitioning the city government. He simply shared the Word, and lives were changed. Of course, the real issue was money, not religion. Paul was wise not to go into the theater, although we admire him for his courage. But the riot only called attention to the gospel and gave the believers more opportunity to witness.

Circumstances that look like obstacles are really opportunities when you let God work.

ACTS 20

The uproars usually cease, so be patient; but be sure to get ready for the next battle.

Paul was going to Jerusalem. Along the way, he met with dear friends, ministered the Word, and even enjoyed a quiet voyage and a refreshing walk (v. 13). God's servants need to get away from people and have time alone to think, meditate, and pray. Paul knew he was facing danger in Jerusalem (vv. 22–23), and he wanted to be prepared spiritually.

In his farewell message to the elders, Paul reviewed his

past ministry (vv. 18–21), shared his present concerns (vv. 22–24), and revealed future dangers (vv. 28–31). If you want to catch the heart of Paul, consider his statements: "Serving the Lord . . . I kept back nothing . . . that I may finish my race with joy. . . . It is more blessed to give than to receive."

One day, life will end, and we will have to give our farewell speech. Can we look back without regret and look ahead without fear? Will we finish our race with joy even while others are weeping?

Paul's Roles

As Paul reviewed his ministry in Acts 20:24–26, he saw himself as an accountant ("I count"), a runner ("I may finish my race"), a steward ("the ministry which I received"), a witness ("to testify"), a herald ("preaching the kingdom"), and a watchman ("innocent of the blood"). What a responsibility it is to be a servant of God!

ACTS 21

The traveler (1–14). This farewell journey brought both joy and sorrow to Paul, but life is like that. He knew what lay ahead of him but kept going (Luke 9:51). Years before, the Lord had told him to get out of Jerusalem (22:18). Was he wrong in going back?

The peacemaker (15–25). Paul moved from "the will of the Lord be done" (v. 14) to "do what we tell you" (v. 23). So anxious was Paul to bring unity to the Jews and Gentiles in the church that he agreed to the plan. Was he following "wisdom from above" or "earthly wisdom" (James 3:13–18)? Not every decision we make turns out to bring peace.

The prisoner (26–40). The plan almost worked; on the last day, however, trouble started (v. 27). Of course, their charges were absurd; yet the mob lives on "suppose" and not fact. Paul had been careful not to cause any unrest in the city (24:10–13), but his efforts had been in vain. He would spend the next five years as a prisoner of Rome.

Sometimes our plans and good intentions seem to bring only trouble. But God is still in control! He used Paul's trials to accomplish His purposes so that His servant got to Rome (23:11). He can do the same for His people today. Walk by faith!

ACTS 22

The *starting point* of Paul's defense was his identification with the Jews (vv. 1–16; 1 Cor. 9:19–23). His birth, training, and early ministry as a rabbi were strictly orthodox. He associated his conversion with Ananias, "a devout man according to the law" (v. 12). He was very tactful, but it takes tact to have contact.

The *turning point* of Paul's defense was his use of the word *Gentiles* (v. 17). Had he not used that word, Paul might have been set free; *but the whole burden of his life was to reach the Gentiles* (Eph. 3:1–13). Paul was arrested because of religious bigotry; his people did not realize that God was doing a new thing in the world.

The *finishing point* was the threat of a scourging, which Paul avoided by asserting his Roman citizenship (vv. 22–29). From then on, it would be one hearing after another and a delay of two years in Caesarea. But God was working out His will in His time, and Paul was willing to wait.

"God is the master of the scenes; we must not choose what part we shall act; it concerns us only to be careful that we do it well, always saying, 'If this please God, let it be as it is.'"

Jeremy Taylor

ACTS 23

Paul was in danger. If the Romans did not imprison him, the Jews would kill him (22:22). What means did God use to help Paul?

Integrity (1–5). Paul had nothing to hide, and his conscience was clear. Ananias was out of line when he had Paul slapped; but Paul showed respect for the office, not the man.

Strategy (6–10). This did not set Paul free, but it did divide the enemy camp and get the Romans to protect their prisoner better.

Advocacy (11). Paul had the best lawyer available! Christ had assured him when he was in Corinth (18:9–11), and He would assure him again (27:21–25; 2 Tim. 4:16–18). Paul knew that "if God is for us, who can be against us?" (Rom. 8:31).

Opportunity (12–22). Paul's nephew lived in the city, and by the providence of God, he discovered the Jewish plot. Only the Lord could have worked that out. We never know what friend or relative God will use to help us.

Authority (23–35). Paul had the protection of 472 Roman soldiers, and the whole authority of the government was behind him. The Romans did not give Paul a fair hearing, but God still used them to protect Paul and get him to Rome.

ACTS 24

How do the unsaved go about opposing the Lord's servants and their work?

Tertullus started with *flattery* (vv. 2–4), knowing that many people in high places are susceptible to it (12:20–24). Flattery appeals to our pride. If we did not flatter ourselves, others could not successfully flatter us. We really *want* to believe what they say!

Then Tertullus used *slander* (vv. 5–8). Napoleon said, "He who knows how to flatter also knows how to slander." As his last weapon, the lawyer called on *false witnesses* (v. 9) who together supported Tertullus's lies about Paul.

Paul's defense was threefold: his life, his faith and his service to his nation. Although his enemies could not prove their accusations, Paul did not go free. *The safest place for Paul was in that prison,* for God had work for him to do in Rome.

You may not understand why God permits lies to triumph, but leave it all in His hands. He is in control, and the final judgment rests with Him.

> ### Don't Delay
>
> *Actually, Felix was the prisoner, and Paul was the prosecutor. Felix knew he was guilty; but instead of accepting Christ, he delayed. The convenient time to be saved is now (2 Cor. 6:1–2; see also Isa. 55: 6–7).*

ACTS 25

Festus tried to use Paul as a political pawn to win favor with the Jews (vv. 3, 9). If he had succeeded and sent Paul to Jerusalem, the apostle would have been killed. Paul did the wise thing: he used his rights as a Roman citizen and appealed to Caesar. There are times when believers must use the law to protect themselves and the ministry.

But now Festus had a problem. How could he send Paul to Caesar when he had no charges against him that could be proved? God's people sometimes are treated like the guilty even though they are innocent. Remember Joseph, David, Daniel, and Jeremiah, not to mention our Lord Jesus Christ.

In all that happened, God was fulfilling His promise to Paul that he would witness before rulers (9:15) and finally get to Rome (23:11). Being a prisoner and enduring the hearings were difficult for Paul, but he used his opportunities wisely. He believed Jesus' words: "But it will turn out for you as an occasion for testimony" (Luke 21:13).

ACTS 26

Paul saw the light. Instead of defending himself, Paul used the opportunity to present the gospel to King Agrippa and others with him (1 Pet. 3:13–17). When Paul met Jesus on the road to Damascus, he made some important and life-changing discoveries: his religion was out-of-date; his zeal for God was only hurting God; Jesus was alive; and Jesus had a job for Paul to do. Talk about a rude awakening!

The Gentiles need the light. Paul's great learning and zeal would be devoted to the spread of the gospel among the Gentiles (vv. 17–18). Lost sinners are in spiritual darkness and only Christ can give them light.

Agrippa rejected the light. He tried to discredit the message by accusing Paul of being mad, and he tried to minimize his own conviction by his nonchalant reply (v. 28). He turned his back on the light; he was "almost" when he might have been "altogether."

" *Almost persuaded to be a Christian is like the man who was almost pardoned, but he was hanged; like the man who was almost rescued, but he was burned in the house. A man that is almost saved is damned.* **"**

Charles Spurgeon

ACTS 27

Rejecting Paul's counsel (1–13). What did a Jewish tent-maker know about sailing a ship? So, the advice of the experts (v. 11) and the vote of the majority (v. 12) carried the day. When you are impatient (v. 7) and uncomfortable (v. 12), and when the golden opportunity seems to come along (v. 13), beware! A storm may be brewing!

Hearing Paul's encouragement (14–26). Paul was right to say, "I told you so!" But he followed it with a word of promise from the Lord and a word of encouragement from his believing heart. At a time like that, people needed promises, not preaching.

Following Paul's example (27–38). Paul publicly gave thanks and directed their hearts to God, which encouraged everybody. The weary passengers needed strength for what lay ahead, and that meant taking time to eat. Paul was practical as well as perceptive.

Although Paul started the voyage as a prisoner and passenger, he ended it as the captain of the ship. The ship was lost; but by the grace of God, Paul's presence saved all the passengers. Can the Lord depend on you to sail by faith when you face the storms? Can others depend on you?

ACTS 28

Does anything in this chapter surprise you?

That the natives were kind (1–2, 7–10)? The natives may have been superstitious, but even unsaved people can show concern for those in need. The pagan sailors worked hard to save Jonah before they threw him into the sea (Jon. 1:11–16).

That Paul picked up sticks (3)? If you had saved 276 people from drowning, would you feel it necessary to do menial labor like picking up sticks? Certainly the grateful passengers would have relieved Paul of the task! But Paul was a servant, and he did the job that needed to be done (Phil. 2:1–11).

That Paul was bitten (3–6)? Had he not already been through enough suffering? When Satan cannot win as the lion (1 Pet. 5:8), then he comes as the serpent (2 Cor. 11:3). We must constantly be on guard and trust the Lord to care for us (Mark 16:18).

Paul's Last Years

Paul was a prisoner in Rome from 61 to 63, and during that time wrote Ephesians, Philippians, Colossians, and Philemon. From 63 to 65, he was free to minister, and he wrote 1 Timothy and Titus. Paul was imprisoned again in 66, wrote 2 Timothy, and was martyred at Rome in late 66 or early 67.

That Paul welcomed encouragement (11–16)? Even an apostle needs to be encouraged at times, and the saints who met Paul did just that. The group at Appii Forum traveled about ten miles farther than the other group. How far would you go to encourage a fellow believer?

That the Jewish leaders rejected the Word (17–31)? God's chosen people should have known the Scriptures; yet when it was time to decide, the group was divided. But Paul kept witnessing and let God bless the Word as He pleased.

ROMANS

◆

Paul was on his third missionary journey when he wrote the epistle to the Romans, probably from Corinth. He had long planned to visit the believers in Rome, many of whom he knew (chap. 16), and this letter prepared the way. In the letter, he answers the false accusations made about him (3:8; 6:1) and explains why he had not visited Rome sooner (15:23–29). He also gives the grandest presentation of Christian doctrine found anywhere in Scripture.

Romans is one of three books written to explain Habakkuk 2:4: "The just shall live by his faith" (Rom. 1:17; Gal. 3:11; Heb. 10:38). The basic theme is "the just," what it means to be justified (declared righteous by God) and to live a righteous life. *Righteousness* is used in one form or another over forty times.

The book easily falls into three parts: God's righteousness and salvation (chaps. 1—8), God's righteousness and Israel (chaps. 9—11), and God's righteousness and practical Christian living (chaps. 12—16). Romans 1:16–17 is a key statement.

Romans is a closely knit argument that defends the righteousness of God. You can summarize the argument by noting the verses containing "therefore" (3:20, 28; 5:1; 8:1; 12:1).

Justification is God's gracious act by which He *declares* the believing sinner righteous in Jesus Christ because of the work of Christ on the cross. When you believe, Christ's righteousness is *imputed,* that is, "put to your account." Sanctification is God's work in the believer whereby He *imparts* His righteousness and develops holy character and conduct. A righteous standing before God leads to a holy life before men. We are not saved by works or by faith plus works; we are saved by a faith that works (James 2:14–26).

ROMANS 1

The gospel of God (1–17). God has good news! It is *promised* in the Old Testament and centered in Jesus Christ. He came to earth a Jew, died, and arose again; and He saves all who will trust in Him. He alone *purchased* salvation, and this message must be *preached* to the whole world. Why? Because the gospel alone is "the *power* of God to salvation" (v. 16, italics added).

Paul was gripped by the gospel; his whole life was controlled by it. Called to be an apostle (v. 1), he felt himself a debtor to the whole world (v. 14). Through His church, God is calling people to Jesus Christ (vv. 5–7). Has the gospel gripped you?

❝*Religions are man's search for God; the Gospel is God's search for man. There are many religions, but one Gospel.***❞**

E. Stanley Jones

Spiritual Debts

God's people are free from the debt of sin, but they are debtors to witness to a lost world (Rom. 1:14), obey the Holy Spirit (8:13), love all people (13:8), encourage their weaker brothers and sisters (15:1), and help the people of Israel (15:25–27). Are you paying your spiritual debts?

The wrath of God (18–32). Paul's main theme is the righteousness of God, but he presents it against the dark background of the judgment of God, *which is going on right now.* Men know God from creation and conscience (vv. 19–20) but refuse to honor Him as God. They live for the creature, not the Creator, and make themselves into gods (v. 25; Gen. 3:4–5). So, God gave them up (vv. 24, 26, 28) and let them suffer the consequences. *The greatest judgment God can inflict on us is to let us have our own way.*

But the same God who delivered up sinners to judgment *delivered up His own Son for lost sinners* (8:32)! That is the gospel. Do you believe it? Are you sharing it?

ROMANS 2

If you know Jesus Christ as your Savior, your sins have already been judged on the cross (John 5:24; Rom. 8:1). But are you ready for the judgment seat of Christ where your works will be judged (Rom. 14:10–12; 2 Cor. 5:10)? Ask yourself the following questions.

Do I judge myself or others (1–3)? How easy it is to cover up my own failures by criticizing others (Matt. 7:1–5)!

Am I grateful for God's goodness (4)? It is not the badness of man but the goodness of God that brings us to repentance (Luke 15:17–19). Do I take God's many blessings for granted?

Is my faith proved by works (5–11)? Paul was not teaching salvation by works but works that prove salvation. Do I obey God's truth and persist in holy living? Do I have a hard heart or a tender heart?

Am I hiding behind religion (12–16, 25–29)? The Jews boasted of their law, but it could not save them. External rituals do not guarantee internal changes. God searches the heart. What does He see in my heart?

> **"**How rarely we weigh our neighbor in the same balance in which we weigh ourselves.**"**
>
> Thomas a Kempis

Do I practice what I profess (17–24)? Do I tell others what is right but then do what is wrong? Do I expect more of others than I do of myself?

God judges honestly (v. 2) and without partiality (v. 11), and no secret is hidden from Him (v. 16). Are you prepared?

ROMANS 3

Paul, the attorney, summarizes his case.

All are condemned (1–19). Both Jews and Gentiles (religious and irreligious) are guilty before God, and one is no better than the other (v. 9). Paul quotes from Psalms and Isaiah to show that, from head to foot, we are all lost sinners. Do you want to argue about this? Then your mouth has not been stopped! God cannot save you until you say, "Guilty!" and shut your mouth.

We cannot save ourselves (20). The law is a mirror that reveals our sin; only the blood of Christ can wash away our sin. It is good to do good works, but good works are not good enough to save us (Eph. 2:8–9).

God's salvation is lawful (21–31). But how can a *holy* God forgive *guilty* people? Is that lawful? If our judges did that, society would fall apart. But God the Law Giver and Judge obeyed His own law, died for us, and paid the penalty for our sins. The Judge is now the Savior!

Have you shut your mouth, trusted Jesus Christ, and heard God say, "Not guilty"?

ROMANS 4

How was Abraham saved (1–4, 9–12)? Not by works, but by faith (Gen. 15:6). Salvation is not like wages that you earn or works that you can boast about. Abraham was not saved by keeping the law because the law had not been given, nor was he saved by obeying a religious ritual. It was all by God's grace!

How was David saved (5–8)? David wrote Psalm 32 after his great sin with Bathsheba (2 Sam. 11). Can God forgive a man who commits adultery, deceit, and murder? Yes! When David repented and turned to God, he was forgiven, even though the Lord allowed David to feel the bitter consequences of his sins (2 Sam. 12). God justifies *the ungodly,* not the righteous (v. 5; Matt. 9:9–13).

How can you be saved (13–25)? Simply by believing God's

promise as Abraham did. *Faith* and *promise* go together just as *law* and *works* go together. Abraham is the father of the Jewish nation physically, but he is the "father" of all believers spiritually (v. 16; Matt. 3:7–9). At Calvary, our sins were put on Christ's account; when you trust Christ, God puts Christ's righteousness on your account (2 Cor. 5:21). What can be more blessed than to know that your sins are forgiven?

Our Sins Are Covered

Because he preached salvation by grace alone, Paul was accused of promoting sin (Rom. 3:5–8), but the accusation was false. Persons who experience the grace of God in forgiveness have no desire to sin; and if they do sin, they confess it to the Lord (1 John 1:5—2:1). They are tempted (1 Cor. 10:13), and sometimes they fall; but they do not stay down (Ps. 37:23-24). Read all of Psalm 32 to see what God does for His own.

ROMANS 5

In chapter 4, Paul went back to Abraham and David to explain how God declares believing sinners righteous; now he goes all the way back to Adam. Adam's sin passed sin and death on to the whole human race, but Christ's obedience gives righteousness and life to all who trust Him. In our first birth, we became condemned children of Adam; but in our second birth, we are the forgiven children of God. Note the blessings of justification.

Riches (1–5). Peace, access into God's grace, joy, hope, love, the Holy Spirit—what riches we have in Christ! And trials work *for* us, not *against* us, and develop Christian character. How rich we are!

Reconciliation (6–11). We are at peace with God and need

not be afraid. If He did so much for us when we were enemies, think what He will do for us now that we are His children!

Reigning (12–21). When we belonged to the old creation under Adam, death and sin reigned; now that we are in Christ in the new creation (2 Cor. 5:17), grace is reigning, *and we are reigning in life* (v. 17). You can live like a king by the grace of God!

ROMANS 6

Being a Christian is *a matter of life or death* (vv. 1–11). Persons who do not understand the grace of God argue, "If God is gracious, then we should sin more so we receive more grace." Those who trust Christ are identified with Him by the Spirit in His death, burial, and resurrection, as pictured in baptism. The old life is buried! We can reckon it dead (v. 11) and walk in newness of resurrection life.

Being a Christian is *a matter of bondage or freedom* (vv. 12–22). Who is your master, Jesus Christ or the old life? You are not under the authority of Moses (v. 15), but that does not mean you have freedom to break God's moral law (8:1–5). Yield yourself to the Lord; He is the most wonderful Master, and the "salary" He pays lasts forever.

"Alive to God"

The most vivid illustration of Romans 6 is Lazarus (John 11). Jesus raised him from the dead and then said, "Loose him, and let him go" (John 11:44). Lazarus left the grave, got rid of the graveclothes, and began a new life (Col. 3:1ff.). God's people are both "dead" and "alive" (v. 11) and by faith must live accordingly.

Being a Christian is *a matter of rewards or wages* (v. 23). We quote this verse as we witness to the lost, and rightly so; but Paul wrote it originally to believers. Although God forgives the sins of His children, He may not stop the painful consequences of sin. The pleasures of sin are never compensated for by the wages of sin. Sinning is not worth it!

ROMANS 7

Believers are not under the law, but that does not give them license to become outlaws. They have a new life (6:1-11) and a new Master (6:12-23), and they also have a new love: they are *married to Christ* (vv. 1-6). If a marriage must be based on laws instead of love, it is going to make for an unhappy home.

If the law cannot change us or control us, what good is it? Its purpose is to reveal sin, and it does its job well (v. 7). Paul learned that the law even aroused evil desires in him (v. 8). If something as holy as God's law (v. 12) can arouse sinful desires, what wicked sinners we must be!

Law brings out the worst in us, but love brings out the best in us. The Holy Spirit within us helps us to do what God wants us to do (Rom. 8:1-5) and to be what God wants us to be (Gal. 5:22-23). Keep your love relationship with the Lord alive and exciting, and you will have righteousness instead of wretchedness.

A Yielded Life

Romans 7:21-25 does not suggest that you live a divided life because that is impossible. You must choose your Master (6:15-23) and be true to your Husband, Jesus Christ (7:1-6). "The mind" refers to the new nature from God and "the body of death" the old nature from Adam. We cannot serve God with an old nature that is sinful (7:18), but the Holy Spirit enables us to do His will as we yield to Him. The human body is not sinful, but human nature is.

ROMANS 8

Paul asked, "Who will deliver me from this body of death?" (7:24). This chapter gives the answer: the Holy Spirit of God. The blessings He brings make us "more than conquerors" (v. 37)!

Life (1–11). When God saved you, He gave you a new life, not a new law; as you yield to that life, you obey His law. Keep your mind centered on the things of the Lord (Col. 3:1–4) and seek to please God in all things. Let the Spirit live His life in you.

Liberty (12–17). We enter God's family by the new birth, not by adoption (John 3); but adoption gives us an adult standing in His family. He deals with us as mature sons and daughters and not as "little children." We can talk ("Abba, Father" [v. 15]), walk, and use our inheritance right now. We are free, but we are still debtors to the Lord (v. 12).

Hope (18–25). We are not frustrated by the suffering we experience or see in our world because we have hope. When Jesus returns, we will enter into glorious liberty! The Spirit is the beginning of the harvest and assures us that the best is yet to come.

The Holy Spirit longs to reveal to you the deeper things of God. He longs to love through you. He longs to work through you. Through the blessed Holy Spirit you may have: strength for every duty, wisdom for every problem, comfort in every sorrow, joy in His overflowing service.

T. J. Bach

Guidance (26–30). God's purpose is to make His children like His Son, and He will succeed. The Spirit intercedes for us and guides us as we pray, and the circumstances of life work for our good, no matter how painful they may be.

Love (31–39). The Spirit of God makes the love of God real to us (5:5; John 14:23–27). The Father is for us (vv. 31–32), the Son is for us (v. 34), and the Spirit is for us (vv. 26–27). Nothing can separate us from His love. Is there any reason why we should not be "more than conquerors"?

God's People

In Romans 9—11, Paul's discussion of Israel is not an interruption but an illustration of his theme. He explains Israel's past election (chap. 9), present rejection (chap. 10), and future reception (chap. 11); and he proves that God has been righteous in all His dealings with Israel. God has not failed to work out His divine purposes for the Jews, nor will He fail to work out His purposes for His church.

ROMANS 9

In a part of the Bible that emphasizes the sovereignty of God, we see Paul sorrowing (9:1–3), praying (10:1), and worshiping (11:33–36). He did not feel that God's sovereignty in any way destroyed man's responsibility. The God who ordains the end (saving the lost) also ordains the means to the end, the prayers and witness of His people. They go together.

God is not obligated to save anybody, for all deserve to be condemned. Even Israel was chosen only because of His grace and love (Deut. 7:6–8). Therefore, nobody can criticize God or say He is unfair. That He is merciful to sinners should make us rejoice!

Israel's rejection of Christ did not ruin God's plan, for He went to the Gentiles (Acts 10:1ff.; 15:14) who gladly received the good news. However, God has a remnant among the Jews (vv. 27–29), and believing Jews and Gentiles are one in the church (Eph. 2:11–22).

His mercy endures forever!

God's Part and Our Part

Charles Spurgeon was asked how he reconciled divine sovereignty and human responsibility, and he replied, "I never try to reconcile friends." Augustine said that we must pray as though it all depended on God and work as though it all depended on us. That biblical balance makes for blessing.

ROMANS 10

Why did Israel stumble over Christ and reject Him? Because they did not understand the kind of righteousness God wanted or how to get it. Like the Pharisees (and many people today), they thought only of righteous *works* and could not comprehend a righteousness that comes by faith (v. 13; Joel 2:32; Acts 2:21).

The missionary heart of Paul comes out in verses 14–17. Salvation is by faith, and faith comes "by hearing . . . the word of God" (v. 17). But unbelieving sinners (including Israel) cannot hear unless we tell them. God needs people with beautiful feet (Isa. 52:7) to carry the gospel to the lost.

Despite Paul's broken heart (v. 1) and God's outstretched hands (v. 21; Isa. 65:2), Israel did not believe; but the Gentiles did believe and God saved them! When you feel discouraged in your witnessing, remember Paul; continue caring, praying, and sharing the good news. Keep those feet beautiful!

ROMANS 11

The theology of Romans 9—11 magnifies God's grace and extols His sovereignty. Never lose the wonder of your salvation or of the greatness of God. No matter how deep the valley or difficult the battle, a vision of God's greatness puts joy in your heart and strength in your soul. God knows what He is doing even if you do not understand it fully.

There is a future for Israel; Paul is proof of that (v. 1; 1 Tim. 1:16), and so is Israel's past history (vv. 2–10). God has always had a believing remnant in Israel, no matter how dark the day. When you become discouraged about the future of the church and feel that you may be the only faithful Christian left, read 1 Kings 19 and focus on God's greatness.

We cannot explain all the purposes and plans of God, but we can worship and praise Him for who He is (vv. 33–36). The end result of all Bible study is worship, and the end result of all worship is service to the God we love.

"Fate says the thing is and must be, so it is decreed. But the true doctrine is—God has appointed this and that, not because it must be, but because it is best that it should be. Fate is blind, but the destiny of Scripture is full of eyes. Fate is stern and adamantine, and has no tears for human sorrow. But the arrangements of providence are kind and good."

Charles Spurgeon

ROMANS 12

The biblical pattern is to relate doctrine and duty, for what you believe must determine how you behave. In these closing chapters, Paul discusses your relationship with the Lord (12:1–2), yourself (12:3), the church (12:4–16), your enemies (12:17–21), government (chap. 13), and believers who disagree (chaps. 14—15).

Transformation (vv. 1–2). The Spirit of God transforms your life by renewing your mind (2 Cor. 3:18), but He cannot do this unless you give Him your body. When you give yourself to God in spiritual worship, you become a living sacrifice to the glory of God.

Evaluation (3). To think more highly of yourself, *or less highly,* is sin, so have a proper estimate of who you are and what God has given you (Gal. 6:3–5).

Cooperation (4–16). You are part of the body of Christ with a ministry to fulfill, so do your part lovingly and joyfully.

Vindication (17–21). If yours is a godly life, you are bound to have enemies (Matt. 5:10–12; 2 Tim. 3:12); but leave all judgment to the Lord. If you let the Lord have His way, He will use your enemies to build you and make you more like Christ.

ROMANS 13

Believers are citizens of heaven, but we must not minimize our responsibilities on earth. We must be exemplary citizens so that the Lord will be glorified (1 Pet. 2:11–17).

Law (1–7). God has established human government because people are sinners and must be controlled. Governmental authority comes from God, so you must respect the office even if you cannot respect the officer. The fear of punishment is not the highest motivation for obedience, but it is better than having chaos.

Love (8–10). Love for God and for your neighbor is the highest motive for obedience. Love does what is right and just and seeks the best for others. By nature, we do not have this kind of love (Titus 3:3); the Lord gives it to us (Rom. 5:5).

Light (vv. 11–14). Christian citizens live in the light of the Lord's return. Paul admonishes, "Wake up—dress up—clean up—look up!" Are you heeding it?

> **❝***Whatever makes men good Christians makes them good citizens.***❞**
>
> Daniel Webster

ROMANS 14

Your love may be tested more by Christians who disagree with you than by unbelievers who persecute you. It takes a diamond to cut a diamond. What should you do when your brother or sister disagrees with you about how God's people ought to live?

Acceptance (1–9). Not all believers are mature, and love demands that the mature members of the family defer to the immature. Love protects people and gives them a chance to grow up. People may be difficult, but we must accept them in love for the Lord's sake.

Accountability (10–12). We have no right to judge and condemn one another because the Judge is the Lord. Each believer will have enough to do in keeping his own account right without interfering with others' accounts!

Ambition (13–23). Our desire must not be to get everybody to agree with us; our desire must be to pursue peace, not cause others to stumble, and help others to mature in Christ. What starts as *grieving* (v. 15) can become *offending* (v. 21), *making weak* (v. 21), and *causing others to stumble and fall* (vv. 13, 21). The result might be *destroying* a brother's or sister's faith (vv. 15, 20). Is destroying another just to have your own way worth it?

Gaining Strength

The weak Christian does not yet understand and practice freedom in Jesus Christ. Jewish believers, raised under the law of Moses, had a difficult time adjusting to their new life. Conscience becomes strong as we accept what God says about us in the Word and act on it by faith. However, it takes time for conscience to develop, and we must be patient with one another.

ROMANS 15

A debt to the weak (1–6). The strong must bear the weak and help them grow, and that takes love and patience. If we live to please ourselves, we will not follow the example of Christ who lived to please the Father and help others.

A debt to the lost (7–21). God saved the Jews so that they might reach the Gentiles and lead them in praising the Lord. God has saved us so that we might win others. We have a debt to pay (1:14).

A debt to Israel (22–33). The Gentiles are indebted to the Jews (John 4:22). And that debt is paid by praying for them (Ps. 122:6), witnessing to them in love, and sharing our material gifts to assist them.

❝To consider persons and events and situations only in the light of their effect upon myself is to live on the doorstep of hell.**❞**

Thomas Merton

ROMANS 16

We are prone to honor Paul and forget the many ordinary people who helped make his ministry possible. Paul was the human author of the epistle to the Romans, but Tertius wrote it down (v. 22), Gaius gave Paul a place to live and work (v. 23), and Phoebe carried the completed letter to Rome. Nobody in God's family is unimportant to Him, and no ministry is insignificant. Find the work He wants you to do and faithfully do it.

There is a "hidden romance of history" that is not recorded in the Bible. When and how did Priscilla and Aquila risk their lives to save Paul (vv. 3–4)? When were Andronicus and Junia in prison with Paul (v. 7)? How was Rufus's mother a mother to Paul (v. 13)? Who were the troublemakers about whom Paul warned the Roman believers (vv. 17–18)? Perhaps one day in heaven we will be given the answers!

Meanwhile, the important thing is that we are obedient to the Lord (v. 19) and lead others into "obedience to the faith"

(v. 26). The God of patience and comfort (15:5), the God of hope (15:13), and the God of peace (16:20) will establish you and enable you (16:25).

> **"**The service we render for others is really the rent we pay for our room on this earth.**"**
>
> Wilfred Grenfell

FIRST CORINTHIANS

◆

Corinth, the capital of Achaia, was perhaps the richest and most important city in Greece. It was also the most corrupt. A center for trade, Corinth was invaded by all kinds of religions and philosophies. Paul founded the Corinthian church during his second missionary journey (Acts 18) and ministered there a year and a half.

After he left, serious problems developed in the church, and Paul wrote the members a stern letter that was not successful (1 Cor. 5:9). He heard that the church was divided (1:11), and then a delegation from the church arrived in Ephesus with a letter asking Paul's help regarding specific questions. First Corinthians was his response.

Paul dealt with sin in the church (chaps. 1—6), and then he answered the questions they asked (chaps. 7—16; note the repeated phrase, "Now concerning . . ."). He discussed marriage (chap. 7), idolatry (chaps. 8—10), public worship (chap. 11), spiritual gifts (chaps. 12—14), the Resurrection (chap. 15), and the special offering he was taking for the Jews (chap. 16).

Paul had planted a church in the city, but the city had gotten into the church; and that explained why there were so many problems. The believers in Corinth needed to heed Romans 12:2, and so do we today.

1 CORINTHIANS 1

Even though believers are "all one in Christ Jesus" (Gal. 3:28), the local church often suffers from division. Why?

For one thing, we forget the calling we have in Christ (vv. 2, 9, 24–29). It is only by God's grace that we have been called, and this fact should humble us and encourage us to love one another (John 15:17).

Another factor is our tendency to follow human leaders and develop a fan club mentality. Christ died for us and lives to bless us, and He must have the preeminence.

A third factor is dependence on human wisdom and philosophies, of which there were many in Corinth. The world's wisdom had crept into the church, and it did not mix with the wisdom of God (Isa. 8:20). Various theologies are the attempts of scholars to interpret the Word of God, but they are not the Word. Never allow them to be a cause of division.

1 CORINTHIANS 2

Power (1–5). Paul did not imitate the itinerant teachers in Corinth who depended on their eloquence and intellectual brilliance. Paul's faith was in God, not in himself (Zech. 4:6). He wanted sinners to trust in Christ's power. You may think you lack ability to serve God, but God can turn your weakness into strength. The gospel still works (Rom. 1:16)!

Wisdom (6–16). The Jews asked for demonstrations of power and the Greeks looked for wisdom, both of which are available in Jesus Christ (1:24). A deeper wisdom of God is available for those who are mature (Heb. 5:12–14). Allow the Spirit of God to teach you about the Son of God from the Word of God, and grow up in Him.

Wisdom and power go together. They need each other, and they keep the Christian life balanced.

1 CORINTHIANS 3

Maturing (1–4). We never outgrow the nourishing milk of the Word (1 Pet. 2:2), but we cannot grow strong unless we also have the "solid food" (Heb. 5:12–14; Matt. 4:4). You grow by eating and exercising (1 Tim. 4:6–8), and it takes both. Age is no guarantee of spiritual maturity.

Harvesting (5–9). Everybody has a place in the Lord's harvest, and all are doing His work (John 4:34–38). There must be no competing or comparing, for the Lord alone recognizes the work and gives the reward. It makes no difference who the servant is so long as Jesus Christ is Lord of the harvest.

Building (10–17). Paul writes about the local church and the materials we put into it as we minister (Prov. 2:1–5; 3:13–

15). Substituting man's wisdom for God's Word means building with perishable materials that will burn up at the judgment seat of Christ.

Glorifying God (18–23). Because the Corinthian believers gloried in human teachers (1:12) and human wisdom, they robbed God of the glory that rightly belonged to Him. "Let no one boast in men" is a command, not a suggestion.

❝If you lack knowledge, go to school. If you lack wisdom, get on your knees! Knowledge is not wisdom. Wisdom is the proper use of knowledge.**❞**

Vance Havner

---

1 CORINTHIANS 4

Life is *a stewardship,* so be faithful (vv. 1–5). We judge ourselves, and others judge us; but the Final Judge is the Lord. Live to please Him alone.

Life is *a gift,* so be humble (vv. 6–9). Your abilities and blessings came from God; you cannot take credit for them. They are God's gift to you, and your use of them is your gift to God. It is sinful to contrast various Christian workers (1:12) because only God knows their hearts.

Life is *a battle,* so be courageous (vv. 9–13). If the apostles were the greatest Christians who ever lived, and they were filth and the scum of the earth, where did that leave the boasting Corinthians?

Life is *a school,* so be teachable (vv. 14–21). Paul saw himself as a father in the Lord who had to instruct and discipline his children. Our Father in heaven uses many hands and voices to teach us, and we must be willing pupils as we go through life.

1 CORINTHIANS 5

Separation (1–7). The background of the chapter is the Passover Feast (Exod. 12). The presence of the immoral man should have turned the feast into a funeral (v. 2), but the church was boasting about the sinner instead of weeping over him. Tolerating known sin in the church is like putting leaven into the Passover Feast: it does not belong.

Celebration (8). Paul saw the Christian life as "keeping the feast" (v. 8), that is, feeding on Christ, being ready to move, and being sure we are not defiled by sin (leaven, yeast). The Lamb has set us free, and we are on our way to our promised inheritance!

Isolation (9-13). Sin in the life of the believer is far worse than sin in the life of an unbeliever. We cannot isolate ourselves from the world, but we can separate ourselves from disobedient believers so that God can discipline them.

Share in Fellowship

The phrase "deliver such a one to Satan" (1 Cor. 5:5) suggests that there is spiritual safety within the fellowship of the local church. To be disciplined and dismissed from fellowship makes us vulnerable to Satan's attacks. Far better to confess our sins, be forgiven, and be restored to fellowship.

1 CORINTHIANS 6

Not only were the Corinthian believers compromising with the world, but they were also losing their testimony before the world by taking each other to court before pagan judges. Paul repeatedly asked, "Do you not know?" (vv. 2, 3, 15, 16, 19). They were ignorant of some basic truths of the Christian life.

We will judge angels (1-8). If God entrusts that great a responsibility to His people, can't He help us with our petty decisions today?

We have been changed (9-12). We are not what we once were, so why should we live as we once lived? It is a matter not of "What is lawful?" but of "What is helpful?"

We belong to the Lord (13–20). He made the human body, He dwells in believers by His Spirit, and He purchased us at the Cross. The believer's body belongs to God and must be used to glorify Him.

Flee These Temptations

"Flee sexual immorality" (1 Cor. 6:18) reminds us of Joseph when he fled from Potiphar's wife (Gen. 39). "Flee also youthful lusts" (2 Tim. 2:22) is a parallel admonition. When it comes to the devil, resist him and he will flee from you (James 4:7); but when it comes to temptations of the flesh, you do the fleeing!

---

1 CORINTHIANS 7

Marriage is *a gift* (vv. 1–9), and not everybody has the same gift. Some people have more self-control than others. People remain unmarried for different reasons (Matt. 19:11–12), and each one must know the will of God.

Marriage is *a ministry* (vv. 10–16). He addressed people who had been converted after marriage and who wondered if they should remain with their unsaved spouses. "Yes," said Paul, "because you might win them to Christ." But even Christian spouses can have a wonderful ministry to each other as they grow in the Lord and love each other (Eph. 5:22ff.).

Marriage is *a calling* (vv. 17–24). When you become a Christian, that does not annul what you were before you trusted Christ. Jews are still Jews, slaves are still slaves, and married people are still married. But now, with the Lord's help, you can fulfill that calling in a greater way.

Marriage is *a challenge* (vv. 25–40). Paul does not deny the blessings of marriage, but he does remind us of the burdens that marriage brings, especially when the times are tough. Building a Christian home is a great ministry, but nobody should enter into it lightly or carelessly.

> **"** *Success in marriage involves much more than finding the right mate. It also requires being the right mate.* **"**

1 CORINTHIANS 8

Life is controlled by conscience. Conscience is the judge within that commends us for doing right and condemns us for doing wrong (Rom. 2:14–15). If we sin against conscience, we do terrible damage to the inner person.

Conscience is strengthened by knowledge. As we grow in spiritual understanding, a weak conscience becomes stronger, and we appreciate our freedom in Christ more and more. The weak believer must not run ahead of his conscience, and the strong believer must never force him to do so.

Knowledge must be balanced by love. Your spiritual knowledge can be either a weapon to hurt people or a tool to build people. If your knowledge puffs you up, it will tear others down. Love knows when and how to yield to others without compromising the truth. Review Romans 14—15.

> **"** *Knowledge is proud that he has learned so much; Wisdom is humble that he knows no more.* **"**
>
> William Cowper

1 CORINTHIANS 9

We do not have the right to give up our freedom, for that was purchased by Christ (Gal. 5:1); *but we do have the freedom to give up our rights.* For the sake of winning the lost (v. 12), Paul gave up his right to receive financial support, and he begged the Corinthians to give up their rights for the sake of the saved.

Christian ministry is like fighting a war, caring for a vineyard, tending a flock, and cultivating a field (vv. 7–11). Meditate on these images, and see what they teach you about serving the Lord.

Ministry is a stewardship (v. 17), and the servant must be faithful (4:2). Ministers of Christ are also like runners who must keep the rules or be disqualified (vv. 24–27).

Verses 19–23 call for courtesy and wisdom in witness, not for compromise. "I have become all things to all men" does not mean Paul had no personal convictions. It means he used his convictions to build bridges, not walls. If he seemed inconsistent, it was only because people did not look deep enough. *His one great desire was to win the lost,* and that governed his every decision.

"*Tact is the art of making a point without making an enemy.***"**

Howard W. Newton

---

1 CORINTHIANS 10

If you insist on using your rights, you may cause a weaker believer to stumble; *and you may also bring trouble on yourself.* When you face difficult decisions, take these factors into consideration.

God's blessing (1–5). The parallel to God's people today is obvious. We have been redeemed from the world, identified with Jesus Christ, and nourished by spiritual food and drink. But these blessings are no guarantee that we will be successful.

God's judgment (6–12). When Israel sinned, God disciplined them; and He will do the same to His people today. Do you practice and tolerate in your life any of the sins named here? God gives His children freedom, but the freedom to sin is not included.

God's promise (13–22). God knows how much we can take and always provides the way of escape. Sometimes the smartest thing to do is to flee (v. 14; 6:18). Always look for the open door and the blessing on the other side.

God's glory (23–33). Two extremes must be avoided: practicing license in the name of Christian freedom, and being so fussy that we cannot live in a real world and make rational decisions. When you seek to edify others and glorify the Lord, you will know what to do.

"*When you flee from temptation, be sure you do not leave a forwarding address behind.***"**

---

1 CORINTHIANS 11

Some matters discussed in this chapter may have only local significance, but the spiritual principles apply to us today. When it comes to sharing in public worship, we must ask ourselves serious questions.

Do I dishonor authority (1–16)? We must be careful not to dishonor the Lord, no matter what the cultural standards may be. God has established headship in creation and in the church, and we must respect it.

Do I despise the church (17–22)? We are one in Christ and in love must honor one another. By the way they ate their love feast, the rich embarrassed the poor and brought shame to the church.

Do I discern the body (23–34)? When we meet to celebrate the Communion service, we must examine ourselves and not one another; and we must be honest with the Lord as we confess our sins. We discern His body in the bread, but we also discern it in the members of the church who eat with us. The Lord's Supper is a family feast. While it must be personal, it must not become so individual that it becomes selfish. It should be a means of promoting the unity of the church.

1 CORINTHIANS 12

The Corinthian believers were especially gifted by God (1:4–7), but some of them were creating problems by using their spiritual gifts in unspiritual ways. Paul reminded those people of three basic truths.

There is one Lord (1–11). The Spirit glorifies Christ (John 16:14), not Himself. The Spirit gives us gifts so that we can serve Christ and His church "for the profit of all" (v. 7) and not for our own selfish enjoyment. Have you discovered what the Spirit has given you? Have you thanked God for it, and are you using your gift(s) under Christ's lordship?

There is one body (12–31). As members of the same body, we belong to one another, and we need one another. The believers you think you can do without may be the ones you need the most! We must minister to one another and care for one another as one body.

There is one danger (25). When a part of your physical body declares independence from the other parts, it starts to die and you have to visit the doctor. Division in the local church brings weakness and pain (1:10–17) because no Christian can go it alone and be successful. Do you thank God for fellow Christians and seek to care for them?

> **❝**None understand better the nature of real distinction than those who have entered into unity.**❞**
>
> Johannes Tauler

---

1 CORINTHIANS 13

This so-called hymn to love was Paul's prescription for solving the sickness in the church body in Corinth. The believers had spiritual gifts, but they lacked spiritual graces and needed to be reminded why love is so important in the Christian life.

Love puts *quality into service* (vv. 1–3). When you have love, your words and actions amount to something and help other people.

Love also puts *maturity into character* (vv. 4–7). The Corinthians were impatient with each other, suing each other, tolerating sin in the church, and creating problems because they did not have love. Whatever qualities you may have, they are nothing without love.

Love puts *eternity into life* (vv. 8–13). Love lasts, and what love does will last. Love is the greatest and does the greatest because "God is love" (1 John 4:8).

" *God hates the great things in which love is not the motive power; but He delights in the little things that are prompted by a feeling of love.* **"**

D. L. Moody

---

1 CORINTHIANS 14

Why go to church? God's people assemble for one purpose: to worship God. They worship Him by their praying and singing (v. 15), teaching and preaching (v. 3). Worship should result in glory to God, blessing for God's people (v. 3), and fear and conviction for sinners (vv. 23–25).

But for these things to happen, Jesus Christ must be Lord of our lives, and we must yield to the Holy Spirit. If we come to church to display our spirituality, we will not only miss the blessing ourselves but also cause others to miss the blessing. We come to honor Him.

A key word in this chapter is *edification* (vv. 3–5, 12, 17, 26), which means "building up." A worship service should lift up the Lord and build up the saints, not puff up the participants.

1 CORINTHIANS 15

We have a living Lord (1–19). Jesus is alive, and the gospel message is true! Witnesses who saw Him have passed along their testimony to us. When you trust Him, you receive resurrection life, eternal life (John 5:24); death can hold you no more.

We have a living hope (20–49). Jesus Christ will come

again, and the dead in Christ will be raised. We will have glorified bodies like Christ's body (1 John 3:1–3). Keep in mind that resurrection is not reconstruction. God does not reassemble the original body that has turned to dust. Like flowers and fruit from the planted seed, the glorified body is related to the "planted" body but different from it.

We have a living dynamic (50–58). We have no reason to give up because Jesus has conquered sin and death! If you really believe in the resurrection and return of Jesus, verse 58 will characterize your life. The best is yet to come, so let us give Him our best now.

"*In God's world, for those who are in earnest, there is no failure. No work truly done, no word earnestly spoken, no sacrifice freely made, was ever made in vain.***"**

F. W. Robertson

---

1 CORINTHIANS 16

Love for the needy (1–4). These instructions concern the offering Paul was taking up from the churches to help the needy believers in Judea (Rom. 15:25–27). The principles involved may be applied to Christian giving in general: our giving should be voluntary, in proportion to God's blessing, systematic, and handled honestly.

Love for leaders (5–12). We have the privilege of encouraging God's work as we pray for His servants. Even men like Paul, Timothy, and Apollos needed the help and encouragement of God's people. Are you praying for leaders?

Love for the church (13–18). Love, steadfastness, and submission make for a strong church. When you have people who are devoted to the work of the Lord, people who refresh you in the Lord, God is going to bless. What a joy to be a part of a church family that ministers in love!

Love for Christ (19–24). "O Lord, come!" is a prayer that reveals Paul's daily anticipation of the return of the Lord. When he made his plans (vv. 5–8), he included the blessed hope. Do you love Him and love His appearing (2 Tim. 4:8)?

How Do You Pray?

"O Lord, come!" (1 Cor. 16:22) is in Aramaic marana tha, often seen as maranatha. In the Lord's Prayer, we pray, "Your kingdom come" (Matt. 6:10); and the apostle John prayed, "Even so, come, Lord Jesus!" (Rev. 22:20). We should long for His coming, not just because we want to escape the trials of life but because we love Him and want to see Him face-to-face.

SECOND CORINTHIANS

◆

The problems in the Corinthian church grew worse, and Paul had to make a painful visit to Corinth to confront the people causing the trouble (2 Cor. 2:1ff.). He then wrote a severe letter and sent it with Titus (2 Cor. 2:4–9; 7:8–12). After some delays, he and Titus finally met; and in response to the good news Titus brought from Corinth, Paul wrote this letter.

First, Paul described his ministry and explained why he had changed his plans (chaps. 1—7). It was a plea for *reconciliation*. Then he detailed the plans for taking up the love offering for the church in Judea (chaps. 8—9). It was a plea for *cooperation*. Because a group in the church questioned his authority, Paul concluded his letter defending his apostleship (chaps. 10—13). It was a plea for *appreciation* and obedience to the Word.

One key word in 2 Corinthians is *comfort* (encouragement), used in one form or another twenty-nine times. Yet there are many references to suffering, too. In this very personal letter Paul opens his heart and shares his deepest joys and sorrows. After all, Christians are human and must be honest in expressing their feelings.

2 CORINTHIANS 1

Christians need comfort. While trying to help the church, Paul experienced suffering so intense that he was almost ready to give up (vv. 8–9). God does not shelter His people from trials, not even gifted apostles who are doing His will. "Be kind," said John Watson, "for everyone you meet is fighting a battle."

Christians receive comfort. Your God is the "God of all comfort" (v. 3), and He will give you the grace you need when you need it. Sufferings are not accidents; they are divine appointments, and your Father is in complete control. You will find comfort in praying, in claiming the promises of the Word (vv. 18–20), and in having deeper fellowship with the Lord.

Christians share comfort. God's comfort is not *given;* it is *loaned,* and you are expected to pass it on to others. The pain you experience now will help you encourage others in their trials. When you suffer, avoid self-pity, for self-pity will make you a reservoir instead of a channel. If you fail to share God's comfort with others, your experience in the furnace will be wasted; and it is a tragic thing to waste your sufferings.

Blessed Be the Lord

What do 2 Corinthians 1:3, Ephesians 1:3, and 1 Peter 1:3 have in common? All three are doxologies, praising the Lord for what He does for His people. They deal with past, present, and future blessings in the Christian life. In your sufferings, take time to praise the Lord. It is good medicine for a hurting heart.

"God does not comfort us to make us comfortable, but to make us comforters.**"**

John Henry Jowett

---

2 CORINTHIANS 2

Feelings (1–5). From a heart of love touched with pain, Paul wrote a severe letter to the church, hoping to correct the problem. It brought grief to his dear friends, and that brought grief to Paul; but they disciplined the man who had caused the trouble. Paul was not afraid to share his feelings with others.

When you are out of touch with your feelings, you are out of touch with reality.

Forgiveness (6–11). When sinners truly repent, we should forgive them and reaffirm our love to them. Otherwise, they might become discouraged and give Satan an opportunity to accuse and attack (Rev. 12:10). Love does not condone sin, but it does cover sin when God has washed it away (James 5:20).

Fragrance (12–17). Paul described a Roman Triumph, the official parade given to a victorious general when he returned to Rome. The incense carried by the priests meant life to the Roman soldiers but death to the prisoners who would end up in the arena with the wild beasts. Christ has conquered, and we are privileged to march in His triumphal procession!

2 CORINTHIANS 3

The legalists who caused trouble in both Antioch and Jerusalem (Acts 15) had come to Corinth and enticed some of the believers into living by the law of Moses. Paul refuted their position by showing the wonders of the new covenant ministry. The background is Exodus 34:29–35.

It changes hearts (1–3). The law only reveals sin; it cannot renew the inner person. The Spirit wants to write a new version of His Word on your heart. Will you let Him?

It gives life (4–6). The law kills, but grace gives life and sustains that life. God's children have a living relationship with Him through the Spirit of life (Rom. 8:2).

It gets more and more glorious (7–16). The glory of the law is gone: the temple, the priesthood, the ceremonies, and the awesome revelations of God's power. But the glory of God's grace remains and grows more glorious (v. 18; Prov. 4:18).

It brings freedom (17–18). The law brings bondage (Acts 15:10), but grace gives glorious freedom that makes us more and more like Jesus Christ. Each day, you can have your own personal transfiguration as you worship the Lord and yield to the Spirit.

2 CORINTHIANS 4

The glory of salvation (1–6). Unlike the legalists who had invaded the church, Paul had nothing to hide. The Jewish religious system veiled the gospel, but Paul sought to reveal the gospel. The image is taken from Genesis 1:1–3 and transferred from the old creation to the new creation (2 Cor. 5:17).

The glory of service (7–12). Paul paid a price for his ministry, but the legalists went about collecting honors (3:1). We are vessels; the treasure of the gospel life within is important. As vessels, we must be clean and available for His use (2 Tim. 2:20–21).

The glory of suffering (13–18). Jesus suffered and turned that suffering into glory; by faith, we can do the same thing. It is not wrong to care for the outward person, so long as you recognize that it is perishing. Concentrate on the inner person. It is the invisible that is imperishable. The best is yet to come!

"Lord, Thou knowest better than I know that I am growing older. Keep me from getting too talkative and thinking I must say something on every subject and on every occasion. Release me from craving to straighten out everybody's affairs. Teach me the glorious lesson that occasionally it is possible that I may be mistaken. Make me thoughtful, but not moody; helpful, but not bossy; Thou knowest, Lord, that what I want is a few friends at the end.**"**

---

2 CORINTHIANS 5

We know (1). This building is our new body that we will receive when we see the Lord (Phil. 3:20–21) because God saves the whole person (1 Cor. 15:42–58).

We groan (2–4). Creation is groaning and God's people also groan (Rom. 8:18–23), yearning for the Lord Jesus to come again. We do not want to die and leave our "houses"; we want these bodies to be "clothed with" the glory of God from heaven (1 John 3:1-2). Paul longed to see Jesus come in his lifetime.

We are confident (5-8). God's Word gives us the truth about death and beyond, and God's Spirit guarantees that God's children will go to heaven. We claim this by faith and walk with confidence, and what peace it gives!

We aim to please Him (9-21). Paul's spiritual motivations for service include the judgment seat of Christ (vv. 9-11), the love of Christ (vv. 12-16), the power of the gospel (v. 17), and the commission of the Lord (vv. 18-21). What motivates you to do His will?

2 CORINTHIANS 6

Acceptance (1-2). Often those in the church who cause problems are people who have never truly been born again. They may think they are saved, but they are not. *Now* is the time to accept God's grace. Tomorrow may be too late.

Appreciation (3-13). It is easy to forget the sacrifices others have made so we can know the Lord. Paul never spoke about his sufferings unless his words helped to protect the ministry (11:16ff.). Do you take your church fellowship for granted? Have you thanked those who came before you and made it possible?

Agreement (14-18). Believers in the church were compromising with the world and not walking in a separated way (Ps. 1:1). God longs to have a closer fellowship with us, but He will not share the yoke with the world.

2 CORINTHIANS 7

Cleansing (1). It is one thing to ask God to cleanse you (Ps. 51:2, 7) and quite something else to cleanse yourself and put away the things that defile (Isa. 1:16). Separation sometimes demands surgery.

Comforting (2-7). The same people who give you joy can also cause you sorrow. When Titus reported that the church had disciplined the offender, the apostle was overjoyed. Have you ever been an answer to somebody's prayers as Titus was?

Clearing (8-11). If we are serious about repentance, we will do everything we can to clear things up. Remorse and regret do not go far enough; there must be repentance followed by restitution.

Caring (12–16). Both Paul and Titus cared about the believers in Corinth, and this love finally won the day. You take a risk when you love others, for they may hurt you; but it is worth the risk to be like Jesus Christ and live a life of love.

True Repentance

Regret *involves the mind primarily, and* remorse *involves the emotions. But* repentance *includes a change of mind, a hatred for sin, and a willingness to make things right. If the will is not touched, conviction has not gone deep enough.*

---

2 CORINTHIANS 8—9

Chapters 8—9 focus on the offering Paul was taking for the needy believers in Judea. The Corinthian church had agreed to share in the collection but had been remiss in doing so. Paul reminded them of their promise and at the same time explained some principles of Christian giving.

It begins with surrender to the Lord (8:1–7). You cannot give your substance until you first give yourself (v. 5; Rom. 12:1–2). When you belong to the Lord, you start looking for opportunities to give instead of excuses not to give.

It is motivated by grace (8:8–9). Jesus was rich in heaven but became poor on earth (even to death on a cross!) that we might share His eternal riches. It was all by grace because *giving is a grace*. Law *commands*, but grace *consents* and does so joyfully.

It requires faith (8:10–15). The example of the manna (Exod. 16) shows that God always provides what we need. Paul also used the image of sowing to encourage generous giving (9:6). God's promises can be trusted.

It also requires faithfulness (8:16–24). Those who handle the Lord's money should be dedicated and faithful, making certain that everything is honest and honorable.

It is a testimony to others (9:1-5). A year before, the zeal of the Corinthians had stirred others to give; now Paul had to stir up the Corinthians! We must not give to be praised by people (Matt. 6:1-4), but we must also be good examples before others. If we make promises, we should keep them.

It must be done gladly (9:6-15). If you want spiritual enrichment from your giving (9:11), you must practice enjoyment and be glad for opportunities to give. Look at God's promises to faithful givers! How can you lose?

" *For the Macedonian Christians, giving was not a chore but a challenge, not a burden but a blessing. Giving was not something to be avoided but a privilege to be desired.* **"**

George Sweeting

---

2 CORINTHIANS 10

Satan seeks to blind minds to God's light (4:3-6), fortify minds against God's truth (vv. 1-6), and seduce minds from God's love (11:1-4). Paul gives some practical counsel for victory in spiritual warfare.

Be Christlike (1). Boldness must be balanced with meekness, for God's power is experienced in humility. Satan is our enemy, not people held by his power.

Use spiritual weapons (2-6). Paul may have had in mind Joshua's victory at Jericho (Josh. 6) when the walls came down because of Israel's faith. Read Ephesians 6:1-20, and be sure you are wearing the whole armor.

Keep your eyes on the Lord (7-11). That the Corinthians accused Paul of inconsistency gave Satan opportunity to work in their lives.

Accept the sphere of service God gives you (12-16). Every Christian soldier has a place to fill; if we are all following His orders, the church will win the battle.

Seek God's glory alone (17–18). How can we boast in victories that God alone can give? Paul quoted Jeremiah 9:24 to remind us where the glory belongs.

2 CORINTHIANS 11

Paul compares himself to a father with obligations to his spiritual children.

Protection (1–4). Spiritual leaders must protect the church from false teachers who are like suitors trying to seduce the church from devotion to Christ. Beware losing your love for Christ and for those who helped you trust the Savior.

Provision (5–15). Paul had the right to receive financial support at Corinth, but he laid it aside and sacrificed for them in love. They did not appreciate it! But do you appreciate the sacrifices others make for you? Are you willing to sacrifice for others even when they do not thank you?

Suffering (16–33). Paul mentioned his sufferings only to defend the gospel and the authority of his ministry. The false teachers bragged about their triumphs, but Paul boasted about his trials.

"*The principle of sacrifice is that we choose to do or to suffer what apart from our love we should not choose to do or to suffer. When love is returned, this sacrifice is the most joyful thing in the world, and heaven is the life of joyful sacrifice. But in a selfish world it must be painful, and the pain is the source of triumph.***"**

William Temple

---

2 CORINTHIANS 12

Permission. Just as God permitted Satan to test Job (Job 1—2) and Peter (Luke 22:31–34), so He permitted Satan to attack Paul. God wanted to keep Paul humble after his exciting visit to heaven. In the loving will of God, suffering has a purpose that can be fulfilled in no other way. Accept it, and it will become a heavenly blessing; fight it, and it will become a heavy burden.

Prayer. Like our Lord in Gethsemane (Matt. 26:44), Paul prayed three times for God to deliver him; but the Lord did not answer that prayer as Paul wanted. However, *God did meet the need* and gave His servant the grace he required. Paul did not simply make the best of it—he made the *most* of it! Grace can do that for you.

Perplexity. Paul was concerned more about the sins of the saints than about his own physical problems. Like a loving father, he wanted to go to Corinth and enjoy his dear children, but they were forcing him to discipline them. Yet, even discipline is an evidence of love (Heb. 12).

We must form our estimate of men less from their achievements and failures and more from their sufferings.

Dietrich Bonhoeffer

---

2 CORINTHIANS 13

As Paul planned his trip to Corinth, he envisioned the different kinds of people he would meet there.

The disobedient (1–4). Why would God's people want to disobey Him (12:20) and create problems for Paul and grief for the Lord, not to speak of problems for their church? Disobedient children must be dealt with, and Paul intended to be a faithful and loving father.

The disqualified (5–10). Some church members have never been born again, and that is why they create problems. Paul urges us to examine our hearts to be sure we are in the faith.

The devoted (11–14). These are the true brothers and sisters in the Lord, the set-apart ones (saints), the people who love one another and promote the peace and purity of the church. They are the mature ones in the fellowship who encourage spiritual growth.

To which group do you belong?

Solutions   *Every local church problem can be solved by being humble and honest and by drawing on the spiritual resources listed in 2 Corinthians 13:14. Do you avail yourself of these riches? Are you a part of the problem or a part of the answer?*

GALATIANS

◆

The churches Paul founded in the Roman province of Galatia (Acts 13—14) were invaded by false teachers like those Paul had refuted in the Jerusalem Council (Acts 15). We call these people "Judaizers" because they tried to bring Christians into bondage to the law of Moses.

Paul wrote this letter to magnify God's grace in salvation and to explain the freedom of God's people because of that grace (Gal. 5:1). It opens with a *personal affirmation* (chaps. 1—2) as Paul explains how God delivered him from bondage through faith in Jesus Christ. He then gives a *doctrinal explanation* and shows the relationship between law and grace (chaps. 3—4). He closes with a *practical application* that tells you how to enjoy grace and freedom in your daily life (chaps. 5—6).

Christian freedom is the liberty to become all that you can in Jesus Christ; it is not the license to do whatever you please. The worst bondage you can experience is living for yourself and yielding to the desires of the old nature (Rom. 6). "We have freedom to do good or evil," wrote St. Francis de Sales, "yet to make choice of evil, is not to use, but to abuse our freedom." Christ did not free us to be our own; He freed us to be His and His alone.

GALATIANS 1

To Paul, the gospel was much more than a message he preached: it was a miracle he had experienced (vv. 1–5). The gospel is "the power of God to salvation" (Rom. 1:16) and it brings freedom. Christ died "that He might deliver us" (v. 4). When Paul trusted Christ, he became a free man. The shackles of sin and legalistic religion were broken!

But the gospel was also a treasure that Paul guarded (vv. 6–17). Paul did not invent the gospel or learn it from others; God gave it to him (1 Cor. 15:1–11). *There is no other gospel.* To add to this message, take from it, or substitute another message is to destroy it. No wonder Paul attacked those who attacked the gospel; when you lose the gospel, you lose everything.

The gospel is a tie that binds God's people together (vv. 18–24). Saul the enemy became Paul the brother, and he was able to fellowship with people he once had persecuted. Christians may disagree on minor matters of interpretation and organization, but they agree on the message of the gospel.

> **"**The gospel is neither a discussion nor a debate.
> It is an announcement.**"**
>
> Paul S. Rees

GALATIANS 2

The runner (1–5). Paul saw himself as a man running a race, and he was sure he was on the right track and headed for the right goal. The Judaizers were trying to move the church into bondage and get them on a detour (5:7; Acts 15).

The steward (6–10). God has committed the gospel to His people, and we must guard it and share it with others. God is not looking for popular celebrities; He is looking for faithful stewards (1 Cor. 4:1–2).

The watchman (11–13). Paul was not afraid to confront the apostle Peter when Peter moved away from the truth of the gospel. "Eternal vigilance is the price of liberty!" said Wendell Phillips, and that applies to our spiritual liberty as well.

The destroyer (14–21). Jesus destroyed the law by fulfilling it (Matt. 5:17–20). His death tore the temple veil (Luke 23:44–45) and removed the wall between Jews and Gentiles (Eph. 2:14–18). To go back to Moses is to rebuild what Jesus tore down and say that He did not really save us when we trusted Him.

> **"** *Whitefield and Wesley might preach the gospel better than I do, but they cannot preach a better gospel.* **"**
>
> Charles Spurgeon

GALATIANS 3

Examination (1–14). It does us good to examine ourselves to make sure our spiritual experience is valid (2 Cor. 13:5). Do you have the Spirit living within? (See Rom. 8:9.) If you began in the Spirit (which is the only way to begin), are you trying to continue in the power of the flesh? Like Abraham, were you saved by faith; and are you now, like Abraham, walking by faith?

Explanation (15–25). The Judaizers wanted the Galatians to go back to Moses, but that was not far enough. *We must go back to Abraham where the promise started*. The law did not annul the promise; the law was given to reveal sin and prepare the way for Christ to come and fulfill the promise. The law is a tutor, not a savior; a mirror, not a cleanser.

Exhortation (26–29). Beware! A false gospel robs you of salvation and of membership in the family of God where all believers are one in Christ. It robs you of your spiritual riches as an heir of the promise. Are you rejoicing in the freedom you have in Christ?

GALATIANS 4

Are you a child of God through faith in Jesus Christ? Then you are also an heir, and all of Christ's riches are yours (Eph. 1:3)! A child must wait until maturity to inherit the family wealth, but God's children can have His wealth now (Phil. 4:19).

Are you a child of God through faith in Jesus Christ? Then you are free! A child is in bondage and must be guarded by adults, but a grown son or daughter enjoys freedom. To live under Law is to be a slave, and God wants His children to enjoy their freedom in Christ.

Are you a child of God through faith in Jesus Christ? Then you can become like Him as you yield to the Spirit (v. 19; 2 Cor. 3:18).

Are you a child of God through faith in Jesus Christ? Then your citizenship is secure in heaven because you are a child of promise (vv. 21–31; Gen. 16). You were born free!

Freedom in Christ

An allegory is a narrative in which people and events teach deeper lessons. John Bunyan's Pilgrim's Progress is a classic example. Paul used Genesis 16 to illustrate your freedom in Christ. Hagar is the law, while Sarah stands for God's grace. Ishmael was born after the flesh (your first birth), while Isaac was born by the power of God (the new birth). Abraham represents faith, so Isaac was born "by grace [Sarah] . . . through faith [Abraham]" (Eph. 2:8). The Judaizers wanted to bring Hagar back again, but she was sent away because law and grace cannot coexist. Like Hagar, the law was a servant that had a temporary ministry. Once the Son arrived, that ministry was fulfilled.

GALATIANS 5

Are you standing free (1)? Your freedom in Christ is a costly thing, for it cost Jesus His life. In Him, you stand free; the yoke of the law has been removed (Acts 15:6–11).

Are you falling (4)? To fall from grace does not mean to lose one's salvation. It means to move out of the sphere of grace into the sphere of law. It means to substitute regulations for a personal relationship with the Lord.

Are you running on course (7)? Or has false teaching gotten you on a detour?

Are you being leavened (9)? Jesus used leaven to picture sin (Matt. 16:6–12). Like yeast, false teaching is introduced quietly, it grows secretly, and soon it affects every part of your life.

Are you serving others (13)? Freedom brings with it the responsibility to serve. Love motivates us to fulfill the law of God (Rom. 13:8–14).

Are you walking in the Spirit (16)? Life, not law, changes behavior; and as you yield to the Spirit, Christ's life is manifest in the fruit of the Spirit.

Law works by compulsion from without, but grace works by compassion from within.

"*Every time we say, 'I believe in the Holy Spirit,' we mean that we believe there is a living God able and willing to enter human personality and change it.***"**

J. B. Phillips

GALATIANS 6

See others humbly (1–2). Your response to another's fall reveals your own walk, whether it is spiritual or not. Pride will make it impossible for you to help the fallen, but humility will bring blessing to you and to them.

See yourself honestly (3–5). Do you use somebody's fall to make yourself look better? Or do you know yourself, accept yourself, and seek to please God alone?

See your leaders appreciatively (6–10). When you give to others whose ministry blesses you, you are sowing seed that will bear fruit. When you use your resources for sinful purposes, you sow to the flesh and will reap a sad harvest.

See the Cross clearly (11–18). The false teachers wanted the world's praise, so they avoided the Cross; but the true believer will glory in the Cross, even if it means suffering the world's enmity.

Faithfully Restore Them

The word translated "restore" in Galatians 6:1 also means "to set a broken bone." How gentle and loving we must be when we seek to help fallen brothers or sisters, for what we do will affect them and the body of Christ.

EPHESIANS

◆

On his second missionary journey, Paul visited Ephesus and left Aquila and Priscilla there (Acts 18:19–21). He returned to Ephesus two years later and ministered for three years, reaching the whole province of Asia with the gospel (Acts 19). Some years later when Paul was a prisoner in Rome (3:1; 4:1; 6:20), he wrote this letter to the believers in Ephesus.

One major theme of Ephesians is that God is at work in this world, through His church, putting things together (1:10). In the first three chapters, Paul explains this as a work of redemption (chap. 1), resurrection (2:1–10), and reconciliation (2:11—3:21). In chapters 4—6, Paul states the responsibilities of believers in the light of God's great purpose. Note the emphasis on the word *walk*.

Ephesus was an important city and boasted of being custodian of the temple of Diana, one of the seven wonders of the ancient world. The city was devoted to idolatry, which explains why Paul had so much to say about defeating the devil (6:10ff.).

The Ephesian letter shows the balance in the Christian life between doctrine (chaps. 1—3) and duty (chaps. 4—6), divine sovereignty and human responsibility. We do not obey God so that He will give us His grace; we obey Him in response to grace already given.

EPHESIANS 1

Salvation is of God. Man does not save himself, for "salvation is of the LORD" (Jon. 2:9). You receive spiritual blessings from the Father (vv. 1–6), the Son (vv. 7–12), and the Spirit (vv. 13–14); and in Jesus Christ, you have all you need for life and service.

Salvation is all of grace. Paul emphasizes this point throughout the letter, especially in 2:1–10. Grace is God's favor bestowed on people who do not and cannot deserve it.

Salvation is for God's glory. God saves sinners not to solve their problems but to bring glory to Himself (vv. 6, 12, 14; 3:21). The church will glorify Him for all eternity!

Salvation reveals God's greatness (15–23). Ask God to open your spiritual eyes to see the greatness of His power. Jesus is alive and has conquered every enemy! You may draw on His power to meet every need in life.

Praying in His Will

The two prayers in Ephesians complement each other. Ephesians 1:15–23 focuses on knowing what God has done for you in Christ, while 3:14–21 emphasizes experiencing His blessings. The first is for enlightenment; the second is for enablement. For other prison prayers of Paul, see Philippians 1:9–11 and Colossians 1:9–12. You may use these prayers for yourself and know that you are praying in the will of God.

EPHESIANS 2

From death to life. Lost sinners are not simply sick people needing help; they are dead people needing life. The Son of God died that we might receive life through faith in Him (John 5:24).

From bondage to freedom. Lost sinners are in bondage to the world, the flesh, and the devil (vv. 1–3) and cannot free themselves. In Christ, you have true freedom (John 12:31–32; Gal. 1:4; 5:24). Now God is working in you and through you to accomplish His great purposes (v. 10).

From the tomb to the throne. God did not give you life and leave you in the cemetery. He lifted you up to sit on the throne with His victorious Son!

From separation to reconciliation. In Jesus Christ, believing Jews and Gentiles are now one; the barriers have been removed. Believers are members of one body, citizens of one holy nation, and living stones in one temple (1 Pet. 2:1–10).

All of this is of God, His marvelous love (v. 4), and His grace and kindness (v. 7). No wonder Paul opened this letter with a doxology (1:3)!

EPHESIANS 3

A purpose. "For this reason" (vv. 1, 14) refers to what Paul wrote at the end of chapter 2, the building of the church. That was the purpose behind his praying and his ministering. Jesus said, "I will build My church" (Matt. 16:18), but He uses people to help get the job done. Is the building of the church your motivation to pray and serve?

A parenthesis. The word *Gentiles* (v. 1) put Paul in prison (Acts 22:21). God gave him a special commission to evangelize the Gentiles and to explain to both Jews and Gentiles God's "mystery" (sacred secret): in Christ, believing Jews and Gentiles are one and share the same spiritual riches. As He builds His church in this world, God is putting things together. Are you helping Him?

A prayer. This prayer is for spiritual vision, to see and lay hold of the greatness of God's love and power. God wants you to be concerned about "the whole building" (2:21), "the whole family" (3:15), "the whole body" (4:16), and "all the saints" (v. 18). Is narrowness in your life leading to shallowness and weakness?

EPHESIANS 4

To "give place to the devil" (v. 27) is to allow unconfessed sin in your life that gives Satan an opportunity to take over. Some sins to avoid are discussed here.

Disunity (1–13). Believers are "all one in Christ Jesus" (Gal. 3:28), but we must endeavor to make that spiritual unity a practical reality in our daily lives. Satan uses people who like to have their own way.

Immaturity (14–16). Spiritual birth must lead to spiritual growth as we become more like Jesus Christ (1 Pet. 1:22—2:3). If we are maturing in Christ, we will show it by being able to speak the truth in love. Satan is a liar and a murderer (John 8:44) and has a difficult time being successful when believers practice truth and love.

Impurity (17–32). You have been set free from the old life, so why live in those old sins anymore? Anything evil from the old life that is brought into the new life will give the devil a beachhead. Paul names such things as lying, losing your temper, stealing, corrupt speech, bitterness, and an unforgiving spirit. These sins invite Satan into your life, and they hurt you, harm the church, and grieve the Spirit of God. Is it worth it?

EPHESIANS 5

As he encourages us to live godly lives, Paul takes us to *the temple* (vv. 1–7) and reminds us of the sacrifice Jesus made for us. If we walk in love, our lives will be living sacrifices (Rom. 12:1–2; Phil. 2:17), fragrant to the Lord (John 12:1–8). Sin is ugly and a stench in God's nostrils (Isa. 3:24).

Then Paul goes to *the field* (vv. 8–14) and reminds us that walking in the light produces spiritual fruit (Gal. 5:22–23). If we walk in the light, we cannot have fellowship with the darkness (2 Cor. 6:14–18).

He takes us to *the marketplace* (vv. 15–17) and exhorts us to be like good merchants who know how to buy up an opportunity. When you walk in wisdom, you use your time wisely.

Then we follow him to *the banqueting hall* (vv. 18–21) and learn to walk in the Spirit (Gal. 5:16–26) and be joyful, thankful, and submissive to one another.

Paul's last visit is to *the home* (vv. 22–33) where he uses marriage as a picture of the relationship between Christ and the church. Christ *loved* us and died for us, but today He *loves* us and cares for us. This intimate life is pictured in the Song of Solomon and can be a reality for all who will yield to Him.

Under the Spirit's Influence

To be "filled with" means "to be controlled by" (Luke 4:28; 5:26). On the day of Pentecost, the believers were filled with the Holy Spirit and were accused of being drunk (Acts 2:13). Just as a drunk is influenced by alcohol, so a believer should be controlled by the Spirit. However, there are important differences. The drunk loses self-control, but the Spirit gives the believer self-control (Gal. 5:23). The drunk has an artificial happiness that does not last, while the Spirit-filled believer has a deep joy in the Lord. Drunken people do stupid things that hurt others and bring them embarrassment, but Spirit-filled believers help others and live to the glory of God.

EPHESIANS 6

Spirit-filled Christians will manifest Christlikeness in the home (vv. 1–4), on the job (vv. 5–9), and on the battlefield (vv. 10–20). If we do not learn to obey at home, we are not likely to be obedient on the job or in the army of the Lord. Likewise, if we have not learned to *take* orders, we will not be too successful at *giving* orders, either as parents or as employers.

The danger in the home is parents who are *authoritarian* but do not exercise loving spiritual *authority*. The danger on the job is the employee who is a clock-watcher and does not obey from the heart, and the "boss" who forgets that he is second in command and must one day give an account to the Lord.

The danger on the battlefield is that we do not take the enemy seriously and therefore fail to put on all of the armor. By faith, you put on the armor through prayer, which must be done at the beginning of every day. Never underestimate the strategy and strength of the devil.

"Stand Up, Stand Up for Jesus"

"Stand up, stand up for Jesus,
Stand in His strength alone;
The arm of flesh will fail you,
You dare not trust your own.
Put on the gospel armor,
Each piece put on with prayer;
Where duty calls or danger,
Be never wanting there."

George Duffield

PHILIPPIANS

◆

Founded on Paul's second missionary journey (Acts 16), the church at Philippi was a source of real joy to him. Hearing that Paul was a prisoner in Rome, the Philippian believers sent a special love offering; and in this letter, Paul wrote to express his thanks. He also wrote to explain why Epaphroditus, their messenger, had been delayed and to encourage the believers to work together to bring unity to the church.

The overriding theme of the letter is Jesus Christ and the ministry of the gospel. Christ is the message of our ministry (chap. 1) as well as the model (chap. 2), the motive (chap. 3), and the means (chap. 4). The theme of joy is also woven throughout the letter. Despite his difficult circumstances, Paul rejoiced in the Lord and urged his readers to do so. After all, the joy of the Lord is the strength of Christian service (Neh. 8:10).

PHILIPPIANS 1

Paul wrote, "For to me, to live is Christ" (v. 21). But he did more than *write* that statement; he *lived* it. Jesus Christ is mentioned eighteen times in this chapter and is seen involved in many aspects of Paul's life.

His friends (1–11). Paul loved the saints in Philippi; he thought about them, prayed for them, and longed to see them. Christ made this fellowship possible.

His circumstances (12–18). He was a prisoner not of Rome but of Jesus Christ, and his chains were "in Christ" (v. 13). Paul was practicing Romans 8:28—and it worked! Do you think first of Christ when circumstances are difficult?

His future (19–26). Paul's life was in danger; if he lost the trial, he could be killed as an enemy of Rome. But when Christ is your life, death is not your enemy; and you have the assurance of being with Christ when life ends.

His enemies (27–30). When you suffer, you suffer for Christ's sake; and you need not fear your enemies. The vital thing is that God's people unite in Christ and oppose the enemy, not one another!

Alive to Christ

"Life is what we are alive to," wrote Maltbie Babcock. Sports fans may be weary, but if they hear of an athletic event taking place, they come alive and want to attend. Hungry people are alive to the mention of food, and avid shoppers come alive at the announcement of a sale. So Christians are alive to all pertaining to Jesus Christ, for Christ is their very life.

PHILIPPIANS 2

Look out (1–11). Christ is the model for Christian life and service because He thought first of others, not of Himself. Do you look out for the interests of others, or do you think only of yourself? Do you have the servant attitude of Jesus Christ, willing to sacrifice for others? Will you empty yourself that others might be filled?

Work out (12–16). As you yield to the Lord, He works in and you work out; in this way, you fulfill His plan for your life (Eph. 2:10). God cannot shine *through* you until He works *in* you, so let Him have His way. You are a light in a dark world, a runner holding forth the living Word to a dead world.

Poured out (17–30). The image is that of the drink offering, poured out on the altar (Num. 15:1–10). Paul was willing to pour out his very life for the sake of the Lord and the church, and to do it *joyfully*. Timothy and Epaphroditus had the same attitude of service and sacrifice, giving themselves for others.

> **❝**I used to think that God's gifts were on shelves one above the other, and that the taller we grew in Christian character the more easily we could reach them. I now find that God's gifts are on shelves one beneath the other and that it is not a question of growing taller but of stooping lower.**❞**
>
> F. B. Meyer

PHILIPPIANS 3

Rejoicing (1). If you cannot rejoice in your circumstances, you can always rejoice in the Lord who controls your circumstances. Fix your attention on Him. He may not change your situation, but He will change you; and that is even better.

Counting (2–11). What is important to you? Do you feel you have made sacrifices to follow the Lord? Paul did not feel he had lost anything worthwhile by trusting Christ. Instead, he gained everything really worth having.

Reaching (12–16). Christians are like runners who refuse to look around or look back but keep running with their eyes on the goal. To look back at past successes or failures, or to look around to see what others are doing or saying, is to invite defeat. Heed Hebrews 12:1–2.

Weeping (17–19). This is the only mention of tears in a letter devoted to joy. Paul wept over professed Christians who lived to please themselves. Instead of having the mind of Christ, they thought like the world, and these people are with us today.

Looking (20–21). Paul looked up and eagerly anticipated the return of the Lord. Christ had taken care of his past (v. 13), and He would also take care of his future. And as for Paul's present, his confidence was knowing that "He is able!" (v. 21).

PHILIPPIANS 4

The message of our ministry is the gospel of Christ (chap. 1). The model for our ministry is the example of Christ (chap. 2). The motive for our ministry is the reward of Christ (chap. 3). The means of our ministry is the provision of Christ (chap. 4).

He provides unity when we disagree with our fellow Christians (vv. 1–5), and peace when we are prone to worry (vv. 6–9). If we pray as we ought to pray and think as we ought to think, the peace of God will guard us, and the God of peace will go with us.

He provides the power we need for life and service (vv. 10–13) and the material needs we have as well (vv. 14–20). Paul did not have a wealthy organization giving him support, but he did have a great God who enabled generous friends to meet his needs. Paul saw their gift as a fragrant sacrifice to the Lord (v. 18), and he rejoiced in the Lord for what they did.

Reach Your Potential

Charles W. Koller affirmed that through Christ you can be what you ought to be (Phil. 4:11), do what you ought to do (v. 13), and have what you ought to have (v. 19), all to the glory of God.

COLOSSIANS

$\mathbf{E}$paphras, one of Paul's converts, founded the church in Colosse (1:7; 4:12–13); Paul had never been there personally (2:1). While imprisoned in Rome, Paul heard that false doctrines were being introduced in the church, so he wrote this letter to warn the believers and to establish them in the faith.

The key theme is the preeminence of Christ (1:18) because the false teachers made Christ one of several emanations from God. They mixed Christian truth with their doctrines of Jewish legalism and Oriental mysticism. Colossians is the perfect answer to the so-called New Age movement today, for Paul affirms that in Jesus Christ believers are complete and have the fullness of God available to them (2:9–10).

Chapters 1–2 are doctrinal and present Jesus Christ as the preeminent Creator, Savior, and Lord. Chapters 3–4 are practical and show how the believer works out the preeminence of Christ in daily living. Because the epistles to the Ephesians and Colossians were written about the same time, you will see parallels; but Ephesians emphasizes the body (the church), while Colossians emphasizes the Head of the body (Jesus Christ). The letters complement each other.

COLOSSIANS 1

The hope before you (1–12). These people were going to heaven! They had heard the Word and trusted the Savior, and they had given evidence of their faith by their love for God and God's people. God qualified them (v. 12); they did not save themselves.

The hope beneath you (13–23). Hope is a foundation on

which you stand when all around you is shaking. The city of Colosse was located in an earthquake area, so Paul's admonition was especially meaningful to them (v. 23). The false teachers wanted the saints to shift their foundation, but Paul pointed the church to Jesus Christ: Savior (vv. 13–14), eternal God (v. 15), Creator (vv. 16–17), and Head of the church (v. 18). What a perfect foundation for your hope!

The hope within you (24–29). Heaven is more than a destination; it is a motivation because Christ lives within. It is a living hope (1 Pet. 1:3) that affects how we think and act all day long. Because Christ is within us, we need not fear what is ahead.

Firstborn

"Firstborn over all creation" (Col. 1:15) does not mean Jesus was a created being and not eternal God, nor does "firstborn from the dead" (v. 18) mean He was the first one raised from the dead. Firstborn is a term of honor and means "the highest, of first rank and importance." Jesus was prior to all creation (John 1:1–3) and is the highest in creation. He is the highest of all who were raised from the dead (Rev. 1:17–18).

Thanksgiving

Note the emphasis on thanksgiving in Colossians (1:3, 12; 2:7; 3:17; 4:2). The more wonderful we see Jesus to be, the more we will be grateful to God for Him and His blessings.

COLOSSIANS 2

Paul wrote to the Colossians, "You must never allow anyone to come between you and Christ. In Him is all wisdom and knowledge (v. 3) and all the fullness of God (v. 9), and you are complete in Him (v. 10). Why accept a substitute?"

Let no one deceive you (4). Religious systems seem so inviting, and their leaders are so persuasive. But if you follow them, you will substitute man's ideas for God's truth.

Let no one cheat you (8). Here the thief is man-made philosophy and tradition, pleasing to the world but rejected by the Lord. If you have all fullness in Christ, why substitute man's empty philosophies?

Let no one judge you (16). Legalism is the robber here (v. 21), stealing your liberty in Christ and making you live by religious regulations instead of by God's grace.

Let no one defraud you (18). Here the culprit is religious mysticism that replaces spiritual nourishment from Christ with empty (but exciting) religious experiences.

You have in Christ all that you need. Beware substitutes!

❝The greatest philosophy ever produced does not come within a thousand leagues of the fathomless profundity of our Lord's statements, e.g., 'Learn of Me, for I am meek and lowly in heart.'**❞**

Oswald Chambers

COLOSSIANS 3

Having laid the doctrinal foundation, Paul now makes the personal application, for truth is something to *live* as well as to *learn*.

Put to death (1–7). In Christ, you have died to the old life and been raised to a new life (Rom. 6:1–14; Eph. 2:1–10), so make the new life the focus of your attention. Set your mind on it; seek to experience all that you have in Christ.

Put off (8-9). Like Lazarus (John 11:44), you must get rid of the graveclothes that belong to the old life. By faith, put off the old sins that bound you; Christ has set you free.

Put on (10-25). God wants you to wear the graceclothes, not the graveclothes! If your focus is on things heavenly, you will obey God in things on earth, especially in your relationships with others.

Filled with the Word

Colossians 3:16—4:1 parallels Ephesians 5:18—6:9, except that the emphasis here is on being filled with the Word of God. When the Word controls your life, you will be joyful (3:16), thankful (3:17), and submissive (3:18—4:1), and these are the same characteristics of the Spirit-filled Christian as explained in Ephesians 5:18—6:9. To be filled with the Spirit of God means to be controlled by the Word of God.

COLOSSIANS 4

Praying (2-4, 12-13). Prayer involves a persevering will, an alert mind, and a grateful heart; and our requests should be specific and related to the ministry of the Word. Paul asked not for an open prison door but for an open door of ministry (1 Cor. 16:9; 2 Cor. 2:12; Rev. 3:7-8).

Witnessing (5-6). The unsaved are outside the family of God, and it is our task to bring them in. Effective witness involves walking wisely, being alert to every opportunity, and being careful in what we say and how we say it (1 Pet. 3:15-17).

Informing (7-9). Paul did not hesitate to share his needs with others, because he depended on their prayer support (Rom. 15:30; Eph. 6:19; Phil. 1:19; 1 Thess. 5:25; Philem. 22). Do you pray for Christian leaders in places of importance? They need it!

Serving (10–18). Paul names six men who were working at his side and encouraging him in the Lord. Even an apostle cannot get the job done alone, and how grateful he was for the saints serving faithfully in Colosse!

Servants of the Lord

Years before, Paul had refused to serve with John Mark (Acts 15:36–41) because Mark had left the work (Acts 13:5–13); but now Paul and John Mark were friends and colaborers. Luke had been a part of Paul's team since their ministry at Philippi (Acts 16:10). Alas, Demas would eventually forsake Paul and the Lord (Philem. 24; 2 Tim. 4:10). Do you pray for the men and women who serve with Christian leaders, that they might be faithful to the Lord?

THE THESSALONIAN EPISTLES

◆

Acts 17:1–15 records the founding of the church in Thessalonica. Paul ministered there a short time, possibly only a month; but the Lord did a great work, and the witness of the church was known far and wide.

Paul had to leave the city and was not able to return, so he sent Timothy to see how things were going. Paul wrote the first letter from Corinth (Acts 18:5) in response to Timothy's report (3:6). He wanted to encourage the saints in their Christian walk and assure them of his love and concern.

The second letter was written a few months later to encourage the church to be steadfast in the midst of persecution. Some of the people thought the "day of the Lord" had come, so Paul dealt with that theme as well. Both letters emphasize the coming of Christ and the practical effect it should have on our lives.

FIRST THESSALONIANS

$\blacklozenge$

1 THESSALONIANS 1

Paul's description of the believers in Thessalonica suggests that they typify an ideal congregation. Ask yourself these questions.

Are others thankful for me (1–4)? Paul was grateful for their faith, hope, and love, and that these Christian qualities revealed themselves in work, labor, and patience. Can others tell that we belong to God? Are they thankful for our spiritual growth?

Jesus' *Return*	Every chapter in 1 Thessalonians ends with a reference to the return of Jesus Christ, and that truth is applied to daily living. An eager looking for His return is an evidence of salvation (1:9–10), a motivation for soul winning (2:17–20), and an encouragement for holy living (3:11–13). This truth is a comfort in sorrow (4:18) and a stimulus to have more confidence in the Lord (5:23–24).

Is God's power seen in my life (5–7)? This comes when you receive the Word of God by faith and allow the Spirit of God to minister to your heart. It also involves suffering for the Lord and letting Him give you His joy.

Do I make it easier for others to talk about Jesus (8–10)? Some believers are such poor examples as Christians that their lives give unbelievers an excuse for rejecting Christ. But the Thessalonian Christians made it easy for Paul to preach the gospel! Their testimony had gone before him and met him wherever he went.

1 THESSALONIANS 2

Faithfulness (1–6). Paul's sufferings in Philippi might have made him hesitate to minister in Thessalonica, but he was a steward who wanted to be faithful to the Lord. His message and motive were pure, and God blessed his ministry. It is better to be approved by God and suffer than to be applauded by men and prosper. When you feel like quitting, keep going (1 Cor. 4:2).

Gentleness (7–9). Young believers need a spiritual parent to lovingly nurture them in the Lord. Paul's ministry was motivated by love, not by pride or the desire for material gain.

Blamelessness (10–12). How important it is to be good examples before young believers! Children do what we do, not what we say. Does your example as a Christian make it easier for others to grow?

Eagerness (13–16). These people had an appetite for the Word of God, and that helped them to grow (Jer. 15:16; 1 Pet. 2:2). When they heard God's Word, they eagerly welcomed it and put it to work immediately.

Hopefulness (17–20). Paul hoped to visit his beloved friends again; but even if they did not meet on earth, he would meet them at the coming of the Lord. When Jesus comes, will you rejoice in His presence because of people you have influenced for Christ?

1 THESSALONIANS 3

What should you do when people you love need your help, but you cannot go to them? The new believers in Thessalonica desperately needed Paul's ministry, but he was not able to return to help them. So, he did what he could.

First, he sent Timothy to minister to the church. If you cannot go, try to get somebody qualified to go in your place.

Then, he prayed for them (v. 10) because prayer is not limited by time or place. Your prayers for your loved ones will do more good than you realize, so keep praying.

Paul encouraged them by writing them at least two letters. His great concern was not their comfort or safety but their faith (vv. 2, 5–7, 10), their love (v. 12), and their obedience to the Lord (v. 13). Perhaps today you could write a letter or send a card to someone who needs your encouragement.

1 THESSALONIANS 4

"More and more" should be the desire of the dedicated Christian (vv. 1, 10).

More holiness (1–8). Your body belongs to God, and His will is that you use it for holy purposes. Christ purchased your body (1 Cor. 6:18–20), the Spirit dwells in your body (v. 8), and the Father has called you to holy living (v. 7). Disobey and the penalties are great!

More love (9–10). You are taught to love by the Father (1 John 4:19), the Son (John 13:34), and the Spirit (Rom. 5:5). Love is one mark of the true believer (1 John 3:14).

More quietness (11–12). Because they expected the Lord to return any day, some believers had quit their jobs and become idlers and meddlers (2 Thess. 3:6–15). What kind of testimony would this be to the lost?

More hope (13–18). Christians sorrow because God made us to weep; but it is not the hopeless sorrow of the world. Jesus is coming again, and that means reunion and eternal rejoicing!

1 THESSALONIANS 5

False peace (1–11). The "day of the Lord" is that time when God will pour out His wrath on the world. God's people have been saved from wrath, so they need not worry (v. 9; 1:10); but the lost world will be caught at a time when they think they are secure. To be ready for Christ's coming, God's people must be sober and live in the light.

Family peace (12–22). The local church fellowship should reflect God's peace; and it will if God's people obey authority, minister to one another, and submit to the Spirit of God.

Verse 21 emphasizes the positive and verse 22 the negative, and both are important.

Faithful peace (23–28). Holiness and peace go together (Isa. 32:17), for the God who quiets the heart also cleanses the heart (James 3:17). A disturbed heart is sometimes evidence of unconfessed sin. God is faithful; let Him bring purity and peace to your heart.

Welcome the Spirit's Ministry

"Do not quench the Spirit" (1 Thess. 5:19) is an admonition to Christians not to resist and reject the ministry of the Spirit. The image is that of fire (Isa. 34:4; Acts 2:3; Rev. 4:5). Just as fire brings light, heat, and cleansing, so the Spirit enlightens, enables, and purifies His people. Paul reminded Timothy to "stir up the gift of God" (2 Tim. 1:6), which means "get the fire burning again." Are you allowing the fire to go out on the altar of your life (Lev. 6:9, 12)?

❝I have noticed this, that when a man is full of the Holy Ghost, he is the very last man to be complaining of other people. He loves everybody too tenderly. He loves even a cold church, and is anxious to lift them up and bring them to a kinder feeling and sympathy.**❞**

D. L. Moody

SECOND
THESSALONIANS

◆

2 THESSALONIANS 1

Along with persecutions on the outside, the church was facing problems on the inside. Some people were suffering great trials for their faith. Others had quit working and were idlers. Still others were harboring the wrong idea that they were experiencing the "day of the Lord." Paul wrote this letter to encourage the suffering (chap. 1), enlighten the confused (chap. 2), and warn the careless (chap. 3).

In times of trial, the essential thing is your faith (v. 3). God will see you through, so trust His promises. Remember that others are watching you and you can encourage them (v. 4). You may be tempted to fight back, but leave that to the Lord (vv. 5–9).

"No pain, no palm; no thorns, no throne; no gall, no glory; no cross, no crown.**"**

William Penn

The lost will be eternally separated from God's glory (v. 9), while the saved will bring glory to the Lord (v. 10). Meanwhile, be sure that God is glorified by your life today (vv. 11–12).

2 THESSALONIANS 2

Satan wants to shake the saints and make them lose their confidence, and one of his chief weapons is deception. Someone claimed to have a letter from Paul saying that the day of the Lord was present, and others said they had messages through the Spirit (1 Thess. 5:21). The believers forgot what Paul had taught them (v. 5), so they were trapped by the lies of the enemy.

The "times and seasons" of God's prophetic plan are in God's hands (Acts 1:6–8), and He has everything in control. A sequence of events is sketched here to assure us that the church is destined for salvation and not judgment (v. 13; 1 Thess. 1:10; 5:9). The Spirit of God in this world is keeping God's program on schedule.

Beware "prophets" who contradict what God has already said in His Word (v. 15). If you stand on the Word, you will not fall for the devil's lies. God's people can face the future with assurance, hope, and comfort because of the unfailing grace of God (vv. 13–17).

2 THESSALONIANS 3

Conflict (1–2). Anyone who seeks to live for the Lord will have enemies (2 Tim. 3:12). The weapon we use is prayer, and the purpose for which we pray is the sharing of the Word of God (Col. 4:2–3). Not everybody in the church at Thessalonica was devoted to the Lord, but Paul still asked for their prayers.

"Work is not primarily a thing one does to live, but the thing one lives to do. It is, or should be, the full expression of the worker's faculties, the thing in which he finds spiritual, mental and bodily satisfaction, and the medium in which he offers himself to God."

Dorothy L. Sayers

Confidence (3–5). God's faithfulness to us is the basis for our faithfulness to Him. If we love Him, we will keep His Word, and we will be patient in times of trial.

Command (6–15). The word *command* (vv. 4, 6, 10, 12) means "a military order." Some of the Christian soldiers in the church were breaking rank and disobeying orders, and Paul had to admonish them. Those who cannot work must be cared for by others, but those who *will not* work must be disciplined. Never let the bad example of others keep you from being a good example.

FIRST TIMOTHY

◆————————

Paul's trial in Rome came out in his favor, and he was released. It is likely he went to Colosse to visit Philemon (Philem. 22). He may have written 1 Timothy from Colosse or from Philippi.

The child of a mixed marriage (Acts 16:1), Timothy was raised in a godly home (2 Tim. 1:5; 3:15) and came to know Christ through Paul's ministry (1 Tim. 1:2). Paul added him to his team at Lystra (Acts 16:1–3) and made him one of his special assistants (Phil. 2:19–22). Timothy eventually was sent to pastor the church in Ephesus (1 Tim. 1:3).

First Timothy is a ministerial letter, telling pastors and people how they should conduct themselves in the local assembly (3:15). Paul stresses preaching the truth (chaps. 1, 4), praying (chap. 2), and appointing qualified leaders (chap. 3). He closes by giving counsel on how to minister to various kinds of people in the church (chaps. 5—6).

1 TIMOTHY 1

The work in Ephesus was not easy, and Timothy wanted a new assignment; but Paul urged him to stay where he was and get the job done (1:3). The next time you want to abandon your assigned place, consider the arguments Paul gave Timothy for staying where he was.

For the work's sake (1–11). What Paul warned the Ephesian elders about had come true: false teachers were in the church (Acts 20:28–30). The pastor's job is to warn them and teach the people the truth. If he abandoned the flock, Timothy would be a hireling and not a shepherd (John 10:12–13).

For the Lord's sake (12–17). Jesus died to save sinners, and

He lives to equip and enable His servants to do the work of the ministry. The same God who empowered Paul could empower Timothy—and can empower us today. God is faithful!

For our own sake (18–20). God had equipped Timothy, called him, and given him a solemn charge. There was a battle to fight, and he dare not run away. If we flee the post of duty, we rob ourselves of opportunities to grow, to serve, and to glorify God.

When the winds of adversity blow, set your sails in the right direction, and let Christ handle the rudder. Otherwise, you may be shipwrecked.

Responsibility   Someone defined responsibility as "our response to God's ability."

1 TIMOTHY 2

What is the most vital ministry of the local church? According to Paul, it is *prayer*. Prayer moves the hand that governs the world. We must pray for government leaders, that the doors of ministry will be kept open and souls will be won to Christ. Because God's people do not pray for people in authority, wars close mission fields, officials do not grant needed visas, and the work of the Lord suffers.

A good woman is the best thing on earth. Women were last at the cross and first at the open tomb. The church owes a debt to her faithful women which she can never estimate, to say nothing of the debt we owe in our homes to godly wives and mothers.

Vance Havner

Paul reminds Christian men that Christian women are important to the Lord and to the work of the church. The gospel brought freedom to women in the Roman Empire, but some of them did not know how to handle it and went to extremes asserting their liberty. Hence, the reminder about the spiritual leadership of the men in the church.

Modesty, true spiritual beauty (1 Pet. 3:1–6), godliness, and good works—these will characterize the woman God blesses.

> **❝**It is in willing submission, rather than grudging
> capitulation, that the woman in the church
> (whether married or single) and the wife
> in the home find their fulfillment.**❞**
>
> Elisabeth Elliot

1 TIMOTHY 3

Being a leader of God's people is a serious task, and no one should accept an office who is not qualified and willing to *use* that office to help the church.

Watching (1–7). The title *bishop* means "overseer" and describes the work of the elder (Acts 20:17, 28). God's people are like sheep; they need shepherds to watch over them, protect them, and lead them. Pray for your spiritual leaders that they might more and more be what God wants them to be.

Working (8–13). The word *deacon* means "servant." The deacons assist the elders in carrying out the work of the church (Acts 6:1–7). As with the elders, the deacons should be qualified spiritually and set the right example in their homes.

Worshiping (14–16). The church is much more than a group of like-minded people who assemble from time to time. The living God is in their midst (Matt. 18:20), and the truth of God has been deposited with them! They worship the Son of God who alone is worthy of praise! Yes, it is a serious thing to be a part of a local church. Do you take it seriously?

1 TIMOTHY 4

Watch yourself (1-5). Satan is at work spreading false doctrine, and his ministers are already in the church (2 Cor. 11:13-15). God's servants must preach the truth and fight the devil's lies. Declaring war may not make us popular, but it will keep us faithful.

Exercise yourself (6-10). If believers would put as much effort into the spiritual life as they do their recreation and hobbies, what a difference it would make! Physical exercise is important, but spiritual exercise is even more essential. Both discipline and devotion are needed to make a winning athlete and an effective Christian.

Give yourself (11-16). It takes real effort to grow in the Christian life and to be successful in Christian service. God asks for our wholehearted surrender, no matter what the cost. Ponder these admonitions that Paul wrote to Timothy and see how they apply in your life.

Advance!

The word translated "progress" in 1 Timothy 4:15 means "pioneer advance." As we walk with the Lord and serve Him, we must move into new territory and not stay the same spiritually. There are new truths to learn, new battles to fight, and new victories to win. "Restlessness is discontent," said Thomas Alva Edison, "and discontent is the first necessity of progress. Show me a thoroughly satisfied man and I will show you a failure."

---

1 TIMOTHY 5

What causes problems in churches? Often, it is people not getting along with each other. Brothers and sisters do not always dwell together in unity (Ps. 133).

Paul suggests that we treat other people the way we would treat members of our own family (vv. 1–2). If the older people complain about things, deal with them as you would your father or mother, and accept the younger believers as brothers and sisters. This is simply a call to love others as God loves you.

Not everybody who asks for help should receive it (vv. 3–16). Charity should begin at home (vv. 4, 16), and church leaders must exercise discernment lest they create more problems than they solve.

Sometimes trouble comes because we believe reports that cannot be verified (v. 19), or we show partiality (v. 21), or we make decisions before getting the facts (v. 22). Not every church member has a character as good as his or her reputation (vv. 24–25), so take care!

1 TIMOTHY 6

Watch your motives (1–2). Be obedient so you do not bring reproach on the Word (v. 1; Titus 2:10) or show disrespect for persons in authority over you (v. 2). Never take advantage of fellow believers; rather, do all you can to help them.

Watch your attitudes (3–5). Do you enjoy arguing about the Bible? Then search your heart to see if any of these sinful attitudes are hiding there. You can never debate people into the kingdom or into a more sanctified life.

Watch your values (6–10, 17–19). Are you content with the necessities of life, or must God give you luxuries? God wants you to enjoy His gifts (v. 17) and employ them for the good of others; but beware when your heart is set on getting rich (Prov. 15:27; Eccles. 5:10).

Watch your testimony (11–16). Know the things you should flee, follow, and fight, and do not confuse them. When you think it too difficult to stand up for the Lord, remember how He stood up for you.

Watch your stewardship (20–21). You have a deposit of spiritual truth to guard and invest (1:18; 2 Tim. 1:14; 2:2), and the enemy wants to take it from you. Beware those who want to give you "new knowledge" beyond what God says in His Word.

Proper Conduct

First Timothy tells you how to "conduct yourself in the house of God" (3:15). This involves exercising yourself (4:7), giving yourself (4:15), taking heed to yourself (4:16), saving yourself (4:16), keeping yourself pure (5:22), and withdrawing yourself from troublemakers (6:5). Are you taking care of yourself as the Lord directs?

SECOND TIMOTHY

$\blacklozenge$

Paul's freedom did not last long. He was arrested again, taken to Rome for trial, and eventually executed. He wrote this letter to his beloved son in the faith to encourage him to remain strong in the Lord (chaps. 1–2), to explain the perilous times (chap. 3), and to urge him to come to Rome as soon as possible (chap. 4). This very personal letter focuses on faithfulness in the ministry.

It was a difficult time for Paul. Not only was he facing trial and almost certain death, but he was abandoned by the believers who should have stood with him (1:15; 4:16). His statement in 4:6–8 is one of the greatest confessions of faith in the Bible.

We are now in those perilous times that Paul wrote about centuries ago. This letter teaches us how to live and serve successfully in them.

2 TIMOTHY 1

Perhaps some of the "enemies" that attacked Timothy are attacking you and making you want to give up.

Self-pity (4). Timothy was having a hard time in Ephesus and wanted to leave (1 Tim. 1:3). Perhaps that caused his tears. When you start feeling sorry for yourself, remember that others are praying for you and that God still honors your faith.

Neglect (6). Timothy had neglected his spiritual life (1 Tim. 4:14), and the flame was low on the altar of his heart. No wonder he needed to exercise himself (1 Tim. 4:7–8)!

Timidity (7). *Fear* in this verse means "cowardice" or "timidity." Timothy was not enthusiastic in his witness or ministry. The Holy Spirit can give us the resources we need to get the job done.

Shame (8, 12, 16). Paul was not ashamed of the gospel (Rom. 1:16) or of the Lord. His friend Onesiphorus was not ashamed of being identified with Paul (v. 16). Timothy should not be ashamed of either the Lord or Paul (v. 8).

Carelessness (13-14). Paul committed the message to Timothy, and Timothy's responsibility was to guard it (1 Tim. 6:20) and share it with others (2 Tim. 2:2). Again, the Spirit of God enables us to be faithful.

2 TIMOTHY 2

God's grace strengthens us and enables us to be faithful teachers (v. 2), soldiers (vv. 3-4), athletes (v. 5), farmers (v. 6), workers (v. 15), vessels (vv. 20-23), and servants (vv. 24-26). The world looks on us as evildoers; but we are God's elect, willing to live and die for Jesus Christ (vv. 8-13).

God's grace enables us to overcome our three great enemies: the world (v. 4), the flesh (v. 22), and the devil (v. 26).

God's grace enables us to endure hardship (vv. 3, 10) as we fight the Lord's battles, so that we do not deny the Lord (vv. 11-13). It helps us do work of which we are not ashamed (v. 15) and deal with problem people of whom we are not afraid (vv. 23-26).

> **"**Grace is but glory begun, and glory is
> but grace perfected.**"**
>
> Jonathan Edwards

2 TIMOTHY 3

Perilous in verse 1 means "difficult," "hard to deal with," or "dangerous." It is the same Greek word used to describe the demoniac in Matthew 8:28 and translated "exceedingly fierce." How do we live for Christ in such terrible times?

Expect them (1-9). The person who is looking for a soon-coming paradise on earth is destined for disappointment. To expect these perilous times is to become not a pessimist but a realist. Note the emphasis on the wrong kind of love (vv. 2, 4).

Follow the right examples (10–12). We tend to emulate the people we admire, so be careful about the heroes you select. Modern-day Christian celebrities may not exemplify the lifestyle God wants us to have.

Stay with the Bible (13–17). Believe God's Word will save you (v. 15), mature you from childhood to adulthood (vv. 15, 17), and equip you to serve the Lord (v. 17). Satanic deception is rampant today and has infected the church (v. 13), and the only weapon that defeats the deceivers is God's inspired Word.

Watch for Counterfeits!

Jannes and Jambres (v. 8) were magicians in Pharaoh's court who imitated the miracles that Moses performed (Exod. 7:8–13). Satan is an imitator who produces counterfeit Christians (vv. 5, 13; 2 Cor. 11:13–15) who infiltrate the church and create divisions. God's people need discernment in these difficult days.

---

2 TIMOTHY 4

Christ is coming (1)! In view of this, we must know our task and be faithful to do it. Review 2 Corinthians 5:9–11, and read 1 John 2:28—3:2.

Apostasy is coming (2–5)! Indeed, it is now here. Many professed Christians have no "ear" for the Word of God. They prefer religious entertainment and sermons that will tickle their ears instead of cut their hearts.

Departure is coming (6–8)! Paul saw his approaching death as the offering of a sacrifice to God (v. 6; Phil. 2:17), the ending of a difficult race (v. 7), and the gaining of a glorious crown (v. 8; Rev. 2:10). This is the victor's crown given to winners at the Greek Olympic Games.

Help is coming (9–22)! Paul was greatly disappointed when the people he had ministered to turned away from him and were ashamed of his bonds. He asked Timothy to come as soon as possible and to bring Mark with him. But best of all, the Lord came to Paul and encouraged him! No matter what His people may do, Jesus will never leave you or forsake you (Acts 18:9–11; Heb. 13:5–6).

Respond to Opportunities

Paul's plea, "Come before winter" (2 Tim. 4:21), is a reminder to us that opportunities do not wait forever. Once the winter season began, Timothy could not travel easily to Rome and see his beloved friend for the last time. "Before winter or never!" said Dr. Clarence Macartney in his famous sermon "Come Before Winter." He continued, "There are some things which will never be done unless they are done 'before winter.'" Are there opportunities you are neglecting today that may soon vanish forever? Are there people you should contact and decisions you should make? Today is yours; tomorrow may be too late. Come before winter!

TITUS

◆

Titus was a Greek (Gal. 2:3) whom Paul won to Christ (Titus 1:4) and enlisted in service. Like Timothy, he became one of Paul's special assistants, sent to the churches to represent the apostle. He was serving in Crete when this letter was written. Paul wrote it, probably from Corinth, after his release from prison.

The letter emphasizes good works (1:16; 2:7, 14; 3:1, 8, 14). We are not saved by good works (3:5), but good works are one evidence of salvation. Apparently the saints on Crete were better at professing the faith than practicing it.

After his greeting (1:1–4), Paul gives the qualifications (1:5–9) and duties (1:10–16) of elders and urges Titus to organize the local churches and deal with the false teachers. He then tells Titus how to minister to various kinds of people in the church (2:1—3:11) and closes the letter with personal information (3:12–14) and a farewell (3:15).

TITUS 1

Titus wanted another assignment from Paul because he was having a hard time ministering in Crete. When you feel like quitting, follow the counsel Paul gave to Titus.

Focus on the privileges of ministry (1–4). God declares His truth through dedicated people, and it is a joy to share the Word with others. The angels in heaven would love to change places with us, so we should never cease to marvel that God would use us!

Obey the Word (5–9). Sometimes there are problems because unqualified people get into places of leadership or because places of leadership have not been filled. The Greek word translated "set in order" is a medical term that means "to set a broken bone." The church body suffers when we avoid facing and solving serious problems.

Face the enemy (10–16). Perhaps like Timothy (2 Tim. 1:7), Titus was too timid to confront the enemy; but it had to be done. "Sound doctrine" (v. 9) means "healthy doctrine," teaching that contributes to the spiritual health of the church. Just as a physician must attack infection and disease, so local church leaders must attack false doctrine.

A Pure Mind

"To the pure all things are pure" (Titus 1:15) concerns false teaching about dietary laws (1 Tim. 4:2–5). It does not mean that a "pure mind" remains pure after beholding what is impure. When God's truth enlightens your conscience, you will know right from wrong and will avoid that which is evil. A defiled conscience is like a dirty window: no light can enter (Matt. 6:22–23).

TITUS 2

Living (1–10). Whether we are young or old, married or single, we are all needed in the local church; and God has a job for us to do. One test of spiritual fellowship is its ability to accept and minister to a variety of people. How we live either blasphemes the Word (v. 5) or beautifies it (v. 10), and those who minister should set the example (vv. 7–8).

Learning (11–12). God's grace not only saves us but also teaches us how to live the Christian life. Those who use God's grace as an excuse for sin have never experienced its saving power (Rom. 6:1; Jude 4). The same grace that redeems us also renews us so that we want to obey His Word (v. 14).

Looking (13–15). What starts with grace will lead to glory! The return of Jesus Christ for His people is more than a blessed hope; it is a joyful hope (Rom. 5:2; 12:12), a unifying hope (Eph. 4:4), a living hope (1 Pet. 1:3), a stabilizing hope (Heb. 6:19), and a purifying hope (1 John 3:3).

"I never begin my work in the morning without thinking that perhaps He may interrupt my work and begin His own. I am not looking for death, I am looking for Him.**"**

G. Campbell Morgan

TITUS 3

We all need frequent reminders!

Remember what you should do (1-2). Christians are citizens of earth as well as citizens of heaven, and they should be the kind of people described in these two brief verses.

Remember what you were (3). God has forgotten our sins, and we should, too; but it does us good to remember what it was like to be a lost sinner. (See Deut. 5:15; 15:15; 24:18, 22; 1 Pet. 4:1-4.)

Remember what God did for you (4-7). Did you deserve to hear the gospel and receive the gift of eternal life? No, it all happened because of God's kindness, love, and grace. "He saved us"—we did not save ourselves. He has washed away our sins; we stand justified in His sight; and we face the future confidently because we are the heirs of God.

Remember what God expects of you (8-11). A major theme in this letter is *good works* (1:16; 2:7, 14; 3:1, 8, 14). People who are busy for the Lord do not have time for useless arguments.

PHILEMON

◆

Providence. While a prisoner in Rome, Paul met Onesimus ("unprofitable" [v. 11]), a runaway slave who belonged to Philemon, a friend Paul had led to Christ (v. 19). Paul won Onesimus to Christ and sent him back to his master in Colosse (Col. 4:7–9). The providence of God is amazing, that Paul and Onesimus should meet in the great city of Rome! Perhaps Philemon's prayers brought the men together (v. 22). Philemon certainly saw Romans 8:28 in action!

Friendship. Paul has so much good to say about Philemon. He was a beloved friend, a man of faith and love, a refreshing Christian, a praying man, a man who obeyed God's will. Can your friends say these things about you?

Accepted and Redeemed	*Two statements in Paul's letter to Philemon remind us of what Jesus did for us. "Receive him [Onesimus] as you would me" (v. 17) reminds us that we are "accepted in the Beloved" (Eph. 1:6). "Put that on my account" (v. 18) reminds us that Jesus paid the price for our redemption (Rom. 4:1–8; 2 Cor. 5:21).*

Reconciliation. According to Roman law, Onesimus could have been executed for his crimes. But he had become a brother in Christ, and Philemon had to forgive him and take him back. True reconciliation is not cheap; there is a price to pay. Paul knew this and was willing to pay the price himself. Can God use you as a reconciler? Are you willing to pay the price?

HEBREWS

◆

The author of Hebrews is unknown to us, but the theme of the book is clear: "Let us go on to perfection [spiritual maturity]" (6:1). The epistle was written to Jewish believers who were tempted to abandon the fullness of Christ and go back to the emptiness of a religious system soon to be destroyed.

Lost people are still "in Egypt" and need to be redeemed through faith in Christ. Those who are redeemed are privileged to enter their spiritual inheritance ("Canaan") and enjoy His "rest" (4:11; Matt. 11:28–30). Entering Canaan is not a type of going to heaven. It is a picture of conquering the enemy and claiming your spiritual inheritance by faith.

But too many believers, like Israel in the Old Testament, are wandering in the wilderness of unbelief and yearning to go back to the old life. The message of Hebrews is especially for them: "Let us go on to maturity!"

Hebrews is one of three New Testament letters written to explain Habakkuk 2:4, "The just shall live by his faith." (See Rom. 1:17; Gal. 3:11; Heb. 10:38.) The emphasis in Hebrews is on "by faith." God has spoken through His Son, and we must respond to that Word. Our response determines the kind of life we live and how much of our spiritual inheritance we claim. We are not only *saved* by faith, but we must *live* by faith.

One key word in Hebrews is *better*. Christ is better than the angels (chaps. 1–2) and better than Moses and Aaron (chaps. 3–6). He has a better priesthood (chap. 7), covenant (chap. 8), sanctuary (chap. 9), and sacrifice (chap. 10); and He gives His people a better life (chaps. 11–13), a life of faith.

As you meditate on this profound letter, ask yourself: Am I looking back and craving the old life, or am I pressing on by faith to claim my inheritance in Christ? Am I wandering in a wilderness of unbelief or resting in His finished work and faithful Word?

HEBREWS 1

"God has spoken to us!" What a tremendous statement, and what a great responsibility it brings to you if you have heard His voice through His Word: "See that you do not refuse Him who speaks" (12:25). What you do with the Word of God determines what you will enjoy of God's will and claim of your inheritance.

Angels   *Jesus is greater than the angels because He is the eternal Son of God Whom the angels worship and serve. Angels serve God's people (Heb. 1:14), even though we may not recognize them (Heb. 13:2; Gen. 18). Angels give special care to children (Matt. 18:10) and intervene in the lives of God's servants when they need special help (Acts 5:17–21; 12:1–10). When believers die, the angels escort them to glory (Luke 16:22); and when Christ returns, angels will accompany Him (Matt. 25:31). We must not worship angels (Rev. 22:9) or pray to them; but we can trust God to send them when we need them most.*

Jesus Christ is the Father's last word. In Him, divine revelation is *seen* and *heard* in its fullness; and in Him, God's revelation is complete. When we see Him, we see the Father (John 14:1–11). Through Christ, we understand where everything came from, where it is going, what keeps it going, and why it is here.

We also understand what He has done for us. *He died for us!* Today He is enthroned in glory, ministering to us and for us (13:20–21). He wants to mature us and teach us how to walk by faith. One day He will defeat all His enemies and bring in His righteous kingdom.

With a Savior like that, why look for a substitute?

"Other men had the threads of truth; but Christ took the threads, and wove them into a glorious robe, put it on, and came forth clothed with every truth of God."

Charles Haddon Spurgeon

HEBREWS 2

Hear Him (1–4). This is the first of five solemn admonitions to believers to pay attention to what God says in His Word. During Old Testament times, God dealt with those who disobeyed His Word. In these last days, we have a greater obligation to obey because we have the complete Scriptures and the full revelation of God in Jesus Christ. Are you serious about what God says to you?

Secure in the Promise

Ponder these verses: "We wish to see Jesus" (John 12:21), "We see Jesus" (Heb. 2:9), and "We shall see Him [Jesus]" (1 John 3:2). The first is the plea of the sinner; the second is the privilege of the saint; the third is the promise of the Scripture.

See Him (5–9). There is a "world to come," and how you live today will help to determine your place in the future kingdom of Christ (1:13; 10:13; 12:28). Today, we see man fallen in Adam; but by faith, we see Christ and His victory. Because He is glorified, we shall be glorified in Him!

Trust Him (10–18). Persons who trust Christ are God's children (v. 13) on their way to glory (v. 10). The Redeemer has defeated death and the devil, and He understands how His people feel as they face the temptations and trials of life. When you come to Him by faith, you come to a sympathetic High Priest who can meet your every need. Trust Him!

A Sensitive Heart

Hebrews is a book of exhortations (13:22). The word means "encouragement" and is a title for the Holy Spirit, the "Comforter, Helper" (John 14:16, 26). The writer encourages us not to neglect the Word (2:1–4), harden our hearts to the Word (3:7–19), become deaf to the Word (5:11–14), defy the Word (10:26–39) or disobey the Word deliberately (12:14–19). God deals in love with His people when they will not listen and obey (12:3ff.), so it pays to have a heart sensitive to God's voice.

HEBREWS 3

Consider Him (1–6). Hebrews focuses on Jesus Christ. The writer wants us to "see" Him (2:9), "consider" Him (3:1), and keep our eyes of faith fixed on Him (12:1–2). Whenever you are tempted to look at your circumstances or at yourself, look to Jesus by faith and rejoice in His faithfulness.

Obey Him (7–15). The writer uses the failure of Israel as a warning against a hard heart. How does a believer's heart become hard? By refusing His words, despising His works, and being ignorant of His ways. Sin is deceitful. You think you are getting away with it, but all the while it is hardening your heart and robbing you of blessing.

Believe Him (16–19). Here is another exhortation to faith. The fact that the Jews were delivered from Egypt was no guarantee they would claim their inheritance. Because of their unbelief, they failed to enter the land (Num. 13). An "evil heart of unbelief" (v. 12) will rob you of what God has planned for you in your Christian life, so pay attention to God's Word. As Paul wrote, "Faith comes by hearing, and hearing by the word of God" (Rom. 10:17).

Are You Hearing?

People with hard hearts know the truth but resist it and refuse to obey it. They know that God chastens disobedient children, but they almost defy God to act. They think they can sin and get away with it. The first step toward a hard heart is neglect of the Word of God (Heb. 2:1–4), not taking it seriously. It is either "hearing" or "hardening." Take your choice (Ps. 95).

HEBREWS 4

His rest (1–10). Three different "rests" are in view: God's Sabbath rest after creation (v. 4; Gen. 2:2); Israel's rest of victory in Canaan (v. 3; Josh. 21:44); and the believer's rest of faith today (vv. 1, 9–10). Israel was delivered from Egypt, but a whole generation failed to enter Canaan and claim their promised inheritance. Why? Because of their unbelief. "Let us fear!" (v. 1).

His sight (11–13). God sees the heart and uses His sword to help us see our true spiritual condition (Jer. 17:9). Spend time daily reading the Word and meditating on it, always applying its truths to your heart. One day you will give account to God of what you have done with His Word, so be faithful.

His throne (14–16). You cannot claim your inheritance in your own power or wisdom. But you have a great High Priest who can give you the mercy and the grace you need just when you need them. He lives to intercede for you (7:25) and to help you do His will (13:20–21).

A Throne of Grace

To the unsaved, God's throne is a throne of judgment (Rev. 20:11–15); but to God's children, it is a throne of grace. When you are tempted, you can come to your great High Priest for mercy and grace. If you sin, you can come to your Advocate for forgiveness (1 John 1:9—2:2). The way is always open.

HEBREWS 5

Selected (1–6). Just as the Jewish high priest was appointed by God, so our great High Priest was appointed by the Father (Ps. 110:4); and He alone is worthy to serve. Never allow anybody to come between you and God, for Christ is the only mediator (1 Tim. 2:5). "The order of Melchizedek" refers to Genesis 14:18–24. Being from the tribe of Judah, Jesus could not serve as priest on earth; but He can serve as priest in heaven. He is there ministering for you today.

Perfected (7–10). Jesus had to prepare for His priestly ministry by experiencing the trials His people experience as they walk by faith (4:15). Because of the life that He lived and the death that He died, He is able to identify with your needs and give you grace to see you through. He understands!

Neglected (11–14). The "milk" of the Word represents the "first principles" of the Christian life, that is, what Jesus Christ did for us when He was on earth. The "meat" of the Word is the teaching about what Jesus is now doing for us in heaven, His ministry as High Priest. How sad it is when Christians neglect God's Word and stop growing in grace.

Mature in Christ	*Mature believers understand the heavenly priesthood of Jesus Christ and know how to come to the throne of grace for help. They are skillful in using God's truth in their personal lives, and they can also teach others. Do you qualify?*

HEBREWS 6

The impossible (1–8). The ABC's of the Christian life are important, but they must be a launching pad and not a parking lot, for the challenge is, "Let us go on to maturity." If we get sluggish (v. 12) and dull (5:11) toward the Word, we may fall by the wayside (v. 6; Gal. 6:1) and stop being fruitful. As long as disobedient believers are bringing shame to Christ, it is impossible to bring them to repentance, and God must deal with them.

The improbable (9–12). But the writer did not believe that his readers were in that condition. Although they had a long way to go in their Christian experience, the fruit was there. Diligence, faith, and patience are required to live the Christian life. Maturity is not automatic.

The immutable (13–20). The chapter ends with one of the greatest statements on security found anywhere in Scripture. God's promise and God's oath assure us that we are His, and God's character backs up His words. Instead of drifting (2:1), we are anchored heavenward where Jesus ministers in the very presence of God, and that anchor will not fail. We are anchored so we can make progress!

HEBREWS 7

With this chapter, the writer begins to explain the better priesthood of Christ; and he begins with the *better order*, the order of Melchizedek (Gen. 14).

Jesus Christ is both King and Priest, and His throne is a throne of grace (4:16). As King, He can control circumstances around you; as Priest, He can change attitudes within you. You will experience righteousness and peace as you yield to Him (v. 2; Pss. 72:7; 85:9–10; Isa. 32:17).

Because He is a Priest forever, He saves forever (vv. 23–25). "To the uttermost" means "completely," "perfectly." You are secure as long as He lives, and He lives eternally. You can live by the power of His endless life!

A perfect salvation should lead to a life of growing maturity. An earthly priesthood can make nothing perfect (v. 11), nor can the law of God (v. 19) or the sacrifices (10:1–2); but Jesus can lead you into spiritual maturity as you walk by faith (13:20–21). He invites you to come to His throne, and He understands you better than you understand yourself.

HEBREWS 8

Finality (1). There were no chairs in the Jewish tabernacle or temple because the priests' work was never finished. But Jesus finished the work of redemption (John 19:30) and sat down on the throne (10:11–14). Rejoice!

Reality (2–6). The Jewish priests in the temple ministered with copies and shadows, but Christ in heaven ministers in the original sanctuary from which the things on earth were copied. When you trust Christ, you enter a life of reality, and you are forever finished with substitutes. Rejoice!

Maturity (7–13). The law of Moses was given to the children of Israel as a tutor to help them grow up and be prepared for their Messiah's coming (Gal. 4:1–7). They were like children; God had to take them by the hand and lead them. But the new covenant, with its heavenly priesthood, leads us to spiritual maturity: God puts His Word in our hearts and transforms our character (2 Cor. 3:1–3, 18).

Rejoice and be exceedingly glad!

HEBREWS 9

A better sanctuary (1–10). In every way, the present heavenly sanctuary is better than any sanctuary on earth, including the temple in Jerusalem. In the earthly temple, the furnishings were only symbols, the work was never finished, and the ministry could never change the human heart. We should be grateful for the price Jesus paid to make His heavenly ministry possible.

A better service (11–15). The Jewish high priest could deal only with externals, but Jesus deals with the heart and conscience. He can purify us and perfect us (13:20–21) so that we can serve God acceptably. Do you come to Him daily and ask for His ministry?

A better sacrifice (16–28). The blood that purchased your eternal redemption came not from unwilling animals but from the Son of God who willingly laid down His life for you (John 10:14–18). The spotless Lamb of God had to die only once; the sacrifice need not be repeated. Have you trusted that blood to save you?

Jesus' Appearings

Hebrews 9:24–28 mentions three "appearings" of Jesus Christ: a past appearing (v. 26) for our salvation, a present appearing (v. 24) for our sanctification, and a future appearing for our glorification (v. 28).

HEBREWS 10

Forgiveness (1–18). The sacrifices under the Old covenant brought a *reminder* of sin, not a *remission* of sin. The blood of God's Son took care of sin once and for all. Because there is no more offering for sin, there is also no more remembrance of sin (v. 17; Jer. 31:34), and we can rejoice that we have a righteous standing before God.

Faithfulness (19–25). The same Savior who died for you now lives for you and invites you to come into His presence to worship and to share your needs. The Old Testament high priest could go behind the veil only once a year, but we can come into God's presence any time. Be sure that you are cleansed and prepared to meet Him. You can trust Him: "He who promised is faithful" (v. 23).

Fearfulness (26–39). The privilege of entering His presence brings with it the responsibility of obeying His precepts. This exhortation applies to those who repeatedly defy God's will and disgrace God's name. God deals with His children; He will not have them acting like rebels. The chapter closes on a note of encouragement. God warns us so that we will not be presumptuous, but He comforts us so that we will not be discouraged. The hard heart needs the warning; the broken heart needs the comfort.

HEBREWS 11

Faith is confidence in God that leads to obedience to God. True faith is based on what God says and is demonstrated in what we do. People with faith *do* things for God, and God does things for them.

Faith is not a luxury; it is a necessity. It is for common people and not just great leaders. We need faith for worshiping (v. 4) as well as for working (v. 7), walking (vv. 8–9), waiting (vv. 10–12), and warring (vv. 30–34). In any area of life where you ignore faith, you will sin (Rom. 14:23).

Steady in the Faith

The great theologian John Calvin defined faith as "a steady and certain knowledge of the Divine benevolence towards us, which, being founded on the truth of the gratuitous promise in Christ, is both revealed to our minds, and confirmed to our hearts, by the Holy Spirit." Note that faith is founded on divine truth (God's promise) and is witnessed to by the Spirit in the heart. It has both objective and subjective aspects, and both are essential.

The phrase "still others" (v. 36) reminds us that we can live by faith and appear to be defeated. Not everybody who trusted God was delivered or protected (vv. 36–40). But the important thing is not God's deliverance; it is God's approval (v. 39). Faith in God gives you the ability to endure when others are giving up.

Where does this faith come from? Read Romans 10:17 and 15:4.

> **❝**Faith makes all things possible;
> love makes all things easy.**❞**
>
> D. L. Moody

HEBREWS 12

Runners (1–4). The people listed in chapter 11 are the "cloud" that witnesses to us, "God can be trusted! Put your faith in His Word and keep running the race!" When you read the Old Testament, your faith should grow, for the account shows what God did in and through people who dared to trust His promises (Rom. 15:4). When you read the Gospels, you see the greatest example of endurance in Jesus Christ.

> **❝**You can judge the quality of their faith from the way
> they behave. Discipline is an index to doctrine.**❞**
>
> Tertullian

Children (5–11). "Chastening" refers to child training, helping the child prepare for adulthood. It does not necessarily mean punishment for disobedience, although that sometimes might be included. The successful runner must exercise discipline and submit to training. Never fear the chastening hand of the Lord; it is controlled by a loving heart. God's goal is your maturity.

Citizens (12–29). The people of Israel had a frightening experience of law at Sinai (Exod. 19), but our experience at Mount Zion is one of grace and glory. We are citizens of the heavenly city and will one day fellowship with patriarchs and angels—and God! But this does not mean we can ignore His solemn voice to us. If God is shaking things in your life, listen to His Word. You will discover the things that cannot be shaken, and you will run the race to the end.

66*We cry too often to be delivered from the punishment, instead of the sin that lies behind it. We are anxious to escape from the things that cause us pain rather than from the things that cause God pain.*99

G. Campbell Morgan

HEBREWS 13

Lest we get the idea that we can run the race successfully alone, the writer closes his letter by reminding us to follow our spiritual leaders. If we do, we will love the brothers and sisters (v. 1), help strangers (v. 2) and prisoners (v. 3), live above lust (v. 4) and covetousness (vv. 5–6), and not be led astray by false doctrines (v. 9).

Remember them (7–8). This may refer to leaders now dead, but their ministry goes on. Remember what they taught you, how they lived, and what they lived for. Church leaders may come and go, but Jesus is the same; and they must fix our eyes on Him.

Obey them (17). If they are faithful to care for your soul and teach you the Word, you have the responsibility to obey. A spiritual leader is not a dictator who drives you from behind. He is a shepherd who goes before and leads the way.

Pray for them (18–19). When you come to the throne of grace, ask God to make His shepherds faithful and fruitful.

Pray that the Great Shepherd will use them to "make you complete in every good work" (vv. 20–21).

Greet them (24). You should know your leaders personally and be on good terms with them. Let nothing come between you that could create problems in the fellowship (12:14–15).

JAMES

$\blacklozenge$

The man who wrote this letter was the half brother of our Lord (Mark 6:3) and the leader of the church in Jerusalem (Acts 1:14; 12:17; 1 Cor. 15:7). He was a devout Jew and wrote to Jewish believers scattered throughout the Roman world. They were troubled by trials and testings as well as by problems in their assemblies; and James wrote to help them mature in their faith (1:4; 2:22; 3:2).

The epistle of James is a practical book that discusses living the faith. It contains echoes of the Sermon on the Mount and the book of Proverbs, both of which are practical.

If we truly practice our faith, it will be seen in how we face trials (chap. 1), in the way we treat people (chap. 2), in what we say (chap. 3), in how we deal with sin in our lives (chap. 4), and in our prayer life (chap. 5).

JAMES 1

Note some essentials for mature living.

The wisdom of God (1–11). You need wisdom in trials so you will not waste your suffering and miss the spiritual growth that should result. When you trust God, trials work for you and not against you; but be sure your heart is wholly yielded to Him. If your heart and mind are divided, trials will tear you apart.

The goodness of God (12–20). When you realize how good God is to you, you will have no interest in the temptations the enemy puts before you. When you are tempted, count your blessings; and you will soon have strength to say no.

The Word of God (21–27). The Word gives us spiritual birth (v. 18; 1 Pet. 1:22–23). It is like seed planted in the heart that produces spiritual fruit (v. 21). It is a mirror that helps us examine ourselves (vv. 23–25) and cleanse our lives. We must *do* the Word of God, not just read it or study it; the blessing is in the *doing*.

> **"**He is already half false who speculates on truth and does not do it. Truth is given, not to be contemplated, but to be done.**"**
>
> F. W. Robertson

Word Pictures

In his letter, James relies on many illustrations from nature. In chapter 1, he compares doubt to the waves of the sea (v. 6), riches to fading flowers (vv. 9–10), and sin to pregnancy (vv. 13–15; Ps. 7:14), weeds (v. 21), and dirt (v. 27). As you continue to read, notice how James uses pictures to make truth vivid and memorable.

JAMES 2

If you have true saving faith, you will practice *impartiality* (vv. 1–13) and see people in terms of character and not clothing. You will not cater to the rich or ignore the poor, but you will love each person for the sake of Jesus Christ. Christian love simply means treating others the way the Lord treats you and doing it in the power of the Spirit.

True saving faith is also seen in *activity* (vv. 14–26). Faith is not something you only talk about; it is something that motivates your life so that you think of others and serve them. Abraham was saved by faith (Gen. 15:6), but he proved that faith by obeying God and offering his son (Gen. 22). Rahab was saved by trusting God (Heb. 11:31), but she showed the reality of her faith by protecting the spies (Josh. 2; 6:17–27).

James and Paul do not contradict each other (Rom. 4:1–5; 5:1); they complement each other. We are justified (declared righteous) before God by faith, but we are justified before men by works. God can see our faith, but men can see only our works.

JAMES 3

The believers James wrote to were having problems with their tongues (1:26; 2:12; 4:1, 11–12). Of course, the tongue is not the problem; it is the *heart* (v. 14; Matt. 12:35–37). But before you say anything, ask yourself some questions.

Who is in control (1–4)? If your tongue is under God's control, you will take what you say seriously (v. 1), and your whole body will be under His discipline (v. 2). Just as a horse needs a rider holding the reins, and a ship needs a pilot at the rudder, so your tongue needs a master; and God is the only one who can do the job. Psalm 141:1–4 is a good prayer if you need help in this area.

"Of your unspoken words, you are the master; of your spoken words, the servant; of your written words, the slave.**"**

Quaker Proverb

What will the consequences be (5–12)? Are you starting a fire that may get out of control and do a lot of damage? Are you turning loose a dangerous beast or poisoning a refreshing spring? Once your words are spoken, you cannot take them back, so look ahead.

What are my motives (13–18)? Is there bitterness in your heart or envy? Are you speaking from God's wisdom or the wisdom of the world? Are you a peacemaker or a troublemaker? If your heart is right before God (Heb. 4:12), He will use your words to produce the right kind of fruit.

JAMES 4

Of the early church, it was said, "Behold how they love one another!" Today, people might say, "Behold how they compete with one another!" Why is it sometimes so difficult for God's people to get along?

Selfishness (1–3). The wars among us are caused by the wars within us. We want to please ourselves, even if it hurts somebody else. If we are not careful, even our prayers can become selfish!

Worldliness (4). Because Abraham was separated from sin, he was the friend of God (2:23); but Lot was the friend of the world (Gen. 13:1–13). Ponder 1 John 2:15–17.

Pride (5–10). Satan knows how to use pride to defeat you as he defeated Eve (Gen. 3:1–6). Are you laughing when you should be weeping over your sins? Are you resisting the devil or resisting the Lord?

"It is right for the church to be in the world; it is wrong for the world to be in the church. A boat in water is good; that is what boats are for. However, water inside the boat causes it to sink.**"**

Harold Lindsell

"A whole new generation of Christians has come up believing that it is possible to 'accept' Christ without forsaking the world.**"**

A. W. Tozer

Criticism (11–12). One of the easiest ways to hide our sins is to expose the sins of others. Gossip and slander grieve the Spirit and divide the family. God called us to be witnesses, not judges!

Boasting (13–17). Life is short and the future unknown, so do the will of God today. When you make plans, always say, "If the Lord wills" (Prov. 27:1).

JAMES 5

In these last days, before the coming of the Lord, what does God want in our lives?

Priorities (1–6). To live only to get wealth is to rob yourself of true riches (1 Tim. 6:6–10, 17–19). It is to worry instead of worship (Matt. 6:19–34). God knows you have needs, and He will meet them if you practice Matthew 6:33.

Patience (7–12). If you have sown the right seed, you will eventually reap a harvest of blessing, so be patient. If others have exploited you, be patient; the Judge is at the door. If you are going through trials, be patient; God is still on the throne.

Prayer (13–18). Many kinds of prayer are named here: prayer for the sick, prayer for forgiveness, prayer for the nation, even prayer about the weather. There is no need that prayer cannot meet and no problem that prayer cannot solve.

Personal concern (19–20). Once again, James emphasizes ministry to individuals (1:27; 2:1–4, 14–16). Can you detect when a fellow believer starts to stray? Are you truly concerned? Will you try to help? Will you wait too long?

FIRST PETER

◆

The apostle Peter was chosen to be the first to take the gospel to the Gentiles (Acts 10; 15:7), but his ministry was primarily to the Jews (Gal. 2:1–10). He wrote these two letters to believers scattered in five areas of the Roman Empire, two of which Paul had not been allowed to enter (Acts 16:7). In writing these letters, Peter fulfilled the commission given him in Luke 22:32 and John 21:15–17.

The theme of the first letter is *the grace of God* (5:12), and Peter tells us how to live as aliens in a hostile world. The theme of the second letter is *spiritual knowledge* (he uses *knowledge* seven times in the letter), and he warns us about false teachers.

Peter opens his first epistle by reminding his readers of what God's grace has done for them in saving them (1:1—2:10). He then points out that God's grace helps them in various relationships of life (2:11—3:12) and in the coming time of persecution (3:13—5:14). Peter sums up the themes of both letters in his benediction in 2 Peter 3:18: "But grow in the grace [1 Pet.] and knowledge [2 Pet.] of our Lord and Savior Jesus Christ." That is the only way to succeed in these last days.

1 PETER 1

Salvation is a calling (1–2, 15). We are chosen by the Father, who gives us the new birth (v. 3). We are set apart by the Spirit, who gave the Word and enables God's servants to declare it (vv. 10–12), and gives sinners the faith to believe the promise (v. 22). We have been purchased by the blood of God's Son (vv. 18–21), who died for us, rose again, and is coming for us to give us our inheritance (vv. 3–4, 13). No wonder Peter opened his letter with a song of praise! (See Eph. 1:3–14.)

Salvation is a birth (3, 23). This is the spiritual birth Jesus tried to explain to Nicodemus (John 3). When you put your *faith* in Jesus Christ (vv. 5, 7, 9, 21), you are born from above. You receive *hope* (vv. 3–4, 13, 21) and *love* for Christ (v. 8) and His people (v. 22). Because we are God's children, we want to obey Him (vv. 14–16).

Salvation is a redemption (17–21). The apostle is referring to the Passover Feast (Exod. 12). Jesus is the Lamb slain for us, and His blood was sprinkled to shelter us (v. 2). The Jews in Egypt had to be ready to depart, and we must have the same attitude (v. 13). When Jesus comes again, we will make our exodus from this world!

And all of this was "for you" (vv. 4, 10, 12, 13, 20, 25). Are you praising Him?

Living Hope

Men's hopes are dead hopes. Like cut flowers, they bloom awhile and then fade and die (1 Pet. 1:24–25). The Christian's hope is fresh and fruitful because it is a "living hope" (v. 3), purchased by the living Christ (v. 3) and promised in the living Word (v. 23).

---

1 PETER 2

Growing (1–3). Just as a baby has an appetite for the mother's milk, so the child of God has an appetite for the Father's Word. If you lose that appetite and stop growing, check to see if any of the sins listed in verse 1 are infecting your life.

Building (4–8). God is building a temple out of living stones (Eph. 2:19–22), and we are privileged to be part of it. We are built on Jesus Christ, so there is no way the temple can be destroyed.

Sacrificing (9–10). Each believer is a priest before God and can bring sacrifices to the Lord through Jesus Christ. As we worship the Lord, we proclaim His virtues to a lost world. That is what God called Israel to do (Exod. 19:1-9), and they failed. Are we also failing?

Abstaining (11-12). As strangers whose citizenship is in heaven, we are carefully watched by the world; and we must live to glorify God. It may be difficult today, but it will be worth it when Jesus returns.

Submitting (13-25). Peter's counsel is that Christians be good citizens and employees so that God will be glorified. (See Jeremiah's advice to the captives [Jer. 29].) The example for us to follow is Jesus Christ who submitted even to death.

1 PETER 3

Peter compared believers to sheep (2:25), and sheep are gentle animals. He then called for Christians to practice gentleness in several areas of life.

In the home (1-7). Christian wives with unsaved husbands should seek to win them to the Lord with true spiritual beauty and not with artificial glamour or nagging. External glamour may fade, but a meek and quiet spirit is incorruptible. Husbands should live as though their wives were priceless porcelain vases and treat them with gentle love.

In the church (8-12). Imagine having to remind Christians to show one another love and courtesy! But as James 4 shows, not every local assembly is a place of peace.

In the world (13-22). Anybody can suffer for doing wrong, but Christians must learn to suffer for doing what is right. Of course, Jesus is the example for us to follow (v. 18; 2:18-25). We witness not by making noise and fighting back but by showing meekness and fear (v. 15). A gentle witness can make a big difference in a violent world.

"Nothing is so strong as gentleness, and nothing so gentle as real strength.**"**

Francis de Sales

<table>
<tr><td>A Godly
Life</td><td>The Christians who received Peter's letter were being slandered by others (2:12, 15, 23; 3:9, 16; 4:4, 14). Peter told them that the best weapon against slander was a godly life that nobody could criticize. H. A. Ironside said, "If what they say about you is true, mend your ways. If it isn't true, forget it, and go on and serve the Lord."</td></tr>
</table>

1 PETER 4

Do not be controlled by the past (1–6). People who have been born again through faith in Christ (1:23) should not allow the old life to control them. The past has been buried, and they are new creatures in Christ. Furthermore, life is too short to waste it on godless living, especially when you realize that one day we will all stand before God.

<table>
<tr><td>Persecution</td><td>Peter said that judgment begins at the house (church) of God (1 Pet. 4:17). The first purpose of persecution is to purify the church so that it will be able to witness to the lost. But it is also a warning to the lost. If God judges His own children for their sins, how much more will He judge lost sinners! (See Prov. 11:31; Ezek. 9.)</td></tr>
</table>

Be serious about the present (7–11). No matter how difficult life may be, there is a job to do; and we must be faithful. Take time to pray. Show love to the saints. Use your gifts and talents to serve others. The Lord who gave you the ability will also give you the strength to use it for His glory.

Be prepared for the future (12–19). A "fiery trial" was about to come to the church. Peter told his readers to expect it, use it as an opportunity to witness for Christ, and in all things seek to glorify God. The trial came under the Roman emperor Nero who accused the Christians of burning Rome. The church today faces persecution. Are you prepared?

1 PETER 5

Even apart from the end-times suffering that the church will experience, believers must face their three great enemies.

The world (1–4). Christian leaders are tempted to act like the world and "lord it over" God's people (Matt. 20:20–28). But leaders are shepherds, and sheep must be *led,* not *driven.* Our service must be willing and humble; we must be eager to help others.

The flesh (5–7). By nature, we do not want to submit to others. The phrase "clothed with humility" reminds us of our Savior when He wore a towel and washed Peter's feet (John 13:1–11). If we are submitted to the Lord, we will submit to His people. Humility leads to honor; pride leads to shame.

The devil (8–14). The devil is an adversary, not a friend; he is a roaring lion, not a playful pet. He wants to devour you, and you had better be on guard. Peter thought he was well able to defeat the enemy, so he did not heed the Lord's warning (Luke 22:31–34). The results were failure and shame. You can resist Satan by faith if you are wearing the armor and trusting the Spirit (Eph. 6:10–20).

SECOND PETER

◆————————

When he wrote 2 Peter, the apostle was conscious that death was near (1:13–14) and that the church was in danger, for false teachers were creeping in. He urged the believers to hold to the precious Word and grow spiritually (chap. 1), to identify and shun false teachers (chap. 2), and to keep the promise of Christ's return uppermost in their hearts (chap. 3). He stressed *spiritual knowledge* that comes from God's Word.

2 PETER 1

Power for the present (1–11). When you trusted Christ, He gave you all that you need for life and godliness. All you have to do is to appropriate what you need from His resources. His Word feeds the divine nature within, and you can grow in knowledge and in grace. This is not automatic; you must be diligent to use the means of grace that God has provided.

Assurance from the past (12–18). Peter would be martyred soon (John 21:18), so he took occasion to remind his readers that they could trust the Word of God. Although Peter's experience on the Mount of Transfiguration was wonderful (Matt. 17:1–13), experiences are not a substitute for the unchanging Word of God.

Hope for the future (19–21). The Word is a light in this dark world, pointing to the return of the Lord. "Private interpretation" means that no prophecy should be isolated from the rest of Scripture or interpreted apart from the leading of the Spirit who gave it to us. The Spirit wrote one Book, and it must be understood as a whole. Believers may differ on individual matters of prophecy, but they all agree on the "one hope" (Eph. 4:4)—Jesus is coming again!

2 PETER 2

The description of the false teachers is clear enough to help you detect them and vivid enough to make you want to avoid them. It is not enough to reject their false teachings. You must also reject their way of life and the hypocrisy behind it.

Their tool is deception, so you must know God's Word and exercise discernment when you hear their impressive language (v. 18) and alluring promises (v. 19). They fellowship with you only to find out what they can get from you (vv. 12–14), and then they will leave you in worse shape than they found you. They are deceptive and destructive, so beware!

Their purpose is personal pleasure and financial gain, and their destiny is judgment. Like Balaam (Num. 22—24), they cause others to sin by using religion for personal gain. They are not God's sheep; they are pigs and dogs in sheep's clothing (Prov. 26:11; Matt. 7:15) and eventually go back to their natural habits. True sheep keep themselves clean because they follow the Shepherd (John 10:27–28).

2 PETER 3

When false teachers cannot accomplish their devious purposes with lies, they start to scoff and ridicule the Word of God. They want you to forget that the very Word they deride is in control of God's universe. God created everything by His Word, and His Word holds it together (Col. 1:16–17; Heb. 1:1–2). His Word caused the Flood (Gen. 6–9), and His Word will one day bring a judgment of fire to the ungodly world (vv. 7–10).

"The Dreadful Day"

"The darkness grows thicker around us, and godly servants of the Most High become rarer and more rare. Impiety and licentiousness are rampant throughout the world, and we live like pigs, like wild beasts, devoid of all reason. But a voice will soon be heard thundering forth: 'Be-

hold, the bridegroom cometh!' God will not be able to bear this wicked world much longer, but will come, with the dreadful day, and chastise the scorners of his Word." Does that sound like a statement by one of our contemporary prophetic preachers? It was said by Martin Luther, who lived from 1483 to 1546. If Luther felt that the Lord's return was near in his day, what should we think today!

Whoever robs you of God's Word robs you of your future. People who have no future hope have no motivation for life today. No wonder Peter closes with "Beloved, be diligent!" (v. 14) and "Beloved, beware!" (v. 17). We live in dangerous days, but the opportunities have never been greater. God is patiently waiting for the lost to trust Christ (v. 15), but he needs you to share the gospel with them.

FIRST JOHN

◆

The apostle wrote this letter to his dear "little children" (the phrase is used nine times) to help them find assurance of personal salvation (5:13). When you are sure of your salvation, you can have fellowship with God and God's people (1:3), experience joy (1:4), and have victory over sin (2:1–2). John also wrote to warn believers about false teachers (2:26–27; 4:1–6). Both Peter and John were concerned about purity of doctrine in the church, and we should be, too.

Chapters 1—2 focus on *fellowship* and contrast *saying* and *doing*. It is easy to talk the Christian life, but God wants the walk. John emphasizes *sonship* in chapters 3—5 (the phrase "born of God" is used several times) and gives three marks of the true child of God: doing God's will (chap. 3), loving the brethren (chap. 4), and believing the truth (chap. 5).

"God is light" (1:5), and His children should walk in the light. "God is love" (4:8, 16), and His children should walk in love. "The Spirit is truth" (5:6), and God's children should believe and obey the truth.

1 JOHN 1

God wants you to have a *living fellowship* (vv. 1–3) with Him and His children. In Jesus Christ, He has revealed what true life really is. Even though you cannot see Him and touch Him as the apostles did centuries ago, He can still be real to you as His Holy Spirit opens the Word to your heart.

He wants you to have a *joyful fellowship* (v. 4). It is not the fellowship of a slave with a master but that of a child with a parent. God delights in His children (Ps. 18:19) and longs to share His love with them (John 14:19–24). When you are happy in the will of God, you are ready to live for Him and serve Him.

He wants you to have an *honest fellowship* (vv. 5–10). This means "walking in the light" and dealing honestly with sin. Salvation is a matter of life or death, but fellowship is a matter of light or darkness. If you lie to God, to others, and to yourselves, you will lose your fellowship with God and your character. A godly character does not develop in the darkness.

" *Some Christians try to go to heaven alone, in solitude. But believers are not compared to bears or lions or other animals that wander alone. Those who belong to Christ are sheep in this respect, that they love to get together. Sheep go in flocks, and so do God's people.* **"**

Charles Haddon Spurgeon

His Life Was Manifested

Manifest *is one of John's favorite words. Jesus was manifested that He might reveal God's life (1 John 1:2), take away our sins (3:5), destroy the devil's works (3:8), and disclose God's love for sinners (4:9).*

1 JOHN 2

In Jesus Christ, you have *an Advocate* (vv. 1–2), representing you before God's throne (Zech. 3). When you sin, confess it to Him, and receive His faithful forgiveness.

In Him, you also have *an example* (vv. 3–6), and you should "walk just as He walked." Ask the indwelling Holy Spirit to make you more like Jesus Christ, and saturate yourself with His life as you read the Gospels.

From Jesus Christ, you have *a commandment* (vv. 7–11) to love God's people. The Father gave this commandment to Israel (Lev. 19:18) and the Son to His disciples (John 13:34), and the Spirit enables us to obey it (Rom. 5:5).

Because of Jesus Christ, you have *a family* (vv. 12–14). The members are at different stages of spiritual development, but all can receive the Word and grow. How wonderful it is when the "little children" become young men and then fathers!

You also have *some enemies* (vv. 15–27), the world and the false teachers. Christians who love the world lose the enjoyment of the Father's love and the desire to do His will. We overcome the world with God's love and the liars with God's truth (vv. 24–27).

You have *a wonderful hope* (vv. 28–29), the coming of Jesus Christ. Abide in Him so you will not be ashamed when He comes.

1 JOHN 3

Deliberate sin is a serious thing. When you deliberately sin, you grieve the heart of the Father who loves you and has a wonderful future planned for you (vv. 1–3). You grieve the Savior who died for you and delivered you from the power of Satan (vv. 4–8).

Deliberate sin grieves the Holy Spirit who lives in you and gave you new birth (vv. 9–15). You have a new nature and a new Father; therefore, you should live a new life. To John, lack of love is the same as hatred; and hatred is the moral equivalent of murder (Matt. 5:21–26).

Deliberate sin also grieves God's people (vv. 16–24) because we cannot minister to them as we should if we are not walking in love and in the light. Strive to have a heart that is right before God and men (Acts 24:16). Ask God to use you to be an encouragement and help to others (James 2). Love is more than a matter of words (v. 18).

1 JOHN 4

Love is evidence of salvation. If you are born of God through faith in Jesus Christ, you have His nature within (2 Pet. 1:4). Since "God is love" (vv. 8, 16), His children who have His nature should also manifest His love. The children should be like the Father!

Our love for others makes God's love real and visible to them (v. 12) so we can better witness to them about Christ. It also makes God real and personal to us. Merely reading in the Bible about God's love is not enough. Seek to *experience* that love in your heart by sharing it with others.

Just as truth is victorious over lies (vv. 1–6), love is victorious over fear (vv. 17–19). As you mature in your love for God, you realize that you have nothing to fear, for your Father has everything under control. You trust those you love, and faith and love will give victory over fear.

1 JOHN 5

When you are born of God, you are born to love (vv. 1–3). You will love the Father who gave you life and the Son who gave His life for you. You will also love His children, for you all belong to the same family.

When you are born of God, you are born to win (vv. 4–5). Your first birth made you a sinner and a loser, but your second birth makes you a conqueror. The world wants to entice you (2:15–17) and the devil wants to seduce you (Gen. 3:6), but Christ will give you the victory you need if you trust Him.

When you are born of God, you are born to assurance (vv. 6–13), and you can know that you have eternal life. You are also born to talk to your Father in prayer and receive from Him what you need (vv. 14–17).

When you are born of God, you are born secure, and the evil one cannot harm you (vv. 18–21). You do not keep yourself saved, for the Father does that (John 10:27–30); but you keep yourself from the clutches of the wicked one. As you abide in Christ, you experience His love and care.

SECOND JOHN

◆

John wrote this letter to an anonymous Christian woman whose home was open for God's people to meet for fellowship and worship. The emphasis is on truth and love, and John points out three dangers believers must avoid.

Knowing the truth but not practicing it (1–6). We must walk in truth and walk according to His commandments. The Word of God is meant for *doing* and not just *knowing*. "If we say" (1 John 1:6, 8, 10) but do not obey, we are hypocrites.

Practicing truth but not defending it (7–8, 10–11). The enemy is busy, and we must oppose him. Love must be balanced by truth (Eph. 4:15), or you will start supporting lies in the name of love (Phil. 1:9–11). It is easy to lose what you have gained by making friends with the wrong people.

Going beyond the truth (9). The word *transgress* means "to go beyond." When you go beyond God's Word, you are going too far. It is not progress but regress. Beware anybody who has something to add to your Bible.

❝Truth is always strong, no matter how weak it looks, and falsehood is always weak, no matter how strong it looks.**❞**

Phillips Brooks

THIRD JOHN

$\blacklozenge$

John wrote this letter to his friend Gaius to encourage him in a difficult situation in his local church. Again, he concentrated on making God's truth a vital part of life.

Walking in truth (1–4). People could see the truth in Gaius because he loved it and walked in obedience to it, and that brought great joy to John. Every Christian parent can echo verse 4 and even make it a prayer.

Working for truth (5–8). When you assist and encourage God's servants, you become a fellow worker with them in spreading the truth. Christian hospitality was important in those days and ought to be revived today.

Welcoming the truth (9–10). Can you imagine Diotrephes rejecting a message from the apostle John! He was so "separated" that he did not even receive John's friends. When we welcome God's people, we welcome God's truth.

Witnessing for the truth (11–14). Not all church members are like Diotrephes; there are people like Demetrius who love the truth and live it. They are the ones who make the local church healthy (v. 2).

JUDE

<hr>

Jude, like James, was a half brother of the Lord Jesus (Mark 6:3). His letter focuses on false teachers and echoes Peter's warnings in 2 Peter 2.

Who they are (1–4). Jude wanted to write about salvation, but the Lord directed him to write about invasion instead. False teachers were creeping into the church and going undetected. These are unsaved people (v. 19), ungodly people, and unprincipled people who use grace as an excuse for sin.

<hr>

Seek Wisdom

In trying to minister to people, we must be careful and exercise discernment lest they do us more harm than we do good (Jude 22–23). Concerning the Pharisees, Jesus said to His disciples, "Let them alone" (Matt. 15:14). God told the prophet Hosea, "Ephraim is joined to idols, let him alone" (Hos. 4:17). And Paul told Timothy to withdraw himself from certain troublemakers (1 Tim. 6:3–5). Ask God for wisdom as you seek to help persons wandering from the faith.

<hr>

What they do (5–11). Like the Jews in the wilderness, the fallen angels, and the evil cities of the plain, they reject the authority of God. Their words are defiant and defiling. Like Cain (Gen. 4), they have no saving faith, but they do have religion. Like Balaam (Num. 22—24), they use religion as a way to make money; and like Korah (Num. 16), they defy the Word of God and the authority of God's chosen servants.

What they are (12–16). False teachers promise much but produce little, like rainless clouds and fruitless trees. Enoch had the best word for them: *ungodly*.

What we must do (17–25). Remember the Word and build yourself up in your Christian faith. True believers are "preserved in Jesus Christ" (v. 1), and they prove this by keeping themselves in God's love (v. 21). Therefore, God can keep them from falling (vv. 24–25).

THE REVELATION OF JESUS CHRIST

◆

John was a Roman prisoner on the Isle of Patmos when God gave him this revelation of Jesus Christ. The book reveals Jesus Christ the Priest-King (chap. 1), the Judge of the churches (chaps. 2—3), the Creator (chap. 4), the Redeemer (chap. 5), the Lord of history (chaps. 6—18), the Conqueror (chaps. 19—20), and the Bridegroom (chaps. 21—22). The key name for Christ in this book is *the Lamb.* John never lets you forget that Jesus died for the sins of the world (John 1:29).

Another key word is *throne,* used over forty times. The Revelation describes the conflict between the throne of the Lamb in heaven and the throne of Satan on earth. As John writes, he depicts worship in heaven and warfare on earth; and the Lord is the victor. No matter how dark the day or how strong the forces of evil, the Lamb of God wins the victory.

The key verse is 1:19. John was told to write "the things which you have seen [chap. 1], and the things which are [chaps. 2—3], and the things which will take place after this [chaps. 4—22]."

Revelation 6—19 parallels Matthew 24 and Mark 13 in describing the day of the Lord or the Tribulation. The first part is described in chapters 6—9; the middle in chapters 10—14; and the last part ("the great tribulation") in chapters 15—19. While good and godly people disagree on the details of interpreting John's numbers and symbols, most agree that the last days will be marked by the increase of evil, the rise of a world government and world ruler, the attempt of Satan to destroy God's people, the pouring out of God's wrath on a rebellious world, and the return of Jesus Christ to deliver His own and establish His kingdom.

As you read, do not get lost in details, but try to see the big picture. And keep in mind that John wrote this book to encourage believers who were going through persecution. Every generation of Christians has had its Antichrist and Babylon, and the hope of the Lord's return has kept the saints going when the going was tough.

Revelation is the climax of the Bible, the fulfillment of what God started in Genesis. Many symbols in Genesis are found in this fascinating book: light and darkness, stars, Babylon, the bride, a garden, a tree of life, a serpent, and so on. He is "the Alpha and the Omega" (1:8). What He starts, He finishes.

REVELATION 1

This book is first of all the revelation of Jesus Christ, not just the revelation of future events. Before John describes end-time events, he describes the Lord Jesus and reminds you of who He is and what He has done.

A Blessed Book	*You will find seven "beatitudes" in Revelation: 1:3; 14:13; 16:15; 19:9; 20:6; 22:7, 14. It is indeed a book with a blessing!*

Let Your Light Shine	*In the Old Testament tabernacle, there was one lampstand with seven branches; but here John saw seven lampstands (Rev. 1:12), symbolizing the seven churches addressed in chapters 2—3 (v. 20). Each local assembly of believers should shine for the Lord (Matt. 5:16) by holding fast the Word of life and proclaiming it in a dark world (Phil. 2:14–16).*

According to verse 5, He is the faithful witness (the Prophet), the firstborn from the dead (the Priest), and the ruler over the kings of the earth (the King). He is also the Savior (vv. 5b–6) who has made His people a kingdom of priests (Exod. 19:1–6; 1 Pet. 2:1–10). Never forget that Jesus shed His blood for you, and that His blood cleanses (1:5; 7:14), redeems (5:9), and overcomes (12:11).

When John was in the Upper Room, he leaned on Jesus' bosom (John 13:23); but when he saw the glorified Christ, he fell at His feet as a dead man (v. 17; 2 Cor. 5:16). Like John, we must begin with worship if God's revelations in this book are to have any meaning to us.

One day "there shall be no more death" (21:4) because Jesus has conquered death (v. 18). When you know Him as Savior and Lord, you need not fear the future; He has the keys in His hand.

REVELATION 2—3

Judgment begins at "the house of God" (1 Pet. 4:17), so Jesus deals with the seven churches before He deals with the lost world. These churches illustrate the good and the bad in churches everywhere and in every age. If you were looking for a church to join, which of these seven would you select and why?

Ephesus (2:1–7). There is so much good in this church that we are surprised to discover they had left (not lost) their first love. The honeymoon was over (Jer. 2:2)! No amount of separation, sacrifice, or service can make up for your lack of love toward the Lord. The word *Nicolaitans* means "conquer the people." Apparently a group in the church lorded it over the people and promoted a separation of "clergy" and "laity." (See Matt. 21:20–27; 23:1–12.)

Smyrna (2:8–11). The name *Smyrna* comes from "myrrh," which is a bitter herb, a suitable name for a church facing persecution. Would the believers be *fearful* or *faithful* (v. 10)? Suffering can enrich us, even if we think we are poor; and what people think is wealth might turn out to be poverty (3:17)! What difference does it make if people slander you so long as you have the Lord's approval?

Pergamos (2:12–17). These believers held to the faith even when it might have cost them their lives. But they were too tolerant of false doctrine and were in danger of having the Lord declare war on the church. Balaam convinced Israel to compromise with their unbelieving neighbors, disobey the Lord, and indulge in immorality (Num. 22—24). Being willing to die for the faith is no substitute for living the faith.

Thyatira (2:18–29). Verse 19 gives you the impression that all is well in the church, but keep reading! Like the saints in Pergamos, the believers in Thyatira tolerated sin in the church. Idolatry and immorality usually go together, and Jezebel personifies both (1 Kings 16:29–34; 21; 2 Kings 9:30–37). Not everybody in the fellowship was guilty of sin, and the Lord did not warn them. Instead, He encouraged them to hold to the truth and be faithful.

Sardis (3:1–6). This church had a great reputation, but close examination showed that its ministry did not live up to its name. In fact, the church was ready to die! What was the cause? Many of the people were defiling themselves by compromising with sin (2 Cor. 6:14–18; James 1:27). The "Book of Life" contains the names of all living persons; and when a person dies without Christ, the name is blotted out. Believers have their names in the Lamb's Book of Life and can never be blotted out.

Philadelphia (3:7–13). The name means "brotherly love," and Jesus had a special love for these people (v. 9). Weak as they were, they were given an open door of service; and the Lord urged them to take advantage of it. When God opens a door for you, nobody can shut it; but you can ignore or neglect it.

Laodicea (3:14–22). This church did not know how bad off it was! It was a working church, but its service was lukewarm. The members lacked spiritual enthusiasm. It was a wealthy church, but it was really poor—and did not know its own sad condition. Worst of all, the Lord was *outside the church trying to get in!* If only one member would yield to Him, the church could be changed.

God's people must be open and honest with the Lord and humbly submit to His spiritual diagnosis. No church or Christian is so far gone that He cannot bring renewal, but we must be willing to repent and return to Him.

To the Overcomers

Each of these messages to the churches ends with a promise to the overcomers. These overcomers are not an elite group in the church but true believers who have trusted Christ (1 John 5:1–5). No matter how unspiritual an assembly may become, Christ will always honor those who belong to Him if they are faithful to His Word. The promises to the overcomers follow Old Testament history, from the Garden of Eden (Rev. 2:7) to the kingdom throne (3:21).

REVELATION 4

A door (1). God will one day open the door, the trumpet will sound, and God's people will be called to heaven (1 Thess. 4:13–18). Meanwhile, we must take advantage of the open door of service that He gives us (3:8).

A throne (2, 4–5). Revelation is the book of the throne. John saw God the Father on the throne and was so overwhelmed that he had to refer to precious stones to describe what he beheld. Satan may have his throne on earth (2:13), but God's throne in heaven rules over all and will not be defeated.

A rainbow (3). This emerald rainbow was *around* the throne, a complete circle and not just an arc. It pictures the grace of God (Gen. 9:11–17). On earth, we see the rainbow *after* the storm; but John saw it *before* the storm of judgment came. God gives His people His gracious promise, and they need not fear the coming storm (3:10; 1 Thess. 1:10; 5:8).

A choir (6–11). The living creatures represent creation praising the Creator (Gen. 1:28–31), and the elders represent God's people worshiping Him. When you lose the wonder of the Creator, you cease to become a good steward of the creation (11:18). All of creation praises the Lord while sinful man praises himself and ignores his Creator.

" *The more I study nature, the more I am amazed at the Creator.* **"**

Louis Pasteur

" *Thus does the world forget You, its Creator, and falls in love with what You have created instead of with You.* **"**

Augustine

REVELATION 5

The scroll (1) represents the title deed to creation, for Jesus Christ alone is the rightful Heir (Ps. 2:8; Heb. 1:2). Satan offered Him the whole world in return for one act of worship (Matt. 4:8–10), but Jesus won the right to receive the scroll when He gave Himself on the cross. Have you placed the scroll of your life in His hands?

The Lamb (5–6) is Jesus Christ who was slain as a sacrifice for sin (1 Pet. 1:18–20); He is both Lamb (John 1:29) and Lion (Gen. 49:8–10), the Savior and the Sovereign. He is also the Root of David, for He existed before David and brought David's kingly line into being. As Lamb, Jesus offers salvation; as Lion, He judges those who reject Him. Marvel at the many aspects of His person and work!

The incense (8) represents prayer (Ps. 141:1–3). For centuries, God's people have been praying, "Thy kingdom come"; and those prayers are about to be answered. Saints on earth do not pray to or through the saints now in heaven; our praying is to the Father and through the Son. But the prayers of God's people play a vital part in God's governing of the world.

The worship (9–14). He is worthy of our worship, not only because He is Creator (chap. 4) but even more because He is our Redeemer. See how the circle of praise grows until every creature worships Him. Heaven is a place of worship, so begin to get ready now to join in the praise!

❝If the veil of the world's machinery were lifted off, how much we would find is done in answer to the prayers of God's children.**❞**

Robert Murray M'Cheyne

REVELATION 6

The world ruler (Antichrist) begins his conquest of the nations by peacefully taking control (vv. 1–2). He has a weapon but no ammunition; and men are saying, "Peace and safety!" (1 Thess. 5:1–3). Satan usually declares peace before he declares war, so beware his offers.

Counterfeit Christ

There are two important riders in Revelation: Antichrist at the opening of the book (6:1–2) and Christ at the close (19:11–16). The prefix anti in Greek means "instead of" as well as "against." The world ruler is a counterfeit Christ, energized by the master counterfeiter, Satan (2 Cor. 11:13–15). John does not use the term Antichrist; instead, he calls him "the beast" (chap. 13). The world would not receive the true Christ, but it will receive the false Christ (John 5:43).

Soon the world is at war (vv. 3–4), and suffering results from famine and plagues (vv. 5–8) and cosmic disturbances (vv. 12–17). Jesus said these things would happen (Matt. 24:4–13).

The martyrs are seen "under the altar" because that is where the blood was placed (Lev. 4:7; 17:11). Death for Jesus' sake is not waste; it is sacrifice and worship. They pray not for personal vengeance but for God's glorification and vindication. When it appears that God is not working as you think He should, be patient and let Him do His will in His time.

"Love makes the whole difference between an execution and a martyrdom."

Evelyn Underhill

REVELATION 7

When the storm starts to get worse, John sees two groups of people and takes courage. Why? Because he realizes that God is at work even in the midst of tribulation.

God has His servants who will proclaim His message and honor His name (vv. 1–8). We are not told what these sealed Jews will do, but we assume they will point people to the Lord. Times of tribulation give opportunities for witness (Matt. 24:14).

"We make a great mistake if we connect with our conception of heaven the thought of rest from work. Rest from toil, from weariness, from exhaustion—yes; rest from work, from productiveness, from service— no. 'They serve God day and night.'"

B. F. Westcott

Apparently the 144,000 Jews will be sealed at the beginning of the Tribulation; and at the end, a great multitude of saved Gentiles will be seen (vv. 9–17). The day of the Lord will bring judgment and destruction, and it will also result in the saving of people. In wrath, God remembers mercy (Hab. 3:2). When you experience trials, ask God to use you to win others to the Savior even in the midst of troubles.

Trials do not last forever. One day, you will come out of tribulation and experience the gracious comforts of God. Wait and be faithful, and He will see you through.

REVELATION 8—9

Incense at the altar (8:1–4). The silence in heaven is the lull before the storm (Hab. 2:20; Zeph. 1:7). Even the heavenly hosts stop their worship as they contemplate the awesome judgments about to fall. But those judgments are the answer to the saints' prayers (5:8), "Thy kingdom come!" Do not stop praying!

Fire from the altar (8:5—9:12). The world will not come to the altar for forgiveness (9:21), so the altar sends forth judgment. Heaven and earth are struck as the trumpets sound, and the bottomless pit belches out demonic creatures to torment mankind. Rather than repent, people will try to commit suicide; but they will not be able to die (9:6). They will continue in their sins: occult practices, murder, immorality, and thievery (9:20–21), all of which sound very contemporary.

A voice from the altar (9:13–21). God has His legions ready to be released at the right time, and torment will be replaced by death. Men have wanted to die, so God will send His servants to do the job. One-third of mankind will be killed (9:15), which means that half of the world's population is now dead (6:8)! The world must make a choice: life or death (Deut. 30:19). Are you offering them the gift of life in Jesus Christ?

REVELATION 10

The voice of the thunders (1–4). We do not know what the angel shouted or what the seven thunders uttered (Ps. 29). God has given sufficient truth in His Word for salvation and godly living, so we must not crave to know the hidden things (Deut.

29:29). The purpose of Scripture is to save sinners and sanctify character, not satisfy curiosity.

The voice of the angel (5–7). The angel said, "There will be delay no longer!" What joy this statement will bring to the martyrs (and others) who ask, "How long?" (6:9–11). God has His times (Eccles. 3:1–8) and will accomplish His purposes on schedule. Our responsibility is to be faithful and not inquisitive (Acts 1:6–8).

The voice of the apostle (8–11). God still needed John to declare His message to the people. No angel could take his place. But to share God's message, we must take the Word, receive it inwardly like food, and let it become part of us (Jer. 15:16; Ezek. 3:1–11; 1 Thess. 2:13). The Word is sweet when you read it (Ps. 119:103) but bitter when it goes deeper and you digest it.

❝*If you conscientiously undertake to walk in the truth revealed, you too will know something of its bitterness. . . . We need the bitter as well as the sweet; and every soul who has walked in the truth, as God has revealed it to him, has found, at last, the blessedness of obedience.***❞**

H. A. Ironside

REVELATION 11

To measure something is to claim it for yourself, as when the new owner of a house measures it for carpets, drapes, and so forth. John claims the temple in Jerusalem for the Lord even though in a short time the Antichrist will take it over (2 Thess. 2:3–4). God may seem to lose some battles, but He will finally win the war. We walk by faith.

We do not know who the two witnesses are, but they encourage us to be faithful to the Lord in difficult times. God protects them and then permits them to be slain (Acts 12:1–10). God's servants are immortal until their work is done. But Satan's victory is short, for God takes the two men to heaven. Satan's victory is defeat, but God's seeming defeat is victory.

No matter what the enemy may do to the temple on earth, he cannot touch the temple in heaven (v. 19). The rejoicing of evil men soon becomes lamentation (vv. 10–14), while the hosts of heaven proclaim the sovereign reign of Jesus Christ (vv. 15–18). Let the nations rage (Ps. 2): Jesus Christ will reign forever and ever!

"No doctrine in the whole Word of God has more excited the hatred of mankind than the truth of the absolute sovereignty of God. The fact that 'the Lord reigneth' is indisputable, and it is this fact that arouses the utmost opposition in the unrenewed human heart."

Charles Haddon Spurgeon

REVELATION 12

The Murderer (1–6). The Child is Jesus Christ, and the woman represents Israel who brought the Savior into the world. The dragon is Satan who tried to keep Jesus from being born and attempted to kill Him after He was born. Satan wants to rule this world, and he will not submit to the King (v. 5; Ps. 2:9).

The Deceiver (7–9). This is a picture of the fall of Satan (Isa. 14:12–17). He was able to deceive one-third of the angels into following him (v. 4), and now he deceives the world into worshiping him.

The Accuser (10–12). Satan has access to God's throne where he accuses God's people (Job 1–2; Zech. 3). The Lamb overcomes him because of His victory at Calvary (Rom. 8:31–34; 1 John 2:1–2) and because of the power of the Word (Eph. 6:17).

The Persecutor (13–17). The war may be over in heaven, but it it getting more intense here on earth. Satan is angry and seeks to destroy the Jews and make war with anyone who trusts the Lord. God is able to shelter His people in spite of Satan's attacks, but be sure you wear the armor (Eph. 6:10–18) and trust the blood of Jesus.

"*I'm not afraid of the devil. The devil can handle me— he's got judo I never heard of. But he can't handle the One to whom I'm joined; he can't handle the One to whom I'm united; he can't handle the One whose nature dwells in my nature.***"**

A. W. Tozer

REVELATION 13

Worship. The beast from the sea is Satan's final and greatest masterpiece—Antichrist, who towers above all the tyrants and dictators of world history. This man accepts the offer that Satan gave to Jesus (v. 2; Matt. 4:8–10). The world worships him as a god, but heaven sees him as a beast (Dan. 7). The counterfeit Christ is now on the scene!

Warfare. The Beast fights God by speaking blasphemous words (Dan. 7:8, 11, 20, 25) and by persecuting the saints (v. 7; Dan. 7:25). It may seem strange that God should permit His people to be defeated, yet this is part of His plan (Heb. 11:35–40). In every age, God's people have had to battle some satanic beast.

Wealth. The Beast's "prime minister" leads the world to worship the Beast by controlling all the wealth. It was a matter of life or death! When you combine political power with economic power and all religion, you have a formula for controlling the whole world. But the lost world worships money and power, so the task will not be too difficult.

Which Riches Are Yours

Since all the riches of this world
May be gifts from the Devil and earthly kings,
I should suspect that I worshiped the Devil
If I thanked God for worldly things.
The countless gold of a merry heart,
The rubies and pearls of a loving eye,
The indolent never can bring to the mart,
Nor the cunning hoard up in his treasury.

William Blake

REVELATION 14

John used agricultural images to tell us that the time was ripe for judgment.

Firstfruits (1–5). God takes the best for Himself before the harvest begins. We met the 144,000 in chapter 7, God's sealed servants who come through the Tribulation and sing the praises of the Lamb. The description in verse 4 should be taken in a spiritual sense: they did not commit fornication by worshiping the Beast or his image (Exod. 34:15; James 4:4).

Wine (6–13). The "cup of wrath" is an image borrowed from Jeremiah 25:15ff. God pours out His wrath on those who follow the Beast and reject God's truth. Although verse 13 may be applied to all believers who die, it will have a special meaning to the martyrs of that evil day.

Reaping (14–20). God is allowing the seeds of sin to grow and produce a harvest (vv. 14–16). One day, the world will reap what it has sown. John also uses the grape harvest to illustrate the coming judgment (vv. 17–20). The "vine of the earth" is ripening, and one day God will apply the sickle. Meanwhile, the branches in the True Vine (John 15:1–8) should be bearing more and more fruit.

REVELATION 15

John reaches back into the Old Testament to teach us about God's judgment and grace. The seven angels have bowls of wrath, plagues to pour on a wicked world. They remind us of the plagues God sent to Egypt in the days of Moses (Exod. 7—12). Note in chapter 16 how the plagues parallel those God sent to Egypt.

God delivered Israel from Egypt, and they sang a song of victory at the Red Sea (Exod. 15). John saw the tribulation victors singing by the heavenly sea of glass. Moses and the Lamb come together in the song of triumph.

The heavenly tabernacle is filled with smoke, just as the glory of God filled both the tabernacle (Exod. 40:34–38) and the temple (1 Kings 8:10–11). But the glory then was a mark of God's presence and blessing. The glory John saw was an announcement that God's wrath was about to be poured out on a wicked world.

Sinners will not learn from the past, but believers can be encouraged by the past. The God of Moses and Israel is still defending His people. There is a new song for you to sing.

REVELATION 16

No matter what the unbelieving world may say, God's judgments are righteous (vv. 1–7). Sinners reap what they sow. Because "righteousness and justice are the foundation of His throne" (Ps. 97:2), nobody can accuse God of being unfair.

God's judgments do not change men's hearts (vv. 8–11). God judges sinners not to reveal His grace but to uphold His holiness. Sinners in the last days will be like Pharaoh in the days of Moses; they will harden their hearts more as God's judgments increase.

Against the dark background of judgment shines the promise of God (vv. 12–16). Christ is coming soon, and we must watch eagerly and walk carefully (3:1–6) so that we will be ready to meet Him (1 John 2:28).

God's judgment will one day be finished (vv. 17–21). God's long-suffering will finally end, and His wrath will be revealed. What holds Him back today? Read 2 Peter 3:9, 15 for the answer.

> **"**In righteousness God reveals chiefly His love of
> holiness; in justice, chiefly his hatred of sin . . .
> Neither justice nor righteousness . . . is a matter of
> arbitrary will. They are revelations of the
> inmost nature of God.**"**

Augustus Hopkins Strong

The Battlefield

Armageddon (Rev. 16:16) is Hebrew for
"the hill of Megiddo"; and Megiddo
means "place of slaughter." It is the plain
in the Holy Land where Barak defeated
the Canaanites (Judg. 5:19) and Gideon
the Midianites (Judg. 7). King Saul
fought his last battle there (1 Sam. 31).
One of the greatest natural battlefields in
the world, it is where the Antichrist will
gather the world's armies to fight against
Jesus Christ (Isa. 24; Joel 3; Zech. 12—
14). Revelation 19:11–21 records the out-
come.

REVELATION 17

Each person must identify with either the harlot or the
bride (21:9); there can be no compromise. The woman represents the ultimate in godless world religion. She is joined with
government (carried by the Beast) and corrupts everything
she touches. The bride is the true church of Jesus Christ,
cleansed by His blood and destined for glory.

Participating in false religion is like committing adultery: you are unfaithful to the one to whom you pledged your love (Isa. 57:3; Jer. 3:8–9; Hos. 2:4). The harlot was popular for a time, but then her "lovers" turned on her and destroyed her. The Antichrist will use a world church to get himself into power and then establish his own religion (13:11–15).

Though Christians must be good citizens and seek to influence government for the Lord, the church must not marry political systems. The systems will only use the church to promote their own plans and then abandon it. Christ's kingdom is not of this world (John 18:33–38), and the enemy is spiritual (Eph. 6:10ff.). We must use spiritual weapons (2 Cor. 10:3–6) to fight spiritual enemies.

REVELATION 18

The harlot and the bride are each identified with a city: the harlot with Babylon and the bride with heavenly Jerusalem (21:9ff.). The heavenly city will be the bride's home for eternity, but Babylon will be destroyed by God. The world's economy will be ruined.

> **"**In our well-intentioned identification with the world, we do not mold it—it molds us. We are not to be isolated but insulated, moving in the midst of evil but untouched by it.**"**
>
> Vance Havner

John certainly had Rome in mind when he wrote this chapter, but his imagery means much more. Babylon symbolizes the whole godless world system that caters to the appetites of sinful men and women (1 John 2:15–17). True believers have nothing in common with the harlot and her city and should be separated from them (v. 4; Jer. 50:8; 51:6; 2 Cor. 6:14–18). In every age, the church has had to identify its Babylon and separate from it.

When God judges sinners, earth laments and heaven rejoices (v. 20). Most people are concerned primarily with satisfying their physical desires; they are not concerned about things spiritual or eternal. They live for the temporary and the immediate, not the eternal.

REVELATION 19

Celebration (1–6). Sinners cry "Alas!" but saints shout "Hallelujah!" at the fall of the godless world system called Babylon. Sin has been judged, God's servants have been vindicated, God has been glorified, and Christ is about to usher in His kingdom. Even as you anticipate these victories, by faith you can shout "Hallelujah!"

Proclamation (7–10, 17–21). Two contrasting suppers are named in this chapter: the marriage supper of the Lamb (v. 9), which brings blessing, and the "supper of the great God" (vv. 17–21), which brings judgment. The bride makes herself ready at the judgment seat of Christ where her "spots and wrinkles" are taken away (Eph. 5:25–27) and she receives rewards for faithful service. In contrast, the godless armies of earth are defeated by the Lord and become food for the birds. This is the battle of Armageddon mentioned in Revelation 16:16.

The Coming Kingdom

His kingdom is coming!
Oh, tell me the story!
God's banner exalted shall be;
The earth shall be filled with His wonder and glory,
As waters that cover the sea.

Anonymous

Revelation (11–16). The conquering Christ comes with His armies and defeats all His enemies! Contrast this with His ride into Jerusalem on Palm Sunday (Matt. 21:1–11), and review the Father's promises in Psalm 2. Also contrast it with the ride of the Antichrist (6:1–2). It encourages us to know that our Savior is *today* King of kings and Lord of lords, and that the future is secure because He is reigning.

REVELATION 20

The lost throne (1–3, 7–10). Since Satan's rebellion (Isa. 14:12–15), God has permitted him to work on this earth, but He has always kept him in control (Job 1–2). Satan will exchange his throne for a bottomless pit, and his final destiny will be the lake of fire where he will spend eternity with the Beast and the false prophet (v. 10; 19:20)—and with those who choose to follow Satan instead of Jesus Christ (Matt. 25:41).

The kingdom thrones (4–6). The first resurrection takes place before Jesus ushers in His kingdom and involves only those who have trusted Christ (John 5:24–29; 1 Thess. 4:13–18). They will reign with Him (Matt. 19:28) and have responsibilities commensurate with their faithful service while living on earth (Matt. 25:14–30).

The great white throne (11–15). This judgment involves only the lost and follows the second resurrection, the resurrection to condemnation. Sinners who rejected Christ will face Him (John 5:22) and hear Him say, "Depart from Me!" (Matt. 7:23; 25:41). This solemn scene ought to move us to pray for the lost and witness to them, and thank the Lord for His grace in saving us!

REVELATION 21

For those who believe in Jesus Christ, the future means "all things new" (v. 5); but for those who reject Him, it means the same old sins for all eternity (vv. 8, 27; 22:11, 15).

Human history begins with a garden (Gen. 2:8–17) and ends with a city that is like a garden. However, the most important thing about the heavenly city is not the absence of sin but the presence of God in all His glory (vv. 3, 11, 23), for His presence makes "all things new."

He is the temple (v. 22) and the light (v. 23); and His presence means there is no more sin, pain, death, sorrow, or crying (v. 4), and no more curse (22:3; Gen. 3:9–19). Heaven is so wonderful that the only way John can describe it is to tell us what will *not* be there! Its beauties and blessings are beyond human words to describe or explain.

Why did Jesus give John this preview of eternal glory? *To encourage His people who go through testing and persecution.* "I go to prepare a place for you" (John 14:1–6) is the best medicine for a broken heart and the best foundation for wavering feet.

> **"**The hope of heaven under troubles is like the wind and sails to the soul.**"**
>
> Samuel Rutherford

> **"**No man ought to look for anything in heaven but what one way or another he has some experience in this life.**"**
>
> John Owen

REVELATION 22

How do you respond to the promise of the Lord's return? John's last chapter can help you take inventory.

Are you treasuring His Word and obeying it (v. 7)? This is *His* message to you (v. 16), and it must not be altered (vv. 18–19). There is a special blessing for the obedient (v. 14).

Are you doing the work He has called you to do (v. 12)? He promises to reward faithful servants (Luke 12:35–48).

Do you really *want* Jesus to return today (v. 20)? Do you "love His appearing" (2 Tim. 4:8)? If Jesus were to come today, would you be disappointed and your plans be upset?

Are you urging lost sinners to trust Him and be ready for His coming (v. 17)? The Holy Spirit works through the church to bring lost people to the Savior. The people described in 21:8

and 22:11 can be saved (1 Cor. 6:9–11) and become new creatures ready for the new heaven and earth (2 Cor. 5:17). Will you tell them?

"Amazing Grace"

Amazing grace! How sweet the sound,
That saved a wretch like me!
I once was lost, but now am found;
Was blind, but now I see!

When we've been there ten thousand years,
Bright shining as the sun,
We've no less days to sing God's praise
Than when we'd first begun.

John Newton